# THE BLUE GUIDES

*Interior of St Sebaldus, Nuremberg*

**BLUE GUIDE**

# Western Germany

**James Bentley**

**A & C Black**
London

**WW Norton**
New York

Second edition 1995

Published by A & C Black (Publishers) Limited
35 Bedford Row, London WC1R 4JH

Maps by Terence Crump.

A CIP catalogue record of this book
is available from the British Library.

ISBN 0-7136-3278-X

Published in the United States of America by
WW Norton and Company, Inc
500 Fifth Avenue, New York, NY 10110

Published simultaneously in Canada by
Penquin Books Canada Limited
10 Alcorn Avenue, Toronto, Ontario M4V 3B2

ISBN 0-393-31196-1 USA

The publishers would like to thank the following for permission to use their photographs: Archiv Fur Kunst und Geschichte, Berlin; Barnaby's Picture Library; Bildarchiv Foto, Marburg; Dacs; A.F. Kersting; Tony Mott; Wim Swaan.

**James Bentley** is an historian and travel writer who wrote the acclaimed biography of Hitler's opponent Pastor Martin Niemöller. He has written numerous travel books about Europe, won the Thomas Cook Travel Award in 1988 and, according to *The Times*, 'is an authoritative guide whose pleasure in the table and command of history gives his work full-bodied value'.

The publishers and the author welcome comments, suggestions and corrections for the next edition of Blue Guide Western Germany. Writers of the most informative letters will be awarded a free Blue Guide of their choice.

# PREFACE

Completely updated, the second edition of Blue Guide Western Germany is the most authoritative guide book in English to a region which includes the entrancing cities of Münich, Heidelberg, Augsburg, Regensburg and Würzburg, as well as such enticing routes as the famous Romantic Road. This too is the part of Germany which incorporates the renowned castles of so-called Mad King Ludwig.

Favourite tourist areas, such as the Rhine and the Mosel, are comprehensively described. At the same time lesser-known regions and cities of Western Germany (such as the cycling country of Münsterland, Thomas Mann's Lübeck, Hamburg and the Pied Piper's Hamelin) are thoroughly covered in James Bentley's new volume.

Special features include information about travel to Western Germany and about hotels, language, food and wine. Comprehensive maps add a further bonus to this edition. Every important art treasure in western German galleries is mentioned. And the many exquisite villages, with their half-timbered houses, superb churches and welcoming inns receive here their due praise.

# Acknowledgments

Lack of space prevents me from, listing the many people—particularly the staff of local tourist offices throughout western Germany—who have helped me in preparing the second edition of this book; but I must especially thank Dr Rudolf Richter, Frau Agatha Suess and Herr Harold Henning of the German National Tourist Office in London, as well as Herr Markus Ruediger, Press and Public Relations Manager, UK and Ireland, Lufthansa German Airlines, and also his colleague Frau Gudrun Gorner. My thanks are also due to Gemma Davies of A & C Black.

James Bentley 1994

# CONTENTS

# AN INTRODUCTION TO WESTERN GERMANY

The contents of this guide cover what was, until German re-unification, the Federal Republic of Germany, whose capital was Bonn until in 1991 the deputies voted by a narrow margin to transfer the seat of government to Berlin.

The region is divided into ten separate *Länder* (or states) of widely different sizes (and including two cities which count as *Länder*), namely: **Baden-Württemberg**, which covers 35,750 square kilometres and has a population of over nine-and-half million, its capital Stuttgart; **Bavaria (Bayern)**, with an area of 70, 547 square kilometres, a population of nearly 11 million and Munich as its capital city; **Rhineland-Palatinate (Rheinland-Pfalz)**, with 19,838 square kilometres, a population of 3,702,000 and as its capital Mainz; **Saarland**, covering 2570 square kilometres, with a population of 1,090,000, its capital city Saarbrücken; **Hesse (Hessen)**, covering 21,112 square kilometres, with a population of 5,660,000 and Wiesbaden as its capital; **North Rhine-Westphalia (Nordrhein-Westfalen)**, its overall area 34,057 square kilometres, its population 17,104,000 and its capital Düsseldorf; **Lower Saxony (Niedersachsen)**, which stretches for 47,408 square kilometres, has a population of 7,284,000 and Hanover (Hannover) as its capital; **Schleswig-Holstein**, its area 15,696 square kilometres, its population 2,595,000 its capital Kiel; as well as the two cities of: **Bremen**, covering 4040 square kilometres, with a population of 674,000; and **Hamburg**, covering 753 square kilometres with a population of 1,626,000.

Each *Land* elects its own parliament, headed by a regional prime minister (or, in the case of Bremen and Hamburg, a Bürgermeister). Head of the whole German state is the Bundespresident, who sits for five years and appoints the Federal chancellor on the advice of the Federal parliament (the *Bundestag*).

Schleswig-Holstein, Hamburg and Bremen, as well as much of Lower Saxony and North Rhine-Westphalia, comprise the North German Lowland, whose clayey soil was laid down in the Ice Age and which includes the forests and heather of Lüneburg Heath. Drained by the rivers Weser and Elbe, these are lands of considerable agricultural and pastoral importance, as well as mineral wealth.

The rest of Lower Saxony and North Rhine-Westphalia combine with Hesse, Rhineland-Palatinate and the Saarland to form the mountainous Central Uplands and include the Harz mountains, the Siebengebirge and the Teutoburg, Odenwald and Spessart forests, as well as the mountain resorts of the Taunus. These uplands also take in the Rhine valley and the Mosel, which border on the Eifel mountains (these last penetrating into Belgium, where they are called the Ardennes).

Finally the River main divides the Central Uplands from the Southern Plateau. Again, here are mountains and rivers, particularly the peaks of the Jural and the River Danube. This is the region of the Bavarian Alps and the Black Forest, which divides the Rhine valley from the fertile countryside of Schwabia.

For the most part western Germany enjoys a mild climate, with average summer temperatures around 22°C, where as the winter temperatures vary from 0°C to 12°C. In consequence, from December to March (and even April in the Alps) many regions relish winter sports.

As for religion, after the Peace of Augsburg in 1555 Germans took as their religious denomination the choice of their temporal ruler, whether Lutheran or Catholic. Today, West Germany consists of roughly half-Lutherans, half-Catholics, with a few members of other denominations and some non-believers (as well as Huguenots who migrated here to escape persecution in the 17C). In the Middle Ages some 800,000 Jews lived in Germany, most of their descendants to be murdered or escape elsewhere during the Hitler Reich. The former Federal Republic is also the home of over five million 'guest workers', 30 per cent of whom are Turks, 10 per cent Italians and 12 per cent workers from the former Yugoslavia.

Among the native German people, regional characteristics are marked, especially where food and drink, traditional dress and dialects are concerned—though all speak the 'High German' which merged as a result of Martin Luther's translation of the Bible.

# History

Prehistoric remains discovered in the present region of West Germany include the skeleton of so-called Neanderthal man (some 100,000 years old), found in the Neander valley near Düsseldorf, and the jaw of so-called 'Homo Heidelbergensis' (500,000 years old), discovered near Heidelberg. Works of Mesolithic art dating from paleolithic times—decorated clay pottery, amber utensils—have been excavated in north and east Germany, and late Iron Age graves have been found containing utensils that have been imported from the Mediterranean.

The art of prehistoric Germany begins with paintings of men and animals from the paleolithic age, followed by neolithic utensils made of fired clay and decorated either by ribbon motifs of whipped cord and ribbon or by incisions. By the Iron Age the predecessors of the Germans were importing goods from the Mediterranean, as well as carving their own stone steles and monuments, though they built in perishable wood.

In AD 9 Arminius, one of the rulers of the Cherusci tribe, fought and defeated three Roman legions at a battle in the Teutoburg forest. Traditionally Arminius is perceived as Germany's first national hero. The word 'Deutsch', however, initially used of a Franconian dialect in the 7C or 8C (and first recorded by Wigbodus as _theoriscus_ in AD 768) did not for many centuries come to be used of the whole of present-day Germany, and the problem of the origins of the German people has not yet been satisfactorily solved.

Two tribes of Indo-European origin, the Teutones and the Cimbri, living west of the River Rhine and north of the River Danube at the end of the 2C BC, invaded Gaul and northern Italy, only to be wiped out by the Romans commanded by Marius in 102 and 101 BC. Julius Caesar next brought under Roman sway such Teutons as were living west of the Rhine, a process continued in 9 BC when the legions penetrated as far east as the River Elbe. Arminius's victory over the army of P. Quinctilius Varus drove them back. Rome retaliated, and during the 1C AD fought numerous battles to control the German tribes.

In 98 AD Tacitus produced his _Germania_, describing in detail (and, most historians, agree, with considerable accuracy) the customs and beliefs of the Germanic people. The Teutons, said Tacitus, with their blue eyes and reddish hair, were 'extremely strong when attacking, but not fitted to the same extent for heavy work'. He wrote of their ancient songs, which claimed that the tribes were descended from the three sons of the god Mannua. Tacitus suggests that only one tribe—the Tungri—was initially known as the Germans, a name which spread to the rest. At this time the Frisii lived in the land between the Ems and the Rhine, the Chatti lived in present-day Hesse, the Suebi (who gave their name to Schwabia) inhabited the region that is now Berlin, the Angles lived in Schleswig, the Chauci occupied the estuary of the River Weser, and Arminius's tribe, the Cherusci, lived further south. Around present-day Regensburg and extending northwards as far as Thuringia lived the Hermunduri.

Both Julius Caesar and Tacitus wrote of a system of periodic land redistribution by the leaders of the German tribes. 'No-one has a fixed measure of land as his own.' wrote Caesar. 'Instead, each year the magistrates and leaders distribute to the tribes and the groups of kinsmen...as much land and in whatever place they consider right. The following year they force the clans and kinsmen to move on'. Tacitus, a century and a half later, described virtually the same system, except that according to him arable land was now being distributed annually to individuals, not to clans or groups of kinsmen. The way was being prepared for the rise of rulers as opposed merely to leaders. At first, however, the Germans elected their chiefs to rule only in wartime. By the time Tacitus wrote, these chiefs were feeding and controlling permanent bands of followers.

After Domitian had fought the Chatti, the Romans began to construct the limes, a series of fortifications 550km long, stetching from the Rhine to the Danube, as a defence against the inroads of the Germanic tribes. Domitian divided the region into two privinces: Germania Superior (whose major castrum was Mongaontiacum, the site of present-day Mainz) and Germania Inferior (whose chief castrum was Colonia Agrippinensis, or Cologne). Modern Germany incorporates altogether sections of four Roman provinces, Raetia (where the Augustus established Augusta Vindelicorum, or Augsburg) and Gallia Belgica (which included Augusta Treverorum, now Trier) as well as Germania Superior and Germania Inferior.

Other Roman garrisons within the confines of present-day western Germany included castra Bonnensia (Bonn, developed on a Celtic site), Borbetomagus (Worms, again set up on a Celtic site), Aquae (Baden-Baden), Novaesium (Neuss), castrum and Confluentes (Koblenz, which Drusus established where the Rhein meets the Mosel) and castra Regina (Regensburg, which the Celts had founded as Radasbona). They prospered so long as the Romans could defend them. Cologne became a centre for glass-production. Under Diocletian, Trier became an imperial residence. Constantine built himself a villa at Neumagen.

When the Romans left Germany the tribes razed the old Roman settlements (for as Tacitus tells us, they preferred to live not in cities but in homesteads). Even where Roman foundations were later rebuilt, few traces remain (outside museums) of the earlier garrisons apart from the street patterns at Cologne and Trier. Exceptions include the Roman amphitheatre at Xanten; traces of Roman baths near the remains of temples to Mithras and Jupiter at Wiesbaden; the remains of Roman fortifications at Boppard; the nine-metre high column erected at Mainz in thanksgiving for the Emperor Nero's recovery from sickness, as well as a 3C Roman arch in the same city and remains of the roman aqueduct in the suburb of Zahlbach; a votive stone dedicated to 'maronae Aufaniae', discovered under Bonn's

Münster and dating from 164 AD; and the baths constructed by the Emperor Caracalla at Baden-Baden in the 3C.

The centuries after the Romans left were marked by remarkable migrations (including the colonisation of England by Angles and Saxons), Franks, Alemanni, Bavarians and Thuringians continued to invade and settle different parts of present-day Germany. Only when the Merovingian king Clovis (481–511) unified the Frankish kingdom and defeated the Alemanni did these extensive migrations come to an end (though some German tribes continued to expand eastwards long after the Carolingian empire had broken up).

These centuries also saw the Germans converted to Christianity (initially to the heretical form known as Arianism). Anglo-Irish missionaries founded the diocese of Konstanz in 613, and monasteries at Echternach in 698 and Reichenau in 724. St Boniface led missions to Bavaria and Hesse, his most important foundation being Fulda in 744, though he also infused new life into moribund bishoprics such as Regensburg.

In 771 Charlemagne (742–814) became king of the Franks. His domains embraced peoples speaking many different languages and dialects, including the Germans. In 800 he became the first western emperor since the Classical era. He converted the Saxons to Christianity, founded monasteries, bishoprics and new ecclesiastical provinces, elevating Trier, Mainz and Cologne to archbishoprics.

In 825 Charlemagne's successor, Louis the Pious, appointed his son, Louis the German, ruler of Bavaria. His sway gradually spread throughout the whole of the German part of the empire, and this separation of most of Germany from the rest of the empire was formalised in 843 at the Treaty of Verdun. The Treaty of Mersen in 870 extended this rule from the River Elbe in the east of Alsace and Lorraine in the west.

Clearly 'Germany' was becoming more of a reality, a development demonstrated linguistically on 14 February 842 when Louis the German and Charles the Bald met at Strasbourg and swore an oath not to plot against each other. Louis swore in the Romance language—his brother's tongue. Charles took the oath in German. Even so, the first ruler whose claim to be truly Germanic makes political and geographical sense was Conrad I, elected king by the Frankish and Saxon dukes assembled at Forchheim in 911. The election was soon accepted by the Schwabians and by Duke Arnulf of Bavaria.

Conrad was succeeded, at his own dying suggestion, by the Saxon duke Henry the Fowler (Henry I, 919–36). Elected by the Saxons and the Franks meeting at Fritzlar, Henry consolidated the realm and took the title king. For the first time Germany was described as a kingdom ('Regnum Teutonicorum'). Lotharingia was brought back under German rule, and in 933 Henry repulsed an attack on Saxony and Thuringia by the Hungarians.

Henry's son, Otto I the Great (ruled 936–73), was crowned emperor in Rome in 962, and vindicated Saxon military prowess by decisively defeating the Hungarians at the Lech in 955. Strong enough to depose Pope John XII and replace him with Leo VII, Otto founded the archbishopric of Magdeburg and built a new imperial residence there in order to extend both Christianity and his own influence beyond the Elbe. In 1007 his successor Henry II consolidated these developments by founding the bishopric of Bamberg. Endlessly travelling with their courts from city to city and from monastery to monastery these rulers had no option but to rely on the German bishops, dukes and counts to govern the various tribes of their kingdom. At the same time as defending their own kingdom against the

Magyars, they pursued military adventures into Italy. During the reign of the first Salian king, Conrad II (1024–39), Burgundy was also incorporated into Germany. Trade flourished: to give one example, 44 mill stones, hewn from volcanic lava in the Rhineland, were transported to London c AD 1000, to be excavated there by archaeologists some ten centuries later.

The 11C witnessed numerous imperial-papal quarrels. Conrad's successor Henry III (1039–56) deposed no fewer than three popes. A reformed papacy fought back. Henry IV (1056–1106), having claimed the right to appoint church leaders in his realms, was excommunicated by Gregory VII (who also absolved the turbulent German princes of their oath of allegiance to the emperor). Henry IV humiliatingly submitted to the pope at Canossa in 1077. And the reforms which Gregory VII and his like demanded in church life had powerful advocates in the Cistercians, who brought a fresh religious impulse from France into 12C Germany, endowing their own distincitive monasteries and churches (amongst them the splendid Kloster Eberbach and the equally superb abbey at Maulbronn).

The Cistercian religious impetus did not wane throughout the 13C, when it was reinforced by that of the Franciscans and then the Dominicans, both orders bringing a sense of magnificent austerity both to the Christian life and to the architecture of their monasteries and churches, an austerity still visible at Esslingen, where the Dominican monastery church of St Paul remains the oldest medicant church in Germany. At the same time secular rulers still took it upon themselves to endow monasteries and bishoprics. Henry the Lion, Duke of Saxony (1142–80) not only brought Mecklenburg and Pomerania under German rule but also founded, for instance, the bishopric of Ratzeburg and its cathedral.

The last Salian king, Henry V (1106–25) died without heirs. The church and the princes of Germany now turned against his nephews, the Hohenstaufen family, and chose instead Duke Lothair of Saxony as emperor. On his death in 1137, they once again displayed their disregard for so-called 'blood rights' and elected the Hohenstaufen Conrad III (1138–52). His successor as Holy Roman Emperor was Frederick I Barbarossa (1152–90), Duke of Schwabia, who agreed to share sovereignty over Germany with his cousin Henry the Lion.

Henry was no firm ally of Barbarossa, refusing to support his Italian adventures. In consequence Barbarossa was defeated by the Lombards at the Battle of Legnano in 1176. The emperor now turned against the Duke of Saxony, who was outlawed, defeated in battle and forced into exile.

Under the rule of Barbarossa's successors the empire gradually disintegrated, so that by the time the Hohenstaufen dynasty came to an end in 1268, subordinate dynasties were ruling their dukedoms virtually unchecked by any sovereign authority.

The advent of the Habsburgs (the first being Rudolf I, 1273–91) began to check this apparent anarchy. Charles IV (1346–78) issued his 'Golden Bull' in 1356, decreeing that seven electors should henceforth apoint the German sovereign. These electors were the archbishops of Mainz, Cologne and Trier, the King of Bohemia, the margrave of Brandenburg, the Duke of Saxony and the Count Palatine of the Rhine. Soon they were invariably electing Habsburgs.

The power of the smaller princelings declined, but stronger rulers arrogated to themselves increasing privileges and rights. At the same time certain cities began to ally themselves in leagues for mutual protection and for the development of trade. On 4 July 1376, 14 imperial cities led by Ulm and Constance formed themselves as the Schwabian Leage, and by 1385 had been joined by 36 other member cities. Even more important from the 13C to the 15C was the Hanseatic League (a title derived from the word *Hanse*, meaning 'association' or 'guild'). Led by Lübeck and Hamburg the Hanseatic League dominated the Baltic from the 14C. In 1368 when the Danish king, Valdemar IV, tried to take command of the Baltic, the League even went to war against and defeated him, for some time ruling Denmark itself. This group of cities remained a powerful force in Germany until the last Hanseatic Diet met in 1699. Meanwhile other powerful cities like Cologne threw out their local lords, recognised the rule only of the emperor and in effect ruled themselves. Collectively the burghers now often equalled in importance members of the formerly dominant nobility.

Lübeck and Bremen were also responsible for the creation of another remarkable German institution, the order of Teutonic Knights. Towards the end of the 12C the two cities set up a hospital at Acre in Palestine. Connected with its was a charitable order which in 1198 took on a military aspect. Its Grand Master Hermann von Salza (1210–39) decided to concentrate the activities of the order on eastern Europe, where the knights supported King Andrew II of Hungary against the heathen Cumans. Next Konrad of Mazovia sought their help in conquering the neighbouring Prussians, who till then had remained pagan. From this base the Teutonic Knights gradually secured a hold over the whole of Prussia, ruthlessly destroying those who stood in their way. Although Prussian towns remained for the most part self-governing and a third of the lands conquered by the Teutonic Knights was handed over to the church, the Teutonic Knights consolidated their position by building castles and endowing Polish noblemen with Prussian estates on condition that they remained subordinate to the order.

The Teutonic Knigths also brought peasants from other parts of Germany into underpopulated Prussia. In 1263 they persuaded the pope to rescind their vow of poverty, so as to exploit the profitable trade in Prussian grain. As the century progressed they fulfilled their debt to Lübeck and Bremen by defending the Hanseatic League. They also expanded into parts of Lithuania and in 1402 bought Neumark in western Pomerania. Poland fought back against the knights, several times defeating the order in the 15C and forcing its grand master to accept Polish suzerainty. When the grand master became a Protestant in 1525, he transformed Prussia into a secular duchy and dissolved the order there. The rest of the Teutonic Knights appointed a *Deutschmeister*, who in 1530 was made a prince of the Holy Roman Empire. He and his successors controlled their pockets of land and property in southern and central Germany until 1809, when Napoleon finally dissolved the order.

The Teutonic Knights represented merely one element in the patchwork quilt of late-medieval Germany. Although the views of the Bohemian reformer Jan Huss (c 1369–1415) were condemned by the Council of Konstanz (Constance) and he met his death at the stake there in 1415, the empire was by then in such disarray that a Hussite army ravaged Saxony, Thuringia and Franconia in 1429 and 1430. To the east the Turks were threatening the empire, a danger exploited by the territorially ambitious Matthias Corvinus, King of Hungary. In three important cities, Speyer, Strasbourg and Nuremberg, the guilds had already revolted against their exclusion from government in the first half of the 14C. Beginning in 1391, the peasants revolted against what they saw as the greed of their lords (which often included the church) with increasing frequency.

In the mid 15C Gutenberg invented printing at Mainz; and capitalism developed rapidly, under the impetus of such rich dynasties as the Fuggers of Augsburg. Maximilian I (1483–1519) fostered new institutions, such as the Reichstag (the imperial parliament) and the Reichskammergericht (the imperial high court) which were to survive until the early 19C. Yet these structures contributed to a separation of powers, in which powerful princes could flaunt the imperial power. Such a system enabled Luther's attack on the Catholic church in the early 16C to survive papal censure. Luther also profited from a long-standing resentment among many German princes at the financial demands of the papacy.

Reformers who did not gain the support of princes were put down as revolutionaries. Such preachers as the Anabaptist Thomas Münzer (1485/90–1525) and Nicholaus Storch took far further than Luther notions of Christian liberty and the personal inner inspiration of every believer. When in 1524 and 1525 the peasants of Hesse, Saxony and Thuringia demanded their ancient rights, appealing to Luther's teachings, Luther himself denounced them, and their revolt was savagely put down. Six years later two princes, Landgraf Philip of Hesse (1504–67) and the elector Johann of Saxony (1458–1532), set up the Schmalkaldic League to defend the Protestant cause. In 1547 the forces of the Catholic emperor Charles V (1519–56) managed to defeat the forces of the league, but the Protestants rallied and drove him out of Germany.

By the time of the Peace of Augsburg in 1555 Catholicism was seriously weakened throughout Germany. The formula 'cuius regio, eius religio' adopted in 1555 decreed that the religion adopted by the prince should be the religion of his territories. Charles V, unable to reconcile himself to tolerating Protestants in one part of his empire while persecuting them in another, abdicated the following year and retired to a monastery in Estramadura.

The Catholic Church fought back, founding in 1609 the Catholic League, led by Maximilian I of Bavaria (1573–1651), in response to the Protestant Union set up in 1608 under the leadership of the Palatinate. In 1618 the Thirty Years War began, creating devastation and poverty as well as bloodthirsty massacres, to be ended only by the Peace of Westphalia in 1648. Now the emperor's position was seriously weakened, his country divided into some 300 virtually independent states and cities, each with a seat in the Reichstag. Realising that the emperor could no longer defend Germany, in 1658 Johann Philip von Schörnborn, Elector of Mainz, managed to persuade both Catholic and Protestant princes to join the Rheinbund (League of the Rhine), pledged to defend each other's territories, to uphold the peace of Westphalia, and to avoid entanglement in foreign wars.

Brandenburg-Prussia now began its rise to power under the Great Elector (1640–88), whose son and successor, Elector Frederick III of Brandenburg (1688–1713), managed to win the emperor's consent to crowning himself King Frederick I of Prussia at Königsberg in 1701. (The emperor needed his support in the forthcoming War of the Spanish Succession.)

Germany increasingly came under the influence of France, partly by conquest, for Louis XIV went so far as to invade the Palatinate (unsuccessfully) on the grounds that it was part of the inheritance of his sister-in-law. In spite of the Sun King's territorial ambitions, German princes, admiring the absolutism of the French court, began to match Louis's aggressiveness. Prussia in particular under Frederick I (king 1701–13) gained part of Pomerania from Sweden, made a temporary alliance with the emperor under Frederick William I (1713–40) to persue her claims to Jülich and Berg on the lower Rhine, and under Frederick the Great (1740–86) obtained Silesia by force from Austria in 1742. As the Comte de Mirabeau observed, war seemed to be Prussia's national industry. Frederick successfully defended his acquisition of Silesia and his own kingdom in the Seven Years War of 1756–63—a war in which he took on Austria, Russia, Saxony, France and Sweden, with Britain and Hanover as his only allies. In the meantime Sweden had been forced to cede Bremen and Verden to Hanover.

Napoleon, as heir to the French Revolution, brought the empire to an end after Prussia and Austria had disastrously attempted to intervene in the affairs of Revolutionary France. By the Peace of Basel (1795) Prussia was forced to promise neutrality and lost the left bank of the Rhine to France. In 1806 the German states neighbouring on France united under Napoleon's protection in the Confederation of the Rhine, the year in which Franz II (ruled 1792–1806) ceased to be Holy Roman Emperor. Napoleon's brother, Jérome, became King of Westphalia. The French emperor proved unstoppable, annihilating the Prussian armies at Jena and Auerstädt on 14 October 1806 and occupying Berlin itself on 27 October. Prussia lost half her territories.

Republicanism or at least new constitutional ideas spread even to Prussia, where the Jews were emancipated and liberal trade laws introduced. Bavaria, Baden, Württemberg and Hesse-Darmstadt all drew up liberal constitutions, allowing propertied voters to elect new assemblies. The Prussians set about transforming a state that was in danger of becoming moribund into a popular monarchy, abolishing serfdom, giving the cities a measure of self-government, embracing the reformist ideals of statesmen-philosophers such as Karl von Stein (1757–1831) and promoting military men of the genius of August Neithardy von Gneisenau (1730–1831) and Garhard von Scharnhorst (1755–1813).

After Napoleon's defeat German rulers turned absolutist again; Liberalism was defeated. The Congress of Vienna promoted the German Confederation, an alliance of 35 princely states and four free cities whose assembly as Frankfurt-am-Main remained dominated by Prussia and Austria. Liberal ideals suffered a further setback as fearful rulers reacted to the July 1830 insurrection against the Bourbons in France.

In 1834, in the first moves towards a united Germany, the German Customs Union (excluding Austria) was established. The railways brought increasing unity. The revolutions of 1848 and 1849 affected every German state, and at Frankfurt an Austrian archduke was appointed administrator of the empire and a national assembly attempted to set up a constitutional monarchy.

The revolutions failed, and Germany restored most of its older institutions. The Frankfurt parliament was dissolved, the German Confederation re-established. In Prussia the vacillating Frederick William IV (1840–61) finally opted for political reaction. Yet paradoxically, the years of political stagnation which followed coincided with a surge towards a new prosperity, as Germany was transformed from a predominantly rural to an industrial economy.

Prussian economic strength continued to increase, translated into political power by Otto von Bismarck (1815–96) who became its prime minister in 1862. In 1864 he gained Schleswig-Holstein as a result of the Danish war, and defeated Austria in 1866 in a war lasting seven weeks. Prussia annexed Nassau, Hesse-Kassel, Hanover, Frankfurt-am-Main and SchleswigHolstein. The North German Federation, with Bismarck as its Chancellor, replaced the old German Confederation.

Next Bismarck led Prussia to victory over the French in 1870–71. The southern states were persuaded to join the North German Federation as one Reich, and on 18 January 1871 at Versailles Wilhelm I of Prussia (1861–88) was proclaimed German emperor. For the next 19 years Bismarck was Imperial Chancellor—the enemy alike of Liberalism, the political aspirations of the workers and social Catholicism.

Wilhelm II (1888–1918) dismissed Bismarck in 1890, but continued to block the hopes of social democracy in his empire. Between 1898 and 1909 the German navy achieved virtual parity with that of the British, to the latter's great concern. International tension increased. In 1914 the assassination of the Archduke Franz Ferdinand of Austria brought Austria and Germany into war against Britain, France, Russia and (eventually) the USA. Although the emperor wished to wage war only on one front, the German officer corps forced him to fight on two. The allies won the war and the rulers of Germany and Austria lost their thrones.

The German Social Democrats, led by Friedrich Ebert, made common cause with Hindenburg, chief of the general staff, in order to prevent an extreme left-wing take-over (incidentally conniving at the murders of the Spartacist leaders Karl Liebknecht and Rosa Luxemburg). For the next 14 years Germany was a republic, ruled from Weimar with a parliament including Social Democrats and the Catholic centre party.

Reparations imposed by the Peace of Versailles after World War I made its economic life precarious. Germany had lost all her colonies, AlsaceLorraine (ceded to France), North Schleswig (ceded to Denmark), upper Silesia, most of Posen, and other parts including West Prussia, EupenMalmedy and Memel. The Saar was under the control of the League of Nations, its coalfields run by the French. The coming years were ones of repeated financial and political instability, and the Weimar Republic finally collapsed as a result of the major economic crises which began in 1929.

By 1932 Adolf Hitler's anti-Semitic National Socialist Party was the strongest in the Reichstag, with 230 seats. Hitler became Chancellor of Germany on 30 January 1933. When the Reichstag building was burned down on 27 February, his government assumed emergency powers, claiming that the fire was part of a Communist plot. Eighty one Communist deputies were either arrested or otherwise excluded from voting so as to enable the Reichstag to pass an enabling act allowing the government to issue legal decrees without consultation. The following year the death of President Hindenburg enabled Hitler to assume the office of President as well as Chancellor.

Soon the trades unions and all rival political parties were suppressed by the National Socialists. The dictatorship of Adolf Hitler saw Germany regain the Saar and the Rhineland as well as march into Austria, the Sudetenland and eventually the whole of Czechoslovakia. It witnessed the virtual extermination of Germany's Jews, as well as other ethnic minorities. On 1 September 1939 Hitler launched an attack on Poland which precipitated World War II. Poland, Denmark, Norway, Holland, Belgium, France, Yugoslavia and Greece were all defeated by Hitler's forces. German troops reached almost as far as Moscow and nearly conquered North Africa. Hitler survived an assassination attempt by German officers, churchmen and politicians on 20 July 1944, and—the war lost—committed suicide on 30 April 1945.

The victorious powers—Britain, the USSR, France and the USA—set up military governors in four German zones. Germany was demilitarised. New political parties were created. At the Potsdam Conference of July and

August 1945, Britain and America accepted the Russian annexation of the northern part of east Prussia. The territories east of the Oder-Neisse line were ceded to Poland.

Increasingly, the Western powers and the Soviet Union grew at odds. In 1948 Russia attempted to prevent all communications between Berlin (in the Russian sector of Germany) and the West, an attempt thwarted by a massive Western air lift. In the same year the Western powers unilaterally set up a democratic West German state with virtually full powers of self-government, of which Konrad Adenauer (1876–1967), former Oberbürgermeister of Cologne, was elected President. Adenauer was elected Chancellor of the Federal German Republic (later known as West Germany) the following year, though the three Western powers ceded full sovereignty to the republic only six years later.

In response, the Russians set up the German Democratic Republic (DDR), known as East Germany. On 17 June 1953 a workers' uprising against this state was put down by Soviet troops. In 1961, after three and a half million refugees had fled from the East to the West, the Russian authorities blocked this escape route by building the Berlin Wall.

In 1954 West Germany became a member of the North Atlantic Treaty Organisation (NATO). The 'occupation' troops at last became troops of friendly powers, stationed by treaty on the soil of a sovereign republic. Three years later the people of Saarland, still under French control, voted overwhelmingly to become a *Land* of West Germany. In the same year the Federal Republic became a founder member of the European Economic Community.

West Germany was experiencing an 'economic miracle', which included full employment. Adenauer was succeeded by Ludwig Erhard (Chancellor 1963–66), who resigned when the 'economic miracle' seemed to be failing in the 1960s. His successor, Kurt George Kiesinger, lasted barely three years (1966–69), to be succeeded as Chancellor by the Social Democrat Willy Brandt, former Oberbürgermeister of West Berlin. Brandt had persuaded the Social Democrats to drop their opposition to conscription and the possible arming of Germany with nuclear weapons. Once in power he inaugurated the controversial 'Ostpolitik'—a policy of cautious rapprochement with the East. Relationships between the two Germanies eased considerably. In 1970 the FDR finally accepted that Poland now possessed the territories east of the Oder-Neisse line. A treaty of 21 December 1971 committed the two republics, West and East Germany, to developing friendly relations.

When Brandt resigned in 1974 (because one of his close colleagues was revealed as an East German spy), he was succeeded by Helmust Schmidt of his own party, who led a coalition with the Free Democratic Party. Schmidt fell from power in 1982, to be replaced by the leader of the Christian Democrats, Helmut Kohl.

Kolh was to preside as Chancellor over the re-unification of Germany, as Soviet Russia proved increasingly unwilling to maintain its power base west of its own borders. On 2 May 1989 Hungary decided to dismantle the iron curtain between herself and Austria. When Hungary opened her frontiers on 11 September, over 10,000 East Germans took the opportunity to cross to the West by way of Austria and Hungary. Opposition parties in the DDR were increasingly vocal, and on 25 September some 6000 people demonstrated at Leipzig in favour of reform. When on the last day of that month the West German foreign minister Hans-Dietrich Genscher announced that

German refugees from the East were welcome to cross into the Federal Republic overnight, around 5500 chose to do so.

By 18 October the East German leader Erich Honecker had been forced to resign. The following month the Berlin Wall was demolished and all East-West frontiers thrown open. Reunion was now only a matter of time but took almost exactly a year to achieve formally. On 24 September 1990 East Germany quitted the Warsaw Pact. On 1 October the allied powers suspended their rights over Germany, including over Berlin. A day later Lufthansa was authorised to begin its first flights over Germany since the Third Reich, and in October Germany was reunited.

The first free elections throughout the whole of Germany since 1932 began on 2 December, four out of the five new *Länder* in the former East Germany having already produced majorities in favour of Kohl as Chancellor. Re-united Germany then settled down to counting the cost of these momentous events which had brought an economically backward East into the embrace of the prosperous West. In the first year after the breach in the Iron Curtain over 720,000 East Germans and *Aussiedler* (that is, Germans from other parts of the former Soviet bloc) had flooded into the West. In 1991 they continued to arrive at over 2000 a day. The overall cost of reunion to the West Germans was estimated at more than 10 billion DM annually (with a bonus that many of the immigrants were young workers, supplying a new life-blood to the aging population that they had joined). Income taxes rose by 7.5 per cent, petrol taxes by 35 per cent and cigarettes by 5 per cent. For many Germans euphoria at re-unification turned to disillusion.

# Art and Architecture

The medieval emperors and princes of Germany, along with the princes of the church, were the earliest patrons of art. Since Germany had no single capital until 1870, the emperors (Carolingians, 768–918; Ottonians, 919–1024; Salians, 1024–1125) were peripatetic. They needed more than one city, with all the customary appurtenances—monasteries, palaces, cathedrals—where they could periodically set up court as they governed their realms. Monasteries, obliged to give hospitality to the emperor and his train, were rewarded with new endowments and in turn established new foundations. Around these grew up the great cities and towns of the empire.

## The Carolingian Revival

The **Carolingian revival** in architecture takes its name and took its impetus from the Emperor Charlemagne (742–814) and after him from the enthusiastic patronage of Emperor Charles II the Bald (823–77). Almost invariably the cities of their empire derived initially from religious colonies, usually constituted according to the rule of St Benedict and in consequence built along the lines laid down by the Benedictines—a church and cloister, cells, a refectory, a chapter house, guest house and an infirmary. A remarkable survival from this period is the so-called *Torhalle* (774–84) at Lorsch, the ceremonial monastery gate through which Charlemagne and his train were received. The churches were often specially built with two chancels, one at the west end (the *Westwerk*) reserved for the Imperial retinue.

Although German museums and ecclesiastical treasures have preserved ravishing examples of Carolingian illumination, much Carolingian architecture in Germany was subsequently rebuilt and substantially altered. The finest of what remains is the court (or palatine) chapel of Charlemagne's favourite city, Aachen, which was consecrated in 805. Here the emperor chose to be buried.

In spite of later additions and restorations, this remains the best preserved example of Carolingian architecture in the country. The *Westwerk* of the former abbey of Corvey in Westphalia, built 873–85, is the second most impressive piece of Carolingian architecture in Germany, its upper sanctuary (known as the *Johanneschor*) spreading over a three-aisled colonnaded entrance hall. Here once stood another Imperial throne.

By no means all Carolingian churches were so imposing. Most were simple, quite small hall churches, of which the 9C chapel of St Sylvester at Goldbach (in Switzerland) on the Bodensee is one of the few surviving examples. In Germany, excavations after World War II revealed that St Willibord, Echternach, and both SS. Petrus and Paulus and the Salvator-kirche were once churches of this type.

At Coplogne and Fulda, as well as Paderborn, superb abbey churches were built at the beginning of the 9C, to be embellished by the masterpieces of goldsmiths and workers in bronze (as witness the bronze doors and grilles of the palatine chapel at Aachen) and also by wall-paintings. Many of the latter have disappeared, though examples survived in the crypt of St Maximin, Trier (now transferred to the Landemuseum), in St Andreas, Fulda, and in the *Torhalle* at Lorsch. This last displays a remarkable ability to employ many-coloured marble slabs, delicate columns and an architrave that give the illusion of opening to the sky. The cult of relics meant that Romanesque shrines (reliquaries) abound from this era. The great medieval abbeys of Germany were not only seats of piety and learning but also workshops for brilliant metalworkers, enamelists and manuscript illuminators.

## The Ottonian Period

Throughout the **Ottonian period** (mid 10C to mid 11C) German art absorbed the powerful influence of Byzantine and Roman originals, both influences transmitted by way of Italy. The first Imperial cathedral was founded at Magdeburg in 955. Mainz cathedral was begun in 975 and Worms cathedral a decade or so later. Four great Ottonian churches retain enough of their original form to exemplify this style of architecture: St Pantaleon, Cologne, and St Cyriakus in Gernrode, both built in the second half of the 10C, the collegiate church of Essen which dates from 971 to 1011, and St Michael, Hildesheim, begun by Bishop Bernward and built between 1010 and 1033.

In all of them strict geometrical forms predominate. Three-aisled naves bisect symmetrical transepts. Three apses embellish the east end, and the choir rises over a crypt. The cubic capitals of the columns are an Ottonian innovation. And Bishop Bernward's bronze door (1015) for St Michael offers the first German sculptured cycle, a series of panels representing scenes from Genesis to the life of Jesus, patterned on models from Carolingian illustrated manuscripts. Comparable are the superb mid 11C wooden doors of St Maria im Kapitol, Cologne. Only three other great doors survive from this period, one in Russia, one in Poland, the third at Augsburg cathedral. St Michael, Hildesheim, is also enriched with an Eastern column, sculpted between 1015 and 1022; and the crucifix of the Catholic parish church at Ringelsheim was probably created a full decade earlier. Lastly, the oldest sculpted Madonna in Germany dates from the late 10C and is housed in the treasury of Essen cathedral.

Ottonian artists included outstanding gold and silversmiths, as well as ivory carvers. They produced the late 10C Gero cross of Cologne and the Gerresheim crucifix. At Reichenau there was a school of manuscript illustrators, patronised by the emperors, and almost matched in skill by those of Regensburg. Working from c 990 from patterns derived from Anglo-Saxon, Greek and Carolingian manuscripts, Kerald and Heribert, two monks at the island monastery of Reichenau, wrote and illustrated a Codex for Bishop Egdbert of Trier (now Codex Egberti, no. 24, in the Stadtbibliothek, Trier) whose 50 miniatures constitute the first complete sequence in German art of the life of Jesus. Among other masterpieces illuminated at Reichenau are the late 10C Codex of the Ottos in Aachen cathedral and the Gero Codex of the same era in the Landesbibliothek of Darmstadt. The tradition was continued in the next century in the Gospel Book of Otto III (now in the Staatsbibliothek, Munich) and in Henry II's Book of Pericope (in the Staatsbibliothek, Bamberg). In the Staatsbibliothek at Munich are also displayed two treasures of Regensburg illumination: Henry II's Gospel Book and his exquisite Sacramentry. As for stained glass, the sole survivor of 10C work is an archaic head of a saint, fragments of which were excavated at Lorsch Abbey in the 1930s and are now displayed in the Hessesches Landemuseum, Darmstadt.

## The Romanesque Period

At the beginning of the 11C no fewer than 85 German monasteries were producing works of art renowned throughout Europe and beyond (the stylistic connection with Byzantium symbolised by Theophano, the Byzantine wife of Otto II). Trier was a major centre of enamel work, again inspired by Byzantine originals. In the cathedral treasury is preserved a reliquary of St Andre from the end of the 10C; in the Residenz, Munich, are displayed the early 11C Gisela cross and the portable altar of Henry II; Essen Cathedral (whose west end and crypt date back to the Salian era) houses two Mithilde crosses, one created in the 970s, the second in the first decade of the 10C; Aachen cathedral boasts the Lothar cross (c 980); and in Hildesheim cathedral is the early 11C Bernward cross. As for wall-paintings, one must either seek out the remarkably preserved frescoes in St George at Reichenau in Switzerland, illustrating Jesus's miracles, or else rest content with the fragmentary remains at Fulda.

Among the glories of **Salian art** in Germany are the magnificent wooden doors (c 1040–60) of St Maria im Kapitol, Cologne, and the equally superb bronze doors (c 1080) of Augsburg cathedral. At Goslar, in spite of later alterations, the *Kaiserpfalz* or Imperial Palace of Heinrich II still boasts its early 12C chapel and the largest imperial hall in Germany.

It is sad that the Arnstein group in the Städelsches Kunstinstitut, Frankfurt-am-Main, represents the only major stained glass in Germany to have survived from the Romanesque period, for its quality is high and it also contains the sole extant Romanesque window (1170/80) signed by its artist. Master Gerlachus even included a self-portrait in one of the windows. (Another self-portrait, sculpted some ten years later, is that of the goldsmith Fridericus, on the shrine of St Maurinus in St Pantaleon, Cologne.) Once five such windows lit the choir of the abbey at Arnstein which had been founded in 1139. The surviving panels enable us to reconstruct a subtle parallelism between Old and New Testament scenes, grouped around a Tree of Jesse.

From the mid 11C to the 13C Romanesque artists continued to produce masterpieces of the quality of the portable altar of Paderborn (now in the cathedral treasury), created by Roger of Helmarshausen c 1100. Another masterpiece attributed to Roger is a portable altar from the monastery of Abdinghof, now in the Franciscan church at Paderborn. Nicholas of Verdun (fl. mid 12C–mid 13C) made the •shrine of the Magi for Cologne cathedral c 1200. In 1181 Nicholas also created the sinuous Klosterneuburg altar. Fine works of monumental sculpture, in particular the tomb of Henry the Lion (c 1240) in Brunswick cathedral, also belong to this period.

Henry the Lion's tomb comes at the end of a stunning outburst of sculptural creativity, still glimpsed for instance in the 'golden portal' of Freiburg (c 1220), in a mid 12C pulpit at Alpirsbach and in the early 13C crucifixion group now housed in the Schnütgenmuseum, Cologne. In this period, just as earlier the self-esteem of the emperor and his retinue had insisted on installing a *Westwerk* in great churches, so now the nobility built two-storeyed churches (such as that founded in 1151 at Schwarz-Rheindorf near Bonn-Beuel by Conrad III's chancellor Arnold or Wied) so as to worship on a higher physical plane than that of their underlings.

In this era stained glass makes its first appearance still in situ in Germany, in the •prophet panes created for Augsburg cathedral in the 1130s (or possibly even earlier). Over 2m high, these remarkable figures once numbered 22 in all. Five remain (that of Moses is a 16C copy), their colourful elements and shading, their monumental design bespeaking a tradition of craftsmanship that survives only here. Fresco painting, too, was blossoming remarkably, as can be seen especially in St Gereon Cologne and St Maria zur Hohe, Soest, as well as in the outstanding series in Arnold of Wied's church at Schwarz-Rheindorf.

The same patterns as Master Gerlachus created for his Arnstein windows have been discerned in the much decayed stained glass in St Patroclus, Soest, and in the magical early 13C windows of St Kunibert, Cologne— again depicting a Tree of Jesse, along with the lives of SS. Kunibert and Clemens as well as in a lower storey a series of female saints. The glass of St Kunibert presaged a blossoming of Gothic glass in mid 13C Germany, following patterns developed at Strasbourg (which was then part of Germany). The glass of St Elisabeth, Marburg, is a major example of a uniquely German style, the scalloped or *Zackenstil*, characterised by agitated broken folds in the painted clothing and vigorously decorated bands surrounding the figures in the glass. The late 13C Bible window in the choir of St Vitus, Münchengladbach, is an impressive example of the development of this style.

A Psalter of Landgrave Hermann of Thuringia, on display in the Landes-bibliothek of Stuttgart, reveals the skills of Saxon illuminators of the early 12C. At Bendiktbeuren in Bavaria monastic illuminators in the 1220s illustrated the Carmina Burana. Fifty years earlier Abess Herrade von Landsberg (fl. c 1170) had written and illuminated her *Garden of Delights* (or *Hortus Deliciarum*). The original was destroyed when the Prussians bombed Strasbourg in 1807, but among the surviving copies are the frescoes of the convent chapel of the Cross on Mont Sainte-Odile, Alsace. Contemporary with this work is the illuminated Prayer Book of St Hildegard von Bingen, now in the Staatsbibliothek, Munich.

The Salian emperors lie in Speyer cathedral, founded in the first half of the 11C. The pattern of its vaults (c 1180) marks a new era of architectural innovation, their bays flanking a single central nave—a pattern soon to be followed in the cathedrals of Worms and Mainz. The triple-apsed St Maria im Kapitol, Cologne, was another much admired prototype (Cologne itself building two other churches, St Aposteln and Gross St Martin, according to this pattern, though the inventiveness of Cologne's Romanesque architects made all three churches individual masterpieces).

At the end of the 12C French sculptors began to influence Germans, the peak of their late-Romanesque achievement being the decorations of Bamberg cathedral, the work of masons from Rheims, c 1230. Surviving Romanesque wall-paintings include those in St Maria in Lyskirche, Cologne (which miraculously escaped destruction during World War II) and those in the cathedral and Marienkirche, Soest.

The 13C witnessed a slow welcome to French Gothic architecture. The church of Our Lady, Trier (finished in 1243) was modelled partly on the choir of Rheims cathedral (completed in 1235) and partly on the choir of St Yved, Braisne; the cathedral of Limburg an der Lahn is recognisably based on the cathedral of Laon in France and boasts an apse and ambulatory borrowed from other French sources; at Marburg between 1235 and 1283 the masons of the church of St Elisabeth, were inspired by their French counterparts to build a masterpiece of German high Gothic.

By the mid 13C French Gothic had at last gained acceptance through most regions of Germany, exemplified above all in Cologne's new cathedral (which was begun in 1248, its choir consecrated in 1322, the whole loosely modelled on Amiens cathedral) as well as in the cathedrals at Regensburg and Freiburg-im-Breisgau. German Gothic, however, never lost its own monumental character, as can be seen for instance at Bamberg, where the sculptor of the Visitation on the cathedral was clearly influenced by the Visitation on the cathedral of Rheims though he retained the patterned folds favoured by his Romanesque predecessors. Similarly the Cistercians, Franciscans and Dominicans continued to build spare basilicas that scarcely acknowledged the rich decoration of French Gothic. Kloster Ebrach is a fine Cistercian example of the persistence of the Romanesque style in architecture. When the Dominicans began to build their earliest churches, for example at Regensburg in 1245, the spare and powerful basilicas strangely contrasted with the exuberant sprouting of the Gothic in the other city churches and cathedrals. Even in these churches, only as the 13C reached its end did the style of German Gothic sculpture (on, for example, the main doorway of the cathedral of Freiburg im Breisgau) finally give way to the gracefulness of French Gothic.

The late 13C and early 14C saw no diminution of the vigour of German stained glass, especially in Schwabia, where the windows in the church of St Dionysius, Esslingen (1290–1310), are both formal and extremely brightly coloured. In the year of their completion, work began installing stained glass in the sacristy of St Gereon, Cologne, displaying delicate grisaille panels flanking figures of saints. Figures of this kind were painted with increasing realism as the 14C progressed, the style reaching its artistic apogee in Ulm Cathedral and in the ˙church of St Jakob, Rothenburg ob der Tauber.

As a new urban bourgeoisie developed in the 14C, these secular patrons began to build impressive town halls as well as fine hall churches. Münster offers the examples both of its town hall (1355) and its cathedral (1225–65). Minden was the first city to build a cathedral (1267 onwards) whose roof covered a nave and aisles which are of precisely the same height. ˙St. Maria zur Wiese, Soest (begun 1343), a square church virtually as wide as it is high, set the pattern for other Westphalian hall churches. Meanwhile towns such as Goslar, Hildesheim and Brunswick built proud half-timbered municipal halls.

In south Germany the Parler dynasty contributed their own decisive Gothic. Heinrich Parler (fl. mid 14C), arrived in Schwäbisch-Gmund from Cologne in 1351 and built there the church of Heiligenkreuz, the prototype for all other south German hall churches. On the north gate of the choir he or one of his pupils carved representations of the prophets and the Wise and Foolish Virgins whose influence can be seen in the near contemporary Madonna and apostles sculpted on the south doorway of Augsburg cathedral. Landshut benefited from the genius of the Austrian Hans von Burghausen (c 1360–1432), generally known as Hans Stethaimer, who built there two hall churches, St Martin, begun in the early 1390s, and the church of the Holy Ghost begun 15 years later. His son carved a study of the architect's head in 1432 for St Martin, Landshut. Straubing owes to Hans Stethaimer its lovely Carmelite church, begun in the late 1380s.

In north Germany (particularly Lübeck and Schleswig) brick Gothic buildings became increasingly fashionable, after the achievement of the Marienkirche, Lübeck, Schleswig cathedral was rebuilt as a Gothic hall church in the mid 15C. While Lübeck benefited from the Gothic genius of the sculptor Johannes Junge (fl. 1406–28), Ulm cathedral (finished 1419) profited from the late-Gothic realism of the sculptor Hans Multscher (c 1400–67). Multscher, who was born in the Allgäu, had travelled widely, bringing to Ulm Dutch and Burgundian influences, and the Man of Sorrows he carved for the cathedral portal has an unsurpassed elegance. To adorn the east side of Ulm hall he carved portraits of Charlemagne and the rulers of Poland and Bohemia. A painter as well as a sculptor, his finest work is probably the altarpiece of the Marienkirche in Dortmund.

In Bavaria the Frauenkirche at Munich (1468–88), the church of St George, Dinkelsbühl, and the choir of St Laurence, Nuremburg, all built in the second half of the 15C, represent a style of late-Gothic hall church that, in spite of its affinities with French Gothic, remains uniquely German. Two important and rare survivals of early 15C Nuremberg sculpture are the Madonna in Glory inside the church of St Sebald and the clay Apostle in the Germanisches Museum, matched in date and importance by the carvings on the portals of the Marienkapelle, Würzburg, and the bishops' tombs inside it.

At this time painting was undergoing a renaissance, with Konrad von Soest (fl. 1402–04) in Westphalia and above all Stephan Lochner (fl. 1442–died 1451) in Cologne. Lochner's superb work is matched by such masters as Martin Schongauer (c 1430–91) of Augsburg (who came from Colmar in Alsace), Hans Holbein the Elder (1460/65–1524), Matthias Grünewald (1470/80–c 1530) and the Lübeck painter and woodcarver Bernt Notke (1430/40–1509). Two other distinguished artists whose talents were to be eclipsed by the genius of Albrecht Dürer (1471–1528) are Konrad von Soest's Dutch contemporary Master Francke (fl. 1st half 15C), who painted the English Pilgrimage Altar in the Johanneskirche, Hamburg, as well as a rich Adoration of the Magi, c 1420, now in the city's Kunsthalle, and Konrad Witz (c 1400–1445/6), born in Rottweil but destined to spend his entire career in Basle and Geneva.

In the 15C we being to learn the names of many German stained glass masters, for their influence throughout Europe now became dominant. Glaziers co-operated creatively with engravers and painters. At Ulm the Acker dynasty of glaziers, established by Jakob Acker c 1430, co-operated with the cartoonist Lukas Moser (fl. 1st half 15C) in producing impressive glass for the Besserer chapel in the cathedral. An Alsatian glazier named Peter Hemmel (1420/25–c 1505) was commissioned to produce windows for the church of St Lorenz, Nuremberg, St Georg, Tübingen, the Frauen-kirche, Munich, and the cathedral at Freiburg im Breisgau. Again the glazier worked hand in glove with engravers. St Lorenz, Nuremberg, is also embellished with some of the most realistic glass produced anywhere in the late 15C, in the massive window on the south side of the choir, a gift of the Rieter family in 1476.

## The Renaissance Period

This collaboration between glazier and artists developed just in time to welcome the supreme genius of Hans Holbein the Elder, Hans Baldung Grien (c 1480–1545) and above all Albrecht Dürer (1471–1528) at the beginning of the 16C. With Dürer the Renaissance began to influence stained glass in Germany. He drew the cartoon for glazing the Schmidt-mayer chapel in St Lorenz, Nuremberg, and Hans Baldung Grien drew those for the choir of the cathedral of Freiburg im Breisgau, glass made in the workshop of Peter Hemmel.

Late Gothic carving also produced supreme masters: Jörg Syrlin (c 1425–91), who carved the entrancing choir stalls of Ulm cathedral, and his son Jörg the Younger (c 1455–1521); Erasmus Grasser (c 1450–1518), who was also a hydraulic engineer and whose celebrated morris dancers, created between 1469 and 1479 for the ballroom of the old town hall of Munich, now adorn the city's Stadtmuseum; Hans Leinberger (fl. 1516–30) of Land-shut, whose masterpiece is the emotionally charged high altar of the collegiate church of Moosburg; Veit Stoss (c 1447–1533), a painter and engraver as well as a sculptor, who was branded on both cheeks for misappropriating money at Nuremberg and has left us the red marble tomb of King Casimir IV in the cathedral there, as well as a massive altarpiece in the church of St Maria; Adam Krafft (c 1455/60–1509), another Nuremberg master who for the cathedral matched an exquisite golden tabernacle in massive stone; the Vischer dynasty, Peter the Elder (c 1460–1529) and Peter the Younger (1487–1528), from whose workshop came the bronze shrine over the sarcophagus of St Sebaldus in Nuremberg; Hans Backhofen (1470–c 1519), the virtuoso of Mainz; Hans Brüggemann (c 1480–1540), who between 1514 and 1521 created a spectacular reredos which is now in Schleswig cathedral; and supremely Tilman Rie-menschneider (c 1460–1531) of Würzburg, the only one of these exceed-ingly gifted men whose skills exceeded even those of Veit Stoss.

The work of these artists looked beyond the boundaries of Germany, and many of them had absorbed the Burgundian-Netherlandish delicacy dis-played in the works of Nicolas Gerhaert of Leyden, (fl. 1462–72) who lived and worked at Trier and at Passau. He died in Vienna. German sculptors also travelled widely. The Czech Anton Pilgram (1450–c 1515), for instance, who in 1487 carved the tabernacle of St Kilian, Heilbronn, worked from 1511 to 1515 as architect at the cathedral of St Stephen, Vienna. Although Veit Stoss is best known for his masterpieces in Nuremberg, he produced a fine altar for Bamberg cathedral (1520–23) and a sensational altar for St Mary's church, Cracow. Riemenschneider moved to Würzburg only after studying in Schwabia and the upper Rhine, and for Bamberg cathedral he created the tomb of Henry II and his queen Kuningunde.

Würzburg is the seat of the Marienburg Schloss, built in the 13C for the prince bishops on the site of a former Celtic hill fort and around Germany's oldest round church (706), enlarged by the Scherenberg family, 1466–95, and again in the early 17C. The German nobility, spiritual and lay, built palaces and Schlösser not simply as dwellings but also to consolidate their power. In 1325 Ludwig the Barbarian built one on an island in the Rhine near Kaub. Many, if not most of these buildings were romantically restored in the 19C. Exceptions are the Schloss at Marburg (13C–16C), Schloss Marksburg (15C and 16C) on the Rhine and Burg Eltz (early 13C–early 16C) on the Mosel which remain today much as when they were built. Burg Eltz is an example of a castle owned by several branches of the same family, each having a separate entrance from the central courtyard.

Although many German secular lords were also princes of the church, secular as well as ecclesiastical architecture now began to flourish in the 16C, and the Augsburg of the Fuggers survives today as a particularly fine example of the civic pride of a rich commercial city. Much other halftimbered architecture throughout the rest of Germany disappeared during World War II, but surviving or restored town halls—especially at Bremen (1405–09), with a Renaissance façade of 1612), Lübeck (1230, decorated 1434, with a loggia of 1570), Marburg (1512–27), Schweinfurt (1572), Rothenburg ob der Tauber (c 1250, sumptuously enlarged 1578 and 1681), Heilbronn (1579–82), Darmstadt (1599), Paderborn (1613–20) and Nuremberg (1616–22)—testify to the continuing wealth of the bourgeoisie.

If the 1939–45 war destroyed for ever thousands of the terraced houses of merchants and artisans which once graced the town and cities of Germany, we can still see in these town halls the ground-level loggias where business was conducted, surmounted by the upper ceremonial rooms. Two outstanding examples are the town halls of Münster and Brunswick. In the former, Gothic gables, ornamented with tracery, rise above the powerful scarcely adorned arches of the loggia. At Brunswick a gable-ended, L-shaped building begun in the late 13C was given a two-storeyed loggia on one side in 1393, matched by a second along the other side in 1447.

The spirit of the Renaissance had already been seen at Augsburg in architecture in the Fugger funeral chapel (in the church of St Anna, 1509–18) and in painting when Hans Burgkmair the Elder (1473–1531) between 1501 and 1504 depicted three Roman basilicas (to be seen today there in the Gemäldegalerie). The building of the Fugger chapel was of extraordinary importance. Dürer sketched for it. Peter Vischer the Elder cast its bronze screen. In the early 16C Holbein the Younger, the sons of Peter Fischer, and Matthias Grünewald (c 1475–1528) brought into Germany the insights and impetus of the Renaissance, a tradition developed by Dürer's pupil Hans Baldung-Grien and by the Cranach family, Lucas the Elder (1472–1553) and Lucas the Younger (1515–86).

These artists often effortlessly absorbed non-German influences. Albrecht Altdorfer (1480–1538), for instance, knew the works of the Paduan Andrea Mantegna, and like Lucas Cranach the Elder had spent time among the humanists of Vienna. Germans were also ready to patronise foreign masters, such as the Dutchman Cornelis Floris (1514–75), who designed the tomb of King Frederick I of Denmark in Schleswig cathedral. Similarly, in the early 16C Duke Ludwig X of Landshut employed Mantuan masons to model his new Residenz on their own Palazzo del Te. The Italian influence spread, seen at its most exuberant in the mid 16C Ottoheinrichsbau of Heidelberg Schloss. Munich architects were now looking for inspiration towards Rome and under its influence built the antiquarium (1569–71) and the church of St Michael (1582–07). Finally German Renaissance architecture reached its apogee in Elias Holl's (1573–1646) masterpiece, Augsburg town hall (finished 1620).

Although some artists managed to continue creating fine work during the Thirty Years War—notably the Swiss brothers Michael (late 16C–mid 17C) and Martin Zürn (fl. 1626–65) at Wasserburg, and Georg Petel (c 1590–1633/4), who lived in Augsburg from 1625 till his death and sculpted a fine Man of Sorrows for the cathedral—the savagery of this conflict resulted in a dearth of German artistic creativity. The Hamelin-born Justus Glesker (c 1616/20–81), having studied in Italy and the Netherlands, settled in Frankfurt-am-Main in 1648, the year the war ended. It is perhaps symptomatic of the devastation of the German economy over the previous three decades that he has left only one known work, a crucifixion group, framed in gold, in Bamberg cathedral.

## Baroque and Rococo

This creative dearth was followed by the extraordinary achievement of German Baroque and Rococo. The enthusiastic and discriminating patronage of two electors in particular, Ernst Augustus the Strong of Saxony (ruled 1679–98) and Maximilian II Emmanuel of Bavaria (ruled 1679–1736) made their respective regions centres of fertile artistic innovation. Both men commissioned not only German architects but also Italians. Ernst August and his successors employed Venetians as well as the German architect Matthäus Daniel Pöppelmann (1662–1736) who had studied in Rome and was also much influenced by the Austrian master Johann Lukas von Hildebrandt (1668–1745).

Italian and to a lesser extent French influences for a time had brought into Germany a pattern of church architecture which exploited domes and two-towered façades, often consciously imitating Roman buildings. Two fine examples are the Theatinerkirche (1663–88) in Munich and the cathedral at Fulda (1704–12), the one partly modelled on Sant' Andrea in Valle, the other on St Peter's, Rome. Soon these influences were overwhelmed by Austrian and Bohemian ones, and German Rococo moved towards its luxurious flowering.

In Bavaria, similarly inspired by such Austrians as Johann Bernhard Fischer von Erlach (1656–1742) and Johann Lukas von Hildebrandt, and by Italians such as Enrico Zuccalli (c 1642–1724) and Agostino Barelli (1627–79), architects of the calibre of the Dientzenhofer dynasty—Georg, (d 1689); Johann (c 1665–1726); Kilian Ignaz (1689–1751) and Josef Effner (1687–1745)—built the cathedral of Fulda (Josef Dientzenhofer, 1704–12), the church of Ettal (Zuccalli, 1710), the Nymphenburg Palace, Munich (Barolli and J. Effner, 1633 and 1728). Two brothers, Cosmas Damian (1686–1739) and Egid Quirin Asam (1692–1750), perfected an unsurpassed blend of architecture, stucco work and painting in their churches (especially St Johann Nepomuk, Munich). Two other brothers, Dominikus (1685–1766) and Johann Baptist Zimmermann (1680–1758), built the remarkable • • • pilgrimage church of Wies (1746–54), the masterpiece of Bavarian religious Baroque. These Baroque architects brilliantly deployed Wessobrunn stucco decoration. At the same time Johann Conrad Schlaun (1694–1773) was introducing the Baroque of South Germany and Rome to Westphalia.

Germany now consisted of over 300 separate principalities, and in consequence this was a period when the princes built palaces consistent with their notions of their proper status: Zuccalli and Barelli, along with the Walloon architect François de Cuvilliés (1695–1768), built Schloss Nymphenburg and Schloss Schleissheim near Munich; Schlaun, Cuvilliés and the Frenchman Robert de Cotte (1656–1753) built Schloss Brühl in 1725 for the archbishop and elector Clemens August. Johann Balthasar Neumann (1687–1753) added a monumental staircase. The masterpiece of south German secular Baroque is the Residenz built by Neumann for the prince-bishops of Würzburg, 1719–44.

The rulers who commissioned such buildings often had a superlative sense of their own importance. When Duke Eberhard Ludwig founded Ludwigsburg in 1709, he commissioned a Schloss and a Schlossgarten huge enough to occupy an entire quarter of the town, a feat matched by the rulers of Stuttgart, Kassel and Bonn. As their town plans tellingly reveal, a new model city (such as Karlsruhe or Mannheim) gave the ruler a unique opportunity to express architecturally how he conceived the proper relationship between himself and his subjects, and indeed the grand ducal Schloss (1720–60) at Mannheim is the largest palace in Germany.

To embellish these residences the richer princes were establishing their own china, tapestry and furniture factories. In the 18C cabinet makers flourished, such as Abraham Roentgen (1711–93) of Neuwied and his son David (1743–1807). The three most important faience and china factories were those at Meissen, Nymphenburg and Berlin. At the same time as fine china adorned the tables of these families, their own portraits adorned their walls. The greatest Italian painter of the 18C, Giovanni Battista Tiepolo (1696–1770), was hired in the 1750s to fresco the vault of the sumptuous staircase designed by Balthasar Neumann for the Würzburg Residenz, and represented there an allegory of heaven and the continents paying homage to the Prince-Bishop of Würzburg in the guise of Maecenas. Courtly portraiture, albeit less flamboyant, was now a common feature of German art. A Parisian named Antoine Pesne (1683–1757) practised portraiture at the court of Berlin, and a Swede named Georg Desmarées (1696–1776) was appointed Bavarian court painter, while Johann George Ziesenis (1716–79) made a profitable living playing the same role in Hanover.

Meanwhile in Prussia Andreas Schlüter (c 1660–1714) was enriching Berlin architecture, followed by the work done by Georg Wenzelslaus von Knobelsdorff (1699–1753) for his patron Frederick the Great (the Berlin opera and part of Schloss Charlottenburg, as well as Schloss Sans-Souci in Potsdam). The importance of courtly patronage, which we have already noted, is symbolised in Berlin by Schlüter's equestrian statue (begun in 1690) of Frederick William, the Great Elector. So much was the art and architecture of Berlin stamped with the personalities of its rulers that in 1779 the English diplomat Sir N. W. Wraxall judged that even 'Peter the Great is not more constantly present to the imagination at Petersburgh, than is the present King of Prussia at Berlin'.

The desire of the German courts to emulate Versailles brought French architects to German courts, especially those of Friedrich II in Berlin and the Rhineland electors. Even the work done by Georg Wenzeslaus von Knobelsdorff reflects French styles. At Karlsruhe between 1751 and 1766 the grand-ducal Schloss, originally erected in 1715, was rebuilt in the Baroque style by Friedrich Kesslau and the French architect Philippe de la Guépierre. As we have seen Robert de Cotte was primarily responsible for the Elector of Cologne's palace at Brühl. The elector also turned to him to design two more palaces, at Poppelsdorf and Bonn.

As the 18C progressed artists of a calibre of Johann Baptist Straub (1704–84), his pupil Ignaz Günther (1725–75), and the Wessobrunn stuc-coworker Joseph Anton Feuchtmayr (1696–1770) developed Baroque art-istry into the often tormented, always sublime Rococo. Neumann matched his Baroque masterpiece at Würzburg with the extraordinary Rococo pilgrimage church of • • • Vierzehnheiligen (1743–72) for the abbey of Langheim in Franconia.

## The Neo-Classical Period

The late 18C and 19C reacted against much of this exuberance. Excavations of Roman and Greek sites and the writings of the archaeologist and architectural historian Johann Joachim Winckelmann (whose *History of ancient Art*, published in 1763 exalted the 'noble simplicity and tranquil greatness' of Greek art) brought a different inspiration. Between 1800 and 1826 the architect Friedrich Weinbrunner (1766–1826) transformed Karlsruhe into a Classical city. The neo-Classical architecture of Leo von Klenze (1784–1864) and Friedrich von Gärtner (1792–1847) in Munich and that of Karl Friedrich Schinkel (1781–1841) and Carl Gotthard Langhans (1732–1808) in Berlin created superb vistas and monumental buildings—all matched by the sculpture of artists of the calibre of Ludwig von Schwanthaler (1802–48), Gotfried Schadow (1764–1850), Christian Rauch (1777–1857), and Reinhold Begas (1831–1911). This was an era of great civic buildings, such as Schinkel's Altes Museum (1822–30) in Berlin, as well as magnificent new streets, triumphal arches and suitably impressive (occasionally pompous) public monuments such as Leo von Klenze's Walhalla (1830–42) or the Feldernhalle (1840–44) in Munich, which Friedrich Andreas Gärtner (1792–1847) modelled on the Loggia dei Lanzi, Florence.

Neo-Classicists and Romantics—in painting among the former the Swiss Henry Fuseli (1741–1825), among the latter Caspar David Friedrich (1774–1840) and Johann Friedrich Overbeck (1789–1869)—both influenced and were soon vying with the Biedermeier school and landscape painters such as Arnold Böcklin (Swiss, 1827–1901), to find new directions in art. The Biedermeier school became immensely popular, celebrating middle-class values, the home, the countryside and piety, exemplified for instance in the Kunstmuseum, Düsseldorf by Wilhelm Joseph Heine's (1813–39) **Service in the Prison Chapel**, in the Neue Pinakothek, Munich, in a painting by Moritz von Schwind (1804–71) of the artist's wife and her friend cosily exulting over a letter, and in the Berlin Natinalgalerie by a portrait by Karl Begas the Elder (1794–1854) of his wife, a work suffused with the influence of Raphael—mediated in part through Overbeck, who died in Rome. The work of Karl Spitzweg, (1808–85) added a welcome touch of humour to the genre.

Overbeck as a young man had helped to form a society in Vienna known as the Nazarenes, since they dressed in pseudo-Biblical ways. On his move to Rome he met a kindred spirit in Peter von Cornelius (1783–1867) who longed to recreate the spirit of the Middle Ages in art, emphasising also its moral purpose and combining this with the heroicism he detected in Michelangelo and the piety he admired in Raphael. Cornelius was summoned to Munich by Crown Prince Ludwig of Bavaria to fresco the Glypothek—a commission then did much to revive the art of fresco painting in Germany. His influence was furthered by his appointment in 1819 as director of the academy at Düsseldorf (where the Kunstmuseum houses his pietistic **Wise and Foolish Virgins**. His Last Judgment in the Ludwigskirche, Munich, is larger than Michelangelo's in the Sistine Chapel, Rome.

## Eclecticism

As in Britain, so in Germany c 1830 neo-Classicism was being challenged by neo-Gothic, to be followed after 1850 by an eclecticism that utilised Renaissance, Classical, Baroque, Gothic and Romanesque elements at will, an eclecticism displayed par excellence in the daring and expensive commissions of 'mad' King Ludwig of Bavaria. Ludwig matched Schloss Neuschwanstein and Schloss Linderhof with a third, modelled on Versailles and situated on an island in Lake Chiemsee.

Seemingly excessive, this passion for romantic castles was not confined to Ludwig II. At Hohenschwangau his father had recreated a Schloss first built by 12C knights. Inspired by the novel *Lichtenstein* by Wilhelm Hauff (1802–27) Duke Wilhelm of Urach built Schloss Lichtenstein (1840–41), its round tower and crenellated walls perched on a rock at Lichtenstein-Honau. At Hechngen ten years later King Frederick Wilhelm IV of Prussia began rebuilding the ancestral seat of his family, Burg Hohenzollern. Finally, to add to this plethora of styles, during the reign of Wilhelm II (1888–1918) neo-Baroque came to be known as the 'Kaiser Wilhelm style', as for example the neo-Baroque Bode Museum (1898–1904) in Berlin, by Ernst von Ihne.

In spite of such monuments as that of Kaiser Wilhelm I at the Porta Westfalica and the countless statues of Bismarck dotting German cities, public sculpture did not glorify solely the rulers of the country. In Bonn's Münsterplatz Ernst Hähnel (1811–91) in 1845 sculpted a forceful statue of Ludwig van Beethoven. In 1868 Ernest Rietschel designed a massive bronze monument to Martin Luther for the Lutherplatz at Worms. (At Luther's feet stand lesser Reformers—Wycliffe, Jan Huss, Philip Melanchthon, Savonarola—as well as statues of the enlightened princelings who protected them.)

After a brief flirtation with Art Nouveau (*Jugendstil*), represented for instance by Joseph Maria Olbrich (1867–1908), the 20C saw another extraordinary flowering of German art. Before World War I two groups of painters and sculptors, *Die Brücke* and *Der Blauer Reiter* developed forms now classified as Expressionism. The former included Ernst Ludwig Kirchner (1880–1938), Karl Schmidt-Rottluff (1884–1976) and Erich Heckel (1883–1970), who founded the movement in 1906, as well as Emil Nolde (1867–1956), Max Pechstein (1881–1955) and Otto Mueller (1874–1930). The latter, based on Munich, included Wassily Kandinsky (1866–1944), Franz Marc (1880–1916), the Russian-born Alexei von Jawlensky (1864–1941) and August Macke (1887–1914). Other artists—such as Oskar Kokoschka (1886–1980), Paula Modersohn-Becker (1876–1907), ˙Max Beckmann (1884–1950) and Ludwig Meidner (1884–1966)—shared some of the aspirations of both groups without ever formally joining either. Ernst Barlach (1870–1938) produced superb Expressionist sculpture. Wilhelm Lehmbruch (1881–1919), the son of a Duisburg miner, sculpted elongated, tragic figures. This tormented man committed suicide at the end of World War I.

In 1916 a group of artists met in Zurich to express their anger and disillusion with the war. Of this group the most important Berlin 'Dadaists' are ˙Georg Grosz (1893–1953), Raoul Hausmann (1886–1971) and Hannah Höch (b 1889). In Hanover Kurt Schwitters (1887–1954) represented the movement. A link between Dadaism and Surrealism was provided by the work of Max Ernst (1891–1976). Meanwhile a group seeking a new objectivity (*Neue Sachlichkeit*) responded to the war in different ways, their chief exponents being *Otto Dix (1891–1969), Christian Schad (b 1894) and Rudolf Schlichter (1890–1955).

These artists flourished during the Weimar Republic, as did the **Bauhaus school** of architecture, painting and arts crafts founded by Walter Gropius (1883–1969) in Weimar in 1919. Its members included Paul Klee (1870—1956) and Oskar Schlemmer (1888–1943). Its architectural manifestations included the Chile Haus (1923), Hamburg, by Fritz Höger (1877–1949), Stuttgart railway station (1914–27) by Paul Bonatz (1877–1951), Gropius's Siemensstadt (1929) in the district of Spandau, Berlin, and the Haus Lange at Krefeld, designed in 1929 by Ludwig Mies van der Rohe (1886–1969), who directed the Bauhaus from 1930 until the Nazis closed it down in 1933.

The Hitler Reich proscribed Dadaists, Expressionists, neo-realists and the members of the Bauhaus alike, the German Führer (who had himself been a painter) patronising a patriotic and heroic style in art, based on an idealogy of 'blood and soil'. In 1927 the Nazis mounted in Munich an infamous exhibition of 'Degenerate Art', and Hitler's artistic minions scoured the country, confiscating in all 15,997 superb paintings, drawings and sculptures. Many artists fled their native Germany, and other endured what became known as 'inner exile', stifling their creative skills for the duration of the Third Reich.

The devastating consequences of the World War II meant that much architectural effort in post-war Germany was dedicated to the heroic and often brilliant restoration of damaged buildings. At the same time some German cities have pioneered new and imaginative projects (such as the Hansa Quarter in Berlin, by such internationally renowned architects as the Brazilian Oscar Niemeyer (b 1907) and the Frenchman Le Corbusier (1887–1965).

Expressionist painters (especially the Dutch artist Jan Thornprykker (1868–1932) who worked in the Cologne region) had sometimes turned their hand to the revived art of staiend glass. Some of these glaziers saw their work destroyed almost as soon as it was created. The first commission of Georg Meistermann (b 1911), the windows of St Engelbert, Solingen, were smashed by air raids in World War II. Meistermann paradoxically profited after the war from the need to replace many a lost medieval window (for instance at St Maria im Kapitol, Cologne) as did, less successfully, Willy Weyres (St. Aposteln, Cologne).

There is a pleasing parallel in the same city in the restaurant Bastei, built by the Expressionist architect Wilhelm Riphahn in 1924, destroyed by allied bombs in 1943 and recreated after the war by Riphahn himself. In a similar fashion a generation of sculptors inspired by Ernst Barlach, especially Ewald Mataré (b 1887) and Gerhard Marcks (b 1889), produced impressive work in a style that had been proscribed during the Third Reich. Cities such as Cologne also made handsome amends to Barlach himself by recasting sculptures that had been destroyed by the Nazis. And the abstract art of such men as Willi Baumeister (1889–55) and Ernst Wilhelm Nay (1920–68), who during World War II had kept their spirits alive by contact with the Parisian avant-garde, triumphantly re-emerged after 1945.

## Developments after World War II

Forbidden to exhibit his paintings from 1933 and deprived of his teaching post at the Frankfurt Art Academy, Baumeister from 1946 taught at the Stuttgart Academy of Art. Nay, who had worked in Paris as early as 1928, before visiting Rome and Norway, returned to Germany after the war and established himself at Cologne as a member of the Zen group, so-called because its members supposed themselves to be expressing the spirit of Zen Buddhism. They included Theordor Werner (1886–1969), another frequent visitor to Paris in the inter-war years, Emil Schumacher (b 1911), a painter whose work was banned by the Nazis and who later was to join the Zero group (see below) and Bernhard Schultze (b 1915), who had served his country in World War II before settling at Frankfurt and paying numerous visits to France. By contrast Hans Hartung (1904–67) fled Germany for Paris in 1935, served in the French Foreign Legion and in 1946 became a French citizen. Nonetheless his influence in his former country remained strong, particularly on a founder member of Zen, Fritz Winter (1905–76), who, though his work too was proscribed by the Hitler régime, had fought on the Polish and Russian fronts and been taken prisoner of war.

Inspired in part by the Bauhaus, the Zero group was founded at Düsseldorf in 1957, its leading members Heinz Mack (b 1931), Otto Piene (b 1928) and Günther Uecker (b 1930). Three editions of its magazine *Zero*, appeared between 1958 and 1961, expounding the notion that shapes and forms in painting should be jettisoned in favour of colour and light. Mack's sculptures utilised curved glass and sheets of polished metal. Piene specialised in reflectors and shadows. Uecker created works of art in which white nails reflect light. In 1966 the Zero group decided to disband itself.

Undoubtedly the most audacious post-Expressionist artist in Germany after World War II was Josef Beuys (1921–86). Beuys had been an air force pilot during the war, crashing in the Crimea and escaping with his life only after his rescuers wrapped his body in fat and felt—not surprisingly, elements subsequently frequently appearing later in his sculpture. An art student at Düsseldorf, by 1961 he was professor of sculpture at the city's Staatliche Kunstakademie, during the next decade leading an international avant-garde group known as Fluxus. Increasingly he devoted himself to 'performance art', assembling and then destroying images (though a considerable collection of his assemblages is preserved in the Darmstadt Museum), as well as exhibiting himself, most notably in 1965 when he paraded through Düsseldorf Art Gallery, his head adorned with gold leaf and honey, explaining the meaning of the exhibits to a dead hare.

This provocative artist was dismissed from his professorship in 1971 but gained increasing international acclaim. Amongst his last pupils at Düsseldorf was Anselm Kiefer (b 1945), whose massive paintings continued the stream of post-Expressionism and also frequently lambasted Germany's Nazi past. Kiefer happily added metals or roots to his paintings, while his sculpture, equally gigantic, is chiefly made of lead.

The tendency to create massive works of art in post-war Germany has been influenced by Documenta, an international exhibition which lasts for 100 days and has been held every four years at Kassel since 1955. Documenta aims to restore to its rightful place the avant-garde art proscribed by Hitler. The Documenta exhibition of 1968 brought to Kassel nearly 60 artists from the USA, many of them given to creating works of tremendous size.

Yet not all modern Düsseldorf artists have shared the anarchism of Beuys. Konrad Klapheck, for example, who was born in the city in 1935 and studied at the Academy of Fine Arts, exhibited at Documenta III and Documenta IV, gaining an international reputation for a deliberately prosaic, objective style of painting, using as his subjects such everyday objects as typewriters, bicycle bells and sewing machines. Similarly Gerd Richter (b 1932) also studied at the Düsseldorf Academy and in 1963 helped to organise an exhibition devoted to 'Capitalist Realism'. His own penchant is for realistic paintings often based on photographs.

Post-1945 architecture in Western Germany has proved equally fecund. Although Mies van der Rohe had fled the Nazis to America, his influence can clearly be seen, for instance in the Thyssen House, built in Düsseldorf in 1960 to the designs of Helmut Hentrich. Munich's 1972 Olympic Games inspired Günter Behnisch to create exhilarating tent-like, meshed structures which are now a major attraction in Munich for sports enthusiasts.

Naturally enough, new museums and art galleries favoured striking designs. Amongst the most acclaimed are the museum Hans Hollein designed for Mönchengladbach in 1982, the Neue Staatsgalerie designed for Stuttgart by James Stirling in 1983, Richard Meier's 1985 Museum für Kunsthandwerk at Frankfurt-am-Main, and Cologne's Wallraff-Richartz Museum/Musem Ludwig (by Gottfried Haberer, 1986).

Many modern architects have renounced avant-garde eccentricity in favour of respect for existing traditions, adding at the same time their own creative flair. The extremely successful Hamburg-based practice of GMP, founded by Meinhard von Gerkan and Volkwyn Marg in 1965, has enhanced that port by basing the design of its own offices, the Elbterrassen building, on ships' architecture, incorporating in the building a luxury restaurant. Enhancing the city with a multi-storey shopping arcade in the Hansaviertel, the partnership took care to use the traditional red-brick pattern of Hamburg architecture, which here supports a glass roof and domes. Designing residential buildings around the Fish Market and the St Pauli area, the same partnership set about matching the long-cherished patterns of Hamburg housing. GMP has also discreetly covered in glass the centre of the celebrated Hamburg Chilehaus of 1923 (which itself mimics the prow of a merchant ship), efficiently enabling the building to serve today as a museum of Hamburg history and also the venue of exhibitions and concerts.

Responsible not only for the new terminal at Hamburg airport and Bielefeld's new city hall, this prolific firm also created both Berlin's Tegal airport and the new terminal of Stuttgart airport. The inspiring playfulness of much of post-war German art and architecture is perfectly symbolised by the fact that the latter has a great hall supported on pillars whose style hints of the trees of the nearby Black Forest.

# Literature

The first recorded language of the Germans, Gothic, survives only in the few sections that remain of a 4C translation of the Bible by a bishop named Ulfilas (who died c 380). This Christian literature initially had to compete with the pagan songs of German folk heroes, songs which Tacitus writes about but have not survived. Around 800 an anonymous author wrote the *Hildebrandslied*, a heroic tale of a father and his son who do battle as the champions of opposing armies. Alas the ending of the *Hildebrandslied* is lost, so that we do not know who won.

In the early 9C German Christians began translating classic works of Christian piety into Old High German, and c 870 Otfrid of Weissenburg wrote a long, intricate poem expounding the life of Jesus and called the *Evengelienbuch*, a rhyming work consisting of 7416 lines. Otfried was a monk at Fulda and had been taught by the brilliant scholar (and pupil of Alcuin) Rabanus Maurus (c 800–856; 5th abbot at Fulda from 822) who had poured out a stream of learned works, none of them in German. Otfrid himself disliked writing in the vernacular and did so, he said, only to counteract contemporary vernacular literature (such as the *Hildebrandslied*) which lauded pagan heroes.

Medieval Germany produced a number of important folk songs and sagas, in particular the 12C *Nibelungenlied, Von des tôdes gehugde* ('Remembrance of Death') written by Heinrich von Melk c 1160, the love poetry of the troubadour Walther von der Vogelweide (1170–1228), Gottfried von Strassburg's (fl. early 12C) *Tristan und Isolde*, and *Parzifal* by Wolfram von Eschenbach (c 1170–1220). Often the courts supported official poets such as Walther von der Vogelweide's master Reinmar von Hagenau (fl. late 13C). A powerful strain of moralising appears both in the mid 11C *Annolied*, which presents Bishop Anno of Cologne as a spiritual hero, and in the mid 12C rhyming history of world rulers since the time of the Roman emperors, the *Kaiserchronik*.

Mystical Christianity inspired remarkable men and women in medieval Germany, among them St Hildegard of Bingen (1098–1179), whose most celebrated writings are the prophetic *Scivias*, denouncing the vices of her time. She also wrote books of medicine and natural science, as well as Biblical commentaries. A fellow Rhinelander and contemporary, Elizabeth of Schönau (1129–64), also excelled at writing visionary treatises. The first mystic to write in German was Mechthild of Magdeburg (1207–82). She was inspired by the Dominicans and called St Dominic himself, 'my beloved father'. As for preachers, the most famous of all in medieval Germany was the Dominican Meister Eckhart (c 1260–1327), who had studied in Paris and produced treatises, sermons and mystical writings in both Latin and German.

In the 12C four major epics, the *Alexanderlied* (c 1150), König Rother (c 1160), the *Rolandslied* (c 1170) and Herzog Ernst (c 1180) brought to the literature of Germany elements derived from the French romances of courtly love. The influence of France can also be detected in medieval German court epics, such as *Tristran und Isolde* (c 1170), in part by the Brunswick poet Eilhart von Oberg, and the sagas *Erec* and *Iwein* which Hartmann von Aue (fl. 1190–1210) modelled on the writings of Chétien de Troyes. Hartmann von Aue also left 16 shorter poems and the epics *Gregorius* and *Der Arme Heinrich*. At the same time German writers showed a lively interest in their own country and its history, witness the *Sachsenspiegel* ('Mirror of Saxony') of c 1225, and even in world history (the *Weltchronik*, also written around that time in Saxony).

In the following three centuries after *Parzifal* a tradition of comic, carnival plays and jokes developed, culminating in the tales of the legendary Brunswick jester Till Eulenspiegel (who died in 1350). Some monarchs still attempted to promulgate a notion of medieval chivalry, and the emperor Maximilian I (1459–1519) even wrote two courtly works of his own, *Weisskunig* (c 1513) and *Theuerdank* (c 1517). In 1401, inspired by Classical models, Johannes von Tepl (c 1350–1415) produced the first major work of German prose, *Ackermann aus Böhmen* ('Death and the Plowman').

Humanism and Christian devotion went hand in hand in Renaissance Germany, seen for example in the writings of Beatus Rhenanus (1485–1547) who edited both the classics and works of the early Christian Fathers as well as writing a masterly study of German antiquities (the *Rerum Germanicarum Libri Tres* of 1531). For a time Beatus Rhenanus was drawn to the ideas of the Protestant Reformation, but he recoiled from its more revolutionary aspects.

Humanists relished satire, and *Reynke de Vos* ('Reynard the Fox', 1498) set out to excoriate the vices of the age in Low German. In this genre Sebastian Brant (1458–1521) achieved lasting fame with his *Narrenschiff* ('Ship of Fools', 1494). A few years later Martin Luther (1483–1546) was creating a classically beautiful language in his hymns, his pamphlets and his translation of the German Bible (finished 1534). Luther was a master of invective. He also realised that drama could further the Reformation, and actively encouraged it. The writings of the Nuremberg cobbler Hans Sachs (1494–1576), the greatest of the Meistersingers, were far less savage than Luther's, though like his they crackled with wit, especially his *Fastnachtsspiel* ('Shrovetide Plays', and were designed to promote a humane, Godly Lutheranism. (Hans Sachs dubbed Luther 'the Wittemberg Nightingale'.)

Luther's enemies turned to satire to attack him, the best writer among them being Thomas Murner (1475–1537) who in 1522 write *Von dem grossen Lutherischen Narren* ('On the great Lutheran Idiot'). In the second half of the 16C Faust makes the first of his entries into German literature with the publication of the anonymous *Historia vom Dr. Johann Faustus* (1587). This too was the age of anonymous folksongs, which were widely popular and in a later age greatly inspired the German Romantics.

In 1618 the 'philosophus Teutonicus' Jakob Boehme (1575–1624), a shepherd and a shoemaker, began writing a series of theosophical Lutheran treatises which he published as *Der Weg zu Christo* ('The Way to Christ') in 1623. This, and several other of Boehme's writings published post humously (such as *Die drei Prinzipien göttlichen Wesens, Von Christi Testamenten* and *Mysterium Magnum*) immensely influenced later German philosophers of the calibre of Georg Wilhelm Friedrich Hegel (1770–1831) and Friedrich Wilhelm Joseph von Schelling (1775–1854), as well as men like William Law in England. In the year of Boehme's death Martin Opitz (1597–1639) set out rules for German poetry in his *Buch von der deutschen Poeterey* ('Book on German Poetry'). The savagery of the Thirty Years War produced a literary masterpiece in Jakob Christoph von Grimmelshausen's (1621/2–1676) equally savage and bitingly satirical *Simplicius Simplicissimus* (1669), almost certainly based on his first hand experience of that war. Grimmelshausen became a Catholic; his contemporary Paul Gerhardt (1607–76) remained a Protestant, writing exquisitely personal hymns.

The next century saw Germany's greatest period of dramatic literature, under the influence of Gotthold Ephraim Lessing (1729–81), whose chief works are *Minna von Barnhelm, Nathan der Weise* and *Emilia Galotti*, all preaching a message of enlightened tolerance. Lessing's genius for drama was matched by that of Friedrich Gottlieb Klopstock (1724–1803) for lyric poetry. In the year of Lessing's death the philosopher Kant (1724–1804) published his *Kritike der reinen Vernunft* ('Critique of Pure Reason'), following it in 1786 by his *Kritike der praktischen Vernunft* ('Critique of Practical Reason'). Both works attacked the philosophical undergirding of Lessing's Enlightenment.

Johann Gottfried Herder (1744–1803), though deeply respectful of Kant, reacted against his extreme rationalism. Herder valued the Bible and Shakespeare, and brought German folk song into literary respectability for the first time. His successors were the group of writers belonging to the *Sturm und Drang* ('Storm and Stress') movement, in particular Johann Wolfgang von Goethe (1749–1832) and Johann Christoph Friedrich

Scholler (1759–1805). The phrase itself derives from a play called *Der Wirrwarr, oder Sturm und Drang* ('Confusion, or Storm and Stress'), written in 1776 by Friedrich Maximilian von Klinger (1752–1831) and glorifying excess and passion.

Both Goethe and Schiller possessed genius that outstripped the other members of the movement. Goethe's epistolary novel *Werther*, and his *Wilhelm Meisters Lehrjahre* ('The apprenticeship of Wilhelm Meister', 1795/6) introduced into Germany a new literary form, the *Bildungsroman* (literally, 'novel of education'). *Die Leiden des jungen Werthers* ('The sorrows of young Werther', 1774), as well as his poems, plays, especially *Goetz von Berlichingen* (1773), *Torquato Tasso* (1790) and *Iphigenia in Tauris*, (1787) and his autobiography (*Dichtung und Wahrheit*); ('Poetry and Truth', 1811/13) culminated in his supreme *Faust* (part 1 published 1808, part 2 1832).

Schiller, influenced by Shakespeare—to whom Germans had already been introduced by Herder and Christoph Martin Wieland (1733–1813) and whom Schiller translated—produced at the age of 20 the tumultuous *Die Räuber* ('The Robbers', 1781), followed by *Kabale und Liebe* ('Cabal and Love', 1784), Don Carlos (1787), the Wallenstein saga (1798–99), a play about Joan of Arc (*Die Jungfrau von Orleans*, 1801) and another about Mary Stuart (1800) as well as *Wilhelm Tell* (1804).

Meanwhile Romanticism was emerging in the lyrics and novels of a group of authors loosely based on Jena: Novalis (the pen-name of Friedrich von Hardenberg, 1772–1801); Johann Ludwig Tieck (1773–1853); and his friend Wilhelm Heinrich Wackenroder (1773–98). These men all derived inspiration from Goethe's *Wilhelm Meisters Lehrjahre*. The Romantic spirit was further developed by the Heidelberg school clustered around Achim von Arnim (1781–1831) and Clemens Brentano (1778–1842). Its offshoots included the fairy-tales (1812–15) of the brothers Wilhelm (1786–1859) and Jacob Grimm (1785–1863) (*Kinder-und Hausmärchen*, 1812–16), the brooding stories of Ernst Theodor 'Amadeus' Hofffmann (1776–1822) and the poems in the anthology *Des Knaben Wunderhorn* ('The young person's magic horn', edited by Achim von Arnim and Clemens Brentano, 1805–08). Heinrich von Kleist (1777–1811) contributed both powerful drama and brooding short stories (*Novellen*). He committed suicide without seeing a single performance of one of his plays. Joseph von Eichendorff (1788–1857) enriched this Romantic tradition with a further element of folk-song in his lyrics and with his novel *Aus dem Leben eines Taugenichts* ('Memoirs of a Good-for-nothing', 1826).

To the names of these Romantics must be added those of Johann Paul Friedrich Richter (1763–1825 and Johann Christian Friedrich Hölderlin (1770–1843). Richter, who liked to be known as Jean Paul (because of his admiration for Jean-Jacques Rousseau), wrote humorous idyllic novels which became immensely popular. Hölderlin, who went insane in 1806, composed exquisite lyrics, hymns, the novel *Hyperion* (1797–99) and a rhyming play named *Empedokles* (1799).

The chief literary organ of the Romantics was the periodical *Das Athenäum* ('The Atheneum'), founded by Friedrich von Schlegel (1772–1829) and his brother August Wilhelm (1767–1845)—another brilliant translator of Shakespeare. For a time Friedrich von Schlegel shared lodgings in Berlin with the theologian and fellow-philologist Friedrich Schleiermacher (1768–1834), whose *Der christliche Glaube* ('The Christian Faith', 1821/22) laid the foundations of 19C and early 20C Protestant theology. In his *über die Religion. Reden an die Gebildeten unter ihren Verächtern* ('On

Religion: speeches to its cultured despisers', 1799) Schleiermacher had already insisted that the Romantics, with their insistence on emotion and feeling and their sense of the infinite expressing itself in the created world, were themselves close to religious belief.

In his *Buch der Lieder* (1827), his *Neue Gedichte* (1854) and his *Romanzero* (1851) the poems of Heinrich Heine (1797–1856) both mocked and furthered Romanticism. Heine also wrote brilliantly satirical prose, and for his pains had his works banned by the federal parliament in 1835. Others suffered censorship at this time, notably the satirical journalist *Ludwig Börne* (1786–1837), who sought exile in Paris, and *Ferdinand Freiligrath* (1810–76), who took refuge in London. Others forced into exile in 19C Germany included Karl Marx (1818–83), who had been fired to write anti-Christian (and anti-Semitic) tracts by Ludwig Feuerbach (1804–72), and his collaborator Friedrich Engels (1820–95). Both men died in England, having collaborated on the *Manifesto der Kommunistischen Partei* ('Communist Manifesto', 1848) and *Das Kapital* (1867, 1885 and 1894). Two novelists and lyric poets who managed to survive and publish in repressive Germany were Eduard Mörike (1804–75) and Annette von Droste-Hülshof (1797–1848).

Contemporary dramatists included Christian Friedrich Hebbel (1813–63) who wrought tragic Schopenhauerean plays (including a Niebelung trilogy) and the revolutionary nihilist George Büchner (1813–37), author of *Dantons Tod* ('Danton's Death', 1835), *Woyzeck* (first published 1879), and *Leonce und Lena* (1836, published 1850) as well as the fragmentary short story *Lenz*. His plays made their impact only when performed 50 years after his death, whereas the narrative verse *Der Trompeter von Säckingen* (1854) by Viktor von Scheffel (1826–86) brought the author instant fame and applause.

As the century progressed Theodor Fontane (1819–98) and Theodor Storm (1817–88) attempted to bring a concentrated poetic realism into their *Novellen* (seen above all in Fontane's ironical *Effi Briest* and in Storm's brooding *Immensee*). Friedrich Nietzsche (1844–1900) introduced a terrifying element of self-analysis and ecstasy into German literature and philosophy, and the experimental plays of Gerhard Hauptmann (1862–1946) successfully pushed the techniques of drama towards symbolism—a major inspiration of the writings of his contemporary Stefan George (1868–1933). Hauptmann's masterpiece was *Till Eulenspiegel* (1928).

The 20C witnessed the careers of the two Mann brothers. Thomas (1875–1955), the most successful, in *Buddenbrooks* (1901) chronicled the decline of bourgeois Lübeck, a decline symbolising that of the bourgeoisie in general, and in *Dr. Faustus* (1947) offered a commentary on the German spirit under Hitler. *Professor Unrat* (1905) by Heinrich Mann (1871–1950) was the basis of the phenomenally successful (and once considered scandalous) film *The Blue Angel*. Another celebrated German book which was made into a yet more celebrated film was *Im Westen Nichts Neues* ('All Quiet on the Western Front', 1929) by Erich Maria Remarque (1898–1970). In the same year appeared Alfred Döblin's (1878–1957) powerfully realistic Berlin *Alexanderplatz*.

As if prophesying the later horrors of 20C Europe, Franz Kafka (1883–1924) was writing his nightmarish *Die Verwandlung* ('Metamorphosis', 1915), *Der Prozess* and *Das Schloss* ('The Trial' and 'The Castle', both published posthumously). These post-World War I years, before Hitler's rise to power, were also an era when some writers were ready to mock militarism, such as Carl Zuckmayer (1896–1977), who wrote *Der*

*Hauptmann von Köpenick* ('The captain of Köpenick') in 1931 and went on to write in exile and as an American citizen *Des Teufels General* ('The Devil's General', 1946).

Like Thomas Mann, the mystical novelist Hermann Hesse (1877–1962) and Heirich Böll (1917–85) both won Nobel prizes. Günther Grass (b 1927), a refugee from the DDR, produced a celebrated series of novels in *Die Blechtrommel* ('The Tin Drum', 1959), *Katz und Maus* ('Cat and Mouse, 1961) and *Hundejahre* ('Dog Years', 1963). The dramatist Rolf Hochhuth (b 1931) caused controversy with his play *Der Stellvertreter* ('The Representative', 1963), which questioned the moral stance taken during World War II by Pope Pius XII, and with his *Soldaten* (1967), which accused Winston Churchill of involvement in the wartime death of General Wladyslav Sikorski, leader of the Polish government-in-exile. German drama continued to agonise over revolutionary ideologies, witness the success of *Marat/Sade* which Peter Weiss (1916–82) published in 1964. His *Die Ermittlung* ('The Investigation') appeared in the following year, a work based on the trial of Auschwitz murderers, and Weiss continued to analyse politics dramatically in his *Trotzky im Exil* ('Trotsky in Exile', 1970).

None of these writers achieved the international success of Bertolt Brecht (1898–1955), author of *Die Dreigroschenoper* ('the Threepenny Opera', 1928) which Kurt Weill set to music. Like Heinrich Mann, after World War II Brecht turned his back on the Western alliance and preferred to return from exile to East Berlin, setting up there his famous Berliner Ensemble (but cautiously keeping bank accounts in the capitalist world) in order to produce his own *Mutter Courage und Ihre Kinder* ('Mother Courage and her children', written in exile in 1941), *Leben des Galilei* ('The Life of Galileo', written 1943), *Der Kaukasische Kreidereis* ('The Caucasian Chalk Circle', 1948) and *Der Gute Mensch von Sezuan* ('The Good Woman of Setzuan', 1943).

# Music

Although Tacitus speaks of the ancestral songs of the Germans as early as 98 AD, detailed history of German music begins only in the early Middle Ages. Christians brought the Gregorian chant to Germany; and because the Imperial court was endlessly traversing the country and thus could scarcely establish schools of music, the art long remained the prerogative of the church (with an Imperial connection through the plainchant espoused in the 9C in Charlemagne's chapel at Aachen). A monk of St Gallen, Notker Balbulus (830–912)—'Balbulus' means 'the stammerer'—is one of the earliest composers of sequences whose name has survived. Musical theory flourished in the German monasteries. Around 900 Regino von Prüm (who died in 915), abbot of the monastery of Prüm near Trier, wrote the first *Tonarius*, a systematic classification of plainsong melodies, as well as an exposition of music as one of the seven liberal arts, entitled *De harmonica institutione*.

This religious tradition, interacting with German folk song, has left us the two earliest vernacular hymns in the language: *Nun bitten wir den heiligen Geist* ('Now we beg the Holy Ghost') and *Christus ist erstanden* ('Christ has risen'), both dating from c 1100. Shortly afterwards extending the range of plain chant, composing an antiphon '*Alma redemptoris mater*' as well as a treatise entitled simply *Musica*.

A monk of St Amand named Huchbald (c 840–c 930) had begun experimenting in music written for more than one voice, developing on the first example of a German polyphonic work that has survived, the *Musica enchiriadis*. In spite of the few vernacular hymns, St Hildegard von Bingen (1098–1179), the 'Sybil of the Rhine', famed for the feat of inventing a language which was a mixture of Latin and German, composed her impressive *Ordo virtutum* in Latin.

Not until the 12C songs of courtly love (*Minne*), of which we still possess some 500 examples, was the German language used in major music. Although patronised by the nobility (especially the Hohenstaufens), many of the Minnesingers themselves—who include Walther von der Vogelweide (died c 1230), Heirich von Morungen (died 1318), Niedhart von Reuenthal (died c 1240) and the nobleman Oswald von Wolkenstein (died 1445)— owed their education to the monasteries.

Their successors were the Meisstersingers, whose first guild was founded in Mainz in 1311 by the Minnesinger Heinrich von Meissen (known as '*Frauenlob*', c 1260–1318). Here again a strong religious bent characterised the finest of them. Many Meistersingers used the Lutheran Bible for their lyrics. Hans Sachs (1494–1576), shoemaker and poet, was the most famous. As we have seen, he dubbed the Protestant reformer Martin Luther (1483–1546) a 'nightingale'. Luther believed that music took second place only to theology, and he was himself was a formidable hymnologist. He probably wrote the music to the hymn '*Ein' feste Burg ist unser Gott*'. The first of his hymn books, the *Geystliches Gesang Büchleyn*, appeared in 1524, its musical settings by Luther's teacher and friend Johann Walther (1496–1570), court composer to the house of Saxony. Meistersingers flourished in Lutheran towns and cities, as well as in Catholic cities such as Augsburg and Regensburg. The organist Paul Hofhaimer (1459–1537), who was active in Augsburg from 1507–19, and supremely Ludwig Senfl (c 1492–c 1555), Kapellmeister at the court of Maximilian I in Vienna and later flourishing in Munich, were the finest song writers in the first half of the 16C. Later, Johannes Eccard (1553–1611), court composer at Königsberg and Berlin, also worked for Jakob Fugger in Augsburg, publishing in 1589 a celebrated set of *Newe Lieder mit fünff und vier Stimmen*. Hans Leo Hassler (1564–1612), who studied in Venice under the organist at St Mark's, Andrea Gabrieli, added Italianate flourishes to this north German Lutheran tradition. He too worked for the Fuggers of Augsburg.

By now musicians were organised in guilds. Cities patronised them, dubbing the musicians' guild the *Stadtpfeifer*. Books of *Lieder* (songs) were becoming popular (in particular the *Lochamer Liederbuch* of 1460, the *Schedel Liederbuch* of 1467 and the *Glogauer Liederbuch* of c 1480).

From the mid 8C organs had been found in royal households and in Imperial cathedrals. In the 15C a group of musicians centred on the blind Nuremberg organist Konrad Paumann (c 1410–73) spread the skills of composition by means of a widely popular *Buxheim Organ Book*. (Its name derives from the Carthusian monastery of Buxheim.) From 1446 he was organist of St Sebaldus, Nuremberg, and became court organist at Munich in 1467. Paumann's gravestone in the Frauenkirche, Munich, depicts him surrounded with a harp, a lute, a *Bockfleute* and a viol, while playing on a portable organ.

Courts as well as monasteries increasingly fostered music. Frederick the Wise of Saxony, for instance, employed Adam von Fulda (c 1445–1505) as his court musician from 1490 and 1502. The composer then moved to the University of Wittenberg, where he soon came to know Martin Luther. Yet instead of developing an authentically German style, these composers remained heavily influenced by foreigners, especially by the Flemish Josquin de Près (c 1435–1521), of whom Martin Luther observed that 'the notes do his bidding, whereas other composers obey what the notes dictate'. In the 17C other non-German influences also came into play. English and Italian composers worked in German courts. The prolific Michael Praetorius (1571–1621), Kapellmeister to the Duke of Brunswick and the court of Saxony, adapted the Venetian style in Germany in a masterly fashion. Heinrich Schütz (1585–1672), Germany's greatest 17C composer, studied in Venice under Giovanni Gabrieli at a time when he dominated Italian music. Schütz's *Dafne* (1627) is the first German opera, commissioned by the Elector of Saxony when opera was 'the rage' in Italy. His contemporary and fellow-Saxon Johann Jacob Froberger (c 1617–67) studied the organ under Frescobaldi in Rome. Bach's contemporaries, the extraordinarily prolific George Philipp Telemann (1681–1767) and Joahann Adolph Hasse (1699–1783) both wrote Italian operas as well as some in German. Bach's great predecessor Dietrich Buxtehude (1637–1707), organist of the Marienkirche in Lübeck, was born not in Germany but in Sweden. Bach trudged 50 miles to listen to Buxtehude play.

One month before Bach, George Frideric Händel (1685–1759) was born. Händel studied first in Italy, before settling permanently in Britain. (He was naturalised in 1726.) Supreme among composers of Biblical oratorios (*Saul, Messiah, Judas Maccabeus, Samson, Israel in Egypt*). Händel was frequently virtually destitute and yet decisively influenced the course of English music.

His contemporary Johann Sebastian Bach (1685–1750) scarcely left Thuringia (for a short time he was an organ scholar at Lübeck), yet he absorbed not only the lessons of his German predecessors, such as Schütz and Buxtehude but also the inspiration of Italian geniuses such as Vivaldi. Prolific at composing sacred and secular music alike, a court official apparently composing to order, Bach succeeded in producing such unequalled masterpieces as the Brandenburg Concertos, the St Matthew Passion and the Mass in B Minor. Sensitive to the tradition of German music he had inherited, he adapted, for instance a song of Hans Leo Hassler ('Mein G'mut ist mir verwirret') to his setting of *'O Haupt voll Blut und Wunden'* in the St Matthew Passion. Bach's life coincided with those of masterly Baroque organ builders, Arp Schnitger (1648–1719) Andreas Silbermann (1678–1734) and his brother Gottfried (1683–1753) in particular. Bach also fathered a dynasty of distinguished composers, including Carl Philipp Emmanuel (1714–88), Wilhelm Friedemann (1710–84) and Johann Christian (1735–82). Carl Philipp Emmanuel, harpsichordist at the court of Frederick the Great, wrote an *Essay on the True Art of Playing Keyboard Instruments* which fathered modern keyboard techniques, and also excelled at daringly mannered improvisations. Dr. Burney, who saw him play at Hamburg, described how he grew as animated as one possessed. 'His eyes were fixed, his underlip fell, and drops of effervescence distilled from his countenance'.

Franz Joseph Haydn (1732–1809) once declared, 'I learned everything I know from Emmanuel Bach'. Basically a Viennese composer, he and the other Austrian genius Mozart managed to rid German music of its dependency on the Italian, as well as extending musical forms further than they had ever reached. Their heir was Ludwig van Beethoven (1770–1827) who, though born in Bonn revered Vienna as his spiritual home. Nonetheless, Beethoven's father and grandfather had both worked as musicians for the elector of Cologne. Haydn taught Beethoven in Vienna, after Beethoven himself had also worked for the elector; but soon he was taking lessons from other Viennese composers without Haydn's knowledge. In 1795 he emerged from Haydn's shadow, making his first public appearance in Vienna as pianist and composer and playing his B flat major piano concerto. His first symphony (1799) confirmed his independent stature. He wrote eight more symphonies, chamber music, five piano concertos, one opera (*Fidelio*, 1805–14) and a violin concerto.

German music was still influenced by foreign composers, and the European musical world still crossed political boundaries with ease. Giacomo Meyerbeer (1791–1864), for instance, though born near Berlin as Jakob Liebmann Beer, lived after 1831 in Paris. Felix Mendelssohn (1809–47) and Robert Schumann (1810–56) remained more closely tied to their native land—though Mendelssohn's inspiration included Shakespeare and Scotland (*A Midsummer Night's Dream* and *Fingal's Cave*). Schumann, whose wife Clara (1819–96) became renowned as the interpreter of her husband's piano works, developed a personal friendship with Johannes Brahms (1822–97) which lasted until her death. Brahms consciously set out to be Beethoven's successor, and was deeply gratified when his first symphony was greeted as 'Beethoven's tenth'.

The international nature of the German musical scene is perfectly displayed in the career of Franz Liszt (1811–86), who was born of a Hungarian father and an Austrian mother, having become famous as a pianist in Paris before settling in Germany as director of music at Weimar. The French composer Hector Berlioz influenced Liszt's own compositions. Liszt created the influential *Allgemeiner Deutscher Musikverein* in 1861. At Weimar he presented the first performance of Wagner's Lohengrin (1846–48), and his daughter Cosima became Wagner's second wife. Wagner's musical debt to Liszt is seen above all in his *Parsifal* (1877–82) and *Tristan and Isolde* (1857–59). Wagner also owed a debt to Carl Maria Ernst von Weber (1786–1826) whose opera *Der Freischütz* ('The Marksman', 1821) romantically glorified the German countryside and German folklore.

Richard Wagner (1813–83) was director of music in such diverse places as Würzburg, Magdeburg, Königsberg and Dresden. After some years of exile (because he espoused the revolutionaries of 1848), he became court musician to King Ludwig of Bavaria, whence he fled first to Switzerland and finally to Bayreuth, where the first performance of his complete *Der Ring des Nibelungen* (1853–74) took place. His *Mastersingers of Nuremberg* (1862–67) exulted in the legacy of Hans Sachs and his fellow musicians.

Between 1885–87 Wagner's assistant at Bayreuth was *Engelbert Humperdinck*, whose six operas, which include the celebrated *Hansel and Gretel* (1893), are themselves distinctly Wagnerian. But Wagner's greatest German successor is undoubtedly Richard Strauss (1864–1949), whose collaboration with Hugo von Hofmannsthal as librettist produced the opulent *Salome* (1905), *Elektra* (1909), *Der Rosenkavalier* (1911) and *Ariadne auf Naxos* (1912). By contrast with Strauss, Hans Pfitzner (1869–1949) strove for a refined, austere classicism.

Thenceforth German music took a new turn under the influence of the atonal works of the Austrian Arnold Schoenberg (1883–1963), whose opera *Mathis der Maler* ('Mathis the Painter') was banned by the Nazis in 1934, and of another Austrian and Schoenberg student, Alban Berg (1885–1935), whose *Wozzeck* was first performed in 1925. Even more avant-garde has been the work of Karlheinz Stockhausen (born 1928 at Mödrath, near Cologne), advocate of the *musique concrète* developed by the French composers Olivier Messiaen and Pierre Boulez, who in 1953 took up a newly created post for creating electronic music established by Cologne radio.

The considerable international impact of these composers failed to match the remarkable success of the oratorio *Carmina Burana* (1937) by Carl Orff (1895–1962) and the still more popular *Dreigroschenoper* ('The Threepenny Opera', 1928) by Engelbert Humperdinck's pupil Kurt Weill (1900–50), whose librettist was Bertolt Brecht, with whom Weill also collaborated in creating the opera *The Rise and Fall of the City of Mahagonny* (1927). As a Jew Weill was obliged to seek refuge from the Nazis in America, where he survived by writing in Hollywood such Broadway musicals as *Knickerbocker Holiday* (1938) and *Lady in the Dark* (1941).

# PRACTICAL INFORMATION

## Planning your trip

### When to visit

Western Germany has a mild, temperate climate, much like that of Great Britain. The average summer temperature is 22°C (70°F) and the average winter temperature varies from 0°C (32°F) to -12°C (10°F). The best time for swimming is between June and August. It is possible to enjoy winter sports from December until March; until April in the Alps.

### Tourist information

The **German National Tourist Board** (DZT) is able to provide general information on all aspects of Germany including maps, brochures on regions, cities and towns, hotels, camping and caravanning holidays and tour operators. Its office in the **UK** is at Nightingale House, 65 Curzon St, London W1Y 7PE (tel. 071-495 3990); in the **USA** at 747 Third Avenue, 33rd Floor, New York, NY 10017 (tel. 212308 330); c/o German American Chamber of Commerce, Chicago, IL 60603-5978 (fax. 312/782-3892); 444 South Flower St, Suite 2230, Los Angeles, CA 90017 (tel. 213-688 7332); in **Canada** at 175 Bloor St East, North Tower, 6th Floor, Toronto, Ontario M4W 3R8 (tel. 416-968 1986); in **Australia** at Lufthansa House, 12th Floor, 143 Macquarie St, Sydney 2000 (tel. 02-367 3890).

### Entry and visa regulations

EC nationals with a valid passport do not need a visa to enter Germany, nor do holders of Australian, Canada, Japanese, New Zealand, South African and United States passports, provided they do not take up employment or stay longer than three months.

Domestic pets brought into the country need evidence that they have been vaccinated against rabies between 12 months and three days before entry.

There are no currency restrictions

### Disabled travellers

Special information for disabled travellers is available from RADAR, 25 Mortimer St, London W1M 8AB (tel. 071-637 5400) or in western Germany from Hilfe für Behinderte, Kirchfeldstrasse 149, D-4000 Düsseldorf 1 (tel. 0211 310060).

### Tour operators

Companies serving western Germany from Britain include **DER Travel Services Ltd**, 18 Conduit St, London W1R 9TD (tel. 071-408 0111), **German Tourist Facilities Ltd**, 182-186 Kensington Church St, London W8 4DP (tel. 071-229 2474) and **German Travel Service**, Bridge House, Ware, Herts SG12 9DW (tel. 0920 485466).

# Getting to western Germany

## By air

**Air services** to western Germany connect major world cities with Bremen, Cologne-Bonn, Düsseldorf, Frankfurt-am-Main, Hamburg, Hanover, Stuttgart, Münster-Osnabrück and Munich. Connecting flights reach Nuremburg from Frankfurt.

The country's leading airline is Lufthansa with offices in the **UK** at 10 Old Bond St, London W1X 4EN (tel. 0345-737747) and in the **USA** at 680 Fifth Avenue, New York, NY 10019 (tel. 718-895 1277), as well as offices in most major cities. National airlines such as British Airways, TWA, United Airlines, Air France and KLM also offer services to airports in western Germany; ask your travel agent for details. Most offer a variety of fares; cheaper charter flights can be found in the small ads in daily newspapers such as *The Times* and *The Guardian* and in the travel sections of Sunday newspapers.

Of the major airports, that at *Munich-II* (otherwise known as Munich Franz Joseph Strauss) is connected to the city centre by S-Bahn 8 which reaches the main railway station in 40 minutes.

**Frankfurt** is connected to the city centre by a metro link (S-Bahn lines 14 and 15) which takes 11 minutes. Frankfurt airport is also connected to Düsseldorf airport (in 2½ hours) by German Railways which calls at the city centres of Cologne-Bonn (2 hours) and Stuttgart (1 hour 25 minutes). This service is available by prior booking by those with airline tickets.

**Cologne-Bonn** airport is 18km from Cologne and 28km from Bonn. Airport bus 170 connects the airport to the centre of Cologne in 20 minutes, while line FL takes another 10 minutes to reach Bonn.

From **Bremen** airport tram 5 reaches the city centre in 15 minutes. Lohausen airport is 8km from **Düsseldorf** and is connected to the city by S-Bahn 7 arriving in the city centre in 13 minutes. **Hamburg-Fulsbüttel** in 8km from Hamburg city centre and is reach in 30 minutes by the Airport City Express bus. **Hanover-Langenhagen** is 11km from Hanover and the city centre can be reached in 20 minutes from the terminal by bus 60. The airport at **Nuremburg** is 7km from the city centre, which can be reached by taking bus 32 to Fritz Münkert Platz and then tram 2 to the main railway station. **Stuttgart** airport is 14km from the city centre; bus A takes 30 minutes to reach the main railway station.

## By sea and car

The only direct sea link between Britain and western Germany is the Harwich–Hamburg route operated by **Scandinavian Seaways**, Scandinavia House, Parkeston Quay, Harwich, Essex (tel. 0255 240240).

All ferry services from the UK, with destinations such as Ostend, Calais, Zeebrugge and the Hook of Holland, leave you with a 2–3 hour road journey to the German border, completing the journey through Belgium and Holland by motorway. **P&O European Ferries**, Channel House, Channel View Road, Dover, Kent CT17 9TJ (tel. 0304 203388) operate crossings to Calais, Ostend and Zeebrugge. By way of Dover to Ostend, a crossing operated by **Belgian Regie Maritime Transport** (tel. 071-233 6480), you can transfer to rail and reach Cologne by way of Brussels and Aachen. **Stena Sealink**, Charter House, Park St, Ashford, Kent TN24 8EX (tel. 0233 647047) operates the service from Harwich to the Hook of Holland, though rail passengers travelling to western Germany must usually change trains in Holland. **Olau Line**, Ferry Terminal, Sheerness, Kent ME12 1SN (tel. 0795 666666) operates a service from Sheerness to Vlissingen (Flushing), from which the rail time to Cologne is five hours. **North Sea Ferries**, King George Dock, Hedon Road, Hull HU9 5QA (tel. 0482 785141) sails from Hull to Rotterdam, where trains continue through Mönchengladbach to Cologne.

**Motorail services** are a very popular way of exploring Germany. An all-in charge is made for car and driver, with reduced rates for accompanying passengers. Concessionary fares are available on various routes within Germany and on all DER (Germany Travel Agency) Motorail services. Detailed information is available in the brochure *Autoreisezüge* (German Motorail) from German tourist offices.

## By rail

Western Germany is easily and speedily reached by rail from Great Britain. Fares are particularly competitive if you are a student or are under 26 or over 60. Contact **Eurotrain** at 52 Grosvenor Gardens, London SW1W 0AG (tel. 071-730 3402).

## By bus

**Eurolines** operate coach services to many cities in western Germany including Berlin (journey time 26 hours), Cologne (13 hours), Frankfurt (18½ hours), Hamburg (22 hours) and Munich (23½ hours). Journey times are long and fares about the same price as the cheapest air fares. Contact Eurolines, 52 Grosvenor Gardens, London SW1W 0AG (tel. 071-730 0202).

# Arriving in western Germany

## Currency

The legal currency, the Deutsche Mark (DM), is divided into 100 Pfennige (Pf). As well as coins the value of 5, 2 and 1 mark, and 50, 10, 5, 2 and Pfenniges, notes are issued, rising from 5 to 1000 DM.

## Accommodation

**Hotels** in western Germany range from the expensive *Luxushotel* to the simple *Gasthof*. The Vereinigung der Berg-und Schlosshotels, D-35260 Trendelburg, publishes an annual brochure *Gast im Schloss*, listing German Châteaux-hotels. Numerous hotel chains offer easy methods of arranging a stay in advance. These include Arabella Hotels (British Sales Office 20 King's Ride, Camberley, Surrey GU15 4HX; tel. 0276- 63513), the usually less expensive Ringhotels (central reservation Belforstrasse 6-8, D-8000 Munich 80: tel. 089 4485959/4470604), and the extensive chain of Best Western Hotels (run from Merganthaler Allee 2-4, D-65760 Eschborn: tel. 06196 47240), whose prices vary. In general the annual red Michelin guide *Deutschland*, which divides hotels into six categories and comments on their cuisine, while inevitably not exhaustive, is invaluable.

Hotel reservations can be made through the Allgemeine Deutsche Zimmerreservierung, Corneliustrasse 34, D-6000 Frankfurt-am-Main 1 (tel. 069-740767). In addition, many major railway stations have information about hotels and will sometimes make reservations for those arriving. Travellers willing to make their own arrangements on the spot will find the cheaper hotels usually close by these stations. In addition the signs *Zimmer Frei* indicate **bed and breakfast** accommodation.

Information on **farming holidays** is available from the Landschriftenverlag, Kurfürstenstrasse 53, D-5300 Bonn, and on camp and caravan sites from the Deutscher Camping Club, Mandlstrasse 23, D-8000 München 28 (tel. 089 3340). Germany boasts some 600 **youth hostels**, listed annually by the Deutsches Jugendherbergswerk, Bülowstrasse 26, D-4930 Detmold 1 (tel. 05321 740114). Information on **mountain holidays** is available from the Deutscher Alpenverein, Praterinsel 5, D-8000 München 22, and from the Verband Deutscher Gebirgs-und Wandervereine, Hospitalstrasse 21, D-7000 Stuttgart 1. Special information for **physically handicapped visitors** is available from Hilfe für Behinderte, Kirchfeldstrasse 149, D-4000 Düsseldorf 1 (tel. 0211 310060).

## Food and drink

German food varies remarkably from region to region—even from town to town. But a typical menu falls into several parts: **Vorspeisen** (first courses) can be smoked salmon or herrings, often salads with mayonnaise; meats and sausages (*Bratwurst* and *Blutwurst*), canapés with paté.

**Suppen** (soups) include asparagus soup with cream (*Spaargelcremesuppe*), vegetable soup (*Gemüsesuppe*), consommé (*Kraftbrühe*) and farmer's broth (*Bauernsuppen*).

**Fische** (fish) invariably included on restaurant menus are trout (*Blaue Forelle*), as well as the ever accessible herrings and often also eel, pike and carp.

**Geflügel** (poultry) often includes duck stuffed with apple and ham, originally deriving from the environs of Hamburg (*Vierländer Ente*), chicken broth (*Kukenragout*), turkey (*Pute*) and at Christmas and New Year goose (*Gans*).

**Fleisch** (meat) includes *Schnitzel* and numerous kinds of sausage (*Wurst*), as well as various forms of pork, such as the version that is smoked and known as *Kassler Rippchen*. Throughout Germany can be found the beef dish called *Sauerbraten*. These dishes are served with inventively cooked potato, cabbage (often in the form of *Sauerkraut*, shredded and pickled), asparagus or *Blindes Huhn* (a mixture of carrots, bacon, green beans and bacon).

A meal usually ends with **Süssspeisen** (dessert), often created with whipped cream and rice. In addition meals often include cakes (*Konditorei*), sometimes enhanced with marzipan, often filled with luscious, fattening cream.

German menus also frequently include beautifully cooked game—*Hirsch* (venison); *Reh* (roebuck); *Wildschwein* (wild boar, either served as haunch, *Keule*, or saddle, *Rücken*); and *Hase* (hare).

Each region has its often seasonal specialties: in Berlin *Kartoffelpuffer* (potato pancakes, which are known as *Reibekuchen* in the Rhineland), *Berliner Pfannkuchen* (doughnuts) relished at New Year, and the *Kasseler Rippespeer*, a lightly smoked Berlin chop; *Himmel und Erde*, which in Cologne means mashed potatoes with black pudding and onions; Rollmops (pickled herrings with onions and gherkins); baked fish with apple wine (*Rippchen mit Kraut*), which you eat in Hessen; *Eisbein* (which derives from the Low German word for a hip-bone), a huge knuckle of pork with

Sauerkraut and pease pudding; skimmed milk cheese (*Handkäse*), served in Mainz *mit Musik*, i.e. garnished with vinegar, chopped onions, salt and pepper; smoked eel (*Räucheraal*), Brunswick style, from the Steinhuder lake; smoked sprats from Kiel, dubbed *Kieler Sprotte*; the Bavarian potato-dumpling seasoned with liver or bilberries or diced bacon or ground calf's liver (known generically as *Knödel*); Nuremberg Christmas *Stollen* and *Baumkuchen* (cakes covered in icing or chocolate); Schwabian sweet bread (*Zuckerbrot*); Westphalian ham (*Schinken*), Westphalian sausages baked in puff pastry (*Würste-Brötchen*) and the local wheat loaf baked in egg and milk and loaded with currants (*Korintenstuten*); soused herring (*Matjes-filet*) served with boiled potatoes and green beans on the Baltic; even the Hamburger, known in Hamburg as the *Hamburger Rundstück*.

Apart from its splendid beers (each person on average drinking 130 litres a year), Germany also devotes 98,386 hectares of its land to vineyards, some 62 per cent of its produce classed as *Qualitätswein* in 1983, 33 per cent classed as *Qualitätswein mit Prädikat* and 5 per cent classed as table wine (*Tafelwein*).

The British have for many years described German Rheinwein as 'Hock', though officially this term may be used only of wine produced from the Sylvaner or Riesling grape. Seven regions produce such wine: Rheinhessen, Rhineland-Palatinate, Rheingau, Nahe, Mosel-Saar-Ruwer, Baden and Franken. In addition the Germans designate as *Liebfraumilch* wines from Rheinhessen, Rhineland-Palatinate, Rheingau and Nahe. Sparkling wines (*Sekt*) are made, following the methods of French champagne vine-yards, with a light variety known as Perlwein.

The denomination of a wine is strictly controlled in Germany (and by the EC), so that *Qualitätswein mit Prädikat* always denotes a wine of choice quality that contains no chemical additions, and *Kabinett* denotes the finest such wines. *Auslese* refers to the finest grapes, while *Spätlese* indicates that these grapes have been gathered in the latest possible moment, when every grape is indubitably ripe.

Wine labels are strictly regulated and give: the year of the vintage; the vineyard; the variety of grape; its harvesting (i.e. *Auslese, Spätlese*); the region of production; a quality control number; and details of the wine merchant.

The words *Erzeuger-Abfüllung* means that the wine had been bottled by the producer.

The regions of Germany differ in alcohol preferences of their citizens. North Germans, in Schleswig-Holstein and along the Baltic coast, are fond of rum, which they liberally add to their coffee. Berlin restaurants serve Schnapps alongside a *Molle* or glass of beer, as well as goblets of foaming *Berliner Weisse*, a pale beer made from wheat and often served *mit Strippe*, that is strengthened with *Kümmel* brandy. Munich beer, being lighter, is usually served in larger quantities, in a Stein known as *die Mass*. At Frankfurt fish dishes are customarily accompanied by dry cider (*Apfelwoi*). In Baden and Württemberg breakfast of rye bread and smoked ham is often accompanied with a glass of *Kirschwasser* (cherry spirit) or else a cup of black coffee laced with *Kirschwasser*, whereas a Westphalian breakfast will usually consist of Pumpernickel, currant loaf (*Korinthenstuten*) and a glass of beer accompanied with Schnapps.

See also **Vocabularies**.

## Tourist Information Offices

The **West German central tourist office**: Deutsche Zentrale für Tourismus e.V., Beethovenstrasse 69, D-6000 Frankfurt-am-Main (tel. 069 75720). **Bavaria**: Fremdenverkehrsverband München-Oberbayern e.V., Sonnenstrasse 10, D-8000 Müchen 2 (tel. 089 598347). Fremdenverkehrsverband Franken e.V., Am Plärrer, D-8500 Nürnberg 81 (tel. 0911 264202). Fremdenverkehrsverband Ostbayern e.V., Richard-Wagnerstrasse 10, D-8400 Regensburg (tel. 0941 560260). Fremdenverkehrsverband SchwabenAllgäu e.V., Fuggerstrasse 9, D-8900 Augsburg (tel. 0821 33335). **Baden-Württemberg**: Fremdenverkehrsverband Schwarzwald-Bodensee e.V., Bertoldstrasse 45, D-7800 Freiburg im Breisgau (tel. 0761 31317-18), Landesverkehrsverband Baden-Württemberg e.V., Esslinger Strasse 8, D-7000 Stuttgart (tel. 0711 247364). **Saarland**: Fremdenverkehrsverband Saarland e.V., Dudweiler Strasse 53, D-6600 Saarbrücken (tel. 0681 35376 and 37088). **Rhineland-Palatinate**: Fremdenverkehrsverband Rheinland-Pfalz, Lörhstrasse 1103-105, D-5400 Koblenz (tel. 0261 31079). **Hesse**: Landesverkehrsverband Hassen, Abraham-Lincoln-Strasse 38-42, D-6200 Wiesbaden (tel. 0611 700361). **The Rhine Valley**: Landesverkehrsverband Rheinland e.V., Rheinallee 69, D-5300 Bonn 2 (tel. 0228 362921-22. **North-Rhine Westphalia**: Landesverkehrsverband Westfalen e.V., Friedensplatz 3, D-4600 Dortmund (tel. 0231 527506-07). **The Weser Hills**: Landesverkehrsverband Weserbergland-Mittelweser e.V., Inselstrasse 3, D-3250 Hameln (tel. 05151 24566). **Lower Saxony and the North Sea**: Fremdenverkehrsverband Nordsee-Niedersachsen-Bremen e.V., Bahnhofstrasse 19-20, D-2900 Oldenburg (tel. 1441 26992). **Lüneberg Heath**: Fremdenverkehrsvervand Lüneburger Heide e.V., Am Sande 5, D-2120 Lüneburg (tel. 04131 42006-07). Harzer Verkehrsverband e.V., Marktstrasse 45, D-338 Goslar. **Schleswig-Holstein**: Fremdemverkehrsverband Schlweswig-Holstein e.V., Niemannsweg 31, D-2300 Kiel (tel. 0431 560025-26).

# Getting around western Germany

## By car

Travel by road is made simple by the extensive system of toll-free motorways (*Autobahn*). Western Germany boasts nearly 40,000km of major roads, including some 5000km of motorways. Lay-bys with notice-boards carrying tourist information, ample service areas and petrol stations provide comprehensive 24-hour facilities for the motorist.

Foreign motorists must take their driving licence, vehicle registration documents and have at least third party vehicle insurance and an International Motor Certificate (Green Card); if you are a member, contact either the Automobile Association (tel. 0256 20123) or the Royal Automobile Club (tel. 0345 3331133) for further information on driving in Germany and for details of reciprocal arrangements with the German motoring organisations.

If you should breakdown call the ADAC (the main German motoring organisation) from their emergency road-side telephones; arrows marked on the verges of the roads indicate the nearest phone. Assistance is free of charge though you must pay for materials. When calling be sure to ask for *Strassenwachthilfe*.

The speed limit outside built-up areas is 100kmph (60mph) and in built-up areas 50kmph (30mph); there is a standard 130kmph (80mph) limit of motorways. Front and rear seat belts must be worn at all times. Children under 12 must travel in the back seats. Driving with dipped headlights is obligatory in the dark and in fog, heavy rain and snow.

**Car hire** is available from all major cities and airports and all the big names—Avis, Hertz, Budget, etc—are represented. Local car hire can sometimes work out cheaper.

The three main motoring organisations are the German General Automobile Club (ADAC), Baumgartnerstrasse, D-8000 München 70, the German Touring Club (DTC), Amalienburgstrasse, D-8000 München 13, and the Automobile Club of Germany (AvD) Niederrad, Lyonerstrasse, D-6 Frankfurt-am-Main.

## By rail

Western Germany's passenger railway system, begun in 1835, today comprises some 29,500 kilometres of track. Germany Railways (DB) are served by three sorts of passenger trains: the fast, international **InterCityExpress** (ICE), with all accommodation first class, as well as a bistro bar and waiter-service dining car; **InterCity** and **EuroCity** (IC/EC) trains, with first and second class seats and a restaurant car. Supplements are payable on all these trains. **City-D-Zug** or **InterRegio** trains are slower, connecting smaller cities and the large towns, offering first and second class accommodation and a bistro café.

**Fares** are charged on a distance-travelled basis. Standard-fare tickets are valid for one day for distances of up to 100km. For longer journeys a single ticket is valid for 4 days and a return ticket for one month. You can break your journey as often as you like and for as long as you like within that period. Children under 4 travel free. Groups of six or more are eligible for reduced fares, with a group of 10 or more adults paying on some trains 30 per cent of the full fare, a group of 25 or more paying 50 per cent.

**Passes**. German railways also offer National and Regional Rail Passes with particularly valuable savings for young or retired people. The **National Rail Pass** gives unlimited travel on 5, 10 or 15 days in one month; the **Regional Pass** offers unlimited travel in various designated regions for 5 or 10 days within a designated period of 21 days. These passes also allow travel on the bus services operated by German railways. The **German Rail Youth Pass**, available to those between 12 and 26, allows travel in second class accommodation only.

The **Euro Domino Pass** can be used on all scheduled trains (except Motorail services) of German railways, including the high-speed InterCityExpress services and the suburban S-Bahn trains serving the airports of Düsseldorf, Frankfurt-am-Main, Munich and Stuttgart. This pass can also be used on the day ships of Köln-Düsseldorfer Deutsche Rheinschiffahrt AG (KD) between Cologne and Mainz but not on KD's hydrofoil or overnight cruise ships. The pass, offered by more than 20 European railways, is valid for 3, 5 or 10 days' unlimited travel for one month within the network. Euro Domino passes can be bought only outside your country or residence. The **Euro Domino Youth Pass** is available to people under 26.

For more information about rail services in the **UK** contact German Rail Services, Suite 4, The Sanctuary, 23 Oakhill Grove, Surbiton, Surrey, KT6 6DU (tel. 081 390 0066) and in the **USA** German Rail R Tours Inc., 9501 West Devon Avenue, Rosemont, LI 60018–4832 (tel. 708 692 6300).

## By bus

The German rail network is so efficient and wide-ranging that a national bus network is rendered unnecessary; the rail and postal authorities network runs buses to town and villages not serviced by the railways. The Europa-Bus Service provides regular trips for tourists along routes of particular interest. The booking office is at Deutsche Touring GmbH, Am Ròmerhof 17, D-6000 Frankfurt-am-Main.

## By boat

There are regular river, lake and coastal services operated by various shipping lines.

**River services**. The great lakes and rivers of the country are well served by water buses. In addition the **Köln-Düsseldorfer** cruise line runs river trips in its floating hotels along the Rhine, the Elbe and the Mosel: head office Frankenwert 115, 5000 Köln 1 (tel. 0221-20818-318 and 319); British Office KD Rhineline, 28 South St, Epsom, Surrey KT18 7PF (tel. 0372 742933); French Office Croisirhin, Karl Noack, 9 rue du Faubourg St. Honoré, 75008 Paris; USA offices 170 Hamilton Avenue, White Plains, New York, NY 10601 (tel. 914-9483600) and 323 Geary St, San Francisco, CA 94102 (tel. 415-3928817).

## By bicycle

Cycling is a delightful way of seeing the German countryside and cyclists are well-provided for with cycle paths in cities, towns (where there are special pedestrian and cycle paths) and regional roads making cycling safe and pleasurable. You can hire bicycles from 260 railway stations if you hold a valid ticket; you are entitled to a discount if you are travelling on a rail pass. German cycling tours can be arranged through Anglo Dutch Sports Ltd., 30a Foxgrove Road, Beckenham, Kent BR3 2BD (081-659 2347; see on this especially Münsterland, Rte 47).

## Maps

Among German publishers, Kümmerly & Frey and Freytag & Berndt produce fine maps of the country, as do Bartholomew in Britain and Michelin in France. Kümmerly & Frey and Michelin also publish regional maps, as do RV Verlag and such Regional Surveying Offices (Landesvermessungsamte) as those of Baden-Württemberg, Bavaria, Lower Saxony, the Rhineland-Palatinate and Schleswig-Holstein, often in considerable detail. For a detailed Wanderkarte of a region, look to those published by Detail Kompass.

The town plans in this book can be supplemented by those published by ADAC Verlag, Munich (which do not confine themselves simply to Bavaria) and by the Euro-Regionalkarte series of RV Verlag.

Regional tourist offices usually stock a selection of these maps, and all can be purchased in Britain from Stanfords, 12-14 Long Acre, London WC2E 9LP.

# General Information

## Public holidays

New Year's Day (1 January); Feast of the Epiphany (6 January), observed in Bavaria and Baden-Württemberg; Good Friday; Easter Sunday and Easter Monday; May Day (1 May); Ascension Day; Whitsunday and Whitmonday; Corpus Christi (18 June); Assumption of the Blessed Virgin Mary (15 August), observed in Bavaria and the Saarland; Day of German Unity (3 October); Day of Repentance and Prayer (18 November); Christmas Day and Boxing Day (25 and 26 December).

## Working hours

**Shops and chemists** usually open from 09.00 to 18.00 or 18.30, closing most Saturday afternoons and Sundays, as well as on public holidays.

**Doctors** can be consulted between 10.00 and 12.00 and 16.00 to 18.00, except on Wednesdays, Saturdays and Sundays, though in hospital outpatients departments it is best to arrive between 07.00 and 08.00. (British visitors carrying a valid form E111 can obtain emergency medical treatment, either free or at reduced cost.)

**Banks** usually open from 08.30 to 13.00 and from 14.20 to 16.00, with and extension to 17:30 on Thursdays. Most banks close on Saturdays and Sundays. Money can be changed at **post offices** which normally open on weekdays from 08.00 to 18.00, closing on Saturdays at noon. The **bureaux de change** at airports and main railway stations open as a rule from 06.00 to 20.00.

The opening times of **churches** varies enormously throughout western Germany, and especially in some Protestant areas you can be sure of seeing the interior of a building only during public worship.

## Telephones

Most public telephones now take phone cards (*Telefonkarte*) which can be bought from post offices; some coin-operated phones are still to be found. You can also make calls from cafés and hotels but rates may be a little higher. Dial 03 for the operator, 1188 for directory enquiries; 00118 for international enquiries. The dialling codes for the UK is 0044 and USA and Canada 001. In the case of emergency dial 110 for police and 112 for an ambulance or fire brigade.

## Further Reading

John Ardagh *Germany and the Germans*, revised edition, Penguin Books 1991.

James Bentley *Bavaria*, Aurum Press, London 1990.

James Bentley *Oberammergau and the Passion Play*, Penguin Books, London 1984.

James Bentley *The Rhine*, George Philip, London 1988.

Julius Baum and Helga Schmidt-Glessner *German Cathedrals*, Thames & Hudson, London 1956.

Philip Bristow *Through the German Waterways*, revised edition, Nautical Books (A & C Black) 1988.

Gordon A. Craig *Germany 1866–1945*, Clarendon Press, Oxford 1978.

Gordon A. Craig *The Germans*, new edition, Penguin 1991.

Gerd Dorr & Karl Kinne *Schwarzwald im Farbbild* (with German, English and French texts), H. Ziehen Verlag, 1987.

Joachim C. Fest *Hitler*, Weidenfeld & Nicolson, London 1987.

Hajo Holborn *A History of Modern Germany 1648–1840*, Eyre & Spottis-woode, London 1965.

Christos M. Joachimides, Norman Rosenthal and Wieland Schmidt *German Art of the Twentieth Century: Painting and Sculpture 1905–1985*, Weidenfeld & Nicolson, London 1985.

Adi Kraus *Tour Guide Germany*, AA Publications 1992.

Gottfried Lindemann *History of German Art*, Pall Mall Press, London 1971.

Golo Mann *The History of Germany since 1789*, Chatto, London 1968.

Agatha Ramm *Germany: 1789–1919, a Political History*, Methuen 1962.

In addition Polyglott-Verlag, Munich, has published an excellent series of slender guides to the various regions of the former Federal Republic, under the general title Polyglott-Reiseführer.

# VOCABULARIES

## Food and Drink

**Suppen** (Soups):

| | |
|---|---|
| Erbsensuppe | pea soup |
| Gulaschsuppe | goulash soup |
| Hühnerbrühe | chicken broth |
| Königssuppe | cream or chicken soup |
| Kraftbrühe | clear beef soup |
| Nudelsuppe | noodle soup |
| Ochsenschwanzsuppe | oxtail soup |
| Rindfleischbrühe | beef broth |
| Schildkrötensuppe | turtle soup |
| Tomatensuppe | tomato soup |

**Vorspeisen** (Hors d'oeuvres):

| | |
|---|---|
| Austern | oysters |
| Gänseleber-Pastete | goose liver pâté/pâté de foie gras |
| Heringssalat | herring salad |
| Kaviar | caviar |
| Räucheraal | smoked eel |
| Räucherlachs | smoked salmon |
| Russische Eier | Russian eggs |
| Weinbergschnecken | snails |

**Salate** (Salads):

| | |
|---|---|
| Gemischter Salat | mixed salad |
| Gurkensalat | cucumber salad |
| Kopfsalat | lettuce |
| Tomatensalat | tomato salad |

**Fische** (Fish)

| | |
|---|---|
| Aal | eel |
| Forelle | trout |
| Hecht | pike |
| Karpfen | carp |
| Krabbe | shrimp/prawn |
| Krebs | crab |
| Makrele | mackerel |
| Schellfisch | haddock |
| Schleie | tench |
| Scholle | plaice |
| Seezunge | sole |
| Steinbutt | turbot |
| Zander | pike/perch |

**Fleisch** (Meat):

| | |
|---|---|
| Bauernschinken | smoked ham |
| Bratwurst | sausage |
| Eisbein | knuckle or pork |
| Filetsteak | fillet steak |
| Hammel | mutton |
| Kalbsschnitzel | veal cutlet |
| Lamm | lamb |
| Leber | liver |
| Ragout | stew |

| | |
|---|---|
| Rind (or Rinder/Ochsen) | beef |
| Rindsfilet | fillet steak |
| Rippchen | slightly cured rib of pork |
| Rumpsteak | rump steak |
| Schweinefleisch | pork |
| Schinken | ham |
| Schnitzel | veal/pork cutlet |
| Schnitzel à la Holstein | Holstein Schnitzel |
| Steak | beefsteak |
| Weißwirst | white Bavarian sausage |
| Wiener Schnitzel | Viennese schnitzel |

**Geflügel** (Poultry):

| | |
|---|---|
| Ente | duck |
| Gans | goose |
| Huhn | chicken |
| Hühnchen | young chicken |
| Kücken/Küken | poussin |
| Pute/Truthahn | turkey |
| Taube | pigeon |

**Wild/Wildflügel** (Game/Venison):

| | |
|---|---|
| Hase | hare |
| Hirsch | venison |
| Reh | roebuck |
| Wildschwein | wild boar |

**Eierspeisen** (Egg dishes):

| | |
|---|---|
| Omelett | omelette |
| Pfannkuchen | pancake |
| Rührei | scrambled eggs |
| Spiegeleier | fried eggs |
| Verlorene Eier | poached eggs |

**Gemüse/Beilagen** (Vegetables):

| | |
|---|---|
| Artischocken | artichokes |
| Artischockenboden | heart of artichokes |
| Blumenkohl | cauliflower |
| Bohne | haricot beans |
| Bratkartoffeln | fried or sautéed potatoes |
| Champignons | mushrooms |
| Grüne Bohnen | runner beans |
| Erbsen | green peas |
| Gurken | cucumbers |
| Karotten | carrots |
| Kartoffelbrei | creamed potatoes |
| Kraut (rot or weiß) | cabbage (red or white) |
| Makkaroni | macaroni |
| Pilz | mushroom |
| Pommes frites | French fries |
| Reis | rice |
| Rosenkohl | brussel sprouts |
| Rote Beete | beetroot |
| Rote Rüben | beetroot |
| Rotkraut | red cabbage |
| Salzkartoffeln | boiled potatoes |
| Sauerkraut | sauerkraut |
| Spaghetti | spaghetti |

| | |
|---|---|
| *Spargel* | asparagus |
| *Spätzle* | spaetzle |
| *Spinat* | spinach |
| *Tomaten* | tomatoes |
| *Weißkraut* | white cabbage |

**Nachtisch** (Dessert)

| | |
|---|---|
| *Apfel* | apple |
| *Apfelsine/Orange* | orange |
| *Apfelstrudel* | apple strudel |
| *Aprikose* | apricot |
| *Eis* | ice cream |
| *Erdbeere* | strawberry |
| *Gefrorenes* | ice cream |
| *Heidelbeer* | myrtil |
| *Käse* | cheese |
| *Kirsche* | cherry |
| *Kompott* | stewed fruit |
| *Konfiture* | jam |
| *Nusstrudel* | nut strudel |
| *Obstsalat* | macedoine |
| *Obst* | fresh fruit |
| *Reisauflauf* | rice pudding |
| *Soufflé* | soufflé |

**Gebäck** (Pastry):

| | |
|---|---|
| *Berliner Pfannkuchen* | Berlin doughnuts |
| *Obstkuchen* | fruit tart |
| *Teegebäck* | tea cakes/sweet biscuits |
| *Torten* | tarts/gâteaux |

**Getränke** (Drinks):

| | |
|---|---|
| *Bowle* | wine cup/alcoholic punch |
| *Dunkles Bier* | dark beer |
| *Helles Bier* | light beer |
| *Kaffee* | coffee |
| *Liköre* | liqueurs |
| *Limonade* | lemonade |
| *Milch* | milk |
| *Mineralwasser* | mineral water |
| *Punsch* | hot punch |
| *Rosé* | rosé wine |
| *Rotwein* | red wine |
| *Schokolade* | chocolate |
| *Sekt* | sparkling wine |
| *Spirituosen* | spirits |
| *Süsswein* | dessert wine |
| *Tee* | tea |
| *Tomatensaft* | tomato juice |
| *Weinbrand* | brandy |
| *Weisswein* | white wine |

## Other words and phrases

**Numbers**

| | |
|---|---|
| *eins* | one |
| *zwei (or zwo)* | two |
| *drei* | three |

| | |
|---|---|
| vier | four |
| fünf | five |
| sechs | six |
| sieben | seven |
| acht | eight |
| neun | nine |
| zehn | ten |
| elf | eleven |
| zwölf | twelve |
| dreizehn | thirteen |
| vierzehn | fourteen |
| fünfzehn | fifteen |
| sechzehn | sixteen |
| siebzehn | seventeen |
| achtzehn | eighteen |
| neunzehn | nineteen |
| zwanzig | twenty |
| einundzwanzig | twenty-one |
| dreissig | thirty |
| vierzig | forty |
| fünfzig | fifty |
| sechzig | sixty |
| siebzig | seventy |
| achtzig | eighty |
| neunzig | ninety |
| hundert | one hundred |
| zweihundert | two hundred |
| tausend | one thousand |

**Days of the week**

| | |
|---|---|
| Sonntag | Sunday |
| Montag | Monday |
| Dienstag | Tuesday |
| Mittwoch | Wednesday |
| Donnerstag | Thursday |
| Freitag | Friday |
| Samstag (or Sonnabend) | Saturday |

**Months of the year**

| | |
|---|---|
| Januar | January |
| Februar | February |
| März | March |
| April | April |
| Mai | May |
| Juni | June |
| Juli | July |
| August | August |
| September | September |
| Oktober | October |
| November | November |
| Dezember | December |

**Basic words and phrases**

| | |
|---|---|
| danke schön | thank you |
| geschlossen | closed |
| groß | large |
| guten Abend | good evening |
| guten Morgen | good morning |

| | |
|---|---|
| *guten Tag (or grüß Gott)* | hello |
| *ja* | yes |
| *nein* | no |
| *kalt* | cold |
| *klein* | small |
| *links* | left |
| *rechts* | right |
| *warm* | warm |
| *können Sie englisch?* | do you speak English? |
| *Ich bin Englischer (Engländerin)* | I am an Englishman (woman) |
| *langsamer bitte* | more slowly please |

## Accommodation

| | |
|---|---|
| *Hotel* | hotel |
| *Gasthof* | small hotel |
| *Jugendherberge* | youth yostel |
| *Zimmer frei* | bed and breakfast |
| *Haben Sie noch ein Zimmer frei?* | have you a room left? |
| *Ich möchte* | I should like |
| *Badezimmer* | bathroom |
| *mit Bad* | with a bath |
| *mit Dusche* | with a shower |
| *Doppelzimmer* | double room |
| *Einzelzimmer* | single room |
| *für eine Nacht* | for one night |
| *Frühstuck* | breakfast |
| *Was kostet?* | how much? |
| *Wo kann ich meine Wagen unterbringen?* | where may I leave my car? |
| *Wo sind die Toiletten?* | where are the toilets? |
| *Damen* | women |
| *Herren* | men |
| *Besetzt* | occupied |
| *Frei* | free |

## The time of day

| | |
|---|---|
| *Heute* | today |
| *Gestern* | yesterday |
| *Morgen* | tomorrow (and also morning) |
| *Mittag* | noon |
| *Nachmittag* | afternoon |
| *Abend* | evening |
| *Mitternacht* | midnight |

## Shopping and other transactions

| | |
|---|---|
| *bitte* | please |
| *billig* | cheap |
| *teuer* | expensive |
| *Wievel kostet?* | how much is? |
| *zu viel* | too much |
| *mehr* | more |
| *Ich möchte einen Reisecheck einlösen?* | may I cash a traveller's cheque? |
| *Hier ist mein Pass* | here is my passport |
| *Postkarte* | postcard |
| *Brief* | letter |
| *Briefmarke* | postage stamp |

**Rail travel**

| | |
|---|---|
| *der Bahnhof* | station |
| *der Zug* | train |
| *die Ankunft* | arrival |
| *die Abfahrt* | departure |
| *die Auskunft* | enquiry office |
| *eine Fahrkarte* | a ticket |
| *eine Ruckfahrkarte* | a return ticket |
| *der Bahnsteig* | platform |
| *das Gleis* | track |
| *das Gepäck* | luggage |
| *das Fundbüro* | lost property office |

**Road travel**

| | |
|---|---|
| *Rechts fahren* | drive on the right |
| *Eintritt verboten* | no entry |
| *Einbahnstrasse* | one way street |
| *Vorsicht!* | take care! |
| *Sackgasse* | cul de sac |
| *Parkplatz* | parking |
| *Umleitung* | diversion |
| *Ich habe eine Panne* | I have broken down |
| *Tankstelle* | petrol station |
| *voll bitte* | please fill the tank |
| *öl* | oil |

# I  BAVARIA

# 1

# Regensburg to Ulm

## A.  Regensburg

**REGENSBURG** (134,000 inhab.; alt. 333m), also called Ratisbon, is situated at the northernmost point of the Danube, at its confluence with the Regen and the Naab. The main city of the Upper Palatinate, the fourth largest in Bavaria and (with some 1400 medieval buildings) the largest surviving medieval city in Germany, Regensburg is superb, completely unscathed by centuries of warfare and unspoiled by its industries (Siemens, Triumph and BMW). 'Regensburg is so exquisitely situated', observed Goethe in 1786, 'that the spot was bound to attract a city'. Regensburg hosts festivals throughout the summer, including a jazz festival at the end of July, as well as a Christkindlmarkt in Advent.

**Main railway station**: Bahnhofstrasse. **Main post office**: Bahnhofstrasse. **Information Office**: Old Town Hall (Altes Rathaus), Kohlenmarkt. **Trains** to Frankfurt, Munich, Ulm, Vienna. **Boats** along the Danube to Passau, taking in Walhalla.

**History**. The Celts founded Radasbona c 500 BC, and were conquered by the Romans in AD 77, when Vespasian had a fortress built here. In AD 179 the legions of Marcus Aurelius constructed a huge camp, *Castra Regina*, large enough for 6000 men and still traceable in the quadrangle of streets at the heart of the city. In the early 6C the Dukes of Bavaria, the Agilolfings, made Regensburg their principal seat. Boniface established a bishopric here in 739. Charlemagne overthrew the Dukes in 788. Regensburg became a Free Imperial City in 1245, whence dates its most flourishing era. From Regensburg Konrad II in 1147 and Frederick Barbarossa in 1189 set out on Crusades.
  In 1541 a conference at Regensburg brought local agreement between Catholics and Protestants. The Swedes besieged the city in 1632. Between 1663 and 1806 Regensburg was the permanent seat of the Imperial Diet. As the emperor's principal representatives at the Diet, the Princes of Thurn und Taxis established themselves here in 1748. Karl von Dalberg, formerly Elector of Mainz, took over as prince in 1803; the French seized the city in 1809 (Napoleon was wounded here: see the plaque where Martin-Luther-Strasse meets Hemauerstrasse); and a year later it became part of Bavaria. Regensburg was the only Gothic city in Germany completely to survive World War II. It has been a university city since 1967. Its sons include the artist Albrecht Altdorfer (c 1480–1538, who was a municipal councillor here), John of Austria (1545–78, illegitimate son of Emperor Charles V and victor over the Turks at the naval battle of Lepanto in 1571), the painter John Zoffany (1733–1810) and the writer Georg Britting (1891–1964).

Maximilianstrasse leads from the railway station N through the park of the Schloss of the Princes of Thurn und Taxis. Turn left along St Petersweg to irregular St Emmeramsplatz, to reach the *Schloss, a former Benedictine monastery, founded by Theodor II and enriched by Charlemagne. The princes took it as their Residenz in 1809. It has a Romanesque doorway, c 1170, and a free-standing bell tower of 1579, while the south wing is neo-Renaissance, built in 1889, and the east wing Baroque. Its library,

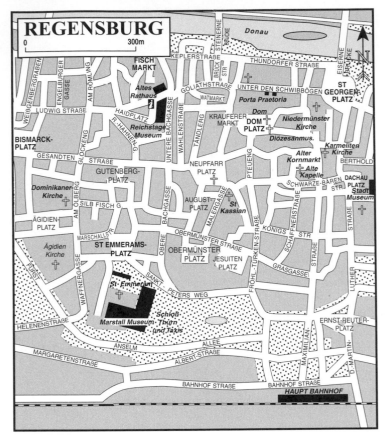

which houses 190,000 volumes, including many manuscripts and incunabula, was frescoed by the Asam brothers in 1737. On the left is the Baroque church of **St Emmeram**, originally built in the Gothic style as the Benedictine's chapel (open weekdays 10.00–16.30). Its free-standing belfry was begun in 1579 and finished in 1777. The 8–12C monastery church has a Baroque interior of 1731, by the brothers E.Q. and C.D. Asam. Three crypts house the tombs of three saints: St Emmeram (9C), St Ramwold (late 10C), St Wolfgang (1052). Other tombs in the main church shelter the remains of Queen Emma (who was executed in 1280), of Emperor Ludwig the Child and Emperor Arnulf of Bavaria. Here too is a monument to the humanist and historian Aventinus, who died in 1534. The stables are now the Marstallmuseum, devoted to the early history of the postal service, which was started by the Thurn und Taxis family, as well as coaches, carriages and sleighs (open for guided tours weekdays except Fri, 14.00–15.15, Sun and holidays 10.40–11.15). Other sights are the mortuary chapel and the Gothic cloisters. The Schloss also houses a museum of Brussels tapestries.

Walking north along Waffnergasse, on the left in tiny Albertus-Magnus-Platz is the 13C early Gothic Dominican church of **St Blasius**. The philosopher Albertus Magnus, who was Bishop of Regensburg, lived in the convent here between 1236 and 1240. On the west façade is a statue of St Dominic (c 1430). Inside are 15C choir stalls; a monument to Lukas Lamprechtshäuser (c 1500); and a Virgin and supplicants (c 1500) on a pillar in the choir. Further N, on the corner of Gesandtenstrasse stands the Protestant Dreieinigkeitskirche, built by the Nuremberg architect Hans Carl (1627–31), with 17C and 18C monuments to famous members of the 'eternal diet' (see below) in the churchyard. Turn W along Gesandtenstrasse to reach the 12C Romanesque **Jakobskirche** founded in 1140 by an Irish Benedictine named Mecherdach (hence its name 'Schottenkirche', Scots church), with a *Romanesque north porch, depicting Christ between SS James and John, Adam, Eve and the twelve Apostles. Look inside for its Romanesque crucifix and the Gothic stone statues on pillars of the choir.

From here Schottenstrasse runs N to reach elegant **Bismarckplatz**, with its fountains, the former palace of the Crown Prince (1702), now the Thurn und Taxis Bank, and a palace (1805) and theatre (1804), both built by Emanuel d'Herigoyen.

Return to Waffnergasse and turn N as far as Ludwigstrasse to reach **Haidplatz**, with its fountain, the Justitiabrunnen (1656). No 1 Haidplatz is the 'Neue Waage' ('New Weigh House'), a former tavern where the protestant Melanchthon disputed with the Catholic Eck in 1541, and No 7 is the Haus zum Goldenen Kreuz, an early Gothic house with a tower. Here in 1546 Emperor Charles V met his future wife Barbara Blömberg. The Renaissance Thon-Dittmer palace, with its classical façade designed by d'Herigoyen in 1810, hosts concerts in summer.

NW in Kohlenmarkt stands the magnificent Old Town Hall (13–18C). In the west wing is the imperial hall (Reichsaal), c 1360, with a timber ceiling of 1408, painted in 1564 by Melchior Bocksberger. The façade is Gothic while the east wing is Baroque, built in 1661. The eight storey tower dates from c 1250. The Venus fountain of 1661 in the courtyard has four stone figures, 1630, from the Dreieinigkeitskirche. The Old Town Hall now houses, along with a courtroom, torture chamber and tapestries, the Museum of the Imperial Diet, for here in the Reichsaal between 1663 and 1806 the emperor, seated under a baldacchino of 1573, presided over electors, princes and the deputies of the imperial cities who made up the so-called perpetual diet (Germany's oldest parliament). The Reichstagsmuseum is open for guided tours May–Sept Mon–Sat at 15.15 in English; otherwise open weekdays and Sat 09.30, 10.30, 11.30, 14.00, 15.00, 16.00; Sun and holidays 10.00, 11.00, 12.00. Across the Kohlenmarkt stands the **Café Prinzess**, established in 1686.

This part of Regensburg boasts merchants' houses, built in the Italian style between the 13C and 16C and fortified with towers. N is Fischmarkt, in which a fish market is held each morning, centred on St George's fountain, c 1600. To the W, at No 5 Keplerstrasse (1540), is a museum devoted to the astronomer Johannes Kepler, who died here in 1630. Nos 1 and 3 Keplerstrasse retain their 13C towers, and No 7, the Blaue Hecht, is a former medieval inn.

Goliathstrasse, with the 13C Goliath haus, frescoed with a picture of David and the giant by Melchior Bocksberger, c 1573, continues E from the Old Town Hall. S of Goliath haus is the Watmarkt, with Regensburg's finest tower house, the seven-storey mid-13C **Baumburgerturm**, and another mid-13C Gothic house, the Bräunelturm, at No 6. Goliathstrasse running into Unter den Schwibbögen, leads past the Bischofshof, which is the bishop's palace from the 11C and now a hotel, and the late 2C Porta

Praetoria, the northern gate of the Roman camp and the only major Roman remain left in Bavaria. South of the Bischofshof are first the 14C church of St Johannes and then the cathedral.

**··Dom St Peter**, famous for its boys' choir, the 'cathedral sparrows' (Domspatzen) was begun in the 10C, damaged by severe fires in the 12C and burnt almost to the ground in 1273. The Eselturm on the north side is all that remains of the old building. Bishop Leo the Thurndorfer began building a new cathedral in 1250. The main choir was vaulted c 1300, the crossing and the first arch of the nave in 1325. Work started on the south tower in 1341, on the north tower in 1383. The whole was completed early in the 16C, apart from the 105m-high towers (1859–69, restored since 1950). The cathedral stands 85.4m long, 34.8m wide and 31.85m from the ground to the highest point of the central of the three naves. Its elaborate west façade and doorway has a rose window behind a crucifix (1480), carvings and statues finished by 1430, including a king riding a curious horned beast and St Martin of Tours (both mid 14C). The southwest porch has a carving of St Peter's release (1360).

Treasures inside include 13C glass in the south transept and 14C glass in the choir; a stone pulpit of 1482; the 15m-high tabernacle of 1493, to the north of the high altar, and a well of 1501, opposite the Eselturm, both by Wolfgang Roritzer. The two west pillars of the crossing carry statues of the Virgin and angel of the Annunciation, c 1280, by the Master of Erminhold. Stone statues include one of the apostle Peter, wearing a conical papal tiara, c 1300, and of Paul, James and Bartholomew, late 14C, early 15C. Amongst the finest tombs are those of Margaretha Tucher by Peter Vischer of Nuremberg, 1521 and of Bishop Philipp Wilhelm, 1598, in the middle of the nave. The high altar in silver of 1785 is by Georg Ignaz Bauer of Augsburg. The silver busts of Mary and Joseph were created c 1695, and those of Peter and Paul in the mid 18C. The altar cross and seven silver lamps date from 1777. The cathedral also houses a damaged memorial to first Prince, Karl von Dalberg.

Its cloisters (guided tours May–Oct, Mon–Sat 10.00, 11.00 and 14.00, Sun and holidays 12,00 and 14.00; Nov–Apr, Mon–Sat 11.00, Sun and holidays 12.00) contain the 12C Romanesque **Allerheiligenkapelle** (All Saints' chapel), built to house the tomb of Bishop Hartwich II (1155–64) with wall paintings, and the Romanesque **Stephanskapelle**, with a 10C altar. The treasury, **Domschatzmuseum**, at No 3 Krautermarkt (entrance from the cathedral) has 11–19C tapestries and vestments as well as goldsmiths' treasures (open Apr–Oct, Tues–Sat 10.00–17.00, Sun from 11.30; Dec–Mar Fri, Sat 10.00–16.30, Sun 11.30–16.30). The **Diözesanmuseum** (open Apr–Nov, except Sat, 10.00–17.00) houses sculpture, paintings and religious works of art from the 11C to the 20C.

Opposite the west façade of the cathedral is the 14C Haus an der Heuport, a gracious patrician house with a courtyard and an open Baroque staircase. Residenzstrasse leads S from the cathedral to the Renaissance Neupfarrkirche, built 1519–40 as a pilgrimage church dedicated to Our Lady. A painting of 'Schöne Maria', over a side altar, is by Hans Leingerger, 1520. This has been a Protestant church since 1542.

South in Kassiansplatz is the Romanesque St Kassian's church, with an 18C Baroque interior. From here Schwarze-Bären-Strasse leads E to the S side of the picturesque Alter Kornmarkt and the **Alte Kapelle**. The chapel was begun in 1002; the choir is mid 15C; and the interior is Bavarian Rococo, with frescoes by the Augsburg painter Christoph Thomas Scheffler. The high altar of 1769–75 is by Simon Sorg of Regensburg, and there is a 13C

*The angel of Regensburg, carved for Regensburg cathedral c 1280*

Italian Madonna in the Lady Chapel. On the NW side of the square stands the 'Roman' (i.e. Romanesque) tower, also the Herzogshof, the palace of the Dukes of Bavaria, which was begun in the late 10C. The present building, however, is c 1200, with the window arcades of the façade c 1220. Behind it rises the Romanesque Ducal Hall. On the W side, and beyond it stands the church of St Ulrich c 1230–50; and on the E side the Baroque church of the Carmelites, 1641–60, with a tower of 1681 and 18C altarpieces from the cathedral.

In Dachauplatz, E of this church, are over 50m of surviving Roman wall and a former 13C and 14C friary now housing the **Stadtmuseum** (City Museum; open Tues–Sat 10.00–16.00, Sun 10.00–13.00), devoted to Bavarian history since the Stone Age. Here are treasures from the city churches, furniture, and on the 2nd floor 16–18C European paintings, including works by Altdorfer and his school. The monks handed over this priory to the city in 1544, and here was built the first Protestant press of Regensburg. The priory church, with its Early Gothic nave of 1260–70, its High Gothic choir 1330–40, and its Late Gothic screen, has Gothic and Renaissance tombs and a Crucifixion group by Erhard Heydenreich, 1513. S of this museum is the new Rathaus, 1936–38.

N of Alter Kornmarkt rises the twin-towered, mid 12C **Niedermünsterkirche** once part of a Benedictine nunnery. Its high altar is by the Salzburg stonemason Jakob Mösl, 1763; the altarpiece of the Assumption dates from 1900. Excavations inside have uncovered buildings dating as far back as the 2C. Here too stands the Bishops' Palace, today housing the Proske Music Library. N of the palace, Donaumarkt leads left into Thundorferstrasse which runs along the river to Germany's oldest surviving stone bridge: the 310m long Steinerne Brücke, 1135–46, a masterpiece of medieval engineering with 16 arches of varying spans. A copy of the Brückenmännchen, or bridge dwarf, is on the west parapet. The Brücktor, sole survivor of three, is 14C. To the right of the bridge is the **Historische Wurstküche**, which for hundreds of years has served up Regensburger pork sausages. Cross the bridge and turn right along Andreasstrasse to find the Baroque church of **St Magnus**.

# B.   Regensburg to Ulm along the River Danube

Total distance 233km. Regensburg—B16, 29km Kelheim—7km Weltenberg—66km Ingolstadt—22km Neuburg—34km Donauwörth—52km Günzburg—B10, 23km Ulm.

Leave Regensburg by Kumpfmühler Strasse to begin a romantic trip along the right bank of the meandering Danube. Turn right before reaching **Bad Abbach**, whose sulphuric baths were reputed in Roman times, today there are three modern rheumatism clinics here. The Emperor Henry II was born in the town's ruined Schloss in 973 AD. Continue along the B16 into the Danube valley to reach after a further 10km the pretty market town of **Saal**. From Saal the B299 runs across the Danube to **Kelheim**, with its 13–14C defences, consisting of three towers and three gates, and its gabled burghers' houses. Situated at a strategic point where the Altmühl meets the Danube, its streets still follow the pattern laid out in the early 13C. Kelheim has a 15C late Gothic parish church, with a Madonna of c 1440 over the south doorway, and the remains of mid-12C towers of the Wittelsbach's Schloss, the rest of the Schloss buildings are used as a school and government offices. Duke Ludwig the Kelheimer was murdered in the chapel in 1231.

Visible on the Michelsberg, 3km out of the town, is the *Befreiungshalle (open Apr–Sept 08.00–18.00, Oct–Mar 09.00–12.00, 13.00–16.00), an extraordinary neo-classical building created by Friedrich Gärtner and Leo von Klenze for Ludwig I of Bavaria in 1842–63 to celebrate the 1813–15 War of Liberation against France. Eighteen massive statues of German maidens, representing the German provinces, adorn the exterior. Inside another 34 marble statues of goddesses of victory, sculpted to the design of Ludwig Schwanthaler, enliven the colossal round hall, which is inscribed, 'Let Germans never forget what made necessary the struggle for freedom'. Between these goddesses are 17 gilded-bronze shields, made from captured French guns and inscribed with the names of the victories of 1813–15.

The area around Kelheim has several caves with stalagmite and stalactite formations, the best known being the **Grosses Schulerloch** and the **Kleine Schulerloch**, close by Oberau and 3km on the road W towards Riedenburg. **Burg Prunn** also rises 100m over the River Altmühl near Kelheim, with a Romanesque keep, Baroque chapel, the rest 16C and 17C. Here in 1577 was discovered a celebrated medieval manuscript of the Lohengrin saga.

Cross the river at Kelheim and follow the wooded Jura heights SW and the Danube gorge to the former Benedictine abbey, founded 620, set among the rocks and woods at **Weltenburg**, with the limestone cliffs of its spectacular river gorge, the 'Donaudurchbruch' and its Baroque *church, 1717–21, by the brothers Asam. The church is built to the plans of Egid Quirin Asam, whose features are depicted as an angel in the ceiling frescoes, and the stuccoed entrance hall is by Cosmas Damian Asam. Within its exquisitely undulating walls is a high altar depicting St George and the dragon. The present monastery buildings date from the same period and were designed by F.P. Blank. Summer visits can be made to the gorge and abbey by boat from Kelheim. The gorge is floodlit in July, known as 'the Danube in flames'.

From Weltenburg follow the signs 8km to Eining, where have been excavated remains of a Roman fort, built 1–3C AD to guard the Limes where these Roman defences reached the Danube. **Neustadt** is 8km further SW and has a 16C Rathaus, the 15C Lorenzkirche, the 16C Annakirche and a 17C cemetery church. The countryside is still wooded and hilly, with fields growing hops. From Neustadt drive 4km E to **Abensberg**, on the River Abens, with parts of its 14–15C fortifications still intact. Its principal sights are the Hofbräuhaus, the birthplace of the historian Johannes Turmair (1477–1534, known as Aventinus), which you find among the gabled houses of the Marktplatz; the 13C church of St Barbara, with wall paintings; the 14C Carmelite church, which has Gothic transepts and later Baroque reordering. The Aventinus Museum is housed in the former monastery. At nearby Allersdorf is a 16C pilgrimage church.

The road SW from Neustadt to Ingolstadt (see Rte 12) leads through Münchsmünster, at the junction with the B300 to Augsburg, with a church belonging to its former Benedictine monastery.

From Ingolstadt continue W along the B16 in the direction of Donauwörth. Continue W to Neuburg an der Donau.

**Neuburg an der Donau** (25,000 inhab.; alt. 403m; Information Office in Luitpoldstrasse) boasts the first Protestant church to be built in Bavaria.

This chapel was built in 1540, with frescoes by Hans Bocksberger the Elder, 1543, for the Renaissance Residenz which is chiefly 1530–45 and was the home of the princes of Neuburg until 1685. Its east wing was built in 1665. Three lines of fortifications and a moat protect the town. In the exquisite **Karlsplatz** stands the court church of Our Lady, built in 1627, with Renaissance furnishings, Wessobrunn stuccoes, an organ gallery of c 1700, a high altar by J.A. Breitenauer, 1752–54, and a pulpit of 1756. Other sights at Neuburg an der Donau are the chapel of St Martin, 1731, now a library, with 18C furnishings; St Peter's church, c 1650, in Amalienstrasse opposite the 13C and 16C town gate, which is known as the Münz, Holy Cross church, with a late 12C crypt, the rest reordered in the Rococo style in 1755–58, with contemporary stucco work, a high altar by J.M. Fischer, paintings and frescoes by J.M. Baumgartner, and a tomb on the south wall by Loy Hering, c 1530. The town hall dates from 1640–42; the Museum of Local History is at 119 Amalienstrasse; and the English Garden is laid out in the NE section of the lower town.

After 5km the road passes through **Oberhausen**. Here a footpath leads left to the 150m-high memorial to the men of the 1st French Grenadiers who fell in the Austro-French war of 1800. Beyond Oberhausen appears on the left bank of the Danube a view of the Baroque Schloss Bertoldsheim.

After 5km driving W from Oberhausen a brief deviation S leads to **Rain**, to find in front of the Rathaus, 1759–62, a bronze statue, 1914, of General Tilly, mortally wounded here in 1632 leading the Imperial and Bavarian troops in defence of the passage of the Lech against the Protestant army of King Gustavus Adolphus of Sweden. Rain has a 14C and 15C church of **St Johann**, alongside the **Allerheiligenkapelle** (Chapel of All Souls), 1471, now a local history museum.

*****Donauwörth** (18,000 inhab.; alt. 403m), 13km from Rain along the B16, at the confluence of the Wörnitz and the Danube, is where this route reaches the Romantische Strasse (see Rte 7B). This Protestant town was mortgaged to the Catholics by Emperor Rudolf II, an act that helped to provoke the Thirty Years War. The island or 'Werth' in the Danube here was colonised in the 6C. Donauwörth was a Free Imperial City from the 13C to 1714, and was savagely bombed in 1945. Its treasures include the late Gothic town hall (at E end of Reichsstrasse, built in 1309, restored in 1853 and now housing the information office). The Renaissance Fuggerhaus, with a grandiose portico, was built for Anton Fugger, 1539, and is at the W end of the celebrated Reichsstrasse, near the Town Hall. The Baroque *****Heilig-Kreuz-Kirche** is by Johann Schmuzer, 1717–22, with 17C and 18C monastery buildings, an early 18C pulpit and stalls, and a high altar of 1724 by Franz Xaver Schmuzer. Look for the early 14C tomb of Mary of Brabant, the wife of Duke Ludwig the Severe, who had her beheaded for allegedly committing adultery in 1256, and in the crypt a relic of the Holy Cross. The late Gothic parish church of Maria Himmelfahrt, 1444–67, houses a tabernacle carved by Gregor Erhart of Augsburg in 1503, medieval frescoes and 15C stained glass. Its belfry supports the 'Pummerin', at 6.55 tonnes the heaviest bell in Schwabia.

Reichstrasse derives its name from the medieval Imperial road between Italy and Bergen in Norway, which passed through the town. The Reichstadt fountain is from 1977. A late Gothic Tanzhaus stands on the corner of Reichsstrasse and Mangoldstrasse, destroyed in World War II and rebuilt in 1974. It now serves as a concert hall and archaeological museum. In Spitalstrasse, SW of the town hall square, stand the Spitalkirche, 1611–12, the Spital, c 1680, and the classical Deutschordenhaus, 1774–78. Spitalstrasse leads to the Riedertor, one of the two remaining gates of the medieval fortifications of Donauwörth.

21km SW along B16 is Höchstädt (alt. 418m) with its turreted Schloss 1589–93, formerly belonging to the Counts of Pfalz-Neuburg and the church of Maria Himmelfahrt, 15C and 16C, with its fine pulpit and high altar. In 1704 during the War of the Spanish Succession Höchstädt was the scene of a decisive battle between the Franco-Bavarian troops and the English and Imperial forces, see the local history museum.

The road continues another 6km to reach **Dillingen** (16,000 inhab.; alt. 433m), formerly the private country seat of the Bishop of Augsburg and seat of a Catholic University from 1551–1803. Dillingen has a 16C Schloss, on Schlossstrasse, frequently enlarged until the 18C. The Catholic church of **St Peter** is from 1619–28. The Peterskirche has a pulpit by Matthias Kager, while the church of Maria Himmelfahrt contains a high altar by J.M. Fischer, with a painting of the Assumption by J.G. Bermüller. Its frescoes by C.T. Scheffler, a pupil of the Asam brothers, include a Virgin surrounded by saints (on the vault of the nave) and a coronation of the Virgin (in the choir). The original university building, 1688–89, on Kardinal-von Waldburgstrasse has a Rococo Golden Room of 1761–64, and a chapel of 1617 with a mid-18C Rococo interior. The former Jesuit College is from 1736–38, with a Baroque library. The Jesuit church is from 1610–17. The parish church of St Peter by J. Alberthal was built in 1619–28; the Church of Our Lady, 1734–40; the church of Christ the King, 1960–62, with a Madonna c 1510 from the workshop of Jörg Syrlin the Younger.

5km W is **Lauingen**, which was the birthplace of Albertus Magnus, 1193–1280; his memorial is beside the 53m-high Schimmel Tower of 1478, whose upper storey was added in 1600. Thirty-eight Wittelsbachs are buried in the parish church of St Martin, 1518. The former Schloss of the Dukes of Pfalz-Neuburg is now a nursing home.

**Günzburg**, known in Roman times as *Guntia*, lies on the River Günz where it joins the Danube, 20km SW of Lauingen along the B16. Dominikus Zimmermann built the Rococo *Liebfrauenkirche between 1736 and 1739; its frescoes are by A. Enderle, 1741. The market square is charming. Also noteworthy are the 16C Renaissance Schloss and the Hofkirche (16–18C). Beside the Schloss is the former mint, by J. Dossenberger. Mid-18C Schloss Autenried dates from 1871.

From here take the B10, driving 23km W to Ulm.

**ULM** (95,000 inhab.; alt. 478m), celebrated for the spire of its cathedral, is situated in Baden-Württemberg at the confluence of the Danube and the Blau, which rises 20km W at Blaubeuren. The town is surrounded by a double set of walls from 14C and 15C, rebuilt in the mid-19C, along the Danube, incorporating the leaning Metzger tower and the Eagle bastion, from which Albrecht Berblinger, the celebrated 'Tailor of Ulm', leapt in 1811 in a vain attempt to fly. Ulm has become the chief city of Upper Württemberg.

**Main railway station**: F-Ebert-Strasse/Bahnhofstrasse. **Post office**: F-Ebert-Strasse. **Information Office**: 51 Münsterplatz.

**History**. Inhabited since the early Stone Age, Ulm became a Carolingian fief in 854, was under the rule of the Salier, 1024–1125, and the Staufen families, 1138–1268, and became a free Imperial city in 1274. The patricians and the merchant guilds agreed on a constitution in 1397, celebrated annually in the swearing-in ceremony (see below). Ulm flourished culturally and commercially in the 14C and 15C, with such masters as Hans Multscher (died here in 1467), Hans Schüchlin (died 1502), his son-in-law Bartholomäus Zeitblom (died c 1520), Martin Schaffner (died c 1540), Jörg

Syrlin the Elder (died 1498) and his son Jörg the Younger (died 1521) forming the nucleus of an important school of artists and architects based in the city. In 1530 Ulm took the side of the Reformers, and work stopped on the cathedral, and resumed only in 1844. Though culturally and commercially harmed by the Thirty Years War, Ulm retained its status as an Imperial city until 1802. Three years later 25,000 Austrians surrendered here to Napoleon Bonaparte. New fortifications were commenced in the 1840s. Nearly three-quarters of the city was detroyed in World War II. The university was rebuilt in 1969. Here was born Albert Einstein (1879–1955). At four yearly intervals Ulm celebrates a traditional fish festival and a coopers' festival.

Follow Bahnhofstrasse SE to the junction with Wengengasse, which leads N to Wengenkirche, a modern building housing the remains of a late-Gothic/Baroque church bombed in 1944. Inside is an 18C altar painting by Franz Martin Kuen.

The continuation of Bahnhofstrasse E is Hirschstrasse, which leads as far as Münsterplatz and the Protestant **Cathedral (Münster)**, begun in 1377 to plans by Heinrich Parler the Elder. After Parler's death building continued

*Pythagoras, inventor of music: a detail of the choir stalls of Ulm cathedral, carved by Jörg Syrlin the Elder between 1469 and 1471*

under Ulrich von Ensingen and Burckhardt Engelberg, and the building finished only in 1890. Among Gothic churches in Germany only the cathedral at Cologne is larger; and at 161m the tower of Ulm is the world's highest—768 steps lead to a superb panorama of the Jura, the Alps when the weather is clear, the Danube and the city itself. It was begun by Ulrich von Ensingen in the 1390s, but the major part was largely the work of Matthäus Böblinger working a hundred years later; the rest including the spires was completed in 1845–90. The cathedral has an arcaded doorway and Renaissance doors, with a statue of *Man of Sorrows by Hans Multscher, 1429, and other early 16C statues by Jörg Syrlin the Younger.

**Interior**. There are five soaring aisles, with no transepts. The choir stalls are by Jörg Syrlin the Elder, 1469–71; note the pagan as well as Biblical motifs, with Greek and Roman sages—Seneca, Cicero, Pythagoras,

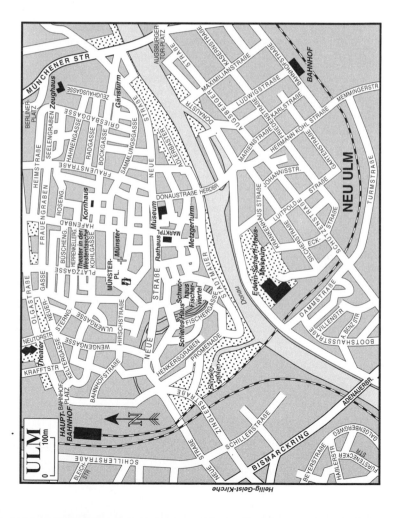

Heilig-Geist-kirche

Ptolemy, and so on—and Apostles and martyrs. Syrlin the Elder also designed the sedilia behind the high altar in 1468. The high altar is by M. Schaffner, 1521, the pulpit by B. Engelberg, 1499, with a canopy by J. Syrlin the Younger, 1510. The cathedral has fan vaulting and a fresco of the Last Judgement, 1471, as well as 14C and 15C glass, and three modern windows, 1956. Its 26m-high *tabernacle of 1464–71 has statues by Multscher, in the upper section, and N. Hagenauer. Major restoration was carried out in 1965–70.

Along the Lautenberg, SW of the Münster, stands the Neuer Bau (1585–93), a former storehouse. In the **Marktplatz** S of the Münster is the Gothic and Renaissance **Rathaus** 1360 and 1420 (restored), with frescoes of 1540; early 15C sculptures of Electors and Emperors by H. Multscher; an astronomical clock of 1520, renovated by L. Habrecht in 1580. Inside is a replica of Berblinger's flying machine. In front of the town hall is the Fischkasten fountain, by Syrlin the Elder, 1482. SW of the town hall is the modern Heiliggeistkirche, with a bizarre, finger-shaped bell tower. To the E of the Rathaus along Neuestrasse is the Taubenplätzle, with a dolphin fountain dated 1585. At 92 Neuestrasse is the **Ulm Museum** (open Tue–Sun 10.00– 12.00, 14.00–1700; no midday break July–Sept). It displays work by local artists, including Martin Schaffner, Hans Multscher and Jörg Syrlin the Elder as well as others who worked on the cathedral, particularly Ulrich von Ensingen and Matthäus Böblinger. Its international modern collection includes 400 major post-1945 works of art donated by the private collector Kurt Fried in 1978.

Walk E along Neuestrasse turning N along Frauenstrasse to reach the old Kornhaus, today a concert hall, by H. Fischer, 1591, with a doorway by C. Bauhofer and staircase tower by P. Schmidt, 1591. The fountain in the courtyard, with its statue of St Hildegard, is a copy of C. Bauhofer's, 1591 original.

**Other sights.** There is the Fishermen's Quarter (Fischerviertel) on the River Blau with the Schiefes Haus (i.e. Crooked House) over the canal, beyond which is the Butchers' Tower (Metzgerturm) of 1340, leaning precariously and a survival from the original city fortifications. The Schwörhaus, in Schwörhausgasse, was built in 1613, reordered in the Baroque style in 1785 and restored in 1954. Here the town officials are annually sworn in, on the festival of Swearing-in-Monday in July. The Dreifaltigkeitskirche in Langestrasse, which was built in 1670 and ruined in World War II, has a 14C sacristy. The handsome former arsenal of 1552 is in Zeughausgasse. There is a theatre at 73 Olgastrasse, 1969, devoted to opera, operetta and drama, including avant-garde works, and the Theatre in der Westentasche in Herren-kellergasse. The city has a Bread and Baking Museum at 17 Fürsteneckerstrasse in the far SW of the city (Deutsches Brotmuseum; open daily except Sat 10.00–12.00, 15.00–17.30); a prehistoric collection at 4 Frauenstrasse (open Mon–Fri 09.00–12.00, 14.00–17.00; Sat, Sun 14.00– 17.00); and a Natural History Museum at 3 Korngasse (open weekdays, except Mon, 10.00–12.00, 14.00–17.00; Sat extension 12.00–13.00).

Cross the Herd bridge to **Neu-Ulm** (which is in Bavaria). Neu-Ulm is enlivened by the modern church of St John Baptist, in Augsburgerstrasse, and the Edwin-Scharff-Museum at 40 Silcherstrasse (open Tue–Sat 14.00– 17.00), devoted to the 20C sculptor Edwin Scharff (1887–1955). Also worth visiting is the city's Heimatmuseum of local mineralogy at 12 Hermann-Köhl-Strasse (open Wed 14.00–17.00, Sat 10.00–12.00).

**Environs. Wiblingen,** 7km S across Adenauer bridge, has a late Baroque abbey church of St Martin by J.G. Specht, 1772–81, with trompe-l'oeil frescoes by Janarius Zick, and a 16C crucifix which once hung in Ulm cathedral. It boasts a Rococo library, built by C. Wiedemann, 1714–60 (open Tue–Sun, Nov–Mar 14.00–16.00, Apr–Oct 10.00–12.00, 14.00–17.00) which has more trompe-l'oeil frescoes and stucco work, as well as symbolic statues, representing mathematics, law, history and natural history as well as the monastic virtues.

At **Erbach,** 7km SW, stands the church of St Martin, which was reordered in 1767–79 by I. and A. Finsterwalder, and frescoed by M. Kuen in 1768. It shelters a Madonna dating from c 1490. The 16C Schloss has a museum.

# 2

# Regensburg and the Upper Palatinate

## A.  Regensburg to Weiden via Amberg

Total distance (without diversions), 177km. Regensburg—B8, 27km Kallmünz—
13km Schmidmühlen—27km Amberg—B85 (or B202), 12km
Sulzbach-Rosenberg—26km Auerbach—36km Kemnath—A93, 36km Weiden.

Leave Regensburg (Rte 1A) by the B8 towards Nuremberg, at Kneiting turning N for an excursion (3km) to Adlersberg, with its 13C early Gothic church which has 14C wall paintings as well as the remains of a medieval Dominican monastery.

Return to Kneiting and drive S to Mariaort, at the confluence of the Danube and the Naab, where you must cross a wooden bridge by foot to visit two tiny Baroque churches, the Calvary church, 1724, and the pilgrimage church of Mariaort, 1774–76. 10km further on is Etterzhausen, with a 16C Schloss and the 12C Romanesque church of St Wolfgang. The B8 follows the Naab to the hamlet of Penk with its 12C Romanesque church, obviously built for defence as well as worship. 6km N is Pielenhofen. Here is a former Cistercian monastery church, 1719, by Franz Beer. Its gable façade with twin, domed towers, gives entry to a Baroque interior, with a shallow cupola by Karl Stauder, 1720, and stucco decoration. The early 18C monastery is now a school.

**Kallmünz** lies 11km N, a 13C fortress town of the Wittelsbachs. The Swedes demolished its Schloss in 1641, though romantic ruins remain. Kallmünz has narrow streets, exquisite squares and old houses, as well as the stone Naab bridge of 1550, a town hall and museum, 1603, and the Rococo parish church of **St Michael,** 1758.

From Kallmünz a brief excursion NE leads to Burglengenfeld, birthplace of the architect Johann Michael Fischer, 1692–1766. Things to see include the remains of its 11C Schloss with a 28m-high keep, walls, 12C towers and a Gothic armoury, also a 16C Altmannsche Schlösschen, a towered and gabled town hall, c 1600, and an 18C Rococo parish church of **St Veit.**

Return to Kallmünz and leave the Naab valley to drive N to Dietldorf, with its Rathaus, built in the style of the late Italian Renaissance between 1700 and 1705, containing Rococo, Empire and Biedermeier furniture. The road leads N (13km from Kallmünz) to Schmidmühlen on the confluence of the Vils and the Lauterach. In the Middle Ages this was one of the richest producers of iron ore in the Upper Palatinate, if not in Europe. Forges and smithies were built on the river and the old smith's mill of 1311 remains. Schmidmühlen was the birthplace of the sculptor Erasmus Grasser (died 1518). The Renaissance upper Rathaus, with its octagonal staircase tower and some 16C wall paintings, and the Baroque lower Schloss have been well renovated.

Two routes now lead further N to delightful Amberg. The westerly route is by way of **Stettkirchen** with its tiny Baroque pilgrimage church, and the market town of **Hohenburg**, which has a ruined Rathaus, once a home of the Margraves of Hohenburg, gabled houses, and a Renaissance town hall, c 1560, with early 18C dormers, now a local museum. Continue NW through Allersburg, where there is a Gothic church, and then through the picturesque narrow Lauerach valley by way of Ransbach as far as (14km) **Kastl**, with a Benedictine abbey founded in 1098, whose Romanesque abbey church was built in 1129. This has a powerful five storey tower and the oldest barrel-vaulting in Germany in the choir. The interior contains a frieze with 69 coats of arms of the founder and patrons of the abbey, as well as fine gravestones in the Gothic vestibule, including some by Loy Hering. From Kastl the route turns E towards (after 20km) Amberg (see below).

The easterly route to Amberg from Schmidmühlen leads by way of Vilshofen and Rieden to **Ensdorf**, with its former Benedictine St Jakobskirche. A fine doorway, with statues, opens into the interior, by Wolfgang Dientzenhofer, c 1700, with early frescoes by C.D. Asam, a high altar painting by Johann Gebhard, a wooden statue of the Madonna and Child, c 1500, and stucco decoration. The monastery is now a Salesian school.

**Theuern** is 6km N, with a Schloss of 1781, displaying a collection of minerals, porcelain and glass and an industrial museum. A water-driven forge has been reconstructed in Theuern, as well as a glass factory and a grain mill.

**·Amberg** (45,000 inhab.; alt. 373m) straddles the River Vils 8km N of Theuern.

**Information Office**: Zeughausstrasse 1a.

**History**. Known as Villa Ammenberg in the early 12C, Amberg received its city charter in 1242. The first ironmasters' guild was founded here in 1387; in the late 14C there were 70 or so ironworks here and the 19C Luipoldhütte remains today one of the largest ironworks in the region, drawing on the mines to the north. Emperor Konrad II gave Amberg to the Bishop of Bamberg in 1034; Duke Ludwig the Severe took control of the town in 1269; and in 1329 it became capital of the Rhineland Palatinate. The town opted for the Reformation in 1538—the first town to do so in the Upper Palatinate. Amberg was added to the territories of Maximilian I of Bavaria in 1628, who restored Catholicism. (The city officially changed its religious adherence no fewer than five times.) In spite of surviving attacks and a severe plague during the Thirty Years War, Amberg was severely reduced.

Amberg's oval-shaped **fortifications** remain largely intact. They include gates and towers, the finest of which are the Renaissance Wingershof Gate of 1580 and the Nabburger Gate, with its polygonal upper storey of 1587. Other sights include the ·Gothic church of **St Martin**, 1421–83. The vault was finished in 1483; the 98m-high west tower, begun in 1534, was finished in the 18C. The Gothic interior contains a sandstone Gothic Annunciation on the N wall, a bronze font of 1417, the *tomb of Count Palatine Rupert Pipan, 1387, behind the high altar, and a red marble relief of Martin Merz, who died 1501, on the S wall.

The 15C Gothic Rathaus, with its 16C Renaissance stairway, arcades and balustrade, dominates the old picturesque market place; its ogival windows were added in 1880; Renaissance panelling decorates the interior. The imposing Gothic church of **St Georg**, founded in 1094 and rebuilt after a fire in 1359, has a Baroque interior and Wessobrunn stucco, 1718–23, as well as frescoes depicting the life of St George, by Josef Adam Müller, 1722. Its Rococo organ case dates from 1767; its high altar with a painting of St George by Johann Nepomuk Schöpf, from 1766.

Other treasures of Amberg are the former Kurfürstliches Schloss by J. Schoch, 1602; the 13–14C Pfalzgrafenschloss, now a museum of local history; the *Baroque library of the Maltesergebäude, formerly the Jesuit college, by Georg Dietzenhofer and Wolfgang Hirschstetter, 1665–89, with stucco by Johann Schmuzer; the present Landsgericht, built by Pfalzgraf Friedrich II, 1545; and the double arched sentry walk across the River Vils, known as the Stadtbrille, or town spectacles, since its arches mirrored in the water form two perfect circles. It was designed to connect the Schloss with the town's arsenal, 1476–1604.

NW of the old town is the Rococo *Schulkirche in Schrannenplatz, by Wolfgang Dietzenhofer, 1693–99; it was enlarged in 1738. Its doorway has statues of SS Augustine and Francis de Sales, while frescoes on the nave vault by Gottfried Bernhard Götz depict the founding of the Salesian order.

3km NE of Amberg (a half hour's walk) is the pilgrimage church on the Mariahilfberg, built as the result of a vow when Amsberg was spared the ravages of a plague and the Thirty Years War in 1634. The stuccoed interior is by Giovanni Battista Carlone; the prophets and saints on the high altar were painted by Carlone's pupil Paul d'Aglio; the ceiling and frescoes in the choir, side chapels and nave were painted by C.D. Asam in 1717.

Travel 12km NW along the main B85 or the quieter B302 to **Sulzbach-Rosenberg** (20,000 inhab.; alt. 450m), dominated by the Ducal Schloss of 1582–1618 (enlarged 1768–94), its main hall dates from 1582, the Prince's wing from 1518; the Schloss fountain is from 1701. The Schloss is now an orphanage. From 1353–73 Sulzbach was the Residence of Emperor Karl IV after his marriage with Anna von der Pfalz. The two towns joined together in 1934. Minerals have been mined here since the late Middle Ages. For centuries Sulzbach prospered from the ore and today has the largest iron and steel works in southern Germany.

Below the Schloss in the Marktplatz is the 14C Gothic Rathaus, with an oriel window in its gabled façade, the Pfalz-Bavarian coat of arms over its clock. Here too is the 13C Catholic church of Maria Himmelfahrt; its nave was rebuilt in 1412. The font is 15C; in the south vestibule is a late Gothic carving c 1480, and in the left side chapel another c 1490; the princes' gallery was added in 1526; the high altar painting is by Hans Georg Asam, 1710. From 1652 Catholics and Protestants shared this church until the protestant Christuskirche, 1955–58, was built. Sulzbach-Rosenberg has numerous 14C gabled houses with oriel windows. The remains of the 14C town walls can be explored, and by foot E of the town can be reached the 17C and 18C pilgrimage church of St Anna at the top of the Annaberg.

Return 4km along the B85 towards Amberg and turn right along the Ammer valley to **Oberammerthal** with its early Romanesque Frauenkirche of 940–1000, with a Gothic tower, choir and vaulting as well as a 15C stone pulpit and baldacchino. The Romanesque parish church of St Nikolaus is 12C. The bottom half of its tower is Romanesque, with a Gothic enlargement; the nave, enlarged in 1800, has Baroque decoration. Opposite the church is the 16C Hofmarktschloss, enriched with an oriel window.

Follow the road W 9km through Götzendorf to Illschwang with a 12C church tower. The road continues towards Weigendorf. From here are short diversions, signposted, to pretty **Fürnried**, dubbed 'the most beautiful village in Upper Palatine', and the ruins of **Burg Lichtenegg** and then onwards to Etzelwang and Rupprechstein. 2km outside these charming spots stands Schloss Neidstein. 20km from Illschwang you reach **Hirschbach** and the climbing country of the Hirschbach valley. **Königstein**, 11km NE, is the centre for climbing the Ossinger (alt. 651m), with its observation tower, the Steinberg (alt. 606m), and the Breitenstein (alt. 612m), with a ruined Burg and a Burg chapel.

The road continues N by way of **Krottensee**, a centre of potholing (especially the Maximilianshöhle), and **Neuhaus** with the medieval Burg Veldenstein, reaching after 27km **Michelfeld**, where in 1697 the Benedictine monastery was reordered to the Baroque plans of Wolfgang Dientzenhofer. 3km E is **Auerbach**, with its Gothic town hall of 1418. Auerbach owes its past fortune to iron ore and to lying on a main merchant route to Nuremberg. The early 15C Rathaus stands on a long market street. Behind is the church of St Johann Baptist, 1445, with Baroque reordering by George Dientzenhofer in 1682. It shelters late Gothic carvings, a stone font of 1525 and a late 18C high altar. The Spitalkirche has Rococo altars. 'Auerbach's Keller' appears in Goethe's Faust.

From Auerbach drive 20km NE along the B470 to **Eschenbach**. Kaiser Karl IV gave it city rights in 1358. The 15C Gothic church of St Laurentius in the Marktplatz was enlarged in 1893. Its tower is Gothic with a cylindrical Renaissance upper part, 1541. Inside are Baroque choir stalls. Close by is the two-storeyed 16C Rathaus. The Maria-Hilf-Kirche, 1771–74, has stucco work and three Rococo altars.

Much of this region is a legally protected nature reserve. Two routes lead to Weiden. The shorter one (33km) runs by way of the B470 E to **Pressath**. The parish church of St Georg was burned down in 1759 and rebuilt 1761–65, and retains old gravestones from the former building. The cemetery chapel of St Stephan dates from 1450 and the Altöttinger chapel from 1754.

3km N of Pressath the 16C Schlösschen Weihersberg stands picturesquely on its hill; its chapel has a Rococo altar. **Parkstein** lies 12km further SE in the direction of Weiden, to the N of the B470 (look for the signs) nestling under the basalt peak of the Parkstein (596m), on which once stood a castle protecting the town. The Berg retains its pilgrimage chapel of 1851. The church of St Pankratius houses the graves of the major families of Parkstein and a Rococo pulpit of 1789. The musician Franz Josef Strauss, the father of Richard Strauss, was born here in 1822 (d 1909).

Follow now the road to Süssenloher Weiher and take the B22 to Weiden.

The longer route from Eschenbach to Weiden leads N to **Speinshart** (5km). Here is a monastery church, dedicated to the Immaculate Conception of Mary, built in the Italian Baroque style by Wolfgang Dientzenhofer in 1696, with paintings by Bartolomeo Lucchese and stucco work by his brother

Carlo Domenico. The depiction of Mary's Immaculate Conception on the overpowering high altar is flanked by statues of SS Norbert and Augustine. 2km E of Speinshart at Baraberg is a 1756 pilgrimage church, restored after World War II.

Continue N to **Neustadt am Kulm** (5km), surrounded by basalt peaks, with its former Carmelite church of 1413 now a Protestant church and reordered magnificently in the Baroque style, with early 18C stucco by Domenico Quadro, and fine 17C tombs. The town hall in the Marktplatz dates from 1611. 7km N lies **Kemnath**, known as Keminata in the 11C, and boasting ancient houses and the late Gothic *Maria Himmelfahrt church, with its 17C side altars, a Baroque high altar, 1739, and a tower of 1854. Other noteworthy sights are St Pirmin's column (1695) and the Sebastian pillar of 1714.

A short diversion E along the B22 leads within 5km to the town of Waldeck, again surrounded by high basalt peaks, with a ruined 12C Schloss on the 641m-high Waldecker Schlossberg. The Rococo church in the Marktplatz was decorated by the brothers Asam in 1731.

Returning to the main route, the charming road leads N through Kulmain to Brand, the birthplace of the composer Max Reger, 1873–1916, and turns right through **Waldershof**, with its Schloss of 1471, and SE through the Stein woods by way of Poppenreuth as far as (18km) **Friedenfels**, with its Renaissance Rathaus. Its Marienkirche, 1877, retains on its outside wall the early 18C tombstone of Georg Rudolf von Nothafft and his wife, from an earlier church on this site. Drive now ENE to **Wiesau**, with a parish church of 1661–63, in front of which is a column to the Virgin Mary; inside are medieval tombs. On the nearby Kreuzberg (627m-high) the Kreuzberg church, 1657, with a Rococo fresco of 1740 on the ceiling. 3km N of Wiesau lies **Fuchsmühl**, whose Baroque pilgrimage church of Mariahilf, 1712–25, retains a chapel of 1688. The Schlossgut of 1510 is south of the village.

**Falkenberg** lies 7km SE of Wiesau in the lovely Waltnaab valley, in the centre of which Burg Falkenberg, founded in 1154, is romantically reflected in water. Its 'Hussite tower' is a reminder that the Hussites took the castle in the 14C, as did the Swedes during the Thirty Years War. Burg Falkenberg was restored in 1934. From here the B299 leads W to **Reuth**, with its Renaissance Schloss and on (14km) to **Erbendorf**, once noted for its silver and zinc works, and with a column dedicated to the Virgin Mary, 1710, and a late Gothic parish church restored after a fire of 1759. The Rococo high altar, 1802, was brought from the Franciscan church at Kemnath after the secularisation of 1802.

**Windischeschenbach**, standing 9km SE of Erbendorf, where the River Fichtelnaab joins the River Waldnaab, is a town devoted to making glass and porcelain. The church of **St Emmeram** is neo-Gothic, like much of Windischeschenbach, rebuilt after a great fire of 1848.

Follow now the A93 19km S to *Weiden, the major town of the northern Upper Palatinate (45,000 inhab., mostly living outside the 1000-year-old inner city; alt. 396m). Porcelain, china, glass (particularly lead crystal) and textiles are made here, and it is a centre for railway repairs.

**History**: Weiden became a city in the mid 13C. It flourished as part of the route to Prague in the next century. Fires in 1536 and 1549, plague and destruction during the Thirty Years War, when the Swedes made the city a centre of their operations, set back its prosperity. In 1777 the city became part of Bavaria. The advent of the railway in 1863 was the beginning of a new prosperity. The composer Max Reger (1873–1916) spent much of his youth here and produced his first important works at Weiden.

The information office is in the town hall. Trains leave for Nuremberg, Regensburg, Munich, Bayreuth, etc.

In Wörthstrasse, E of the railway station, stands the Oberen Tor, put up in 1911 on the site of the original city gate. From here walk E to the Rathaus, passing left the protestant church of **St Michael** in the Oberen Markt. This Gothic church was reordered in Baroque in the 18C and has a late Baroque onion-domed five-storey tower. Inside are the remains of late Gothic fan vaulting, also a Baroque high altar of 1791, a pulpit of 1787, and an organ case which derives from 1565. The Rathaus in the Unteren Markt, with its 16C and 17C burghers' houses, was built between 1539 and 1545 in the Renaissance style by Hans Nopl of Weiden. The outdoor staircase and the gable end, with the arms of the seven regional districts of Bavaria, date from 1915. Note the carved hand—symbol of tax collection—and the scales—symbol of justice. Over the gable a mosaic depicts the first historical documentation of Weiden, under Emperor Konrad IV in 1241. The other gable has an eight-sided Renaissance tower.

Follow Unteren Markt to the Unteren Tor, a late Romanesque gateway despoiled by soldiers in 1635 and rebuilt in 1698, surrounded by medieval houses. Narrow streets lead from here to the remains of the city walls. Go through the Unteren Tor to Schlörplatz, with a monument to the last Bavarian trade minister, Gustav von Schlör (1820–83). From here a narrow street leads into Bürgermeister-Prechtl-Strasse. Turn right and walk along Sebastianstrasse to the 15C church of St Sebastian (restored 1697), with a memorial to the twin children of Count Palatine Friedrich von Vohenstrauss, 1590.

Return to 31 Bürgermeister-Prechtl-Strasse, now the Max-Reger-Haus, where the composer was taught by Albert Lindner and created celebrated organ works between 1898 and 1901.

Scheibenstrasse leads NW from Bürgermeister-Prechtl-Strasse to Weiden's only Baroque building, the Waldsassener Getreidekasten. This was built by the monk Philipp Muttone in 1739–42, and was where the monks of Waldsassen collected their tithes. From here walk SW along Luitpoldstrasse to the neo-Romanesque Catholic church of **St Josef** 1899–1900, with a Jugendstil interior. Kirchenstrasse leads S from here into Schulstrasse with, right at 4 Pfarrplatz, the seven-storeyed Old Schoolhouse (Altes Schulhaus), 1566, the two corner houses known respectively as the German school and the Latin school, with the teachers' and clergy quarters in between. The Old Schoolhouse is now a cultural centre, containing the city archive, library, museum and Max Reger collection (open Mon–Fri 10.00–11.00, 15.00–16.00).

A gentle walk leads to the Max-Reger-Park on the River Naab, with a memorial to the composer.

# B. Regensburg to Furth-im-Wald and north along the Czech border

Total distance 177km. Regensburg—11km Walhalla—13km Wörth an der Donau—20km Falkenstein—15km Roding—B85, 15km Cham—38km Lam—21km Furth im Wald—44km Stamsried.

At Regensburg cross N of the Danube and the Regen by the Nibelungen bridge and drive E along the Landtrasse for 9km to Donaustauf, with a Schloss that was left in ruins in 1634. Turn by the Salvator church for (after 2km) *Walhalla, its name deriving from the Nordic resting place for the souls of heroes. This is a marble temple of fame, modelled on the Parthenon and set 96m above the river. It was dedicated by Ludwig I to the memory of eminent Germans and built in 1830–41 to designs by Leo von Klenze. Either drive to the well-signposted parking place or climb the 240 steps to the 32m by 67m temple, with its 52 Doric columns and 118 busts of the great. The statues of Ludwig I and six valkyries were added after World War II. (Open 10.00–16.00; closed in winter 12.00–14.00.)

The road continues along the left bank of the Danube to Sulzbach. NE is the Thurn und Taxis zoo, the largest in south Germany. Continue 13km E through Bach and Kruckenberg, the latter with a Weinstube for tasting and buying local wines, and **Wiesent**, with its Schloss of 1695 and an 18C onion-domed church, to **Wörth an der Donau**, the towers of whose Schloss, once the bishop's palace, appear long before you reach the town. The main gate dates from 1525, the Renaissance chapel from 1616, while the 'Roundell' and the princely bedroom retain their 18C decorations. The rest of the old town virtually disappeared in a fire of 1841.

Return to Wiesent and turn N for a drive of 18km by way of **Frauenzell**, to visit its former Benedictine abbey and the church with its massive medieval tower, which was restored by the brothers Asam in 1747 and has a Baroque façade, a late 17C pulpit and a roof painting by Otto Gebhard, 1752. Then on to **Brennberg**, with its ruined 14C Rathaus, as far as **Falkenstein**. The Schloss, high on a granite peak, was founded in the 11C and belonged initially to the Bishop of Regensburg. It was given to the town by the Fürst von Thurn and Taxis in 1967. The whole complex, with its chapel and lodgings, has been exceptionally well restored.

Continue 6km to Michelsneukirchen and turn left to reach after 9km **Roding**, a town founded in 844 whose medieval walls and towers partly remain. The Renaissance Rathaus in the Marktplatz carries a Baroque bell tower. Note the pillory. The parish church of St Pankratius is Baroque; inside are a Romanesque stone font and a Madonna of 1320.

The B85 leads E for 15km to **Cham** (17,500 inhab.; alt. 465m). Around three of its sides flows the River Regen. The 14C and 15C Gothic Rathaus bears an oriel window and a tablet commemorating the expulsion of the Jews from Regensburg in 1519, and is now a museum of local culture. The 14C Biertor, a defensive gate with two round towers, and the Straubinger Tor (once the city jail) remain from the old fortifications. A 15C inn, the 'Krone', in the Marktplatz has 16C battlements. The Spitalkirche of 1519 was reordered in the Baroque style in 1750. The late Gothic parish church of St Jakob has an 18C Baroque and Rococo interior, with a roof painting by Johann Gebhard. Cham was the birthplace of Count Nicolas von Luckner, Marshall of France, who was guillotined in 1794.

At Chammünster, 4km E of Cham is a church founded in the 9C, with a 12C charnel house. The present parish church of Maria Himmelfahrt is basically 15C, with a 13C choir and north tower, two 12C Romanesque fonts and an interior reordered in the 18C.

Leave the B85 12km SE at Miltach, with a 17C Rathaus, and travel E for 6km to **Blaibach** at the confluence of the Weisser Regen and the Schwarzer Regen, with its Schloss of 1604 and 18C Rococo church of St Elisabeth. N of the town of Kötzting, 4km E at the foot of the Keitersberg, is an 18C Rococo pilgrimage church, the Weissenregen, with a 14C picture of the Virgin Mary and a pulpit like a fishing smack. **Kötzting** itself boasts a Baroque parish church with a Rococo high altar, and a Baroque Rathaus. Each Whitsun Kötzting stages a religious horseback procession, the Kötztinger Pfingstritt.

The route continues along the river valley through the mountains as far as Lam on the Weisser Regen, a tourist centre that is popular with mountaineers and walkers, with an early 18C church dedicated to St Ulrich.

Lam is 21km SE of Furth im Wald. The road runs parallel to the border with the Czech Republic and through **Neukirchen bei Heilig Blut**, with its impressive Baroque double church of 1720, built in honour of a statue of the Madonna from which blood is reputed to have flowed when a Protestant cut off its head. At **Furth im Wald** is a rail and road pass into the Czech Republic. The Baroque parish church of 1727 was reordered in the late 19C. The Stadtturm of 1866 now houses a local museum. The statue of St John Nepomuk was erected in the Stadtplatz in 1767. Furth im Wald is the chief centre for tourism in the forests of Bavaria and the Upper Palatinate. On the second Sunday in August a 500-year-old festival depicts the slaying of the dragon by St George.

Continue 18km NW to **Waldmünchen**, a town founded in the 10C by monks from Chammünster and now boasting the 15C Pflegamtsschloss. The destruction of the town in 1742 during the War of the Austrian Succession is commemorated by an annual pageant in July and August. The much rebuilt church of St Stephan was founded in 1660. The statue of St John Nepomuk and the two fountains were erected in the Marktplatz in the mid 18C. The cemetery chapel dates from 1712, the Spitalkirche from 1767. There are water sports at the nearby Perl Lake.

From here the route passes through **Ast** with its 13C early Gothic pilgrimage church, with Baroque reordering. Note the branch ('Ast') on the old pulpit. Continue W through Schönthal, which has a former Augustinian monastery, founded 1255 and closed 1803; and a Baroque parish church, c 1700. After 15km you reach **Rötz**, which became a city in 1495. The ruined Schloss Schwarzenburg towers 706m high on the Schwarzwihrberg—a 30-minute walk from the Marktplatz. The parish church at Rötz, mostly 1850, has a Gothic choir, 1401, and a tower built in 1552.

The route ends at Stamsried, 10km due S of Rötz, a town razed by the Swedes in the Thirty Years War but retaining its medieval Schloss. E of the town (signposted) are extensive remains of Burg Kürnburg. A column bearing the statue of the Virgin Mary was erected in the Marktplatz in 1729.

# C.  North of Schwandorf and along the border of the Czech Republic

Total distance 234km. Schwandorf—18km Nabburg—11km Wernberg—
Köblitz—B14, 10km Wieselrieth—20km Tännesberg—B22, 11km
Oberviechtach—12km Schönsee—18km Moosbach—24km Neustadt an der
Waldnaab—B15, 35km Mitterteich—B299, 7km Waldsassen—68km Pleystein.

**Schwandorf** (17,000 inhab.; alt. 365km) has a Baroque pilgrimage church
of 1678, which was rebuilt in 1950–52, after three-quarters of the city was
destroyed in 1945. The 15C tower survives from the town's old fortifications.
The medieval houses make the Marktplatz particularly attractive. To the N
of the city is the Renaissance Schloss Fronberg, which was finished in the
mid 17C. 9km N lies Schwarzenfeld, with a pilgrimage church of 1720,
housing a Baroque high altar and a Rococo pulpit, the mid 18C Rococo
parish church of St Dionysius and St Ägidius, and a 19C Rathaus.

**Nabburg** lies 9km further N. Founded in 929, though much was destroyed
in the Middle Ages and the Thirty Years War, the town retains its walls,
gates and towers. The *basilica of St Johann Baptist dates from the 14C.
The sculpted reliefs on its south doorway date from c 1350; 14C glass fills
the north windows; the 'Nabburg Madonna', c 1470, is on the left side altar.
Nabburg also has a Renaissance Rathaus of 1550, and the 12C Romanesque
church of St Nikolaus. The 18C cemetery chapel of St Georg in the lower
town has a Romanesque tower.

The way to Pfreimd, 5km N, leads through **Perschen**, which has a 12C
cemetery chapel and the 13C late Romanesque basilica of St Peter and St
Paul, with Gothic vaults and choir, and a Baroque nave of 1752–53. Here is
the Upper Palatinate rural museum (closed Mon), in a 12C farmhouse. At
the confluence of the Nab and the Pfreimd is Pfreimd, where the Counts of
Leuchtenberg lived from 1332 to 1646. The spot retains part of its medieval
Rathaus, with two Renaissance doorways, and the church of the former
Franciscan monastery, 1593. Johann Schmuzer built the church of Maria
Himmelfahrt, 1681–88, which retains by the high altar a marble epitaph of
Count Leopold von Leuchtenberg (d. 1463). Close by, though a stiff climb,
is the Eixlberg (517m) with a pilgrimage church and Loretto chapel.

Continue 6km to Wernberg-Köblitz, with a 12C Schloss. The B14 leads
10km NE to Wieselrieth, where a brief diversion N reaches Leuchtenberg,
founded in 1124. **Burg Leuchtenberg** preserves its 14C inner wall, a 15C
chapel and its keep (restored). Return to Wieselrieth and continue SW for
10km to Trausnitz, with its 13C keep, where Duke Friedrich the Beautiful
was imprisoned in 1322 after his defeat by Ludwig the Bavarian at the battle
of Mühldorf. Due E, after 10km, is Tännesberg, close by which is the
Baroque pilgrimage church of St Jodok, 1689, with a 'plague cross', brought
here from Vienna in 1690. Following a vow of 1796, costumed farmers and
horsemen process here on the second Sunday in July.

The B22 now leads SE 8km to **Teunz**, whose Baroque church of St Lambert
has a classical tower and a Rococo high altar, and another 3km to
**Oberviechtach**. The formerly Gothic church of St Johann Baptist now has
a splendid Rococo interior, 1775. From here the route leads NE 12km to
Schönsee, once part of Bohemia and known as Kronlehen. Here a double
statue of St John Nepomuk, 1791, looks towards both Bavaria and Bohemia.
The present form of the parish church dates from 1868; the chapel of the
Fourteen Helpers from 1799. The Hunting Museum is close to the Hotel St

Hubertus. An excursion 7km E reaches the pilgrimage church of Our Lady and St Michael at Stadlern, with late Gothic statues of Mary and Children on a Baroque choir altar, and St Michael fighting the dragon on a side altar.

The picturesque road N from Schönsee reaches Eslarn after 9km. Here the early Baroque church of Our Lady, 1685–87, has a Rococo pulpit. To continue N brings you by way of the nature reserve of Pfrentsch after 8km to the border crossing at Waidhaus, with a 1754 statue of St John Nepomuk in the Marktplatz. Turning W at Eslarn the route leads after 9km to **Moosbach**, whose pilgrimage church of 1769 has a Rococo altar, confessionals and pulpit. The route continues through (2km) Burgtreswitz with a 13C Schloss as far (4km) as **Vohenstrauss**. The most imposing building in the town is the Renaissance Burg, with its six round towers, gable and high saddle roof, 1586–90. The church of St Johann Baptist, c 1350, survived a fire of 1839 which destroyed much of the old town. There is a museum of local history in the 1911 Rathaus.

Continue 20km NW to **Neustadt an der Waldnaab**, a town prospering on lead crystal ware, and boasting many fine gabled houses in the Marktplatz. The church of St Georg, built 1607–66, has been rendered Rococo. Here rises the Alte Schloss of 1543 and the Italianate Baroque Neue Schloss by Antonio Porta and Anton Ritz, 1702. The nearby **Altenstadt an der Waldnaab** has a Romanesque church of Maria Himmelfahrt, with a late Gothic tower and choir and a Rococo high altar.

Follow the B15 NE for 24km to **Tirschenreuth**, which retains the 1330 Klettnersturm from its old fortifications. Sights include the 12C Fischhof, the stone bridge of 1750 (modelled on that of Regensburg), the Rathaus of 1583, with an oriel festooned with coats of arms, and the memorial in the Marktplatz to the linguist Johann Andreas Schmeller (1785–1852). The B15 continues NW to **Mitterteich** (11km). Its Rathaus of 1731 shades the Marktplatz; alongside are statues of St John Nepomuk and a Virgin Mary column. A dance of death can be seen inside the Maria Hilf cemetery chapel of 1780. Attached to the 1891 church of St Jakobus is a 17C tower.

Now take the B299 for 7km through **Bad Kondrau**, with its medicinal waters, to **Waldsassen**, founded by the Cistercian monk Gerwig von Wohmundstein in 1133. The superb Baroque *church of Maria Himmelfahrt and St Johann was built between 1681 and 1704 by Abraham Leuthner of Prague, aided by Georg Dientzenhofer and the brothers Jakob and Bernhard Schiesser. The frescoes are by the Prague artist Jakob Steinfels, the stucco work by the Italian G.B. Carlone, the choir stalls of 1696 by the local woodcarver Martin Hirsch. Karl Stilp created the marble Annunciation and the tabernacle on the high altar. The *Stiftsbibliothek, a late Baroque library, also possesses rich, often humorous carvings by Stilp, with stucco work by Peter Appiani.

A picturesque wooded route now travels S virtually alongside the Czech border for 68km through a nature conservancy area as far as **Pleystein**, with its cemetery chapel of 1750 and a Baroque column of St John Nepomuk in the Marktplatz. The Kreuzberg dominates the town, with the neo-Baroque Kreuzbergkirche.

# D.  Neumarkt to Walderbach via Regensburg

Total distance 157km. Neumarkt—24km Sulzbürg—B299, 20km Beilngries—
29km Parsberg—E5, 36km Regensburg—B15, 15km Regenstauf—33km
Walderbach.

**Neumarkt** (30,000 inhab.; alt. 425m) is first documented in 1160 and
became a city in 1235. At the very end of World War II the inner city was
virtually destroyed and has since been well restored. Two churches and a
Rathaus, 1520, are the major sights of the city. The Catholic parish church
of St Johannes, built out of sandstone, begun in 1404 and finished in the
mid 15C, has three fine doorways of which the western is famous for its
carvings. The early Gothic stone font dates from c 1200, the gravestones
and remains of frescoes from the 15C and 16C.

The sandstone Gothic church of Maria Himmelfahrt was built by Count
Johann von Wittelsbach in 1410, and the nave was rebuilt in the Baroque
style by Jakob Engel in 1702. The late Gothic red marble tomb of Count
Palatine Otto II dates from c 1499. The Schloss was burnt down in 1520 and
rebuilt in 1539 in the Renaissance style. The parish church of St Johann
dates from 1404 to mid 15C. Two other sights are the ruined Burg Wolfstein,
with a fine view of the city, and the pilgrimage church of Mariahilfberg
(585m high), 1718, with an altar painting of 1478, depicting the life of the
Virgin Mary. The Heimatmuseum at 7 Weiherstrasse displays weapons,
local art, fossils, and so on, and opens Thur 16.30–18.00, Fri 17.00–19.30.

Leave Neumarkt SW towards Freystadt, making a brief excursion (right)
after 9km to **Seligenporten** where the powerful 15C tower of its gate
remains from the old fortifications. The 16C east wing remains from the
former Cistercian monastery, as well the 13C monastery church, with its
14C choir and stalls. **Freystadt**, with its long market street, burghers' houses
and 1550 Rathaus, possesses an early 18C domed pilgrimage church, by
Antonio Viscardi stuccoed by Francesco Appiani in 1708, with wall paintings by C.D. Asam. See also the 1750 parish church, with a 13C Gothic
tower and 16C carvings.

E of Freystadt by way of Rocksdorf and then S is (9km) Sulzbürg, notable
for its Jewish cemetery, the synagogue was destroyed in 1938 during the
Hitler Reich. Continue S along the B299 for 12km to reach **Berching**, which
retains its 6m-high walls incorporating 12 towers and the city gates, built
1464–94, and many old burghers' houses. Its important churches are the
11C St Lorenz with a relief of c 1220 on the north doorway, side altar
paintings c 1515, and a Gothic high altar 1500–29, and the early Gothic
Maria Himmelfahrt, enriched with Rococo stucco, c 1750. **Plankstetten** lies
4km to the S along the B299, with a Benedictine church of 1138 whose tower
has a Baroque cap, while inside is a 15C transept with late Gothic stellar
vaulting and three mid 12C windows, a Baroque pulpit of 1651, early
Rococo stucco work, c 1730, and a *Rococo Heilig-Geist-Kapelle, c 1760,
by Johann Jakob Berg.

The B299 continues S with (right) Schloss Hirschberg, once the summer
retreat of the Bishops of Eichstätt, built in the early 14C and much enriched
in the 18C. **Beilngreis**, 4km S, at the confluence of the Sulz and the Altmühl,
and also on the Ludwigskanal, retains much of its 15C city wall, as well as
fine gabled houses with Baroque façades and the 15C town hall. The late
Gothic cemetery chapel dates from the 1470s, the Rococo Frauenkirche
from the 18C, by Maurizio Pedetti, and the church of St Walburga from
1913.

The Route leads E for 4km to Kottingwörth. Its medieval parish church, with early 15C wall paintings, was mostly rebuilt in 1760. After 6km more you reach **Dietfurt**, with its 17C Rathaus, faced by a 'Chinese' fountain, its Baroque church of St Ägidius, 1660, which was altered in the 19C, and boasts a 65m high tower. Continue NE for 7km to **Breitenbrunn**, lying in the middle of peaks and woods. It has the 16C Gasthof Post; the pilgrimage church of St Sebastian, with two onion-domed towers, first built 1386 and rebuilt 1702–08; and two 18C Schlösschen. 12km further NE is Parsberg, with a 16C Upper Schloss and a Lower Schloss c 1600.

Join the E5 just N of Parsberg and drive SE for 36km to Regensburg (see Rte 1A). Take the B15 N for 13km to **Regenstauf**, where the Schlossberg (436m, with a viewing tower) offers a superb panorama. At Ramspau, 4km further N, is a Baroque Schloss, and at Hirschling, 6km further N, a medieval Schloss. The Route continues N along the bank of the River Regen, which bends right (as does the road) at Marienthal, where the ruins of 13C Burg Stockenfels stand on a high rock. As the Route continues E towards Nittenau the 10C Burg Stefling (restored 1748) and the medieval Burg Hof appear.

**Nittenau** 22km from Regenstauf retains parts of its old walls and towers, and a modern parish church, which incorporates a Gothic choir and tower with a Baroque dome. From Nittenau the road leads ESE for 9km to Reichenbach, whose Romanesque monastery church of c 1130 has a Gothic choir; the tomb of Markgraf Diepold II, 1304; a sandstone Madonna, 1420; and a Baroque interior, with frescoes by Andreas Gebhard.

The Route ends 2km E at **Walderbach**, with a 12C Romanesque church, formerly part of a Cistercian monastery, whose choir, tower and nave windows date from the 18C. The geometric decoration was added in 1888.

# 3

# Regensburg to Füssen via Augsburg

Total distance 237km. Regensburg—B16, 49km Münchsmünster—B300, 43km Schrobenhaunsen—43km Augsburg—B17, 38km Landsberg—27km Schöngau—15km Steingaden and the Wieskirche—22km Füssen.

Leave Regensburg by the Kumpfmühlerstrasse to take the B16 SW for 49km as far as Münchsmünster, with the church of a former Benedictine monastery, for the junction with the B300. The B300 continues SW through the Dürnbucher Forest for 21km, through Geisenfeld, where you cross the valley of the Ilm before traversing the Feilen Forest to reach Langenbrück and the junction with the Nuremberg–Munich motorway. After 5km the B16 reaches Pörnbach and the junction with the B13 from Ingolstadt to Munich.

Continue 17km SW to reach **Schrobenhausen**, a town at least 1100 years old, with remains of the 15C walls. Here the artist Franz Lenbach (1836–1904) was born and is commemorated in a museum at 1 Ulrich-Preisse-Gasse (open daily 09.00–11.00, 13.00–16.00). The late Gothic basilica of St Jakob dates from 1425–80 (there are wall paintings in the choir and nave, and a crucifixion group and calvary of c 1500). The church of St Salvator was built in the 15C. The museum of local history, 22 Lenbachplatz, opens daily 09.00–11.00, 13.00–16.00. An excursion 7km W leads to Sandizell, with an 18C Rococo parish church by E.Q. Asam and a mid 18C burg.

14km further is **Unterwittelsbach**, its church dating from 1418. Here once stood the family castle of the Wittelsbachs, which was demolished in 1209 after an imperial ban on Count Palatine Otto von Wittelsbach. In 2km is **Aichach**, with its early 16C late Gothic parish church. After 11km you reach the Stuttgart–Munich motorway, but continue SW along the B300 for 7km to Friedberg.

Shortly before the town of Friedberg, to the left is the pilgrimage church of **Herrgottruh** built in 1730–53, its stuccoed interior designed by Franz Xavier Feuchtmayr, the frescoes in the nave painted by Matthias Günther, the ceiling in the choir painted by C.D. Asam. **Friedberg** on the Lain, once a stronghold of the Wittelsbachs in their opposition to Augsburg, possesses a Schloss, with 13C walls, a tower of 1552, and the rest 17C, which houses a museum of local history, its Rathaus is from 1680. In the neo-Romanesque parish church, 1872, is a memorial stone of Duke Ludwig the Bearded (died 1409).

Augsburg lies 9km SW, entered by joining the B2 from Munich.

•••**AUGSBURG** (245,000 inhab.; alt. 496m). Still moated, Augsburg is the chief city of the Bavarian regional district of Schwabia. The city lies in the foothills of the Alps where the River Lech meets the River Wertach. An important trading post with Italy (especially Verona) in Roman times, Augsburg developed a textile industry that still fourishes. By the Middle Ages the city was the seat of important banking families, such as the Welsers and the Fuggers.

**Main railway station**: Bahnhofstrasse. **Information Office**: 7 Bahnhofstrasse. **Travel Office**: main railway station. **Trains** to Munich, Nuremberg, Stuttgart, Würzburg. **Coach trips** to the 'Romantische Strasse' (see Rte 5B).

**History**. Drusus, a relative of the Emperor Augustus, established a Roman camp here in 15 BC and in the next century Augsburg (then called *Augusta Vindelicorum*) became the capital of the Roman province of SS Raetia. St Afra was martyred here in 304. With the support of St Ulrich, bishop of the city, who died here 973, Otto I defeated the Hungarians at Lechfeld near Augsburg in 955. Augsburg received its town charter in the 11C. Fortified in the 12C, in 1276 it became a Free Imperial City. Luther took refuge in the Carmelite monastery of St Anne (see below) in 1518. The Augsburg Confession of 1530, drawn up here by Martin Luther and his ally Philipp Melanchthon, set out the fundamentals of European protestantism in 1530. The Peace of Augsburg (1555) granted a limited freedom of worship to Protestants, and an Imperial Diet presided over by the Emperor Charles V's successor Ferdinand I declared that each prince should decide whether his territory was to be Catholic or Protestant. Prussia and Austria joined with the League of Augsburg in the 17C against Louis XIV's pretentions. After the problems caused by the Thirty Years War, Augsburg continued as a Free Imperial City until 1805, being incorporated into the Kingdom of Bavaria the following year.

Augsburg was the home of the Habsburg's bankers Jakob Fugger II (1459–1525) and his nephew Anton Fugger (1495–1560), of the finest local architect, Elias Holl (1573–1646) and the birthplace of Hans Holbein the Elder (c 1460–1524), his son Hans the Younger (1497–1543), Leopold (1719–87), the father of Wolfgang Amadeus Mozart, and Bertolt Brecht (1896–1956). Hans Burgkmair (1473–1531) flourished here and his house still stands in the Mauerberg. Almost equal in wealth to the Fuggers were the Welsers; in 1528 Bartholomäus Welser set sail with a squadron to conquer Venezuela ('Welserland'), which was then run as a family colony; his niece Philippine Welser married Archduke Ferdinand of Austria in 1557. Another daughter of an Augsburg merchant, Agnes Bernauer, married Duke Albrecht III of Bavaria (see Straubing, Rte 6).

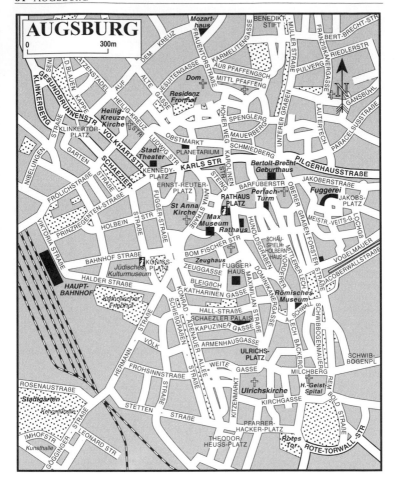

Here in the 1890s was produced the first diesel engine, named after the engineer Rudolf Diesel (1858–1913) in whose Augsburg factory it was developed. Half the city suffered severe destruction in World War II. Today Augsburg prospers on the manufacture of diesel engines as well as aircraft and electrical machinery. Augsburg has in part preserved its medieval fortifications.

From the main railway station follow Prinzregentenstrasse into Grottenau to find the Theatre at 1 Kennedyplatz which seats nearly 1000. Turn left from Grottenau along Heilige-Kreuz-Strasse where Emperor Maximilian I lived at No. 4 from 1504 to 1519, to reach the **Heilig-Kreuz-Kirche**. Beautifully restored in 1981, it was built in 1653 by Johann Jakob Krauss, a pupil of Elias Holl, on the site of a 12C chapel. Attached to an Augustinian monastery, it was the natural refuge from his enemies of the Augustinian monk Luther, and today it belongs to the Lutherans. It features a flat wooden roof; classical galleries on three sides; an organ of 1730–31; a triptych of angels worshipping the Infant Jesus, 1515, in the Grosse Sakristei, as well as contemporary portraits by an unkown hand of Luther and Melanchthon. In the Kleine Sakristei hangs a series of scenes from Luther's life and of the presentation of the Confession of Augsburg to Charles V in 1530, painted in 1730 by Johann August Corvinus. On the west wall of the church hang an Adoration of the Shepherds by Friedrich Sustris, c 1570, Jesus preaching from a boat by Johann Heinrich Schönfeld, 1670, a late 17C Annunciation by Johann Heiss and a Trinity by Johann Georg Bergmüller, 1730. On the north wall hang paintings of Jesus carrying his cross and a Deposition by J.H. Schönfeld, both c 1660, and Ernst Philipp von Hagelstein's picture of Jesus using a child as an example of humility, 1712. On the N wall hangs von Hagelstein's Marriage at Cana and Tintoretto's *Baptism of John the Baptist, c 1570.

Adjoining Heilig-Kreuz-Kirche is a late Gothic Catholic church, 1492, with Baroque decoration. Kohler-Gasse leads NE from here into Jesuiten gasse as far as Frauentorstrasse. Turn N along Frauentorstrasse to find (at No. 30) **Mozarthaus**, where the composer's father was born (museum open weekdays except Tue 10.00–12.00, 14.00–17.00, Sat, Sun 10.00–12.00). It houses original scores and W.A. Mozart's Stein piano. SE along Frauentorstrasse you reach *St Mary's Cathedral (Dom), built on 10C foundations, enlarged by Bishop Heinrich II, 1047–63 and Gothicised in the 14C. Twin copper spires rise from brick and stone towers. The Romanesque west end contrasts with the Gothic choir, built 1326–1431. Its exterior is enhanced by the 11C Romanesque *south doorway and 32 bronze Romanesque panels depicting Old Testament and mythological scenes. The interior has five **12C windows depicting Jonah, Daniel, Hosea, Moses and David (south side), the oldest important stained glass in Germany, with other medieval glass in the south aisle. The cathedral has a Romanesque crypt of 1060; a bishop's throne, c 1100; the bronze tomb of Bishop Wolfhart Rot, 1302; a huge wall painting of St Christopher in the south transept, 1491; nave pillars with paintings of the life of the Blessed Virgin Mary by Hans Holbein the Elder, 1493; and a modern bronze group of crucified Christ with the twelve Apostles, in the east choir, by Josef Henselmann, 1962.

Follow Karolinenstrasse S from the cathedral to the spacious **Rathausplatz**, with the Renaissance *Rathaus, by Elias Holl, 1615–20, seven storeys high, with onion domes. (Open daily 10.00–18.00.) Note the town symbol of a pine cone on the gable. The whole was built under the influence of Palladio and Sansovino. Its Goldener Saal was restored in 1985, after the destruction of World War II. Rathausplatz is cooled by the **Augustusbrunnen** by H. Gerhard, 1598–94, the bronze figures of the fountain representing the rivers Lech, Wertach, Brunnenbach and Singold; and it is enlivened by the **Perlachturm**, a Romanesque watch tower, 78m high, transformed into a belfry by Elias Holl in 1614. It is open daily and there is a fine view from the top. W stands the 12C St Peterskirke.

Beside the Rathaus Am Perlachberg leads E to the **Bertolt Brecht Haus** (open Tue–Sun 10.00–17.00) and the *Fuggerei. Here in 1519 Jakob Fugger the Elder (known as 'the Rich') founded a little town for the poor. Still in use, the Fuggerei has four gates, 53 gabled houses and eight streets, its inhabitants still living virtually rent free. At the north gate stands St Jakobkirche, 1355–1533.

S from the Rathaus, the exquisite, curving Maximilianstrasse, with several Renaissance burgher's houses, leads to the church of St Moritz, 14–15C brick Gothic, with Baroque decoration of 1714 and a statue of St Sebastian in the choir by Hans Leonhard Gemelich, c 1627. In front is the Mercury Fountain by Adriaen de Vries, 1599, a copy of Giambologna's Mercury in Florence and the 14C old Weavers' House Weberzunfthaus. At 24 Philippine-Welser-Strasse NW of St Moritz is the **Maximilian Museum**, in two burghers' houses, built in the late 15C–early 16C and originally the house of the Welsers (see above), transformed into a museum in the early 20C by Gabriel von Seidl (open Tue–Sun 10.00–17.00, Oct–Apr 10.00–16.00) with goldsmiths' works of 16–18C, sculpture, including a Virgin Mary by Hans Multscher c 1440 and Georg Petel's Hercules fighting the Hydra 1626; firearms; the history of Augsburg; and architectural models by E. Holl. The statue of Jakob Fugger was erected in front of the museum in 1857. Nearly opposite the museum is 13 Philippine-Welser-Strasse where Philippine Welser (see above) spent her childhood.

W of the museum in Annastrasse is the **St Annakirche**, formerly part of a Carmelite monastery, a Gothic church, founded in 1321, enlarged in the late 15C, rebuilt by Elias Holl in 1602–16, and decorated with Rococo stucco work and frescoes of 1747–49. Its Gothic Goldsmith's Chapel has late 15C wall paintings; its Renaissance **•Fuggerkapelle** was built in 1509–12 (restored 1947) and was the first Renaissance building in Germany, with reliefs on the tombs of Jakob and Ulrich Fugger to drawings by Dürer, statues by Sebastian Loscher and Hans Daucher; portrait of Luther and painting of Jesus as the Children's Friend, both by Cranach the Elder; an altar by Hans Daucher; double organ of 1512, with wings painted by Jörg Breu the Elder. In 1518 Martin Luther was living here when he refused to recant before the Papal Legate Cardinal Cajetan.

S of the church is the Fuggerhaus, built for Jakob Fugger the Rich, 1512–15. To the W is the **Zeughaus** (city Arsenal), built by Elias Holl with a bronze of St Michael, and east façade, by Hans Reichle, 1603–06.

Still further S, at 46 Maximilianstrasse, is the Rococo **Schaezlerpalais**, built for the banker von Liebert by K.A. von Lespilliez, 1765–67. It has a Baroque banqueting hall, with mirrors, Rococo gilding and a ceiling fresco of the four continents. The Palais houses the Staatsgalerie, with its Baroque masters (open Tue–Sun 10.00–17.00, to 16.00 Oct–Apr) and also the Altdeutschegalerie with works by Dürer and Hans Holbein the Elder. In front of the Schaezlerpalais is the **Herkulesbrunnen** by Adriaen de Vries, 1602.

E of the Fuggerhaus stands the former Dominkanerkriche 1513–15, its Rococo stucco work by F.X. and J.M. Feuchtmayer, 1716–49. This is now the Römisches Museum (open daily Tue–Sun 10.00–16.00), and displays valuable archaeological finds. Follow Maximilianstrasse further S to reach the Catholic Munster of SS Ulrich and Afra. This was formerly a Benedictine abbey, founded by Maximilian I to replace a church over the tomb of Saints Afra and Ulrich. The nave, begun in 1474, was completed by the architect Burkhard Engelberger between 1477 and 1500; its pentagonal north entrance dates from 1481; the 93m-high tower with an onion dome was finished in 1594; the choir, with a foundation stone laid by Maximilian I in 1500, was consecrated in 1607. The interior was reordered in the 17C; the Baroque grille and three Baroque altars are by J. Degler the Elder, 1604–07; the cross and bronze figures of the altar are by H. Reichle, c 1605; the stations of the cross is by Januarius Zick; and a Crucifixion of 1607. The chapel to St Simpert is on the north side, with a Gothic baldacchino and terracotta saints; St Afra's vault has the saint's Romanesque sarcophagus; St Ulrich's vault has Rococo decoration by P. Verhelst, 1762; the **•burial chapel** of Jakob Fugger dates from 1580, with the tomb of Hans Fugger by

*The opulent Rococo ballroom of the Schaezlerpalais at Augsburg*

Hubert Gerhard and Alexander Colin, 1584–87, and a screen of 1588; and stained glass by Hans Holbein the Elder in the sacristy.

Adjacent is the Protestant church of St Ulrich, 1458, remodelled in 1710, with a pulpit of 1714. SE of St Ulrich in Eserwallstrasse stands the brick and golden stone Red Gate, or **Rotes Tor**, a 16C fortified building, with a tower by Elias Holl, 1622. Next to the Red Gate, is the open-air theatre, which seats 2400 people, and Elias Holl's last work, the **Heilig-Geist-Spital** of 1625–30, which stands to the N.

**Other sights**. The city garden (Stadtgarten) is laid out S of the main railway station and has a congress hall built in 1974, with a restaurant and the 117m-high Hotel Tower. The canoe slalom stadium, by Hochablass, 1972; a renowned marionette theatre, the Augsburger Puppenkiste at 15 Spital-gasse, and the M.A.N.-Werkmuseum, with the first diesel engine and printing presses at 28 Heinrich-von-Buz-Strasse (open Mon–Fri 08.00–16.00) round up Augsburg's special treats.

Leave Augsburg by Haunstetter Strasse and travel S on the B17. After Haunstetten you pass through countryside bordered by the Rivers Wertach and Lech in the neighbourhood of which a battle was fought between Emperor Otto I and the Hungarians in 955. After 24km you reach **Kloster-lechfeld**. Next to the Franciscan monastery of 1604 (enlarged in 1669 and

1738) Elias Holl built in 1604, for Regina Imhoff, widow of an Augsburg patrician, a cylindrical and domed pilgrimage church based on the Pantheon in Rome. Its nave dates from 1659; two chapels from 1691; and the stuccoed Rococo interior is by J.G. Lederer, 1733–41.

14km S, the B17 reaches **Landsberg**, on the banks of the River Lech, where Henry the Lion built a Schloss in the mid 12C to guard the river crossing. The walls and towers derive from the 13C, the Bavarian Gate from 1425. The architect Dominikus Zimmermann was Bürgermeister here from 1749–50, and he enriched the early 18C **Rathaus** with its stupendous façade, in front of which a fountain and statue of the Virgin Mary by J. Streiter, 1783, adorn the lovely Marktplatz. The town hall houses works by the artist Hubert von Herkomer (1849–1914), born in nearby Waal.

Zimmermann also created the Rococo decor and the horseshoe-shaped chancel of the St Johanneskirche, 1752, on the Vorderanger. The parish church of **Maria Himmelfahrt** in Georg-Hellmair-Platz dates from 1458–88, and was designed by V. Kindlin of Strasbourg. The Baroque interior includes stained glass of 1450, by Wolfgang Prielmayr, behind the *high altar by J. Pfeiffer, 1680, as well as a 1437 Madonna in the rosary altar by Hans Multscher. Behind the high altar is a monument to Cyriacus Weber by H. Reichle, 1575; the organ case was built by the local artist L. Luidl in 1696. See also the Malteser church of 1754 which adjoins the former Jesuit college. The stucco decoration in the sacristy is by D. Zimmermann; the roof painting by C.D. Asam's pupil Christoph Thomas Scheffler and by G.B. Götz; the altar painting by J.B. Bader. The Stadtmuseum exhibits local history, including prehistoric finds, paintings and sculpture (open Tue–Sun 10.00–12.00, also 14.00–16.00 Fri, Sat). Other treats at Landsberg are the Baroque Heilig Kreuz Kirche of 1754, in Helfsteingasse, and the Bayertor of 1425, one of Bavaria's best-preserved town gates. The town also has a heated swimming pool with artificial waves.

The B17 now follows roughly the Roman *Via Claudia Augusta* and the medieval trade route from Augsburg to Italy. At Epfach was the Roman camp *Abodiacum* during the era of Augustus. Close by Hohenfurch (23km) stands (right) the Romanesque *basilica of St Michael at **Altenstadt**, built c 1200, its two towers much the same as then. Its frescoes were discovered in 1938; the building was restored, first under Ludwig I in 1826, then in 1936 and most recently 1961–63. It has a Romanesque sandstone font with carvings of the Baptist, Jesus's baptism, the Virgin Mary and the Archangel Michael; in the north aisle is a Madonna of c 1330; the remarkably stern crucifix dates from 1540. Altenstadt was a seat of the Knights Templar, who in 1289 brought to the basilica the almost 3.5m-high wooden Romanesque crucifix in the main apse, known as the 'Great God of Altenstadt'. The flanking statues of St John and the Virgin are copies of originals now in the Bavarian National Museum, Munich. Note the 14C frescoes of the Annunciation and the Archangel Michael with saints, and the 15C fresco of Mary and St John beneath the cross.

**Hohenfurch** itself has a parish church of Maria Himmelfahrt with an interior of c 1750, and a late Gothic Madonna of 1420. SE of the town on a peak is the chapel of St Ursula (1520), with a fine contemporary carved altarpiece.

Within 2km the route S reaches **Schongau**. The town is ringed by virtually intact walls from the 15C to 17C. The parish church of Maria Himmelfahrt was rebuilt in the 18C with an onion-domed tower to replace one that fell down in 1667; its chancel stucco is by Dominikus Zimmermann, 1748, its frescoes by M. Günther and F.A. Wassermann, its statues by F.X. Schmädl, its high altar c 1760. The Rathaus, on Marienplatz though modified in the 19C, dates from 1515. See also the Steingadenes Ritterhaus of 1493; the Heilig Geistkirche of the 16C and 17C, the cemetery chapel of the 16C–18C and the Heilig Kreuz Kapelle of 1689, as well as several burghers' houses. The city museum, at 6 Karmeliterstrasse, opens at present only on Wed 10.00–12.00.

Schongau is the tourist centre of the region known as the Pfaffenwinkel (clergymen's corner), with hiking maps (Wanderkarten) available from the tourist office at 1 Schlossplatz, there is a ski school and sailing on the Schongauer See.

Continue S to **Peiting**, a winter sports and convalescence centre, with its parish church of **St Michael** boasting a Romanesque tower and crypt, a late Gothic choir, a Rococo pulpit and a high altar of 1758 with carvings by F.X. Schmädl. Peiting also has a pilgrimage church, Maria unter dem Egg, c 1650. A Way of the Cross leads to the Kalvarienberg, with a superb panorama of the surrounding mountains.

An **excursion** 9km SE along the B23 reaches the Augustinian (later Benedictine) monastery of **Rottenbuch**, founded in the 11C. Franz Xaver Schmädl and Josef Schmuzer of Wessobrun created the Rococo interior of the church—its superb high altar, choir stalls, cherubs and musicians and the statues of the apse designed by Schmädl; its ceiling fresco of the death of St Augustine by Matthäus Günther, 1741; its organ by Balthasa Frewiss, 1747; its late Gothic Madonna by Erasmus Grasser, 1483. A Wanderkarte outlines the König-Ludwig-Wanderweg between Peiting and Rottenbuch. 3km S is the Echelsbacher Brücke, arching 89m above the River Ammer and Germany's first bridge of reinforced concrete (1929).

From Peiting the route continues for 9km S to **Ilgen** with its late Renaissance pilgrimage church of Maria Heimsuchung, by Johann Schmuzer, 1676. After 3km more the route reaches **Steingaden**, where in 1147 Welf VI established a Premonstratensian abbey, dedicated to St Johann Baptist, whose twin-towered Romanesque sandstone basilica of 1176 still remains. The late Romanesque transept now boasts a 15C Gothic vault. Frescoes of 1580 decorate the vestibule. The Johannes Kapelle dates from the 12C. The chancel is Baroque, 1663. The vaulted nave of 1729–45 was decorated in the Rococo style by Johann Georg Bergmüller with scenes from the life of St Norbert, the founder of the Premonstratensians, and with stucco work by the younger Schmuzer. J.C. Storer created the high altar painting in 1663. The monastery cloister, in which Dominikus Zimmermann, the architect, is buried, retains 13C Romanesque columns. See also at Steingaden the 13C cemetery chapel of St Johannes, with lions guarding its doorway.

Two hour-long **excursions** may be made from Steingaden. SE lies **Wies**, whose • • • **Wieskirche** (Meadow Church) is the richest Rococo church in the whole region. In 1730 a farmer found an apparently weeping statue of the scourged Jesus. When a small church was built to house this statue, the spot became the centre of a remarkable cult, and Dominikus Zimmermann was commissioned with the building of a new, totally Rococo church. Zimmermann made sure even that the line of the roof of his remarkable oval building (19m long and 24m wide) matched the nearby mountain ridge. The high altar was painted by B.A. Albrecht; Ägid Verhelst the Elder designed the figures of the evangelists that frame it; Johann Baptist Zimmermann took responsibility for painting the ceilings, his masterpiece being the Last Judgement on the flattened dome; J.G. Bergmüller designed the altars of St Margaret and St Mary Magdalene; Anton Sturm created

*In a ruggedly magnificent setting above the Pöllat gorge, King Ludwig II's Neuschwanstein rises to 970 metres*

remarkably vivacious statues of the four doctors of the church; Dominikus Zimmermann himself created a trompe l'oeil impression of arches that bend not upwards but downwards! Zimmermann chose to spend the last years of his life in a house next to his masterpiece.

The second **excursion** goes W from Steingaden to **Urspring**, with its Romanesque church, reordered as late Gothic and then given a Baroque decor in the 18C.

Returning to the main routes, 8km S of Steingaden is another holiday resort, **Trauchgau**, at the foot of the Trauchberg (1638m). Schwangau lies 19km SW of Steingaden along the B17. Shortly before the town signposts direct towards the **royal Schlösser of Hohenschwangau** and **Neuschwanstein**. Hohenschwangau was constructed in the 12C near the blue-green waters of the Alp See by the Swan Knights, whose line died out in the 16C. In 1567 the Schloss became the property of the Dukes of Bavaria. A park lies to the S. Much damaged during the Napoleonic wars and sold in 1820, it was bought 12 years later by King Maximilian II (then Crown Prince), under whose patronage the Schloss was restored as a medieval dream castle by architects and artists including Moritz von Schwind and Domenico Quaglio. Gothic tracery, pseudo-medieval stained glass, coats of arms and suits of armour, triptychs and paintings of medieval legends give the Schloss its present character. Legends of the Swan Knights are painted on the walls of the dining room. The centrepiece of the 'Hall of Heroes' is a massive gilded bronze of the Nibelungen saga. Other rooms depict the exploits of Charlemagne, Charles Martel, King Theodoric of the Ostrogoths, the Lombardic King Authori and his bride Theodelinde, Martin Luther. In a hall built for Maximilian's Queen Friederike, medieval women are painted hunting with falcons, reading to children, and playing the harp. In marked contrast is Friederike's bedroom, furnished with oriental gifts from Sultan Muhammed II after the Crown Prince's visit to Turkey in 1833.

At Hohenschwangau Maximilian's son, the future King Ludwig II of Bavaria, entertained Richard Wagner; and you can see Wagner's piano, bust and other memorabilia of the two men. In 1868, after a visit to the Wartburg, Ludwig told Wagner, 'I plan to rebuild the ancient ruined Schloss [of Neuschwanstein] in the true style of a fortress of the old German knights'. Though only 15 out of the projected 65 rooms of this neo-Romanesque and neo-Gothic Schloss had been completed when Ludwig was declared unfit to rule on 13 June 1886, it remains a bizarre masterpiece. The chief artists included August Spiess and Ferdinand von Piloty. Decorations testify to the king's devotion to Wagner before their quarrel with scenes from 'Tannhäuser' in the king's study; from 'Tristan and Isolde' and 'Lohengrin' in his dining room; a Singers' Hall with scenes from 'Parzifal'. Over Ludwig's bed is a canopy evidently modelled on those of medieval tombs. His private chapel has Munich stained glass and a triptych carved by the Munich sculptor Josef Hofmann. Two and a half million pieces of inlaid marble form the floor of the Byzantine basilica planned for the throne room, though the throne was never installed. Annual concerts take place here each September. Both Schlösser are open Apr–Sept 09.00–17.00, in winter 10.00–16.00.

Nearby is the Marienbrücke, bridging the **Poellat gorge** at a height of c 100m and built in 1866. A funicular railway runs to a restaurant/hunting lodge on the 1707m-high Tegelberg.

W of Schwangau is the resort of **Füssen/Bad Faulenberg** (13,000 inhab.; alt. 800m), with its narrow streets, a spa (mud baths, massage), winter sports and sailing on the artificial lake the Forggensee, which takes its name from the village it submerged when the Lech was dammed. The Romans called Füssen *Foetibus*. The **Hohes Schloss** is the former summer retreat of the Bishops of Augsburg, built between the 13C and 16C, its knights' hall with paintings by Jörg Lederer, c 1500, and a Gothic chapel with a wooden relief of the coronation of the Virgin. The Schloss is now the town gallery, with late Gothic works and masterpieces by Jörg Lederer and Stefan Mair (open May–Oct daily 10.00–12.00, 14.00–16.00, closed Sat afternoon, Nov–Apr Thur 10.00–12.00).

The Baroque monastery of **St Mang**, by Johann Jakob Herkomer, 1701–17, displays Venetian traits—Herkomer had worked in Venice—and was built on the site of the late 8C chapel, and later 12C Romanesque church, set over St Magnus's tomb. The statues on the high altar are by Anton Sturm. The abbey buildings, with trompe-l'oeil paintings in the cloister, incorporate a museum of local history, with a musical collection (open weekdays at 10.30, Nov–Apr only Wed). The façade of the **Spital-kirche**, designed by Herkomer's great-nephew Franz Karl Fischer, 1749, on the

Lech bridge is superbly painted in the 18C 'Lüftlmalerei' fashion. The town boasts numerous picturesque burghers' houses. S of the spa is the **Lech gorge**, the St Mang falls and the 955m-high Kalvarienberg, with a panorama of Füssen, Hohenschwangau, Neuschwanstein and the mountains.

# 4

# Regensburg to Munich via Landshut

Total distance 118km. Regensburg—B15, 48km Landshut—B11, 37km Freisang—33km—Munich.

Leave Regensburg S by the B15 to reach after 14km **Alteglofsheim**, with its fine 18C Schloss of the Thurn und Taxis, built on a former medieval castle, later enriched in the Rococo style by J.B. Zimmermann, Cosmas Damien Asam and others. **Hagelstadt** lies 3km S, with a Baroque church by J.M. Fischer. 14km further S the route turns left at Oberlindhart to reach after 6km **Mallersdorf-Pfaffenberg** where the monastery church has an altar by Ignaz Günther. Return to Oberlindhart and travel S for 17km to Landshut.

••**LANDSHUT** (52,0000 inhab.; alt. 393m) set between wooded hills and the Isar is the capital of Lower Bavaria.

**Information Office** is at 315 Altstadt.

**History.** 'Hut' means 'protection' and the town appears as 'protecting' the surrounding countryside in 1150. In the following century Duke Otto II made it the chief town of his duchy. In 1255 upper and lower Bavaria were divided and Heinrich XIII made Landshut his capital. The history of Landshut was subsequently turbulent, the citizens revolting against their lord in 1409, a plague decimating Landshut in 1444 and another ravaging the region 55 years later. During the struggle for the lordship of the town in 1504–05, when the upper Bavarian Wittelsbachs disputed the succession, Götz von Berlichingen lost his right hand and obtained an iron one from the forges of Landshut. The lower Bavarian Duke Albrecht IV won the battle and made Landshut his second capital. Gustavus Adolphus savaged the town in 1632; plague again scourged the citizens in 1648; Turenne caused much damage in the early 18C; the Austrians occupied the town in 1742.

Yet still much survived and was embellished. The 14C and 15C were especially happy ones for Landshut. The future Duke Georg the Rich married a Polish princess here in 1475. The wedding took place amidst scenes of unparalleled splendour, and for seven days the tradesmen and guesthouses of the town served every visitor at the duke's expense. This marriage is still celebrated here in a regular three-yearly festival, the *Landshuter Hochzeit*, with some 2000 costumed participants and medieval music in Burg Trausnitz and in the Residenz of Duke Ludwig X, who lived at Landshut from 1514–45. Crown Prince Wilhelm V lived in and enhanced the Burg Trausnitz. Landshut was the seat of a university from 1800–25.

The exquisite, gently curving street or long square known as the **Altstadt** has a series of splendid gabled burghers' houses many of them painted green, pink, white or yellow. Note in particular Nos 69, Haus Altstadt, 81, the Papperbergerhaus, c 1400, arcaded in 1681, and where Emperor Friedrich III stayed for the wedding; 299, the late Gothic Grasbergerhaus, arcaded in 1453 and given a 19C façade, there is a church at either end of the street. The Altstadt also houses the triple-gabled **Rathaus**, assembled out of three 14C and 15C houses, with a Renaissance oriel window of 1570, a Gothic façade of 1860 and the **Prunksaal** (state hall) with wall paintings of the wedding of 1475 (see above) commissioned c 1880 by Ludwig II of Bavaria from the Munich artists Rudolf Seitz, August Spiess, Konrad Weigand and Ludwig Löfftz (open weekdays 14.00–15.00). This hall, with a massive tiled fireplace, wooden beams and chandeliers, derives from a house built after a fire of 1342, acquired by Landshut in 1386 and widened for the marriage celebrations. The Gothic architect Georg Hauberisser restored the whole in 1880.

Almost opposite is the **Residenz**, built for Duke Ludwig X between 1536 and 1543, commissioned after the duke's visit to Mantua and the earliest Italian palace on German soil (and half of it still emphatically German). The inner courtyard is arcaded, with pink round columns and murals. Among its 40 rooms the great hall is frescoed and stuccoed, Thomas Hering carving limestone medallions depicting the Labours of Hercules, Ludwig Raufinger decorating the ceiling with paintings of Holy Scripture and Greek mythology. The living rooms are now an art gallery and regional museum (open daily 09.00–12.00, 13.00–17.00 in season, 13.00–16.00 Oct–Mar), with early Stone Age finds; local artists and traditions, *European Baroque art.

The finest of the two churches on the Altstadt is the basilica of *St Martin, where the Archbishop of Salzburg conducted the 1475 wedding. Its 130.6m-high tower, the 'Stethaimer', is the tallest brick-built tower in the world. It is named after Hans Stethaimer, also known as Hans von Burghausen, after Burghausen, the town where he was born, who began it in 1399. Two crowns of thorns circle the top of the spire, which was finished in 1500. St Martin's basilica has five Flamboyant Gothic porches sheltering earlier Gothic doorways. The outside walls are partly covered with tombstones and epitaphs including on the south side between two porches that of the *architect (died 1631), the oldest self-portrait bust in German art, though perhaps the work of Stethaimer's son. The bust is on a corbel holding up a carving of the suffering Jesus. Underneath is Stethaimer's coat of arms (two set-squares), flanked by those of his two wives, with an inscription listing his masterpieces—his two Landshut churches, the choir of the Franciscan church in Salzburg, the parish churches of Neuötting and Wasserburg, the Carmelite church at Straubing.

The **interior** displays two rows of slender octagonal columns, each 22m high, the vaults springing directly from them; the aisles equal the nave in length. Other features are a stone high altar of 1424, by Hans Stethaimer, given a Baroque superstructure in 1664 with rows of saints including St Martin; a stone pulpit of 1429; in the aisles coloured terracotta figures, 1460–80, which are sheltered by Gothic canopies; choir stalls of c 1500; a crucifix by Michael Erhart, 1495; the organ screen of 1620; fragments of 15C and Baroque frescoes; tombstones, including that of Martin Vair, co-founder of the University of Ingolstadt (who died in 1481); stained glass by Franz Högner, 1945; and a famous *Madonna and Child* by Hans Leinberger, c 1518. A circular staircase leads down to the remains of the earlier 13C Romanesque church. Theatinerstrasse, next to St Martin, leads to the 15C Landtor a defensive gateway, with two square, battlemented towers, in the medieval fortifications of Landshut. In Ländtorplatz is a theatre of 1836, reordered in 1947 and seating 806.

Beyond St Martin **Burg Trausnitz**, partly restored after a fire of 1961, rises above the town. Ludwig the Kelheimer (Second Wittelsbach Duke of Bavaria) built it in 1204. When Duke Albrecht IV died in 1508, his sons Ludwig X and Wilhelm IV ruled the duchy jointly, and Ludwig and his successors transformed the Burg into a Renaissance Schloss, making it the seat of their court. On the way up to the Schloss is a statue of Duke Ludwig the Rich, ruler 1450–79 and founder in 1472 of Bavaria's first university. The Burg houses the Lower Bavarian state archive (open Apr–Sept except Mon 09.00–12.00, 13.00–17.00, closing 16.00 Oct–Mar); see also a 13C late Romanesque chapel of St Georg, with a 15C high altar, Gothic vaulting and early 16C statues; the commedia dell'arte figures painted in the Narren-treppe (or 'fools' staircase) in the Burg courtyard by the Italian A. Scalzi; and a superb view of the town.

At the opposite end of the Altstadt is the **Heilig-Geist-Kirche**, which Hans von Burghausen began in 1407. It has another brick spire, this one set beside the church, whereas that of St Martin rises from the west end. The architect's son took over the work, and the church was finished in 1462, a year after his death. Opposite across the street is the Heilig-Geist-Spital, a 13C hospice, rebuilt by Johann G.G. Hirchstetten, 1722–28, the Holy Trinity in heaven is frescoed on the façade and dated 1728.

Walk NW along Zweibrückenstrasse, so called because the Isar divides into two at Landshut and must be crossed by two bridges. In between the streams is the church of **St Sebastian**, built in the late 15C, with a Baroque reordering in the early 1660s. Beyond is the 1870–71 war memorial, Bismarckplatz and the Cistercian abbey of Seligenthal, founded in 1232 by Ludmilla von Bogen, the widow of Ludwig I the Kelheimer. The present monastic buildings date from the 19C and 20C. The monastery church is a Rococo building by Johann Baptist Gunetzrhainer of Munich, erected on the walls of the mid 13C church and incorporating a 1232 chapel of St Afra, in which are the tombs of the founders, their statues carved in wood. The church is the last resting place of Duke Ludwig X who died in 1545, with a notable grave-stone and statue of Ludwig. The mid 18C frescoes and stucco work on the vault and choir are by Johann Baptist Zimmermann and Egid Quirin Asam, mid 18C, with a coronation of the Virgin by Zimmer-mann on the dome. See also the mid 13C crucifix in the Nonnenchor of Jesus hanging on a tree; the Rococo altars; early 15C carvings of the Deposition and Last Supper in the chapel of St Agatha underneath the Nuns' Choir; and a 13C fresco of the Coronation of the Virgin in the refectory.

Narrow cobbled streets join the Altstadt with the **Neustadt**, founded to complement the Altstadt in 1338. Herrngasse leads to it from the Heilig-Geist Kirche to the church of the Ursulines. At the far end, past gabled Gothic houses, some with Baroque façades, is the barrel-vaulted, classical Jesuit church which Johann Holl built in 1613–41; its Wessobrunn stucco is by M. Schmuzer, 1640–41. Half-way along the Neustadt stands the 1914–18 war memorial. From close by, Regierungstrasse leads to the former Dominican monastery, founded in 1271, rebuilt in the 14C and again in 1802, with a late 19C classical façade. The church was given a Rococo aspect by J.B. Zimmermann in 1749. Forcibly dissolved at the secularisation of Bavaria in 1803, the monastery now houses the state administrators. Beyond rises the huge, brick hall-church of St Jodok, possibly an early work by Hans Stethaimer, begun in 1338, expanded after a 15C fire, and housing the tomb of Peter von Altenhaus by Stephan Rottaler, c 1513.

From Landshut follow the B11 SW towards Munich, reaching after 10km Kronwinkl, with its Schloss of the 11C, 17C and 18C, the family seat of the Counts Preysing, and with fine views back towards Landshut of the tower of St Martin's basilica and Burg Trausnitz. The road reaches **Moosburg an**

**der Isar** after another 9km. Moosburg, which retains fragments of its old walls, was founded in the mid 8C, and developed around the relics of a Roman martyr, St Kastulus. Its greatest treasure is the 12C Romanesque basilica of **St Kastulus**, containing a marvellous 15m-high, late Gothic main altar by Hans Leinberger, 1515, and the medieval shrine of the saint. Other sights are the 13C cemetery church of St Michael; the 14C and 15C church of St Johann; its medieval houses; and the 16C Schloss Asch.

18km from Moosburg stands **Freising** (32,000 inhab.; alt. 421m), a city founded as the result of the work of 8C missionaries, amongst them Boniface and Korbinian. Freising flourished in the 14C under Bishop Otto, the historian and uncle of Barbarossa. Its chief treasure is the brick 12C double-towered *Dom*—Freising was the seat of the bishops of Bavaria from 724 until the see transferred to Munich in 1817. The cathedral has a 13C crypt, late 15C vaulting, Gothic choir stalls of 1448, and an interior by the brothers Asam, 1724. The relics of St Korbinian are venerated in the crypt, with Romanesque animals carved on the crypt columns. Other important buildings include the 13C Benedictine church, which was rebuilt in the mid 14C; the church of St Johann, which dates from 1359 and is filled with painting and sculpture; and the Spital Kirche dating from 1607. Freising is further enriched by the 14C to 18C Bishops' Palace and a monastery church by Giovanni Antonio Viscardi, 1705–15, with decoration by F.X. Feichtmayr and J.B. Zimmermann and a *high altar of 1765 by Ignaz Günther.

The B11 continues for 33km as far as Munich (see Rte 11) by way of the Isar Valley and Freimann (where the road joins the motorway for Berlin). The route enters Munich by the Ludwigstrasse, Leopoldstrasse and Ungererstrasse.

# 5

# Würzburg and the 'Romantische Strasse'

## A.  Würzburg

**WÜRZBURG** (126,000 inhab.; alt. 182m), beautifully situated amidst vine-clad hills on the River Main, is an old university city, the seat of a Catholic bishopric, and the administrative centre of Lower Franconia. It lies on motorway B8 midway between Nuremberg (102km) and Frankfurt-am-Main (117km) and at the start of the Romantische Strasse. Three bridges cross the river: from N to S the Friedensbrücke, the Alte Mainbrücke and the Ludwigsbrücke.

**Main railway station**: Haugerglacisstrasse. **Tourist offices**: Falkenhaus in the Marktplatz; opposite the main railway station. **Tramway** system. **Trains** to Aschaffenburg, Bamberg, Frankfurt, Ingolstadt, Munich, Nuremberg, Regensburg, Stuttgart. **Boats** along the River Main to Veitshöchheim.

**WÜRZBURG**

0  300m

HAUPTBAHNHOF

BISMARCK STRAßE

RING

Messe
gelände

RÖNTGEN

KAISER
PLATZ

HAUGER GLACISSTR

N

FRIEDENS BRÜCKE

KOELLIKER STRAßE

KLINIK

MAHCUS
STR

HAUGER RING

WALLGASSE

Congreß
centrum

PLEICHERWALL

NEUTORSTR

VIEHMARKT
PLATZ

PLEICHER-
KIRCHPLATZ

KAISER STRAßE

BAHNHOF STRAßE

TEXFORD STR

Stift
Haug

KRANENKAI

GERBER STRAße

Main

BACHG

Julius
spital

BARBAROSSA-
PLATZ

HEINESTRAßE

Alter
Kranen

JULIUSPROMENADE

GRABEN

STR

GRABENBERG

OBERTHUR STR

SEMMEL STRAße

HAND

KARTAUSE

INN

BRONNBACHER GASSE

KARMELITENSTRAße

HERZOGEN STRAßE

STR

Bürger
spital

STRAße

GASSE

LUDWIG

STRAße

HOFSTALL STR

ELSTERG

LAUFERG

MAINKAI

Falkenhaus

EICHHORN

SPIEGELSTR

THEATER STRAße

K-FAULHABER
PLATZ

KAPUZINER

ZELLER STRAße

BURKARDER STR

Marien
kapelle

Rat-
haus

MARKT
PLATZ

SCHÖNBORN

Otto
Richter
halle

MAT STR

A KASERNENSTR

Alte Main
brücke

DOMSTRAße

Neu
Münster

Stadt
Galerie

HOFSTRAße

Fürsten-
garten

BUTTNERSTRAße

Dom

RENNWEG

RESIDENZ
PLATZ

Festung
Marien-
berg

AUGUSTINERSTRAße

URSULINERG

FRANZISKANERG

FRANZISKANER-
PLATZ

DOMERSCHULSTR

BIBRA STRAße

KETTENGASSE

BALTH-NEUMANN-PROM

Residenz
M. von
Wagner
museum

St
Burkard

SAALGASSE

MAINKAI

Alte
universität

Hofgarten

Mainfrän-
kisches
Museum

OBERER

REIBELTG

JOHANN-
PLATZ

JOHANNITERGASSE

SANDER

NEUBAUSTRAße

STEFANSTR

OTTO-STRAße

Main

ROSENG

St Peter

PETERS
PLATZ

KORNG

LANDWEHR STR

MÜNSTRAße

STRAße

ZWINGER

Geschw-
Scholl-Platz

Universität

EBERT RING

TIEPOLOSTRAße

SANDER RING

Käppele

LUDWIGS BRÜCKE

SANDER RING

**History**. There was a Bronze Age settlement here c 1000 BC, where later the Celts settled at a spot where the Main could be forded. Irish monks brought Christianity in the 7C; three of them, SS Kilian, Kolonat and Totnan, were martyred in 689. 'Castellum Virteburch' was well established high on the left bank of the Main by the early 8C, and St Boniface founded a bishopric here in 742. The first bishop was Burkart, and pilgrims increasingly visited the tomb of Kilian. Charlemagne's court was at Würzburg in 788 (when the cathedral was consecrated in his presence) and in 793. Würzburg prospered further after 1030, when the bishops gained the right to mint coins, to oversee markets and to charge tolls.

The marriage of Frederick Barbarossa and Beatrix of Burgundy was celebrated here in 1156. Twelve years later Barbarossa made the bishops Dukes of Franconia, and they then ruled the city until 1802 (in spite of numerous uprisings against them by the burghers, particularly that of 1397). The citizens supported the peasants during the Peasants' Revolt of 1525. In the late 16C and the 17C the city expanded, especially under the Prince-Bishop Julius Echter von Mespelbrunn (1573–1617), who re-endowed the university, 1582. In spite of its capture by Gustavus Adolphus during the Thirty Years War, Würzburg continued to prosper in the 17C and 18C, especially under the Prince-Bishops Johann Philipp von Schönborn (1642–73), Johann Philipp Franz von Schönborn (1719–24) and Friedrich Karl von Schönborn (1729–46). From 1802–05 the city was part of the Electorate of Bavaria, and then was ruled as a Grand Duchy under Ferdinand of Tuscany.

Tilman Riemenschneider (c 1460–1531), the greatest limewood sculptor of the Renaissance, was mayor of Würzburg. The painter Matthias Grünewald was born here, c 1465. Distinguished 19C savants at the university (founded 1420) included the philosopher F.W.J. Schelling, the physicist Wilhelm Konrad von Röntgen, who discovered X-rays, and Gladstone's friend the theologian Ignatius Döllinger, 'a remarkable and a very pleasing man'. Würzburg suffered a devastating air raid on 16 March 1945. In the 1970s the city began to spread into the new town of Heuchelhof, and the New University was founded in the suburbs.

Candlelit Mozart concerts are held in the Residenz each June, and there is an autumn wine festival.

From the main railway station follow Bahnhofstrasse to the twin-spired **Stift Haug**, the first significant Baroque church in Franconia, by the Italian Antonio Petrini, 1670–91. Its dome is impressive. The interior was destroyed in 1945; over the high altar is a crucifixion of 1583 by Jacopo Tintoretto.

A few metres to the W Juliuspromenade leads W past the Baroque **Juliusspital**, part of which is now a Weinstube, part serving the university founded by Prince-Bishop Julius Echter in 1576. The prince's building (Fürstenbau) boasts a Rococo apothecary, still in use. Its garden wing was built by Antonio Petrini in 1699, the wing facing the street by Geigel in 1789. Behind is a park with a pavilion (used as the university anatomy room in the 19C) designed by Joseph Greising in 1714, and a Baroque fountain of 1706 by Jakob van der Auvera. Juliuspromenade continues W to the **Alter Kranen** (old crane) on the riverside, built by Franz Ignaz Neumann (Balthasar's son), c 1770. Through the alleyway is an impressive view of the Marienberg fortress across the river; see below. N of Juliuspromenade is the 1611 church of **St Gertraud**, with a modern interior.

S along the river bank and first left leads into Bronnbachergasse, with the **Fichtelhof**, the house of Court Chancellor Fichter, 1724, with a superb doorway and staircase. Continue W across Schönbornstrasse to reach the former Dominican **Augustinerkirche** with a Gothic choir of c 1250; a central aisle by Balthasar Neumann, 1741; and stucco work by Antonio Bossi. Continue as far as Eichhornstrasse, turning left here to reach Theaterstrasse. NW along Theaterstrasse at No. 4 is an ornamental doorway with a statue of the Virgin Mary. Immediately opposite the corner of Eichhornstrasse, where Theaterstrasse meets Semmelstrasse, is the **Bürgerspital**, today a Weinstube. Built in 1319, the arcaded courtyard is by Müller, 1717; there are statues in the Gothic chapel; the Glockenspiel is 20C.

Return along Eichhornstrasse to cross Schönbornstrasse into the **Marktplatz** to find the finest burgher's house in Würzburg, the Rococo **Falkenhaus**. A former inn with stucco decoration dating from 1752, the whole was meticulously restored after World War II and today is the city's tourist office. Here the burghers built a late Gothic hall-church, the **Marienkapelle**, on the site of a synagogue, having held the Jews responsible for the plague of 1347–52 and driven them away (1377–1481): of its sculpted doorway the famous figures of Adam and Eve by Riemenschneider are now in the city museum. The interior, renewed after 1945, houses on the south wall of the nave a Madonna c 1430, which was formerly part of the west doorway, as well as tombs of knights and townsmen, including the *tomb of Konrad von Schaumberg sculpted by Riemenschneider in 1502, and Balthasar Neumann's tombstone.

S of the Marktplatz is visible the Romanesque tower of the **Rathaus**, reached by the Marktgasse, the Gressengasse and then the Langgasse, formerly the Hof zum Grafen Eckhart. It has a Romanesque ground floor; the 13C Wenceslas Hall on the first floor; and two upper storeys dating from the 16C. The lower half of its tower was built c 1300, the upper half in 1453. N of the town hall, in both Gressengasse and Rückermainstrasse, is the Baroque **Rückermainhof** (1715–23). Abutting the town hall is the late Renaissance **Red Building** by Preiss and Villinger, 1659. Facing the town hall to the S is the Baroque **Vierrohrren** fountain by Lukas van der Auvera and Peter Wagner (1763–66).

Walk E along Domstrasse to the cathedral of **St Kilian (Dom)**, the fourth largest Romanesque church in Germany, begun in 1045 on the site of a 9C building; the E towers dated to 1237. All were destroyed in 1945, rebuilt and rededicated in 1967. **Interior**: high Baroque, early 18C stucco work is by Pietro Magno; the ceiling of the central aisle was painted by F. Nagel; bishops' tombstones, including the earliest, for Gottfried von Spitzenberg (d. 1190), and *Riemenschneider's red marble tombstones for Rudolf von Scherenberg (who died in 1495) and Lorenz von Bibra (who died in 1519); a pulpit by Michael Kern (1609–10, saved in 1945); the Rococo **Schönbornkapelle**, which was the burial place of the Prince-Bishops and was built by Balthasar Neumann and M. von Welsch, 1721–36, its frescoes painted by Byss, its sculpture by Claude Curé; a late Gothic sepulchre, with modern windows by Georg Meistermann; and finally the modern altar, tabernacle and bishop's throne by A. Schilling, 1966–67. The cloisters date from 1034, with a crucifixion group by Lukas van der Auvera (1761–63).

N of the cathedral stands the **Neumünster** on the spot where St Kilian was martyred and buried (his shrine is in the crypt). This church is 11C Romanesque, with a 13C choir and tower. The dome and Baroque façade are by V. Pezani and Johann Dientzenhofer, 1710–16. Inside seek out Riemenschneider's *Madonna (in the SW niche of the rotunda) and the tombstone of the humanist abbot Johannes Trithemius, who died in 1516. The Baroque reordering of the Neumünster (restored after 1945) is by Joseph Griesing, Nikolaus Stuber and J.-B. Zimmermann, with stucco by Dominikus Zimmermann. In the little garden (**Lusamgärtlein**) is the grave of the minnesinger Walther von der Vogelweide (who died in 1230). The cloisters, c 1170, have a garden. E at 1 Maxstrasse is the **Otto-Richter-Halle**, the home of modern art exhibitions. In this area some burghers' houses and courtyards escaped destruction in 1945, including the Renaissance **Hof Conti** in Herrenstrasse, now the bishop's palace, of 1609, with a Renaissance balcony, and the classical **Hof Rannenberg** at 3 Hofstrasse, restored 1965–69. The Städt Galerie (City Art Gallery) is to the S. Open Tue–Fri 10.00–17.00, Sat, Sun and holidays 10.00–13.00, it displays 19C and 20C Franconian painters.

Follow Hofstrasse E to reach the Residenzplatz and the Baroque **•*Residenz** (open 09.00–12.00, 13.00–17.00; varying times for court church and gardens), built in 1719–44 as the palace of the Prince-Bishops to the plans of Balthasar Neumann, though these were modified by Johann Lukas von Hildebrandt and Maximilian von Welsch. In the courtyard gushes a fountain, 1894, with statues of the minnesinger Walther von der Vogelweide, the painter Matthias Grünewald and the sculptor Tilman Riemenschneider. Neumann's magnificent staircase and cupola has a ceiling painted by Giambattista Tiepolo, 1750–53. At 540 sq m this, the largest fresco in the world, depicts God in his heaven ruling the world: note the portrait of Neumann as an artillery officer, in the representation of

Europe. The Weisser Saal has stucco by Antonio Bossi; the Kaisersaal is by Neumann and Hildebrandt, with stucco by Bossi and frescoes by Tiepolo, 1752, depicting the history of Würzburg, chiefly the marriage of Barbarossa and Beatrix of Burgundy. The ceiling fresco of the Garden Hall was painted by Johannes Zick and stuccoed by Antonio Bossi. The Residenz also boast a Rococo Parade Room of 1740–70, very seriously damaged 1945, and a court chapel by Neumann (note the light coming from one side only), with frescoes by Johann Rudolf Byss and a side altar painting by Tiepolo. As for the gardens (Hotgarten), they are defended by Baroque bastions, and ornamented with cherubs by P. Wagner and elaborate wrought-iron Rococo gates by J. G. Oegg.

Würzburg's **Martin-von-Wagner-Museum** has a picture gallery open Tue–Sat 09.30–13,00, and displays its antiquities Tue–Sat 14.00–17.00; both galleries open Sun, 10.00–13.00; do not miss the antiques and copperplates. In the N wing are the Bavarian national archives; the garden is lovely—the garden front of the Residenz is 167m long. The Residenz has a Weinstube in the Hofkellerei. NE of the Residenz is the neo-Gothic Protestant church of **St Johannes**, 1895, restored after World War II.

From Residenzplatz Balthasar-Neumann-Promenade leads SW to the corner of Neubaustrasse. To the S is the church of **St Stephan**, which J.P. Geigel built in 1789 above an 11C crypt; the crucifixion group above the high altar is by Helmut Ammann, 1955. W along Neubaustrasse rise the restored late Baroque Jesuit church of **St Michael**, 1765–98, the **Priests' Seminary** by Joseph Greising of 1715–19, the Renaissance **Alte Universität** buildings, begun by Georg Robin in 1582, and the Renaissance **Neubau church** begun in 1586, with a tower by Petrini, 1696. A little further W is the **Franciscan church**, built in 1221, and restored after World War II as were its cloisters, with a doorway carved with St Francis receiving the stigmata, by Michael Kern, 1st half 17C, and *Riemenschneider's Pietà and then (No. 7) the noble house **Zum Rebstock**, decorated with Rococo stucco work.

From Neubaustrasse Münzstrasse leads S to **St Peter's church** built by Greising in 1717, and retaining two towers from the 12C Romanesque church that earlier stood here; its Rococo pulpit is by Auvera. To the W you can see across Sanderstrasse the **Carmelite** church built by Antonio Petrini, 1662, the first Italian Baroque church in Würzburg. From here a short walk leads to the river bank. Walk N alongside the river to the **Alte Mainbrücke**, first built in 1133, rebuilt between 1474 and 1543, adorned with Baroque sandstone statues (the originals c 1730) of rulers and saints, including Barbarossa and the Irish missionaries of Würzburg; the present statues are copies sculpted by Claud Curé, a Frenchman who made his home in Würzburg, and the brothers Volkmar and Johann Sebastian Becker. Across the bridge stands the late Gothic **Hospital Church**, with its neo-Classical façade. The church now serves as an art gallery of contemporary works (open Wed–Mon, 10.00–12.00, 13.00–17.00). From here Zellerstrasse leads NW to the former church of the order of Teutonic Knights, the **Deutschhaus-kirke**, today used for Protestant worship. Its style is early Gothic, mostly dating from 1296, though the church retains a late Romanesque tower.

S of the Alte Mainbrücke on the W side of the river stands the Roman-esque basilica of **St Burkard**. Consecrated in 1140, it has late Gothic transepts and a late Gothic choir of 1493, as well as early Gothic capitals, a Gothic statue of the Virgin, a 14C relief of the crucifixion, a bust of the Madonna by Riemenschneider in the south aisle, and Baroque altars by the workshop of Auvera.

NW of St Burkard is the church of a former Irish monastery, dedicated to St John Bosco, a post World War II replacement for the destroyed St Jakob's church. W of this church is the dominating **Festung Marienberg**. This fortress, founded in 1201, grew around a church consecrated to St Mary, c 706, the oldest round church in Germany, its interior much altered and housing a Baroque altar and tombstones of bishops. The Marienberg in turn is dominated by its Bergfried (the Round Tower, c 1200) and centres on the Brunnenhaus (1601). The Prince-Bishops lived here from 1253 to 1719. The main castle dates from 1482, as do the walls, though the Scherenberg gate was not built until c 1600. Julius Echter transformed the fortress into a Renaissance palace, his Echter bastion and temple rising above a 104m-deep well. The palace became a Baroque fortress again, after Gustavus Adolphus's victory over Würzburg in 1631. From the Princes' Garden there is a panorama of the city; the Baroque armoury (1702–12) is now the **Mainfränkisches Museum** (open daily 10.00–17.00; Nov–Mar closes 16.00). On display are sculpture by Veit Stoss, Ferdinand Dietz, Peter Wagner and, especially, **Riemenschneider, plus an exhibition devoted to regional wines and a prehistoric collection.

S of the Marienberg is the pilgrims' **Käpelle** with its lovely spires and domes, surrounded by vineyards and standing 359m high on the Nikolausberg. Built by Balthasâr Neumann, c 1748, its interior has frescoes by Feichtmayr, stucco by Matthias Günther, a Rococo organ case, c 1750, and a classical high altar of 1797–99. The life-size stations of the cross on the way to the church are by P. Wagner, 1767–75, and the view from the terrace provides a splendid panorama.

**Other sights.** The **Huttenschlösschen**, outside the city walls to the S, was built by Beyer, c 1720, for the Prince-Bishop of Hutten. The **Am Hubland** (University Mineral Museum) opens Sat 14.00–17.00, and the **Civic Theatre** of 1966 is at 21 Theaterstrasse.

# B.  Würzburg to Augsburg: the 'Romantische Strasse'

Total distance 233km. Würzburg—B27, 35km Tauberbischofsheim—B290, 18km Bad Mergentheim—45km Rothenburg ob der Tauber—B25, 43km Dinkelsbühl—B25, 31km Nördlingen—B25, 28km Donauwörth—B2, 45km Augsburg.

Leave Würzburg by way of the Alte Mainbrücke and make for the B27, which runs SW to reach after 32km picturesque **Tauberbischofsheim** (inhab. 12,300; alt. 180–230m), lying amid vineyards in the Tauber valley. Cross the bridge over the River Tauber and continue along the Hauptstrasse to the Marktplatz, which houses the Rathaus and the Baroque church of St Lioba. The town takes its name from the missionary, Bishop Boniface, to whom it was presented in the year 725. The name of the River Tauber was added only in 1806. Around the Marktplatz are numerous well-restored half-timbered houses (especially the Baroque Haus Mackert of 1744 and the Sternapotheke opposite). Some of them are carved with mermaids, allegorising the importance of the river to Tauberbishofsheim. Numerous metal plates indicate the level to which the Tauber rose when it flooded the town in 1985.

S of the pedestrian zone is the Schlossplatz, with its 14–16C Schloss, incorporating the older Türmers tower. Today this serves as the Tauber-fränkisches Landschaftsmuseum with Gothic paintings and woodcarvings of the school of Riemenschneider (open Easter–mid-Oct, Tue–Sat, 14.30–16.30; Sun and holidays also 10.00–12.00). N of the pedestrian zone is the neo-Gothic church of St Martin (1910–14) which still possesses its old Gothic furnishings, including the Marienaltar, part of which is by Tilman Riemenschneider, and the 1761 altar of the cross. Its chapel of St Sebastian, formerly the charnel house, displays a Last Judgement over its door, painted in 1476.

The Romantische Strasse now follows the B290 and the right bank of the river SE under the Heilbronn–Würzburg motorway through **Distelhausen** with a Baroque parish church, perhaps by Balthasar Neumann, 1731–38, reaching after 6km **Gerlachsheim**, which has a former monastery church of 1725–30, with stucco work, a high altar painting by Johann Zick and a Rococo pulpit of 1788. The mid 18C statue of Mary comforting the distressed in the centre of the town was restored in 1878.

From here a short **excursion** NE takes in **Grünsfeld**, with a half-timbered town hall c 1580 and a parish church dedicated to SS Peter and Paul, dating from the 14C to the 18C and containing Riemenschneider tombs (including that of *Countess Dorothea von Wertheim, who died in 1503). Continue NE to **Grünsfeldhausen** with its 12C eight-sided chapel of St Achatius, to which is attached another smaller eight-sided chapel and a 19C tower. Inside are 12C wall paintings. Further NE lies **Ilmspan**, with an elegantly stuccoed Rococo church designed by Johann Michael Fischer in 1766. The excursion now runs SE to Oberwittighausen, with just outside the town an eight-sided chapel, St Sigismund, topped by a Gothic belfry, comparable to that of Grünsfeldhausen. Return SW to **Zimmern**, with its church of 1768 by J.M. Fischer, and continue back through Grünsfeld to Gerlachsheim.

**Lauda**, the next place on the Romantische Strasse and another wine-growing town, appears almost immediately, at the other side of the river (crossed by a bridge of 1510–12). A history of the town is laid out in the local history museum (May–Oct 15.00–17.00, Sun and holidays) at 25 Rathausstrasse, which is a restored farmhouse of 1551. The town hall dates from 1591, there are fine 17C and 18C houses and the church of St Jakob dates from c 1700 (restored 1954). Close by is the sizeable new town of Lauda–Königshofen.

**Bad Mergentheim** (inhab. 20,000; alt. 410m; tourist office 3 Marktplatz), 50km S of Würzburg, is where the Romantische Strasse begins to be signposted with green signs (lettered in yellow). 'Mergentheim' derives from the name of a Duchess, 'Marigund', who ran her son's realm when he was a minor. The Catholic branch of the Teutonic Knights established an important headquarters here in 1526 when they lost their Prussian territories, for they had already invested much in the town. They fortified the town in 1330 and their traces are found throughout Bad Mergentheim and above all in their Deutschordensschloss (1568–1628), on the E side of the town. The grand master had his seat here from 1526 to 1809, when the knights were dispossessed by Napoleon. The Schloss, boasting Renaissance spiral staircases in its corner towers, now houses a museum of the Order (open Tue–Sat 14.30–17.30, Sun and holidays and Nov–Feb 10.00–12.00), with portraits of the Teutonic Knights, their robes, a number of dolls' houses and peasant costumes. Over its main doorway is sculpted the coat of arms of the Teutonic Knights. The Schloss is also the venue for numerous concerts and son et lumière displays. Its Schlosskirke dates from 1730–36, partly the work of Balthasar Neumann and François Cuvilliés. Inside are tombs of knights and 1734 frescoes by Nikolaus Stuber.

In addition, the magnesium sulphate springs at Bad Mergentheim have made it famous for over a century and a half, since a shepherd re-discovered these medicinal waters in 1826. Medicinal fountains and a pump room were first constructed in 1829, and the town today attracts many to its sanatoria and pump room. The name 'Bad' was added only in 1926. Bad Mergentheim has fine patrician and half-timbered houses and a town hall of 1564 in the Marktplatz along with the Michling fountain topped by a statue of Wilhelm Schutzbar, the Teutonic Knight who brought his section of the Order to Bad Mergentheim. S of the Marktplatz stands the 14C Dominican Marienkirche, with early 14C wall paintings and a bronze memorial by Hans Vischer of Grand Master Walther von Cronberg, who died in 1543. On the N side of the Marktplatz an alley leads to the 13C church of St Johannes, built by the Knights of St John of Jerusalem, with an early 17C gravestone of the Teutonic Knight, the Marquardt von Eck. Nearby is the frescoed chapel of the Hospice of the Holy Ghost. Nos 2–4 Burgstrasse, connecting the Marktplatz and the Schloss, house the Automobil Museum.

The poet Eduard Mörike (1804–75) lived here from 1844 to 1851 and married a girl of the town.

10km SW of Bad Mergentheim lies **Stuppach**. The late Gothic church of 1607 was extended in 1930 to house the *****Stuppacher Madonna** or St Mary of the Snows, by Matthias Grünewald, painted c 1519, which came here in 1812—from the triptych on the Maria-Schnee altar of the Aschaffenburg hospice church—and was recognised as Grünewald's in 1900. Another short excursion W from Bad Mergentheim leads to **Boxberg**, with a Baroque church by Balthasar Neumann, to **Boxberg-Wölchingen**, with a 13C late Romanesque church, and to **Boxberg-Unterschüpf**, whose church is part 13C Gothic, part early 17C Renaissance, with 15C wall paintings and a Rococo altar.

From Bad Mergentheim the route runs 11km E to **Weikersheim** (7400 inhab.; alt. 223m), a tiny town with a moated Renaissance schoss built by the princes of Hohenlohe between the 16C and the 18C, incorporating a 12C keep and now the Tauberländer Museum. Its glories include a banqueting hall with a coffered ceiling 35m by 12m designed by E. Gunzenhaüser and painted with hunting scenes by Balthasar Katzenberger, as well as life-sized plaster sculptures of emperors and empresses in the *****Rittersaal**, which is half-Renaissance, half-Baroque and dates from 1603. The Baroque park, laid out in 1710, the orangery of 1719 and the Schloss are open 09.00–18.00 Mar–Oct (otherwise Tue–Sun 10.00–12.00, 14.00–16.00). In the graceful, semi-circular Marktplatz stands the late Gothic parish church of 1518. The Neptune-fountain here dates from 1768. On the W side are the so-called 'Zirkelhäusern' (compass houses) of 1520. Between these is the way to the Schloss.

4km to the SE is the small town of **Weikersheim-Laudenbach**, with a late 15C Gothic pilgrimage chapel, altered in the 17C. In the crypt chapel is an alabaster tomb of Fieldmarshal Melchior von Hatzfeld, who died in 1658. From Weikersheim the Romantische Strasse continues E through rolling country to Röttingen with its medieval town walls, and a wine festival in October, shortly afterwards turning S to reach after 11km **Bieberehren**. Admirers of Tilman Riemenschneider will make a diversion NE to **Aub**, whose parish church has a crucifixion group partly by him, sculpted c 1500.

*St Mary of the Snows, the Stuppach altarpiece painted by Matthias Grünewald in 1519*

The Rathaus, built in 1482, fronts a square with a Baroque pillar topped by a gilded statue of the Virgin Mary.

From Aub the route runs S to reach **Creglingen** where, 2km outside the town, the Herrgottskirche, built by the Hohenlohe family in 1380, houses Riemenschneider's 7m-high **\* \* \*Marienaltar** (c 1505). The wings of the altar depict the life of the Virgin; the centre her assumption—this piece is certainly by the master himself. The church (open Apr–Oct 08.00–18.00, otherwise except Mon 10.00–12.00, 13.00–16.00) was built to celebrate the discovery of a sacred Host by a 14C ploughman. The high altar was constructed c 1510, the side altars c 1460. Opposite the church is a museum of thimbles. The town of Creglingen itself has fine houses, and a Riemenschneider crucifix in its church.

The Romantische Strasse now runs 18km SE to **\* \* \*Rothenburg ob der Tauber** (inhab. 12,000; alt. 426m), passing through Detwang en route, where the basically Romanesque parish church possesses a crucifixion altar c 1515, in part by Riemenschneider. Rothenburg is a virtually unspoilt medieval town, preserving its 2.5km walls intact and standing some 100m above the right bank of the River Tauber. It is situated where the Romantische Strasse crosses the Burgenstrasse (castle route) between Nuremberg and Heildelberg.

**Trains** to Steinach; **buses** to Steinach, Füssen, Creglingen, Würzburg and Schilling-fürst. The **information office** is in the town hall.

During the tourist season Rothenburg runs a riding school, and the region has fine hill-walking country. The nearest motorway is the Würzburg-Randersacker Autobahn, 5.5km from the town.

Annual events include the renactment of the 'Meistertrunk', when the Bürgermeister of the town persuaded the Catholic General Tilly not to raze Rothenburg by accepting and winning a challenge to drink at one gulp a huge draught of wine. Other events are the Schäfertanz ('shepherds' dance') on Whit Sunday and during the summer, and the Hans Sachs festival (Easter and during the summer season).

**History**. The Celts built a small fortress here, dominating a meander of the River Tauber. The Franks made the town the capital of the Duchy of Franconia. In 1115 the emperor gave Rothenburg to his nephew, Conrad von Hohenstaufen, who became Emperor Conrad III in 1138. By the mid 12C the Hohenstaufens owned two castles here, which an earthquake destroyed in 1356. From their chief burg the main street of Rothenburg led to the Marktplatz. The lords of the town fortified Rothenburg in the 12C, from which epoch remain the Markus Turm and the Weisser Turm. By the end of the 13C it had become a Free Imperial City. Rothenburg became Protestant at the Reformation, and barely escaped destruction in 1631 for taking the side of Gustavus Adolphus during the Thirty Years War (see below). The Peace of Westphalia confirmed its Free status. Apart from its incorporation into Bavaria in 1802, the town slept during the late 17C, 18C and 19C and was deliberately spared during World War II by orders of the American General Devers, hence its present unspoilt aspect. Today one and a half million tourists pass annually through its gates.

Begin a tour of Rothenburg in the Marktplatz, with its **Rathaus**, half-Gothic, c 1250, half-Renaissance, dating from 1578, with a balcony of 1681 and vaulted halls, decorated with scenes from the Thirty Years War (open daily Apr–Oct). The 55m high tower was built in the 16C. An open-air staircase leads into the Renaissance wing and the imperial hall. To the right of the town hall is the **Ratstrinkstube** of 1446, where daily on the hour from 11.00–15.00 and 21.00–22.00 a window of a clock opens for a puppet representation of the 'Meistertrunk'. Opposite is the fountain of St Georg, 1446, reordered in the Renaissance style in 1608.

**Obere Schmiedgasse** leads from the Marktplaz S. The street comprises fine patrician houses. No. 21, the **Roter Hahn**, was the home of Bürgermeister Nusch who saved the town from Tilly's wrath in 1631; No. 3, the **Baumeisterhaus**, is a Renaissance building with a sandstone façade, by the town architect L. Weidmann, 1596, now a restaurant, its statues represent on the first floor the seven cardinal virtues, and on the second the seven deadly sins. Next to it stands the **Gasthof zum Greifen**, once the home of Bürgermeister Heinrich Toppler, who led Rothenburg to its greatest prosperity in the 14C, and died in the town gaol. Next to Nusch's house is the church of **St Johannes**, 1311–1471, with early 17C modifications. (The Puppet and Doll Museum (Puppen-und-Spielzeugmuseum) at 13 Hofbronnengasse, which leads S of Marktplatz, is a private collection dating from 1780 to 1940; open daily 09.30–18.00.)

Leave here W by Rothenburg's oldest street, the Burggasse, which boasts at No. 3 the **Kriminalsmuseum**, a criminals' museum and torture chamber (open daily Apr–Oct 09.30–18.00; otherwise 14.00–16.00). Follow Burggasse as far as Herrngasse, which includes the 14C Gothic **Franziskanerkirche**, with a late Gothic rood screen and 15C and 16C tombstones, as well as the 16C Herrn fountain, and leads to the 13C Burg gate.

Beyond this gate is the **Burggarten**, which houses the **Blasiuskapelle**, c 1200, all that remains of the old castle and today serving as a war memorial. From the Burggarten you can see across the river as far as Detwang. Return to the church of St Johannes and walk S as far as the picturesque corner known as **Plönlein**, from which two streets each lead to a fortified gate. From here continue either right to the **Kobolzellertor**, by way of Kobolzellertsteig, or left by way of Untere Schmiedgasse to the **Siebersturm** c 1385, en route for the hospice quarter. This was created in the late 13C though—apart from the 14C Heiliggeistkirche—the present buildings date from the 2nd half of the 16C. Especially notable is the turretted Hegereiterhaus, i.e. horse-breaker's house, of 1591. Spitalgasse leads from here to the imposing 17C **Spitalbastein**.

Return from here to the Marktplatz. Pass between the town hall and the Ratstrinkstube to reach the Grünen Markt and then the **Kirchplatz**, on the W side of which is the 14C and 15C basilica of ˚**St Jakob**. Inside are a stone Virgin, c 1360; 14C stained glass; an early 15C aumbry; the mid 15C high altar, with sculpture by H. Waidenlich and painted panels by Friedrich Herlin—note the depiction of Rothenburg itself; and Tilman Riemenschneider's ˚˚˚**Holy Blood altar**, 1501–04, which depicts the Last Supper and incorporates a crystal said to contain a drop of the blood of Jesus.

On the N side of the square is the three-storeyed Renaissance former secondary school, built by L. Weidmann in 1581. Continue N from the church along Klingengasse and then W at Feuerleinserker to reach the **Reichsstadtmuseum** at 5 Klosterhof, in a 12C former Dominican monastery, open Apr–Oct 10.00–17.00; otherwise guided tours 13.00–16.00. It contains Bürgermeister Nusch's famous flagon, twelve paintings of 1494 making up the 'Rothenburg Passion' and what is claimed as the oldest kitchen in Germany. Also from the church of St Georg, Georgengasse leads E to the 12C White Tower. N of here is the former Jewish quarter, with the grain store of 1588 in **Schrannenplatz**. Two other remains of the 12C fortifications —the Markus Tower and the **Röderbogen**—are found by following Pfarrgasse (right from the White Tower), and then the Pfeiffergässchen and Rödergasse. Follow Hafengasse from Röderbogen back to the Marktplatz.

A tour along and outside the 13C and 14C **walls** of Rothenburg ob der Tauber is rewarding. Through the Burg gate, W of the town, and the Burggarten the route crosses the 14C Doppelbrücke 'Double Bridge' (restored after destruction in World War II) by way of the Kobolzeller church (1479), to the W of which stands the Toppler Schloss, 1338. Rödergasse leads E of Rothenburg to the Rödertor, from which you walk N to the Würzburger Tor, formerly the site of the town gallows and then W to the late 16C Klingentor, into which is built the fortified St Wolfgangs-Kirche, the 'Shepherds' Church'. Erected c 1490, it houses a statue of St Wolfgang, sculpted in 1489, a high altar of 1514 by Wilhelm Ziegler and the 1515 Marienaltar also by Ziegler; open Apr–Oct 10.00–12.00, 14.00–16.00.

*Jesus and His apostles before His Passion: the Holy Blood altar carved by Tilman Riemenschneider for the church of St Jacob, Rothenburg ob der Tauber*

**Other museums**. The **Topplerschlösschen**, 100 Taubertalweg, built for Bürgermeister Toppler in the mid 14C, so as to allow him to supervise the town mills on the Tauber, open Apr–Oct daily 10.00–12.00, 14.00–17.00, otherwise 13.00–16.00; the Rothenburg **Handwerkerhaus** and local history museum, 26 Alte Stadtgraben in a restored half-timbered house of 1270, open Easter–Oct daily 09.00–18.00, 20.00–21.00.

Leave Rothenburg ob der Tauber S by the B25 , crossing the A7 motorway and reaching Feuchtwangen after 31km.

A brief detour E, 12km S of Rothenburg, leads to **Schillingsfürst**, sign-posted, reveals an early 18C Baroque Schloss, once the home of the Hohenlohe–Schillingsfürst family (open Mar–Oct weekdays 18.30–11.30, 14.00–17.30; Sun and holidays 10.00–12.00, 14.00–17.00). Its outbuildings display an oxen-treadmill. Franz Liszt (1811–86) lived here and his statue is in the Schlosspark.

**Feuchtwangen** (10,500 inhab.; alt. 460m) developed in the neighbourhood of an 8C Benedictine monastery allegedly founded by Charlemagne who was led here by a dove—hence the dove fountain in the Marktplatz. On the N side of the Marktplatz is the 13–14C Stiftskirche, much renewed in the 20C, with a fine interior. Its high altar of 1484 is in part by Michael Wohlgemut of Nuremberg. Alongside early 16C choir stalls and a 17C crucifix, the church also houses a 15C font, tabernacle and pulpit, and notable tombs, including the life-size figure of the Knight of the Swan Sixt von Ehenheim, 1504, and its companion for his wife Anna, and that of Lucas Freyer sculpted by Loy Hering in 1523. The west wing of the church is a museum of local crafts. S of the church are a calvary and Romanesque cloisters, where plays are held in summer. Nearby at 19 Museumstrasse is the Heimatmuseum, which includes local history and a collection of fire-fighting equipment from the 18C onwards (open by request 10.00–12.00, 14.00–17.00). The Romanesque church of St Johann lies to the N of the Stiftskirche, with a fine hall (the 'Kasten', 1565) adjoining.

An **excursion** from Feuchtwangen follows the B14 for 25km NE to **Ansbach**—home of the Hohenzollerns from 1331—to see its Italian Baroque Markgrafenschloss (for full details, see end Rte 21). SE of Ansbach, off the B13, is **Wolframs-Eschenbach**, the birthplace of the medieval author of Parzifal, Wolfram von Eschenbach, who is buried in its 13C church of Maria Himmelfahrt. This church was remodelled in the 18C Baroque style, its Lady Chapel dating from 1751. The 17C Schloss of the Teutonic Knights today serves as the Rathaus, and is surrounded by half-timbered houses. The former town hall is 15C. On the way back to Feuchtwangen make a brief excursion S to **Herrieden** to see its 15C former Stiftskirche of St Veit, with a Baroque interior.

From Feuchtwangen follow the B25 13km S to *Dinkelsbühl (10,000 inhab.; alt. 445m) on the River Wörnitz. The medieval town, including its complex fortifications with 20 towers, is completely unchanged, having survived eight sieges in the Thirty Years War before being taken by Gustavus Adolphus. Because the town's children are said to have saved it in 1632, each summer (mid-July) the 'Kinderzeche' is performed in thanksgiving (see below).

Enter moated Dinkelsbühl by the 13C Wörnitz Tor, to reach the oldest part of the town, with its late 12C 'Burgus Tinkelspuhel', crossing the Altrathausplatz with its old town hall, 1350 and lion fountains (Löwenbrunnen) to reach the Marktplatz. To the E stands the 15C parish church of *St Georg, a hall-church whose three aisles, each 22.5m high, match the width of the church and virtually match its 77m length. The interior and fan vaulting are sumptuous late Gothic, and the ciborium at the chancel dates from 1480. Most of the church is the work of Nikolaus Eseler and his son Nikolaus (1448–99) though its portal is Romanesque. Three 15C statues (St Bartholomew, the Virgin Mary and St George) decorate the pillars of the apse. The high altar, dating from 1892, incorporates a late Gothic crucifix.

Past the present town hall Föhrenberggasse leads to the Schloss of the Teutonic Knights (1761–64). Follow the route for the Rothenburger Tor, passing the half-timbered 15C *Deutsches Haus in Dr Martin-Luther-Strass, with a fine 16C Renaissance façade and a late 17C statue of the Virgin Mary above the entrance. Then pass the former cornhouse (c 1600) and former hospice, No. 6, now a local history museum, open daily 09.00–12.00, 13.30–17.00, and still housing a few elderly residents. At the Rothen-burger Tor, c 1380, take the Obere Schmiedgasse to the walls and then walk along them by way of Kapuzinerweg, to reach the former Capuchin monastery. Close by is a granary (Kornhaus) of 1378. Pass the Segringer Tor, rebuilt in 1655, to reach the mid-16C chapel of the Magi (now a war memorial).

From the pre-1425 Segringer Tor Oberer Mauerweg follows the town wall to the late 15C Nördlinger Tor, outside which is the late 15C town mill. To walk outside the walls is rewarding—with parks and a large sports centre to the W. Beside the Nördlinger Tor is an ancient fortified town mill.

Other churches in Dinkelsbühl are the 14C Dreikönigskapelle, the 17C Capuchin church, and the early 18C St Ulrich.

Dinkelsbühl is also celebrated for a boys' band of 50 musicians who dress in Rococo uniforms, and for the children's festival (Kinderzeche) in the third week of July celebrating both St George's slaying of the dragon and the reprieve given to the town by the Swedish Colonel Klaus Dietrich von Sperreuth in 1632 when the children of the town, bearing only flowers, marched out to his army to beg mercy.

The route now travels E through Gerolfingen to **Wassertrüdingen**, with the remains of medieval walls and a former Benedictine monastery church, with a Renaissance tabernacle by Loy Hering, 1512, and an altar by Hans Schäufelin, 1513, dedicated to the Virgin Mary. Continue S to **Oettingen**, which retains part of the chapel of its former Schloss and its 'new', 17C Schloss (restored in the early 19C), as well as the parish church of St Jakob, which has stucco work by Matthias Schmuzer.

Travel SW to *Nördlingen (20,000 inhab.; alt. 430m; tourist office 2 Markplatz) with its perfectly preserved town walls, which have eleven towers and five gates.

Nördlingen was a Carolingian court in the late 9C; it prospered and was built lavishly during the 14C and 15C. The Imperial forces captured the town in 1634, but outside its walls in 1645 Turenne defeated the forces of the emperor. The town became part of Bavaria in 1803 and lost its status as a Free Imperial City.

The Salvatorkirche of 1385 preserves 15C frescoes and a high altar of 1497. Close by is the Winter-Haus, 1677. The 13C Rathaus in the Marktplatz has a defensive tower of 1509, an open-air Renaissance flight of steps added in 1618 and, on the second floor, a huge wall painting by Hans Schäufelin, 1515, which depicts the beheading of Holofernes. The bookshop, 1552, E of the town hall was formerly a pawnshop.

On the W side of the Marktplatz is the Brothaus (or Tanzhaus) of 1444 (now the information office), with a statue of Emperor Maximilian I on the façade. On the S side of the Marktplatz is the 93m long late Gothic church of St Georg, 1427–1519, with an 89m-high tower, finished in 1539 when the Renaissance copper dome known as 'Daniel' was added, with 365 steps to the summit; a Baroque high altar; a pulpit of 1499; a sandstone tabernacle of 1525, a Baroque organ gallery of 1610, and 16–18C funerary motifs on the walls. The Baroque high altar incorporates five Gothic statues representing the crucified Jesus, his mother, St John and two angels. These are flanked by statues of St George and St Mary Magdalen. The church tower gives superb views of the surrounding landscape, including a crater in which the town lies, some 25km in diameter, created by a meteorite 15 million years ago.

Other sights include the nine-storey Hohes Haus of 1442. In the tanners' quarter many houses still retain balconies from which hides were hung for ventilation. The 'Klösterle' is the former Franciscan church of 1420; its doorway dates from 1686. The complex 16C Spital, or town hospital, preserves its 13C church, restored in the mid 19C, with late 14C frescoes, and now houses the Stadtmuseum (open daily 09.00–12.00, 14.00–17.00; Sun and holidays opens an hour later and closes an hour earlier); with works by Friedrich Herlin, who lived here from 1462 to 1477, including panels he painted for the high altar of the church of St Georg. The 15C Carmelite monastery church of St Salvator in Salvatorgasse has contemporary wall paintings and a high altar of 1497 by H. Nussbaum.

At Nördlingen the oldest steeplechase in Germany takes place each September; each June a fair and festival commemorate the granting of the right to hold a Whitsun market to the town in 1219; plays are performed in the open-air theatre in July and August. Trains link Nördlingen with Füssen and Donauwörth.

Leave Nördlingen by the Reimlinger Tor and follow Augsburger Strasse to take the B25 SE for 17km to picturesque **Harburg** (5600 inhab.; alt. 413m) nestling beside the River Wörnitz. The Felsenburg, built by the princes of Oettingen 12C to 16C, which dominates the town is south Germany's largest surviving castle. Its princely collection displays fine works by Riemenschneider, Gobelin tapestries and a superb library (open daily for guided tours, Mar–Oct 19.00–11.30, 13.30–17.30). Harburg retains its Romanesque Schloss church of **St Barbara**, extended in the 14C, with a carved Madonna, 1480, and the church of St Michael, 1510. The town hosts an annual Bockfest in June. Leisure pursuits here include fishing on the Wörnitz and relaxing in the Ozon-Hallenbad. After 25km the route reaches Donauwörth (see Rte 1B). The B2 now runs 36 km S to Augsburg (see Rte 3).

# 6

# Würzburg to Passau via Nuremberg and Regensburg

## A.  Würzburg to Nuremberg

Total distance 100km. Würzburg—B8, 19km Kitzingen—41km Neustadt— 40km Nuremberg.—Leave Würzburg (see Rte 5) SE by the B8, crossing the Frankfurt–Nuremberg motorway, to reach after 12km **Bibelried**, with a crucifix by Riemenschneider in its parish church, and after a further 7km Kitzingen, on the right bank of the River Main.

*Kitzingen (18,400 inhab.; alt. 200m) with its noted Falterturm (crooked tower, 1496), which derives from the second ring of walls thrown around the town, gained its charter as a city around 1300. Also preserved are some of its 13C walls, especially in Kapuzinerstrasse, and an ancient stone bridge, partly rebuilt in the 17C and 18C, which spans the Main to reach the suburb of Etwashausen and the Baroque *Heilige-Kreuz-Kirche by Balthasar Neumann, 1741–45. In Kitzingen itself the Catholic St Johannis-

Kirche dates from the 15C and has a tall tabernacle of c 1470. At the heart of the Altstadt is the Renaissance Rathaus (1561, restored in 1977), near which rises the 15C Marktturm. In Gustav-Adolf-Platz stands the Italian Baroque Protestant parish church, an 18C building by Antonio Petrini. Trains run from Kitzingen to Würzburg and Nuremberg.

As this is the centre of the Franconian vineyards, **wine tours** are available (tourist office at 34 Markstrasse, Kitzingen), visiting 13km S (along the Bocksbeutelstrasse or 'round bottle road') **Sommerhausen**, with its Renaissance Schloss and town hall, and medieval walls; **Marktbreit**, with lovely houses, a Black Tower, a town hall of 1579 and a parish church with an early Gothic tower; and **\*Ochsenfurt**, approached across an old bridge, whose 14C parish church boasts a statue of St Nicholas by Riemenschneider—and a high altar of 1612—and whose late Gothic town hall, 1487, sports a clock with mechanical figures added in 1560. Next to the parish church is the mid-15C Michaelskapelle, formerly the cemetery chapel. There is a town museum in the Schloss.

From Kitzingen continue 10km SE along the B8 to the little wine-producing town of **\*Iphofen**, its 14C and 15C fortifications perfectly preserved with gates and towers. The mid-14C church of St Veit houses \*sculpture by Riemenschneider; the town hall is Baroque. Continue through the Steigerwald 14km to **Markt Bibart**, close by the 17C Schloss Schwarzenberg, by Elias Holl, and a further 17km to **Neustadt an der Aisch**. Again the town walls are preserved along with a church of 1434, as well as a Baroque Rathaus, 1711, on which a model goat bleats the hour of noon.

18km further SE the route reaches **Langenzenn**, with its early 15C parish church, housing wall paintings c 1470, a Renaissance pulpit and an Annunciation by Veit Stoss. Langenzenn has also preserved cloisters from an Augustinian monastery and a Baroque Rathaus rebuilt after a fire of 1727. A further 15km on lies **Fürth**, with a population of 94,000, near where Gustavus Adolphus fought against Wallenstein in 1632 and where the first German railway—to Nuremberg, with a locomotive built by George Stephenson at Newcastle-upon-Tyne—started in 1835. The town has a 14C Gothic church of St Michael, with an 8m-high tabernacle from the workshop of Adam Krafft; and a mid 19C Rathaus, modelled on the Palazzo Vecchio, Florence. 7km further the route reaches Nuremberg.

**NUREMBERG**, German NÜRNBERG (490,000 inhab.; alt. 310m). Situated on the River Pegnitz and the Rhine–Main–Danube canal, opened in 1972, Nuremberg is the major city of northern Bavaria and the second largest in Bavaria. The city was savagely damaged in World War II, though preserving most of its medieval fortifications and some old buildings. Much has been restored, plus a new wing added to the National Museum, 1958–59. This is the seat of the Nuremberg–Erlangen University. Nuremberg's month-long Christkindelsmarkt in Advent is the finest in the whole of Germany.

**Main railway station**: Bahnhofsplatz. **Main post office**: Bahnhofsplatz. **Tourist Information**: main railway station; 18 Hauptmarkt. **Airport**: N of the city, 5km from the city centre. **Trains** to Bamberg, Bayreuth, Berlin, Frankfurt, Munich and Stuttgart.

**History**. An 11C royal Schloss on the River Pegnitz was the basis of the city, which developed in the mid 11C, virtually as two separate settlements on either side of the river. Frederick II granted various charters, early 13C, and Frederick III gave the city Free Imperial status in 1216 and, in 1256, Nuremberg became one of the Rhenish League of commercial cities. The city's ramparts, round which you can walk, were

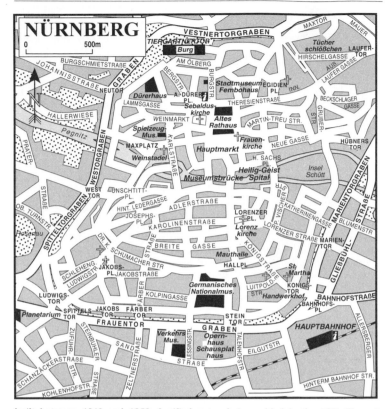

NÜRNBERG
0    500m

built between 1346 and 1352, fortified gates being added in the 16C. The arts flourished in the late Middle Ages—Nuremberg attracted and bred remarkable artists, while from 1578 the church of St Martha was the home of the celebrated Mastersingers, whose most famous member was the poet Hans Sachs (1494–1576). Nuremberg opted for the teaching of Luther in 1525 and declared for religious toleration in 1532. Goldsmiths flourished in the 16C and 17C, leading artists being Ludwig Krug, Melchior Bayer and Christoph and Wenzel Jamnitzer. With the discovery of the Cape of Good Hope, Nuremberg's trading connections with the East became less important, and the city went into a slow decline, hastened by the ravages of the Thirty Years War, during which Gustavus Adolphus occupied the city. In 1806 Nuremberg was incorporated into Bavaria. The first German railway line, 1835, ran between Nuremberg and Fürth, and the city took a lead in the industrialisation of the 19C, becoming the toy-making capital of Europe. At the same time 19C Romanticism flourished (supremely expressed in Wagner's 'Mastersingers of Nuremberg').

The Nazis chose Nuremberg as the venue of their annual rallies, including the notoriously successful rally of 1926, and during World War II the Allies destroyed 90 per cent of the city. After the war Nuremberg was chosen as the seat of the Nazi war crimes tribunal. Rebuilding, matching the old pattern of the streets in the Altstadt, took some 20 years, but today once again the city is ringed by walls first built in the Middle Ages, from which rise some 80 towers, medieval and Renaissance façades mingling harmoniously with modern shopping precincts.

Citizens have included St Edmund, King of the East Angles (born here by chance 841, martyred by the Danes 870), the mathematician Johann Müller (known as Regiomontanus, 1436–76), the sculptors Veit Stoss (1445–1533) and Adam Krafft (c 1455–1508), the cosmographer Martin Behaim (1459–1507), the painter Michael Wolgemut (1434–1519) and his pupil the painter and engraver Albrecht Dürer (1471–1528), the humanist Willibald Pirckheimer (1470–1530) and Peter Henlein (who invented the pocket watch in 1500).

Nuremberg hosts international organ concerts in July, concerts by the Nuremberg Symphony Orchestra from May to September and an International Toy Fair.

At Bahnhofsplatz in front of the main railway station stands the old city arsenal courtyard, with the craftsmen's alleys of the **Handwerkerhof**—restored half-timbered houses, used by 20C craftsmen making dolls, pewter work, gold, glassware (open weekdays 10.00–18.30, Sat 10.00–12.00). From here Königstrasse leads past the Gothic church of **St Martha** (right), home of the mastersingers' school, 1578–1620. Left at the corner of Luitpoldstrasse is the **Klara-Kirche**, its choir dating from 1273, its nave rebuilt in the early 15C. Further NW along Königstrasse stands the imposing former granary or **Mauthalle**, built by Hans Beheim, 1489–1502, later the city customs house, now a restaurant.

Continue along Königstrasse to reach Lorenzer Platz and the **St Lorenzkirche**, with its 13C nave and 15C Gothic choir. The north tower was finished in 1332, the south tower in 1400, both six storeys high. Notable elements are the Gothic doorway and *rose window in the W façade; the stained glass in the choir, fired 1476–83 and depicting a Jesse tree; *Veit Stoss's Annunciation (the Englischer Gruss, with Mary and Gabriel garlanded with medallions depicting her seven joys) and his crucifix over the high altar, created 1517–18; a limestone tabernacle by Adam Krafft, with nearly 100 figures, supported statues of the sculptor himself and two assistants, 1493–96; the Haller altar, in the Haller chapel, built for Ulrich V. Haller, d 1456, with a painting of the crucifixion c 1450.

N of this church is the **Tugendbrunnen**, the Fountain of Virtue, by Benedikt Wurzelbauer 1585–89. W of the church is the oldest house in Nuremberg, the **Nassauer Haus**—its cellar, ground floor and first floor are 13C, its upper storey c 1421; it is now a restaurant. Here in the early 15C Emperor Sigismund pledged his crown to the owner in return for 1500 guilders.

Pedestrianised Königstrasse leads directly N across the **Museumsbrücke** (restored in 1954). It offers a view to the W of the **Fleischbrücke** of 1598, a copy of the Rialto Bridge in Venice, and over the river to the Hauptmarkt, with the **Schöner Brunnen**, the Beautiful Fountain, nearly 20m high, created by Heinrich Parler 1385–96, and bearing statues of seven Electors and nine Old Testament heroes. On the way can be seen to the right the **Heilig-Geist-Spital**, built on two arches over a branch of the River Pegnitz in 1331, enlarged in 1447–1527, and rebuilt after World War II. It now contains an old people's home and a Weinstube. The crucifixion in the courtyard is by Adam Krafft. North of this almshouse across Spitalbrücke in Hans-Sachs-Platz is the **Hans Sachs Memorial**.

On the E side of the Hauptmarkt stands the 14C Gothic **Frauenkirke**, rebuilt after World War II. A clock, 1509, over the main door, with mechanical figures representing the seven Electors and Emperor Charles IV, performs daily at 12.00, in commemoration of a bull issued by Charles IV in 1356 undertaking to hold his first Diet in Nuremberg. Inside are the Tucher altar—a triptych of the Annunciation, Crucifixion and Resurrection, c 1445—and works by Adam Krafft.

On the N side stand both the **Neues Rathaus**, 1954, and the **Altes Rathaus** by Jakob Wolff, 1616–22, incorporating two earlier buildings of 1332–40 and 1520, three turrets and superb west doorways. The **Lochgefängnisse**, or torture chambers, are open May–Sept weekdays 10.00–16.00, weekends 10.00–13.00. Behind the Altes Rathaus is the **Gänsernännchen Brunnen**, depicting a peasant carrying two water-spouting geese and sculpted by Pankraz Labenwolf c 1555.

NE at 26 Winklerstrasse stands *St Sebaldus-Kirche, Nuremberg's oldest, 1225–1273. Its 79m-high towers were finished in the late 15C; in the west façade are Romanesque doorways; the Gothic choir dates from 1379 with— on the outside—the Schreyer-Landauer tomb by Adam Krafft, 1492. On a pillar in the north aisle is a Madonna, c 1425; in the choir is the *tomb of St Sebaldus, the supreme masterpiece by Peter Vischer and his sons, 1508–09, which incorporates the saint's silver sarcophagus of 1397 (note P. Vischer's self-portrait, chiselling). St Sebaldus also has a 6000 pipe organ,

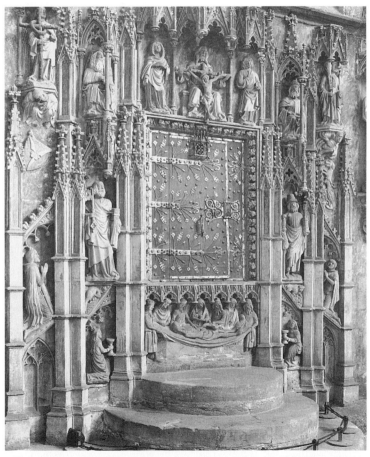

*The shrine of the Holy Sacrament was created for St Sebaldus, Nuremberg, in the late 14C*

and a bronze font by Peter Vischer's father. N of this church stands the **Stadtmuseum Fembohaus** in a gabled home built for the merchant Philip Oyrl 1590–1600; open weekdays, except Mon, in summer 10.00–17.00, closing winter 13.00. Its exhibition is devoted to the history of Nuremberg. W of the Fembohaus in Albrecht-Dürer-Platz is the Dürer Monument of 1840, by D. Rauch, cast by D. Burgschmiet.

Go E along Theresienstrasse from the Fembohaus. No. 21 is the only remaining Baroque house in Nuremberg. Continue along this street and along Theresien-Inn to turn N into Egidienplatz. Here is the Baroque **Egidienkirche**; 1711–18, incorporating the Romanesque Wolfgang chapel—with a mid-15C Entombment, the Romanesque-Gothic Eucharius chapel of c 1140, the mid 14C Tetzel chapel and the Landau tomb by Adam Krafft, c 1500. At the north side of Egidienplatz is the arcaded courtyard (1605) of the former **Pellerhaus**, destroyed in World War II and faithfully restored. The Pellerhaus now houses the State archives and library. Walk E from here to find, in Hirschelgasse, the Renaissance **Tucherschlösschen**, 1533–44, open weekdays 14.00–16.00, Sun 10.00–11.00. On display are Renaissance and Baroque furniture, and paintings, including glass paintings from the workshop of Augustin Hirschvogel.

Return to Egidienplatz and walk W into Tetzelgasse; turn here NE to the junction with Paniersplatz, where you turn left to reach the **Kaiserstallung**, 1595, now a youth hostel. Here too is the **Graphische Sammlung**, open weekdays 09.00–16.00; prints and original drawings . Adjoining to the W is the five-cornered tower (**Fünfeckigen Turm**, c 1040) and the 12C **Kaiserburg** (open daily Apr–Sept 09.00–17.00, Oct–Mar 10.00–12.00, 13.00–16.00). Its delights include the 12C chapel of St Margaret; the courtyard with its well; the panorama; and the 12C round **Sinwellturm**. From the five-cornered tower, Johannisstrasse leads some distance W to the medieval **Johannisfriedhof**, where Dürer, Pirckheimer, Stoss and Hans Sachs are buried. Here is the 14C St Johannis chapel and a 1513 rotunda. Adam Krafft designed the stations of the cross, the present statues are copies, leading from here to the **Tiergärtnertor**, with its unspoiled medieval square and the 15C **Pilatushaus**, its timbered upper storey—five of them—rising from a red-sandstone ground floor, with a statue of St George on the corner.

Directly S at 39 Albrecht-Dürer-Strasse is the 15C **Dürer-Haus**, the sole totally preserved Gothic house in the city and the artist's home from 1509 until his death. It now contains an exhibition devoted to Dürer, open daily Tue–Sun 10.00–16.00. The line of the city walls leads SW to the **Neue Tor**. These walls, built in the 14C and 15C with 80 towers, are the third to have surrounded the city. From Dürer-Haus follow Albrecht-Dürer-Strasse S into **Weinmarkt**, where No. 2 is a Gothic house dating from the 14C and 15C. Continue S to the **Spielzeugmuseum** at 13 Karslstrasse, in a 17C building (open Tue–Sun 10.00– 17.00, Wed to 21.00). The toys on display include dolls and dolls' houses. SW of the museum is the former wine depot, the **Weinstadel**.

From here **Henkerstag** leads SW across the river to the **Unschlitthaus** ('Tallow House') of 1491, another former granary. Follow Grillenberger-Strasse SW to reach Karl-Kappenstrasse, where you turn left to reach the neo-classical church of **St Elisabeth**, once the church of the Teutonic Knights, part 18C, by the younger Neumann, and part 19C. This church is directly north of Jakobsplatz, reached by way of Ludwigstrasse, and the 14C Gothic church of St Jakob. Follow Ludwigstrasse SW to **Ludwigstor**, passing through the gate in the city walls to turn right to reach the **Planetarium**. S of the Planetarium is the **St Roch cemetery**.

Frauentorgraben leads E from Ludwigstor to the **Schauspielhaus**, the civic theatre, seating 900 in Richard-Wagner-Platz. Here too is the **Opernhaus** seating 1100. Lessingstrasse leads due S to the **Verkehrsmuseum** at No. 6; open weekdays 10.00–17.00, Oct–Mar closes at 16.00. This museum of transport includes 'Adler', the first German steam locomotive, archives, etc. of the first German railway, model railways, stamp collection.

Due N the *Germanisches Nationalmuseum** is at 1 Kornmarkt, in the former Carthusian monastery buildings (open Tue–Sun 10.00–17.00; Thu also 20.00–21.30). Based on the collection of Hans Freiherr von und zu Aufsess, but enormously expanded since it was opened in 1832, the museum houses works of art from prehistory to the 20C; it begins with over 10,000 prehistoric finds, followed by German painting and sculpture from the earliest to modern times. Masterpieces of sculpture include works by Adam Krafft (**Jesus's Passion), Veit Stoss (**Tobias and the angel) and Tilman Riemenschneider (**St Elisabeth). The collection of paintings includes works by Dürer (including a *Lamentation and a **portrait of Martin Wolgemut), Lucas Cranach the Elder's **portrait of Martin Luther, and a remarkable nude **Judith with the head of Holofernes by Hans Baldung Grien. Non-German masters include superb paintings by Rembrandt. Caspar David Friedrich, Liebermann, Slevogt and Kirchner are among those representing the 19C and 20C. The decorative arts include such rarities as the late 9C binding of the Echternach Codex Aureus and the jewellery which was a speciality of Nuremberg in the 16C.

**Other museums**. The **'Mensch und Natur' Museum** at 4 Gewerbenmuseumsplatz; open weekdays except Wed 10.00–17.00, Sat 09.00–12.00, is devoted to geology and prehistory. **Kunsthalle**, 32 Lorenzstrasse, open daily except Mon 10.00–17.00, Wed also to 21.00, hosts exhibitions of modern art. The **Centrum Industriekultur** (Industrial Museum) is at 45 Guntherstrasse. The **Spielzeug Museum** (Toy Museum, also known as the Museum Lydia Baker) is at 13 Karlstrasse (open Tue–Sun 10.00–17.00, Wed 10.00–12.00).

**Other sights**. **Meistersingerhalle**, in Luitpoldhain, built in 1963 and the Kongresshalle. The Sports Stadium is impressive. The **Trödelmarkt**, i.e. junk market, opens up on an island where the river divides near the 14C 'Man's Guilt' Tower. The **Zoo** (open Mar, Oct 08.00–17.30, Apr–Sep 08.00–19.30, Nov–Feb 09.00–17.00) with its dolphinarium and restaurant, is 4400m E of the city along Bahnhofstrasse. Nuremberg also has a major harbour of the Rhine-Main-Danube-Canal, 5km SW of the city.

Leave Nuremberg SE by the Allersbergerstrasse to follow after 9km a brief stretch of motorway as far as Feucht. Continue on the B8 to 23km Neumarkt in der Oberpfalz, much destroyed in World War II and now restored. See Rte 2D for its attractions and the rest of the 64km route to Regensburg.

Two routes lead from Regensburg to Passau. The motorway A3 leads 58km E to Bogen (a town known in the 8C) and another 30km to **Deggendorf** which lies on the Danube just N of the motorway. Five kilometres before of Deggendorf is **Metten**, whose Benedictine abbey was founded in 770. Its Baroque church of 1715 has an altar with a painting by C.D. Asam of the Archangel Michael slaying Lucifer, and stucco work of 1722 by F.J. Holzinger. Its library, also decorated by Holzinger (1724–26) with stucco and frescoes of the Beatitudes, the seven deadly sins and the figure of Theology, flanked by SS Thomas Aquinas and Bonaventura, counts as one of the masterpieces of German Baroque decoration. The town hall of 1535

*At Metten near Deggendorf survives this superb library, decorated by F.J. Holzinger in the mid 1720s for Benedictine Monks*

of **Deggendorf** stands in Luitpold-strasse; two fountains (16C and 20C) gush in the Marktplatz; the mid-14C church rises to the S of the Markplatz, (its Baroque tower of 1727 by J.B. Gunetzrhainer and J.M. Fischer). Further S is the parish church of Maria Himmelfahrt, built in the 17C, with 19C restored façade, and inside a Rococo high altar by M. Seybold, 1749. Nearby is the 15C Wasserkapelle. Deggendorf's local history museum is in the Oberer Stadtplatz (open Mon–Fri 09.00–12.00, 14.00–16.00, Sun 09.00–

12.00). From Deggendorf the motorway continues through Hengersberg for 30km to Passau.

The route by the B8 leads after 35km to **Straubing**. Settled by the Celts and the Romans, Straubing was refounded by Ludwig the Kelheimer in 1270 and soon became a dukedom. Here Agnes Bernauer, wife of Duke Albrecht III of Bavaria, was falsely accused of witchcraft and ceremonially drowned in the river (see Augsburg, Rte 3). Her tombstone is in the Agnes-Bauer-Kapelle, built in atonement for her death by the Duke in the graveyard of the pillared Romanesque basilica of St Peter, c 1200, with contemporary west and south *portals, and W towers finished in 1886. A dance of death and a Baroque mural decorate the late Gothic Liebfrauenkapelle in the same cemetery. Straubing also has gabled houses in the broad Stadtplatz, along with a Renaissance fountain and the 14C town tower.

Its churches include two by Hans Stethaimer: the finest is the huge brick St Jakob, a hall-church with a tower capped by a Baroque spire in 1780. Its interior was glamorised by the Asam brothers, who retained its 15C furnishings, including 15C stained glass and frescoes in the Maria-Hilf-Kapelle, and the 1430 tomb of Ulrich Kastenmayer, 1430. The Baroque pulpit dates from 1753, and the neo-Gothic high altar incorporates earlier statues of 1590. Hans Stethaimer's second church at Straubing is the Karmeliten-Kirche in Albrechtgasse, its interior given an early 18C Baroque rendering by W. Dientzenhofer. Inside, behind the high altar, is the red-marble tombstone of Duke Albrecht II, who died in 1397. The massive Baroque high altar was created c 1740.

The Ursulinen-Kirche, 1728, in Burggasse is by E.Q. Asam, decorated by C.D. Asam. In the courtyard of the medieval Schloss—originally 14C, but much altered, with a 15C chapel—Friedrich Hebbel's drama of the life and death of Agnes Bernauer (written in 1852) is performed at four-yearly intervals (1997, etc.), and each August Straubing hosts a beer festival, the Gäuboden.

Beside the River Isar, 16km SE of Straubing, is **Plattling**, with a Romanesque church of St Jakob with a Gothic choir. Much of medieval Plattling was destroyed in a fire of 1633. The road now leads 19km SE to **Osterhofen**, where Benedictine monks founded a monastery in the 8C and J.M. Fischer rebuilt part of the present church of *St Margaretha between 1726 and 1731. Its nave has rounded angles, oval side chapels, Rococo decoration by the Asam brothers, and a high altar by E.Q. Asam. After 13km the route reaches picturesque **Vilshofen**, its defensive gateway, the Stadtorturm of 1642, deriving from the former fortifications. The town's most imposing building is the late Baroque church of St Johannes der Täufer (St John the Baptist) of 1803, with an early 18C high altar by J. Hartmann and side altars by M. Götz, brought from St Nikolai, Passau, in 1803; its next is the Italian Baroque church of **Mariahilf**. Domed and built in the shape of a Greek cross, it shelters a high altar sculpted by Andrea Solari.

**Passau** (32,000 inhab.; alt. 320m) is 23km further, in a superb setting at the confluence of the Danube, Ilz and Inn, a city founded by the Celts in the 1C BC. The city was next a Roman camp and then became the seat of a bishop in the 5C. Bishop Ulrich acquired the rank of a prince in 1217 and two years later built the powerful Veste Oberhaus. As a staging post on several trade routes the city flourished in the Middle Ages. The treaty of Passau, concluded in 1552 between the Emperor Charles V and the Elector Maurice of Saxony, was a milestone in the reconciliation of Protestants and Catholics and a predecessor of the Peace of Augsburg. Passau's leanings towards Protestantism were vigorously opposed by the Counter-Reformation Bishop Urban von Trennenbach, 1561–98. Although Passau survived the Thirty Years War intact, the city suffered two severe fires in 1662 and 1680. Secularisation drove out religious orders in 1803 and suppressed the bishopric, but this was restored in 1827.

A tour of Passau, beginning on the banks of the Inn, would encompass, in Innstrasse, the 14C church of St Nikola, with stuccos and frescoes c 1720. Built for Augustinian canons, who left at the secularisation of 1803, it has an 11C crypt. NW of this in Neuburgerstrasse is the Nibelungenhalle, built in 1935 as an exhibition hall and seating 6000 people. Neuburgerstrasse joins Nikolastrasse, with its Heilig-Geist-Kirche, built in the 14C, enlarged in 1442, much restored in the 19C, but incorporating a 14C nuns' gallery at the west end; and to the NW stands the formerly Franciscan Votivskirche, 1613–19. Follow Ludwigstrasse NE to find remains of the old city walls, tracing their origin back to the Romans. Directly E stands the church of St Paul, rebuilt in 1678 after a fire, with 20C stucco decor.

Immediately E is the Domplatz, dominated by a statue of King Maximilian I, by Christian Jodhan, 1824. The square is bordered by the Lambergpalais of 1724, where the 1552 treaty was signed, the 16C and 17C cathedral canonry, the Renaissance Herberstainpalais and the **\*\*Cathedral of St Stephan**.

This cathedral was founded in the 14C, but only its choir, by Hans Krumenauer, 1407–1520, is Gothic; as a result of a conflagration in 1662, the rest is late 17C Baroque, by the Italian Carlo Lurago, 1677, with a lavish stucco decor by Giovanni Battista Carlone, 1677–86. The side aisles were stuccoed equally lavishly by Carlo Antonio Bussi; the domes were frescoed by Carpoforo Tencalla of Lugano between 1679 and 1684; the Viennese-style pulpit was created in 1722; in the chapels are paintings by the Austrian Johann Michael Rottmayr, 1654–73; the high altar is the work of Josef Henselmann, 1953. Its tower, a pastiche of that of Salzburg cathedral, was finished in 1896. The cathedral possesses the largest church organ in the world. Built in 1928 with 230 stops and 17,000 pipes, recitals are held May–Oct on weekdays, 12.00–12.30; Thu 19.30–20.00. In the cloister is the mid-15C \*tomb of Heinrich von Ortenburg.

The former bishops' palace, restored in 1680, is S of the cathedral. E in Residenzplatz is the present three-storeyed half Baroque, half Rococo bishops' palace, built from 1712 to 1771, possibly to the plans of Domenico d'Angeli, with a superb staircase of 1768. NE stands the Rathaus, mostly late 19C, with a late Gothic doorway of 1683. From here walk SE to St Michael-Kirche, of 1678, by G.B. Carlone, formerly the church of the Jesuit college of 1664, which is now a high school and a theological college. Then follow the lanes to the Niedernburg convent. This is the burial place of the foundress, the widowed Queen Gisela of Hungary, who died in 1060 and was its first abbess; her memorial dates from the 15C. Cross the Luitpold-brücke to the N to reach the late Gothic Salvatorkirche of 1478, with a Romanesque crucifix, sculpted c 1200. This church is set into the hillside on the site of a former synagogue. Nearby rises the majestic Veste Oberhaus (fortress), 408m high (a 15 minute walk), housing a Gothic chapel, later reordered in the Baroque style, the city art gallery, a museum devoted to the Bohemian forest, and a local customs and fireman's museum (open Mar–Oct 09.00–17.00, except Mon). Connected to it by a rampart is the 14C Veste Niederhaus. The city theatre was built by G. Hagenauer in 1783.

The environs of Passau include the Renaissance pilgrimage church of **Mariahilf** (1624–27), from which are views of Veste Oberhaus and the city.

**Wanderkarten** (bought at the tourist office in the Nibelungenhalle or at local bookshops) open up the **Bavarian Forest** which, along with its contiguous neighbour across the Czech border, is the largest in Europe and includes some 1300 sq km of National Park, whose national park house is due N of Passau at Grafenau.

# 7

# Würzburg to Hof via Bamberg and Coburg

Total distance 234km. Würzburg—B22, 45km Ebrach—45km Bamberg—B173, 34km Vierzehnheiligen—B289, 29km Coburg—B303, 30km Kronach [B85, 20km—Kulmbach]—B173, 51km Hof.

Leave Würzburg by the Nürnbergerstrasse and take the B22 E for 18km as far as **Dettelbach**, which is protected by 15C walls, with 36 towers, and has a late Gothic 16C town hall. Its most interesting building is the pilgrimage church of **Maria im Sand**, 1505–1520, where the porch is carved with an Annunciation, the pulpit depicts the genealogy of Jesus and the Rococo altar of grace dates from 1778. Its organ was built by Peter Scholl in 1569.

Dettelbach offers a fine view of the Steigerwald, by which the route continues for another 27km to **Ebrach**. Here is one of the best preserved monastic churches in the region, a three-aisled basilica formerly belonging to a Cistercian abbey founded in 1127 and suppressed in 1803. It boasts a Romanesque chapel of St Michael, 1207; early Gothic features; a magnificent rose window of around 1280; an alabaster Bernardus altar by V. Dümpel, 1626; a sacristy by J.L. Brenno, 1696; and a classical, stuccoed interior by Materno Bossi, 1773–93. The Baroque monastic buildings were converted by J.L. Dientzenhofer, Balthasar Neumann and J. Greising from 1716 onwards. About 14km S of Ebrach, the fairytale park of **Geiselwind** has some 1000 exotic birds.

After 22km from Ebrach the route reaches Unterneuses, 9km S of which is the Baroque **\*Schloss Pommersfelden**. Also known as Schloss Weissenstein, it was built by J.L. Dientzenhofer, Maximilian von Welsch and J.L. von Hildebrandt, court architect at Vienna, for Lothar Franz von Schönborn, who was Elector of Mainz and Bishop of Bamberg. Its main building, wings and curved mews are set in a splendid park. Inside are a monumental double staircase; a trompe l'oeil painting by J.R. Byss, 1718, depicting the four continents and the gods of Olympus; a room designed as a grotto; the marble Herrensaal—the venue of summer concerts—with portraits of members of the Schönborn family and a ceiling painted by J.F. Rottmayr, 1717 (the triumph of virtue). The rooms house paintings by Rubens, Titian, Cranach and Breughel (open Apr–Oct 08.00–12.00, 14.00–17.00, except Mon).

8km further the route reaches Bamberg (see Rte 8). 4km N of Bamberg along the B4 lies **Hallstadt**, a modern industrial town with a late Gothic church, a Renaissance Rathaus and a Baroque government building. At Breitengüssbach the road meets the B173, which leads directly NE, by way of **Unterleiterbach** with its Schloss, for 34km to reach the pilgrimage church of ***Vierzehnheiligen**.

On this spot in the mid 15C 14 particular saints ('Vierzehnheiligen'), a group held in Bavaria to be specially concerned with succouring the devout, had, accompanied by the Infant Jesus, repeatedly appeared to a pious shepherd. The visions took place on the left bank of the River Main, on the opposite bank of the fortress-like, yellow sandstone abbey of Banz (see below).

In the 18C the monastic community commissioned the building of a pilgrimage church on the spot where the visions had occurred. When Balthasar Neumann and his pupil Johann Michael Küchel were brought into the project in the 1740s, the monks had already received plans by the Weimar Court architect Heinrich Krohne. In spite of the fact that the

*Marble and stucco create a dizzily Baroque exuberance for the interior of the church of Vierzehnheiligen*

prince-bishop favoured Neumann's proposals, Krohne managed to have them completely changed when work began. Neumann's response produced a masterpiece. He made the Gnadenaltar (altar of Grace), which was to be the church's spiritual centre, into its physical centre as well. He incorporated this altar in a pattern of vaults that does not correspond with the ground plan but consists instead of three ovals running along the length of the church, the two centre ovals larger than the others. Smaller spaces, topped by cupolas, create a transept where the ovals converge at the east. Over the crossing transverse arches fail to meet, rising towards each other and then following their own spherical ways, the form of these spheres deliberately and tantalisingly conflicting with that of the ovals.

Küchel designed the Gnadenaltar, dedicated to the 14 saints, enlisting artists of the calibre of the Feuchtmayr brothers to help him decorate it. J.G. Üblherr was responsible for the stucco work. J.I. Appiani frescoed the ceiling. Küchel also designed the nearby priory (1746).

Shortly beyond Vierzehnheiligen, turn NW along the B289 to reach after 29km Coburg. On the way, just across the River Main, a brief detour left brings you to **Banz** and the former Benedictine abbey dedicated to St Denis, founded in 1071 by Countess Alberada of Schweinfurt. Severely damaged in the Thirty Years War, it was rebuilt first by Johann Leonhard Dientzenhofer, 1695 onwards, and then by his brother J. Dientzenhofer, 1710–19. In the mid 18C Balthasar Neumann designed its courtyard and the corner pavilions. Today the abbey church boasts twin-onion domed spires, and a complex west façade with saints by B. Esterbauer, 1713.

Return to the B289 and continue to ***Coburg** (42,000 inhab.; alt. 300m), a former capital of Saxe-Coburg, which nestles in the Iltz valley under its 460m-high Schloss. The name Koburk first appears in 1056. Coburg alternated with Gotha as the main residence of the Dukes of Saxe-Coburg-Gotha, whose family proved remarkable at forming dynastic links with the other great houses of Europe. In 1830 Leopold of Saxe-Coburg acceded to the throne of Belgium. He married Princess Charlotte of Great Britain, and a widowed Coburg princess married the Duke of Kent, whose daughter Victoria ascended to the British throne in 1837. The Coburg family next managed to marry Prince Albert of Saxe-Coburg to his royal cousin. In addition the family married into the Bulgarian and Portuguese royal families.

Massive Veste Coburg, the fortress towering over the city, was begun in the 11C, from which also dates its chapel. The Fürstenbau was built in the 12C and 13C and the rest was added in the 16C and 17C, much of it under the Elector of Saxony Frederick the Wise (1463–1525) after a fire of 1500. In consequence the architecture is complex, the Blaue Turn Romanesque, much else Gothic, including the late Gothic Eisenofen, Germany's oldest extant cast-iron stove, and the Ziehbrunnen Renaissance in style. Duke Ernst I von Saxe-Coburg (1806–44) was responsible for rebuilding some of the fortress in the neo-Gothic style. Between 23 April and 5 October 1530 Martin Luther took refuge here during the Diet of Augsburg, protected from his Catholic enemies by Frederick the Wise. (Luther was assigned the Fürstenbau and preached his Reformation doctrines of salvation on Easter Day and the following week.) Today the fortress displays many Luther memorabilia, 16C and 17C sleighs and carriages, an extensive collection of arms and armour, paintings by *Lucas Cranach the Elder, court painter to Frederick the Wise—see especially his naked Lucretia of 1518, and his Madonna, Jesus and St John of 1539—Dürer and Rembrandt engravings.

The Luther chapel opens Apr–Oct 09.30–12.00, 14.00–16.00, except Mon; winter 14.00–15.30; the art gallery stays open till 17.00.

In the Marktplatz is a statue of Queen Victoria's consort Albert, who was born here, and the late 16C Stadthaus, which boasts two corner towers and five rich gables. The late Gothic Moritzkirche (St Moritz is the patron saint of Coburg) has a portal with carvings of Adam and Eve, a Baroque interior, 1701, and the alabaster tomb of Duke Johann Friedrich II by Nikolaus Bergner, 1595. Opposite the church, Coburg's Renaissance secondary school of 1605, includes a statue of its founder, Duke Johann Casimir (1586–1633). Schloss Ehrenburg in Steingasse, based on a mid-13C Franciscan monastery, was mostly rebuilt in 1816–38 to the neo-Gothic plans of K.F. Schinkel, and has a huge library, a giants' gallery (named after 28 stuccoed figures), a rich court chapel of 1701, an early 19C gilded classical throne room, French tapestries in the Gobelin Room, a portrait gallery and a local history museum (open Tue–Sun, 09.00, 10.00, 11.00, 13.30, 14.30 and 15.30). In its park is a natural history museum and 8000 species of bird (open summer 09.00–18.00, closing at 17.00 in winter). Coburg's theatre dates from 1840. The Congress Hall was built in 1962.

Continue E along the B303 by way of Neustadt bei Coburg and **Mitwitz**—early 16C Schloss with a Baroque Oberes Schloss, to 36km **Kronach**, Lucas Cranach the Elder's birthplace. The parish church is 15C; the town hall of 1583 has three works by Cranach; the Rosenberg Schloss dominates the town.

An **excursion** SE by the B85 after 20km reaches **Kulmbach** (29,000 inhab; alt. 306m), on the Weisser Main, a town long celebrated for its beer and overlooked from the Burgberg by **\*Schloss Plassenburg**. Begun early in the 12C for Count Berthold II von Andechs, it was rebuilt, after a fire, between 1559 and 1569, by G. Beck and C. Fischer. Its inner Renaissance courtyard (the Schöner Hof), has a double gallery on three sides, sculpted decorations and medallions relating to the Hohenzollerns who inherited the Schloss. Exhibitions inside occupy 12 Renaissance rooms and include paintings and especially tin figurines depicting battles and other historic events (open Tue–Sun 10.00–14.30, closing 13.30 Oct–Mar). In the town rises the late Gothic Petri-Kirche with a lantern tower and mid-17C furnishings; the Klosterhof of 1695; and the 16C Rathaus with a delightful Rococo façade of 1752.

From Kronach the B173 runs 43km NE to Hof through the Franconian woods and past the 795m-high **Döbraberg**—reached by foot from Schwarzenbach in 20 minutes. **Hof** is the most important industrial town (textiles) in Upper Franconia. It has an 11C to 13C church of St Lorenz, with a 16C wooden cross and the 15C winged Hertnid altar, the gift of Dean Hertnid von Stein of Bamberg; a 13C twin-towered church of St Michael, much restored by G. Saher in the early 19C after a fire of 1834 and, like St Lorenz, boasting a 15C wooden cross; a 13C Spitalkirche, with a neo-Gothic exterior of 1836, restored in the 20C—its treasures include a late Gothic altarpiece, a late 17C ceiling painting by H.A. Löhe and a pulpit by J.N. Knoll, 1693. The Martin-Luther-Kirche was built by R. Reissinger in 1936. Hof also has its own city theatre; the Theresienpark, laid out in 1815, with its botanical garden; swimming pools; and a symphony orchestra. The information office is in the three-storeyed Rathaus of 1563–66, with a staircase tower; the whole restored in 1823.

# 8

# Bamberg to Lindau

## A. Bamberg

**\*\*BAMBERG** (74,000 inhab.; alt. 262m), a city built on seven hills, preserves
a remarkable number of buildings from the era of the Holy Roman Emperor
Henry II (see below), who made the city an Imperial residence. The River
Regnitz on its way to the River Main divides into two at Bamberg, embracing the old burghers' city, which developed from the 12C. The older
ecclesiastical city stands on the W bank of the left branch of the river. A
market was founded between the two branches of the Regnitz c 1100 and
became the centre of the secular city. Today Bamberg also derives trade by
way of the Rhine–Main–Danube Canal—the harbour, with its grain eleva-
tors, was opened in 1962. A Bamberg speciality is beer brewed from
smoked malt (Rauchbier). Bamberg sponsors a celebrated symphony orchestra.

**Main railway station**, Luitpoldstrasse. **Information Offices**: at the main railway station
and at 6 Geyerswörthstrasse; site of the vegetable and flower market. **Trains** and **buses**
run to Coburg, Erlangen, Nuremberg and Würzburg.

**History**. The Badenbergs established themselves here sometime before the 10C,
building a castle on the rise now occupied by the cathedral. Their revolt against the
Carolingians led to the confiscation of their lands. Duke Henry the Quarrelsome of
Bavaria took over their Schloss in 973, and under his son, the Emperor Henry II (the
sole canonised German emperor, 973–1024), the bishopric was set up in 1007. Henry
II also founded the cathedral and made the Schloss into a royal palace. In the Middle
Ages churchmen and burghers frequently quarrelled, especially over the former's
claim to taxes. The city remained predominantly Catholic during the Reformation.
Bamberg sided with the Catholic League in the Thirty Years War and suffered at the
hands of the Swedes in 1632. In 1648 Bishop Melchior founded a university which was
closed down in 1803. The city was attacked by the Prussians in the Seven Year War.
In the 18C two prince-bishops—Lothar Franz and Friedrich Carl von Schönborn—were
largely responsible for the Baroque richness of the city, deploying the brilliant brothers
Georg and J.L. Dientzenhofer. Between 1808–13 the musician and writer, E.T.A.
Hoffmann, was director of the city theatre. In 1818 the bishops were elevated to
archbishops. Happily, damage during World War II was remarkably slight. Bamberg
became a university city again in 1979.

Follow Luitpoldstrasse SW from the main railway station, turning left at
Königstrasse to find (left, in Theuerstrasse) the church of **St Gangolf**.
Consecrated in 1063, it was enlarged in the 15C and later centuries. From
here walk SE to the Protestant **Erlöserkirche**, an octagonal church with a
free-standing tower, by Bestelmeyer, 1930. Walk along Kunigundendamm
NW along the river bank, crossing the river at Luitpoldbrücke, and then
turning right along the river to reach Hauptwachstrasse. Hauptwachstrasse
leads SW into Maximiliansplatz, where you find the **Neues Rathaus** (1733–
36).

   SW from here, along Grüner Markt, is the Baroque, Jesuit church of **St
Martin**, 1689–91, partly by Georg Dientzenhofer, partly by his son Johann
Leonhard, with a 55m-high tower, a waggon-vaulted nave and a trompe

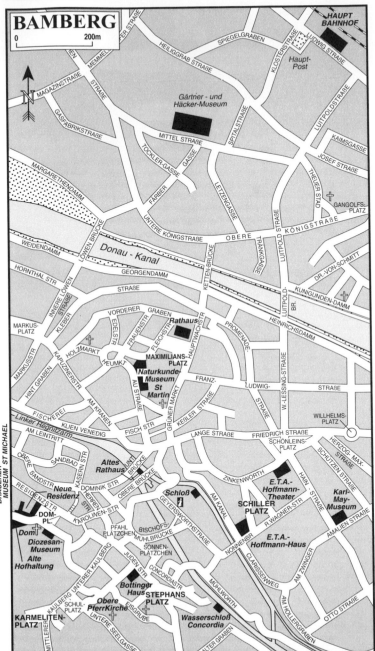

# BAMBERG

0       200m

**HAUPT BAHNHOF**

MEMMELS STRAßE

SPIEGELGRABEN

KLOSTERSTRAßE

LUDWIG STRAßE

HEILIGGRAB STRAßE

Haupt-Post

MAGAZINSTRAßE

STRAßE

Gärtner - und Häcker-Museum

LUITPOLDSTRAßE

KAIMSGASSE

GASFABRIKSTRAßE

MITTEL STRAßE

SPITALSTRAßE

JOSEF STRAßE

TÖCKLER-GASSE

GASSE

THEUER STAD

GANGOLFS-PLATZ

MARGARETHENDAMM

FARBER

LETZENGASSE

UNTERE KÖNIGSTRAßE

OBERE KÖNIGSTRAßE

LUITPOLD STRAßE

WEIDENDAMM

LÖWEN BRÜCKE

**Donau - Kanal**

TRANKGASSE

KETTEN-BRÜCKE

HORNTHAL STR

GEORGENDAMM

STRAßE

KUNIGUNDEN-DAMM

DR.-VON-SCHMITT

INNERE LÖWEN STRAßE

KLEBER STR

VORDERER GRABEN

**Rathaus**

PROMENADE-

HEINRICHSDAMM

LUITPOLD-BR.

MARKUS-PLATZ

EDELSTR

FRAUENSTR

FLEICHSTR

HAUPTWACH-STR

MAXIMILIANS-PLATZ

MARKUSSTR

KAPUZINERSTR

HINT GRABEN

HOLZMARKT

HEUMKT

AU STRAßE

**Naturkunde-Museum**

FRANZ-

LUDWIG-

STRAßE

W.-LESSING-STRAßE

FISCHEREI

AM KRANEN

**St Martin**

GRÜNER MARKT

KEßLER STRAßE

WILLHELMS-PLATZ

Linker Regnitzarm

KLIEN VENEDIG

FISCH STR

LANGE STRAßE

FRIEDRICH STRAßE

AM LEINTRITT

SCHÖNLEINS-PLATZ

HERZOG. MAX. STRAßE

OBERE SANDSTR

SANDBAD

**Altes Rathaus**

UNT. BRÜCKE

OBERE BRÜCKE

ZINKENWORTH

**E.T.A.-Hoffmann-Theater**

SCHÜTZEN STRAßE

**Karl-May-Museum**

RESIDENZSTR

KASERN STR

DOMINIK STR

HERREN STR

**Schloß**

GEYERSWORTHSTR

AM KANAL

**SCHILLER PLATZ**

R.WAGNER-STR

HAIN STRAßE

AMALIEN STRAßE

**FRÄNKISCHES BRAUERER-MUSEUM ST MICHAEL**

**Neue Residenz**

KAROLINEN-STR

**DOM-PL.**

PFAHL PLÄTZCHEN

BISCHOFS-

MÜHLBRÜCKE

**E.T.A.-Hoffmann-Haus**

NONNENBR

CLARISSENWEG

AM ZWINGER

**Dom**

**Diozesan-Museum**

**Alte Hofhaltung**

UNTERER KAULBERG

JUDEN STR

SONNEN-PLÄTZCHEN

CONCORDIASTR

MÜHLWORTH

AM HOLLERGRABEN

OTTO STRAßE

KAULBERG

**Bottinger Haus**

**STEPHANS PLATZ**

**Wasserschloß Concordia**

**KARMELITEN-PLATZ**

SCHUL-PLATZ

**Obere PfarrKirche**

FISGRUBE

MITTLERER KAULBERG

UNTERE SEELGASSE

ALTER GRABEN

l'oeil fresco on the dome. Close by is a Neptune fountain by J.K. Metzner, 1698. Behind is the former Jesuit College, now the university faculty of theology. Continue as far as the Obstmarkt. Cross into Karolinenstrasse. Where Karolinenstrasse crosses the river, by the **Obere Brücke**, 1453–56, is the **Altes Rathaus** of 1453, rebuilt by J.M. Küchel, 1744–56, standing on piles set in the river bed. Its charms include trompe l'oeil painted façades and a half-timbered Häuslein leaning over a pier of the bridge. The area around the Old Town Hall, with its fishermen's houses, is known as Klein-Venedig (Little Venice) and is entrancingly viewed from the Untere Brücke. South of the Old Town Hall stands the former palace of the prince-bishops, the **Geyerswörth Schloss**, 1585–86. From the Schloss Geyerswörthstrasse leads SE. Turn right to cross the other arm of the River Regnitz at Bischofsmühlbrücke, leading into Judenstrasse, along which stands the **Böttingerhaus**, a Baroque palace in the Venetian style of 1707–13, built for the rich Privy Councillor Böttinger. Judenstrasse runs SE into Concordiastrasse, at the end of which stands the Baroque **Concordia** palace, 1716–22, Privy Councillor Böttinger's second palace in Bamberg.

Walk back along Concordiastrasse to turn almost immediately W and reach Stephansplatz and the church of **St Stephan**, built in 1020, with 17C Baroque reordering and late Romanesque/early Gothic towers, which is now the chief Protestant church of Bamberg. NW of St Stephan, on the Unterer Kaulberg, stands the 14C **Obere Pfarrkirche**. Its choir is by Parler, 1375–87; it has a Gothic ambulatory, while the rest of the interior is now Baroque. The portrait of the Madonna on the high altar dates from 1320. A font of 1520 is carved with the seven sacraments. On the N side of the church the so-called 'Marriage doorway' is sculpted with an apotheosis of Mary and wise and foolish Virgins c 1330. Close by is the Baroque courtyard by M. Küchel of Ebrach monastery.

From here Unterer Kaulberg leads S to Karmelitenplatz and the **Karmelitenkloster**, which belonged to the Benedictines until 1553. This Romanesque building was reordered in the Baroque era—façade by J.L. Dientzenhofer and others—but has preserved its 14C transept with fine capitals. From here take the street named Sutte NW to reach the 12C **St Jakob's** church, which is Romanesque with a Baroque façade. Obere Karolinenstrasse leads from this church E to the Domplatz. No. 5 Obere Karolinenstrasse is the Baroque archbishop's palace; the entrance to its inner courtyard is from 7 Domstrasse.

Dominating the Domplatz is the **\*\*Dom**. After a fire of 1081 had destroyed the building founded by Henry II, Bishop Otto rebuilt it, but his new cathedral was again burnt down in 1185. A third cathedral was begun early in the 13C, with a raised Gothic Westwerk complementing its terraced apse. It features a Romanesque east apse, 1215–20, while on the north side, on the Fürstenportal (Princes' Doorway), with its ten slender receding pillars and arches, is a Last Judgement, apostles and prophets. The sculpture carved c 1210 on the Marienportal on the N side of the choir includes the Apostles' frieze, with the Apostles symbolically borne on the shoulders of the Prophets. On the south side of the choir the Adam's door, with its dog-toothed pattern, once carried statues of Adam, Eve, St Peter, St Stephen, Henry II and his wife Kunigunde, c 1235, but these have been removed to the diocesan museum (see below; Adam and Eve are the first life-size nude statues to have been sculpted since Classical times). The cloisters date from 1457, while the stone terrace at the east end (the 'Domkranz') was added 1508–11, for the exhibition of the cathedral's relics. Spires to the towers were added by J.M. Küchel in 1766–68.

The **interior**—restored 1828–37 by K. Rupprecht, K.A. von Heideloff and F. Gärtner, with a second restoration 1969–74—is packed with masterpieces of religious art, beginning with the **\*\*tomb of Henry II and Kunigunde** in front of the choir, by Tilman Riemenschneider, begun in 1499. Henry and Kunigunde, lying on the tomb, were sculpted in 15C costume out of limestone with other carvings depicting the emperor's death, the weighing of his soul, St Benedict miraculously removing his gall-stones, Kunigunde dismissing dishonest servants and her ordeal by fire, suspected of adultery. The celebrated **\*\*\*Bamberg Rider**, an equestrian statue depicting an idealised medieval monarch or knight, based perhaps on a French original, dates from c 1240. The tomb of Friedrich I von Hohenlohe is by the Master

*An image of chivalry from the high Middle Ages, the 13C Bamberg Rider*

of Wolfskehl, like Riemenschneider, from Würzburg, c 1352. Look out for the late Romanesque stone sculptures of apostles and prophets, by the Master of the Georgenchor, with female statues depicting Christianity and the Jewish faith, a blindfolded woman, beside the apostles and statues of Mary and Elizabeth between the prophets, statues which probably once graced the Fürstenportal. A crucifixion group of 1650 over the neo-Romanesque altar is by the Frankfurt artist Justus Glesker. The cathedral's 14C choir stalls were restored 1835–38. In the west choir is the marble tomb of Pope Clement II, former Bishop of Bamberg, d 1047, dated c 1450, with reliefs depicting the pope's death and the four virtues (Fortitude, Prudence, Justice, Temperance). The north aisle houses the late Gothic Gattendorf altar, the third altar from the east, while further west in the north aisle are reliquary busts of Henry II and Kunigunde, and statues of St Lawrence, by H. Nussbaum c 1500, and St Sebastian, from Riemenschneider's workshop. In the chapel of the Blessed Sacrament, south aisle, a painting of heaven enclosed in a rosary has been attributed to Lucas Cranach, c 1520. The *Christmas Altar by Veit Stoss, 1520–24, depicting the Nativity, is set against the west wall of the south transept.

Modern works are the stations of the cross in the south aisle by F. Baumhauer, 1921; an apse painting of Christ with St Peter and St George, by K. Caspar, 1928; a modern altar, with bronze scenes from the life of Christ, by Klaus Backmund, 1974; the four-manual organ (77 registers), by Rieger & Co., 1976, with sculptures by Backmund. The cathedral crypt (early Gothic, extended in the mid 15C) contains the sarcophagus of Konrad III, who died in 1153, bronze slabs commemorating the cathedral canons, and three altars, namely: the triptych altar with apostles, by H. Nussbaum c 1500; an altar with a crucifix, by F. Theiler 1675—secondary figures by T. Buscher 1917; and the war memorial altar, by G. Busch, 1921.

On the N side of the Domplatz stands the Baroque *Neue Residenz with a rose garden in its courtyard. In the early 17C the Prince-Elector commissioned a Renaissance palace, whose two aisles still stretch along Karolinenstrasse. A century later it was enlarged by the addition of two more wings in the Baroque style, built on behalf of Lothar von Schönborn in the 1690s and early 18C by the architect Johann Leonhard Dientzenhofer. Dientzenhofer's Rococo pavilion, with its 24 apartments, includes the Kaisersaal, now an art gallery, the **Staatsgalerie Bamberg** (open 09.00–12.00, 13.30–17.00, closes 16.00 Oct–Mar) with paintings by Lucas Cranach the Elder and Hans Baldung Grien, Baroque furniture, Gobelin tapestries and exquisite parquet floors. On the W side of the Domplatz stands the Renaissance *Alte Hofhalttung, 1571–76, formerly the episcopal palace, its Renaissance façade incorporates the sculpted Renaissance Reiche Tor, which gives access to the inner courtyard surrounded with Gothic, half-timbered buildings. The Domplatz also houses the gabled Renaissance **Ratstube**, which now houses the **Historisches Museum** (open May–Oct Tue–Sun 09.00–12.00, 14.00–17.00, Sun and holidays 10.00–13.00) displaying Franconian art, paintings from the late Middle Ages to the Biedermeier era (with works by Lucas Cranach the Elder and Carl Rupprecht), as well as pottery, porcelain, glassware and musical instruments; the Domherrenhöfe (canons' residences), decorated with their coats of arms, and the chapter house by Balthasar Neumann, 1730–33, now the **Diözsan-Museum** (open weekdays 10.00–12.00, 14.20–18.00; Sat, Sun 10.00–13.00) with statues from cathedral, vestments, stained glass and Baroque art. No. 8 Domplatz is the National Library, with 3400 incunabula (open weekdays 10.00–12.00, 14.30–17.30, Sat 09.00–12.00, Sun 10.00–13.00).

A stiff walk from here leads W along Aufsessstrasse, to the N of the cathedral, and then NW along Michaelsberg up to the former Benedictine abbey (now an old people's home) of Michaelsberg, founded 1009, with the abbey church of **St Michael**, boasting twin Gothic towers and pointed spires, finished 1610. Its 17C Baroque *façade is approached by a magnificent flight of steps, by Leonhard Dientzenhofer, 1697, with a balustrade of 1723. Inside are the Gothic tomb of St Otto (Bishop of Bamberg 1102–39); a carving of the Man of Sorrows c 1350; a vaulted ceiling and flower paintings c 1610; the Renaissance wall memorial to Johann Philipp von Gebsattel who died in 1609, by Michael Kern; a statue of the grieving Virgin Mary, c 1720; choir stalls, by F.A.T. Böhm, Servatius Brickhard and others c 1726; Baroque statues of Henry II and Kunigunde, by Peter Benkert 1726; a *Rococo pulpit by Goerg Adam Reuss, 1751; the sepulchral chapel on the south side, painted with a Dance of Death and enlivened by Rococo stucco work. As for the monastery buildings, these are by J.L Dientzenhofer, 1696–1702, and by Balthasar Neumann, 1742. At 10f Michaelsberg is the Frankisches Brauereimuseum, a museum of brewing, open weekdays, except Mon 13.00–16.30, Sat, Sun and holidays 13.30–16.00.

From here you have an impressive panorama of the city. Follow St Getreu-Strasse W to the Baroque church of **St Getreu** (now a clinic for nervous diseases), which contains an Entombment of Christ, c 1500, and eight late Gothic panels depicting the Passion.

**Other museums**: National Archives, 39 Hainstrasse (open weekdays 08.00–18.15, Wed till 20.00, Fri till 15.00); **Naturkundemuseum**, 2 Fleischstrasse (open Mon–Fri 08.00–12.00, 13.00–17.00); **Karl-May-Museum**, 2 E.T.A. Hoffmann-Strasse (open Wed–Sat 09.00–13.00). In the last, alongside the novelist's study (whose furnishings came to here from Radebeul near Dresden) are many works, his own included, about the North American Indians.

**Other sights**: Schillerplatz houses both the **E.T.A. Hoffmann-Theater** and at No. 26 the **house** in which E.T.A. Hoffmann lived (open weekdays 16.30–17.30, Sat, Sun 09.30–10.30: here the novelist composed 'Der goldene Topf' (The Golden Pot). The City stadium and cycle track are in the **Volkspark**.

**Environs**. **Altenburg**, 3km SW, has a 387m-high Schloss, a moated fortress belonging to the bishops since 1251, which was destroyed by the Margrave Albrecht Alcibiades of Brandenburg-Kulmbach in 1553 and rebuilt in 1901. The site offers another lovely panorama of Bamberg.

# B. Bamberg to Lindau via Nuremberg and Augsburg

Total distance 366 km. Bamberg—A73, 25km Forchheim—15km Erlangen—19km Nuremberg—A2, 16km Schwabach—31km Weissenburg—40km Donauwörth—36km Augsburg—B17, 36km Landsberg—B12, 9km Buchloe—59km Ottobeuren—9km Memmingen—29km Leutkirch—42km Lindau.

The A73 leads SE from **Bamberg** (see Rte 8A) and travels through the Franconian basin close by the River Regnitz and the Ludwig Canal, which joined the Main to the Danube in 1855. Set beside the Wiesent close to its confluence with the Regnitz, **Forchheim** (29,000 inhab.; alt. 265m) lies 25km SE. Still following the contours of its former fortifications, Forchheim was a Carolingian palatinate in the 9C and the seat of several Imperial diets. Its Gothic **Pfarrkirche** was domed in 1670. Inside on the pillars are eight 15C altar paintings of the Passion and the life of the patron, from the school of Martin Wohlgemut. Close by stands the moated Pfalz (1353–83), built chiefly by Lampert von Brunn and formerly an episcopal palace, with two frescoed rooms, one by the Parler family, c 1370, the other by Jakob Ziegler, 1559. It is now a museum of local history and art (70 modern works by Georg Mayer-Franken, 1870–1926; open May–Oct 10.00–12.30, 14.00–16.30, except Mon). The half-timbered Rathaus and many burghers' houses, especially in the Marktplatz, date from the 14C to the 16C. From the Pfalz the nearby Saltertum leads to the Renaissance and Baroque fortifications. NE of Forchheim beer cellars have been cut into the rocks.

15km S lies ***Erlangen** (100,000 inhab.; alt. 280m; information office: 1 Rathausplatz), a city developed by Huguenot refugees, sheltered by the Margrave Christian Ernst of Kulmbach-Bayreuth, who laid out the new Baroque town for them, to plans by Johann Moritz Richter, after the Revocation of the Edict of Nantes by Louis XIV of France in 1685. Their memorials include the Huguenot fountain, 1706, in the Schloss garden, with statuettes of the original refugees. Erlangen was first mentioned in written history in 1002 and by 1017 belonged to the bishops of Bamberg. Emperor Karl IV granted it city rights in the 14C. From this era dates the Altstadt. In 1440 the city passed into the hands of the Margraves. Erlangen became part of Prussia in 1791 and part of Bavaria in 1810. Johann Gottlieb Fichte (1805–06), Friedrich Rückert (1826–41) and Ludwig Feuerbach (1828) taught at the university. The physicist Georg Ohm (1789–1854) was born here and the city, which is the HQ of Siemens & Co., still prospers on electronics and electrical engineering.

Churches include the 13C SS Peter and Paul, with its huge tower and Baroque interior, the ceiling painted by C. Leinberger; the church of St Martin, basically the oldest church in the city; the church of St Xystus late-Gothic, reordered in the Baroque style; the 13C Kriegenbrunn church, housing late-Gothic frescoes; the former Dominican monastery church of St Matthew, with a Romanesque porch; and the Hugenottenkirche of 1686–93. Its university, founded 1743, now has its administration in the Schloss, by G. von Gerdeler, 1700–04. Schwanthaler sculpted the statue of Margrave Friedrich Wilhelm in front in 1843. The Schloss garden has an orangery by the same architect, 1706–08, a statue of Friedrich Rückert and at the NE corner the oldest Baroque theatre—the Markgrafentheater—still in use in western Germany. It was built for Margrave Friedrich Wilhelm, 1517–19 and refurbished by the Venetian G.P. Gasperi in 1742. In the Marktplatz is the Stutterheimsches Palais (1730), now the city library. The Baroque Rathaus of 1731 on Martin-Luther-Platz, in the Altstadt, now houses the city museum (open Mon–Fri 08.00–12.00; Sun 10.00–13.00, and some afternoons). The Neues Rathaus is by H. Loebermann, 1971. The university has noted anthropological, mineralogical and zoological collections, as well as an art gallery—its gems include self-portraits by Grünewald and Dürer; open Mon–Fri 09.30–12.00, 14.00–16.00).

19km S of Erlangen is Nuremberg (see Rte 6). Leave Nuremberg by the Schweinauer Hauptstrasse and travel 16km S along the B2 to **Schwabach**, a town of 35,000 inhab., specialising in tobacco-growing and work with gold leaf, with a late Gothic St Johanniskirche. Built 1469–95, it was enlarged in the 16C; its late Gothic high altar was painted by Martin

Wohlgemut in 1508, with panels depicting SS Barbara and Catherine by Hans Baldung Grien. The church tower reaches 72m, carrying a bell founded in 1415. Schwabach has half-timbered houses, a Baroque fountain of 1716 by J.W. von Zocha and another classical one, both are in Königsplatz, as well as a town hall of 1509, its upper storey half-timbered in 1799. Articles drawn up at Schwabach in 1528–29 formed the basis of the first section of the Confession of Augsburg.

The route after 12km passes through **Roth bei Nürnberg** at the confluence of the Roth, the Rednitz and the Aurach. The 16C early Renaissance Schloss Ratibor, built for Margrave Georg the Pious and renovated in the 19C, has a courtyard with an ancient lime tree and a huntsman fountain, and is matched by another hunting Schloss on a peak outside the town. The Marktplatz has half-timbered houses, including the exquisite Riffelmacher-Haus, and a Rococo fountain of 1757.

Continue as far as **Ellingen**, with its Rococo town hall of 1746; its Schloss, once belonging to the Teutonic Knights (their largest) and rebuilt in the Baroque style by Franz Keller, 1718–25; its church lavishly decorated by C.D. Asam; and remnants of fortifications.

**Weissenburg**, 3km S, a Free Imperial City from 1360 to 1802, has a late Gothic town hall of 1476—the tower dates from 1567; a Roman fort (*castrum Biriciana*) and baths, part of the Limes, and discovered in 1977; an open-air theatre; and the church of St Andreas, which was finished in 1520, with three altars c 1500. The town is ringed with medieval *fortifications built of mellow yellow stone, with 32 inhabited towers and, especially, the 14C Spital and Ellinger Gates. Nearby on its 630m peak stands the 16C **Schloss Wülzburg**, built for the Margrave von Ansbach by G. and B. Bernwart. Inside is the deepest rock well in western Germany. An important Roman Museum is at 3 Martin-Luther-Platz.

The route now leads 40km S to **Donauwörth** (see Rte 1B) and 36km S to **Augsburg** (see Rte 3). Continue S along the B17 for 38km to **Landsberg** (see Rte 3). Continue W for 9km along the B12 to **Buchloe**, whose parish church was built in 1400 and reordered c 1700, with a rosary picture by Matthias Kager, 1626. The administration centre of the diocese of Augsburg is here, in a building of 1729 by J.G. Fischer.

For an excursion, from here the B12 runs S for 18km to **Kaufbeuren**. Five towers remain of its 13C to 14C fortifications. Equally defensive is the fortress-like church of St Blasius NW of the town, built in the 15C and sheltering a crucifix c 1350, a sculpted and winged high altar of 1436 by J. Lederer and late Gothic wall paintings. In the town itself the church SS Cosmas and Damian dates from 1494, reordered inside in the 17C and 18C, and the Rathaus dates from 1888 by Hauberrisser. Kaufbeuren was the birthplace of the novelist Ludwig Ganghofer (1855–1920), commemorated with a room in the Heimatmuseum at 12–14 Kaisergässchen (open Tue–Sat 09.00–11.00, 13.00–16.00, Sun 09.00–12.00). The older road runs slightly E of this road to **Ketterschwang** (14km), with its mid-18C Rococo parish church by Joseph Fischer, with wall and ceiling painting by Johannes Baptist Enderle.

The B18 leads 20km W from Buchloe to Mindelheim. En route a brief diversion S leads to **Bad Wörifshofen**, where the parish priest Sebastian Kneipp (1821–97) so developed thermal treatment—hot and cold baths, massages, mud packs, etc.—that today there are 7500 beds here for those seeking cures, and spa rooms built in 1905 and modernised in 1954. The late Gothic church was enriched by Franz Beer, 1722, and has stucco work by Dominikus Zimmermann. **Mindelheim** is dominated by Schloss Mindelsburg, seat of the legendary knight Georg von Fundsberg, 1473–1528, who formed the mercenary Landsknechte in the 16C. The 13C Jesuit church was later reordered in the Baroque style (inside is a Madonna of 1670); see also the Liebfraukirche of 1510. Gates and towers, c 1400, still surround the town.

Leave the B18 and take the route WSW for 10km to reach **Mussenhausen**, with its mid-18C pilgrimage church of Our Lady of Mount Carmel, by Thomas Natterer, its ceiling fresco by J.B. Enderle. After 15km the road reaches **Ottobeuren**, another Kneipp health resort. Its *Benedictine abbey, founded 764, was rebuilt 1711–31, most of it the achievement of J.M. Fischer; the monastic buildings are complex and rich, with frescoes in the Benedictuskapelle and the Abtkapelle by the Venetian J. Amigoni. J.M. Fischer built its **Baroque church, 1737–96, which has two 86m-high towers. Inside over the tabernacle is a 12C cross, choir stalls of 1760 by Martin Hermann, and gilded limewood reliefs of the life of St Benedict and scriptural scenes by Joseph Christian. The frescoes are by Amigoni, J.J. Zeiller and J.B. Zimmermann; the stucco work by J.M. Feuchtmayr. Karl Joseph Riepp, a pupil of the Silbermann family, built the *Baroque organ of 1756–66. The abbey, suppressed in 1803 and restored to the Benedictines in 1918, is open weekdays 10.00–12.00, 14.00–17.00; Sun and holidays 10.00–12.00, 13.00–17.00; Nov–Mar 14.00–17.00, including the monastery museum).

9km NW is **Memmingen** (38,000 inhab., alt. 601m), founded in the mid 13C by Duke Welf VI, which became a free town in 1268 and flourished in the 14C and 15C, trading with France, Spain and Flanders, and in the 16C with India and Venezuela. Here in 1525 the manifesto (the Bauernartikel) of the Peasant's Uprising was drawn up. Today the town's industries include foam rubber, textiles, machinery and cosmetics.

Walled with towers, Memmingen has a tax-collection building of 1495; a town hall of 1589 with a façade of 1765, which stands in the Marktplatz along with the arcaded Steuerhaus of 1495. There are important *wall paintings, c 1470, in the Gothic Liebfrauenkirche. Two other majestic buildings are the Kinderlehr church, with its late Gothic courtyard and frescoes by B. Strigel, and the Gothic church of St Martin by Matthäus Böblinger, 1499. The latter has choir stalls of 1506 by Heinrich Stark and Hans Dapratzhauser (see his name and the date in the choir). But Memmingen's chief attraction is the *Siebendächerhaus (1601), built by tanners, with seven overlapping roofs designed for drying pelts. Modern churches are St Joseph by (Michael Kurz and Thomas Wechs, 1927–30), and Maria Himmelfahrt by Thomas Wechs, 1956, with sculpture by Josef Henselmann and glass by Franz Nagel. The city museum at 8 Zangmeisterstrasse is housed in a Rococo palace of 1736, designed by Benedikt von Herman (open Tue–Fri, Sun 10.00–12.00, 14.00–16.00). After 1km follow the signs 9km S for the Maria Steinbach pilgrimage church, by D. Zimmermann, enriched by Franz Georg Feuchtmayr.

20km SW **Leutkirch**, at the heart of the Württemberg Allgaü and a centre of winter sports, was a Free Imperial Town from 1293 to 1802. Its Catholic church of St Martin is Gothic, 1514, and a hall-church—as is the Protestant Dreifaltigkeitskirche of 1613–15 with Gothic decoration of 1860. Leutkirch's arcaded town hall is Baroque, 1739–41, with a stuccoed room by Johann Schütz). Its Marktplatz is surrounded by burghers' houses, and part of the old fortifications and towers have been preserved. See also the church of Maria Himmelfahrt, built in 1612, though its interior is 18C. Two other sights are the 1636 Schloss Hummelsberg, SE of the town, and the Heimat-museum in the Kornhaus of c 1500, with cribs, handiworks and paintings by Hans Multscher (1400–59), Konrad Hegenauer (1737–1803) and Benedikt König (1863–1904) (open Mon 10.00–12.00, Thu, Sun 15.00–18.00; fewer unspecified hours in winter).

From here after 23km the route reaches the health resort of **Wangen** (24,500 inhab.; alt. 402m), at the centre of which is a charming old town, with walls and towers and a Baroque Rathaus of 1721. Follow the B18 a further 19km to **Lindau** on Lake Constance (26,500 inhab.; alt. 402m). Fishermen founded the town on an island in the late 8C and Count Adalbert of Rhaetia established a Benedictine convent here in 810. Fortified as a Free Imperial City in the 13C, Lindau profited from the trade route into Italy. It became briefly Austrian in 1804 and Bavarian the following year. In 1899, westward along the lake shore, at Friedrichshafen (see Rte 18), Count Ferdinand von Zeppelin (1838–1917), a native of Lindau, built his first airship hangar and the first Zeppelin.

Today Lindau is a thriving tourist resort, standing at the beginning of the Deutsche Alpenstrasse, a spectacular tourist route, the old town connected to the mainland by a road and a railway and a Gartenstadt with beaches and sports facilities stretching along the shore of the lake. In 1852 a 700-year-old monastic church was transformed into the civic theatre. Close by are the springs of Bad Schachen, renowned since 1474. Railways connect with Singen and Bregenz, ships with Constance, Bregenz and Rorschach, and buses with Bregenz, Wangen and Friedrichshafen. Tourist information offices are opposite and inside the main railway station.

Leave the main railway station and walk NE along Hafenplatz to the Mangturm, part of the old early 13C fortifications. Towards the harbour can be seen the 13C lighthouse and the 6m-high Bavarian lion, by Johann von Halbig, placed on the Löwenmole in the 19C. In the distance are the Voralberg and Appenzeller Alps. Continue as far as the Reichsplatz, with the Altes Rathaus of 1422–46, a late Gothic building with Renaissance elements, which was the seat of an Imperial Diet in 1496. An open-air staircase climbs to its upper storey. The paintings on the façade were done in the 1970s to designs by Josef Widmann. Nearby at 3 Bismarckstrasse is the Baroque Neues Rathaus, 1706–17. In Reichsplatz is the Lindavia fountain of 1884.

Follow Ludwigstrasse E to find the theatre, which stands on the founda-tions of a 13C church—and has been, amongst other things, an arsenal and a gaol. Continue NE along Fischergasse to find first the Catholic church of St Maria, a Baroque building by Johann Caspar Bagnato, 1748–51, its stucco work mostly renewed in 1925, and next the Gothic Protestant church of St Stephan, reordered in the Baroque style in the early 1780s. The former monastery buildings connected with St Maria, 1730–36, are now the offices of the town council; its ceiling fresco is by F.J. Spiegler. N is the Heiden wall, the remains of a Carolingian watch tower, to the E of which are the town gardens.

Return to the two churches of St Stephan and St Maria and continue W across the Marktplatz to find the *Haus zum Cavazzen, a Baroque building of 1729 that now houses the town museum (open Tue–Sat 09.00–12.00, 14.00–17.00; Sun 10.00–12.00). This area is now a pedestrianised zone with charming alleyways and, at 8 Lingg-Strasse, the home of the poet Hermann von Lingg (1820–1905). Walk W along Maximilianstrasse and N along

Zeppelinstrasse to reach the oldest church in Lindau, the basically early 11C St Peter, its tower dating from 1425, which boasts among the 13–16C frescoes the only surviving wall painting (the 'Lindau Passion') by Hans Holbein the Elder. Beside it rises the Brigands' Tower (Diebsturm) of 1380. The earliest 'Peace museum' in Europe is housed in the classical Linden-hofvilla at 24 Lindenhofweg (open mid-Apr–mid-Oct Tue, Sat 10.00–12.00, 14.00–16.00, Sun 10.00–12.00).

# 9

# Bamberg to Frankfurt-am-Main along the river Main

Total distance 178km. Bamberg—B26, 61km Schweinfurt—38km Karlstadt—52km Aschaffenburg—B8, 27km Frankfurt.

Leave **Bamberg** (see Rte 8A) by the Schweinfurter Strasse and take the B26 for 19km W to **Eltmann** on the left bank of the Main, a centre of quarrying, overlooked by the 13C Wallburg fortress, with a 19C parish church by Leo von Klenze. 2km further on is **Ebelsbach**, with a Schloss built between 1564 and 1569, and after 6km the route reaches the walled **Zeil am Main**, with a pilgrimage church on the peak of the Käppelsberg. On the way to Zeil am Main make a **detour** to the pilgrimage church of **Maria Limbach**, built by Balthasar Neumann in 1755. After 9km the route passes through **Hassfurt**, another walled town of half-timbered buildings, whose Knights Chapel—the Ritterkapelle, in the Obere Vorstadt—of 1390–1506, which was restored in the mid 19C, has nearly 300 knightly coats of arms inside and outside. Hassfurt also boasts a late Gothic parish church on the N side of the Marktplatz containing work by Riemenschneider and his colleagues—the statues of St John the Baptist and the Madonna are both probably by Riemenschneider himself.

Continue along the B26, passing the Schlösser at **Untertheres** and **Obertheres**. The second Schloss was formerly a Benedictine monastery, with a Baroque chapel and a Rococo parsonage. Drive on through the Steiger woods by way of Mainberg (dominated by a privately owned Schloss) to reach Schweinfurt in 29km.

\***Schweinfurt** (60,000 inhab.; alt. 218m), which appears in history c 900 as the seat of a Margrave and from 1254 till 1802 was a Free Imperial City, today makes ball-bearings and engines. Much was destroyed in World War II. The Renaissance town hall of 1572, by Nicolaus Hoffmann, has been well restored. The choir of the Gothic church of St Johann dates from 1554–62, the rest incorporating a Romanesque doorway on the south side, a transept of c 1225 and a nave that is partly late 13C. The font dates to 1367, with contemporary painting, and there are 14C tombs and a pulpit of 1684. The former secondary school (Altes Gymnasium at 12 Martin-Luther-Platz) from the early 1580s and founded by Gustavus Adolphus, now houses a museum (with irregular opening times), partly of scientific instruments and partly devoted to the local poet and Orientalist Friedrich Rückert (1788–1866, born at 2 Am Markt). There is a Rückert memorial in the

Marktplatz, and the modern Friedrich-Rückert building houses the city library. Post-war buildings include the Catholic church of St Kilian by Hans Schädel and the Protestant church of the resurrection by Olav Gulbransson and Wilhelm Wirth. The theatre at 2 Rossbrunnstrasse was built in 1966.

From here the River Main winds S to Würzburg. Continue W for 12km to Werneck and **Schloss Werneck** with its twin onion domes, set in an English park, built in the 16C for Prince-Bishop Julius Echter von Mespelbrunn, with two wings added by Balthasar Neumann, 1733–45, to transform the Schloss into a summer retreat for Friedrich Carl von Schönborn, Prince-Bishop of Würzburg. 9km further W is the pilgrimage church of **Maria Sondheim**, containing a Baroque ceiling painting depicting the battle of Lepanto, a 14C crucifix, a Pietà of 1470, stained glass of 1480 and the tomb of Philipp von Hutten by Loy Hering. Close by, after 3km, is **Arnstein**, with its half-timbered houses, a hospital founded in 1558 and the church of St Nikolaus, with a Baroque altar by Jacob van der Auvera, 1710; the ceiling painting dates to 1726. 20km further, by way of **Trappstadt**, a town of half-timbered houses and an onion-domed church, is **Karlstadt**—at a junction with the B27, which follows the River Main S for 24km to Würzburg, see Rte 5A. A modern industrial town, Karlstadt has a walled inner quarter containing 15C half-timbered houses, a gabled Rathaus of 1422, inside which is an inn of 1605 and a Renaissance hall, and the late Gothic church of St Andreas, housing work by Riemenschneider, Renaissance frescoes in its south transept and a Romanesque Christ. This town was the birthplace of one of the most extreme Protestant reformers, Andreas Bodenstein (c 1480–1541), who took the name Karlstadt and sufficiently offended Martin Luther for the latter to dub him 'Judas'. Continue along the B26 15km W to **Steinbach**, with a Schloss of 1725, much damaged in 1945, and a parish church of the same date, both by Balthasar Neumann.

The road crosses the Main again and after 4km reaches \***Lohr am Main**, a town specialising in glass-making and ironworks, with fine half-timbered houses (shops with golden signs depict their goods) in the pedestrianised Altstadt. One of these, the Gasth of Schönbrunnen, is fronted by a sandstone fountain set up in 1936 to mark the 800th anniversary of the town's foundation. Beside it rises the Renaissance Altes Rathaus, with Corinthian columns, by the local architect Michael Imkelling, 1599–1602. The Gothic church of St Michael, with 15C and 16C tombs of the Counts of Rieneck, has a curly parapet below its spire. From Marktplatz, on the other side of the Rathaus from the fountain, Kellereigasse leads to a turretted Schloss built for the Electors of Mainz, 1561—1611. It now houses the interesting museum of local arts (open Tue–Sat 10.00–12.00, 14.00–16.00; Sun and holidays 10.00–13.00).

After travelling 35km W—through **Laufach**, whose modern parish church houses work from Riemenschneider's studio—the route passes through forests to reach \***Aschaffenburg** (59,000 inhab.; alt. 130m; information office: 15 Dalbergstrasse), set among the Spessart hills on the right bank of the Main at its confluence with the Aschaff, and where the B8 meets the B26 and by the Frankfurt–Nuremberg motorway. For many years Aschaffenburg was ruled by the bishops of Mainz. Between 1803 and 1810 it was capital of one of Napoleon's German principalities. Archbishop Carl Theodor von Dalberg founded a university here in 1808. The town became part of Bavaria in 1814, and 30 years later the opening of the railway to Bamberg and Frankfurt increased its prosperity. Trains connect with Frankfurt, Ulm, Mainz/Wiesbaden, Nuremberg and Darmstadt.

The 12C and 13C collegiate church of *SS **Peter and Alexander** possesses fine Romanesque cloisters, a 13C portal and a gable end dating from 1870. The sole of two projected towers is late Gothic (begun 1415, finished 1490). Inside this pillared basilica the nave and aisles are 12C and the choir is early Gothic; there is an early 12C crucifix; also a stone font of 1487; the Maria-Schnee chapel of 1516; a Resurrection by Lucas Cranach the Elder, 1520; *Matthias Grünewald's Lamentation, c 1525 (Grünewald lived in the town); a Renaissance pulpit, 1602; a Mary Magdalen altar 1620, by Hans Juncker; a bronze canopy by Hans Vischer, 1536, for the tomb of St Margaret; west gallery, 1618, supported on 16 Romanesque pillars brought from the Burg at Babenhausen; and a high altar of 1772. The founder of the church in 950, Otto von Schwaben, is buried here. The fountain in Stiftsplatz dates from 1882.

The sandstone Renaissance Schloss Johannisburg, by Georg Ridinger of Strasbourg, 1615–14, built for Archbishop Schweickard von Kronberg, is now an art gallery and library (open Tue–Sun 09.00–12.00, 13.00–17.00; Oct–Mar 10.00–16.00), with 13C Mainz gospels; the MS of Schiller's 'Wilhelm Tell', with the author's autograph dedication to Karl von Dalberg, 1804; cork models; and devotional works by Lucas Cranach the Elder. The Schloss is 85.5m square, and sports four corner lantern towers, each rising to 59.5m. A 14C watchtower guards the entrance to the courtyard, which was remodelled in the 18C. The Schönbusch park (open summer 08.00–13.00, 14.00–18.00, except Mon) has a classical Schloss by E.J. d'Herigoyen, lakes, a maze and a temple of joy, 1778–89, the whole landscaped by Franz Ludwig von Sckell. The Pompejanum is a reproduction of the temple of Castor and Pollux at Pompeii, built for Ludwig I by F. Gärtner, 1842–49. The 'English' Park Schöntal of 1780 houses a ruined abbey and a pheasant house.

The town hall by Diez Brandi dates from 1958. Its bronze doorway decorations are by Ursula Ullrich. The parish church zu Unserer Lieben Frau, with its early Gothic tower and reordering by Franz Bockorni, 1768–75, was damaged in World War II. A theatre by the Spaniard E.J. d'Herigoyen, 1810, was restored in 1960. The Stiftsmuseum displays religious art (open mid-Apr to mid-Oct daily, except Tue 10.00–13.00, 14.00–17.00). The Natural History museum (in Schönborner Hof, 15 Wermbachstrasse) opens weekdays, except Wed, 10.00–12.00; also 14.00–16.00 at weekends. In the Rosso Bianco Sports Car Museum, 125 Obernauer Strasse are displayed some 200 classic sports cars; open Apr–Oct, except Mon, 11.00–18.00. Aschaffenburg hosts an annual festival in June. Clemens Brentano, the Romantic author and folklorist, 1778–1842, lies in the town cemetery.

The B8 leads 16km NW to Kahl, on the Bavarian border, and crosses into Hesse to reach after a further 11km **Hanau**, where the brothers Jakob and Wilhelm Grimm were born, Schloss Philippsruhe and Wilhelmsbad (for details of all three, see beginning of Rte 36).

The route now runs W for 19km to **Frankfurt-am-Main** (see Rte 34A), passing after 10km, on the opposite bank of the canal, Schloss Rumpenheim, 1680.

# 10

# Bayreuth to Heidelberg via Bamberg and Würzburg

Total distance 298km. Bayreuth—B22, 61km Bamberg—B22, 86km Würzburg—B27, 90km Mosbach—61km Heidelberg.

The holiday resort of **BAYREUTH** (67,000 inhab.; alt. 345m; information office: 7 Luitpoldplatz) sits between 'Franconian Switzerland' and the Fichtelgebirge mountain chain. Celebrated today above all for its association with Richard Wagner, the town is much older, as is its musical tradition. Bayreuth appears in documented history in the late 12C (as Baierrute), was given its charter in 1231 and came into the hands of Friedrich III von Hohenzollern, remaining in the hands of the Franconian branch of the same family until 1791. In 1361 the blossoming town, set in the wide valley of the Roter Main and on the trade routes between Nuremberg, north Bohemia and Saxony, began to mint its own coinage. Hussites ravaged the settlement in 1430.

When Margrave Christian von Kulmbach made Bayreuth his principal seat in 1603, the town began an extraordinary period of artistic and architectural expansion. Margrave Christian-Ernst (1661–1712) inaugurated an era of sumptuous Baroque architecture, his ambitions for the town carried on by his successors Georg Wilhelm (died 1726) and Friedrich (died 1763), who was married to the talented and creative Princess Wilhelmine (1709–58), sister of Frederick the Great. The town was annexed to Prussia in 1791, was under French suzerainty from 1806 and became Bavarian in 1810. Richard Wagner came here in 1872, making the town his home until his death in 1883, and in 1876 his 'Ring' began the performances that have made Bayreuth internationally famous through the series of **festivals** held annually from the end of July to the end of August (other music festivals take place in spring).

Air traffic connects Bayreuth with Frankfurt, and railways to Nuremberg and Neuenmarkt–Wirsberg open up the rest of Germany. Coaches also travel as far as Berlin, Munich, Bamberg and Würzburg. The novelist and humorist Johann Paul Freidrich Richter (known as Jean-Paul, 1763–1825) lived here from 1804 (see below), as did Houston Stewart Chamberlain (1885–1926) after his marriage to Wagner's daughter Eva in 1908. Richter, Wagner's son and grandson, Siegfried and Wieland, and Franz Liszt (1811–86) are buried in the town cemetery.

From the main railway station follow Bahnhofstrasse S to Luitpoldplatz and the information office. S of the square, in Maximilianstrasse, is the 16C Altes Schloss, much rebuilt after a mid 17C fire, its octagonal tower and spiral ramp (designed to take horses) by Caspar Vischer, 1566. The medallions are by E. Räntz, 1691, the Rococo Schlosskirche by the French architect Joseph Saint-Pierre, 1753–56. Inside are the tombs of Margrave Friedrich and his wife Wilhelmine, while in the courtyard is a statue of Maximilian II. The Schloss is open Apr–Sept 09.00–11.30, 13.00–16.00; otherwise 10.00–11.30, 13.00–14.30.

W, on the corner of Opernstrasse, stands the Markgräfliches Opernhaus, again built by the court architect Joseph Saint-Pierre for Wilhelmine between 1745 and 1748. Its severe façade contrasts with the Baroque interior designed by the Bolognese architects Giuseppe and Carlo Galli-Bibiena, who made the court box a rival attraction to the stage.

Follow Opernstrasse and then Ludwigstrasse S to find the mid 18C Neues Schloss by Joseph Saint-Pierre, with its garden landscaped in 1726. Its delights include the Rococo rooms, a Japanese room, the mirror gallery, the palm room and a museum (open daily except Mon 10.00–12.00, 13.30–17.00; in winter closes one hour earlier). In front of the Neues Schloss is a fountain by Elias Räntz, 1700, with an equestrian statue of Margrave Christian-Ernst, which is the home of part of the Bavarian collection of paintings, as well as the town museum.

To the E of the Schloss garden is the neo-classical Haus Wahnfried, built for Richard Wagner by J. Wölfel, 1874, and now a museum (open daily, except religious holidays, 09.00–17.00) with manuscripts, mementoes of the composer and his entourage, including such luminaries as Ludwig II and Mathilde Wesendonck. Wahnfried means 'peace from torment', and the inscription in the house reads *Hier, wo mein Wähnen Frieden fand, Wahnfried sei dieses Haus von mir benannt* ('Here where my fancies first found peace I call this house Wahnfried'). Above is depicted Wotan the Wanderer. In front of the house is a bronze bust of Wagner's patron, King Ludwig II of Bavaria. Richard and Cosima Wagner are buried in the garden.

The oldest church in Bayreuth is the late Gothic *Holy Trinity in Kanzleistrasse, which M. Mebart restored in 1611–14, with massive twin towers, flying buttresses, five fine doorways (including the Renaissance sacristy door) and a high altar by H. Werner, c 1615. The town has old half-timbered houses, especially in Friedrichstrasse and Maxstrasse.

Just S of the railway station Tunnelstrasse leads E from Bahnhofstrasse and then N to Markgrafenalle, on which are the early Baroque church of St Georg (1705–11) and the little Schloss by Johann David Räntz, c 1730. N of the town lies the Richard-Wagner-Park with Gottfried Semper's 1876 Festspielhaus, seating 9000 spectators. NE stands the fanciful Eremitage, built 1715–50 according to the French fashion, with a rotunda 'dedicated' as a temple of the Sun, a dragon's cave, a couple of fanciful Schlösschen and a small hermit's chapel. (Visits to the Altes Schloss Eremitage summer 09.00–11.30, 13.00–16.30, except Mon; winter opening one hour later and closing two hours earlier.) Bayreuth also has a museum devoted to German Freemasonry, the Deutsches-Freimaurer-Museum at 1 Wahnfriedstrasse (open weekdays 10.00–12.00, 14.00–16.00, weekends only mornings), and a museum of typewriters at 11 Bernecker Strasse (open Mon–Fri 14.00–17.00). The Jean-Paul museum is in his former home at 84 Königsallee (opening times vary). Maisels' Brewery and Coopers' Museum at 40 Kulmbacher Strasse has guided tours Mon–Thu from 10.00.

From Bayreuth the B505 is a fast route of 75km to Bamberg. The more picturesque route of 61km is the B22, leaving Bayreuth by the Erlanger Strasse and travelling 24km W (through Donndorf, with its Schloss Fantasie of 1765) to Hollfeld, where there are a Rococo Schloss and a parish church which was once part of a Dominican monastery, as well as the church of St Salvator, 1704. Further on is **Würgau**, a centre of walks and rock climbing. 20km from Hollfeld the B22 reaches **Schesslitz**, with its 15C Gothic church of St Kilian, whose interior is late Baroque, and a pilgrimage church on the peak of the Gügel (523m high). The Dillinger Haus of 1692 was built by the brewers' and coopers' guilds. The remaining 9km to **Bamberg** (see Rte 8A) pass the towers of Schloss Seehof, 1695–1711, the early Baroque summer retreat of the prince-bishops.

Follow the B22 86km W to **Würzburg** (see Rte 5A) and the B27 30km SW into Baden-Württemberg to reach **Tauberbischofsheim** (see Rte 5B). From Tauberbischofsheim the route leads 17km W to **Hardheim**, with its 16C Schloss and the 15C keep of an earlier one, and another 9km W to Walldürn whose Schloss dates from 1492 and whose pilgrimage church of the Holy Blood was built from 1698 to 1728. Here the local history and pilgrimage museum in the patrician house Zum Güldenen Engal, 1588, opens Wed and Sun 14.00–16.00. Follow the road 8km S to **Buchen**, with its late Gothic parish church of St Oswald, 1503–07, enlarged 1922; its half-timbered houses; a fortified gateway remaining from the 15C walls; and a Baroque town hall of 1732. After 26km the B22 reaches **Mosbach**, with more half-timbered houses, especially the *Palmsches Haus of 1610, a Rathaus of 1558 and a 15C parish church of St Juliana whose choir has been used by Catholics since 1707 while Protestants worship in the nave. Mosbach is a holiday resort, with outdoor and indoor swimming pools, sauna baths, tennis and riding schools and a narrow gauge railway to Mudau.

3km SW lies **Neckarelz**, at the junction with the B37 from Frankfurt to Stuttgart and the confluence of the Elz and the Neckar. Neckarelz has a late Gothic Schloss built by the Teutonic Knights. Close by is the ruined Schloss of Götz von Berlichingen (1480–1562), the Hornberg, with its round tower. From Neckarelz, the B27 continues 26km SW to Sinsheim, where the motorways A6 followed by the A67 lead to Heidelberg. A more picturesque route is to take the minor road W from Neckarelz, to cross the border into Baden-Württemberg thus reaching Heidelberg by means of the B37.

**\*\*HEIDELBERG** (130,000 inhab.; alt 245m) situated at the entrance to the Neckar valley, dominated by its Schloss, by the 568m-high Königstuhl and by the 440m-high Heiligenberg, is the home of one of the oldest German universities and today profits from its electrical, optical, metal and leather industries and above all from tourism. The Altstadt is particularly romantic, the setting is superb, amidst green hills; and the city was given a new aura when Sigmund Romberg chose it as the venue of his Student Prince.

The **information office** is situated in the **main railway station** to the W of the town centre. **Trains** connect Heidelberg with Dortmund, Basel, Munich, Ludwigshafen, Mannheim and Würzburg.

**History**. For the Celts this was a holy mountain site. The Romans built a camp on the right bank of the Neckar in the 1C BC, with a temple dedicated to Mithras and Mercury. The Roman settlement was destroyed by the Alemmani in the 3C AD. In the early 11C the Bishop of Worms built a castle here, which Konrad von Hohenstaufen (step-brother of Frederick Barbarossa) chose as his chief residence in 1155. He and his successors enriched the town, which remained the capital of the Rhine Palatinate until the Elector Charles Philipp transferred his capital to Mannheim. In 1802 Heidelberg was incorporated in the Grand Duchy of Baden. Ruprecht I von der Pfalz founded the university in 1386, modelled on that of Paris. The Reformation greatly divided Heidelberg. At the head of the Catholic League, Tilly devastated the town in 1622. Heidelberg was then much damaged in the Thirty Years War, but recovered, especially when Elizabeth Charlotte, the daughter of Elector Karl Ludwig von der Pfalz, married the Duke of Orleans, brother of Louis XIV of France, in 1671. When the electors' line died out in 1685 the French claimed the town, and the struggles over the succession again destroyed much of Heidelberg. The old pattern of streets was retained when rebuilding began.

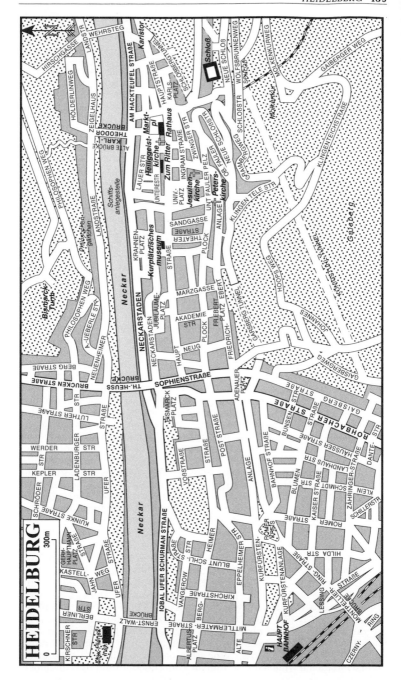

In 1805 Achim von Arnim and Clemens Brentano published here their 'Des Knaben Wunderhorn' ('Child with the Magic Horn'). Friedrich Ebert (1871–1925), first president of the post World War I German republic, was born here. In the inter-war years D.H. Lawrence had a premonition of the bleak future for Germany under the Third Reich when he saw here, 'Students the same, youths with rucksacks the same, boys and maidens in gangs come down from the hills', yet, he added, 'not the same', for they were young Nazis. (Lawrence's report ends presciently *Quos vult perdere Deus, dementat prius*/Whom God wishes to destroy, he first drives mad.)

Yet the city itself escaped injury during World War II, after which it became the US European Military HQ. In summer parts of the new university and the Schloss are used for open-air performances. Heidelberg hosts a glove fair each June.

To reach the Schloss from the modern (1955) main railway station take the tram to Kornmarkt and then the funicular railway. By foot, which takes 35 minutes, follow Neuestrasse from the station, and then take the Friedrich-Ebert-Anlage, crossing Friedrich-Ebert-Platz and leaving right to reach the church of St Peter. The late Gothic **Peterskirche**—15C and 16C, restored 1865, retaining a Romanesque tower from a previous church and housing the university chapel of 1489—contains tombs dating from the 16C to the 19C. The new and old university buildings, incorporating the 13C **Hexen tower** and the '**Domus Wilhelmiana**' of 1712–28 by Johann Adam Breunig, lie to the E.

Follow the arrows above the church to the **··Schloss**, which towers c 80m above the town on a spur of the Königstuhl. Its Rondell, formerly where the artillery was stationed, offers an entrancing view of Heidelberg. Begun in the 14C, this castle was virtually destroyed by the French in 1689 when they evacuated Heidelberg in the face of the approaching German troops. In the 19C a French immigrant, the Count de Graimberg, restored the ruins. (Guided tours 09.00–16.00; a tour takes at least an hour. Gardens open 09.00–dusk.) The oldest surviving parts are 9C granite pillars brought from Charlemagne's palace at Ingelheim and now in the Brunnenhalle. Elector Ruprecht I (1398–1414) added three towers to the east and the Ruprecht building, designed by M. Gertener; note its imperial eagle. All was redone in the Renaissance style in the 16C, with a particularly fine ·fireplace on the second floor. Friedrich II (Elector from 1544–56) commissioned a Hall of Mirrors in 1549, whose architecture is a delicious blend of the Gothic and the Renaissance styles. The library and Frauenzimmer building, or 'Womens' Wing', date from the 16C, along with the first Renaissance palace in Germany, the ·Otteinrichbau ('Otto Heinrich wing'), named after and built by the elector who ruled Heidelberg, 1556–59. This is a part-Italian, part-German, part-Dutch masterpiece, with a doorway designed by Alexandre Colin of Malines (1526–1612). Three-storeyed, partly Ionic in style and partly Corinthian, its façade is decorated with sculptures and medallions. The wing now houses the **Deutsches Apotheken-Museum** (open Apr–Oct 10.00–17.00; Sat, Sun opens at 11.00). Opposite is a monument to the Heidelberg physicist Robert Wilhelm Bunsen (1811–99).

The late Renaissance Friedrich wing was added 1601–07 (by Johann Schoch of Strasbourg), with its statues in niches depicting rulers from Charlemagne to its builder, Elector Friedrich IV; these are replicas of the originals by Sebastian Götz). The three storeys display Doric, Tuscan and Ionic styles. Its rich chapel was restored in 1959. Friedrich V built an 'English Wing' (1612) for his English wife (Elizabeth, daughter of James I). For the 19th birthday of Elizabeth he commissioned the lovely Elizabeth Gate (Elisabethentor). His English gardener laid out an Italian Renaissance garden, the Hortus Palatinus. When the electors claimed a tithe of the annual Palatinate wine harvest, Elector Karl Theodor built the Heidelberg

Tun here, capable of holding 220,000 litres of wine. The tun supports a platform for wine-tasting.

There is a fine view of Heidelberg from the terrace, laid out, like the gardens, under Friedrich V, 1616–19. Descend from here to the Kornmarkt, and on to the Karlstor at the E end of the Hauptstrasse. The **Karlstor** is a classical gate, designed 1775–81 by the French architect Nicolas de Pigage. From here walk back along Hauptstrasse. No. 235 is the **Palais Weimar** by Johann Adam Breunig, c 1715. Housed here is the museum of ethnology, the **Völkerkunde Museum**, displaying the art and culture of non-European people (open weekdays, except Mon, 15.00–17.00, Sun 11.00–13.00). Opposite (Nos 132–4) is the early 18C **Haus Bruhl**, by Johann Jakob Rischer. Nos 207–9 is the **Palais Boiserée** of 1742.

Continue W along Hauptstrasse to the **Marktplatz** with its Baroque **Rathaus**—1701, partly burned down 1909 and restored 1924, with more recent restoration 1960–61. The carved façade is by the Hungarian Heinrich Charrasky, who worked in Heidelberg c 1700–20. Here also stands the 15C Gothic **Heiliggeistkirche**, housing the tomb of Ruprecht III von der Pfalz, d 1410, and his wife Elisabeth von Hohenzollern. The tower was finished in 1544, save for its 1709 summit; the saddle roof dates from 1698. N of the church is the **Fischmarkt**; note the Madonna in the corner of the 18C house at No. 4. In Hauptstrasse, opposite the church, at No. 178 is the *Gasthof **Zum Ritter**, built by a French Huguenot immigrant, Charles Bélier, in 1592. The 'Ritter' on the pediment is St George. A little further on is the early 18C **Jesuitenkirche**, built to the designs of Johann Adam Breunig, finished in 1759, apart from the three upper storeys of the tower, 1868–70. Part of the church now houses the old university library. The Jesuits also built a seminary here (by Breunig, 1715) and a college of 1750–65 by Franz Wilhelm Rabaliatti. At No. 97 is the Baroque **Palais Morass** of 1712, housing the **Kurpfälzisches Museum** of late Gothic religious and secular art, Riemenschneider's **Windsheim altar and local artists (open Tue–Sun 10.00–13.00, and 14.00–17.00). Close by is the **Providenz** church of 1658–61, with a mid 18C tower. No. 52 is the Baroque **Haus Zum Riesen**, 1707, where in 1859 Bunsen and G.R. Kirchoff (1824–87) succeeded in separating the colours of the spectrum. This is now the university museum of geology and palaeontology (open weekdays 09.00–12.00 and containing part of the skull of *Homo heidelbergiensis*).

Return along the Hauptstrasse to the Providenz church and then N to the river bank. E stand the 15C stables and 1510 city arsenal. Further E is the **Brückentor**, a classical gateway of 1768–88, with statues on the pillars of Elector Karl Theodor and the goddess Pallas Athene (by Franz Konrad Linck). The gateway leads onto the **Alte Brücke** (also known as the Karl-Theodor Brücke, from the Brückentor, built for Elector Karl Theodor. Cross the bridge for the **Philosophenweg** (Philosophers' Walk), taking about half an hour on foot, which passes the **Bismarck** monument and the **Heiligen** watch-tower (375m, built 1885), and then climbs to the **Heiligenberg**, with its ruined 11C monastery and 11C basilica of St Michael. A bus also runs from Bismarckplatz to this 440m-high peak.

See also the St Anna-Kirche in Friedrich-Ebert-Anlage, begun 1714 by Johann Adam Breunig, finished 1753 by Franz Wilhelm Rabaliatti, and Friedrich Ebert's home, at No. 18 Pfaffengasse, now a museum with documents relating to his life and a reconstruction of the room in which he was born and spent his youth (open Tues–Sun 10.00–18.00, closing Thu 20.00).

# 11

# Munich

•••**MUNICH**, in German München (1,350,000 inhab.; alt. 520m), situated on a plateau, straddles the River Isar. As Thomas Mann observed, 'At Munich a radiant sky of blue silk looks down on festive squares and white, columned temples, on neo-classical monuments and Baroque churches, on gushing fountains and on the palaces and gardens of the Residenz'.

The city's proximity to the Alps influences its climate, giving the city cold winters and variable summers. The capital of Bavaria and seat of both a Protestant bishop and a Catholic archbishop, Munich has been a university city since 1826—the Ludwig-Maximilians-University today has c 42,000 students, the Technical University more than 16,000. The philosopher F.-W. von Schelling was professor here, 1826–40. Other academics were the scientist Georg Simon Ohm (1787–1854) and the discoverer of X-rays, Wilhelm Conrad Röntgen (1845–1923). Ibsen lived here, 1875–91, and the city saw the first performances of his 'Hedda Gabler' and five other works. Thomas Mann, 1893–1933, who found the city 'scintillating', came to Munich after the death of his father in 1891, wrote here his 'Death in Venice' and in 1933 left for exile in France and then Switzerland. Lenin lived in Munich from 1900 to 1902. The Munich 'Blaue Reiter' artists included Franz Marc, Paul Klee and Wassily Kandinsky. Richard Strauss was musical director at Munich, 1895–98.

Annual festivals include **Fasching** (7 January to Ash Wednesday with the main events, on the Sunday before Lent, taking place between Karlstor and Marienplatz, and on Shrove Tuesday in the Viktualienmarkt) and the feast of **Corpus Christi**, both occasions of notable celebrations. The Catholic churches have a joint act of worship followed by processions in Marienplatz on the second Sunday after Whitsun. Marienplatz is also the site of Munich's 600-year-old **Christkindlmarkt**, whose stalls sell Christmas decorations, presents, carvings of the Christmas crèche, mulled wine and punch. Operas, concerts, ballet and theatre create the '**Festspielzeit**' of July and August, with performances by the Munich Philharmonic orchestra.

Munich's celebrated **Oktoberfest** takes place in October on the Theresienwiese and lasts 16 days, during which four million litres of beer, 720,000 barbecued chickens, 70 or so roast oxen and over 320,000 pairs of pork sausages are consumed by over five million guests. The festival was initiated in 1810 with the celebrations for the marriage of Crown-Prince Ludwig and Therese von Sachsen-Hildburghausen. Today the event begins on Saturday with a parade of decorated beer-floats and bands, followed the next day by a 6.5km-long parade with participants in oldfashioned costumes typifying not only Bavaria but also the rest of Germany and neighbouring countries. When the Bürgermeister of Munich taps open the first barrel, he cries in the local dialect 'Ozapft is!' to declare the Oktoberfest open. (Contact the tourist office, tel. 239 12 66.) Other beer festivals, for which particularly strong beer is brewed, are the Starkbierzeit in March and the Maibock in May.

**Beer** in Munich is sold in measures of a 'Quartel' or 'Schoppen' (c ¼ litre), 'eine Halbe' (c ½ litre) and 'die Mass' (c 1 litre). The city has six major breweries: Augustiner Brewery, 35 Landsbergerstrasse, Hacker-Pschorr

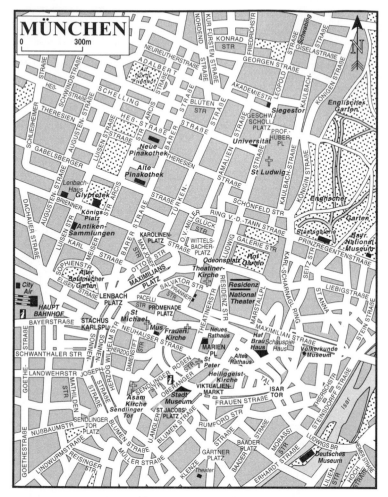

Brewery, 34 Bayerstrasse, Löwenbräu Brewery, 4 Nymphenburgerstrasse, Hofbräuhaus in Haidhausen Brewery, 6 Innere Wienerstrasse, Spaten-Franziskaner Brewery, 46–48 Marsstrasse and Paulaner-Salvator-Thomas-bräu Brewery, 75 Hochstrasse. All which welcome visitors who make prior appointments.

The city's main **markets** are the Viktualienmarkt (see below), the Pasingermarkt (Bäckerstrasse), the Haidhausermarkt (Wienerplatz) and the Schwabingermarkt (Elisabethplatz).

**Main railway station**: Bahnhofsplatz. **Main post offices**: inside the main railway station, 1 Bahnhofsplatz; 2 Residenzstrasse; Airport. **Tourist Information**: in the railway station complex on Bayerstrasse, open 08.00–23.00 daily, tel. 23 91 256; at the airport entrance hall, open Mon–Sat 08.30–22.00, tel. 90 72 56, and in the Rathaus, open Mon–Fri 09.00–17.00, tel. 23 91 272. Tourist offices and many hotels distribute a free monthly magazine in English ('Munich Found'), and the Theater-Fibel gives monthly details of theatre and music in the city. The Fremdenverkehrsamt, Zimmer-vermittlung, Postfach 8000, München 1, will arrange hotel reservations by post, and there are accommodation bureaux at the airport and at the main railway station.

**Transport**: The city has an excellent underground railway integrated with a bus and tramway system. Munich's newly built airport is called Munich 2 (and also Munich Franz Joseph Strauss; flight information tel. 975 213 13). Expensive taxis ferry passengers to the city's main railway station, along with a much cheaper airport bus, which runs at 20-minute intervals. The journey by road can take half-an-hour—or much longer, depending on the traffic. The most reliable, speedy transport (taking around 40 minutes) is by S-Bahn 8, whose trains run every 20 minutes between the airport and Munich's main railway station.

**Banks** open on weekdays 10.30–12.30, 13.45–16.00; Thu extension until 17.30. Money can be changed at the main railway station 16.30–23.00 (as well as at post offices, and at the airport from 17.00–20.30). **Train information** and tickets are obtainable opposite platform 20. **Shops** in Munich open Mon–Fri, 08.30–18.30, almost all closing on Sat at 14.00.

**History**. The capital of Bavaria makes its first appearance in the early 12C. Its monastic origins have bequeathed the figure of a monk (St Benno) to the city's arms. Duke Henry the Lion (Heinrich der Löwer) fortified a monastic village here in the mid 12C, bridged the River Isar and exploited a salt market which had developed early in that century. Count Otto of Wittelsbach took possession of Bavaria in 1180, and after Ludwig II had granted the city a town charter in 1253 the Wittelsbachs settled permanently in Munich. Emperor Ludwig the Bavarian (Ludwig der Bayer) built another ring of walls and the present city gates between 1285 and 1315, and the imposing Frauenkirche built in the second half of the 15C indicates the growing importance of the city and its bourgeoisie. In the next century the Dukes of Bavaria set about extending their Munich Residenz. Munich suffered greatly during the Thirty Years War and was occupied by Gustavus Adolphus of "Sweden in 1632. The citizens paid the Swedes 300,000 Reichsthalers to prevent their troops from sacking their city. Then the plague years took off a third of the whole population.

Revival came in the 18C under the patronage of the court, with the city taking on first an Italianate aspect, under the influence of the architects Enrico Zuccalli and Agostino Barelli, and then a French aspect, especially influenced by François de Cuvilliés. Johann Michael Fischer and the Asam brothers helped to transform Munich into a Baroque gem. After Napoleon Bonaparte had entered Munich in 1805 and raised Bavaria to a kingdom the following year, the monarchs decided to make the city a capital worthy of their new status. King Maximilian I (1806–25, formerly the Elector Max Joseph) and King Ludwig I (reigned 1825–48, abdicated in the face of the scandal caused by his relationship with Lola Montez and died 1868) developed and extended the city, opening out wide streets and squares outside the medieval walls, such as Ludwigstrasse and Königsplatz. The neo-classical architect Leo von Klenze (1784–1864) built most of Ludwigstrasse and extended the Residenz. Along with Berlin, Munich in consequence boasts the finest of Germany's 19C architecture, and von Klenze's legacy was augmented by the buildings of the Romanticist architect Friedrich Gärtner (1792–1847). Ludwig II patronised Richard Wagner, who lived here from 1864 to 1865. When Ludwig II was drowned in 1886, Prince Luitpold, acting as regent from 1886 to 1912 for Ludwig's mad brother Otto, put through an impressive scheme of civic building and design, creating Prinzregentenstrasse and the city museum. In 1918 his son Ludwig III was forced to abandon his throne by Munich revolutionaries, who set up a short-lived Socialist republic the following year.

In the same year the Nazis established their headquarters in Munich. Hitler at-tempted and failed to seize power here in 1923. Ten years later the brownshirts were in control of Germany, and in 1928 the Führer met Chamberlain, Mussolini and Daladier in Munich, securing their agreement to Germany's annexation of Sudeten-land. The city was savagely bombed in World War II, suffering no fewer than 66 raids which cost Munich 60 per cent of its buildings. The city has since been substantially restored, the centre virtually traffic-free. Munich staged the Summer Olympics of 1972. Post World War II buildings include Wassili Luckhardt's Social Insurance Building, 1959, Otto Kirchenhofer's Centre for Atomic Research, 1959 and Gustav Grassener's

Protestant church of St Matthäus, 1944–45. Bavarian state radio and TV are based in Munich.

# A. Bahnhofsplatz to the Alte Pinakothek

From **Bahnhofsplatz**, Luisenstrasse leads NE from in front of the main railway station towards Alte Pinakothek (see below), crossing Elisenstrasse and reaching Karlstrasse. Turn right here for half a kilometre to find on the left the basilica of **St Bonifaz**, by Georg Friedrich Ziebland, 1835–47, who had been sent to Italy by Ludwig I to study early Christian architecture. St Bonifaz is a columned basilica with five naves supported by 66 columns of grey Tyrolese marble, the whole modelled on San Paolo fuori le mura, Rome, which was built for the Emperor Constantine in 390. Inside is Ludwig I's grey marble mausoleum. In the vault below rests his queen, who died in 1854.

Return to Luisenstrasse and turn right to reach the **Alte Botanischer Garten**, so-called to distinguish it from the 'new' botanical garden of Schloss Nymphenburg. The garden was created by Ludwig von Sckell between 1808 and 1814, and completely remodelled in the 1930s. Its neo-classical entrance is by Emanuel Josef von Herigoyen, 1812, and inside citizens and visitors can rest on seats set out around a Baroque fountain of Neptune designed in 1937 by Joseph Wackerle.

No. 33 Luisenstrasse is the **Städtische Galerie im Lenbachhaus**, a golden-yellow building of 1887–91 with a charming formal garden and sunken lake, designed in the style of a Florentine Renaissance villa for the painter Franz von Lenbach (1836–1904) by Gabriel von Seidl, assisted by Lenbach himself. Lenbach was celebrated for his portraits of leading contemporaries, and the gallery, open Tue–Sun 09.00–16.30, houses many of his works. The collection also ranges from the Middle Ages but includes mostly 19C and 20C Munich artists: Karl Spitzweg (1808–85), Wilhelm Leibl (1844–1900), Johann Georg Dillis (1759–1841), Wilhelm Kobell 1766–1829), and also works by Wassily Kandinsky (1966–1944; some 1000 paintings are housed here), Franz Marc (1880–1916), a Blue Horse of 1911, August Macke (1887–1914), Lovis Corinth (1858–1925) and other members of Die Blaue Reiter school. Lenbach's own rooms remain intact, displaying his furnishings and his own paintings. The north wing, added by Hans Grässl, 1927–29, houses changing exhibitions.

Continue along Luisenstrasse to the impressive **Königsplatz**, which Leo von Klenze laid out for Ludwig I, following an original conception of Karl von Fischer. On the north side of the square at No. 3, Leo von Klenze built the neo-classical **Glypothek** for Ludwig, 1816–30, after a design by Carl von Fischer. Restored by Josef Wiedemann, 1972, it opens Tue–Sun 10.00–16.30; Thu 12.00–20.30, displaying Greek and Roman ˙sculpture, including statues by Praxiteles, a torso of Apollo by Polyclitus and two sets of 5C BC sculptures depicting the struggles between the Trojans and the Greeks which came from the temple of Aphaia at Aegina. Discovered in fragments in 1811, these were restored for Ludwig I by the Danish sculptor Bertel Thorwaldsen.

On the opposite side of the square at No. 1 stands the **Staatliche Antikensammlung**. The building was designed by G.F. Ziebland, 1838–48, to house the royal collection of Classical art (open Tue–Sun 10.00–16.30; Wed also 12.00–20.30). The frescoes in the upper storey are by Carl Rottmann; on display are Greek, Etruscan and Roman treasures, mostly derived from the collection of Ludwig I. On the western side of the square stands the **Propyläen** 1854–62, modelled on the Acropolis by Leo von Klenze. In the gable are sculptures, by Ludwig Schwanthaler, honouring King Otto of Greece—the son of Ludwig I, who was elected king in 1832 and expelled in 1862—and the Greek struggle against Turkey.

This is an area of great public galleries. From Königsplatz turn right along Briennerstrasse, which was laid out by Karl von Fischer in 1808 and completed by Leo von Klenze, to the junction of Arcisstrasse and Meiserstrasse. Immediately to your right at 10 Meiserstrasse is the **Haus der Kulturinstitut**, which houses the **Staatliche Graphische Sammlung** (opens Mon–Fri 09.00–13.00, 14.00–16.30). Founded in Mannheim in 1758 by the Elector Karl Theodor, it was transferred to Munich in 1794. It displays over 300,000 14–20C European prints and drawings, including works by German Expressionists, and masterpieces by Rembrandt (1606–69), Paul Klee (1879–1940) and Ernst Ludwig Kirchner (1880–1938). It also houses the Central Institute for Art History, with an extensive library, and visitors can gain access to a collection of casts made from antique sculpture (admission Tue–Sun 10.00–16.30, Thu 12.00–20.30). Opposite is the Musikhochschule venue of the fateful meeting in 1938—when it was the Braunhaus, the local Nazi headquarters—between Hitler, Daladier, Chamberlain and Mussolini. Further NE, along Arcisstrasse, the continuation of Meiserstrasse, you reach on the left the Technical University and on the right first the Alte Pinakothek and then the Neue Pinakothek.

The ••**Alte Pinakothek** at 27 Barerstrasse (open Tue–Sun 09.00–16.30, Tue–Thu 19.00–21.00). Built by Leo van Klenze, 1826–36—rebuilt under the supervision of Hans Döllgarr, 1952–57) in the Venetian classical style—to house the Wittelsbach collection. This was enriched by Herzog Wilhelm IV (1493–1550), Elector Maximilian I (1597–1651, who contributed the Dürers), Elector Max Emmanuel (1679–1726, who contributed 12 works by Rubens and 15 by Van Dyck) and Ludwig I (1825–48, whose chief legacy consists of the Raphaels, Murillos and Titians). The collection was further enriched by the purchase in 1827 of works rescued by the brothers Sulpiz and Melchior Boisserée from Cologne churches and convents after their suppression at the beginning of the 19C. Although the Alte Pinakothek was burnt out during World War II, the magnificent collection had been removed to a place of safety and survives intact. Though occasional variations in the hanging occur, the collection principally consists of: **Ground floor Rooms I–III and 1–10**: early German painting, many of the works derived from churches and monasteries after the secularisation of 1806, though also including several portraits, including Count Philip the Warlike of the Palatinate by Hans Baldung Grien (1517). Here are also an •altarpiece by Michel Pacher depicting the four church fathers, with on the wings scenes from the life of St Wolfgang (c 1475), and a Crucifixion by Lucas Cranach the Elder (1503). **Rooms XI–XIII and 19–23**: 16C and 17C Netherlandish paintings, including works by Jan Breughel the Elder and Pieter Breughel the Elder (especially The Land of Cockayne, 1567) and an Altar of the Crucifixion by Hans Burgmaier (1519).

**Upper floor Rooms I–IIa**: early Netherlandish paintings, including an •Altarpiece of the Magi by Roger van der Weyden (c 1460) and works by Hans Memling (The Seven Joys of Mary, 1480) and Dirk Bouts, as well as a Madonna by Lucas van Leyden and Jan Gossaert's Danae (1527). These paintings come from a collection bought by Ludwig I in 1827. **Rooms II–III**:

early German paintings, a collection based partly on the acquisitions of the Wittelsbachs and partly on treasures derived fom the secularisation of the churches in 1806. They include The Battle of Alexander the Great by Albrecht Altdorfer (1529), two panels depicting the **Four Apostles by Albrecht Dürer (his last work, 1529), as well as a self-portrait in a fur coat (c 1500?), and A Disputation between SS Erasmus and Maurice by Matthias Grünewald (early 16C).

**Rooms IV–V–XXIb and 1–6, 23**: Italian painting, a collection built up by Crown Prince Ludwig under the influence of the Nazarenes. It includes Raphael's Casa Tempi Madonna (c 1507), his Canigiani Holy Family (1506) and a Virgin and Child by Leonardo da Vinci. The Wittelsbach collection contributed an unfinished painting by Titian of Christ crowned with thorns (done when the artist was over 90) and his portrait of the Emperor Charles V (1548), while an Adoration of the Magi by Giovanni Battista Tiepolo (1753) came from the monastery of Münsterschwarzach outside Würzburg. **Room 11**: 16C and 17C German painting includes works by Johann Rottenhammer (1564–1625) and Adam Elsheimer (1578–1610). **Rooms VI–VIII and 7–10, 12**: *Flemish painting, a superb collection, based on 101 paintings acquired in 1698 by Elector Max Emanuel when he was governor of the Netherlands. These include 12 paintings by Rubens and 15 by Anthony Van Dyck. The collection was further enriched in 1806 when paintings belonging to the Palatine branch of the Wittelsbachs were transferred from Düsseldorf to Munich, bringing here for instance Rubens's portrait of himself and his first wife Isabella Brant, painted shortly after their marriage in 1609. In these rooms hang also Rubens's Drunken Silenus (begun 1618), portrait of Helene Fourment and her son (c 1635), Castor and Pollux carrying off the daughters of King Leucippus (1618) and Lion hunt, painted with the help of Van Dyck (c 1617).

**Rooms IX and 13–22**: Dutch painting, including a Descent from the Cross (one of five, all here, commissioned by the Calvinist Prince Frederick Henry of Orange in 1632) and a self-portrait, aged 23 (1629), by Rembrandt. Here also are a portrait of the merchant Willem van Heythusen by Frans Hals (1629) and works by Holland's second great genre painter Jan Steen (1626–79). **Rooms XI–XIIa**: French painting, including a Lamentation by Nicolas Poussin, a Seaport at Sunrise by Claude Lorrain (1674) and among several works by François Boucher, a portrait of Louis XV's mistress Madame de Pompadour and an erotic nude lying on her stomach (1752), said to be a portrait of another of Louis XV's mistresses, Louisa O'Murphy. **Room XII**: Spanish painting, the finest collection in Germany, which includes a Disrobing of Christ by El Greco (1577–79), five genre paintings by Bartolomé Esteban Murillo, beginning with his Melon and grape eaters (1645), and an unfinished Portrait of a young nobleman by Diego Velázquez (undated, bought for the Elector Palatine in 1694).

# B.   Neue Pinakothek to Karlsplatz

To the N of the Alte Pinakothek, at 29 Barerstrasse, stands the **Neue Pinakothek**, the home of Munich's main collection of 19C and 20C art (open Tue 09.00–21.00, Wed–Sun 09.00–16.30; the Sun and Tue of Fasching and 31 Dec 09.00–12.00). In 1809 Crown Prince Ludwig bought his first modern painting, the Penitent Magdalen by H.F. Füger. Twenty years later Ludwig I began a systematic collection of contemporary art, which he enriched in

1841 by buying over a 100 contemporary paintings which had been acquired by Leo von Klenze. In 1846 the foundation stone of the Neue Pinakothek was laid, to provide a home for these works. The building, designed by August von Voit, was finished in 1853. Of its directors the most discerning was Hugo Tschudi (appointed 1909), who between 1911 and 1913 raised private finance to buy important works by, among others, Gauguin, van Gogh, Manet, Monet and Cézanne. The Neue Pinakothek was destroyed by bombing in 1944 and 1945, but the pictures had been transferred elsewhere for safety. They now hang in a building of 1975–81 by Alexander Freiherr von Branca.

As with the Alte Pinakothek, the pictures on display in the Neue Pinakothek are not invariably hung in the same rooms, but the usual order is as follows: **Rooms 1, 2, 2a**: international art c 1800, including a portrait of Marquise de Sorcy de Thélusson by Jacques-Louis David (1790), a Landscape by Thomas Gainsborough (1783) and Francisco Goya's Outing in the Country (c 1788). **Rooms 3, 3a**: Early Romanticism, with paintings by Caspar David Friedrich (Landscape in the Riesengebirge, c 1800) and his colleague and friend Kersting (Woman sewing by the light of a lamp, 1825), as well as a Landscape by the Tegernsee by Wilhelm von Kobell (1833) and Joseph Karl Stieler's celebrated portrait of Goethe (1828). **Rooms 5, 5a**: German neo-classicists in Rome. **Room 6**: the Georg Schäfer collection, with works of the early German Romantics and Biedermeer paintings. **Room 7**: works by the Nazarenes, of which the most important painting is Italia and Germania by Friedrich Overbeck (1828). **Rooms 8, 9**: Biedermeier paintings, including The visit by Moritz von Schwind (c 1852) and The awaited one by Georg Waldmüller (1860). **Rooms 10, 10a**: French late Romantics and Realists, a collection which includes a Heroic Landscape by Théodore Géricault (1816–17), Lake Garda near Riva by Jean-Baptiste-Camille Corot (1835), Clorinde rescuing Olindo and Sophronia from the stake by Eugène Delacroix (1854–55), Le Greffeur by Jean-François Millet (1855), The drama by Honoré Daumier (c 1860) and A sluice near Optevoz by Gustave Courbet (c 1860). **Rooms 11, 11a**: German late Romantics and Realists, including the Poor poet by Karl von Spitzweg (1839) and Living room with the artist's sister by Adolph von Menzel (1847). **Room 12**: the drawings for a series of frescoes by Wilhelm von Kaulbach which in 1853 were painted by Friedrich Christoph Nilson as a frieze around the upper storey of the original Neue Pinakothek.

**Rooms 13, 13a**: historical paintings of the Second Empire (the 'Gründerzeit'), including Seni with the corpse of Wallenstein by Karl von Piloty (1855). **Rooms 14, 14a**: the 'Gründerzeit', social representations by Franz von Lenbach, Albert von Keller, Hans Makart. Mihaly von Munkacsy and others, including The last volunteers by Franz Defregger (1872). **Room 15**: 19 works by the intensely mythological Hans von Marées, given to the Neue Pinakothek by his patron, Konrad Fiedler, in 1891. **Room 16**: paintings by Arnold Böcklin (Pan among the reeds, 1859), Anselm Feuerbach (Medea, 1870) and Hans Thoma. **Room 17**: Wilhelm Leibl and his circle, a group which helped to bring into German paintings the insights of the French Impressionists.

**Room 18**: French Impressionists, including a Bridge over the Seine at Argenteuil by Claude Monet (1874), a Woman ironing by Edgar Degas (1869) and Édouard Manet's Breakfast in the studio (1868–69). **Room 19**: Paul Cézanne, Vincent Van Gogh and Paul Gauguin, including a Railway cutting by Cézanne (1870), a View of Arles by Van Gogh (1889) and The Nativity by Gauguin (1896). **Rooms 20, 21**: Social Realism and German

Impressionism, including Woman with goats by Max Liebermann (1890) and a portrait of Eduard Graf von Keyserling by Lovis Corinth (1900). **Room 21a**: the Munich Secessionists, who came together in 1892, the first of a succession of groups of artists (including artists in Vienna and Berlin) who 'seceded' from the official academies. **Rooms 22, 22a**: Symbolism and Jugendstil (Art Nouveau), with works by Gustav Klimt (portrait of Margarethe Stonborough-Wittgenstein, 1905), the Belgian Fernand Khnopff (I lock my door upon myself, a painting based on a poem by Christina Rossetti, 1891) and Max Klinger.

Leaving the gallery walk SW along Barerstrasse (E of the Neue Pinokathek) through **Karolinenplatz**, in the centre of which rises a bronze obelisk erected in 1833 to the designs of Leo von Klenze and commissioned by Ludwig I in honour of Bavarian soldiers killed fighting against Russia. From here Max-Joseph-Strasse leads SE to the rectangular **Maximiliansplatz**, with tree-shaded statues in a garden created by Karl von Effner, the Wittelsbach fountain, 1895, by Adolf von Hildebrandt and the Norwen fountain by Hubert Netzner, 1907. The statues are of the chemist Julius Liebig (died 1873), by Ferdinand Wagmüller, and the hygienist Max von Pettenkofer (died 1901), by W. Ruemann. This is the area of fashionable shops, particularly clothes, footwear and art, with antique shops in Ottostrasse. At the NE side of Maximiliansplatz the bust of Schiller by Ferdinand Miller, 1863, looks out across Briennerstrasse to the Almeida-Palais (by Métivier, 1824, its classical façade restored after World War II). Across Briennerplatz is the Bavarian Kulturministerium.

Return along Maximiliansplatz to Max-Joseph-Strasse. Across the square a classical gateway leads into Prannerstrasse, and its antique shops. On the right-hand side stand the Rococo **Palais Guise** by Karl Albert Lespilliez, c 1760, and the Rococo **Palais Sensheim** (architect unknown, again c 1760). On the left hand side at No. 10 is the fascinating **Siemens Museum**, exhibiting the history of the communications and electrical engineering company, open weekdays 09.00–16.00, weekends 10.00–14.00. No. 2 Prannerstrasse is the Rococo **Palais Preysing** by François Cuvilliés the elder (c 1750).

Turn into **Kardinal-Faulhaberstrasse**, named after a doughty opponent of Adolf Hitler, to find the **Palais Porcia**, commissioned by the Fugger family from Enrico Zuccalli in 1697, with a façade by Cuvilliés, c 1731. Retrace your steps S along Kardinal-Faulhaberstrasse past the Rococo **Erzbishöfliches-Palais**. Its Cuvilliés façade was enriched by Johann Baptist Zimmermann. 1733–37, and the building has been occupied by the archbishops since 1818. Beyond it is Salvatorplatz and the **Salvatorkirche** with its six-storey tower (1494, by Lukas Rottaler—Jörg von Halspach's successor as city architect) built as a cemetery chapel attached to the cathedral and used by Greek Orthodox Christians since 1829.

Walk E from Salvatorplatz to **Theatinerstrasse**, filled with more elegant clothes and leather shops, shoeshops and art dealers, and turn right to find the **Theatinerkirche** or parish church of St Cajetan. It was built for Theatine monks as a thanks offering for the birth in 1662 to the Electress Henrietta Adelaide of Savoy of an heir to the throne, Crown Prince Max Emmanuel. Work began in 1663 under the Italian Agostino Barelli, to be continued in 1674 by Enrico Zuccalli, who built the dome and the towers—the whole inspired by the church of S Andrea della Valle in Rome. François Cuvilliés the elder added the Rococo façade in 1765–68. Anton Boos designed the marble figures of SS Cajetan, Adelheid, Ferdinand and Maximilian.

Inside, the elaborate stucco work is by Nicolo Petri (1685–86); the three chief altars are by Barelli; the pulpit is by Andreas Faistenberger (1681); the Lady altar with a painting of the Holy Family was designed by Carlo Cignani in 1676. The St Cajetan altar (with a painting of the saint interceding during a plague at Naples), designed by Joachim Sandrart in 1671, stands in the south transept. Here are buried many Electors (including Ferdinand Maria, husband of the foundress), King Max I, King Otto of Greece, Crown Prince Ruprecht and Prince Regent Luitpold. Dominican monks now live in the Theatiner monastery, next to the church.

A few metres further S along Theatinerstrasse rise the Feldherrnhalle and the Preysing-Palais. The **Feldherrnhalle** is by Andreas Gärtner, 1840–44, inspired by the Loggia dei Lanzi, Florence. Its bronze statues of General Tilly (Bavarian general in the Thirty Years War) and Count Wrede (who fought in the campaign of 1814) were designed by Ludwig von Schwanthaler; between them is a memorial, 1892, by Ferdinand von Miller to the Bavarian dead in the Franco-Prussian War of 1870–71. The Rococo **Preysing-Palais** at 27 Residenzstrasse, situated behind the Feldherrnhalle, was built by Joseph Effner for Graf Maximilian von Preysing, 1723–28. The first Rococo palace of Munich, today it retains from the original building only the façades along Residenzstrasse and Viscardistrasse.

Follow Theatinerstrasse, turning right into **Maffeistrasse**, with similar establishments to Theatainerstrasse and pedestrianised (save for trams). Passing under the arch of the Bayerische Vereinsbank you reach **Promenadeplatz**, for which Ludwig I commissioned statues of Orlando di Lasso (1839), Christoph Wilhelm von Gluck (1850) and Max Emanuel, Kurfürst of Bavaria (1861). To the S of the square stands the **Gunetzrhainerhaus**, which the court architect J.B. Gunetzrhainer built for himself in 1733.

To the W in Pacellistrasse—another street of art dealers—stands Munich's oldest Baroque church, the **Karmeliterkirche** (the former Carmelite church), which was begun in 1654 to plans by the court architect H.K. Asper. Its classical façade was added 1802–22 by N. Schedel von Greiffenstein. The adjoining monastery was destroyed in World War II and the deconsecrated church is now a library. Beyond it, at the other side of Pacellistrae, is the **Dreifaltigkeitskirche** of 1718, the church of the Holy Trinity. The city paid for the building of this church, designed in the Italian Baroque style by Johann Georg Ettenhofer and Enrico Zuccalli to plans of Giovanni Antonio Viscardi. Inside, the dome fresco, depicting the Trinity in glory, is by Cosmas Damian Asam, 1715, the stucco by Johann Georg Bader, 1715, the tabernacle relief of the high altar by J.B. Straub, 1760. Building was prompted by a woman named Anna Lindmayr who predicted great misfortune unless the Holy Trinity were thus honoured. In the gable is a bronze statue of St Michael by J. Fichtl, 1726.

Pacellistrasse leads on into **Lenbachplatz**, SW of which is **Karlsplatz**—known to the citizens of Munich as the 'Stachus', the nickname of Eustachius Föderl who ran a Gasthaus here from the mid 18C. The square today houses a shopping centre. In creating this square Elector Karl Theodor demolished part of the city walls and filled in the moat. The city courts of justice—late Renaissance style, by Friedrich von Thiersch, 1891–97—are on the N side of the square. Close by is another gate of the old Botanical Garden, by Emanuel Joseph von Herigoyen, 1812.

# C. Karlsplatz to the Theresienwiese

Continue to the modern fountain in Karlsplatz and by way of the 1302 **Karlstor**, the former W gate of the city. Much restored, it was Gothicised in 1791. Passing a comical fountain of a Herm spitting on a naked boy, once through the gate you enter the extremely lively pedestrian zone. E along Neuhauserstrasse stands the **Bürgersaal**, a Baroque and Rococo church which was built for the Marianists by Georg Ettenhofer, to plans by Giovanni Antonio Viscardi in 1709–10. The Madonna on a crescent moon over the doorway is by Andreas Fainstenberger. Inside, to see the building from the best vantage point, climb the stairs. The Bürgersaal is adorned by frescoes by Johann Anton Gumpp (18C, restored 1971–80); a Baroque oratory; statues of angels (under the organ) by Ignaz Günther (1762); and 14 oil paintings of Bavarian pilgrimage sites dedicated to the Virgin Mary, by Franz Joachim Bleich, 1719. An Annunciation by Ignaz Günther remains from the bombed high altar by Andreas Faistenberger, who also designed the silver bust on the altar. The Marienaltar is by Franz Dexler, c 1925. Look out for the memorial to the Jesuit priest and resistance hero Fr. Rupert Mayer, who died in Sachsenhausen concentration camp in 1945 and was beatified in 1987. He is buried in the vault.

Further E, at No. 51, is the **Alte Akademie**, which was built as a school and seminary for the Jesuits by the architect Friedrich Sustris between 1585 and 1597. It became successively the university and the city library. Restored after World War II, it has a *Renaissance façade. In front is the sensual **Richard-Strauss-Brunnen**, sculpted in bas-relief by Hans Wimmer in 1962 and depicting the composer's opera 'Salome'. On the opposite side of Neuhauserstrasse, just before you reach the Salome fountain, rises the **Augustiner-Bräu-Auschank**, founded in 1803. Its restaurant is dated 1897.

Immediately E in Neuhauserstrasse stands **Michaelskirche**, built for the Jesuits by Herzog Wilhelm V, 1583–90, and modelled in part on the church of the Gesù, Rome. In part Renaissance, later transformed in the Baroque style, its first architects were Wendel Dietrich and Wolfgang Müller. The tower fell down in 1590, ruining the choir, and the reconstruction was effected by Sustris; the façade was restored in 1972. The sculpture (restored) on the gable depicts Christ presiding over Otto's victory at the Lech in 955, with portraits of successive emperors and dukes of Bavaria, including the founder, in the second row of figures, third from right, holding a model of the church. Between the main doors the bronze Archangel Michael killing the dragon is by Hubert Gerhardt, cast by Martin Frey, 1592; the angel on the stoop inside is also by Gerhardt, same date.

Inside, a massive Renaissance barrel vault—the largest in Europe after St Peter's in Rome—shelters ten altars; the high altar is by Wendel Dietrich, 1586–89, its painting by Christoph Schwarz, 1587; in the right transept is a crucifixion from the school of Giambologna; the pulpit dates from 1610. Here too is a memorial to Eugène de Beauharnais (Napoleon's stepson and the son-in-law of Max I Joseph) by Bertel Thorwaldsen, 1830, and in the vault are the tombs of 40 Wittelsbachs. They include Wilhelm V who commissioned this church; the tomb base has four statues representing Bavaria, Franconia, Schwabia and the Rhineland Palatinate, over which he ruled.

E of St Michael's church, at No. 53, is the former Augustinerkirche. This Gothic Augustinian monastery church was first built 1291–94, outside the city walls, enlarged in the 14C and 15C and again 1618–21. Deconsecrated in 1803, it has housed the **Deutsches Jagd-und-Fischereimuseum** since 1966, filled with hunting and fishing memorabilia (open daily, May–Oct 09.30–17.00). Its walls also shelter shops selling coffee, cakes, watches and tobacco.

Augustinerstrasse curves left into Frauenplatz, where rises the red brick Dom and city parish church of Our Lady, the **\*\*Frauenkirche**, in front of which is a fountain constructed from blocks of granite in 1972 by Bernhard Winkler. Duke Sigismund laid the first stone of this late Gothic building in 1468, on the site of a demolished Romanesque basilica. The architect was Jörg von Halspach (known as Ganghofer), replaced after his death in 1488 by Lukas Rottaler. The copper-capped towers (99m and 100m high, with an elevator in the south tower) were finished in 1525. Tombstones from the old cemetery are incorporated in the walls. All five doorways are by Ignaz Günther (1770s). The main, west doorway incorporates statues of Christ and a Madonna, c 1340, from the former basilica; the Arsatius doorway (first on south side) has a 15C statue of St Rasso; the Bride's doorway (also south side) carries statues of Christ and Mary, 1430; the Benno doorway (opposite, north side) has 15C statues of Christ and Mary and (inside) one of St Sebastian by Andreas Faistenberger; the Sixtus doorway (west end of north side) has a 16C statue of St George. The cathedral's eight bells, date from 1441 to 1958.

The interior (restored 1980–81 after war damage), is lofty, wide (41.5m) and long (109m), its three aisles, each 31m high, separated by two rows of eleven octagonal columns, with \*statues by Erasmus Grasser on the third one from the east end, 1502. The choir has stained glass—the finest, the middle window by Peter Hemmel of Andlau, 1493—while the window depicting the Annunciation dates from 1392 and the Three Kings window from 1430. The restored \*choir stalls were designed by Erasmus Grasser in 1502. The whole cathedral is crammed with artistic treasures: a splendid wooden statue of St Christopher of 1520 at the west end; a bas-relief of a Lamentation by Hans Krumper, 1618; the \*memorial tomb of Emperor Ludwig the Bavarian in the S aisle, designed by Peter Candid and Hans Krumper, 1619–22; bronze allegorical figures and statues of Wittelsbachs by H. Gerhardt and D. Frey, c 1595; the cross in the middle nave by Josef Henselmann, 1954; the pulpit by Blasius Spreng, 1957.

Statues and memorials in the side chapels, beginning east of the Arsatius doorway include the tombstone of J.M. Fischer; in the third chapel east of the doorway, the patron saint of bakers, 16C; next east, a mid 17C carving of the Magi; east of the Bride's doorway is the baptistery; the next but one chapel houses the Ligsalz tombstone of 1360; the chapel to the right of the high altar has a mid 15C crucifixion. On the high altar the depiction of the Virgin Mary sheltering Christians under her cloak is by Jan Pollack c 1500; left of the high altar you find a baptism of Jesus, c 1510; east of the Benno doorway is a 1620 Assumption; west of the Benno doorway the painting of Christ with his crown of thorns dates from 1640. Next west is the tombstone of the first priest of the new Frauenkirche, 1520; the north chapel at the west end has a Mariahilf altar, c 1475; and the monument to Julius Cardinal Döpfner by Hans Wimmer, 1981, is in the former Appolonia chapel. In the northern tower chapel is stained glass by Richard Holzner, 1931.

In the pavement under the organ loft is a shallow imprint, said to be that of the devil's foot. The crypts (entered behind the choir stalls) shelter tombs of archbishops of Munich and of Wittelsbachs (from the son of Ludwig the Bavarian to Albrecht V), as well as of the last King of Bavaria, Ludwig III.

Return to the Alte Akademie and cross Neuhauserstrasse to follow **Damen-stiftstrasse** SE. No. 1 is the St Anna-Kirche, built in 1733 by the Gunetzrhainer brothers, its interior sumptuously decorated by the Asam brothers. Among the fine buildings of this part of the city, which is known as the Altes Hackenviertel, two stand in **Herzogspitalstrasse** which leads W from St Anna-Kirche: the **Herzogspitalkirche**, inside which is a wooden statue of the Sorrowing Virgin by T. Pader, 1651, and the former Gregorian seminary at No. 12, 1574, its façade added in 1808. Brunnenstrasse, further S along Damenstifstrasse and then E, leads to 7 Hackenstrasse, once the home of Heinrich Heine, 1827–28, with a classical façade (1817, by Jean-Baptiste Métivier); opposite at No. 110 stands the Rococo façade, 1741, of the former home of Johann Baptist Straub; on the corner of Hackenstrasse and Hotterstrasse is Munich's oldest inn, 'Zur Hundskugel' (1440), deriving its name from the six dogs playing with a ball, over the doorway of the Rococo 10 Hackenstrasse, 1741.

Reaching the corner of Brunnenstrasse, Damenstiftstrasse becomes Kreuzstrasse, named after the **Kreuzkirche** which stands on the right. This brick Gothic church, possibly designed by Ganghofer, has a Rococo interior of 1770 containing a crucifix by H. Leinberger, early 16C, a tabernacle of 1779 from the former Carmelite church, and the 18C so-called Rotenhamm Madonna over the high altar. The church was until recently used by Czech Christians.

Kreuzstrasse meets Herzog-Wilhelmstrasse, where you turn left to reach the **Sendlinger Tor**, an arched gateway flanked by two towers which derives from the 1318 fortifications of Ludwig the Bavarian. Nussbaum-strasse leads SW from Sendlinger Tor to the protestant church of **St Matthäus** (Gustav Grassener, 1954–55).

Continue SW across Kaiser-Ludwig-Platz for a fairly lengthy walk to **Theresienwiese**, scene of the horse race on 17 October 1810 celebrating the marriage of the Crown Prince and inaugurating the annual Munich Oktoberfest still held on this site. On the W side of the Theresienwiese towers the massive figure of **Bavaria**, dressed in a bear skin with a lion at her side, by Ludwig Schwanthaler (1844–50) cast by Ferdinand von Miller; 130 steps inside lead to the statue's eyes and three other lookouts, for fine views of the city. Behind is the huge Hall of Fame, the **Ruhmeshalle**, built in the Doric style by Leo von Klenze 1843–53 and commissioned by Ludwig I, inside which are busts of great Bavarians. On the south side of Theresianwiese rises the Gothic church of **St Pal**, built between 1892 and 1906 by Georg Hauberisser, its spires and walls softly illuminated after dark. Nearby, on the corner of Martin-Greif-Strasse and Schwantaler-strasse, stands the Tudor-style house the architect built for himself in 1878 and 1879. Further on, across Theresienhöhe, is the city exhibition centre (**Messe**). Its 330,000 sq m and 20 halls cope with over 30 annual trade fairs.

# D.   Sendlingertor to the Hofbräuhaus

Return to Sendlingertor. Running NE from Sendlinger Tor, traffic-free **Sendlingerstrasse** houses the church of **••St Johann-Nepomuk**, built in 1733–46 by the Asam brothers at their own expense on their own land—and known as the **Asamkirche**. The Baroque/Rococo façade has portrait medallions of Pope Benedict XIII and Bishop Johann Theodor of Freising.

A statue of St Johannn Nepomuk is over the main door, which is carved with scenes from his life. The oval-shaped entrance hall has Rococo confessionals, one of them decorated with white and winged skulls—one, wrapped with a gilded snake, depicting sinfulness, the other, with a gilded laurel wreath, representing saintliness. The interior is long and narrow, with red stucco marble walls and a high altar, enriched with twisted columns, and a wax model of Johann Nepomuk in a glass sarcophagus, its tabernacle by Roman Anton Boos. On either side are medallions of the architects. In a niche to the left of the high altar is a Virgin Mary by E.Q. Asam. The two angels of the Bruderschaftsaltar in the gallery are by Ignaz Günther, 1767.

To the right of the Asamkirche is the rectory of 1771, designed by E.Q. Asam and completed after his death, to the left a house built for himself by E.Q. Asam in 1733. Its richly stuccoed façade has allegorical figures setting side by side the Ancient world and the Christian world, the whole scene presided over by a figure of the Virgin Mary on a crescent moon. From here through a secret window the architect was able to look into his own church.

Turn right where Sendlingerstrasse meets Hackenstrae to reach Oberanger and **St Jakob's** church, by F. Haindl, 1956, replacing a 13C monastery church. Across the street at 1 Jakobsplatz **Münchner Stadt-museum**, or city museum, in the former Zeughaus (arsenal) of 1526 (open Tue 09.00–16.30, Sun and holidays 10.00–18.00, Thu–Sun 10.00–17.00). It houses photography exhibitions; a film institute; a puppet museum, with 25,000 European puppets; a collection devoted to the history and culture of Munich including ten of the 16 celebrated *Morris Dancers, carved by Erasmus Grasser for the Rathaus, 1480; 200,000 prints of old Munich; a museum of brewing; a collection of musical instruments and 16C music; and a restaurant. N of this is the **Ignaz-Günther-Haus** of 1761, Rococo, on a Gothic base, restored in 1977. Here is a small exhibition devoted to the sculptor Günther.

To reach the **Viktualienmarkt** take Oberanger and turn right into Rosental. In the market square are figures of six Munich theatre artists: Elise Aulinger (1881–1965, by Toni Ruckel); Karl Valentin (1882–1948, by Andreas Rauch); his partner Liesl Karlstadt (1892–1960, by Hans Osel); Weiss Ferdl (1883–1949, by Josef Erber); Ida Schumacher (1895–1956, by Marlene Neubauer-Wörner); and Roider Jackl (1906–75, by Hans Osel).

To the N is **Heiliggeistkirche** (Church of the Holy Spirit), standing where Duke Otto founded a hospital c 1250. This church was rebuilt 1723–30 by Georg Ettenhofer; its Baroque ordering is by the Asam brothers. Almost all of the present church is a restoration, after damage in World War II. The high altar is the work of Nikolas Stuber and Antonio Matteo, 1728–30, the John the Baptist altar (to the right of the high altar) by Matteo. The picture of Christ's baptism is by Melchior Steidl, 1731; other paintings are by Ulrich Loth, 1661; the angels are by J.G. Greiff, 1730. The so-called Hammerthal Madonna, on the middle altar on the north side, dates from the mid 15C and was brought here from a monastery at Tegernsee. The war memorial chapel has a late Gothic crucifix of 1501; and the church houses a copy of a bronze memorial to Herzog Ferdinand by Hans Krumper, 1588.

To the W stands the 90m-long parish church of **St Peter**. One of two claiming the status of oldest parish church in the city (see St Stephan in Berg am Laim, below), the church has a famous 90m-high tower, domed, completed in 1386 and known as Alter Peter with views of the city from its platform (open weekdays 09.00–17.00; Sun 10.00–17.00). St Peter was first a Romanesque church, rebuilt in the late 12C and again, after a catastrophic fire of 1327, in 1368. The interior, with its Baroque choir and Rococo decor, has many masterpieces: the stone Schrenkaltar, 1407; the red marble tomb designed by Erasmus Grasser for Dr Ulrich Aresinger, 1482; a high altar by Nikolaus Stuber of 1720, 20m-tall, with a statue of St Peter carved in wood, 1492, also by Erasmus Grasser; late Gothic altar paintings (now in the presbytery) by Jan Pollack, 1517; a font by Hans Krumper, 1620; a high altar by Nikolas Stuber, 1730; statues of the four doctors of the church, by E.Q. Asam, 1732; and a Corpus-Christi altar by Ignaz Günther, 1770.

E of this church stands the **Isartor**, the east gate of the walls built by Ludwig the Bavarian, restored in 1972. The fresco of Ludwig returning from the battle of Mühldorf in 1322 (when he defeated the Habsburgs) is by Bernhard Neher, 1835. The tower houses a museum devoted to the comedian Karl Valentin (1882–1948; open Mon, Tue, Sat 11.00–17.30, Sun opens 10.00). Continue SE along Zweibrückenstrasse and across Ludwigsbrücke, 1934–35, to find a notice pointing right to the huge **Deutsches Museum**, founded by the scientist and engineer Oskar von Miller (1855–1934) and devoted to 'masterpieces of natural science and technology'. The museum (open daily 09.00–17.00) has a library of nearly 700,000 volumes, mostly of a technical, scientific nature, and is one of greatest scientific/technical museums of the world. Built by Gabriel von Seidl and his brother Emanuel, it opened in 1925 and was restored after World War II. The 'museum island' also encloses a Congress Centre.

Returning to the church of St Peter, pass through the Isartor into **Marien-platz**. Here are both the Old and the New Town Halls. The *Altes Rathaus** was built by Jörg von Halspach, 1470–80. The tower of the Altes Rathaus now houses the Toy Museum (Spielzeug Museum, open Mon–Sat 10.00–17.30; Sun 10.00–18.00). Its barrel vaulted council chamber has 99 coats of arms and medallions. The tower and much else were rebuilt after World War II, 1953–58. The **Neues Rathaus** is by Georg Hauberisser. The east building dates from 1867–74, the limestone section from 1888–93 and 1889–1908. On the 85m-high tower a Glockenspiel—with 43 bells, covering three octaves; the fourth largest in Europe—plays at 11.00 (and in summer at 17.00), its mechanical figures depicting the joust which took place at the marriage of Herzog Wilhelm V and Renate von Lothringen in 1568, while other mechanical dancers celebrate the deliverance from a plague in 1517. Lullabies are played at 21.00. This Glockenspiel was the gift in 1904 of a citizen named Karl Rosipal, who was celebrating the 100th anniversary of his furniture firm. On top of the tower perches a statue of the Münchner Kindl (i.e. the monk from whom Munich derives its name), blessing the city. The centre of Marienplatz is adorned by the **Mariensäule**, with a statue of the crowned and sceptred Madonna, created by Herbert Gerhard in 1594 for the Frauenkirche. She stands on a column set up in 1638 by Elector Maximilian I to commemorate Munich's escape from the plague. On its plinth four armed cherubs slay mythical beasts representing plague, war, heresy and hunger. The **Fischbrunnen**, at the NE corner of the Marienplatz, was created by Konrad Knoll in the 1860s and restored/recreated by Josef Henselmann in 1954.

Burgstrasse leads N to the Alter Hof. At No. 5 is the best-preserved late Gothic house in Munich, c 1550; of especial note are the courtyard, staircase tower and façade. At No. 6 in 1781 Mozart composed 'Idomeneo'. The court architect François Cuvilliés died at No. 11 in 1768; the Bavarian jurist Wigläus von Kreitmayr (d. 1790) lived at No. 12. The **Alter Hof** at No. 8, the former court of the Wittelsbachs from 1253 until they moved to the Residenz (see below) in 1474, was situated in the 13C at the W extremity

Its late Gothic west wing was built under Herzog Sigismund, c 1460. Half demolished in the 19C—in 1815 the complex lost a church dedicated to St Laurence and built for Ludwig the Strong—and badly bombed in World War II, it was restored between 1946 and 1968. Since 1816 the Alter Hof has served as offices of the Bavarian government, today housing the Munich finance department. Its courtyard, with a fountain and tree-shaded seats, is peaceful. Next to the main tower is an exquisite oriel window topped by a spire. An ancient crane still protrudes from one of the dormer windows. In front of the Alter Hof is an equestrian statue of Ludwig the Bavarian by Hans Wimmer, 1947.

Across Hofgraben stands the **Postamt**, originally built by the Gunetzrhainer brothers for Count von Törring-Jettenbach between 1747 and 1754. Leo von Klenze transformed this building into the chief post office, 1834–36, adding a loggia on the north side (the whole restored in 1953 after war damage). To the E in Residenzstrasse stands the Bavarian Hauptmünzamt or **Münzhof**, the Central Mint. Formerly the ducal stables and next to the ducal library, it has a lovely fine Renaissance courtyard, three-storeyed and arcaded. The early classical west side, adjoining the Hofgraben, is by Andreas Gärtner and Franz Thurm, 1809, and bears the legend MONETA REGIA; the façade facing Maximilianstrasse is by Friedrich Bürklein, 1859–63.

E again along Pfisterstrasse stands the celebrated **Hofbräuhaus**, successively a ducal, royal and state brewery. Founded in 1589, it reached its present location in 1644, though the present building, the work of G. Maxon and Max Littmann, dates from 1896–97 and the brewery itself was transferred to Innere Wienerstrasse in 1890. Enlivened today by a maypole, the Hofbräuhaus is the venue of daily music and beer drinking, and of brass band concerts. This is an area selling many tourist souvenirs and trinkets; and opposite the Hofbräuhaus the **Platzl** stages folk theatre.

# E.   The Hofbräuhaus to the Residenz

Orlandostrasse leads NE from the Hofbräuhaus into **Maximilianstrasse**, which was designed by Friedrich Bürklein in 1852 at the behest of Maximilian II (king from 1813–72). It constitutes a fascinating development in urban planning, for the monarch demanded 'ein die Kultur der Gegenwart repräsentierender Stil', that is to say an archictectural style mirroring contemporary culture. Bürklein responded with an eclectic but basically Gothic pattern, which later became known as the Maximilian style. Later additions diluted, and sometimes decisively contradicted, the concept, but elements of this style are still recognisable as you proceed along the street.

On the N side of Maximilianstrasse stands the **Hotel Vierjahreszeiten**, built in 1856–58 by Rudolf Wilhelm Gottgetreu, a disciple of the Berlin architect Karl Friedrich Schinkel. A little further E and S of the street stands the Art Nouveau studio theatre built by Max Littmann and Richard Riemerschmid of 1900–01, excellently restored after World War II and one of the few theatres in this style to have survived in western Germany. Continue E to find (N of Maximilianstrasse) the government offices of Bavaria, built by Bürklein under the influence of 19C English Gothic, 1856–64, though modified by him to represent one of the finest extant examples of the Maximilian style. Almost directly opposite at No. 42, is the **Völkerkundemuseum** (Museum of Folk Art), built in the 19C English

Gothic style, by Eduard Riedel, 1858–65, and housing some 300,000 examples of the ethnology of non-European peoples. Changing exhibitions augment the permanent display; admission Tue–Sun 09.30–16.30.

The area is dotted with bronze statues: the Bavarian general General Deroy (who lived from 1743 to 1812, when he met his death at Poloczk); the American landscape artist Benjamin Thompson, who called himself Count Rumford (1753–1814); the philosopher Friedrich Wilhelm Schelling (1775–1854); and the astronomer Josef Fraunhofer (1787–1826).

Still further E along Maximilianstrasse is the **Max-Monument**, set up in 1875 in honour of King Maximilian II Joseph and known to the people of Munich as 'Max-Zwo'. Designed by Kaspar von Zumbusch, its allegorical figures represent the four virtues of a sovereign; four cherubs display the coats of arms of Bavaria, Franconia, Schwabia and the Rhineland Palatinate, over which he ruled. En route, Sankt-Anna-strasse leads N to the Rococo Franciscan church of **St-Anna-im-Lehel** of 1737, by J.M. Fischer, rebuilt after World War II. Its ceiling, painted by C.D. Asam, was restored 1971–72; its pulpit is by J.D. Straub, with altars by the brothers Asam. Opposite the church is the neo-Romanesque **St Anna** church by G. von Seidl of 1887–92.

Return to Maximilianstrasse and cross the Maximiliansbrücke (built in the Jugendstil by Friedrich Thiersch, 1903–05, with a stone statue of Pallas Athene) to reach the **Maximilianum**. Friedrich Bürklein began the building in 1857, and after his death Gottfried Semper completed it in 1874, hence its odd mixture of Gothic and Renaissance styles. Though planned to give free accommodation to exceptional students, hence the educational statues on its façade, which include Duke Ludwig the Rich founding the university of Ingolstadt, the Maximilianum now serves as the home of the Bavarian parliament and senate house. The building is flanked by (S) the Maximilian gardens and (N) a Ludwig II memorial by T. Rückel of 1967.

Return along Maximilianstrasse to **Max-Joseph-Platz**—with its 1835 memorial to Maximilian II Joseph, designed by the Berlin sculptor Christian Daniel Rauch and cast by J.B. Stigmaier—passing en route the neo-classical **Nationaltheater** on the right. The theatre (faithfully rebuilt under the direction of Leo von Klenze in 1825 after a fire had demolished the original building of Karl von Fischer) was restored after World War II at a cost of 63 million DM. It houses the Bavarian state opera and ballet. The statues on the lower of the two pediments, representing Apollo and the muses, were sculpted by Georg Brenninger in 1972. The mosaic on the façade is by Leo Schwanthaler. The buildings on the other side of the street were designed by Bürklein between 1859 and 1863. Next to the Nationaltheater is the **Residenztheater**, 1948–51, by Karl Hocheder, which houses the Bavarian state theatre. The loggia of the post office on the S side of the platz was added by Leo von Klenze in 1834 to an 18C palace of the Gunetzrhainer brothers.

N of Max-Joseph-Platz is the **\*\*Residenz** (enter from Max-Joseph-Platz), which owes its origin to the decision of the Wittelsbachs in 1385 to leave their Alter Hof in Burgstrasse and build a new palace. Today it consists of eight courtyards joining together seven buildings: the late Renaissance **\*Altes Residenz** by Hans Krumper, 1611–19, the banqueting hall, the Rococo **\*\*Cuvilliés Theater**, a masterpiece by François Cuvilliés, of 1731–77 (open Mon–Sat 10.00–16.30, Sun and holidays 10.00–17.00), whose exquisite interior decor had been hidden during World War II and thus survives in the post-war reconstruction, and the ruined church of the Holy Spirit (neo-classical, by Leo von Klenze).

The main courtyard, the Königsbauhof, is dominated by a statue of Neptune (G. Petel, 1641), and the Königsbau itself, modelled on the Pitti Palace in Florence, houses the Wittelsbach treasury, consisting of ten rooms of over 1250 items, including a Carolingian prayer book of Charles the Bald, the crown of Empress Kunigunde, c 1010, and the Bavarian royal crown, made in Paris in 1806. The arcaded Grottenhof was built 1581–86. Its bronze fountain with a Perseus group was cast by Hubert Gerhardt in 1590. Of the four other courtyards the octagonal *Brunnenhof boasts a fountain surmounted by Otto von Wittelsbach and depicting the four main Bavarian rivers (Danube, Isar, Lech and Inn), as well as gods, goddesses, cherubs and beasts. Its creator was Hubert Gerhardt, 1611–14. The Apothekenhof (Leo von Klenze, 1832–42) contains the remains of the earliest building, the Neufeste (begun 1385, burned down 1750). East of this courtyard, the Apotheken Wing houses the Munich Science Academy. The Antiquarium was constructed by Wilhelm Egkl and Jacopo Strada of Mantua between 1559 and 1571 on behalf of Albrecht V (1550–79) and is the oldest German museum of Greek 'antiques', most of them in fact Roman or Renaissance copies.

Since 1920 the Residenz has been a **museum**, open Tue–Sat 10.00–16.30, Sun 10.00–13.00 and visited by means of two separate tours of rooms 1 to 81 and rooms 82 to 112. Apart from the antiquities (Antiquarium, above), it displays porcelain, weapons, reliquaries, 'the Nibelungenrooms' (by Leo von Klenze, 1827–34, decorated with paintings of the Nibelung saga by Julius Schnorr von Carolsfeld), the Court chapel (1601–03), the Golden Room (Cuvilliés, c 1730), the Baroque Papal Rooms (Agostino Barelli, 1665–67, named after Pope Pius VI who stayed here 1782), the early Rococo *Rich Rooms (Joseph Effner and Johann Baptist Zimmermann, 1729) and Maximilian's private chapel, designed by Hans Krumper in 1607 and furnished with Rococo chapels by J.B. Zimmermann in 1708. Portraits of 121 Wittelsbachs are on display in the Ancestors' Hall, the Silver Chamber exhibits 3500 pieces of their silver tableware, and the Renaissance wing of the Residenz also houses the State Collection of Egyptian art (Staatliche Sammlung Ägyptischer Kunst).

The Baroque additions to the Residenz are the legacy of Max Emmanuel II (1679–1726). The 19C added further legacies. Leo von Klenze built the Königsbau, N of Max-Joseph-Platz, in 1826–35, and the 250m-long Festsaal N of the Apothekenhof, in 1832–42, with bronze statues and figures by Ludwig Schwanthaler. The Maximilianische Residenz, adjoining Residenzstrasse, was built by Hans Krumper and Heinrich Schön between 1611 and 1619; its Renaissance façade was restored after World War II. The bronze Madonna between the doorways is by Krumper, 1616, and the armorial lions by Gerhardt. To the N lies the Kaiserhof, with a façade by Hermann Kaspar.

# F.   The Hofgarten to the Englischer Garten

North of the Residenz is the **Hofgarten**, laid out in the French style by Heinrich Schön in 1613–17 for Herzog Maximilian I, with elegant arcades (restored in 1950). Its Temple has copies of work both by Hubert Gerhard and cherubs by H. Krumper. You gain entrance through the **Hofgartenertor** (Leo Von Klenze, 1816). At the E end is the grave of the unknown soldier by Bernhard Bleeker, of 1924. At the NE corner of the Hofgarten stands

Munich's finest early 19C classical building, now the official residence of the Bavarian Ministerpresident, the **Prinz-Carl-Palais** of 1803–05, designed by Karl von Fischer, with a west wing by J.-B. Métivier of 1826. To the W of the Hofgarten lies **Odeonsplatz**, laid out by Leo von Klenze, who also built the **Odeon** 1826–28, to the N; originally a music school, it is now the seat of the Bavarian ministry of home affairs. Opposite is the equestrian memorial statue of Ludwig I by Max von Widenmann, 1862. Further N along Ludwigstrasse, constructed under Ludwig I, 1816–50, is (left) the **Leuchtenberg-Palais** of 1816–21, built for Eugène de Beauharnais, Napoleon's stepson, who was living in exile in Munich as the Duke of Leuchtenberg. Now the Bavarian finance ministry, it was patterned by Leo von Klenze on the Palazzo Farnese, Rome. Opposite is the classical **Bazargebäude** by Leo von Klenze, 1824–26. Still further along Ludwigstrasse on the right stands the former Bavarian war office, 1826–30, now the **Staatsarchiv** and the home of the Institute for Bavarian History, the last building in Ludwigstrasse by von Klenze.

From here most of Ludwigstrasse is the work of Friedrich von Gärtner. N stands his brick-built Bavarian state library of 1832–39, the **Staatsbibliothek**, with statues of Homer, Thucydides, Aristotle and Hippocrates, modelled on the early Renaissance Palazzo Strozzi, Florence. Amongst its treasures is the Carmina Burana, 13C Latin poems (interspersed with French and old German) celebrating love, drink and other secular pleasures. Opposite Gärtner built the former Damenstiftsgebäude, a charitable hostel for ladies, and the former Blind Institute, both 1840–43. Continuing N along Ludwigstrasse you reach the twin-towered church of **St Ludwig**, a three-aisled basilica built at the expense of Ludwig I by Gärtner, 1829–44, and rebuilt by Erwin Schleich after World War II. Ludwig Schwanthaler was responsible for the statue of Jesus and the four evangelists on the façade, and the frescoes of the Romanesque interior are by Peter Cornelius, including a monumental Last Judgement, 1836–40. On the left of Ludwigstrasse now appears the **Universität** by F. von Gärtner, 1835–40 built in the classical style; the fountain of 1840 is also by von Gärtner. Gärtner's Catholic seminary, 1834–42, stands opposite. To the N is the former Max-Joseph-Foundation for young ladies, which was founded in 1809.

Still further N, on the corner of Akademiestrasse, rises the **Siegestor** based on the Arch of Constantine, Rome, by Friedrich von Gärtner and finished by his pupil Eduard Metzger, 1843–52, to celebrate Bavaria's part in the Wars of Liberation, 1814–15. Its inscription reads, 'Dedicated to victory—destroyed by war—an exhortation to peace'. Over its middle arch a statue of Bavaria rides in a chariot drawn by four lions, the work of Martin von Wagner.

N of the Siegestor is the residential and artists' quarter called **Schwabing**. Once the home of Paul Klee, Wassily Kandinsky and Thomas Mann, Schwabing remains one of the best places in Munch to shop for antiques, especially in Türkenstrasse and seek out fashionable boutiques, notably in Türkenstrasse, Hohenzollernstrasse, Amalienstrasse and Leopoldstrasse. Some of its early 20C apartments have dates inscribed on their façades, as, for example, in Hainstrasse, and around little Wedekindplatz is a cluster of cabarets, a reminder of the pre-eminence in this field of Schwabing in past years.

Near the Siegestor stands the Academy of Fine Arts, a Venetian Renaissance building designed by Gottfried Neurather, 1874–87. From here follow Ludwigstrasse SE to the corner of Veterinärstrasse, where you turn left to find the *Englischer Garten, which is nearly 192 sq m in dimension. Four weeks after the French Revolution, the Elector Karl Theodor, possibly fearful for his own position, decreed that he 'no longer wished to withhold this most beautiful natural park from the general public in its leisure hours'. Laid out by Ludwig von Sckell, 1789–95, to plans by Benjamin Thompson (Count Rumford, who was born in North Woburn, Massachusetts), the garden derives its name from the tree-shaded informality which was commonly attributed to English gardens in the late 18C and early 19C. Crossing the ice-stream (Eisbach), the route reaches the Monopteros, a classical Rotunda set on an artificial hill with splendid vistas, built by von Klenze, 1833, in memory of the Elector Carl Theodor. The garden also has an artificial lake, a Chinese Tower by Joseph Frey, 1790, restored 1952, and a Chinese Inn by Joseph Baptist Lechner, also 1790; a monument to Benjamin Thompson (Lechner, 1790) and Elector Carl Theodor (a classical temple by Leo von Klenze, 1833); the Ökonomiegebaude by Lechner, 1790, now a restaurant; and a Japanese Teahouse, given to the city by Mitsuo Nomura after the 1972 summer Olympics. Boating is permitted on the Kleinhesseloher See, with its café and beer-garden, and nude sunbathing has been allowed at marked FFK spots in this park since 1982. A recent innovation is a tree-trail, starting at the bus stop near the Chinese Tower, the trees identified with little plaques, their names in German and Latin.

From the English Garden the Max-Joseph-bridge, built by T. Fischer in 1902, leads across the River Isar to the suburb of **Bogenhausen**. The route enters Montgelas Strasse, from which you turn right into Möhlstrasse, to find by way of Neubergstrasse the splendid Baroque church of **St Georg** in Bogenhauserkirchplatz. Rising in a quiet square, its pink walls and copper onion dome are surrounded by a small graveyard. Initially the parish church of Bogenhausen was Romanesque; the present building was totally redesigned in the mid-18C by the Baroque architect Johann Michael Fischer. Fischer, however, died in 1766, two months after work began, and the job was completed in 1777 by Balthasar Trischberger, while Josef Mahl built the dome of the tower in 1771.

An exquisite ceiling fresco depicts the martyrdom of St George and was painted by Johann Philipp Helterhof. On the high altar is a dramatic statue by Johann Baptist Straub, in which a moustachioed St George on a white charger slays a dragon. Two side altars enshrine works by Ignaz Günther, one depicting the Madonna and Child standing on a horned moon—with the face of the man-in-the-moon realistically portrayed—the other depicting SS Korbinian and Leonhard. Günther also designed the Baroque pulpit, with its languid angel.

Amongst the tombs of celebrated men and women in the graveyard is the one of Maria Josepha von Törring by Johann Baptist Straub. Here also lie the earthly remains of the conductor Hans Knappertsbusch, of the comedienne Liesl Karlstadt and of the writer Erich Kästner, author of 'Emil and the Detectives'.

A little further S, at 22 Maria-Theresia-Strasse, stands **Hildebrandt's Haus**. The sculptor Adolf von Hildebrandt, who designed the Wittelsbach fountain in Maximiliansplatz and Munich's Father Rhine fountain on the Kalk island in the River Isar, had this house built for himself between 1897 and 1898. He modelled it on Bavarian Baroque country villas and enlivened it by fanciful late 19C ironwork and 'Egyptian-style' mosaics, as well as the motto ART IMPENTIERE VITAM. Hildebrandt's Haus now serves as part of the Max-Planck-Institute.

Walking (or taking the tram) up Montgelas Strasse you shortly reach **Arabella Park**, a district named after the 1933 musical comedy 'Arabella' by Richard Strauss and the librettist Hugo von Hofmannstal. Arabella Park is criss-crossed by other streets and a square dedicated to Strauss and his works: Richard-Strauss-Strasse, Elektrastrasse and Rosenkavalierplatz. Though inclined to 1960s and 1970s architectural brutalism, the glass and steel buildings of Arabella Park are humanised by trees and soft lighting at dusk. The park's three most important buildings are the concrete **Sheraton Hotel**, built by Edgar Frasch from 1969 to 1971, the less brutal 22-storey-high **Arabella Hotel Bogenhausen**, created by Tobias Schmidtbauer in 1969, and—the finest of these modernistic buildings—the **Hypo-Haus**, whose glittering, cylindrical towers were built by Bea and Walter Betz between 1975 and 1981.

# G.   The Englischer Garten to Haidhausen

South of the English Garden, at 1 Prinzregentenstrasse, is the **Haus der Kunst**, built by Paul Ludwig Troost in the monumental style of the Third Reich, 1933–37 to replace a glass pavilion burnt down in 1931. Now the **Staatsgalerie Moderner Kunst** (open daily, except Mon 09.00–16.30; Thu 19.00–21.00), it houses a rich collection of 20C art, beginning with the Fauves and the Expressionists and ending with American Pop Art and a room devoted to Josef Beuys (1921–86). Its collection of works by such artists as Ernst Ludwig Kirchner and Max Beckmann is unrivalled, and no other German museum matches its collection of Cubist paintings (Georges Braque, Pablo Picasso).

**Prinzregentenstrasse**, laid out between 1891 and 1912, is Munich's last monumental thoroughfare. At No. 3, further E from the Haus der Kunst, stands the **Bayerisches Nationalmuseum**, founded by Maximilian II in 1855 and today housed in a building by G. von Seidl, 1894–1900, its façade a bewildering mix of styles from Romanesque through Renaissance to Baroque and Rococo. Opening daily except Mon (the times vary with the season, summer admission from 09.30–17.30), it displays arts and crafts from the Middle Ages to 1900, including a *Wessobrunn exhibition in room 1 (devoted to the school of stucco artists based on the upper Bavarian village of Wessbrun, who worked in Bavaria and Schabia from c 1600 to c 1800 and did their finest work from 1625 to 1720), **works by Riemenschneider in room 16, a Leinberger room (21) and downstairs an extraordinary collection of Christmas cribs dating from the 17C to the 19C.

Still further E, at No. 9, is the **Schackgalerie**, which Kaiser Wilhelm II commissioned from Max Littmann, 1907–09. Open daily, except Tue 09.00–14.30, the gallery houses a rich private collection made by Adolf Friedrich von Schack, 1815–94, of 19C Bavarian paintings (amongst the finest works by Johann Georg Dillis, Carl Rottmann, Moritz von Schwind, Carl Spitzweg, Anselm Feuerbach, Franz von Lenbach and Arnold Böcklin). If you turn NE at the Schackgalerie along Oettingenstrasse and left along Himbselstrasse you reach the **Prähistorische Staatssammlung** at 2 Lerchenfeldstrasse (open daily Tue–Sat 10.00–16.00, Sun 10.00–20.00) with prehistorical collection.

Walk on towards Europaplatz to find at 60 Prinzregentenstrasse the **Villa Stuck**, an Art Nouveau treasure house (open daily 10.00–17.00, Thu until 21.00). The painter and sculptor Franz von Stuck (1863–1928), who helped

*The entrance hall of the 'Roman' villa which Franz von Stuck built at Munich at the end of the 19C*

to found the Munich secession movement in 1893 in protest against prevailing artistic orthodoxies, designed this villa for himself in 1897. He too designed the bronze figure over the main doorway of an Amazon throwing a lance. Although its Doric portico is neo-classical in style, basically this is a Jugendstil building. The core of its artistic collection is also Jugendstil. It includes works by Franz von Stuck himself, which were once considered daring, as well as paintings by his contemporaries, murals, mosaics and copies of antique statues.

300m E, at Prinzregentenplatz, stands the **Prinzregententheater**, 1899–1901, built in the Renaissance style by Gottfried Semper at the behest of Ludwig II to host the operas of his beloved Richard Wagner. From here Prinzregentenstrasse runs E over the Luitpoldbrücke—adorned with statues of Bavaria, Franconia, Schwabia and the Palatinate—as far as the 23m-high **Friedensengel**, a monument supposedly representing the angel of peace, erected in 1895 to celebrate the Treaty of Versailles and 25 years without war. Its creators were Joseph Bühlmann, Max Heilmaier, Georg Pezold and Heinrich Düll, and the monument was restored in 1983. The statue is in fact a copy of the Greek goddess of victory, Nike, at Olympia, and the column rests on a structure modelled on part of the Acropolis.

South-west of Prinzregentenplatz is **Haidhausen**, a beguiling quarter on the right bank of the Isar. Not so expensive as Bogenhausen to the N, Haidhausen, formerly a suburb housing Munich's impoverished and lowly paid workers, is now far more fashionable than Schwabing (see above), in part because its attractions include cabarets, and the Philharmonic Hall (the **Gasteig Philharmonie**), which was built in 1986. In Haidhausen also look out for the **Herberghäuser**, an ensemble of picturesque 18C houses between Max-Weber-Platz and Wiener Platz, and the 'French quarter', built after Germany's victory in the Franco-Prussian War in 1871, with French neo-Baroque style houses lining streets named after great French cities. A museum devoted to the history of Haidhausen is at 24 Kirchenstrasse (open Mon–Wed 16.00–18.00, Sun 14.00–18.00).

# H.   Other churches, museums and Schlösser

## Churches

Holy Cross, in Forstenried Forstenrieder Allee, is late Gothic (early 15C), with Baroque reordering by Gasparo Zuccalli, 1672. On the high altar is a late Romanesque wooden crucifix, c 1200, reputed to have miraculous powers.

**St Johann Baptist** Gleissenbachstrasse (in Johanneskirchen), was built in the 13C and has 14C frescoes and a doorway of 1520. Its stuccoed dome dates from 1688, and the statues on the high altar are by Ignaz Günther.

**St Lorenz** Muspillistrasse (in Oberföhrung) is the work of Wolfgang Zwerger, 1680. His Baroque church was built on the site of a Romanesque one (1315–1678) which itself stood on the foundations of an earlier church first mentioned in 822.

**\*\*St Maria** in Ramersdorf, which is generally known as the **Ramersdor-fkircherl**, is one of Bavaria's oldest pilgrimage churches. On this spot a church has existed since the 11C, though the present entrancing building dates from 1399, its Baroque décor dating from 1675. Surmounting its ancient belfry is a Baroque onion dome. Inside, the ceiling motifs are picked out in gold, and the thrust of the church converges on the Baroque high altar, with its miracle-working Madonna and Child, sculpted by Erasmus Grasser around 1480. Flanking the high altar are two other Baroque ones. The pews are also Baroque, while a modern organ rises above the Gothic choir gallery. Another masterpiece created by Erasmus Grasser for this church is a crucifixion, a multitude of expressive figures beneath the cross and four side panels depicting Jesus's passion. The paintings on this crucifixion are by Jan Pollack. Another painting of 1635 shows 42 Munich hostages taken in the Thirty Years War, with Munich itself depicted in the background.

**St Maria** Frauenbergplatz (in Thalkirchen), was built in the 14C, with a Baroque reordering of 1692. Gabriel von Seidl widened the church in 1906; its high altar of 1432 is by Gregor Erhart.

**St Martin** in Untermenzing, is a late Gothic church built by Ulrich Randeck in 1499, which houses a 17C high altar.

**\*\*St Michael** in Berg am Laim was built between 1738 and 1751 by the architect Johann Michael Fischer on behalf of the Wittelsbach Clemens August, who had become both Archbishop and Elector of Cologne. This superb church lay close to Clemens August's family seat in what was then the village of Berg am Laim outside Munich. The high altar and six other altars are the work of Johann Baptist Straub, the frescoes and stucco the work of Johann Baptist Zimmermann. The pulpit of 1745 is by Benedikt Hassler.

**St Stephan** Baumkirchnerstrasse (in Berg am Laim), is possibly Munich's oldest church (but see St Peter, above). The present building is by Lukas Rottaler, c 1510, with Baroque reordering of 1713.

**St Ulrich** in Laim (Agnes-Bernauer-Strasse) is a 15C late Gothic church.

**St Wolfgang** in Pipping (Pippingerstrasse) is a perfectly preserved late Gothic (1478) church with wall paintings by Jan Pollack, 1479, and a carved wooden altar.

## Other museums, exhibition and concert halls

**Architektursammlung** (Technical University), 21 Arcistrasse; open Mon–Thu 09.00–12.30, 14.00–17.00, Fri 09.00–12.30, 16.00–19.00, Sat 14.00–19.00: architectural drawings.

**Nachttopf-Museum** or Chamber-pot Museum, is the world's first devoted to this subject; 30 Böcklinstrasse, open Sun 10.00–13.00, Thu 14.00–18.00.

**Die Neue Sammlung** (3 Prinzregentenstrae; open 10.00–17.00 except Mon) displays applied art and a historical/cultural collection from the 19C to the present day.

**Mineralogische Staatssammlung**, 41 Theresienstrasse, entrance Barerstrasse; open daily, except Mon, 13.00–17.00, Sat, Sun, to 18.00: minerals.

Munich's **Feuerwehrmuseum**, 34 Blumenstrasse, displays the history of the Munich fire service, and can be visted on Sat 09.00–16.00 or by prior arrangement.

The **Museum of Railway Technology**, Munich-Passing Station, 19 Hildachstrasse; opens Wed 08.00–12.00.

The **Music Museum**, 31 Metzstrasse is open Fri–Sun 16.00–20.00; see also the collection of musical instruments in the Stadtmuseum.

Munich's **Sewing-Machine Museum**, at the firm J. Strobel & Son, Ltd, 68–70 Heimeranstrasse is open Mon–Fri 10.00–16.00.

The *Bavaria Filmstadt** or film centre at 7 Bavariafilmplatz in Geiselgasteig (tel. 64 90 67), reached by Tram 25 covers some 365,000 sq m. Munich's 'film city' began producing distinguished films in 1919. In the 1920s the young Alfred Hitchcock worked in the city. Later Max Ophuls directed Karl Valentin in 'Die verkaufte Braut'. The Hitler years saw the studios given over to brilliant propaganda. In the post-war years under American occupation the studios flowered anew, when such directors as Anatol Litvak and Elia Kazan worked here. From 1 March–31 October daily from 09.00–16.00 you can pay for a tour of the studios on a little train known as the Filmexpress. During part of this period the studios mount 'Stuntshows', with actors impersonating famous film stars. Secrets of film-making are revealed, and historic relics (such as the U-boat from the celebrated film 'Das Boot') are on display. You are encouraged to wander on foot, for example through the model streets of Berlin built for Ingmar Bergman's film 'Schlangenei'.

N of Munich's city centre the **Olympic Park** (covering 2.8 sq km and reached by U-Bahn 3 from Marienplatz to Olympiazentrum) was laid out S of Georg-Brauchle-Ring for the 20th summer Olympics of 1972 and still hosts international and national sporting events. Its creators were the firm of G. Behnisch and Partners, and its 289.53m-high television tower is the highest in western Germany—open 09.00–24.00 with a viewing platform and revolving restaurant. The park includes the Schuttberg, a hill made out of rubble from houses destroyed in World War II. Sports centres are sheltered by a sinuous tent-like roof made of steel netting and acrylic panels. The sports hall (also by Behnisch and Partners, 1968–72) seats 40,000 and is used for concerts and the six-day races at Fasching. The Olympic stadium, the home of the Bayern–München football club, has room for 78,000 spectators. The ice rink, with room for 7200 spectators, was designed by R. Schütze, the cycle stadium, with room for 5000 spectators, by H. Schürmann. The Olympic lake, fed by the Nymphenburg Canal, is equipped with a floating stage for concerts. Of the former Olympic village, the men's quarters, by Heinle, Wischer and Partners, are now residential flats and the women's quarters, by Eckert and Wirsing, serve as students' hostels. You can hire boats on the lake, or use the skating rink and the swimming hall (with its sauna, solarium and sunbathing area) as well as the tennis court, bowling alley and fitness and recreation centre. The Olympic Park also has a tennis snack bar and a beer-garden (with a second beer-garden in Coubertinplatz).

Nearby, at 130 Peteulring, is the **BMW museum** (open daily 09.00–17.00) with exhibition of automobiles since 1919.

### Schlösser

The **Asam Schlössen** in Benediktbeurerstrasse was built by Cosmas Damian Asam for himself, 1729–32.

**Schloss Blutenburg** in the Obermenzing district of Munich was begun by the Wittelsbachs in the early 15C and surrounded by powerful walls. On the site of a former fortress, Duke Albrecht III had built a small hunting lodge, with defensive walls and water. In 1488 his son Duke Sigismund added a late Gothic *chapel (open daily 14.00–17.00) which still has 32 stained glass windows and three altar paintings by Jan Pollack in 1491. There are also carvings of the apostles by an unknown master (perhaps Erasmus Grasser). Later the Schloss was given a Baroque tower. Inside are also frescoes with the Wittelsbach coat of arms. The Schloss now houses an international young persons' library.

The former hunting-lodge of **Schloss Fürstenried**, Forst-Kasten-Allee, by Joseph Effner, 1715–17, is approached by an alley of lime trees.

The **Suresnes-Schlössen** (Werneckstrasse, in Schwabing) was built by Johann Baptist Gunetzrhainer, 1715–18.

# I.  Environs of Munich

**Schloss Nymphenburg**, 8km NW from the centre of Munich (U-Bahn service no. 1 to Rotkreuzplatz, followed by tram 12 to the Schloss), which along with the Amalienburg, stables and porcelain museum, are open Tue–Sun, 09.00–12.30, 13.30–17.00; the other buildings open at 10.00. The Schloss opens one hour later 1 Oct–31 Mar, when the others buildings are open 10.00–16.00.

Begun in 1664 and finished only in 1758, Schloss Nymphenburg is the sumptuous former summer residence of the Wittelsbachs. You approach it walking around an artificial lake with wildfowl. The whole building aims at symmetry and is long and low. Its central pavilion, begun by Agostino Barelli in 1664, was continued by Enrico Zuccalli 1673–75, and was the Elector's gift to Henriette Adelaide of Savoy after the birth of their son Max Emanuel. Under Elector Maximilian Emanuel, Giovanni Antonio Viscardi added the four cube-shaped side pavilions and the connecting buildings (to Zuccalli's plans, 1702).

The Schloss chapel in the second pavilion to the N was built by G.A. Viscardi in 1715. Joseph Mölck painted its Rococo ceiling in 1759; its statue of Jesus is attributed to Andreas Faistenberger. Semi-circular wings, modelled on Versailles, were added in 1715–16 by Joseph Effner. François Cuvilliés remodelled the ballroom, with stucco and frescoes by J.B. and F. Zimmermann, 1756–57; the great Roundel to the north-side (home of the Nymphenburg Porcelain Factory) is also by Cuvilliés, 1729–58. Special delights are the Hall of Mirrors, by Cuvilliés and J.B. Zimmermann, 1755–57, and the gallery of beauties—contemporary ladies, including the dancer Lola Montez, all painted for Ludwig I by Josef Stieler, 1827–50. In the south wing of the palace is housed the museum of the Royal Stables (the **Marstallmuseum**) of 1719, with is state coaches, carriages, sedan chairs, sleighs and sumptuous harnesses.

The Schloss park, covering 221 hectares, was redesigned in the 'English' style by the landscape gardener Friedrich Ludwig von Sckell in 1805. For this park Effner designed an octagonal Chinese-style Pagoda, begun in 1716, finished in 1719, to stand beside one of the two lakes in the park. François Cuvilliés the Elder decorated the Pagodaburg in 1767, though the upper ceiling was frescoed by Johann Anton Gumpp. Effner next designed the Badenburg, a bathing lodge at the corner of the larger lake, completing the work in 1721, with 18C Chinese wallpaper and stucco work by Charles Claude Dubut. Each building has a Baroque parterre with waterworks. Finally Effner built the artificially ruined hermitage known as the Magdalenenklause. Finished in 1728, it has a grotto chapel and a statue of St Mary Magdalen by Giuseppe Volpini, 1726, and a ceiling painted by Nikolaus Gottfried Stuber, 1725–28.

Another superb Rococo building in the park is the *Amalienburg, a hunting lodge and gift of Karl Albrecht to his wife Maria Amalia, by Cuvilliés and J.B. Zimmermann with carvings by J. Dietrich and paintings by P. Moretti, G. Desmarées and P. Hörmannstorffer. It incorporates a hall of mirrors, the blue bedroom and a hunting room. The temple of Apollo is by Leo von Klenze, with another temple by K. Mühlthaler, 1865. Garden sculpture in the Greek style includes works by Ignaz Günther, Roman Anton Boos, J.B. Straub. A waterfall, built by Dominique Girard in 1731, was designed by J. Effner. Other features are the Orangerie, which dates from 1723–24, and the botanical garden, which was laid out 1909–14 (alpine plants, rhododendrons: open summer 09.00–19.00, winter 09.00–17.00—the greenhouses close half an hour earlier.

**Hellabrunn Zoo** lies in the Isar valley (at 6 Siebenbrunnerstrasse; admission, summer 08.00–18.00, winter 09.00–17.00) is 6km S of the city. Designed by E. Seidl and opened in 1911, the park shelters over 5600 animals, mostly roaming free-range and all arranged by geographical origin, including amongst several extremely rare species 96 pure-blooded prehistoric horses, edmi gazelles and mhorr antelopes. Landscaped to reproduce the regions from which the animals derive, the zoo's park offers, for instance, a miniature Serengeti for its zebras, antelopes and gazelles, and a polar landscape for its polar bears.

**Schloss** (or **Burg**) **Grünwald**, at 3 Zellerstrasse, Grünwald, 13km S of Munich, began life as a 13C Gothic fortress. Parts of the building, including its tower, remain medieval. After coming into the possession of the Wittelsbachs, the Schloss was enlarged in the 1480s, with the addition of a

*Rococo playfulness: François Cuvilliés' Amalienburg, Munich*

splendid porch, decorated with coats of arms. It has been both a prison and an armoury. Today it shelters part of Munich's prehistoric collection as well as an historical survey of the Schloss's history and an exhibition of Roman antiquities (open 15 Mar–30 Nov 10.00–18.30 except Mon).

**Shäftlern Abbey** in the Isar valley (25km S of Munich by B11) was founded in 762 and rebuilt by Giovanni Antonion Viscardi between 1702 and 1707. The abbey church was begun by François Cuvilliés the Elder in 1733, completed by Johann Michael Fischer in 1751 and frescoed by Johann Baptist Zimmermann.

18km NW of Munich (S-Bahn service No. 2), on the left bank of the River Amper, lies the picturesque old town of **Dachau** (inhab. 35,000; alt. 505m), which was granted a market in 1391. The Renaissance parish church is by Hans Krumper, 1624. Here are remains of a Renaissance Schloss by Heinrich Schöttl with a staircase by Joseph Effner, who was born at Dachau. The town hall was rebuilt in 1934–35 as it formerly stood in 1615. The former concentration camp, now a memorial to the dead, has a grim museum (95 Alte Römerstrasse, open daily 09.00–17.00).

# 12

# Munich to Fulda via Ingolstadt, Würzburg and Brückenau

Total distance 340km. Munich—B13, 58km Ingolstadt—B13, 51km Weissenburg—44km Ansbach—78km Würzburg—B27, 51km Hammelburg—25km, Bad Brückenau—33km Fulda.

Leave Munich N by the Leopoldstrasse and after 16km on the B13 make a brief diversion 3km W to **Schleissheim**, to see the Altes Schloss, the Schloss Lustheim, and the 330m-long Neues Schloss of 1701–27. Built from 1597 to 1626 for Duke Maximilian I by the architect Heinrich Schön, the Renaissance **Altes Schloss**, was decorated by Peter Candid. Today it is a gallery devoted to the Christian year and to world-wide religious folk art (open daily 10.00–17.00).

At the far side of the Baroque park of the Altes Schloss is **Schloss Lustheim**, an Italian Baroque palace by Enrico Zuccalli, built in 1684 to mark the marriage of Max Emanuel of Bavaria to Maria Antonia, daughter of the Emperor Leopold I. Zuccalli himself initially laid out the park. Schloss Lustheim stands amidst a circular canal, adding to the east a couple of orangeries. The pillars of this two-storey building rise alongside windows with pediments that are alternately triangular and curved. Inside is a festival hall with a mirrored vault, painted Atlantes and rich stucco. Francesco Rosa, Johann Trubillo and Johann Gumpp painted frescoes dedicated to Diana the Huntress, while a massive oil painting depicts scenes from the life of Max Emanuel. In 1968 the philanthropist Ernst Schneider donated a splendid collection of Meissen porcelain to the Bavarian state on condition that it was exhibited in a Baroque palace, and his legacy of almost 2000 pieces, the majority created between 1710 and 1800, is displayed in 15 rooms at Lustheim. Open Tue–Sun 10.00–12.30, 13.30–17.00, closing at 16.00 from 1 Oct–31 Mar.

The **\*\*Neues Schloss** rivals Versailles. Max Emanuel, the Great Elector, commissioned the building in 1701, from the Italian architect Enrico Zuccalli. During the War of the Spanish Succession, when the Elector was defeated at the battle of Höchstädt, he fled to France, and no work was done on his Schloss from 1704 to 1719. The Bavarian architect Joseph Effner finally completed the building in 1725; he also designed the cascade in the garden. The long white façade of the Neues Schloss, reflected in a spacious, round artificial pond, has windows and arches picked out in yellow, with elegant pediments above the windows on the ground floor. Corinthian pilasters enliven the second floor of the main façade, which rises to a smaller, more elaborate third storey, while arcades extend the wings to smaller, delicate outbuildings. Ignaz Günther created the east portal in 1763. Leo von Klenze reconstructed the façade in 1848, and completed the great staircase.

Inside, the staircase vault was frescoed by C.D. Asam, who also decorated the Elector's chapel with scenes from the life of St Maximilian. J.B. Zimmermann provided stucco work and decorated the dining hall. The Festival Hall has a ceiling fresco by the Italian Jacopo Amigoni, depicting the exploits of Aeneas. Today the Neues Schloss (open Tue–Sun 10.00–12.30, 13.30–17.00; closing 16.00 Nov–Mar) houses a collection of Italian and French Baroque paintings from the Bavarian National Collection, alongside Dutch and Flemish works.

The B13 continues for 31km through hilly country to **Pfaffenhofen**—its Gothic church of St Johann has early Baroque decor and a high altar of 1672, and then for 3km to **Haimpertshofen**, whose church has a high altar of the 16C. Continue for 8km to the junction with the B300 at Pörnbach and for another 21km to Ingolstadt. Straddling the Danube, **INGOLSTADT** (90,000 inhab.; alt. 365m), though deriving its wealth today from oil refineries, assembling motor cars and spinning machinery, retains a fascinating historic centre and much of its 600 year old fortifications (and the gateway in Heiligkreuzstrasse) which protect the old town on the left bank of the river.

**Main railway station**: Bahnhofstrasse. **Information Office**: 1 Schrannenstrasse, in the late 17C Kurfürstlichem Universitäts riding school.

**History**. Ingolstadt began as a Frankish court estate in the 8C. Its first historical mention occurs in 806, when the Holy Roman Empire was partitioned. The Carolingian monarchs ruled the town as their personal fief. The settlement was destroyed by the Magyars and rebuilt in the 11C. The Wittelsbachs took possession of the town in 1228. Ludwig II fortified it in the mid 13C. Duke Ludwig the Severe built a Schloss at Ingolstadt in 1260, Duke Ludwig the Bearded founded the Münster in 1425 and in 1472 Duke Ludwig the Rich founded a university, amongst whose professors was the Catholic controversialist Johann Mayer von Eck (1486–1543). The Jesuit college, founded in 1555, was the first in Germany. The Swedish king Gustavus Adolphus besieged the town in 1632 and his general, Tilly, was mortally wounded beneath its walls, dying on 23 April; there is a plaque on the Renaissance house in Johannesstrasse. Only in the 19C, when the university moved to Landshut and the monasteries were secularised, did Ingolstadt begin to decline. King Ludwig I refortified the town in 1828 and the coming of the railway began to revive its fortunes. After World War II, which destroyed a fifth of the town, Ingolstadt rebuilt and expanded, until today it constitutes the second largest town in Upper Bavaria. An Ingolstadt professor, Adam Weishaupt, founded the secret society of the Illuminati in 1776.

The Spitalkirche (in its present form dating from 1460), in the Rathausplatz in the centre of the old town, has 16C frescoes, 17C altarpieces and Baroque decoration of 1720. An inscription reads, 'This church was founded by Duke Ludwig the Bavarian in the year 1319'. Inside, ten round pillars support Gothic arches, the whole intricately patterned and picked out in gold leaf. In the same square is the Altes Rathaus. Though created out of four Gothic houses, it was modified by Gabriel Seidl in 1882 in the German Renaissance style. The inscriptions and escutcheons in the arcades are from the old town gates. Nearby stands the Neues Rathaus of 1959.

Follow pedestrianised Theresienstrasse W noting the 16C oriel window at No. 26; that the inn opposite still preserves its warehouse crane; and the modern stone fountain, as far as the late Gothic, twin-towered •Liebfrauen-münster, 1425–1500, which is built of brick with stone facings. Particularly fine features of the exterior and the southeast porch are the carvings of the Annunciation, the Magi, the Twelve Apostles, the Virgin Mary, and the coats of arms of Bavaria and Ingolstadt. Inside, the high altar has 91 paintings by Hans Mielich in 1572, celebrating the Virgin Mary as patroness of Bavaria. There is a bronze memorial to Johannes Eck and the tombs of General Tilly (died 1632) and Fieldmarshal Mercy (died 1645). Exquisite Gothic tracery decorates the side chapels. The Renaissance stained glass in the east window is by Hans Wertingerr, 1527, while that in the first chapel on the south side is by Hans von Krumbach, 1511; amongst the sculptures is a 15C Virgin on the pulpit.

North rises the Rococo chapel of Maria de Victoria, 1732–35, by the brothers Asam. Its treasures include a 'Lepantomonstrance' created by J. Zeckl in 1708. The altar of 1763, and the allegorical statues of theology, medicine, law and philosophy, are by J.M. Fischer. C.D. Asam decorated the ceiling with a trompe l'oeil fresco of 'The Virgin Mary spreading Christianity'. The southwest tower (the Pfeifturm) was initially the town watchtower. To the W of the church is a seven-towered, fortified gateway, the Kreuztor of 1385. A museum of the history of anatomy and medicine, the Deutsches Medizinhistorisches Museum, is in Anatomiestrasse close by, in a delightful 18C building with an arcaded courtyard (open Tue–Sun 10.00–12.00, 14.00–17.00; Nov–Mar closes Thu and Fri afternoons).

East from Rathausplatz, Ludwigstrasse—note at No. 5 the delicately stuccoed and painted 18C Ickstatthaus—leads to the moated Neues Schloss, now a town and the Bayrisches Armeemuseum (Bavarian military museum; open Tue–Sun 09.30–16.30). Begun in 1418 for Ludwig the Bearded, its gatehouse dates from 1558, its clock tower from 1771. Its late Gothic interiors include a twisting central pillar in the Schöner Saal. To the S is the Herzogkasten or Altes Schloss, built c 1225 by Ludwig I.

Other notable buildings in Ingolstadt include the Franziskanerkirche, an early Gothic church of 1380, which houses the •'Schutter Virgin', 1350, on the altar of the first chapel on the S side; woodcarvings of 1613 in the choir; a 1755 altarpiece on the high altar; many 16C and 17C tombstones, especially the Tettenhammer and Helmshauser tombs by Loy Hering (1543 and 1548); and a Renaissance Holy Trinity (the Esterreicher-Epitaph). The St Moritz-Kirche, founded in the 9C and successively rebuilt in the 13C, 14C and 15C, has a Romanesque north tower and a stone Virgin in the north porch of c 1320. Inside are a font of 1608; statues of the Madonna, c 1350, and of Christ the King, 1450, which were placed in the reordered choir after war damage in April 1945; stucco by J.B. Zimmermann; a silver Madonna by Ignaz Günther; and a statue of the Immaculate Virgin by J.F. Canzler, 1760. Ingolstadt also has preserved the remains of the Jesuit College—the Canisius seminary of 1582, named after the apostle of the CounterRefor-mation St Peter Canisius, 1521–97, and the Orbansaal, with a stucco ceiling of 1732. The mid-1840s brick Protestant church of St Matthäus stands in Schrannenstrasse. H.W. Hämer built the town theatre in 1966.

The triple medieval walls and fortifications dating to 1368–1434 mostly survive, and are now laid out as gardens, with semi-circular brick towers. Also surviving are the Renaissance fortress and the neo-classical fortifica-tions by Leo von Klenze south of the river.

Ingolstadt celebrates an annual Bürgenfest on the first Friday and Satur-day of July and hosts concerts from May to September—the annual Kultursommer. Most Sundays a fleamarket sets itself up either by the

Kreuztor or in Manchinger Strasse. The city museum (with varying opening times) is in the 1838–43 Kavalier Hepp building, 45 Auf der Schanz.

Romantic-looking **Neuburg an der Donau** lies 22km W of Ingolstadt, along the B16, standing 403m above the Danube, defended by walls, a moat and outer fortifications. The 1520 Residenz with its arcaded Renaissance court-yard, of the Fürst von Pfalz-Neuburg, stands on a rock in the upper town, above the S bank of the river. The Schloss chapel is the oldest Protestant church in Bavaria, and was frescoed by H. Boxberger in 1543. In the Hofkirche, 1627, are stucco decorations by Michele and Antonio Castelli. The Rococo Heilig-Kreuz-Kirche of 1755–58 has a 12C crypt; the tomb of W. von Muhr by Loy Hering, c 1535; stucco work frescoed by J.W. Baumgartner; and a high altar by J.M. Fischer. In the church of St Peter (by J. Serro, 1641–47) look for the mid-18C high altar. Neuburg's Martin-skapelle, 1731, with its Rococo stucco is now a library of incunabula and humanist works, shelved on 18C bookshelves. The medieval Stadtburg today serves as the town museum. The town has a Baroque Rathaus of 1613, with a double staircase.

From Neuburg travel directly N for 23km to the walled city of **˙˙Eichstätt** (14,000 inhab.; alt 388m), situated at the foot of the Jura. In 741 St Boniface founded a bishopric here, where prehistoric man had settled, and the first bishop, Boniface's nephew St Willibald, built a monastery and cathedral here. In 1817 the whole diocese was sold to Napoleon's stepson, Eugène de Beauharnais, who took the title Duke of Leuchtenberg and Prince of Eichstätt. The bishopric was restored in 1821 and Eichstätt became Bavarian in 1859. Eichstätt has been a university city since 1980. Its entrancing Baroque character derives from the rebuilding necessitated by a severe fire in 1634.

The present **˙Dom**, consecrated by Bishop Gundeker II (whose tomb is to the left of the high altar) in 1060, boasts an 11C Romanesque east tower and a west façade of 1718 by the Baroque masters Jakob Engel and Gabriel de Gabrieli. The early Gothic west choir dates from 1269 and shelters a 16C statue of Willibald in old age by Loy Hering and a Rococo altar by Matthias Seynold. Hering also created the Wolfstein altar on the west side of the south aisle. The east choir and nave are late 14C and the high altar is late 15C (much restored), by Meister Hans of Eichstätt and decorated with statues of St Richard of Wessex, and his children SS Wunebald, Walpurga and Willibald, all patrons of the bishopric. A ˙stone Madonna of 1297 is in the Willibald choir, as well as St Willibald's mid 13C tomb. In the north transept is a huge altar given by Canon Kaspar von Pappenheim in 1489, and probably made by V. Wirsberger of Munich. The present double-sto-reyed cloisters date from the 15C. Other tombs are in the so-called Mortu-arium, a late 15C Gothic funeral chapel west of the cloisters, filled with grave-stones, with a 16C crucifix, twisted columns and groined vaulting as well as stained glass of the Last Judgment by Hans Holbein the elder.

The Baroque **bishop's palace**, 1704–91, adjoins the cathedral, and is fronted by an 18m-high column of the Virgin Mary of 1780, with a gilded copper statue, rising from a fountain. Residenzplatz is surrounded by Baroque buildings by G. Gabrieli. St Willibald is commemorated by a 17C statue and fountain by Jakob Engel, 1695, in the Marktplatz, which is also the site of the 15C town hall (restored 19C), with a 34m high tower. Another episcopal palace (18C) stands in the Leonrodplatz, as well as the Baroque Schutzengelkirche, the Jesuit church, begun 1620, mostly late 17C, with stucco by F. Gabrieli and a 17C priory. Other important religious buildings are the Benedictine abbey and church of St Walburga, 1631, with Wesso-brun stucco of 1706 and a high altar painting by Jakob Sandrart; the huge former summer palace of the bishops, built by G. Gebrich in the early 18C; and the 11–16C Capuchin monastery, all in Ostenstrasse. In Westenstrasse stands the 17C Mariahilfskapelle. Also worth seeing are the Dominican church of 1723, the 17C Kapuzinerkirche, which houses a 12C model of the Holy Sepulchre of Jerusalem, the former Augustinian monastic church—its west end is Romanesque, the rest was built in 1734, with a few buildings remaining from the former monastery—and the Hofgarten, a park laid out for Eugène de Beauharnais.

On the right bank of the Altmühl NW of the railway station stands the Renaissance Willibaldsburg, the former main residence of the prince-bishops (half an hour uphill by foot), commanding magnificent views. Begun in the 14C, it was extended by Elias Holl 1609–19 for Bishop Konrad von Gemmingen, and now houses the archaeological, Jura and city museum (open summer 19.00–12.00 and 13.00–17.00; Oct–Mar 10.00–12.00, 14.00–16.00, Sun 11.00–17.00) with late Gothic and Baroque sculpture and paintings. Close by is the Frauenberg Chapel of 1739.

Other museums include the fossil collection, with a skeleton of *Archaeopteryx*, in the Bergér museum at the Hartburg (open weekdays 13.00–17.00, Sun 10.00–12.00, 13.00–17.00) and the Diocesan museum at 7 Residenzplatz, entry through the Mortuarium (open Tue–Sun 09.30–13.00, 14.00–17.00, Sun 11.00–17.00), which is devoted to religious art and the history of the diocese. In the former chapter house is an 18C fresco.

From here the B13 follows the Altmühl valley NW for 26km to **Weissenburg** (see Rte 8), continuing for another 3km to reach **Ellingen** (3200 inhab.; alt. 398m), once a town of the Teutonic Knights, given to them by Emperor Friedrich II in 1216, and still retaining their Schloss by Franz Keller, 1718–25. Its Baroque chapel has wall paintings by C.D. Asam, 1718; its main staircase is superb; the stucco work is by F. Roth. In the Schloss is a museum of the history of the Teutonic Knights; open except Mon summer 09.00–12.00, 13.00–17.00; winter 10.00–12.00, 14.00–16.00. Ellingen also has a Baroque town hall by F. Roth, 1746, the church of St Georg of 1731, the Pleinfelder Tor (part of the largely disappeared fortifications, 1660) and Baroque town houses.

**Gunzenhausen** (15,000 inhab.; alt. 420m), on the Altmmühl 18km further along the B13, was a prehistoric settlement—some remains are displayed in the local history museum, as well as other artefacts, at 12, Rathausstrasse—and now boasts a 15C Gothic church and the remains of its medieval walls and towers. After 11km the B13 reaches **Merkendorf**, whose old town is still ringed by medieval walls. 4km N of the town, off the B13, stands *Wolframs-Eschenbach*, again completely ringed by medieval walls and gates, with a former town hall dating from 1471, numerous old houses, the Schloss of the Teutonic Knights, 1608, with 18C alterations, and a 13C Romanesque-Gothic hall-church badly restored in 1878. The fountain of 1861 is in memory of the Minnesinger Wolfram von Eschenbach, who was born here c 1170 (died c 1220).

Return to Merkendorf and continue by way of **Triesdorf**, with the 'White Schloss' of 1692, which was the former summer residence of the Margraves of Ansbach, to reach after 17km **Ansbach** (see Rte 20). The B13 continues NE for 29km to Uffenheim, which retains its 14C walls and defences as well as half-timbered houses.

A **detour** 11km to the SW, turning off the B13 some 11km NW from Uffenheim, brings you to the 13C and 17C church at **Aub** which boasts a wooden *Riemenschneider crucifixion, c 1515. Aub also retains some of its former fortifications, a 17C town hall, law courts of 1580–1620 and the ruined Schloss Reichelberg, demolished during the Peasants' War.

The main route brings you into ***Ochsenfurt** (11,500 inhab.; alt. 192m), on the River Main 19km along the B13 from Uffenheim, which is still ringed by its medieval walls and retains fine half-timbered houses as well as a 17C bridge spanning the river. Its *Rathaus (main building c 1500, east wing c 1520, all further embellished in 1531) has a notable chiming clock, 1560, and a splendid open-air Gothic staircase. It contains an interesting local history museum (open May–Sept, Sun and holidays 10.00–12.00, 14.00–16.00). The lofty parish church of St Andreas, begun in 1288, was finished in the 15C and hosts a bronze font of c 1520, a statue of St Nicholas by Rimenschneider and a high altar of 1612 by G. Brenck. The church also boasts an early 14C sculpted Adoration of the Magi; an octagonal early 16C bronze font; late Gothic choir stalls; and the 18C St Johann Nepomuk chapel. Nearby is the mid-15C cemetery chapel of St Michael. See also the Spitalkirche of 1500.

6km further along the B13 lies **Sommerhausen**, surrounded by its old walls and towers, which embrace an 18C church and the Schlösschen of the Counts of Rechtern. After 3 more km you reach the walled wine-village of **Eibelstadt**, where the crucifixion group in the parish church is by the school of Riemenschneider. The B13 runs for a further 9km along the right bank of the Main to reach **Würzburg** (see Rte 5A), passing en route through the medieval wine-town of **Randersacker**, with its Romanesque-Gothic church set in a 17C defensive courtyard, an 18C garden pavilion by Balthasar Neumann and several 16C and 17C houses.

The motorway A7 is the fast route from Würzburg to Fulda. To take the B27 N leave Würzburg by the Veitshöchheimer Strasse and travel 6km to **Veitshöchheim**, to visit above all its superb Rococo Hofgarten, laid out 1763–75, with a lake, grottoes and sculpture by J.W. van der Auvera, J.P. Wagner and Ferdinand Dietz. (The original sculptures) are in the Mainfränkische Museum at Würzburg.) The garden cascade was created by J. Philipp Geigel. (Visits in summer, Tue–Sun 09.00–12.00, 13.00–17.30.) Its Schloss was built to plans by Antonio Petrini and Heinrich Zimmer, 1680–82, on behalf of Peter Philipp von Dernbach, Prince-Bishop of Würzburg. Rococo wings were added by Balthasar Neumann, 1749–53, for Prince-Bishop Carl Philipp von Greiffenclau.

After 18km the road reaches **Karlstadt** (see Rte 9) by way of **Thüngersheim**, walled, with its three defensive towers, its 16C parish church and its half-timbered houses) and **Retzbach**, whose 16C Rathaus has a staircase tower. Here is a church of 1738 by Balthasar Neumann, and a pilgrimage church of Maria in Grünen Tal, founded in 1229 in the valley outside the town.

After 27km NE along the B27 the route reaches ***Hammelburg** (12,500 inhab.; alt. 183m), lying on the right bank of the Saale, reputed for its wines in the 7C and still retaining parts of its 13C fortifications, including three towers. Dominating the town from the other side of the river, perched 281m high, is Schloss Saaleck, founded in the 13C and now devoted to selling wine. The Gothic Catholic church boasts a Madonna by Jakob von Auvera. The Renaissance Rathaus dates from 1526 (and was in part gothicised in the 19C), in front of which is a fountain of 1541. The Bavarian Academy of

Music, formerly a Franciscan abbey, derives its present buildings from 1649. The modern Protestant church is the last work of the Norwegian Olaf Andreas Gulbransson, 1962–63. On the nearby Sodenberg (506m high) is the family seat of the Thüngen family, the Rote Schloss, a Baroque building by Andreas Gallasini, 1731, where Götz von Berlichingen, a German mercenary (1480–1562), reputed for having a steel replacement for his right hand, spent some of his youth. Continue 25km N to **Bad Brückenau**, set among extensive forests in the Sinn valley, whose three mineral springs (the Stahl, the Sinnberger and the Wernarzer) are therapeutically reputed. The main sights are the Fürstenhof Pavilion of 1775; Kursaal, 1827–33; and the 1900 Kurhaus.

33km NNW, over the border in Hessen, lies **∗∗Fulda** (60,000 inhab.; alt. 261m), the economic centre of eastern Hessen and the seat of the conference of German Catholic bishops. A speciality is its wax candles.

**Main railway station**: Bahnhofstrasse. **Information Office**: 5 Karlstrasse. **Railways** connect with Kassel and Frankfurt, and **buses** with the Rhön and the spa of Salzschirf on the Voralberg.

**History**. In 744 the English missionary St Boniface founded a monastery here which became pre-eminent in the conversion of Germany to Christianity. In the next century the monastery developed an extraordinary range of learned activity, particularly in copying and illuminating manuscripts. Fulda was chosen for the historic meeting between Pope Benedict VIII and the Emperor Henry II in 1020. The city which grew up around the monastery was given many privileges, receiving its city charter in 1114. Its abbots became prince-abbots in 1220, and Fulda became an independent principality in the 18C, when its architecture received the Baroque character it wears today. In 1734 Abbot Adolf von Dalberg founded a university (which closed in 1805). The abbots became bishops in 1752. Fulda became part of Prussia in 1866 and part of Hesse in 1945. Charlemagne's biographer Einhard (c 770–840) was born here.

Walk SW from the main railway station along Bahnhofstrasse to reach the city museum in Universitätsplatz (its speciality is fire-fighting equipment from the 14C). Close by stands the Altes Rathaus, basically 16C but founded in the 13C. Friedrichstrasse and Pauluspromenade lead NW to Schlossstrasse (right) with the former Abbots' Palace, a Renaissance building transformed into Baroque by Johannes Dientzenhofer, 1703–34, now housing the city offices and also part of the Vonderau museum. The acme of its sumptuously decorated interior are the Kaisersaal, the ∗Spiegelkabinett and the Fürstensaal; open Mon–Thu 10.00–12.30, 14.30–17.00, Fri 14.00–17.00, Sat, Sun 10.00–12.30, 14.00–16.30.

Pauluspromenade continues NW to meet Kastanienallee, which runs SW to the Baroque Dom of SS Salvador and Boniface, by Johannes Dientzenhofer, 1704–12, partly modelled on St Peter's, Rome, and replacing an early 9C Romanesque basilica. Inside is a Baroque organ; early 18C high and side altars; and Italianate statues. The tomb of Boniface (martyred in 754) is in the crypt. The cathedral museum (2 Domplatz) opens Apr–Oct weekdays 10.00–17.00, Sat 10.00–14.00, Sun 12.30–17.00, otherwise weekdays 09.30–12.00, 13.30–16.00, Sat 09.30–14.00, Sun 12.30–16.00; its treasure is the codex sliced by the murderers of Boniface.

Continue NW along Pauluspromenade, passing on the right the Schloss park, laid out between 1714 and 1726, with its Baroque ∗orangery by Maximilian von Welsch, 1724. The ceiling was painted by Emmanuel Wohlhaubter and the stucco is by Andreas Schwarzmann and Andrea Pozzi; on its terrace the baroque 'Flora' vase of 1728 is by J.F. Humbach. On the left of Pauluspromenade is the Carolingian ∗church of St Michael, by the monk Racholf, 820–22, inspired by the Church of the Holy Sepulchre,

Jerusalem. The crypt too is Carolingian, while the roof is a Baroque
addition. Continue through the Paulustor (brought here in 1771) and turn
left along Am Frauenberg for a quarter of an hour's walk up to the
Franciscan monastery of 1760, with superb views.

Alternatively (c 30 minutes walk) turn left at Paulustor along Eichsfeld,
walk S along Kronstrasse to turn right and continue along Langenbrück-
strasse across the river to Bardostrasse. Bardostrasse leads S to the frescoed
late Ottonian church of St Andreas. A bus reaches the church from the bus
station S of the Schloss. Another bus runs NE of the city under the railway
bridge and along Magdeburgerstrasse to the 9C church of St Lioba, built
at the time of Abbot Rabanus Maurus; in the crypt are wall paintings of
836–47.

OTHER SIGHTS are the Palais Buseck of 1732, the Palais Altenstein of
1752, and the old guard house (Hauptwache) of 1757–59.

6km S of the city (leaving by the junction of Bardostrasse and Löherstrasse
is *__Schloss Fasanerie__, the abbots' summer retreat, 1730–56, in a superbly
wooded setting, built mostly by Andreas Gallasini, with a Baroque façade
by Johann Conrad Bromeis, 1825–27. Its museum houses the collection of
the Landgraves of Hessen; antiquities, 18C and 19C furniture, paintings
including works by Jacob van Ruisdael (1628–82), sketches by G.B. Tiepolo,
idyllic rustic scenes by Johann Heinrich Tischbein the Elder (1722–89),
portraits by Franz Xaver Winterhalter (1806–1873) and Meissen porcelain
(open Apr–Oct 10.00–16.00, except Mon).

# 13

# Munich to Garmisch-Partenkirchen and Oberammergau

Total distance 178km. Munich—A95, 15km Percha (excursion around the
Starnberger See (50km)—B2, 45km Murnau—25km Garmisch-Partenkirchen—
round trip back to Murnau by way of Ettal, Schloss Linderhof, Oberammergau
and Bad Kohlgrub (43km).

Leave Munich (see Rte 11) SW by way of the A95 motorway (the so-called
'Olympia Strasse', taking the spur towards Starnberg. The route passes
through the Forstenrieder Park, once a motor racing circuit, and **Forstenried**. Here is a 15C pilgrimage church, dedicated to the Holy Cross and
possessing a Romanesque wooden crucifix. The church has an octagonal
onion-domed tower. Christian Strasser decorated the interior in the Rococo
style. Fourteen life-size wooden statues date from 1670 and the silver
tabernacle from 1700. After 15km the route, passing through Wangen,
reaches **Percha** at the northern tip of the Starnberg Lake.

### Excursion around the Starnberger See (50km)

This is the second biggest stretch of water in Bavaria, 20km long, between 2km and 5km wide, reaching a depth of 123m, created by the basin of a glacier and surrounded by peaks. Popularised among the nobility in the 17C by Kurfürst Ferdinand Maria and his wife Henriette Adelheid of Savoy, today the lake is criss-crossed by passenger boats and surrounded by holiday resorts, filled with yachts.

Just W of Percha at the N end of the lake is the chief holiday resort, **Starnberg**, with beaches, promenades and swimming pools. The information bureau is at 3 Kirchplatz. Trains connect with Munich and Garmisch-Partenkirchen. On the Schlossberg the Schloss dates back to the 13C. An arched bridge joins this Schloss with the Rococo church of St Joseph, 1770, with a high altar by Ignaz Günther, and a splendid pulpit, with the symbols of the four Evangelists. In a 16C wooden house nearby at 9 Possenhofener Strasse, is a museum of local history, with an attached art gallery, including work by Ignaz Günther (open Tue–Sun 10.00–17.00; closed winter).

Leave Starnberg by the Possenhofener Strasse and follow the W coast of the See to reach in 5km **Possenhofen**, with a sailing school and a privately owned Schloss. At **Pöcking**, some 5km along a road W of the lake, is a 17C church with an onion dome. Return to Possenhofen and continue S through Feldafing, with its golf links, its 'English Park', the Rose Island with a villa built by Maximilian II and a rose garden given by Ludwig II, as far as Tutzing (7km). The peaks of the **Johannishügel** and the 729m-high **Ilkanhöhe**—from which can be seen the Alps from the Watzmann to the Grünten—picturesque ravines and Schloss Garatshausen, 1532, now a Protestant academy, add charm to this second largest town on the lake. Follow the coast road for 6km through **Unterzeismering**, whose chapel has a 16C wooden statue of the coronation of the Virgin, past Schloss Höhenried (now a clinic) to **Bernried**, with its park, the gift of Wilhelmine Busch-Woods, its former Augustinian monastery (founded 1121), the church of St Martin, with a 1484 altar and a Rococo tabernacle, and the parish church of St Maria, with a crucifix and a Virgin with the Rosary, both 16C, as well as altars by Tassilo Zöpf, 1769.

6km further, through Seeseiten lies **Seeshaupt**, with fine alpine vistas and an onion-domed parish church. Continue round the bottom end of the lake and N along the E coast, through the fishing villages of St Heinrich and Ambach, as far (10km) as **Holzhausen**, with its pilgrimage church sheltering a 15C monstrance. 3km further is **Münsing**, a centre for mountain walks. To reach Berg, 8km N, the route passes through **Allmannshausen**, with a Schloss and the church of St Valentin by Kaspar Feuchtmayr, and **Assenhausen**, whose most notable monument is the Bismarck gate. At **Berg** is the Schloss of 1640 where in 1876 King Ludwig II of Bavaria built a neo-Gothic chapel. Here the mentally deranged king was later put under house arrest, and close by is the spot where on 13 June 1886 he and his doctor were drowned. A plaque marks the place where their bodies were brought ashore, and a neo-Romanesque chapel was built here as a memorial for the king in 1900. The late Romanesque church of St Johann Baptist at Berg is worthy of note. 2km SE of Berg lies **Aufkirchen**, whose 15C pilgrims' church of Maria Himmelfahrt has life-size figures of Jesus, Mary and the Apostles, 1626, and 28 frescoes painted by Ignaz Biderman in 1704.

From Berg the route N reaches Starnberg within 5km, by way of Kempfenhausen, with its Rococo church, and Percha.

To follow the main route from Percha, take the B2 SW for 16km to charming **Weilheim** in the Ammer valley (see Rte 14B). The B2 now runs 20km S to Murnau, with the landscape, as well as villages such as **Etting** (a church of 1526 with a Rococo decor) and **Obersöchering** (a late Gothic Madonna in the Frauenkirche) enriching the journey. **Murnau** lies at 629m on the warm **Staffelsee**, 4km long, 3.5km wide and 35m deep, with seven islands, a favourite bathing resort and health centre, at the start of the Bavarian Alps. Many walls of its houses are painted in the traditional fashion of Bavaria. Its treasures include a 15C and 16C Schloss, the church of Mariahilf (1734), the neo-Gothic town hall (1842) and, especially, the church of St Nikolaus, built in 1734 with Rococo decor, and sheltering statues of SS Anne, Joseph and Joachim by F.X. Schmädl, 1751. On the feast of Corpus Christi is held a procession of boats, and another on 6 November (the 'Leonhardifahrt').

Continue S for 8km to **Ohlstadt**, at the foot of the 1790m-high Heimgarten. Here stand fine 17C and 18C houses, and the St Laurentius church, 1759–62, with paintings by Franz Zwinck, the 'Lüftlmaler'. There is a ski lift to Walchensee. **Eschenlohe**, from which the plague came to Oberammergau in 1633, is reached 2km S. Its parish church of St Clemens was designed by J.M. Fischer in 1773 and has a Rococo tabernacle by J.B. Straub. On its peak remains the chapel of the ruined Burg. The route continues S through **Oberau**, a winter sports centre, with the churches of St Ludwig and St Georg (16C ceiling-fresco) and **Farchant**, with its picturesque farmhouses and the church of St Andreas, 1728 (whose high altar dates from 1779), to reach after 15km Garmisch-Partenkirchen.

Lying at the foot of the highest peak in Germany, the 2963m-high Zugspitze, and at the confluence of the Partnach and the Loisach, **Garmisch-Partenkirchen** (28,000 inhab.; alt. 798m; tourist office: 34 Bahnhofstrasse) is the country's chief winter sports centre. This is a region of cable cars and mountain railways; theatres; indoor swimming pools (one with artificial waves, next to the ice rink, see below); canoing; horse- and pony-trekking; concerts; and tennis courts. Garmisch-Partenkirchen has a golf course. Its health centres, clinics and health park operate in summer as well as winter. There are more than 300km of mountain paths around the town. The cable cars reach the heights of Eckbauer (1239m), Oster-felderkopf (2050m), Wank (1780m) and from the Hotel Schneefernerhaus (2650m, reached by mountain railway) to the peak of the Zugspitze. Railways connect with Munich and Innsbruck.

**History**. The two separate communities of Garmisch and Partenkirchen (which still retain their village charm) joined together in 1935 in preparation for the following year's Olympic Games. Garmisch has existed since the early 9C at least; Partenkirchen derives from the Roman camp *Partanum* and prospered in the Middle Ages from its market, granted in 1361, and its position on the trade route between Augsburg and Venice. Richard Strauss (1864–1949) spent most of his long working life here.

For a tour of what was formerly **Partenkirchen**, beginning at the railway station follow Bahnhofsstrasse E to the Rathausplatz, whose town hall of 1935, by O. Bieber, is decorated with frescoes by J. Wackerle. Cross E over Hauptstrasse into Ludwigstrasse, with at No. 45 the peasant theatre in the Gasthof 'Zum Rasen' and at No. 47 the Wackerle House, now a museum of woodcarving and cabinet making (open Tue–Friday 10.00–13.00, 15.00–18.00; Sat, Sunday only 10.00–13.00). N of Ludwigstrasse stands the 1634 'plague chapel' of St Sebastian and St Roch, both saints having been reputed to be able to protect the faithful against plagues, set in the plague cemetery, which was created in 1776 and made into a war memorial by J.

Wackerle in 1924. Return S along Münchener Strasse to find on the corner of Sonnenbergstrasse the parish church of Maria Himmelfahrt, rebuilt after a fire, 1865–71, but retaining a 16C statue of St Rochus and paintings by the Venetian B. Letterini, 1731. Due NE of this church, along St-Anton-Strasse stands the elliptical pilgrimage church of St Anton, 1704, enlarged by J. Schmuzer, 1738, who added an oval dome, which J.E. Holzer frescoed in 1739; the stucco decor of the high altar is by B. Letterini. Continue S along Ludwigstrasse and then along Mittenwalder Strasse and Wildenauer Strasse to the Olympic ski stadium of 1936, which has space for 70,000 spectators, 3000 of them seated.

To visit what was formerly **Garmisch**, start again at the railway station. Bahnhofstrasse leads N and then W to Richard-Strauss-Platz, the centre of the theatre (in a park) and health complex. N in Burgstrasse is the formerly Romanesque church of St Martin. Inside is a St Christopher of 1350, along with 14C and 15C Gothic wall paintings of the crucifixion and Last Judgment, stained glass of 1400, late Gothic carvings on the choir stalls, a 15C Passion group, and paintings of Christ crucified, St Erhardt and Popes Urban and Gregory, 1450. The high altar dates from 1670 and the ceiling frescoes are by Mattäus Günther. Continue E along Frühlingstrasse and Zoeppritzstrasse to find the villa of Richard Strauss, who died here in 1949, exclaiming that the experience exactly matched his own tone-poem 'Death and Transfiguration'. Return E along Richard-Strauss-Strasse and Maximilianstrasse to the so-called 'new' parish church of St Martin, by J. Schmuzer, 1730–34. Its ceiling was frescoed by Matthias Günther in 1733. Statues by Anton Sturm on the high altar date from 1734. On either side of the organ are paintings of 1774 by F. Zwinck. Return along Bahnhofstrasse, turning S at Olympiastrasse to find the Olympic Ice Rink, the largest in Europe, built in 1936, roofed in 1964 and seating 12,000 spectators. The Congress Hall stands in Richard-Strauss-Platz.

## Round trip to Ettal, Schloss Linderhof, Oberammergau and Bad Kohlgrub (45km)

Drive 9km back along the B2 from Garmisch-Partenkirchen to Oberau and take the B23 W (the 'Deutsche Alpenstrasse') for another 6km to **Ettal**, where a Benedictine monastery was founded by Emperor Ludwig the Bavarian in 1330. The present superbly sited monastery buildings date from the 18C, when to Baroque plans by Enrico Zuccalli the Gothic church of St Maria was first transformed, 1710–26, and then, after a fire of 1744, redone in the Rococo style of J. Schmuzer. Johann Jakob Zeiller painted an apotheosis of the Trinity on the 85m-high dome in 1746, the stucco work and organ gallery are by J.B. Zimmermann, the organ case by S. Gantner and the pulpit by J.B. Straub, c 1760. The fresco on the chancel dome is by M. Knoller, 1786, the woodcarvings in the choir by Roman Anton Boos. The marble statue of the Madonna in the tabernacle was brought by Ludwig the Bavarian in 1330 and may be by Giovanni Pisano. The monks sell Etalkloster liqueur (their rebuilt monastery, as Jerome K. Jerome cynically observed, rather than acting as a house of prayer, serving 'the more useful purpose of a brewery').

A 10km **excursion** due E from Ettal leads to *Schloss Linderhof (open 09.00–12.15, 12.45–17.00; Oct–Mar closes at 16.00). The site once sheltered a farm belonging to the Ettal monastery and, from the 15C, the home of the Linder family. In 1870–78 Georg Dollmann built here an Italianate Schloss for Ludwig II, loosely based on the Petit-Trianon at Versailles. The entrance hall has a bronze statue of Ludwig's exemplar, the Sun King Louis XIV.

*Schloss Linderhof, deliciously situated amidst formal French gardens at the foot of the Bavarian Alps*

Every detail pays homage to the French 18C court, with portraits of Mme de Pompadour, Louis XV and the rest and a hall of mirrors. Ludwig even called the building 'Meicost Ettal', an anagram of Louis XIV's 'L'état c'est moi'. Karl Effner laid out 52 hectares of garden, with pools, cascades and fountains, a grotto—based on the Venusberg of Wagner's Tannhäuser—a Moorish pavilion and a temple of Venus, everywhere adorned with sculpture by J. Hautmann and M. Wagmüller. Ludwig II continued to extend and alter this Schloss, using the architect Julius Hofmann, until his death, when Hofmann was engaged on refurbishing the royal bedchamber.

Return to Ettal and drive 5km NW to **Oberammergau**, where the miraculous lifting of a plague in 1633 led to the thanksgiving performance every ten years (with some additions, such as 1934 and 1984) of the now world-famous Passion Play. The present text, with some anti-Semitisms expunged, is by two parish priests, Othmar Weiss and J.A. Daisenberger, the early 19C music by the local schoolmaster Rochus Dedler. Oberammergau, dominated by the 1343m-high Kofel with its huge cross, is also a centre for winter sports, its amenities including an open-air swimming pool, with artificial waves, and a cable-car to the 1400m-high Kolbensattel. Some of its craftsmen practise glass painting, while others are skilled woodcarvers— a carving school was established in 1878, and the work is displayed in the local museum at 8 Dorfstrasse (open 10.00–12.00, 14.00–17.00). In the Middle Ages the town belonged to the Hohenstaufen and after 1269 to the Dukes of Bavaria. It prospered, being on the trade route from Italy through Augsburg to the Rhineland. In 1736–42 J. Schmuzer rebuilt its parish church, with stucco work by his son Franz Xavier Schmuzer, and frescoes by M. Günther. The Rococo altars are by F.X. Schmädl. The 18C 'Lüftl-malerei' painted on the outsides of the Pilatushaus and the Geroldhaus is by Franz Zwinck, a tradition continued today on other houses (e.g. in the Hansel and Gretel house, painted by Max Strauss in the 1920s). The severely functional Passionspielhaus is based on a theatre built in 1890 by Lautenschlager, stage manager of the Munich Court Theatre.

4km further NE lies the charming village of **Unterammergau**, with an onion-towered parish church of St Nikolaus basically built in the first two decades of the 18C. Its ceiling was frescoed by Johann Jakob Würmseer of Oberammergau. Unterammergau's chapel of the Holy Blood has a relic of the Holy Blood brought from Italy in 1734, and a Baroque organ of 1777. This chapel was plundered in 1704 during the War of the Spanish Succession and later restored, with stucco work and a new painted ceiling by J.J. Schmuzer, 1750–51.

The route leads NE for 6km to Saulgraub and turns E to reach in 3km more **Bad Kohlgrub**, Germany's highest Alpine resort. Its baths are reputed to cure numerous ailments. The nearby Hörnlegebirge rises to 1565m. The town has numerous painted houses, and its onion-towered parish church dates from 1729. From Bad Kohlgrub the road leads 12km directly E to Murnau.

# 14

# The Country Around the Chiemsee

## A.  The Chiemsee to Ulm

Total distance 237km. The Chiemsee—A8, 19km Rosenheim —62km Munich— B2, 26km Fürstenfeldbruck—42km Augsburg—B10, 54km Burgau—34km Ulm.

The Chiemsee is a lake lying 503m above sea level and dominated by the Chiemgau mountains, with the 1669m-high Kampenwand (whose summit you can reach by cable car) as their highest peak. Covering 80 sq m, and reaching a depth of 73m, the lake is a haven for fishermen and water sports.

The Romans settled on its banks, and legend has it that Pontius Pilate came here for a cure and died. One of its islands, Herreninsel, was the centre of a bishopric from the Middle Ages until 1805.

On the E bank of the lake is the little resort of **Chieming**, whose presbytery dates from c 1530 and the neo-Gothic church of Maria Himmelfahrt from 1882. 4km NE along the lakeside sits **Ising**, with a Gothic church dedicated to Maria Himmelfahrt. The interior, which was remodelled in 1751, has a marble altar. Ising also has a neo-Gothic Schloss. At the northern tip of the lake is the sports and holiday resort of **Seebruck**. Once the Roman camp of *Bedaium*, its local history museum displays Roman remains. The road now follows the lake SW through Mittendorf to **Gstadt**, which has a late Gothic church of St Peter and Paul and a bathing beach, and is also the stopping point for the lake steamers. The route then turns W and again S to reach •**Prien an Chiemsee** (8950 inhab.; alt. 532m; information offices: Bahnhofsplatz).

Dedicated to the mud baths and mineral water cures invented by the Revd Sebastian Kneipp in the 19C, Prien am Chiemsee is a health resort which also boasts the sumptuously decorated parish church of Maria Himmelfarht, first built in the late Gothic style in 1472, then half-demolished and refurbished in the late Baroque style of the 1730s by Johann Steinpeiss of Wasserburg. It houses blue-canopied altars with stucco work by Johann Baptist Zimmermann. He and his son Joseph also painted the frescoes, depicting in the presbytery the Holy Trinity, surveying the earth from their heavenly seat, and on the main ceiling the battle of Lepanto of 1571, when Spanish and Venetian galleys destroyed the Turkish fleet. Included in this fresco are Pope Pius V, who commissioned the Catholic fleet, and its commander Don John of Austria, as well as the inscription 'Joh. Zimmermann pinxit anno 1738'. The Baroque organ is by Sebastian Mayr of Prien.

Next to the parish church stands the Gothic baptistry, again with an onion dome. This dome carries a bell of 1773 weighing 55 kilos, and in the entrance are superb Renaissance tombstones. In 1923 a war memorial gallery was added on three sides, designed by Otto Riemenschmid (and restored in 1952). The adjoining fountain and statue of St Catherine are by Friedrich Lommel. North of the baptistry a traffic free zone leads to the local history museum, in a pretty three-storeyed house built in 1837 (open Apr–Oct, except Mon 10.00–12.00, 15.00–17.00, Sat 10.00–12.00). The former town hall is also a museum and art gallery, the Galerie im Alten Rathaus, with varying exhibitions (open except Mon and Thu 10.00–12.00, 15.00–17.00).

Trains connect Prien with Munich, Bad Reichehall and Salzburg. Two 19C steam locomotives ply along a single track from the railway station to Priem Stock, from where ferries sail to the islands of the Chiemsee. The writer Ludwig Thoma spent his youth at 23 Seestrasse, now a school.

To the N of Prien, close by the source of the river from which the town takes its name, lie first **Aschau** (reached by rail), with a Gothic church richly rebuilt in the Baroque style in 1702, and the Renaissance Schloss Hohenaschau, followed by **Sachrang** on the Austrian border, which is graced by a late 17C church built by the Italian Lorenzo Scisca. 2.5km W of Prien is **Urschalling**, whose small, basically Romanesque parish church of St Jakobus is decorated with late 14C frescoes depicting scenes from the Old and New Testaments, Jesus blessing the world from a mandorla (flanked by the symbols of the Evangelists) and a charming naive depiction of the Holy Trinity.

The steamers from **Prien Stock** which serve the islands of the Chiemsee also stop at various landing stages around the lake. A fishermen's colony has been established on one of the islands of the lake, the **··Fraueninsel**, on which stands the former Benedictine monastery of Frauenwörth, founded in 766 by the last Agilofinger, Duke Tassilo III, and rebuilt in the 12C. Its church, a three-aisled basilica, though altered in the 15C, boasts a 12C choir and Romanesque wall paintings, and its main entrance preserves a Romanesque door-knocker. Because these Romanesque frescoes are in the roof space of the church and thus inaccessible to visitors, meticulous copies have been made of them and are displayed in the Torhalle N of the church (see below). Master Jörg of Schnaitsee built the nuns' choir at the west end of the church in the late 15C. The delicate tracery of the nave, as well as the double-storeyed choir, were created at the same time by Hans Lauffer of Landshut. The nave was painted with its delicate foliage in 1606. All eleven altars are late Gothic, dating from 1468 to 1476, with Baroque retables from between 1688 to 1702. The high altar was made by Matthias Piechlinger in 1694. Its painting of the risen Jesus appearing to his mother is by Jacopo Amigoni, done between 1717 and 1720.

Blessed Irmengard of Fraueninsel was the daughter of Charlemagne's grandson Ludwig the German, who installed her as abbess here. Her body lies in the chapel of Blessed Irmengard, under an altar whose retable is by Piechlinger. The church also possesses numerous fine Renaissance tombstones and, in the chapel of Our Lady of Compassion, Rococo frescoes by Balthasar Furthner.

In 1983 Benedictines established on Fraueninsel a school and a seminary for women's work. (The neighbouring Krautinsel, now uninhabited, was once the site of the monastery garden.) The free-standing octagonal belfry—with five bells, two of them cast in 1573 by Hans Christoph Löffler of Innsbruck—was originally quite separate from the monastery and probably served as a watchtower. Its lower part dates from the late 9C or early 10C, its onion dome from the 1570s. Close by is the Torhalle, once the gateway to the monastery and built around 860. In its upper storey is a chapel, dedicated to St Michael and decorated with copies of the Carolingian frescoes mentioned above. Today the Torhalle serves as a museum (open daily Whitsun–end Sept 11.00–18.00), exhibiting archaeological finds connected with the monastery and exact replicas of masterpieces by Romanesque Bavarian goldsmiths which are now in other treasuries and museums.

On the **·Herreninsel** King Ludwig II commissioned Georg Dollmann to build **·Schloss Herrenchiemsee** (open summer 10.00–17.00, winter 10.00–16.00), 1878–85, modelled on Versailles, and decked out with chandeliers, Boulle cabinets and an equestrian statue of Louis XIV. The Schlosspark is also modelled on that of Versailles. Inside the Schloss you can visit the 'ambassadors staircase', based on one demolished at Versailles in 1752, with a fountain of Diana by Philipp Perron; ante-chambers, one with oval-shaped windows (as at Versailles); a bedroom for the monarch's lover; a conference hall, with a portrait of Louis XIV and a ceiling painted with the gods of Olympus; the **·hall of mirrors**, 77m long, with 52 candelabras and 33 crystal lustres; state apartments, especially the Rococo one by Julius Hofmann and Franz Paul Stulberger); the blue bedroom—Ludwig slept here for only 23 nights; Ludwig's 'cabinet de travail' (where he never worked), with a portrait of Louis XV, an astronomical clock and the elephant clock by Carl Schweizer of Munich; the rich blue salon; the porcelain salon; Ludwig's dining room, designed after a salon of the Hôtel de Soubise, Paris, with a 'Tischlein-dech-dich' or a table that apparently sets itself; a small gallery; the bathroom; and the unfinished north gallery, with a statue of Ludwig II by Elisabeth Ney, 1870. An Augustinian monastery was founded on Herreninsel in 1130. Its church, by Lorenzo Sciasca, 1684, was the cathedral until 1805.

On the lake SW of Prien am Chiemsee is the holiday resort of **Bernau** with its ski lift, steamers, sauna and indoor swimming pool. Its Gasthof zum Alten Wirt dates from 1697. From Bernau the A8 motorway runs directly W from the Chiemsee to Munich (see Rte 11) and continues to Ulm (see Rte 1B).

After 19km take the exit N for the resort of **Rosenheim** (52,000 inhab. alt. 450m; tourist office: in the Stadthalle at 4 Kufsteinerstrasse), which, lying on the River Inn, boasts a college of woodcarvers, parks, a botanic garden and a concert hall, as well as old burghers' houses, especially around the pedestrianised, arcaded Max-Josefs-Platz, where there is a fountain of St Johann Nepomuk. Here the Romans bridged the river in 15 BC. The parish church of St Nikolaus was rebuilt after a fire of 1469 rased an earlier building—and much of Rosenheim, too. A second fire in 1641 destroyed part of the 15C tower, which was rebuilt with a Baroque onion dome in 1656. The rest of the church is late Gothic, restored in the 19C, from which era dates the Nazarene mosaic of the Blessed Virgin on the south façade. St Nikolaus' modern altar cross is by Josef Hamburger, 1963, over which is a painting dated 1667. Pedestrianised Heilig-Geist-Strasse leads from Max-Josefs-Platz to the Heiliggeistkirche, 1449. Other important churches are the Baroque Loretto chapel, 1635, the church of St Joseph, built by a Rosenheim merchant named Simon Peer in 1619, and the Rossacker chapel dated 1737. Its frescoes include a late Gothic Annunciation and an Entombment of the same date. To find the 17C Baroque Heilig-Blut-Kirche follow Kufsteinerstrasse to the town boundary.

The imposing 14C Mittertor, the sole suviving town gate after the fire of 1641, now houses the local history museum (open weekdays, except Mon 09.00–12.00, 14.00–17.00; weekends 10.00–12.00). The work of regional artists is displayed in the Max Bram gallery (at 2 Max-Bram-Platz, open daily, except Mon and holidays, 09.00–13.00, 14.00–17.00, Sun opens at 10.00). The Inn museum, at 74 Innstrasse, opens from Apr–Oct 09.00–12.00, and the town's exhibition hall is at Lokschuppen am Rathaus. A daily fruit and vegetable market takes place E of the church of St Nikolaus. Rosenheim has an ice-stadium and hosts an annual beer festival at the end of August.

4km N lies **Westerndorf**, with a Baroque round church of the Holy Cross, built in 1691. 12km W is **Bad Aibling**, with its peat baths and lake. Its finest church is Maria Himmelfahrt, reached along Kirchzeile and rising from a hill which was once the site of a Celtic oppidum and then of a palace built in 855 by Kaiser Ludwig the German. In 1754 Joseph Michael Fisher transformed the Gothic Maria Himmelfahrt into a Baroque church. The Rococo stucco work is by Thomas Schwarzenberger, the frescoes by Martin Heigl. Under an altar bearing a crucifixion group by Josef Götz is a skeleton, said to be that of St Honoratus and brought here from the catacombs of Rome. To the N side of this hill, the Hofberg, stands Schloss Prantseck, 1564. Bad Aibling's other fine church is in the Marienplatz. St Sebastian, first built as a thank-offering by those spared the plague of 1634, was rebuilt in 1789, after a fire of 1765 had destroyed much of the old church. The Baroque high altar enshrines a Renaissance statue of the patron saint.

The motorway continues 31km W from the Rosenheim junction by way of Irschenberg, lying at the foot of the 751m-high Irschenberg peak, to the exit for **Holzkirchen**, close by which is the deep river bed known as the Devil's Ditch. This market town has a late Baroque church of St Laurentius, built in 1711. Inside, two statues, both dating from around 1500, depict the patron saint, and the Virgin Mary, her child and her mother. Continue along the A8 31km NW to Munich (see Rte 11).

Leave Munich and travel W along the B2 for 26km to the attractive town of **Fürstenfeldbruck** (29,000 inhab.; alt. 528m). At the entrance to the town you find the late Gothic church of St Leonhard, built and frescoed around 1440 and now a war memorial. Then cross the River Amper into the Haupstrasse to find the former Rathaus, designed in the 1660s by J. Marggraff and bearing two medallions, the work of F. von Müller, one depicting Kaiser Ludwig the Bavarian, the other Duke Ludwig II the Severe. The fountain nearby was set up after the First World War in honour of the dead sons of Fürstenfeldbruck.

Kirchstrasse leads N from the Altes Rathaus to the Baroque church of St Maria Magdalena, built beside the river by K. Pader in the 1770s on the site of a church first constructed in 1286. Its stucco work is by Theodor Jipf; the frescoes by Ignaz Baldauf; the modern organ by Dieter Ott of Göttingen. The town has 17C and 18C burghers' houses around the Marktplatz, and half-way down Hauptstrasse the Klosterrichterhaus built for Abbot Leonhard von Inchenhofen in 1621. At the far end of Hauptstrasse rises the present town hall, a classical building of 1700 enlarged in the 19C.

Follow the notice on the church of St Leonhard to find the *church and former Fürstenried monastery in the town park. Built for the Cistercians by Johann Georg Ettenhofer to designs by G.A. Viscardi, 1718–36, the monastery is today the home of the Fürstenfeldbruck art collection. The Baroque façade of the monastery church bears statues of Jesus, St Benedict and St Bernard. Cosmas Damian Asam frescoed the choir and nave. His brother Egid Quirin created the side altars. An unknown master made the imposing Rococo high altar. An early Gothic Madonna graces the Liebfraualtar; a late Gothic Madonna is attributed to Ulrich Neeunhauser, c 1470. Johann Georg Fux built the early 18C organ. The intricate Rococo metalwork of 1780 is by Anton Oberögger. 3km further W of Fürstenfeldbruck is **Puch**, with a memorial, 1808, to Emperor Ludwig the Bavarian, killed while hunting here in 1347. The road travels for 39km through the industrial town of Mehring as far as Augsburg (see Rte 3).

Leave Augsburg W by the B10, reaching after 54km **Burgau** with its two schlösser, one of which, dated 1787, houses the local history museum. The city fountain was put up in 1728, and the parish church dates from 1791. Burgau also has a museum of vintage motor cars. Just off the motorway SW is **Wettenhausen**, with an Augustinian monastery founded in 1130. Its church has a late Gothic choir, 1523, a coronation of the Virgin by Martin Schaffner, 1524, the tomb of Provost Ulrich, 1532, a Baroque nave by M. Thumb, 1670–83, with stucco work by M. Gigl of Wessonbrunn, 1680, and an organ chamber of 1700. By way of Günzburg (see Rte 1B) the B10 reaches Ulm (see Rte 1B) after a further 34km.

# B.  Prien am Chiemsee to Kloster Andechs

Total distance 173km. Prien am Chiemsee—23km Rosenheim—11km Bad
Aibling—11km Feldkirchen-Westerham—22km Holzkirchen—B13, 12km Bad
Tölz—B472, 14km Benediktbeuern—B472/B2, 33km Weilheim—12km Wesso-
brunn—24km Diessen am Ammersee—11km Kloster Andechs.

Drive due W from Prien am Chiemsee (see Rte 14A) through wooded
countryside, passing the waters of the Simsee, to reach after 14km a
signpost directing you left up Neukirchenerstrasse to the pilgrimage church
of Maria Stern at **Neukirchen am Simsee**. The stern exterior of the church
strikingly contrasts with its rich Baroque and Rococo interior.

Although a church has stood here since the 8C, the present building
basically dates from the mid 15C, with an 18C tower and interior and a 19C
spire. The frescoes of 1730 were painted by the Tirol master Joseph Adam
Mölck (and restored in 1880). On the reredos of the early Rococo high altar
is a 17C painting of the Madonna, brought here in 1710 when the church
became a pilgrimage centre. She stands between statues of St John the
Baptist and St John the Evangelist. The statue is painted in the numerous
ex voto panels hanging on the side walls of the church.

Return to the Rosenheim road, crossing the river Inn after 9km to enter
Rosenheim (see Rte 14A). 11km further W is Bad Aibling (see Rte 14A).
From here drive 11km NW to **Feldkirchen-Westerham**, whose massive
classical church of St Laurentius was built in the late 19C and early 20C
and furnished with elaborate Gothic altarpieces of a similar date. A
kilometre out of Feldkirchen-Westerham turn SW and wind for 12km more
through woodlands and farming villages to reach Holzkirchen (see Rte
14A).

The B13 leads from Holzkirchen SW towards Bad Tölz. After 12km a
signpost points W towards **Sachsenkam** and Kloster Reutberg, which lie
1km off the main road and are a rewarding diversion. Beside the old
monastic buildings is the former monastic brewery, the Bräuerei Genossen-
schaft Reutberg, founded in 1677, with a nearby Bräustüberl. The chief
treasure of the Rococo church, 1729–35, is a Madonna and Child brought
here in 1616 from Loreto in Italy. Over the clock above the entrance to the
apse is a fresco depicting the miraculous transfer from Nazareth to Loreto
of the house in which the Virgin Mary was born. Still used by Franciscan
nuns, the monastery possesses a Baroque apothecary.

**Bad Tölz** (13,000 inhab.; alt. 670m; information office (Kurverwaltung); 1
Ludwigstrasse) is just ahead, an idyllic spa washed by the Stausee and the
river Isar. An iodine spring was discovered here in 1846, and like the peat
baths of Bad Tölz its waters are reputed to improve the circulation, to cure
bronchial asthma, to relieve rheumatic fever and to ameliorate spinal
deficiencies. Drive into the town's Altstadt (signposted) through a gate
dated 1353 (restored 1969). The traffic-free Marktstrasse runs down from
here, flanked by elegantly façaded houses with overhanging roofs. In the
centre of Marktstrasse is a memorial to the dead of the Franco-Prussian
War, decorated with panels showing the death of Kaspar von Winzerer, who
perished in a joust with Jörg Frondsberg of Brandenburg on 25 October
1552, as well as the same hero fighting a tourney against Kaiser Max I at
Vienna in 1515 and the episode when he and Frondberg took King François
I of France prisoner at Pavia in 1515. A final panel shows Napoleon III
fleeing from Sedan in September 1870.

Half-way down Marktstrasse, Schulgasse leads left to the church of Maria Himmelfahrt, rebuilt in the late Gothic style after a fire on 4 May 1453. Amongst the delights inside is stained glass c 1500 in the aisles and a Baroque Madonna carved in 1611 by Bartholomäus Steinle for the arch of the choir. The Winzererkapelle, added in the 16C, has an entrance frescoed with both St Sebastian and St Roch, defenders against the plague. Further along Marktstrasse is a modern Maria fountain. The street runs down to the river, where high ahead you see the Franziskanerkirche, its date (1735) painted on the west wall. Built by A. Holzleithner, with a high altar by F.J. Winter, it stands in the town's war memorial gardens and houses fine 18C altars as well as a 16C statue of the death of the Virgin. Beyond it is laid out one of the three spa parks. NW of the spa, stations of the cross lead up to Kalvarienberg.

At nearby Eichmühle is an open-air swimming pool. Bad Tölz itself boasts the 'Alpamare', a pool with artificial surf waves and thermal bubble pools, the Blombergbahn chair lift rising up to mountain walks in summer and ski runs in winter—as well as a celebrated boys' choir. On 6 November the town celebrates the Tölzer Leonhardifahrt, when the citizens dress in traditional costumes, and enjoy the music of brass bands and horses pulling decorated carts through the streets. The former Rathaus of Bad Tölz was built by G. von Seidl in 1903 and is now the local history museum. The Mühlfeldkirche of Maria-Hilf, along Salzstrasse, was built in the 1730s by L. Reiter to plans by J. Schmuzer. Its choir frescoes are by Matthäus Günther. The Protestant church dates from 1880.

To reach the celebrated monastic village of Benediktbeuern from Bad Tölz, cross the river Isar and take the B472 in the direction of Schongau (see Rte 3). After 13km you reach Bichl by way of Bad Heilbrunn. Turn left along the B11 and find **Benediktbeuern** after 1km. Here is the oldest monastery in upper Bavaria, founded in 789. Invading Hungarians destroyed the first cloister in 955. Here in the 13C was written the *Carmina Burana*. A signpost marked 'Kloster-Basilica' points to the place from the crossroads in the middle of the village. The 18C monastery buildings now house a philosophical and theology high school, an institute for young people, a glassworks museum and a youth hostel. Within the huge cloister grow a massive copper beech and roses, alongside a fountain. From here you enter the twin-towered, onion-domed Baroque abbey church, built between 1680 and 1686, and crammed with elaborate stucco work. The ceiling frescoes are by H.G. Asam, and the painting on the Antoninus altar by his son Cosmas Damian; a reliquary of St Anastasia is by E.Q. Asam; and the Baroque Anastasia chapel was built 1750–58 by J.M. Fischer.

Return to the village of Benediktbeuern and drive back to Bichl, taking the B472 from there W towards Peissenheim. After 20km a T-junction sends you N 13km to reach **Weilheim** (16,000 inhab.; alt. 565m) in the Ammer valley. (Trains connect Weilheim with Munich, Augsburg, GarmischPartenkichen and Landsber.) In the 17C Weilheim became famous for its woodcarvers and goldsmiths. Its early Baroque parish church of Maria Himmelfahrt in Marienplatz, standing on the site of a former hospice, boasts some of their work, for example, a monstrance of 1698 by Josef Anton Kipfinger, in the form of a tree of Jesse, and a crucifix which he created a year later. This Gothic church was transformed by Georg Praun and Bartholomäus Steinle into a Baroque one, 1624–28, though they preserved an early Gothic tower. The date 1573 on one side of the tower relates to the addition of the dome and cupola after lightning had destroyed the earlier Gothic spire; on the other side the date 1975 refers to the restoration. The high altar painting is by Ulrich Loth, 1641, the 'Rastaltar' by Franz Xaver Schmädl, 1760. Schmädl also sculpted St Michael slaying Lucifer. See also an Astkreuz (a branch crucifix, with Jesus hanging on two leafy tree branches) of 1350. The font is Gothic, 1547, on a Romanesque base. A 'Lamentation' was painted by Martin Knoller for the middle altar on the south side in 1790; and the *fresco of 1761 in the Anger chapel of Judith with the Head of Holofernes, is by Johann Baptist Baader. Jörg Schmuzer, the stucco master from nearby Wessobrun (see below), enriched the rest.

In pedestrianised Marienplatz a statue of the Virgin Mary stands on a red marble column (a thank-offering erected by Ignaz Degler after the plague of 1698), alongside a stone fountain, with rustic children at play, copied in the 18C from one in the monastery at Steingaden. In the same square is the civic museum, in the former Rathaus of 1553 (restored 1788), containing *Hans Leinberger's 'Man of Sorrows' and many cribs (open Sat–Thu 10.00–12.00, 14.00–17.00). Walk on past the Rathaus to the end of the street to find a plaque declaring that the Oberer Tor stood here from 1238 until it was smashed down in 1871. Weilheim's Gothic cemetery chapel of St Salvator dates from 1449, its tower from 1584. Inside are frescoes of 1591 by Elias Greither, and a shrine and altar of 1470. The church of St Johann at Töllern dates from 1490 and has 15C and 17C frescoes. The chapel of the Sorrows of Our Lady, 1761, was frescoed by J.B. Baader.

The celebrated village of Wessobrunn lies 12km from Weilheim on the tree-lined road to Landsberg. En route at **Polling bei Weilheim**, stands a 15C church formerly belonging to Augustinian canons with a tower added by Hans Krumper in the 17C. Its high altar is by B. Steinle, 1623; an enthroned Madonna was carved by Hans Leinberger in 1526; trompe-l'oeil arches are frescoed at the entrance to the sacristy, with another fresco depicting the flight into Egypt, and a fresco of Jesus's resurrection, with the skeleton of death falling defeated, all painted by Johann Baptist Baader.

**Wessobrunn** became famous in the 18C for producing an astonishing number of brilliant craftsmen and artists: stucco workers such as the Feuchtmayr brothers and J.G. Üblherr; Franz Xaver and Johann Schmuzer and Johann's son Josef; and the Zimmermanns. At the entrance to the village a notice points to the right towards the Kloster-Pfarrkirche, which was founded as a Benedictine monastery in 753 by Duke Tassilo III and three noble brothers. Tassilo dreamed that angels were ascending and descending a ladder to a holy well discovered on this spot by a huntsman named Wezzo—hence he called the site Wezzo's well or 'Wezzobrunnen'.

In 955, the Hungarians razed the monastery, slaughtering the abbot and six monks. It was refounded in the mid 11C. Apart from the fortified 12C belfry, the monastery buildings today date from the late 17C and early 18C and are largely the work of the Schmuzer family. The plasterwork is lavish, the hunting scenes in the Hall of Tassilo particularly opulent. In the forerunner of this monastery, around the year 814, the oldest document in the German tongue was composed, the Wessobrunn prayer. The surviving manuscript (now in the Bavarian state library, Munich) contains 18 pen-drawings, thus making Wessobrunn also the source of the earliest Christian paintings in Bavaria. Benedictine nuns returned to Wessobrunn in 1913, and visits to their cloister are allowed only with a guided tour (on weekdays at 10.00, 15.00, 16.00; on Sun and festivals at 15.00, 16.00). The church of St Johann Baptist is open throughout the day. In the mid 18C F.J. Schmuzer transformed the interior into a Rococo masterpiece. The frescoes of 1759 are by Johann Baptist Baader (1717–80), who painted here part of his signature—the letters 'Baa'—on the collar of a little dog. The Romanesque Wessobrunn cross, carved in the mid 13C, hangs on the north wall. A nearby lime tree with a circumference of 13.17m, the 'Tassilolinde', is said to be 700 years old. As for Wezzo's well, Josef Schmuzer in 1735 built a well house which still stands to the E of the church and encloses three springs.

**Diessen am Ammersee** (8500 inhab.; alt. 540m) lies 24km away, reached by turning right at Rott, 6km from Wessobrunn. The first half of the road is wooded, until it emerges into open countryside with glimpses of the lake ahead. Some 16km long, 6km wide, plied with steamers, the lake has contributed greatly to Diessen's popularity as a holiday resort. The impressive Klosterkirche of Diessen is signposted to the right at the entrance to the town. Flanked by monastic buildings, its Baroque façade is curved and gilded. Next door is the monastic Chorherrstüberl. Inside the church, which was designed by Johann Michael Fischer between 1732 and 1739 and then decorated by the Feuchtmayr brothers and François Cuvilliés the elder, Baroque ironwork and gates separate the nave from the entrance hall. Cupolas extend eastward towards Cuvilliés's high altar, which was sculpted by J. Dietrich showing the four doctors of the church. Above this altar the Holy Trinity is depicted welcoming into heaven the ascending Virgin Mary, painted by Giovanni Battista Tiepolo. An earlier treasure is a 15C statue of St Peter by Erasmus Grasser. Note too an angel by Ignaz Günther, and the pulpit and organ loft by J.B. Straub. Diessen also boasts the church of St Georg, first set up in the 15C and embellished by Baroque masters, particularly Matthias Günther and F.X. Feuchtmayr, in the mid 18C. On Ascension Day potters from throughout Bavaria arrive at the town for the annual Diessen pot market or Töpfermarkt.

An **excursion** to **Kloster Andechs** from Diessen can be made by turning right at the T-junction at the bottom of the hill from Maria Himmelfahrt and following the signs for another 11km. For centuries Andechs has been famous for its cheese and its beer. Founded in the Middle Ages on the Heiliger Berg, a holy mountain 711m above sea level, the monastery church was rebuilt many times and remains, after Altötting (see Rte 15), one of Bavaria's most celebrated places of pilgrimage. Its style remains partly mid-15C Gothic and partly Johann Baptist Zimmermann's Rococo. Inside, Zimmermann in 1755 frescoed the Törringkapelle with a painting of Duke Tassilo and his three noble friends deciding to found the monastery at Wessobrunn beside Wezzo's well.

# 15

# Wasserburg to Neumarkt-Sankt Veit via Altötting

Total distance 188km. Wasserburg am Inn—B304, 21km Ebersberg—20km Munich by-pass—8km Aschheim—B388, 23km Erding—20km Dorfing—B15, 16km Haag—B12, 45km Mühldorf am Inn—10km—Altötting—3km Neuötting—B299, 22km Neumarkt-Sankt Veit.

The walled town of ***Wasserburg** (13,000 inhab.; alt. 421m) rises exquisitely on a strip of land that juts out into the River Inn, opposite the Schloss which Ludwig the Bearded built in the early 15C and Duke Wilhelm IV of Munich enlarged in 1526, adding the late Gothic Schloss chapel of St Agidien. Wasserburg had been given the right to hold a market in 1201, and was raised to the status of a town by Kaiser Ludwig the Bavarian. In 1503, during the struggles over the succession to the dukedom of Landshut, the town was taken by Pfalzgraf Ruprecht, passing at the end of the dispute into the hands of Duke Wilhelm IV.

Enter Wasserburg by crossing the river bridge and passing through the battlemented Brucktor of 1374, which was renewed by Wolfgang Wieser in 1470 and decorated with paintings of knights in 1568. This gate incorporates the former late Gothic Heiliggeist-Spital, founded in 1341, part of which is now an art gallery containing the collection of Günter Dietz, ranging from the Romanesque to the 20C and including some impeccable reproductions of original paintings (open Tue–Sun 11.00–17.00 May–Sept; otherwise 13.00–17.00). The Spitalkirche dates from the 15C.

In Kirchplatz just E of the Schloss and reached by steps is the impressive parish church of St Jakob, a Romanesque 12C building, rebuilt in the Gothic style in the 15C first by Hans Stethainer, who began work in 1410 and had rebuilt the nave by the time of his death in 1432, and next by Stephan Krumenauer. After Krumenauer's own death the work was continued by Wolfgang Wieser and finished in 1478 when the tower was completed. Today the church boasts a brick nave and a stone apse, with statues of SS Peter and Paul over the entrance. The Baroque interior dates from 1639–63, enriched in 1879–80. Inside is a *pulpit of 1639 by the brothers Martin and Michael Zürn, and Baroque side altars. At the age of seven Mozart first played the pedals of an organ in this church. Close by is the presbytery, 1496, with a modern statue of St James, 1988, in its courtyard.

Leave Kirchplatz S by way of the arcaded Herrengasse whose picturesque houses include at No. 15 the late Gothic Herrenhaus, now the town museum (opening times vary; it specialises in farmhouse furniture). Turn right around Alte Schranne into the Marienplatz, dominated by the Frauenkirche, 1324–86, on whose high altar is a late Gothic picture of the Madonna, carrying grapes as well as her Child. The church has a font of 1520, and late 15C statues of SS Blasius and Apollonaria. Its 65m belfry (by Wolfgang Wieser) was once the town watchtower. An inscription declares that both church and tower survived a conflagration of 1874 due to the intervention of the Blessed Virgin Mary. Further E across the square stands the Rathaus, two mid-15C buildings joined together, the present ensemble mostly the work of Jörg Tünzl, with a Ratsstube of 1564. Nearby is the

Kernhaus—its name deriving from the patrician Kern family who once owned it—with a stuccoed Rococo *façade added by J.B. Zimmermann in 1738. Marienplatz also houses the former tollhouse, built in 1497 but deriving its Renaissance façade and oriel windows from 1530. At No. 23 a plaque declares that in 1779 this was the birthplace of the religious poet Johann Kaspar Aiblinger. Continue S through the Brucktor and across the river to find on the Mühldorf road Wolfgang Wieser's church of St Achatz, built in 1485. It stands outside Wasserburg since its purpose was to serve an isolated leper colony.

The information office is in the Rathaus. Trains connect the town with Munich, Mühldorf, Rosenheim and Ebersberg. Annual events include the February pigeon fair, the Whitsuntide fair, a July wine festival and a flea market on the first Saturday in August.

Follow the B304 W for 21km to **Ebersberg** (8800 inhab.; alt. 520m) at the foot of the 620m-high Lugwigshöhe—a favoured spot for hikers. The town has a Rococo monastery church of St Sebastian built on a foundation of 1312 by J.G. Ettenhofer in 1734 to plans by G.A. Viscardi. The church contains a Romanesque reliquary sheltering the patron saint's alleged skull, and tombs from an earlier building, including the red marble *memorial to Graf Ulrich and Gräfin Richardis von Sempt-Ebersberg. Sculpted by Wolfgang Leb in 1501, it depicts the founders of the original church, with a heavenly Madonna, angels and a model of the building. Their former gravestone lies in the Chapel of the Sacred Heart. Nearby is the sumptuously stuccoed Baroque chapel of St Sebastian designed by Heinrich Mayer in 1689. In the Marktplatz is the Rathaus of 1529. Ebersberg lies at the end of S-Bahn line 4 from Munich. The B304 continues W through the Ebersberg forest for 20km by way of **Zorneding**, with its Rococo church of St Martin, 1719, crossing the ring road E of Munich (see Rte 11) to reach **Haar**, where the church of St Nikolaus has a 13C apse.

Take the ring road N around Munich for 8km to **Aschheim** (4200 inhab.; alt. 510m), an ancient town with a church attested here at the end of the 7C (and the burial place of St Emmeram before his translation to Regensburg). Continue along the B388 NE for 23km through **Niederneuching** with its Baroque church of 1693 as far as **Erding** (24,000 inhab.; alt. 462m). Of its fortifications remains the 15C so-called beautiful gate or 'Schöne Turm' with a dome of 1660. Much of medieval and Renaissance Erding was destroyed in a fire of 1648, and today its finest secular buildings date from the late 17C and 18C. Cross Schrannenplatz from the Schöne Turm and walk along Landshuterstrasse to find at No. 1 the former residence of the Counts of Preysing, built in 1648 and now the town hall. Erding also has an impressive late Gothic church, St Johannes der Täufer, with a crucifix by Hans Leinberger, 1525 and a fine 19C reredos. As with the Frauenkirche at Wasserburg, its free-standing belfry was once the town watchtower. The church of the Holy Blood, 1675, was stuccoed in 1704; and the late Gothic Heiliggeistkirche (whose high altar dates from 1793) was reordered in the Baroque style in 1688. Heiliggeistspital, 1444, stands to the S of the Schöne Turm, with an archway leading between it and the Heiliggeistkirche into a courtyard surrounded by remains of the 14C town walls. The church was originally late Gothic in style, rendered Baroque in 1688 and provided with a new altar in 1793. In Schrannenplatz the deconsecrated church of Our Lady, built in the 14C and restored in 1665, today serves as the town's art gallery (opening irregularly and displaying local handicrafts, sculpture and paintings from the 14C to the 18C).

E of Erding is the Baroque pilgrimage church of **Maria Verkündigung**.
Continue 20km directly E and then S to **Dorfen** (10,500 inhab.; alt.
464m) on the River Isen, with its classical pilgrimage church of Maria-Dorfen,
1782–86, one of the earliest churches in this style in Bavaria, the ceiling,
painted by Johann Huber in 1786, sheltering a 15C miracle-working statue
of the Virgin Mary. Take the B15 S for 1.5km and make an **excursion** E to
visit the mid-13C Romanesque church of St Johann Baptist at **Rottenbuch**.
Return to the B15 and continue S for 14.5km to **Haag** (inhab, 5000; alt.
560m), which still retains the powerful tower, c 1200, of its medieval Schloss.
From Haag the B12 runs E. After 6km make a short **excursion** S for **Gars**,
where the Baroque church of St Maria, buit by Gasparo and Domenico
Zuccalli in 1661, has a Pietà c 1425 and **Au am Inn**, where you find another
church of St Maria to plans by Domenico Zuccalli, built 1708–17, inside
which is the tomb of Gräfin Törring by J.B. Straub.

Continue NE along the B12 for 45km to walled, moated **Mühldorf am Inn**
(15,000 inhab.; alt. 383m), whose spacious *Stadtplatz is surrounded by
houses with arcades and the old city tower, and contains four Baroque
fountains. The late Gothic Rathaus to the N of the Stadtplatz, comprising
three buildings in all, has a mid-17C façade. Nearby is the Frauenkirche,
1640–43, once belonging to a Capuchin monastery (note the monk on its
weather vane). The 35m-high tower was added in 1856. Leave by the N
side of the Stadtplatz àlong Kirchgasse to find the Rococo church of St
Nikolaus, built to plans of Alois Mair between 1769 and 1775, with a ceiling
fresco of 1772 by Martin Heigl, depicting the life of the patron saint. Mair
preserved the Romanesque church tower and medieval entrance, which
has signs of the zodiac and faded frescoes. The relic in the glass case on
the north side of the church is said to be the corpse of St Deodoratus. The
nearby octagonal cemetery chapel of St Johannes dates from the mid 14C,
with a tower of 1450. Inside are 15C frescoes and a Gothic winged
altarpiece. Other sights are the late Baroque Maria-Eich chapel, 1699; the
late Gothic St Katharin Kirche, whose 18C interior houses 16C monuments;
the city library in the 16C Kornkasten; and the museum in the Lodronhaus
(7 Tuchmacherstrasse, open Tue 14.00–19.00, Wed, Thu, 14.00–16.00, Sun
10.00–12.00, 14.00–16.00). Trains connect with Munich, Landshut, Burghausen, Rosenheim and Traunstein.

From Mühldorf the B12 leads for 10km directly E to ***Altötting** (10,000
inhab.; alt. 402m), which possesses in the inner octagon of its Heilige
Kapelle one of Germany's oldest churches, possibly deriving from a 7C
pagan temple. Standing in Kapellplatz, the Heilige Kapelle contains a
miraculous Black Madonna, c 1300, carved in limewood, brought here from
Lorraine and enshrined in a late 17C altar of grace. The statue has been
venerated since 1489 as miracle-working, and the little chapel is covered
with numerous ex voto paintings, the earliest deriving from 1520. These
paintings stretch around the covered ambulatory of the chapel, which was
added in 1494. Before the Black Madonna kneels an 18C silver figure (by
the Rococo sculptor Wilhelm de Groff) of the ten-year-old Kurprinz Maximilian of Bavaria, who was cured of a mortal illness in 1737 after interces-
sions before the statue. On the left is a 1931 statue by Georg Busch of St
Konrad of Parzham (1818–94), beatified in 1934 after spending 41 years of
austerity and charity at Altötting. The inner octagon of this chapel dates
from the 8C, housed in a 14C late Gothic church. Inside are more votive
pictures and rich gifts, with the hearts of dead Bavarian monarchs (those
of Kaiser Albrecht VII and Kaiserin Maria Amalie in an urn of 1745 by
Johann Baptist Straub, and Ludwig II of Bavaria in a heart-shaped urn of

1886), as well as the heart of Field Marshal Johann Tserclaes Tilly (1559–1632). The fame of the Black Madonna has made Altötting Bavaria's foremost pilgrimage centre, visited annually by half a million worshippers. Processions take place each Sunday evening in summer and on 15 August (the feast of the Assumption). To cope with the press of pilgrims, Johann Schott of Munich in 1910 designed the huge neo-Baroque church of St Anne, now a papal basilica, which stands to the NW of Kapellplatz.

To the S of the Heilige Kapelle rises the double-steepled collegiate church of SS Philipp and Jakob, the third one on this site, begun by the architect Jörg Perger in 1499 and finished in 1511. The building incorporates a late 15C cloister, a 12C font and another font of 1501 and a Romanesque doorway of 1254. Inside the church, the a chapel of St Sebastian was designed by Domenico Zuccalli in 1680. Its altar relief is by Andreas Faistenberger, 1690. The organ gallery and organ date from 1724–55. The most macabre item is a clockwork statue of a skeleton, set here in 1634, symbolically scything a person to death once every second. The coffin of Field-Marshal Tilly lies in the chapel of St Peter. The most celebrated item in the church treasury (opening times vary) is the *golden horse of 1392, the work of French goldsmiths.

Opposite the Heilige Kapelle stands the church of St Magdalena, 1593, with Baroque reordering of 1697. Other features of Kapellplatz are the 18C church of St Maria Magdalena (with a statue on the wall of Pope John Paul II) and the Rathaus, dating from 1908, with a double onion dome and a tower. This adjoins the Hotel Zur Post, once the guesthouse of the monastery on the opposite side of the square and still retaining a couple of medieval rooms. Enrico Zuccalli designed the present monastic buildings in the late 1670s. Alongside them is the cemetery (with 20C stations of the cross). Close by is the local history museum (4 Kapellplatz, open daily in summer).

Kapuzinerberg leads W from Kapellplatz to the Bruder-Konrad church, built in 1657, widened in 1754, with a modern interior. Originally dedicated to St Anne, it now houses the mortal remains of St Konrad of Parzham, and adjoins the fountain fronting the entrance to the Capuchin monastery of Altötting.

Trains connect the town with Munich and Burghausen. Altötting is a centre for none-too-strenuous walks. The Information Office is in the town hall (open Mon–Sat 08.00–12.00, 14.00–17.00).

3km N of Altötting is **Neuötting am Inn** (5800 inhab.; alt. 392m), walled and rising on a cliff above the river. First appearing in written history in 1231, as *forum novum Oldingen*, Neuötting consists of a long, wide and arcaded Marktplatz closed at each end by a medieval gateway. The southern one is painted with a coat of arms of 1792. Another ancient tower, the 13C Pfennigturm, once housed the mint. The hall-church of St Nikolaus stands at the N end of Marktplatz, begun under the direction of Hans Stethaimer in 1410, though the ogival vaulting inside was finished only in the 1620s. Its spire reaches 78m. Inside, the Chapel of the Holy Cross dates from 1440; the Chapel of the Twelve Apostles from 1446, with frescoes of 1586; the clock from 1588; and the organ case from 1642. Look out for the Rococo statue of St Nicholas. Many of the church furnishings were Gothicised in the 19C, so that the high altar dates from 1896, though an altar of 1776 survives in the chapel of St Sebastian. See also the church of St Anna, built in 1511, its high altar depicting the Holy Family, carved three years later.

Follow the B299 NW for 22km to reach **Neumarkt-Sankt Veit**, another
Bavarian market town whose Stadtplatz is guarded at each end by fortified
gateways (the Unteres Tor specifically dated 1542). The church of St Johann
Baptist in the Stadtplatz dates from c 1450, with ogival arches inside, as
well as wall paintings of 1578 on either side of the high altar. The road
through the Unteres Tor climbs gently up to the church of St Veit, the largest
Gothic church in the region with an onion dome added by Johann Michael
Fischer in 1765. Its late 18C high altar is by Johann Nepomuk della Croce.

# 16

# Berchtesgaden and its Region

Total distance 167km. Traunstein—B304, 28km Freilassing—B20, 17km Bad
Reichenhall—18km Berchtesgaden—9km Ramsau—39km Ruhpolding
(excursion to Inzell)—37km Marquartstein—19km Prien am Chiemsee.

The winter sports and health resort of **Traunstein** (17,000 inhab.; alt. 600m)
lies on the B304, superbly situated in the Alps c 7km E of the Chiemsee
(see Rte 13), overlooked by the 900m-high Hochberg and where the old
Roman road from Salzburg to Augsburg crossed the River Traun. In the
Stadtplatz rises an externally classical church, St Oswald, with a high altar
of 1731 and a 19C interior. The basic form of the church dates from a
rebuilding after a fire in 1321, but the whole was repeatedly rebuilt over
subsequent centuries (with the late-17C hand of Kaspar Zuccalli particularly evident in the interior) to produce a three-aisled hall-church, with a
tower of 1597. Lorenzo Sciasci helped to remodelled the choir. A second
fire of 1701 gave the opportunity for further enrichment of the interior by
Philipp Köglsperger, Antonio Coralla and Matthias Pöllner. Among the
treasures which escaped a third fire in 1851 are a Baroque monstrance in
the form of a Jesse tree, by the Augsburg goldsmith Gregor Leider, 1648,
a Baroque statue of John the Baptist over the font, early 18C Baroque altars
and a Rococo Maria Immaculata. The Trinity group above the high altar is
by Ernst Fischer, 1909. The organ of 1856 (by Ehrlich, a firm from Landshut)
was transformed into a two manual instrument in 1929.

In the same square gushes the St Leonhard or Liendl-brunnen of 1525,
and here too is the arcaded medieval local history museum (opening times
vary). Abutting onto this museum is a house dating from 1541, rebuilt in
1794. Other churches are the chapel of St Rupert, c 1630, with contemporary frescoes discovered in 1928, and (in the Stadtpark) the church of St
Georg and Katharina, still Gothic in spite of being built in 1639. The town
park houses a culture centre. Each Easter Monday the St Georgtritt (St
George's ride), with sword dancing, takes place from here to Ettendorf and
back. Traunstein has three Kneipp establishments and is the second biggest
Kreisstadt in Bavaria. Trains connect the town with Salzburg and Munich.
Local information office Am Stadtpark (open Mon–Fri 08.00–12.00, 13.00–
17.00).

The B304 crosses the River Traun and leads E through the hilly land of
'Rupertiwinkel' (so named after St Rupert, first bishop of Salzburg, c

650–718) for 18km through Teisendorf to Freilassing on the Austrian border (and 7km from Salzburg). Just before Freilassing the B20 leads S along the left bank of the Saalach (with on the left the peaks of the the Gaisberg and Untersberg) crossing the Munich–Salzburg motorway to reach after 17km the winter sports centre and health resort of *Bad Reichenhall (18,500 inhab.; alt. 470km; tourist office: 15 Wittelsbacherstrasse). This celebrated spa and ski resort was famous for its salt mines in Celtic times ('Hall' is Celtic for salt). Thermal springs supply the health centres of the Kurpark (where you can also indulge in roulette and baccarat). A cable car reaches the 1614m-high Predigtstuhl.

In the centre of Rathausplatz is a lion fountain, 1905. The former town hall was burnt down on the night of 8/9 November 1834, replaced by today's Altes Rathaus in 1849. The Altes Brodhaus with a fine oriel window rises on the NW corner of Rathausplatz, rebuilt to reproduce a gutted 14C building. Follow Poststrasse past the Altes Brodhaus to reach the Carmelite church of St Ägidien—Romanesque 1159, partly Gothicised 15C, tower rebuilt after falling down in 1978. Inside on the south wall is a painting of its anti-Nazi parish priest, who died in Dachau concentration camp in 1942. On the outside of the apse wall another painting depicts the four horsemen of the Apocalypse riding above the town, commemorating an allied air attack of 25 April 1945 which killed 224 citizens. At the end of Postrasse rises the Romanesque church of St Johannes.

From Rathausplatz Salinenstrasse leads to the former early 16C salt works ('Alte Saline'), which received the salt-water poured along pipes from Berchtesgaden. Visits to the underground springs and pump rooms of the former salt works (which were considerably rebuilt under Ludwig I in 1834) take place most days in summer 10.00–11.30, 14.00–16.00. Moritz von Schwind frescoed the salt works chapel. Schloss Gruttenstein rises nearby (13C to 17C). Walk SE past the salt works towards the Altstadt, turning right along Kirchgasse to reach the Romanesque basilica of St Nikolaus of 1181, widened in 1860, when the tower was added; the frescoes are by Moritz von Schwind. From here stretch the early medieval town walls, with the remains of the Tyroler gate. Part of the former convent has been transformed into the St-Ägidi-Keller restaurant. On the opposite side of the street rise the 15C former offices of the salt works. Getreidegasse leads left by this 'Salzmaierampt' to the 14C granary, the 'Städtischer Getreidesaal', now the local history museum of Bad Reichenhall, open May–Oct weekdays except Mon 14.00–18.00, first Sun in the month 10.00–12.00.

Bad Reichenhall's finest Romanesque church, *St Zeno, stands to the NE of the town and is the largest Romanesque basilica in Upper Bavaria. Founded for Augustinian canons by Archbishop Konrad I of Salzburg in 1208, part of the monastic church was rebuilt in the late Gothic style after a fire of 1512. The cloisters and *superb red and grey marble Romanesque doorway survived intact—on the doorway are carvings of the Madonna, SS Zeno and Rupertus. The chapel in the east wing of the cloister is inscribed FRIDERICUS IMP, a reference to Frederick Barbarossa, one of the monastery's patrons.

Continue 18km SE to Berchtesgaden by way of **Bischofswiesen** (8000 inhab.; alt. 700m), with its clinics, heated swimming pools, tennis courts, winter sports facilities and a network of 90km of marked paths and walks. This is one of the five towns that make up the Berchtesgadener Land, the others being Markt Schellenberg, Ramsau, Schönau am Königsee and Berchtesgaden itself. Bischofswiesen means 'bishop's fields' and derives its name from land owned by the Bishops of Salzburg when they ruled the Berchtesgadener Land. Here a sign points left for the 5km drive to the early 18C pilgrimage church of **Maria Gern**, which stands above a village of 500 persons and was built to house a miracle-working statue of the Virgin, 1666. Gabriel Wenig and Jacob Hilliprant, both of the Berchtesgaden court, designed the church, with stucco work by Joseph Schmidt of Salzburg. Christoph Lehrl painted on the ceiling the cycle depicting episodes in the life of the Virgin Mary, 1710, and frescoed the side altars and the organ gallery. The high altar is by Caspar Schneider. The statue of St Michael slaying Lucifer is by Andrä Stangaster. On either side of the Baroque high altar stand SS Anna and Joachim, the parents of the Blessed Virgin. The side altars of the Holy Cross and the Josephsaltar date from the late 1730s, each flanked by angel-herms carrying medallions. The Munich court painter Johannes Zwick signed and dated the painting over the Josephsaltar, 'Jo: Zwick inv. e pin: Monachi 1740'.

Return to Bischofswiesen and drive on to **\*\*Berchtesgaden** (22,000 inhab.; alt. 530–1170m), superbly situated at the foot of the Untersberg (1973m), Höher Göll (2522m), Hochkalter (2607m), Watzmann (2714m) and the little Watzmann (2307m). Cable cars reach Obersalzberg (1020m) and the Jenner (1874m) with **\*views**, skiing and a toboggan run. The Hirscheck chair-lift carries visitors to the Hochschwarzeck, lying at the foot of a mountain called the 'Toter Mann'. The Obersalzberg lift rises from near the main railway station to a height of c 1000m.

**Information Office** and **Kurdirektion** 2 Königseestrasse opposite the railway station (open 6 June–29 Oct Mon–Fri 08.15–18.00, Sat 08.00–17.00, Sun and festivals 09.00–15.00; at other times in the year Mon–Fri 08.00–12.00, Sat 08.00–12.00, Sun and festivals 09.00–12.00). **Trains** connect Berchtesgaden with Munich and Freilassing; **buses** with Bad Reichenhall and Salzburg (a mere 20 minutes away).

Celtic tribes already mined salt in the region of Berchtesgaden in the 5C BC, using it to preserve food throughout the moist winters. Around AD 1000 a man named Perther built here a hunting lodge (or 'Gaden' in Middle High German, hence 'Berchtesgaden'). Soon Augustinian monks were mining salt in this region, persuading Emperor Frederick Barbarossa to confirm their exclusive rights to excavate it. Salt is still being mined at Berchtesgaden, and the clergy bless the mines on the feast of the Epiphany. Salt miners in traditional costume parade the streets on Whit Monday. The present-day salt mines began working in 1517. Visits to this 'Salzbergwerk' last around 1½ hours, with a film-show, rides in miners' cages, down chutes and on underground railways, with simultaneous translations of the guided tours (open daily 08.00–17.00, May–mid Oct; winter 13.00–15.30).

Start a tour of Berchtesgaden in the **\*Schlossplatz**, with its fountain and the former granary and teller's house, founded 1458, arcaded c 100 years later, its outer wall painted by J. Hengge as a World War I memorial in 1929. The late Gothic monastery church of SS Peter and Johannes was founded in the second half of the 12C, and retains Romanesque features—the west doorway, **\*transepts** and part of the south tower, though the two 13C towers were mostly rebuilt in 1866 and the western façade is almost entirely 19C Romanesque, including the two statues of SS Peter and John the Baptist. The tympanum on the north side is decorated with a painting by Rueland Fruehauf the elder of God the Father leaning from heaven to raise Jesus from the tomb. Jesus is flanked by his mother and St John, besides whom are the patrons of this church and also Propst Erasmus Pretschlaiper, who commissioned the painting in 1474. Inside in the entrance is a late Gothic, early 16C crucifixion, while the nave is Romanesque c 1200, the choir c 1300; also to be seen are Gothic net vaulting of 1515; a sculpted Romanesque bucket designed for carrying holy water; an early Baroque Madonna;

red marble tombs of the provosts (or 'Propsts') who ruled both the monastery and also the Berchtesgadener Land, including that of *Fürstpropst Gregor Rainer (to the left of the main entrance); mid-14C oak choir stalls, 1436–43; a Baroque high altar by Bartholomäus von Opstal; and a silver tabernacle by Franz Thaddäus Lang, 1735.

On the southern side stand the convent and cloisters which became the seat of the prince-abbot, next the residence of the Wittelsbachs when the town became Bavarian in 1810 and finally a museum and art gallery. The Romanesque cloister has contemporary carved capitals. The Gothic dormitory now houses woodcarvings by Erasmus Grasser, Veit Stoss and Tilman Riemenschneider. See also works by Lucas Cranach the Elder and portraits of the Wittelsbachs, Meissen pottery and a room devoted to prince-regent Luitpold (tours Sun–Fri 10.00–13.00, 14.00–17.00).

NW of the Stiftskirche of SS Peter and John the Baptist stands the church of St Andreas, begun 1396, rebuilt in the Baroque style 1698–1700, though the Baroque tower still rises from a late Gothic base. Standing opposite the west end of this church is Berchtesgaden's town hall. Walk through the SW archway of the Schlossplatz to the Renaissance and Baroque Marktplatz. The inscription on the fountain declares that it was set up in 1860 to mark the fiftieth anniversary of the union of Berchtesgaden and Bavaria. It stands on the site of a fountain set up by Churfürst Maximilian Heinrich in 1677. Maximilian Heinrich's portrait is painted on the façade of the nearby Hirchenhaus (1584, save for the 19C tower), built by Georg Inbermann who is also portrayed. Walk on past the burghers' houses and the shops of Marktplatz to Ludwig-Ganghofer-Strasse, named after the Bavarian novelist who once said of the Berchtesadener Land, 'Lord, let the one you love fall into this country', turning left out of Ludwig-Ganghofer-Strasse into Dr-Imhof-Strasse. This street leads as far as Am Anger, at the end of which stands the Franciscan church of St Maria-am-Anger by P. Kitzinger, 1488–1519; tower 1682. Otherwise known as the Frauenkirche, it has two arched aisles bisected by five round pillars, but no centre aisle. At the east end the two aisles meet in the Marienkapelle of 1688. Over the altar of this chapel is the statue of Unsere Liebe Frau am Anger, copied in Italy c 1500 from the statue of the Madonna in Milan cathedral. See also the carving of Christ in captivity, 1689, and the grim tomb of Maria Honorata, 1713.

To the N side of the church is Berchtesgaden's cemetery, the first tomb on the right through the gate that of its longest-lived citizen, Anton Adner (1705–1822). On the S side stands the National Park House (exhibition open daily 09.30–17.30, except for Nov–mid-Dec, outlining the history and aims of the Berchtesgaden National Park). This 21,000-ha park was founded in 1978. (Detailed plans of suggested tours, especially along the *Wimbach valley, which consists of constantly moving stones and pebbles, and information about guided tours are available at the National Park House.) **Königssee** is also part of Berchtesgaden's National Park, the ships that ply it driven by electricity so as to avoid pollution. Buses to the lake leave from the main railway station, parking at the village of **Königssee** from where the boat trip to and from **Schönau am Königssee** takes 1¼ hours, with views of the 400m-high Röthbach waterfall and the Baroque pilgrimage church of St Bartholomä at Schönau am Königssee, where there is also a restaurant, the haunt of the artist Caspar David Friedrich and the composer Max Reger. Continuing to the end of the lake, you can walk on to **Obersee**, from which run extensive mountain hikes.

Nonntal, the oldest street in the town, leads to the local history museum (woodcarvings) in Schloss Adelsheim at 6 Schroffenbergallee (guided tours

Mon–Fri at 10.00 and 15.00). Berchtesgaden also has a mid-19C royal villa, built for King Max II and his wife Marie by Friedrich von Gärtner. The Augustinan canons founded a brewery in the early 17C; visits to this 'Hofbräuhaus' take place on weekdays 08.00–19.00, Sat 08.00–12.00, 16.00–19.00, Sun 10.00–12.00, 16.00–19.00. The Bräustübl dates to 1910. In the 17C the Grassl family was granted the right to distil a liqueur from gentian plants and still does so. For a guided tour of the modern factory and the 'Enzian' museum drive along Bergwerkstrasse, turning left at the sign for Gewerbegebiet Gartenau.

Berchtesgaden both profits and suffers from its connection with the Nazi dictator Adolf Hitler. In 1937 Albert Speer designed for Berchtesgaden its present monumental railway station, at which Hitler received a succession of visiting dignitaries, including the Duke and Duchess of Windsor, exiled from Great Britain after his abdication, Mussolini's son-in-law Count Ciano, the British foreign minister Lord Halifax, the Austrian chancellor Kurt von Schuschnigg, the British prime minister Neville Chamberlain, the Japanese ambassador, Crown Prince Umberto of Italy, King Carol of Romania and the foreign minister of Poland. Speer's railway station remains, but after World War II the Americans demolished most of the villas built by the Nazis on the Obersalzberg, though they kept Hitler's guesthouse, the 'Platterhof', as a rest-home for American servicemen, renaming it the General Walker Hotel.

As a fiftieth birthday present the people of the town built for Hitler the remarkably sited **Kehlstein** or Eagle's Nest, which stands 1834m-high on a spur of the Höher Goll. Despite the extraordinary feat of engineering necessary to give access to this spot, Hitler scarcely ever visited it. Nothing connected with the dictator can be seen there now, and the Eagle's Nest today boasts only its daring site, *panoramas of Bavaria and Austria and a restaurant. To reach the Eagle's Nest drive for 5km from Berchtesgaden railway station, following the signs for Obersalzberg-Kehlstein and parking at Hintereck. Buses then take you for 6½km along a spectacular private road, through five tunnels and then directly up the north face of the mountain. The road is impassible in winter, open only from mid-May to mid-October. The final tunnel reaches a lift taking fewer than two minutes to arrive at the Kehlsteinhaus itself. A second legacy of 1930s engineering is the **Rossfeld Höhenringstrasse**, a toll road winding for 16km around the mountainside from Berchtesgaden and back, dotted with mountain inns (all of which close around 21.00).

Berchtesgaden festivals include the midsummer celebration of 'Johann-istag', with clog-dancing, bands and yodelling in local restaurants and hotels. On the evening of 5/6 December St Nicholas is depicted fighting against 12 evil spirits known as Butt'nmandln. On the four Thursdays before Christmas children dress as shepherds, wandering around, singing and receiving presents. The Schlossplatz at Berchtesgaden houses an Advent Christkindlmarkt, with small wooden huts selling presents.

9km W along the Bavarian Alpenstrasse lies the holiday resort of **Ramsau** (1800 inhab.; alt. 668m), approached through a tunnel hung with a mass of icicles in winter and lying by the stream known as the Ramsauer Ache. Its 16C parish church has a bulbous 18C dome on its spire. Inside, family names are still let into personal pews and there are 15C Gothic statues of Jesus and the 12 apostles on the organ loft, plus a high altar of 1680 and a Rococo side altar of 1745. The pilgrimage church of Maria Kunterweg on the slope of a nearby hill has a miraculous picture of the Virgin, 1690, in a high altar of 1750. The route leads NW to reach after 39km the health and winter sports resort of **Ruhpolding** (7000 inhab.; alt. 691m), with—up Kirchbergasse—the *parish church of St Georg, with a double onion dome a Romanesque west end and a panorama of the valley. Its architect was Johann Gunetzrhainer, 1738–57. Inside are the Romanesque Ruhpolding Madonna, c 1230, a mid-18C pulpit and choir stalls and a modern, jewelled cross over the high altar by Professor Karl B. Berthold. The local history museum is at 2 Schlossstrasse, in a Renaissance hunting lodge of 1587 (open weekdays 10.00–12.30, Fri also 14.30–17.00). Climb further to reach the 17C cemetery chapel, tomb-slabs on its walls. Ruhpolding is surrounded by 200km of summer walking routes and more than 50km of winter walking routes, the snow cleared by the tourist board. The Rauschberg cable car and the Unternberg ski-lift cater for skiers. The Kurverwaltung is at 60 Hauptstrasse, tel. 08 663 1268.

**Excursion**. The holiday and health resort of **Inzell** (3650 inhab.; alt. 692m) lies 13km E of Ruhpolding. The church of St Michael, founded by Archbishop Albrecht II of Salzburg, 1190, burnt down save for its tower, 1724, was rebuilt from 1727 and in the 19C and 1930s, restored 1985. Town hall with a table tennis room, a reading room and a salon showing video films, as well as the information office (open Mon–Fri 08.00–12.00, 14.00–18.00, Sat 08.00–12.00, Sun and holidays 09.30–11.30).

From Ruhpolding the Bavarian Alpenstrasse winds SW as far as **Reit im Winkl**, with an artificial ski run, decorated houses and views from the Grünbügel, and then NW by way of Unterwössen to reach after 37km **Marquartstein** at the foot of a 1743m-high peak. The 11C Burg Marquartstein is in private hands. Not far up Burgstrasse is the house called 'die Ahna', home of Richard Strauss, 1894–1907, where he composed songs, symphonic poems and the two operas 'Salome' and 'Feuersnot'. Marquartstein also has a parish church built in the 1930s, with contemporary wall paintings and reredos. From this church a signpost directs you along Loitshauserstrasse towards a fairy-tale and nature park.

The route now leads 19km NW to Prien am Chiemsee (see Rte 14A) by way of **Grassau**, with a late Gothic parish church of Maria Himmelfahrt, 1491, with a Romanesque tower topped by an onion dome, 1737 and a Corpus Christi procession painted over the entrance, 1700. The interior was remodelled in the Baroque style during the pastorate of Pfarrer Matthias Winkler, 1695–1707, whose tomb of 1715 is in the church. The frescoes are by Johann Peter della Croce of Burghausen and the statues of the four Evangelists on the pulpit are by Melchior Hofmayr, 1654).

# 17

## The Black Forest

### A.  Basel to Freiburg im Breisgau, and on to Breisach am Rhein

Total distance 108km. Basel—22km along the Landstrasse to Badenweiler—56km Freiburg im Breisgau—B31, 30km—to Breisach am Rhein. The Landstrasse as far as Freiburg is 78km long.

Quicker routes: the A5 motorway between Basel and Freiburg is 73km, passing alongside the Rhein and by Neuenberg.

From Basel to Freiburg on the B3 is 72km, reaching after 40km Mülheim, the centre of the region's wine trade. 17km further lies the spa of Bad Krozingen, with a Schloss of 1579. To follow this extremely scenic route, take the Landstrasse out of **Basel**, which after 3km crosses the SwissGerman frontier at Weil am Rhein (26,500 inhab.; alt. 261m). Here the River Rhine veers N to flow for some 300km through the wide, fertile rift valley known as Graben. Weil am Rhein, set where Switzerland, France and Germany converge, was called Willa in the 8C when it was a fief of the monks of St Gallen. Its Vitra Design Museum was designed by Frank Gehry and built between 1986 and 1989. 7km later the route reaches Binzen by way of the B3.

Drive N to **Kandern** (6000 inhab.; alt. 400m), a summer tourist resort devoted to hikers, which lies in the valley of the River Kandern. The town is also celebrated for its ceramics and pretzels. Its other treats include a museum of local history; the 15C former Rathaus; mills, including the Fischermühle of 1452; a hunting lodge of 1589; and the parish church built by Friedrich Weinbrenner in the 1820s. Local ceramics are displayed in an old Gothic house at 20 Ziegmerstrasse (open Apr–Nov, Sun 10.00–12.30 and Wed 15.00–17.30). Its most celebrated potter was Max Laueger, who died at 88 in 1952, leaving a legacy of Art Nouveau work. Johann Peter Hebel said of the local wine: 'Jetzt schwingen wir den Hut, Der Wein, der war so gut': 'Now we raise our hats at this splendid wine'.

2km after Kandern a detour right steeply reaches the Rococo *Schloss **Bürgeln** of 1762, with a restaurant and guided tours. Two-storeyed, its yellow walls contrast with its white shutters. Rising from the park, with its superb views, the Schloss has a Rococo staircase, lacy ironwork balconies and a stuccoed interior. From the tower of the nearby ruined Sausenburg you can see into Switzerland.

After 12km of vineyards the road reaches the thermal resort of **Badenweiler** (1500 inhab.; alt. 425m–449m) set in a huge plain, with vineyards and a view of the Vosges. Badenweiler was known for its curative waters to the Romans and has preserved Roman baths of 1C AD, covering nearly

3000 sq m, which were discovered in 1784 in the Kurpark. The baths display four bathing halls, each heated, the women's baths separated from the men's (guided tours Tue at 17.00, Sun at 11.00). Around the Schlossberg, with its old Schloss, is a sub-tropical park of 16 hectares. Badenweiler's Kurmittelhaus, designed in 1875 in the style of the ancient Roman baths, was considerably extended several times in the 20C. Its Kurhaus dates from 1972. Noteworthy are the 15C fragmentary wall paintings in the Protestant church, which was built by J. Durm between 1892 and 1897. The Renaissance Grand-Ducal palace of 1586 was remodelled in 1887–88. In the Kurpark are remains of the 10C and 12C Romanesque fortress, built by the Dukes of Zähringen and despoiled by the French in 1678. Anton Pavlovitch Chekhov (1860–1904) died here; his memorial is in the Kurpark. Walking tours are detailed in maps available at the Kurverwaltung. Badenweiler has preserved some of the ramparts built during the Thirty Years War. Open-air concerts take place in the bandstand of the Kurpark.

This is now the Baden wine road. At **Müllheim** (13,000 inhab.; alt. 250m), NW of Badenweiler, the oldest wine fair of the region is held annually in the third week of April, followed by a wine festival at the end of June. The town also boasts 18C vintners' houses, a Gothic parish church of St Martin, built in the 16C, and a wine and local history museum at 7 Wilhelmstrasse.

9km N of Badenweiler lies the spa of **Sulzburg**, which the Margraves of Baden-Durlach made their chief residence in the 16C. Here still stand a white and pink medieval gateway, a lime tree with a circumference of 4m and the 10C monastery church of St Cyriak which was founded by Birchtilo, Count of Breisgau, in 993. Well-restored in 1964, this three-aisled basilica, with a crypt, is noted for the 13C relief of Jesus Christ and the two founders on its portal; the founder's tomb in the apse; a tower begun in 1280; and its Gothic windows. In the Marktplatz the former Schloss church houses a regional mining museum, the Bergbaumuseum des Landes Baden-Württemberg (open daily except Mon, 14.00–17.00). Enquire here to visit the nearby former salt, lead and silver mines. The Rathaus is in the sole remaining wing of the 1515 Schloss. Streams flow on either side of the main street.

Sulzburg is followed after 5km by delightful **Staufen** (7400 inhab.; alt. 290–715m), picturesquely set on a hillock amidst its vineyards at the start of the valley of the Münster. Its glory is the late Gothic church of St Martin, built in 1485, with a 16C Pietà and crucifix, which is almost matched by the ruined Schloss Staufenberg, built in the 12C and razed by the Swedes in 1632. In the Marktplatz rise the three-storeyed, gabled and irregularly arched Rathaus of 1546 which is covered in coats of arms, a 16C fountain and the Gasthaus Löwen where Dr Faust on whom Goethe based his play is said to have been taken by the devil in 1539. Opposite the Gasthaus is a house with a courtyard, dated 1736. In the 16C and 18C Unteres Schloss is the forestry commission. Staufen derives from Stouf, early German for an upturned chalice, which the hill on which the Schloss stands supposedly resembles.

The route continues for 23km to Freiburg through the wine centre of Ehrenkirchen and then past (a short detour right) the former Cluniac monastery church of **St Ulrich**, a lovely Baroque building of 1740 by Peter Thumb, with a Romanesque font in the presbytery garden.

**\*\*FREIBURG IM BREISGAU** (180,000 inhab.; alt. 269m), still 'antique, irregular and picturesque' as Mary Shelley described it, is situated on the River Dreisam between the Kaiserstuhl (see below) and the Black Forest at

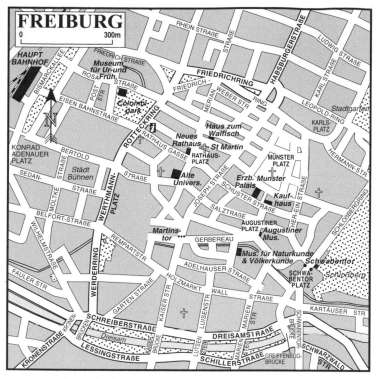

the start of the Höllental. Capital of the Black Forest, the city now dominates an important crossroads on the borders of France and Germany and is the seat of the regional government of South Baden.

**Main railway station**: Bismarckallee. **Main post office**: 58–62 Eisenbahstrasse. **Information Office**: 14 Rotteckring. **Trains** to Frankfurt, Basel, Holland.

**History**. A stronghold was founded by Duke Berthold II of Zähringen c 1091. This Freiburg was developed by Berthold's brother, Duke Konrad, 1118–20, as an oval town with streets crossing the oval in the fashion favoured by his dynasty (cf. Villingen-Schwenningen, Freiburg in Switzerland, Bern, Solothurn and Offenburg). The city was walled c 1200, when the cathedral was begun. Five monasteries arose here in the 13C, when Freiburg was at its richest, from its position on the Schwabian-Alsace trade route, and from silver mined in the Black Forest. In 1368 the Habsburgs became lords of Freiburg—by peaceful agreement with the citizens who had bought their freedom from their unpopular ruler Count Egino III, whose Schloss they had destroyed—and the university was founded in 1457 by Archduke Albrecht VI of Austria. Freiburg became a centre of learning. In 1507 the cosmographer Martin Waldseemüller (c 1480–c 1521) published here a book of maps which was the first to call the newly discovered continent 'America'. The peasants took the city in 1515, and in 1564 2000 inhabitants died of the plague. Freiburg never converted to Protestantism and became a refuge for persecuted Catholics.

In spite of several sieges during the Thirty Years War, when the Swedes captured Freiburg in 1632 and 1638, the city retained much of its character and buildings intact. Between 1677 and 1697 Freiburg belonged to the French, its defences strengthened by Vauban to make it one of the safest in Germany. The city became Austrian again with the Peace of Ryswijk, 1697, though the French twice recaptured the city—in 1713 and 1744, destroying all the city fortresses when they were driven out the following year. In 1805 Napoleon insisted that Austria transfer all her territories in Baden to a newly established Grand Duchy, and following the Treaty of Pressburg in 1806, Freiburg became part of the Grand-Duchy of Baden, an entity destroyed by the victors of World War I. Twenty-one years later its bishops became archbishops. When the call for a revolution was made in 1918, the city became a republic. Much was destroyed in World War II (the German air force killing 57 citizens in an erroneous attack of 1940, the allies killing some 3000 in a bombing raid on 27 November 1944), but much has been restored; the open medieval sewage streams (the 'Bächle') still flow through the city.

Each year Freiburg hosts processions on the Monday before Lent and on Corpus Christi. As well as its June wine festival the city holds a beer festival in early August. Freiburg flea markets are held on the second Sunday in May and on the second Sunday in September. Each Christmas a fair lasting four weeks is held in the Rathausplatz.

**Eisenbahnstrasse** leads from the main railway station as far as the **Colombipark** with its late-19C neo-Gothic **Colombischlössle**—it is now a museum of prehistory and early history—**Museum füt Ur-und Früageschichte**—built in the English Gothic revival style for the Duchess Maria Gertrud von Zea Bermudez und Columbi in 1859 on the site of one of Vauban's former fortresses (open daily 09.00–19.00). Cross the Rotteckring, with the Raufbuben fountain of 1931, to reach the church of **St Ursula** with its 18C Baroque chapel. The church interior was finished in 1710. Its ceiling is stuccoed, and the building is graced with a Rococo pulpit and sounding board, and a double-storeyed choir gallery with a Rococo balustrade. St Ursula is used for Anglican and Old Catholic worship. The narrow **Rathausgasse** has medieval houses, particularly Zum Biber ('At the Beaver's'), 1460; Zum Geilen Fisch ('At the Merry Fish'), 1390; Zum Blauen Sperber ('At the Blue Sparrow-Hawk'), late 14C. It leads to the chestnut-shaded **Rathausplatz**.

Here is a fountain with a monument to the monk Berthold Schwarz who discovered gunpowder in 1353. To the left is the **Neues Rathaus**, created in 1856 by the union of two 16C Renaissance houses. It has richly decorated oriel windows, a fine courtyard and a carillon in the clock tower, playing folk-songs daily at 12.03. Adjacent is the **Altes Rathaus**, with a Renaissance gable and in the courtyard, where there are open-air concerts in summer, the restored courthouse. Over its clock tower are the coats of arms of the former Habsburg rulers (1368–1806). In front of the Neues Rathaus a mosaic pavement displays the escutcheons of Besançon (France), Guildford (UK), Innsbruck (Austria) and Padua (Italy), all twinned with Freiburg, while on the front of the Altes Rathaus is the coat of arms of the city itself.

To the right of Rathausplatz is the Gothic church of **St Martin**, with three naves, built for Franciscan monks and dating in part from the 13C. It was bombed in 1944 and restored in 1953 and again in 1974. St Martin has a Baroque porch (the Sonntagsportal of 1719), a crossing of 1246, the tomb of the writer Heinrich Hans Jakob (died 1916) and, abutting, a Gothic cloister from the former Franciscan monastery. Inside is a fresco of 1480 whose background is the oldest depiction of the city.

Follow Franziskanerstrasse to the restored **Haus zum Walfisch** ('House of the Whale'), built by the Emperor Maximilian I in 1516 for his retirement and incorporating two flamboyant oriels, a wrought iron gate of 1911, a gargoyle with a goitre and a graceful alcove/canopy decorated with sculpted milk-wort and tendrils. Maximilian died here in 1519. A plaque records that Erasmus of Rotterdam lived here from 1529 to 1531, having found the Protestants of Basel little to his taste.

The route reaches the arcaded main street of Freiburg, pedestrianised **Kaiser-Joseph-Strasse**, which once had the less pompous name Langgasse until Kaiser Joseph II visited Freiburg in 1777. This is a venue for street theatre on Saturdays. On the right you find the **Baseler Hof** (known as the Stürtzelches Haus, from Konrad Stürtzel von Buchheim, who commissioned the building in 1500). From 1588 till 1677 it became the home of the cathedral chapter of Basel, fleeing the Reformation. Today it serves as the seat of the regional administration. Finished in 1510, this gracious building has a doorway of 1588 and a staircase tower in its courtyard. On the façade a splendid Renaissance carving of 1593 depicts the patron and patron saints of Freiburg, Emperor Heinrich II, the Virgin Mary and St Pantalus.

Turn into **Münsterplatz** (market) to find the red sandstone **\*\*Münster** (or Dom) of Unserer Lieben Frau, built in four distinct architectural phases between c 1170 and the early 16C. The earliest parts consist of the

*Standing 115m-high, the fretted Gothic spire of the münster of Freiburg im Breisgau*

Romanesque crossing with its frescoes, and the early 13C Hahnentürme ('Cock Towers', with later Gothic superstructures, so-called after their weather vanes). The Gothic central nave and the two side aisles date from the mid 13C. The next period of building produced the 115m-high west tower, begun in 1250 as a square base by Master Gerhard of Strasbourg, which by way of an octagon becomes a delicate open-tracery pyramid (built by Master Heinrich Müller, c 1275–98, and finished in 1350 by Master Peter of Basel). From the top, reached by 328 steps, is a panorama of the Kaiserstuhl, the Rhine valley and the Tuniberg and Vosges mountains; entrance in the aisle beside the west porch (open weekdays, except Mon 10.00–17.00, Sun and holidays 13.00–17.00).

Among its 16 bronze bells the oldest single spire of its kind in Germany carries one of Germany's oldest, the 'Hosanna' of 1258, which rings every Friday at 11.00. Below is the great door, with statues of SS Lambert and Alexander flanking the Virgin Mary, along with late 13C sculptures of the wise and foolish virgins, sin and voluptuousness, the demon prince, and friezes depicting the life of Jesus, the Last Judgment and the 12 apostles. The church and synagogue are also represented, the synagogue blindfolded. In the porch, once used as a courtroom, are stone benches, and set beside the entrance are the measures for an ell and a barrel as well as the contours of loaves of bread. The late Gothic chancel, begun 1354, was designed by Johannes Parker of Gmünd, and is encircled by a polygon of chapels. Work was suspended c 1370. At the expense of the Emperor Maximilian I and other patrons, Hans Niesenberger took over the project in 1471, and the cathedral was finished in 1513.

**Interior**. 125m long, 30m wide, 27m high, the cathedral has some 13C–15C stained glass, incorporating inscriptions and coats of arms of the donors, who included the various craftsmen's guilds of Freiburg. The nave has a Gothic pulpit by Jörg Kempf, 1561, with the sculptor—perhaps—portrayed by himself underneath the steps. Its canopy is by Franz Xaver Hauser, 1705. The nave also has a fresco by Ludwig Seitz, 1877 of the coronation of the Virgin Mary. The allegorical friezes at the entrance to the Hahnenturm-Kapelle depict mythical and medieval scenes. On the altar in the transept is an Adoration of the Magi by Hans Wydyz, 1505. The high altar of 1511 carries Hans Baldung Grien's lovely *Coronation of the Virgin, each of the wings painted with six apostles, led by SS Peter and Paul. Other paintings include Grien's Schnewlin altar, depicting Jesus's baptism and St John the Divine on Patmos; a Man of Sorrows by Lucas Cranach the Elder, 1524, in the sacristy; and the Oberried altar by Hans Holbein the Younger, 1521, which depicts the adoration of the Magi, the Shepherds and the donors.

The Rococo font in the Cyriak chapel is by Christoph Wenzinger, 1768. In the Bocklin-Kapelle is a silver-gilt crucifix, c 1180. The chapel of the tomb dates from 1340, with a recumbent Jesus, watched over by his disciples and the holy women. The Locherer chapel contains a Virgin of Mercy, carved in 1524 by J. Sixt. Do not miss the remains of a 14C fresco in the chapel of SS Peter and Paul, and the round 14C window in the nave.

Münsterplatz is cooled by Freiburg's oldest fountain, the Gothic **Fischbrunnen** by Hans von Basel, 1483, as well as by the modern successful pastiche of a Gothic fountain, the Georgsbrunnen. North of the cathedral square is the former granary, the **Kornhalle**, with its steep recessed gable. Destroyed in 1944 and since restored to its original state of 1497, this is now the home of Benedictine nuns. To the S is the Baroque **Erzbischöfliches Palais**, built in 1756 and decorated by a wrought-iron balcony and the episcopal coats of arms. Next to it rises the half-Gothic, half-Renaissance **Kaufhaus** (the merchants' house of c 1520), arcaded, with a balcony and two corner turrets at its gabled ends, and decorated with statues of Maximilian I, his son Philip I of Spain, his grandsons Emperor Charles I and Ferdinand I, carved by S. von Staufen, 1530. Inside is the stuccoed Kaisersaal with wooden pillars.

The northern part of Münsterplatz houses a daily market selling vegetables, eggs and fruit, while the southern section has a daily market selling ham, bacon, pottery, honey, olives, woodcarvings and straw footwear. Flower stalls set up W of the cathedral. This platz is the annual scene of Freiburg's wine festival, held over the last weekend in June. From here a little street leads to the baroque **Haus zum Schönen Eck**, built by Christian Wenzinger for his own use, 1755–65, with a staircase well in the courtyard; it is now a music school. Wenzinger's bust is on the balcony, and inside the house he appears on the frescoed ceiling of the staircase welcoming Hercules into Olympus.

Of Freiburg's fortifications remain the much altered **Martinstor**, originally 13C, enlarged with a turreted roof in 1905 to reach 63m. Behind it are ancient streets still bearing the name of craftsmen who worked there: Gerberau (the tanners, now filled with antique shops), Fischerau (the fishermen), Metzgerau (the butchers). The 12C **Schwabentor**, restored 1901, with a fresco of the peasant who came with a pot of gold to buy the city, now houses a museum of 5000 tin figures, laid out to represent battles, as well as a diorama of Luther's entry into Worms (open Jun–Aug daily 10.00–12.00, 16.00–18.00, Sun 11.00–13.00; May, Sept, Oct, Sat 10.00–12.00, 16.00–18.00, Sun 11.00–13.00).

The **\*\*Augustinermuseum** stands in Augustinerplatz, housed in the ochre-coloured former Augustinian monastery founded in 1278, with 14C cloisters. Its treasures include works by Grien and Grünewald—especially the latter's 'Miracle of the Snow', as well as other art connected with the city and the Upper Rhine, beginning c 800 with the Aldelhauser Tragaltar or 'portable altar'. Next door, at 32 Gerberau, are the **Museum für Naturkunde** and the **Museum für Völkerkunder**, housed in the Baroque former Adelhauser Kloster.

Beyond the Martinstor is the Catholic **St Johannes-Kirche**, 1894–99, modelled on the Romanesque cathedral of Bamberg. Around the Schwabentor is situated the old Bürgers' quarter of Oberlinden, incorporating Germany's oldest inn, **Zum Roten Bären** ('At the Red Bear') of 1311 or even earlier. In its square rises the Baroque **Marien** fountain, and the house **Zum alten Kameltier** ('At the Old Camel') is decorated on its façade with regency stucco. The nearby **Schwabentorbrücke** has on its S side a monument to the battle of Sempach, 1336, between the Swiss and the troops of Archduke Leopold III of Austria. Opposite the Tor is a statue of St Albertus Magnus, the 13C provincial of the Freiburg Dominicans. From here rises the 430m-high **Schlossberg**, with its vineyards, a Bismarck monument of 1900, the Greiffenegg Schlössle, built in 1805 for the last Austrian district president Hermann von Greiffenegg and now a restaurant, and from the top a \*panorama. (A chair-lift reaches its peak from the Stadtgarten.) Freiburg's other notable peak, the 1284m-high **Schauinsland** (which means 'Look into the country') can also be reached by cable car, from the suburb of Horbern, or by an excellent road used biennially in summer as a race track. It has marked hiking routes, and views of the highest Black Forest peak, the 1493m-high Feldberg and into the Swiss Alps and the French Vosges.

OTHER SIGHTS: municipal theatre of 1910, rebuilt 1963; the university buildings of 1911; the former university, dating from the 17C and 18C; Jesuit church in Bertholdstrasse, 1685–1705, which was destroyed in World War II and rebuilt rather spartanly. The Museum of Mechanical Musical Instruments; the Museum of Folksong, No. 12 Silberbachstrasse; and the Museum für Neue Kunst, No. 10a Marienstrasse (all open Tue–Sun 10.00–17.00, closing Wed at 20.00). A Stucco Museum (Kleines Stuckmuseum), No. 11 Liebigstrasse, opens weekdays 13.00–18.00, Sat 09.00–13.00.

East of the city, in the **Moselpark**, boats ply the Waldsee in summer, which becomes a natural skating rink in winter. In this suburb also stands the **Stadthalle** (at 80 Schwarzwaldstrasse), with seats for 4000 spectators. The Mösle sports stadium in the same suburb accommodates 22,000, the Dreisam Stadium (at 193 Scharzwaldstrasse) 14,000, and the Eissporthalle (in Ensisheimer Strasse W of Freiburg) 6000 spectators.

Leave Freiburg NW along the B31 by way of **Umkirch**, with its Hohenzollern Schloss and **Ihringen** (Germany's warmest town and a great wine centre) to reach after 30km the fortified town of *'Breisach am Rhein** (9500 inhab.; alt. 190–240m). On its steep promontory overlooking the Rhine, this spot was inhabited in the Bronze Age, fortified by the Romans and is now a wine and Sekt centre. The Zähringen family built a fortress here in the 12C. Breisach was an Austrian stronghold from 1331, after which for centuries the Habsburgs and the French disputed its possession.

The road to the heart of Breisach winds upwards through the 16C walls, past Vauban's Rheintor of 1670, with portrait medallions of Louis XIV and his queen, to the grey-walled *'münster of St Stephan, half Romanesque, half Gothic, built from the 10C to the 15C and today surrounded by a garden. One tower is Romanesque, the other 13C Gothic. On the tympanum of the west façade is a Gothic carving of St Stephen. Inside, do not miss the Gothic *'high altar, carved out of limewood by Hans Liefrink, 1527. It depicts the Coronation of Mary, who is surrounded by the Holy Trinity, while on the wings are SS Stephen and Laurence, SS Gervase and Protase. The Münster has a fresco, c 1490, by Martin Schongauer of the Last Judgment; a late Gothic *'choir screen, c 1500, with the Madonna, SS Joseph and Stephen and the Magi; late 15C choir stalls with grotesques; a 15C tabernacle; in the north transept an early 16C Deposition; and a silver reliquary, 1496, with the relics of SS Gervase and Protase. Breisach is the border town at the crossing of the Rhine for Colmar in Alsace. The pre- and early history museum at 21 Münsterbergstrasse, opens weekends from 14.00–16.00. The Galerie Kroner in the early classical Schloss Rimsingen (1773, by F.A. Bagnato) open Tue–Sun 10.00–19.00. The anti-pope John XXIII, c 1370–1419, deposed in 1415 by the Council of Constance, fled to Freiburg disguised as a groom and travelled on to Breisach, where he was captured.

About 10km NE is the **Kaiserstuhl**, formed from a range of vine-covered black volcanic hills where, according to legend, the emperors would meet the people to settle their subjects' grievances. Here the principal wine town is **Endingen**, with its gabled Kornhaus and Rathaus, both dating from the 16C.

# B.  Ettlingen to Freiburg im Breisgau

Total distance, by way of the B3, 121km. Ettlingen—18km Rastatt—15km Steinbach—3km Bühl—10km Achern—9km Offenburg—20km Lahr—10km Ettenheim—9km Kenzingen—11km Emmendingen—16km Freiburg.
The motorway from Ettlingen to Offenburg is 74km.

The old town of **Ettlingen** (37,000 inhab.; alt. 340m) lies 8km S of Karlsruhe
(see Rte 17D) on the River Alb. Although it retains some medieval fortifications, Ettlingen was largely rebuilt as a Baroque town after the War of
the Spanish Succession. Its Rathaus has a Baroque façade, 1737–38, by J.P.
Rohrer of Baden-Baden; in its wall is set the Roman Neptune stone
recovered from the river in 1480. Ettlingen's four-winged Renaissance
Markgravenschloss (16C and early 18C) is fronted by a well topped by the
Narrenbrunnen dated 1549. Today the Schloss serves as the Information
Office and houses regional museums with exhibits ranging from Roman
times to the 20C (open Sat 14.00–17.00, Sun 10.00–12.00, 14.00–17.00). The
coat of arms on the balcony is that of Markgräfin Sibylla Augusta von
Sachsen-Lauenburg, who around 1730 commissioned J.M.L. Rohrer to
build the fourth wing and the two great round towers of the Schloss. Its
*Hofkapelle, built and decorated with trompe l'oeil frescoes of the life of
St Johann Nepomuk by Cosmas Damien Asam in 1732, is now a concert
hall belonging to South German TV, and in the courtyard is a dolphin
fountain of 1612. Other sights are the Lantern Tower, which survives from
the old town defences, and the 18C Catholic parish church of St Martin,
with a 12C (in part) sacristy, a 13C choir and mid-15C vaulting. It rests on
Carolingian foundations. J.M.L. Rohrer rebuilt the nave in the Baroque
style in 1733.

The B3 leads 18km SW to the industrial town of **Rastatt** (40,000 inhab.;
alt. 120m), near where the River Murg joins the Rhine. Burnt down by the
French in 1689, Rastatt was rebuilt by Markgraf Ludwig Wilhelm von
Baden (known as 'Türkenlouis' because of his victories over the Turks) and
after his death in 1707 by his widow Sibylla Augusta von Sachsen-Lauenburg, who particularly exploited the Baroque skills of the Rohrer brothers.
This was the principal residence of the Margraves of Baden from 1707 to
1771. Here in 1713 and 1715 Prince Eugene of Savoy and the Marshal de
Villars met to bring an end to the War of the Spanish Succession. An
abortive meeting at Rastatt between the French and their enemies in 1799
led to a massacre of the French. The town became a garrison in 1811 and
was fortified in 1840.

The red sandstone *Schloss, 1697–1707, is the first in Germany in the
Baroque style of Versailles, built under the direction of the Viennese
architect Domenico Egidio Rossi with a garden front 230m long and a
courtyard dominated by a balustrade with Baroque statues. Over the
central wing rises a statue of Jupiter known as the Goldenen Mann. Sibylla
Augusta's tomb is in the Baroque Schloss chapel, designed by Michael
Ludwig Rohrer, its rich decoration, by J. Hiebal and J. Ongers, reminiscent
of Sibylla's Bohemian origins. The Schloss now houses a regional and
military museum as well as a museum of the German freedom movement,
with special reference to the historic events of 1848/9 (open respectively
Tue–Sun  10.00–12.00,  14.00–17.00,  and  Good  Friday–31  Oct  Tue–Sun
10.00–17.00). Its finest room is the frescoed Festsaal. In the gardens rises
the polygonal Pagodenburg, 1722, by J. Effner, modelled on the Nymphenburg at Munich, and the chapel of Maria Einsiedeln, built in 1715. This is

modelled on the pilgrimage chapel of the same name in Switzerland, where Sibylla went to pray before a Black Madonna on behalf her son, who had been born dumb. Opposite the Schloss stands the Ludwig Wilhelm Gymnasium, built in 1739 as a monastery, and beside it is the Protestant parish church of 1701–17.

Rossi designed the Marktplatz of Rastatt, now dominated by the Rathaus, with its Baroque façade of 1750, and the onion-domed Catholic parish church of 1764, by J.P. Rohrer. These buildings overlook two fountains by J.P. Rohrer, the St Johannes Nepomuk Brunnen of 1734 and the Alexis Brunnen of 1738. The local history museum is in Herrenstrasse (open Wed, Fri, Sun and holidays 10.00–12.00, 15.00–17.00).

5km S in the direction of Baden Baden is **Schloss Favorite**, which Michael Ludwig Rohrer built for Sibylla Augusta in 1711. It houses valuable porcelain and stucco, and is decorated with silks and Chinese wallpaper, and Venetian looking glasses (the Spiegelkabinett has 330 mirrors) and marble; hourly visits from 09.00 to 17.00 in summer, closing at 16.00 Oct, Nov; otherwise closed). Its model was the Bohemian Schloss Schlackenwerth. Its gardens and lake are enhanced with Cavaliers' Houses, an Orangery and a Hermitage.

The route continues S, passing near 13C ruins of **Ebersteinburg** (see Rte 17D) and **Hohenbaden**, with its Altes Schloss on the left. Now mostly ruined, its earliest part, the early 12C Hermannsbau, with its fountain and belfry, takes its name from Margrave Hermann I, who built it. The other Gothic parts date from the 14C and 15C. Pass through Baden-Oos (see Rte 17C for Baden-Baden) to reach **Steinbach** (3500 inhab.; alt. 142m), with its open-air swimming pool. Here was born Erwin von Steinbach (died 1318) architect of Strasbourg cathedral. A statue in his honour stands on a nearby hill.

3km S of Steinbach is **Bühl** (22,000 inhab.; alt. 136m) on the edge of the Black Forest, at the mouth of the Bühl valley and famous for its fruits; the town hosts a fruit tart festival each September. Bühl has an 1877 Gothic church of SS Peter and Paul (with 1950s stained glass by Albert Burkart) and a Corn Hall. Its Rathaus preserves an early 16C eight-sided tower from the former parish church. The Heimatmuseum at 2 Luisenstrasse, open first Sun in month, 14.00–18.00, displays Celtic and Roman finds. Further S, on the outskirts of **Ottersweier**, is the Baroque pilgrimage church of Maria Linden. The Rathaus is in the former Jesuits' College. The present parish church is 19C neo-Gothic, and beside it is a modern fountain-statue of St John the Baptist.

An **excursion** from Bühl takes you 9km NW to **Schwarzach**, with its Benedictine abbey church, dedicated to SS Peter and Paul, begun in the late 12C. The three-aisled, late Romanesque church culminates in a Romanesque apse and carries on its portal sculptures of Jesus and the two patron saints. Ogival Gothic vaults top the aisles. The organ is by J.-A. Rohrer (or, say some, by Gottfried Silbermann); the Baroque high altar was carved by Martin Eigler in 1752. For this monastery Peter Thumb created Baroque conventual buildings between 1724 and 1736, of which a few traces remain.

4km S of Bühl on the main route are the half-timbered houses of the small town of **Sasbach**, near where the French Marshal Henri de la Tour d'Auvergne, Vicomte de Turenne, was killed by a bullet on 27 July 1675, while leading his troops against the Imperial forces under General Montecuccoli. On the spot where he fell is a granite obelisk of 1829, 12m high, decorated with a medallion inscribed 'La France à Turenne' and approached by an avenue of pine trees. Scottish and Irish monks founded a monastery at Sasbach in 750, and the town's parish church, dedicated to St Brigid of Kildare, was built by Anton Schmidt, though designed by Kaspar Waldner, between 1774 and 1776. Schmidt retained parts of the late Gothic predecessor, including a relief of St Brigid, c 1480, while the interior is Rococo, save for the classical altars by Peter Wagner, court-sculptor of Würzburg. A Turenne museum is at 3 Schwarzwaldstrasse, open Mon–Sat 09.00–12.00, 14.00–17.00.

After 6km you reach **Achern** (22,000 inhab; alt. 143m) at the beginning of the valley of the Acher. The slightly unsightly Nikolaus Kapelle, 14C, has a 16C tower. Achern's pedestrianised shopping square is cooled by a fountain. The monument in the marketplace is to the Grand Duke Leopold who ruled Baden from 1830 to 1852—and annoyed Mary Shelley when she reached Darmstadt in 1842 when she found that he had booked every decent room in the city, relegating the English visitors to 'the common eating room—of course, redolent with smoke'. This is a centre of the brandy industry and of glass blowing, as well as tourism (golf, tennis, camping). A local history museum in Berliner Strasse opens on Sun 14.00–18.00 and by appointment.

The road continues through **Renchen**, which has two statues of the poet and author Johann Jakob Christoph von Grimmelshausen, born 1621, who died here in 1676, and the railway junction of **Appenweier**. Here is the Rococo St Michael's church, designed by Franz Ignaz Ritter and built by J. Ellmenreich between 1748 and 1752, with an onion dome and a splendid *interior, including a marble pulpit by Johannes Schütz and a late Gothic panel depicting the Virgin Mary presenting the Infant Jesus to St Anne. The Franco-Prussian war memorial in the centre of the town has a bust of Kaiser Wilhelm I.

Beyond Appenweier the route reaches Offenburg, lying at the centre of the Ortenau vineyards.

**Offenburg** (51,000 inhab.; alt. 140–690m) was founded by the Zähringer family in the 12C and in the next century became a Free City. Almost entirely destroyed by the ravages of the French troops in 1689, it boasts in the pedestrianised Hauptstrasse the Baroque Heilig-Kreuz-Kirche, by Franz Beer and Leonhard Albrecht, begun in 1700 and finished in 1790. Their building retains a late Gothic choir, a crucifix of 1521—on the left side altar—and, outside, a Mount of Olives group of 1524 and 16C tombstones. Inside are also a Baroque high altar of 1740 by F. Lichtenauer; choir stalls of 1740; a pulpit of 1790; and an 18C organ. Also in Hauptstrasse stands the double-storey, Baroque Rathaus, created in 1741 by Matthias Fuchs out of an earlier Renaissance building. Nearby, at No. 96, is M. Rohrer's Baroque Landratsamt of 1717. At 10 Ritterstrasse is the Ritterhausmuseum of 1775, with a Grimmelshausen archive, and another devoted to the naturalist Lorenz Oken (1779–1851). Offenburg also offers the Baroque Palais Rieneck, and a late 13C Jewish bath, at 6 Glaserstrasse. Offenburg's former Franciscan monastery stands in Lange Strasse, dates from 1717 and shelters an organ by the Silbermann family. Close by, across what remains of the cloister, stands the funeral chapel of 1515, with a Virgin sculpted in wood in the early 16C. E. Eiermann built the Verlagshaus Burda in 1954.

On the way to the industrial town of Lahr, 20km S of Offenburg, make a **detour** SE to **Gengenbach**, once a Free Imperial City, which has halftimbered houses, two medieval gates (the 13C Haigeracher Tor and the 14C Kinzigtor) and three medieval towers (the Schwedenturm, the Niggelturm and the Prälatenturm). In the Marktplatz, which centres on a fountain of 1572, rise the gabled Pfaffsche Haus, decorated with a statue of the Madonna and built by Franz Beer, the Rathaus of 1784, ornamented with statues of wisdom and justice, and the Kauf-und Kornhaus of 1696. Another Madonna is sculpted on the façade of the five-aisled church of St-Marien, which was begun in the 12C and frequently rebuilt, being topped with its Baroque tower in 1716. Square pillars and columns alternate in its Romanesque interior. The neo-Romanesque frescoes date from the 19C.

**Lahr** (37,000 inhab.; alt. 170m) stands on the N bank of the River Schutter, close by the 300m-high Schutterlindenberg and in the pleasant Schutter valley. At the E end of the Kaiserstrasse stands the Altes Rathaus of 1608, restored by Friedrich Weinbrenner in the 19C and adorned with belfry, Gothic staircase, gable and arcades. Pedestrianised Markstrasse leads from here S to the remains of the 13C burg of the lords of Geroldseck, the Storchen Tor, which now houses the Geroldsecker Museum (town history; open Wed, Sat 16.00–18.00, Sun and holidays 11.00–12.00, 16.00–18.00).

S too, in Bismarckstrasse, lies the 13C Gothic Stiftskirche, also restored in the mid 19C (by J.-F. Eisenlohr), though its choir remained relatively untouched. The façade of 1874 incorporates three flamboyant Gothic portals. Inside, the pulpit is an 1850 copy of a Gothic original. The Neue Rathaus dates from 1808. In the park is a museum of local history and art (open Wed, Sat 15.00–17.00, Sun and holidays 10.00–12.00, 14.00–17.00, closing an hour earlier in winter), and the museum of pre- and early history is at 54 Dinglinger Hauptstrasse (open Wed, Sat 16.00–18.00, Sun and holidays 10.00–12.00). The poet L. Eichrodt (1827–92) lived at Lahr. In the suburb of Burgheim is the restored 11C Romanesque church of St Peter, with 15C wall paintings.

A brief **excursion** E reaches **Reichenbach**, with the ruined Schloss Hohengeroldseck, 526m-high, while some 15km SW of Lahr is the **Europa-Park**, a leisure and family centre, with Mississippi steamers and the like.

Continue S from Lahr to **Mahlberg**, with its tobacco museum, mid-13C Schloss, restored in the 17C, and an eight-sided chapel of St Catherine (with 17C and 18C stucco and decoration). After Mahlberg the B3 reaches **Ettenheim**. Ettiko II, Duke of Alsace, and his son Bishop Etto of Strasbourg, founded this town in the early 8C. Here on 14 March 1804, Napoleon arrested the conspirator d'Enghien (who was executed at Vincennes six days later). Here lived Cardinal de Rohan during the French Revolution, in the present administrative offices, 1790–1803. The parish church dates from 1777, with the cardinal's tomb in the chancel, and two town gates survive from the 18C. The half-timbered and Baroque houses at the heart of Ettenheim form a fine ensemble. **Ettenheimmünster**, 4km E of the town, retains only the walls, a mill and a few other traces of its former Benedictine monastery, as well as a richly decorated Baroque church of St Landolin, built by Peter Thumb in 1783. Landolin was an Irish monk and missionary, killed here by a pagan huntsman in 640. Inside are a silver bust of Landolin, 1509; Rococo frescoes of the life of the saint; Rococo furnishings, including confessionals; and an *organ by Johann Andreas Silbermann.

The road from Ettenheim passes S through **Herbolzheim**, where a 45-minute climb rises to the panoramas from the 310m-high Kahlenberg, to reach **Emmendingen** (25,000 inhab.; alt. 201m). Goethe's sister Cornelia married J.G. Schlosser, a town magistrate, and is buried in the cemetery here. Here too died the writer Alfred Döblin, author of 'Berlin Alexanderplatz' (1929), and the painter Fritz Boehle (1873–1916) was a native of the town. The Markgrafen Schloss, 1574, is now a local history museum, including memorabilia of the Goethe family and Boehle (open May–Oct Wed, 15.00–17.00, Sat 10.00–12.00). The town retains a Rathaus of 1729 and the Neue Schloss of 1789. The church of St Boniface, the 1815 work of Weinbrenner save for its 15C Gothic choir, boasts a late 15C Gothic altarpiece by Friedrich Herlin. Beside it is the Renaissance Schloss built for Christoph II von Baden-Hachberg in 1588 and now the local history museum (open mid-May to mid-Oct, Wed–Sat 08.00–12,00, 14.00–17.00). In the railway station the Bahnhofsmuseum (open Sat 08.00–12.00, 14.00–17.00) displays steam trains. Emmendingen's wine festival takes place on the third Sunday in August. 4km from the town on a 345m hill are the ruins of the 11C Schloss Hachberg, demolished by the French in 1689. The road travels S from here to reach after 16km Freiburg (see Rte 17A).

## Picturesque alternative route from Offenburg to Freiburg

Total distance 137km. Offenburg—39km Gutach—10km Elzach—15km Triberg—15km Furtwangen—20km St Märgen—6km St Peter—32km Freiburg.

Leave **Offenburg** by the B33, SE in the direction of Donauschingen, travelling along the valley of the Kinzig through **Gutach** devoted to the silk industry, where traditionally single women wear red straw hats, married women black ones. Its church of St Peter has a Gothic tower of 1467, while the nave and pulpit date from 1743. At Gutach is the Schwarzwälder Frelichtmuseum of traditional farming, which incorporates three farms— the thatched Vogtsbauernhof of 1570, the Lorenzenhof, built around 1540, and the Hinterseppenhof of 1599 (visits daily Apr–Oct 08.00–18.00).

Turn W along the road to **Elzach**, the route passes the Landwassereck (630m high, with panoramas) and reaches after 4km the tourist resort of **Oberprechtal**, which offers fishing, hunting, miniature golf and a spa. Then rejoin the B33 and travel S through the ski country (the Rohrhardsberg peak is 1152m high) and the winter sports town of **Schonach** (4200 inhab.; alt. 885m) where you can enjoy a late Rococo church dedicated to St Urban and the Blinder Lake, to reach after 15km Triberg.

**Triberg** (7500 inhab.; alt. 700–1001m) is situated at the junction of the valleys of the Gutach, Schonach and Prisenach and takes its name from three pine covered hills—the 847m Kapellenberg, 948m Kroneck and 1006m Sterenberg. Nearby are the spectacular Gutach waterfalls, at 136m the highest in Germany. The spa is open all the year round, and the town specialises both in winter sports and cuckoo clocks. The Black Forest railway passes here, and its constructor, the engineer Robert Gerwig (1820–85), has a granite monument in the Hauptstrasse. Inside the riotous Baroque pilgrimage church of Maria in der Tannen, 1705, is a silver antependium before the high altar, given by Louis the Turk in 1706, as well as the miraculous statue Maria in der Tannen by A.J. Schupp of Villingen, 1645. Another altar, on the right, enshrines the relics of St Serena, who died in 408. The spa boasts a fine park. The administrative offices were built in 1697. At 4 Wallfahrtstrasse is the Schwarzwald Museum (open mid-May to end Sept 08.00–18.00, otherwise 09.00–12.00, 14.00–17.00) displaying a remarkable collection of clocks. The Rathaus of 1828 has a chamber decorated in wood in 1926.

The route travels S, along the B500, to the spa of **Schönwald**, with its covered and open-air, heated swimming pools, and numerous other sports facilities, reaching after 15km **Furtwangen** (11,000 inhab.; alt. 850–1150m), the main regional centre for clock-making, with a clock museum, the Deutsches Uhrenmuseum in the Gewerbehalle at 11 Gerwigstrasse (open daily Apr–Nov 09.00–17.00), and on a railway line from Freiburg and Donauschingen. Nearby is the 1149m summit of the **Brend** and, 6km NW of Furtwangen, the 1100m-high main source of the Danube, the **Donauquelle**.

Drive SW through Neukirch to for 20km **St Märgen**. The former Augustinian church of St Maria dates from 1725; its interior was restored in 1907. Look in the Lady Chapel for a 14C painting of the Virgin Mary. The monastery it once served was founded in 1118. Much of its decor is 18C. 6km NW lies **St Peter**, at the start of the wine-blessed Glotter valley. Here are well-preserved remains of a former Benedictine monastery founded by Duke Berthold II of Zähringen in 1093—its chief delight a *Rococo library (guided tours, Thu at 14.30, and Sun at 11.30) its ceiling painted by B. Gambs, 1751, the allegorical statues of the arts and sciences by Matthias Faller. Today the monastery serves as the theological college for the diocese of Freiburg. The twin-domed, Baroque monastery church is by Peter Thumb, 1724–77, with statues on the high altar by J.A. Feuchtmayer, a Baroque organ, a painting by S.C. Storer and tombs of the Dukes of Zähringen. Frescoes by F.J. Spielger illustrate the life of St Peter. A short excursion N along a new road leads to the **Kandel**, the highest peak of the central Black Forest region (1241m).

The route E from St Peter passes through the Glottertal wine centre and reaches after 15km Denzlingen before turning S along the B294 and running 17km into Freiburg (see Rte 17A).

# C.  Freiburg im Breisgau through Freudenstadt to Baden-Baden

Total distance 177km. Freiburg—16km Waldkirch—39km Wolfach—10km Schiltach—10km Alpirsbach—27km Freudenstadt—13km Bad Rippolsau-Schapbach—46km Kurhaus Bühlerhöhe—16km Baden-Baden.

Leave Freiburg (see Rte 17A) travelling NE for 16km by the B294 through Denzlingen as far as Waldkirch at the foot of the 1240m-high Kandel, which can be reached by a good road (13km). Situated in the valley of the Elz, **Waldkirch** (18,600 inhab.; alt. 263m) is a health resort offering excellent swimming pools, a landscaped park, sports facilities and concerts. The town grew up around a nunnery founded in 918. Its Baroque 18C church of St Margaret by Peter Thumb houses Rococo stucco, as well as a font of the same style and a pulpit, all by J.C. Christian. Nearby, in the former provost's house, is the regional museum (open Thu, Sat, 15.00–17.00, Sun 10.00–13.00). NW of the town, on the 369m-high Schlossberg, stands the ruined Kastelburg.

Continue along the B294 through Elzach, turning NE at Haslach and continuing by way of **Hausach**, where there are many good walking routes, to reach after 39km **Wolfach**, at the confluence of the Kinzig and the Wolf, where the 15–17C Schloss, once the home of the Princes of Fürstenberg, is now a museum with a mineral collection, with a renovated Schloss chapel (open May–Sept, Tue, Thu, Sat 14.00–17.00, Sun also 10.00–12.00; for rest of year Thu 14.00–17.00). Some of the medieval defences of Wolfach still stand. The Gothic parish church dates from 1473–1515. Wolfach is also a health centre.

The road continues for 10km to **Schiltach** (4000 inhab.; alt. 325m), situated where the River Schiltach flows into the Kinzig. This health resort is guarded by the ruined Schloss Schiltach (418m), and boasts in its Marktplatz of mostly 18C houses a Rathaus dated 1593. The route passes **Schenkenzell**, which has a sports centre, and the ruined Schloss Schenkenburg, 390m, and then traverses the gorge known as the Devil's Kitchen to reach after 10km **Alpirsbach** (7000 inhab.; alt. 325m), a health resort with a Rathaus of 1566 and a partly *Romanesque church dating from 1099 and housing several Hohenzollern tombs. The lower part of the massive church tower is Romanesque; the Gothic choir and crossing date from the 15C; Jesus in glory, with angels and the church founders, are sculpted on the Romanesque portal. Other fine features are late Gothic cloisters (guided tours), 12C wall paintings, and an altarpiece of the Coronation of the Virgin, c 1520, possibly by Jörg Syrlin the Younger. This was once the house of God of a monastery, which was restored 1879–92 and today is the venue in summer of concerts by internationally renowned orchestras. Alpirsbach is also renowned for its beer.

After 27km this route, known here as the 'Schwarzwald-Tälerstrasse' ('Black Forest Valley Road') reaches the winter sports and congress centre of ***Freudenstadt** (20,000 inhab.; alt. 740m), the second most popular health centre of the region after Baden-Baden.

**Tourist Office**: in the Kurhaus, 5 Lauterbastrasse. **Trains** connect Freudenstadt with Stuttgart, Rastatt and Offenburg; **buses** with Stuttgart, Baden-Baden and Freiburg.

**History**. Herzog Friedrich I of Württemberg founded Freudenstadt in 1599 as a town for silver miners. Later, Protestant refugees from Austria established themselves here. The imperial forces sacked and burned Freudenstadt in the Thirty Years War. Almost 50 per cent of the newly built town was destroyed in World War II. The town has been brilliantly rebuilt (according to the original plans of the ducal architect H. Schickhardt).

The arcaded Marktplatz, which stretches 219m by 216m, has at its centre the Rococo Wachhausbrunnen of 1763, plus another two fountains, and houses the Stadthaus (with a local history museum). The Rathaus and Schickhardt's Protestant church of 1608, restored 1951, are found at the NE and SW corners of the square. The church, whose wings meet at right angles, because of its position in the square, now houses treasures from other sacred buildings throughout the region, including a *lectern c 1180, an early 12C font and carved choir stalls of 1488. The Catholic church was built in 1929, the Kurhaus in 1951 and the Kurgarten laid out in 1971. A forest of pine trees covering 2500 hectares surrounds the town.

From Freudenstadt the 'Schwarzwald-Hochstrasse' ('Black Forest Highway') leads for 85km to Baden-Baden.

13km W of Freudenstadt lies **Bad Rippoldsau-Schapbach**, known for its curative waters in the Middle Ages, when the Benedictines developed and exploited them. The route here turns N along the B500 and reaches the village spas of **Kniebis** and **Allerheiligen**, with the ruins of a monastery founded in 1196 and a modern church of 1960, climbing to another spa, **Ruhestein**, and a further 250m to reach **Hornisgrinde** (alt. 1164m, ski lift), before beginning to descend again and reach after 46km the renowned Kurhaus and sanatorium of **Bühlerhöhe**. Bühlerhöhe is 16km from Baden-Baden which is reached by way of Baden-Lichtental. **Baden-Baden** itself

(53,000 inhab.; alt. 150–1002m), surrounded by wooded hills and lying in the valley of the Oosbach, has been known for its curative waters since Roman times.

**Tourist Office**: Haus des Kurgastes, 8 Augustaplatz. **Trains** connect with Paris, Vienna, Italy, Frankfurt, Holland and Basel; **Buses** run from Baden-Baden into France and into the Black Forest. A **funicular** rises 668m above the town. There is an **airport**. **Horse-racing** takes place at Iffezheim, 5km NW.

**History**. The Emperor Caracalla (211–17) constructed baths here that can still be seen in 'Römerplatz' (open Apr–Oct, Tue–Sun 10.00–12.00, 14.00–17.30). Known initially as *Aquae Aureliae*, the name Baden appears for the first time in the late 10C in a charter of Otto III, long after the Romans had left and the town had enormously declined. The spot was invested by the Alemanni and then by the Franks. The Zähringen family acquired the town and built a Schloss here in the early 12C, and Duke Hermann II became the first margrave of Baden in 1112. So severely did Baden-Baden suffer during the Thirty Years War and in 1689, when the town was almost totally destroyed, that in 1705 the margraves transferred their Residenz to Rastatt.

The first Kurhaus since the Romans was built here in 1765 and is the basis of the present building of 1824. The vogue for visiting the town reached its apogee under Napoleon III and has scarcely declined since: 350,000 visitors a year play blackjack, baccarat and roulette in its Casino. One past visitor, Mark Twain, commented that at Baden-Baden, 'The shopkeeper there swindles you if he can, and insults you whether he succeeds in swindling you or not'.

The thermal quarter of the town, served by a score of springs with temperatures ranging from 45–69°C, consists of a fine park of over 200 species of trees with the 90m-long arcaded Trinkhalle of 1842, designed by F. Hübsch and frescoed by Götzenberger with the 'Fourteen Legends of the Black Forest', the vast Kurhaus by Friedrich Weinbrenner, 1822–24 with its Corinthian façade, which incorporates restaurants and the Casino designed in 1854 by Jacques and Edouard Bénazet. NW of the Trinkhalle on the 210m-high Michaelsberg is the Byzantine-style Stourdza Chapel, built in 1866 by Leo von Klenze to house the body of a Romanian prince who had died in Paris at the age 17 (open daily 10.00–18.00). The neo-Renaissance Friedrichsbad, designed in 1873, is sumptuous.

In the Kurgarten is also the Baroque theatre designed by Edouard Bénazet, 1862, from which begins the Lichtentaler Allee, an exotic creation by Bénazet inspired by English parks, housing at No. 8a the art gallery displays 20C art; open Tue–Sun 10.00–18.00, and shaded by over 300 species of tree and shrub, some of them rare. It leads to Kloster Lichtental at 40, Hauptstrasse, a Cistercian abbey founded in 1245 by Irmengard, the widow of Hermann V of Baden, whose present buildings date from the 14C and 15C. In the courtyard is a fountain dated 1602. The church, built in 1330 and restored c 1960, contains numerous treasures—frescoes c 1330; the tomb of the foundress, died 1260, by Wölflin von Ruffach; an altar of 1486; and a pulpit of 1606 by Thomas König. Adjoining the church the Fürstenkapelle contains the graves of Margraves, and rising behind it is the 230m-high Cäcilienberg.

In Schlossstrasse is the 16C Niederbaden Neues Schloss, by the Munich architect Kaspar Weinhart, now incorporating the Kavalierbau of 1709 and the Küchenbau of 1572—and housing Baden-Baden's history museum, with a huge collection of porcelain (open Mar–Oct Tue–Sun 10.00–18.00). The main Schloss contains thermal baths. In the Marktplatz is the late Gothic Marienkirche, built over the ruined Roman baths, with a medieval tabernacle, a late Gothic sandstone crucifix by Nicolaus von Leyden, 1467, and several tombs of the margraves and their families, including those of Bernhard I (died 1431), Bishop Friedrich of Utrecht (died 1517) and the

Rococo portrait tomb of 'Türkenlouis' (Margrave Ludwig Wilhelm I, died 1707). Opposite the church rises the Rathaus, in what was once a Jesuit College of 1632, in part transformed by Friedrich Weinbrenner in 1809.

The Kurhaus is celebrated for its concerts as well as its waters. Amongst composers who have been inspired by Baden-Baden was Brahms who lived here from 1865 to 1874. The Brahmshaus, 85 Maximilianstrasse is a museum, open Mon, Wed, Fri 15.00–17.00, Sun 10.00–13.00. And in earlier times Baden-Baden was the home of the noted doctor Paracelsus (Theophrastus Bombastus von Hohenheim, 1493–1541.

# D. Karlsruhe to Kehl via Rastatt and Freudenstadt

Total distance 172km. Karlsruhe—29km Rastatt—18km Gernsbach—22km Forbach—29km Klosterreichenbach—10km Freudenstadt—20km Bad Peterstal-Griesbach—24km Oberkirch—20km Kehl.

**\*KARLSRUHE** (276,000 inhab.; alt. 116m), close to the Rhine and a major port, is the centre of important industries and refineries and was thus a key target in World War II, when much of the old city was destroyed.

**Main railway station**: Bahnhofsplatz. **Main post office**: Kaiserstrasse. **Information Office**: 8 Bahnhofsplatz. **Trains** connect with Heidelberg, Ettlingen, Stuttgart, Mannheim, Heilbronn, buses with Heilbronn and Pforzheim.

**History**. Established by Margrave Karl Wilhelm of Baden-Durbach in 1715, Karlsruhe (i.e. 'Karl's rest') was laid out in the shape of a fan, along roads radiating from the new Schloss. In 1800 Friedrich Weinbrenner (1766–1826; born and died in the city) was engaged to lay out the rest of the city, as he did with classical regularity. Karlsruhe possesses Germany's oldest technical university, and is the centre of the country's atomic research as well as the home of EURATOM. The city is also the seat of western Germany's supreme courts and the Federal High Court.

Karl von Drais, inventor of the bicycle, was born here in 1785, as was Carl Benz, creator of the first vehicle driven by petrol, in 1844. Here Heinrich Hertz made discoveries in the field of electro-magnetics; between 1852 and 1870 Edward Devrient dominated German theatre from Karlsruhe; and here lived the authors Johann Peter Hebel (1760–1826) and Joseph Viktor von Scheffel (1826–86), author of 'Der Trompeter von Säckingen'.

From **Bahnhofsplatz** take the underground passage to the **Stadtgarten**, with its swimming pool, waterfalls and zoo (entrance on Ettlinge Strasse) and cross it to the Festplatz, with the Stadthalle (built in 1915 and now a conference centre), the Schwarzwaldhalle (1953), the Gartenhalle (1965) and the Nancyhalle (1967). From here **Ettlingerstrasse** (becoming Karl-Friedrich-Strasse) leads N by way of the circular **Rondellplatz**, with its pink sandstone **Verfassungssäule**, or column of the constitution, flanked by griffins. It was set up in 1826 to commemorate the liberal constitution granted to Baden by Grand-Duke Karl in 1818; he is represented in a medallion on the base of the column. E of the Rondellplatz rises what remains of the central wing (restored after World War II) of Weinbrenner's 1803–14 Margrave's **Palais**. Continue along **Karl-Friedrich-Strasse** to the **Marktplatz**, in the centre of which is a red sandstone pyramid, 6.5m high, enclosing the grave of Friedrich-Wilhelm, founder of the city (died 1738).

On the left is the **Rathaus** with its square belfry, 1815–25, on the right the **Stadtkirche**, 1807–16, resembling a Greek temple with a portico carried on six Corinthian columns, inside which is buried the designer of both buildings, Weinbrenner, who died in 1826. The interior was not restored to its original style after World War II, but given a concrete aspect by the architect H. Linde. Cross Kaiserstrasse to reach the huge triangular **Schlossplatz**, whose apex is the octagonal tower of the yellow and white **Schloss**, 1715, and its sweetly angled wings, 1749–81, following the original ground pattern of Friedrich von Kesslau and Philippe de la Guèpière, and in part, perhaps, the work of Balthasar Neumann. Much damaged in World War II, these buildings were restored externally in 1966 to incorporate the Badische Landesmuseum, ranging from prehistory through Egyptian, Greek, Etruscan and Roman sculpture and medieval art to the present, and including *a Madonna and Child of c 1515 by Tilman Riemenschneider of Würzburg (open Tue–Sun 10.00–22.00, closing Thu at 17.30). In the centre of the Schlossplatz is a statue of the Grand Duke Karl Friedrich by Ludwig Schwanthaler, 1844, the original design by H. Hübsch. The end of the central parterre is dignified by a series of statues of classical figures, including Hercules, Venus and Pan, sculpted by Ignaz Lengelacher in 1782.

Enter the vast semi-circular **Schlossgarten** by the arcade at the end of the left wing of the Schloss: here are a statue of J.P. Hebel by Steinhüser, 1836; the Wildpark stadium of 1930 (holding 55,000 spectators); tennis and other sports facilities; the **botanical gardens**, with glasshouses (open weekdays 19.00–16.00; Sat, Sun 09.00–12.00, 13.00–17.00); the **Margraves' Mausoleum** of 1889; and the ornamental Hirsch Gate of 1759 leading to the Fasanenschlösschen of 1765 by Kesslau. To the left of the Schlossgarten, along Moltkestrasse, is the city's youth hostel.

*At Karlsruhe the 18C Schloss today houses the Landesmuseum of Baden*

Return to Schlossplatz and by way of Waldstrasse reach the **Staatliche Kunsthalle**, at 2 Hans-Thoma-Strasse, built in the Florentine Renaissance style between 1837 and 1846 (east wing 1896, north wing 1908) with a national collection chiefly built up by the Margraves, Grand Dukes from 1806, of Baden, and including Mathias Grünewald's painting of Jesus carrying his cross, as well as his Crucifixion where Jesus is flanked by Mary and St John. Here also are works by Dürer, Grien, Cranach and Holbein amongst the Germans, and a Rembrandt self-portrait, plus works by Rubens and Lucas van Leyden among the Dutch, as well as modern works by Max Beckmann, Schmidt-Rottlufff, Kandinsky, Kokoschka, etc. (open Tue–Sun 10.00–13.00, 14.00–17.00). The building was designed by Heinrich Hübsch, with a fresco on the monumental staircase by Moritz von Schwind depicting the consecration of the cathedral of Freiburg im Breisgau, 1840–42.

Opposite the Orangerie attached to the gallery **Stephanienstrasse**, begun in 1806, leads to Weinbrenner's last work, the **Münze** (at No. 28) of 1826, which served as the mint of the Federal Republic from 1948. **Karlstrasse** leads S from the Münze, with on the left at No. 10 the former **Prinz-Max-Palais**, built for the banker August Schmieder, 1881–84, and so named because it was the home of the last Imperial chancellor, Prinz Max von Baden (1867-1929). It now houses the city art gallery and the museum of the city's history (open Tue–Sun 10.00–13.00, 14.00–18.00, Wed also 19.00–21.00). Turn left at the main post office from Karlstrasse along **Kaiserstrasse**, N of which lies the semi-circular **Zirkel**, built of identical 19C (well restored) houses for court officials. The university, 1826, is housed at the far end (E) of Kaiserstrasse.

Only a short way from the post office along Kaiserstrasse is (right) **Ritterstrasse**, which leads to the Catholic church of **St Stephan** in Erbprinzenstrasse, by Weinbrenner, 1808–14, inspired by the Pantheon, Rome, and housing a Silbermann organ from the abbey of Sankt-Blasien. The post-war restoration has slightly simplified the building, leaving it with a reinforced concrete dome. Opposite the church is the **Landesbibliothek**. Next door is the **Museum am Friedrichsplatz** (natural history; open Tue 10.00–20.00, Wed–Sat 10.00–, Sun 10.00–17.00). Ritterstrasse also contains the former **Erbgrossherzogliches Palais** by J. Durm, 1891, now the seat of the supreme court.

OTHER SIGHTS: the **Karpatendeutsches Museum** (of local history), 223 Kaiserstrasse (open Mon–Fri 09.00–15.00); the Transport Museum, 63 Werderstrasse (open Wed 15.00–20.00, Sun 10.00–13.00); the Staatstheater (1975), No. 11 Baumeisterstrasse, with two auditoria of 1002 and 550 seats, stages opera as well as drama; the Kammertheater is at No. 79 Waldstrasse; Die Insel is at Nos 14–16 Wilhelmstrasse.

**Environs**. At **Karlsruhe-Durlach** (5km E along Durlacher Allee), where the Margraves lived until 1715, is their former Schloss (16C–18C), one of whose wings, the Prinzessinenbau, houses a museum. It exhibits pottery produced at Durlach between 1723 and 1840 and documents on the Revolution of 1848 (open Sat 14.00–17.00, Sun 10.00–12.00, 14.00–17.00). The town possesses richly decorated houses c 1700 and from the fortifications the 16C Basler gate (rebuilt 18C). In Pfinztalstrasse stands the Rathaus of 1845 and the Protestant parish church, whose tower dates from the 12C. The vine-clad Turmberg, E of Durlach, rises to 265m, its funicular railway of 1888 one of the oldest in Germany, its former observatory offering in fine weather views of the cathedrals of Strasbourg and Speyer.

At **Grötzingen**, 3km NE, are half-timbered houses, including the Rathaus of 1688, as well as half-timbered Schloss Augustenburg of 1564, with two staircase towers, and a 16C parish church with a 14C choir. 15km NE is Bruchsal, on the way to which, to the right at the wine village of Obergrombach are the ruins of 13C **Burg Obergrombach**. At **Bruchsal** is a superb Schloss of 1720–60, in part by Balthasar Neumann and now the venue for concerts; visits daily except Mondays. Bruchsal also has a Baroque St-Peters-Kirche with an onion-domed tower, designed by Neumann and built 1738–43.

The Rhine **harbour**, 3.5km W of Karslruhe, was created by Max Honsell in 1902. Comprising 16 docks and a basin opening into the river itself, it is the third largest port in Germany and the first petroleum port in Europe, with an annual tonnage of nearly 10 million.

From Karlsruhe take the B3 29km SW to Rastatt (see Rte 17B). Leave Rastatt SW by way of Niederbühl, passing under the the Basel–Karlsruhe motorway to reach after 4km Schloss Favorite (see Rte 17B). From here the B462 passes through the village of Gaggenau to reach after 14km the health resort of **Gernsbach** (14,000 inhab.; alt. 185m), situated on both sides of the River Murg. Gernsbach has a Renaissance Rathaus, built of sandstone in 1617; the church of Our Lady, 14C and 19C, with 16C decoration and a stained glass window of 1460; timbered houses and fountains, including one in the Marktplatz of 1541; the Jakobskirche with a Gothic tabernacle; the Storchen tower—the remains of the old Schloss and a Kurpark.

2km S is the 13C **Ebersteinburg**, rebuilt 1798 and restored again by F. Weinbrenner in 1803, now housing a restaurant and overlooking the Murg valley. After another 20km appears the village of **Forbach**, set amid forests on the right bank of the Murg, whose covered wooden bridge of 1778 was restored in 1955. The route continues S through the village of **Raumünzach** (with its indoor swimming pool), at the confluence of the Murg and the Raumünzach, to reach the health resort of **Schönmünzach**, situated at the confluence of the Murg and the Schönmünzach and, after another 27km, **Klosterreichenbach**, once the site of a Benedictine monastery, whose buildings were restored in the late 19C. Klosterreichenbach is now an enterprising health resort. The route continues E to **Baiersbronn**, another health resort, and reaches Freudenstadt (see Rte 17C) to the S after 10km.

The B28 now winds W to the border crossing of the Rhine into Alsace. After 20km it reaches **Bad Peterstal-Griesbach**, whose springs have been reputed since the 16C. The parish church has altars from the former abbey at Allerheiligen. Nearby is **Bad Freyersbach**, noted for its mineral water. The road continues to **Oppenau**, situated at the confluence of the Rench and the Lierbach. As well as its old town gate, the Lieberbachertor, rebuilt in the 18C and its cemetery chapel of 1464, Oppenau has a local history museum displaying Alemannic arms and jewellery, in the Rathaus. Travel further along the River Rench to reach **Lautenbach**, with a late Gothic pilgrimage church, *Maria Krönung, built 1471–83 by Hertwig von Bergzabern, slightly altered in 1900 by the addition of two bays and a tower. The ogival vaulted interior shelters a choir screen; a *high altar of c 1580, with pictures perhaps by Grünewald and a Madonna flanked by SS John the Baptist and John the Evangelist; a winged altar of 1521 with statues and paintings of SS Martin and Wolfgang; another made at the same time with a Pietà and SS Catherine and Barbara; an 18C Baroque pulpit; and glass in the choir from the abbey of Allerheiligen. The latter's evocative remains lie 11km N of Oppenau (see Rte 17D).

After another 4km the road reaches **Oberkirch** (17,000 inhab.; alt. 194m), whose September wine festival indicates its importance for that industry. The town is also reputed for its cherry liqueur. In the Altstadt are numerous half-timbered houses, including the Amthaus of 1758–72, once the mint and residence of the bishops of Strasbourg, the former Hotel Zum Greifen of 1738, fronted by a lion fountain, and the Hotel Obere Linde, 1692–1702. The Baroque Schloss dates from 1743. This was the home of J.C. von Grimmelshausen from 1650 to 1667, and his life is celebrated in the local history museum at 7 Kirchplatz (open Wed and Sun mornings). The classical Rathaus was built in 1802. Nearby are two ruined schlösser: **Fürsteneck**, 2km SW, built in 1263, and the 11C and 13C **Schauenburg**, 2km NE.

**Appenweier** is 9km W, its Rococo, onion-domed church dedicated to St Michael and built by Johann Ellmenreich between 1748 and 1752 (perhaps to plans by Frantz Ignaz Krohner). Inside there is stucco by Johann Schütz, as well as the Rococo high altar, angels on its canopy and statues of SS Sebastian and Wendeln; a painting by J. Plummer of Michael driving Lucifer from heaven; and beside the pulpit a late Gothic panel of 1510, depicting the Madonna and her mother St Anne, who offers the infant Jesus a pomegranate. Appenweier has a late Baroque Rathaus, and a Franco-Prussian war memorial with a bust of Kaiser Wilhelm I, opposite a fountain.

5km further W at **Willstätt** are half-timbered houses and a Baroque church of 1756 by Johann Ellmenreich, with the arms of the landgraves of Hesse-Darmstadt on its porch. And after another 5km the route reaches **Kehl** (30,000 inhab.; alt. 140m), where the Kinzig and the Schutter flow into the Rhine and which Vauban fortified in 1681. Much destroyed during World War II, Kehl has been rebuilt as a modern town, with a town hall of 1969 that also serves as a festival hall. The regional Hanauer Museum at 5 Friedhofstrasse opens Sun 14.00–17.00. Kehl offers fine views of the river, which the Europa Bridge crosses on the way to Strasbourg.

# E.   Freiburg im Breisgau to Titisee, Donauschingen, Waldshut, St Blasien, Lörrach and Bad Säckingen

Total distance 218km. Freiburg—B31, 12km Himmelreich—18km Titisee—30km Donauschingen—B70 and B314, 29km Waldshut—B500, 24km St Blasien—23km Bärental—B317, 40km Schopfheim—12km Lörrach—B317 and B518, 30km Bad Säckingen.

Leave Freiburg (see Rte 17A) E by the Schwardzwalderstrasse, passing the sports stadia and through the suburb of Wiehe to join the B31 and the picturesque valley of the **Dreisam** (known as the 'Valley of Hell' and leading appropriately to Himmelreich, the 'Kingdom of Heaven'), reaching **Ebnet** after 4km. The town has a Schloss of 1748–49, in whose park are sandstone figures of the four seasons by Christian Wenzinger. After a further 4km you reach **Zarten** (mentioned 1C AD by Ptolemy as 'Tardunum'), with its notable Zartener House. To the S of Zarten is **Kirchzarten** (8000 inhab.; alt. 400m), a health resort, whose 16C church has a Romanesque tower.

Continue SE from Zarten to Himmelreich (14km S of St Märgen) and on through **Falkensteig**, with the remains of its old Schloss to the left, as far as the picturesque defile known as the **Höllental**, where, at **Hirschsprung** a bronze statue of a deer celebrates the legend of a beast which escaped its hunters by springing across the valley in one leap. A little further on is **St Oswald's chapel**, 1148, the oldest still-standing chapel in the Black Forest; restored 1952. Beside the waterfall at the magnificent gorge known as **Ravennaschlucht** is a pathway climbable (up and down) in about half an hour.

Further E, 18km from Zarten, the route reaches the health and winter sports resort of **Hinterzarten**, where you can enjoy camping, tennis, mud bath cures, miniature golf, swimming pools, mountain walks and skislopes. Though modernised, its old parish church retains its onion dome. From here the pass (915m) takes you on to the health resort of Titisee (with a local history museum; information office in the town hall; see below), situated 858m high between the 2km long lake from which it takes its name and the 947m Hirschbühl.

4km further along the B31 lies another health resort, **Neustadt**, founded in the mid 13C (then called *Nova Civitas*). Its charms are the church of 1797, cuckoo clocks, papermaking and forestry. Its parish church of St Jakobus is neo Gothic. The local history museum (the Heimatstube) opens from mid-May to mid-September Mon–Fri 14.00–17.00, Sun 10.00–12.00; otherwise Sun 10.00–12.00, Thu 14.00–17.00).

The road continues E to **Löffingen** (whose game park is open to the public) and through Döggingen to reach after 12km *Donauschingen** (18,000 inhab.; alt. 677m; information office: 41 Karlstrasse), close by the confluence of the Brigach and the Breg which here become the Danube. The town was once the seat of the Princes von Fürstenberg. The 'schingen' part of its name derives from a corruption of Esko, an Alemannic ruler of these parts. Donauschingen has a superb park, and a Schloss of 1772 built by Prince Friedrich Ferdinand von Fürstenberg, whose family became rulers of Donauschingen in 1653. Altered in 1894, it shelters sumptuous earlier furnishings (open Apr–Oct except Tue 09.00–12.00, 14.00–17.00). Here too stands the Baroque, twin-towered church of St Johann der Taufer, 1724–47, housing the relics of St Valentine and a Madonna c 1525. J.V. von Scheffell (1826–86) was court librarian at Donauschingen, and the court library, at 5 Haldenstrasse, holds 140,000 works including 1600 medieval German manuscripts and c 500 incunabula. The source of the Danube is by the Schloss, hence the 1826 Donauquelle fountain (see also Rte 17B) and statues by Adolf Weinbrenner and Adolf Heer. Behind the Schloss at 7 Karlsplatz, in the Karlsbau of 1868, is the former princely art collection, the Fürstenburg-Sammlungen, begun by Prince Karl Egon III (1796–1854), which includes paintings by Lucas Cranach the Elder and Younger, Hans Holbein the Elder, especially his 'Grauen Passionaltar', Matthias Grünewald and Bartholomäus Zeitblom (open except Mon and Nov, 09.00–12.00, 13.30–17.00). Donauschingen runs a music festival each August and an international music festival in October. Trains run to Freiburg, Ulm, Stuttgart and Konstanz.

4km SE of Donauschingen, en route to Geisingen, is **Neudingen** where Charlemagne died (888), close by the Fürstenberg (795m high), the origin of the name of the noble family, some of whom are buried in the vault of Neudingen church (T. Diebold, 1853–56).

From Donauschingen the E70 leads 17km SE to join the B314 which runs 43km SW along the Swiss border to Waldshut, passing through **Stühlingen**, with its former Capuchin monastery and Schloss Hohenlupfen, and

**Tiengen**. This spot has been inhabited since the Stone Age. Of its medieval ramparts remains the Storchenturm, c 1300. Peter Thumb designed the Baroque church of Maria Himmelfahrt in 1753, incorporating a Gothic tower. The Schloss was built between 1571 and 1619; the Hauptstrasse has two stone fountains of 1735 and 16C houses.

**Waldshut** (23,000 inhab.; alt. 300m), on the right bank of the Rhine, with fine views into Switzerland, is where the peasants' revolt of 1524 broke out. The old town, built by the Counts of Zähringen on a Carolingian fortress, preserves two 13C tower-gates (the Oberes Tor and the Unteres Tor). The Baroque Rathaus was built c 1770. The Heimatmuseum is located in a 16C building (the former abbatoir or Alte Mertig) at 62 Kaiserstrasse (open Jun–Oct Sun 10.00–12.00, additionally Tue 10.00–12.00 July–Sept). Beside the Oberes Tor rises the Liebfrauenkirche, 19C with a Gothic choir. Other sights are the 15C Greiffenegg Schlösschen in Johannisplatz and the 16C Königsfelder Hof. Annually on the first Sunday after the feast of the Ascenscion Waldshut's Chilbi festival celebrates the lifting of a siege by the Swiss in 1468.

The B500 now runs 25km N to St Blasien, passing through the health resort of **Höchenschwand**, at 1015m the highest village in the Black Forest, with superb views in fine weather from nearby peaks as far as Mont Blanc and the Jura mountains.

Surrounded by wooded hills, **˙St Blasien** (4500 inhab.; alt. 760m) is the site of a celebrated Benedictine abbey, founded in the 9C. After its medieval buildings had been replaced by a huge Baroque group in 1727–48, a disastrous fire in 1768 meant that almost all had to be rebuilt, by the French architect Pierre Michel d'Ixnard, much of whose work, in the early classical style under the influence of the Pantheon, Rome, completed in 1772, remains. The Rococo high altar is by C. Wenzinger. The copper dome of the church, 72m high and 34m in diameter inside, is supported on 20 columns and was finished by Nicolas de Pigage in 1781, who respected the plans of d'Ixnard. In the crypt lie the ancestors of the Habsburgs. The monks left St Blasien in 1806. In consequence many of the treasures of the church have disappeared. The monastery library perished (in Karlsruhe) in World War II. The town today houses a noted Jesuit college in the abbey buildings. Here was born the painter Hans Thoma (1839–1924), whose work is displayed in the town hall.

The **Titisee**, 34km N of St Blasien, is reached by way of lakes and health and sports resorts: Seebrugg, Schluchsee—whose once tiny lake has become, at 5 sq km, the largest in the Black Forest through damming in 1932, Windfällweiher, Altglashütten, where glass has been made since the 17C, and (after 23km) Bärental. At Bärental turn left along the B317 and travel SW through **Todtnau** (5300 inhab.; alt. 600m), situated in healthy winter sports country. Here a cable chair rises to the 1158m-high Hesselhorn, and the 95m Todtnauberg waterfall. 8km SW lies **Schönau**, with an altar c 1530 in the parish church. This was the birthplace in 1894 of the German patriot Albert Leo Schlageter, who was executed by the French in 1923. An **excursion** 13km NE leads to the **Belchen**, 1414m high, with an orientation table. After another 19km the route (B317) reaches Schopfheim, whose Höckling chapel, c 1400, has wall paintings. Schopfheim also has a late Gothic church of St Michael, 1482, built on Romanesque foundations, with some traces of early 14C wall paintings, and a classical town hall, built 1820–30.

12km W is **Lörrach** (43,000 inhab.; alt. 296m) close where the Rhine is crossed into Basel, Switzerland; trains run into Basel. Lörrach boasts fine wines, a Protestant parish church by Weinbrenner, (1815–17) and a statue of Hebel, who was professor here 1783–91, set up in 1910. Its classical Protestant parish church, 1817, incorporates a tower of 1514. The 1822 church of St Fridolin is by C. Arnold. In the Museum am Berghof, at 143 Basler Strasse, are displayed ceramics, weapons, history and prehistory, literature, and paintings, as well as works by Hans Thoma (open Wed 14.30–17.30, 19.30–21.30, Sat 14.30–17.30, Sun 10.00–12.00, 14.30–17.30). In the suburb of Haagen stands the Schloss Rötteln, the second oldest fortress in south Germany—built in the 12C, half ruined 1678, but retaining its Romanesque keep—and in the suburb of Tüllingen rises a late Gothic church with frescoes and a tabernacle of 1474. 4km S is the moated **Schloss Inzlingen** of 1563.

Return from Lörrach to Schopfheim and follow the B518 for 18km to Bad Säckingen. On the way you pass **Wehr**, with the early medieval ruins of Burg Werrach and NE the ruins of the 12C Burg Bärenfels. 4km N is the pothole known as the Haseler Tropfsteinhöhle; tours in summer. **Bad Säckingen** was made famous by Joseph Viktor von Scheffel's 'Trumpeter of Säckingen'. Scheffel lived between 1850 and 1852 in the house belonging to the Teutonic Knights at the end of the 200m-long covered wooden bridge of 1580 which spans the Rhine. From the old fortifications remain the 14C Gallus and Diebs towers. The Gothic münster of St Fridolin, 14–17C, is dedicated to the town's patron saint, an Irishman who founded a monastery here in the 6C; his statue and that of Count Ursi of Glarus (whom he restored to life) are carved over the porch. On the exterior of the choir is the tomb of Werner Kirchofer and his wife Maria Ursula (died 1690 and 1691), on whose history Scheffel based his tale. The Rococo decoration of the church is by J.M. Feuchtmayer, the high altar by J.P. Pfeiffer, 1721. The silver shrine of St Fridolin dates from 1764, while the crypt dates from the Carolingian foundation. Each March a festival is held to honour St Fridolin. Bad Säckingen is also a health resort, with swimming pools, mineral springs and clinics. The Hochrhein museum (in Schloss Schönau, c 1600, much rebuilt 1964–68) contains prehistoric finds, as well as exhibitions connected with the painter Hans Thoma (1839–1924) and Scheffel (open Tue, Thu, Sun 15.00–17.00). Religious art is displayed in the Münster Schatzkammer, at 8 Münsterplatz.

From Bad Säckingen the B34 runs for 28km E to Waldshut (see above).

# 18

# Karlsruhe to Ulm via Stuttgart

Total distance 137km. Karlsruhe—B10, 27km Pforzheim—17km Vaihingen—
22km Stuttgart—29km Göppingen—18km Geislingen an der Steige—24km
Ulm.

Leave **Karlsruhe** (see Rte 17D) by the Durlacher Allee and by way of
Durlach through Grötzingen (see Rte 17E) under the Munich–Salzburg
motorway just before reaching **Pforzheim** (106,000 inhab.; alt. 275m; tourist
office: 1 Marktplatz). Once a Roman colony, *Porta Hetcyniae*, Pforzheim
was the birthplace of the humanist and Hebrew scholar Johann Reuchlin
(1455–1522). Situated at the confluence of the Rivers Enz, Nagold and
Würm, it developed jewellery making and goldsmiths' ware in the 18C—and
is as a result dubbed Goldstadt. Much of the town was destroyed in World
War II by an aerial bombardment of 23 February 1945. The finest monuments of the town rise in the Schlossberg quarter, the most important being
the (rebuilt) monastic church of St Michael, which has a west end begun
in 1225 and a Gothic choir of 1460. Ogival vaulting covers the nave, which
shelters the funeral monuments of Margrave Albert Alcibiades of Branden-
burg-Bayreuth (died 1557), and Princes Albert (died 1574) and Karl II (died
1577). Beside it rises the Archiv tower, part of the former Schloss, as well
as the Blumenhof park.

The oldest church of Pforzheim, St Martin in the old town (in Aldstädter-
strasse) on the bank of the Enz, is a 12C basilica which retains a Romanesque doorway (finely carved with the temptations which beset men and
women) and in its mid-14C choir late Gothic wall paintings, including one
of the Last Judgment.

To the S of the town the Reuchlinhaus at 42 Jahnstrasse houses a museum
of 4000 years of jewellery (open weekdays 09.00–12.00, 14.00–18.00; Sat
09.00–12.00). At 243 Karl-Friedrich-Strasse is a local history museum (open
first and third Sun in month 10.00–12.00, 15.00–17.00, Tue, Thu 14.00–
17.00). Another jewellery museum, in Bleichstrasse, opens Wed
09.00–12.00, 15.00–18.00 and the fourth Sun in month 10.00–12.00, 14.00–
17.00. The town theatre is in Osterfeldstrasse. The Wildpark in
Tiefenbroner Strasse is Pforzheim's zoo. Its Alpengarten, 4km SE, was laid
out from 1927 by the nurseryman and plant breeder Karl Förster (1874–
1970), whose aim was to integrate natural plants with landscape design.
Open daily, Apr–Oct, it displays some 100,000 plants.

The routes from Pforzheim to Freudenstadt (see Rte 17C), some 90km S,
pass through the health and winter sports resorts of the northern part of the
Black Forest. From Pforzheim the B10 runs NE for 17km to **Vaihingen**
(23,000 inhab.; alt. 103m), dominated by the 12C and 16C Schloss Kalten-
stein (on a 270m peak) and retaining the Haspel and Pulver towers from its
old fortifications. Its Swabian beer museum, at 12 Robert-Koch-Strasse is
open Tue–Sun 10.30–17.30.

## An alternative route (45km) from Karlsruhe to Vaihingen by way of Bretten and Maulbronn

Leave **Karlsruhe** for Durlach. At Durlach drive 20km NE to **Bretten**, birthplace of the humanist and Protestant reformer Philipp Schwarzherd, known as Melanchthon (1497–1560), whose statue is in the Marktplatz. A new Melanchthon House, 1897–1903, at 1 Melanchthonstrasse, replaces his birthplace (which was destroyed in 1689) and houses the Melanchthon museum with 450 manuscripts in his hand, 800 of his works and 5500 books on the Reformation (open 15 Mar–30 Sept daily 09.00–11.00, 14.00–16.00). The Protestant parish church dates from the 14C and 18C. Two towers remains from the old town fortifications: the 14C Simmelturm and the 16C Pfeifferturm.

The B35 leads from here E through Knittlingen, birthplace in the 16C of Johannes Faust, the inspirer of Goethe's drama. The Altes Rathaus, a building near the church, said to be where he was born, is now a museum to him, open weekdays, except Mon, 09.30–12.00, 13.30–17.00), weekends 10.00–18.00). 6km from Bretton, the B35 reaches **Maulbronn**, where a Cistercian abbey was founded in 1146. Its Romanesque *church, consecrated 1178, has early 15C Gothic chapels, a crucifixion group by the Parler family, c 1370, choir stalls c 1470 and a crucifix of 1473. Its early 13C portal—the 'Paradise'—on the west side, is 22m in length and 7.5m wide. A 13C Romanesque-Gothic cloister rises on the north side, with a monks' refectory c 1225 with seven central columns, an early 12C lay refectory divided by seven double columns, a late 13C chapter house and a fine fountain-lavabo, c 1350 (open summer 08.30–17.30, winter 09.30–17.00). In 1556 this abbey became (and still) remains a Protestant seminary, where between 1786 and 1788 Friedrich Hölderlin and between 1891 and 1892 Hermann Hesse were educated. A fountain plays in the church square, shaded by half-timbered houses. The B35 continues SE from here to **Vaihingen** (see above).

Continue SE along the B10 to reach shortly *Markgröningen (inhab. 12,500; alt. 114m), an attractive little town which sits beside the River Glems just off the main road to the left and is blessed with numerous half-timbered houses. Its medieval Marktplatz has a fountain of 1580 and the massive, half-timbered 15–17C town hall. The town's Protestant parish church of St Bartholomew c 1300, has 14C and 15C wall and roof paintings and choir stalls c 1300, a font of 1426, and the tombs of Hartmann von Gröningen and Walburga von Risenach. Its huge W towers were finished by Alberlin Jörg in 1472. The Catholic parish church (the former Spitalskirche) with a choir c 1300, stands next to the 15C and 16C hospital. A Shepherd's Race, held here on the weekend after St Bartholomew's day (24 August), dates from 1443.

After 22km the B10 reaches **STUTTGART (inhab. 600,000; alt. 207m), beautifully sited amidst a garland of hills. Lying on the W side of the River Neckar, Stuttgart is the capital of Baden-Württemberg and—at the heart of a wine producing and agricultural region, with mineral water springs, as well as a centre for printing, textiles, cameras and car manufacture—of economic importance for the whole Federal Republic.

**Main railway station**: Arnulf-Klett-Platz. Trains connect with all the other major cities of West Germany and with France and Switzerland. Passenger boats ply the Neckar.

**Tourist information**: at the main railway station and at No. 5 Lautenschlagerstrasse.

**Airport**: at Echterdingen, 14km S of the city.

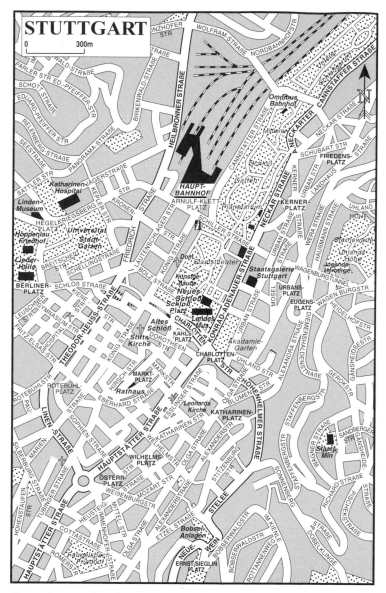

**History**. Stone-age people lived here, witnessed by the tombs discovered in the suburb of Bad Cannstatt. Alemannic tribes, then the Romans and then the Franks invested the site. Here in the mid 10C Duke Luitolf (son of the Emperor Otto I) set up a stud farm (hence 'Stuttgart', which first appears in a document of 1229, hence also the black horse on the city's coat of arms). The city greatly developed after Ulrich I built here a Schloss (124–65). In 1321 the city became the seat of the counts of Württemberg, whose illustrious Count Eberhard the Bearded was raised to the status of a duke by the Emperor in 1495. The Habsburgs captured Stuttgart during the Thirty Years War. Duke Karl Eugen (1737–93) founded a famous school (where Schiller was educated) here. In 1803 the Duke became an elector and two years later Napoleon made him King. Stuttgart expanded greatly under King Wilhelm I (1816–64) who saw the first railway reach the city in 1845. In consequence the city prospered, setting up its stock exchange in 1861, profiting from automobile geniuses such as Gottlieb Daimler, Carl Benz and Ferdinand Porsche (the last designing the Volkswagen in 1934). Württemberg became a free state in 1918, with Stuttgart as its capital. Though savagely bombed in 1944 (losing 60% of its buildings) much of Stuttgart has been restored.

Stuttgart was also the native town of the philosopher George Wilhelm Friedrich Hegel (1770–1831); his birthplace at No. 53 Eberhardtstrasse still standing. The city has a university, the Württemberg State Library and a renowned orchestra. In 1985 the Nobel Prize for physics was awarded to Klaus von Klitzing of its Max-PlanckInstitut. Its 217m-high TV tower (built in the mid-1950s by Fritz Leonhardt, Rolf Gutbrid and Erwin Heinle on the wooded Hoher Bopser, itself 482m high) has an observation platform and restaurant at 150m. Stuttgart's beers are stronger than those of Munich, and its Canstatter Volkfest, which takes up to 15 days from the end of September to the beginning of October, celebrates them, attracting annually some 4 million visitors.

The main railway station (by Paul Bonatz and E.F. Scholer, 1914–27, with an observation tower 58m high and a lift to the top) stands in Arnulf-Klett-Platz (named after the Oberbürgermeister of Stuttgart from 1945 to 1974). Cannstatterstrasse divides the main railway station from the vast **Schlossgarten**, well laid out with fountains and cafés. At the NE end of the park is found Schloss Rosenstein (1823–29), close by the Neckar. Here on the corner of Ehmannstrasse is the Post Office, and to the NW the Wilhelma botanical and zoological gardens, laid out in the Moorish style from 1837–53 (with Moorish buildings by L.W. von Zanth, built between 1842 and 1853) for Wilhelm I of Württemberg. The garden was remodelled and the addition of a zoo, with over 8000 animals of some 1000 species, after World War II. It has the largest magnolia grove in Europe; camellias and azaleas; and orchid conservatories; open daily, in summer 07.00–19.30, winter 08.00–16.00.

Returning to the main railway station (in front of which is the Hindenburg building of 1928 and the underground Klettpassage shopping mall), take the Königstrasse (its shops and other buildings almost entirely rebuilt since World War II) SW from the station. To the left is the modern Schloss garden building fronting this part of the Schlossgarten (with a monument to the victims of fascism by Elmar Daucher, its inscription by the Marxist philosopher Ernst Block). Here are to be found the classical **Neues Schloss** (by Leopoldo Retti, Philippe de la Guêpière, Reinhard Ferdinand Heinrich Fischer and Nikolaus Friedrich von Thouret, 1746–1807, restored 1961, and based on the palace of Versailles). Once the home of the monarchs, it now serves as the ministry of finance and culture). Stuttgart's **Art Gallery** (Kunstgebäude), by Theodor Fischer, 1910–13, has a cupola adorned by a gilded deer. The gallery was rebuilt 1959–61 by Paul Bonatz and Günther Wilhelm; see below). Here too are the **State Opera House**; the parliament building of Baden-Württemberg (by Viertel, Linde and Heinle, 1961); and the State Theatre (1962).

Stuttgart's Kunstgebäude incorporates the **\*\*City Art Gallery**, (the Galerie der Stadt; open daily except Mon 10.00–17.00, closes Wed 19.00), which possesses a remarkable collection of works by the foremost exponent of 20C German realism (Neue Sachlichkeit), Otto Dix (1891–1969), including his most notorious work, the triptych Metropolis (Grossstadt) of 1928. Here too hang his Salon I of 1921 (depicting four prostitutes, which led to his trial for pornography), three repulsive nude women painted in 1926, his Skat Players (1920, who include cripples of World War I), several selfportraits, the viciously satirical Prager Strasse, the yet more vicious Odd Couple (Ungleichliches Liebespaar) of 1928, in which a young woman wearing only boots sits on an old man's knee, still lifes, and a series of poignant portraits including those of the sad aristocratic poet Uvar van Lücken, 1825, and that of the family of Dr Paul Ferdinand Schmidt (1921), his hands crazily clenched.

Königstrasse continues SW to pass, on the left, the modern church of St Eberhard (1955) to reach the Schlossplatz, with its chestnut trees, which has two fountains and the 30m-high granite Jubilee Column (with statues by Wagner, the whole crowned with a bronze statue of Concord) erected in 1841 to commemorate the 25th anniversary of the accession of Wilhelm I. Here too stands a monument to Duke Christoph von Württemberg (died 1568) by Paul Müller, 1889, and two 1863 fountains. To the right is the Königsbau with its two Corinthian porticos and 26 Ionic columns including a 135m-long colonnade (built by Johann Michael Knapp and Christian F. Leins, 1856–60; restored and now housing shops and cafés). The Kleiner Schlossplatz, further on, is where the former Palais of the Crown Prince stood until 1944.

Left of the Schlossplatz stands the Neues Schloss (see above) and to the SW the irregular **Altes Schloss** with its round pepperpot towers and dormer windows peeping from its tiled roof. Begun in 1320 as a moated castle, it was mostly rebuilt for Duke Christoph by Alberlin Tretsch, and Martin and Blasius Berwart, 1553–78, and was restored after World War II. Its finest feature is a splendid interior, arcaded three storey courtyard, with Corinthian columns (the venue of concerts and the opening of the Christmas market). The equestrian statue of Eberhard V, Duke of Württemberg who was known as the bearded (died 1496) is by Ludwig Hofer and was raised here in 1859. The Altes Schloss now houses the **Land Museum**, with treasures depicting the history of Baden-Württemberg from prehistoric times to the 19C (open daily except Mon 10.00–17.00, closing 19.00 on Wed).

The Altes Schloss faces onto **Schillerplatz** (with a statue of the poet by Bertel Thorwaldsen, 1839), close by which is a Mercury column, set up in 1598 (the golden figure of Mercury was added in 1862). On the NE side of the square rises the former Ducal Chancellery (1541–43, restored 1952). To the N stands the Palladian Prinzenbau by Heinrich Schickardt. Finished by Matthias Weiss and Johann Friedrich Nette, 1715, today it houses the ministry of justice. On the SW side rises the late-Gothic **Fruchtkastern**, with its Renaissance gable, built between 1578 and 1596 as a granary and for the collection of tithes and now a museum of musical instruments. The ensemble is completed by the late-Gothic **\*Stiftskirche** (by Hänslin and Alberlin Jörg, 1433–56; rebuilt in 1964 by Hans Seytter). Its W tower was finished in 1531. On the tympanum is a carving of Jesus crucified between John the Baptist and the Virgin Mary, sculpted in 1320. The restored interior has, amongst the tombs, a monument commissioned by Herzog Ludwig III from Sem Schlör, 1576–1608, depicting eleven of his ancestors as Renaissance warriors.

To the E is Stuttgart's **market hall**, an art nouveau building of 1915 by Martin Elsaesser, its frescoes by Greff and Häbich. Kirchstrasse leads from Schillerplatz S to the marktplatz, with Stuttgart's new town hall (by H.P. Schmohl and P. Stohrer, 1954–56, boasting in its 60m-high tower a 30-bell Glockenspiel, which plays Swabian folk songs at 11.06, 12.06, 14.36 and

21.36 daily). The Platz has a fountain, and hosts a produce and flower market on Tuesdays, Thursdays and Saturdays 07.00–12.30. Markstrasse runs SE from the Marktplatz to Leonhardsplatz and the flamboyant Gothic church of **St Leonhard**, by Alberlin Jörg, 1463–74, the tower completed in 1491. Its crucifixion scene is a copy of that by Seyffer in the Hospitalkirche, see below. The early 16C sculpted stalls are also from the Hospitalkirche. The church's modern crucifix was created in 1957 by K. Hemeter. Here is the grave of the humanist Johannes Reuchlin, 1455–1522. The modern stained glass is by Kohler, while the fountain by the church depicting evening is by Fremd (1900).

NW from Königstrasse (just SW of Kirchstrasse) Büchsenstrasse leads past, on the left, the **Hospitalkirche** by A. Jörg, 1471–93, of which only the later tower, 1729–38, and the choir remain. Its choir shelters a crucifixion group by Hans Seyffer, 1501. At the end of Büchsenstrasse is found Stuttgart's Liederhalle (by A. Abel, R. Gutbrod and B. Spreng, 1956, with three concert halls, holding respectively 2000, 750 and 350 listeners, and a restaurant). From here Holzgartenstrasse runs N to Hegelplatz and the *Linden Folk Museum, which was founded in 1884 (ethnography, particularly a collection of African art from the Sudan and the Congo, as well as artifacts from North America and Melanesia).

In 1927 Mies van der Rohe brought together 16 European architects to design houses for an international exhibition. These, by Mies and by such architects as Le Corbusier, are found (many restored after World War II) in the **Weissenhofsiedlung**.

W of the city centre is the 50 hectare **Höhenpark Killesberg**, designed by Hermann Mattern (1902–71, Professor of Garden and Landscape design at Berlin) for the Reich Garden exhibition in 1936. Destroyed in World War II, it was reconstructed by Mattern in 1950. Its features include a parterre, naturalised bulbs, a rose garden, a marsh and water-lily pond and a miniature railway (open daily May–Sept 08.00–20.00, otherwise 08.00–sunset).

The Carl-Zeiss **Planetarium** (at No. 47 Neckarstrasse) has performances daily except Mon. The youth hostel is at No. 27 Haussmannstrasse.

THEATRES. Staatstheater, at No. 6 Oberer Schlossgarten; Komödie im Marquardt, at Nos 4–6 Bolzstrasse; Altes Schauspielhaus, Kleine Königstrasse; Theater der Altstadt, Charlottenplatz; Wilhelma-Theater for music and the performing arts, at No. 9 Neckartalstrasse; International Bach Academy, at No. 1 Johann-Sebastian-Bach-Platz.

OTHER GALLERIES. The **Neue Staatsgalerie**, by James Stirling and Michael Wilford, 1977–82, No. 32 Konrad-Adenauer-Strasse, has a superb collection of paintings and prints (open daily except Mon 10.00–17.00; to 20.00 Tue and Thur). The masterpieces begin with German primitives (Ratgeb's Herrenberger altar of 1519), continuing through Italian works of art (Tiepolo's Rest before the flight into Egypt) and Dutch paintings (*Rembrandt's St Paul in Prison). The 19C German section includes works by Caspar David Friedrich and Feuerbach, the French Impressionists represented by superb works by Manet, Monet, Pissaro, Sisley and Renoir. Here too are displayed paintings by Cézanne, Gaugin and the Nabis, and a good handful of works by Picasso, Dufy, Matisse, Vlaminque and Roualt. Twentieth century German and Austrian masters are represented amongst others by Egon Schiele, Maholy-Nagy and Max Ernst, as well as the Dadaists, surrealists and constructivists.

The **Landesmuseum** is in the Altes Schloss, Schillerplatz, and displays sculpture, weapons, musical instruments, textiles, church art, porcelain, etc. (open daily except Mon 10.00–17.00). See also the Porsche motor museum, No. 42 Porschestrasse (open weekdays, except for holidays, 09.00–12.00 and 13.30–16.00); the Linden Museum (see above, at present closed); the German Bible Society collection, at No. 31 Balinger Strasse (open weekdays 08.00–16.00); Bad Cannstatt Heimatmuseum at No. 7 Wilhelmstrasse (open weekends 10.00–12.000 and Apr–Oct also Wed 15.00–17.00); Playing Card Museum, at No. 32 Schönbuchstrasse in Lein-felden-Echterdinger (S of the city), open weekdays except Mon 14.00–17.00 and Sun 10.00–13.00); the Wine Museum is in the suburb of Uhlbach (open Apr–Oct Sat 14.00–18.00, Sun and holidays 10.00–12.00).

Stuttgart's spring festival takes place at the end of April and the beginning of May; its wine festival, in Marktplatz, Schillerplatz and Kirchstrasse, begins on the last Fri in Aug; a 300-year-old Christmas market, in same squares, runs from the end November till 23 December.

## Environs

At **Rotenburg**, W of the city, is the Rococo **Lustschloss Solitude** (now a hotel). Built for Herzog Karl Eugen, 1763–67 by Johann Friedrich Weyhing (and stuccoed by Louis-Philippe de la Guêpière), its massive central dome is flanked by gentle white wings and approached by monumental flights of steps. Here is the mausoleum (1824) of Wilhelm I's queen, Katharine of Russia (died 1819). Wilhelm also lies here. The Schloss chapel is classical, decorated by Nicholas Guibal, who also decorated the interior of the central Weisse Saal of the Schloss. 4km S is the Solitude racetrack.

For Ludwigsburg see Rte 19. On the NE side of the city (reached along Cannstatder Strasse) lies the spa of **Bad Cannstadt**. In this suburb the Kurpark covers a vast 17 hectares and surrounds the Kursaal, originally built by Thouret in 1825. The mineral bath at Canstatt is next to the Kursaal and offers guests hydro-electric therapy, mud baths, massages and Turkish baths. The Rathaus of 1491 faces the Gothic parish church, the work of Alberlin Jörg (who built on an earlier 12C and 13C church). The local museum opens at weekends and is situated in the barn of the former convent. Similar health treatments as those of Bad Cannstadt are available at the Mineralbad Leuze (on the König-Karls-Brücke) and the Mineralbad Berg (at No. 9 Am Schwanenplatz). A Canstatt folk festival, inaugurated 1818 by King Wilhelm I, takes place during the last week in September and the 1st fortnight in October, with beer tents and the world's largest mobile Ferris wheel.

Leave Stuttgart by taking Cannstatterstrasse NE and turning right across the Neckar bridge. The route now runs SE through Untertürkheim, where the Daimler-Benz motor museum is found at No. 137a Mercedes-Strasse (open weekdays except Mon 08.00–12.00 and 13.30–16.30; 2nd Sat in month 08.00–12.00), with its 150 models, beginning with the three-wheeled Reitwagen of 1886, and by Rotenberg (see above) to reach after 12km **'Esslingen am Neckar** (inhab. 96,000; alt. 240m; **information office** at No. 16 Marktplatz). Trains connect with Stuttgart, Tübingen and Ulm and buses with Plochingen.

Situated on the Neckar, surrounded by vineyards, Esslingen was settled in the Bronze Age and appears first in written history in 777 AD. Its oldest gate (the Wolfstor, c 1220, on the SE side of the still partly fortified town) carried the Hohenstaufen coat of arms. Grown rich on its wines, Esslingen became a free imperial city in 1219, and here in 1488 the Swabian League was formed. Esslingen became part of Württemberg in 1802, and the town's industries started to develop. The firm of Kessler began producing Sekt here in 1826 and remains the oldest Sekt producer in Germany. The late 13C Pliensau bridge is the oldest stone bridge in Baden-Württemberg.

The old town centre remains intact. Here the Neckar canal is spanned by the Innere Brücke, which incorporates a chapel of 1430. 80m above the town stands the **Burg**, a walled Hohenstaufen fortress with defensive towers. The late-Gothic **old town hall** (c 1430), once the tax house, has a Renaissance gable and north façade (by Heinrich Schickhardt, 1586, with a Glockenspiel and astronomical clock of 1592 by Jacob Diem) and now is the town museum (open Mon–Sat 14.00–16.00, Sun and holidays 10.30–12.00, its finest room the Bürgersaal of 1430). The Baroque **new town hall** opposite dates from 1746, and was built for the imperial counsellor Franz von Palm.

**St Dionysius's church** in the Hafenmarkt (13C and 14C) spans the change between Romanesque and Gothic, its twin towers bizarrely bridged. Inside the basilica with its seven bays are a choir screen of 1486 and a tabernacle and font of 1496 by Lorenz Lechler of Heidelberg, as well as stained glass in the choir, 1290–1310. The church houses a museum, and its high altar of 1604 is by Peter Riedlinger and David Mieser. Outside, by the choir, is the 13C Romanesque Kesslerhouse, close by which (along Archivstrasse) is the 13C Totenkapelle. N of the Hafenmarkt stands the Gothic church of **St Paul**, dating from 1233–68, once belonging to a Dominican monastery and the oldest church of a mendicant order in Germany. A bridge leads W over Augustinerstrasse to the **Marienkirche** (1321–1516), close by the old city gate, which has a 75m-high tower by the Ulm architect Ulrich von Ensingen and exceedingly fine stained glass (1320–30) in the choir. Hans and Matthäus Böblinger, who also worked on this church in the 15C, lie buried inside it. Esslingen is further enhanced by half-timbered buildings, particularly Nos 6, 8 and 10 in Hafenmarkt (these amongst the oldest in Germany, dating from the 14C). In Webereg is the Konstanzer Pfflegehof of 1327.

A brief **excursion** S reaches **Denkendorf**, with a Romanesque church (late 12C and early 13C, rebuilt 1377). In the crypt are 15C wall paintings of St Martin, Herod and Salome and the beheading of John the Baptist. The church also has a late-Gothic altar in the choir, and early 16C tombstones.

Leave Esslingen by the B10 to reach **Plochingen** (with its fortified parish church, 1488 with a Renaissance pulpit) and then, 39km from Esslingen, Göppingen by way of **Ebersbach** (which has a fortified Gothic church dedicated to St Guy), **Uhingen** (where there is a 17C Schloss) and **Faurndau** (which has a 13C church, with contemporary frescoes). **Göppingen** (inhab. 54,000; alt. 408m) lies at the foot of the 684m-high Hohenstaufen with its ruined Imperial Schloss (1079). Most of the old town was destroyed in a fire of 1782, but there is still much to enchant a visitor. The town has a **Schloss** of 1560 (by Alberlin Tresch and Martin Berwart, notable for its decorated staircases), to the E of which are the former 16C half-timbered stables. The parish church of 1619, designed by H. Schickhardt, has a Baroque interior and a tower of 1838. Nearby is the half-timbered 16C Schloss of the barons of Liebenstein (now the **town museum**, open weekdays except Mon 14.00–17.00 and weekends also 10.00–12.00). NE of the town at **Oberhofen** is a 15C church with a late-Gothic choir, wall paintings of 1499 including a view of the Hohenstaufen fortress, choir stalls 1500 and a crucifix c 1520. The town hall was built in 1783, the theatre (by Schnitger) in 1890. Göppingen's town **museum** at No. 36 Wühlerstrasse is housed in a stone and half-timbered building of 1536 (open mid-Mar to mid-Nov daily except Sun 10.00–12.00 and 14.00–17.00). Information office at No. 1 Bahnhofstrasse.

10km S of the city is **Bad Boll**, with a celebrated Evangelische Acadamie (made famous by the Protestant Pastor Johann Christoph Blumhardt, 1805–80, and his son Pastor Christoph Friedrich Blumhardt, 1842–1919).

The B10 continues SE of Göppingen, reaching after 18km **Geislingen an der Steige** (inhab. 28,000; alt. 44m), where five valleys meet. Apart from the setting, its finest features are the 15C town hall; a fortified tower (the Odenturm); ruined Schloss Helfenstein; the 15C late-Gothic church (with stalls by Jörg Syrlin the Younger, a high alter of 1525, and a Renaissance wooden pulpit by Daniel Hendenberger, 1621); the former customs house (15C and 1593) among many fine half-timbered houses; and a local history museum at No. 11 Moltkestrasse, open May–Oct Tue–Sat 15.00–17.00, Sun 10.00–12.00. Tourist information at No. 19 Hauptstrasse. From here the Rte runs S for 36km to Ulm (see Rte 1B).

# 19

# Ulm to Lindau via Friedrichshafen

Total distance 156km. Ulm—B28, 20km Blaubeuren—B492, 18km Ehingen— llkm Laupheim—B30, 18km Biberach an der Riss—B30 23km Bad Waldsee—17km Weingarten—4km Ravensburg—20km Friedrichshafen (B31 Meersburg, Salem, Überlingen—B34 Bodman)—B31, 25km Lindau.

Leave **Ulm** (see Rte 1B) E, crossing the Fahrbrücke and continuing along the valley of the Blau. After 8km the road passes through Klingstein with a 15C Schlösschen on the left, arriving 12km later at **Blaubeuren** (12,000 inhab.; alt. 520m), where you find Benedictine monastic buildings (now a Protestant seminary), dating from 1466 to 1510. The interior of the former monastery church is by P. Koblenz, 1499, and its choir stalls were designed by Jörg Syrlin the Younger, 1493. A late Gothic, double-winged and painted **high altar was worked on by Georg Erhart in 1494, and by Bartholomäus Zeitblom and Bernhard Striegel. See also the 15C Protestant church and the town hall of 1593. The Heimatmuseum is in the Klosterhof. Marked walks lead to the Blautopf, a deep glacial pool an hour or so away.

Turn S along the B492 for 18km to **Ehingen** (22,000 inhab.; alt. 511m), where the River Schmiech joins the Danube. In the 13C Ehingen was already an Alemannic settlement and became prosperous in the 15C and 16C. In spite of several damaging fires, especially in 1688 and 1749, and the ravages of the Thirty Years War, Ehingen has retained many architectural treasures: the Ritterhaus of 1692; the late Gothic parish church of St Blasius set on a rocky spur, with 18C transformations, a Pietà of 1520 and classical and Baroque statues; the former Franciscan church of Our Lady, founded in 1239, rebuilt in 1725, and housing a 15C Madonna; and the Baroque *Konviktskirche of 1719. Built in the form of a Greek cross, it has stucco decoration and on the high altar a Falling Asleep of the Blessed Virgin by Johann Georg Bergmüller. Trains connect Ehingen with Ulm, buses with Tübingen, Lindau and Ulm.

From Ehingen travel 11km SE to pretty **Laupheim** (15,000 inhab.; alt. 515m), which is washed by the Rottum. Its treasures include Schloss Gross Laupheim, 16C and 18C, set in a park and rose garden. Part of it is now the local history museum (open first Sun in month, 14.00–17.00). The 17C Baroque church of SS Peter and Paul, with its Baroque interior, has an equally fine setting on the Kirchberg. Visitors are offered swimming and camping, parks and walks, as well as processions on the third Sun in July. Here are bred Pinsgau horses. Close by at Rottum is Schloss Kleim Laupheim, 1789, now the local history museum, opening first Sun in month, 14.00–17.00.

Follow the B30 18km S to ***Biberach an der Riss** (29,000 inhab.; alt. 532m). Of the fortifications remain the Gigel tower, 1373, the Ulm gate, 1410 and the White tower, 1480, enfolding numerous half-timbered houses. The Marktplatz houses the 15C Rathaus, and at No. 2 the Wieland museum (open Sat, Sun 10.00–12.00, 14.00–17.00; Wed 10.00–12.00, 14.00–18.00). The late Gothic parish church of St Martin has a Baroque interior, with a pulpit, 1511; a high altar, 1720, by J.E. Hermann; a trompe l'oeil fresco in the nave by Johannes Zick and Joseph Mehringer, 1746; and an elaborate choir screen of 1768. Here in 1655 was founded a theatre which Christoph Martin Wieland (1733–1813, born close by at Oberholzeim) took over in 1760, to direct the following year his own translation of Shakespeare. Other noted artists working here were the composer Justin Heinrich Knecht (1752–1817) and the goldsmith Johann Michel Dinglinger (1664–1731). A Children's and Marksmen's festival takes place in July. The Art and Local History Gallery, 6 Museumstrasse, has a room devoted to the Expressionist painter Ernst Ludwig Kirchner (1880–1938), as well as animal paintings by Anton Braith (1836–1905) and Christian Mali (1832–1906), open Tue–Sun 10.00–12.00, 14.00–17.00. Trains connect with Ulm and Friedrichshafen, buses with more local spots.

An **excursion** for 11km E along the B312 leads to **Ochsenhausen** (6500 inhab.; alt. 612m). Its Benedictine abbey, founded 1100, became a centre of learning and culture in the 18C, when the buildings, partly destroyed during the Thirty Years War, were reconstructed in the Baroque style. Inside are choir stalls of 1686 and frescoes by Josef Gabler and J.B. Bergmüller, 1728–36. Gabler also designed the organ, with its 49 voices.The stucco is by the Italian Gaspare Mola. The church has a Rococo high altar and a pulpit by Ägid Verhelst, 1741. Beside the church are extensive monastic buildings (now in part a school), begun 1583–91, including the chapter house of 1785 and the classical library of 1785–91 which was frescoed by J.A. Huber and stuccoed by T. Schaldhof. This library was restored in 1984.

Another 11km SE is **Rot an der Rot**, where in 1126 St Norbert, the founder of the Premonstratensian order, established its first church in Germany. Today its monastery (1682–98) serves as a diocesan hospice for young people. Behind it rises the former parish church of St Verena and Maria-Himmelfahrt, built in 1693, rebuilt between 1777 and 1796, its style is part Baroque, in part classical. In the crypt are the relics of St Verena. Januaris Zick frescoed the nave in 1784; M. Schister created the stalls in the early 1690s; A. Meinrad van Au frescoed the choir in 1780; and the high altar and baldacchino are the work of Franz Xaver and Simpert Feuchtmayer.

From Biberach an der Riss the B30 continued S for 23km to **Bad Waldsee** (inhab. 15,000; alt. 600m), a spa with mud baths, picturesquely situated between two lakes which are known as the Schlossee and the Stadtsee (beach and boating). Here is a Gothic town hall by Ulrich Kuderer, 1426, with a tall and impressive gable of 1657 (and inside a council chamber with a coffered ceiling), which stands opposite the 15C town ·granary (Kornhaus), now a local history museum opening Sundays in summer 10.00–12.00. The 15C parish church of St Peter once belonged to an Augustinian priory and was much rebuilt in the Baroque style in the 18C. Its high altar is by D. Zimmermann, 1715, and it also boasts side altars of the 1720s and a sacristy whose ceiling was frescoed by Zimmermann. Other attractive buildings in Bad Waldsee are the 16C and 18C Schloss Waldburg-Wolfegg and parts of the 13C town wall.

The route now continues S to Revensburg (21km), passing through **Bad Waldsee-Gaisburen**, with its tiny Romanesque chapel of St Leonhard, and Baindt, whose Romanesque-Gothic church was decorated inside by F.M. Kuen, c 1763 and has a 14C Gothic crucifix and a Rococo high altar of 1764 by Johann George Dirr.

Next on the way to Ravensburg follows *Weingarten, celebrated for its Benedictine abbey, which was founded for women in the 10C and taken over by men in the next. In 1715 Abbot Sebastian Hyller demolished the 12C and 13C abbey church, replacing it with the present one, which was begun by Franz Beer and finished by Christoph Thumb, Andreas Schreck and above all by Donato Giuseppe Frisoni (who was responsible for the dome and the high altar as well as much of the Italianate interior decoration). It is the longest Baroque church in Germany (interior of the nave 102m by 29m, the vault rising 28m, the dome 66m). Its frescoes are by Cosmas Damian Asam, the stucco by Franz Schmuzer, 1718. Inside are 42 marquetry choir stalls by J.A. Feuchtmayr, 1730; an organ case (4 keyboards and 741 pipes) by Josef Gabler, 1737–50; a high altar of 1718, built by G.A. Corbellini to Frisoni's design, with sculpture by Diego Carlone; and a Rococo pulpit by F. Sporer, 1765. The monastic buildings to the N of the church date from the 18C, while from earlier monastic buildings on the S side remains a Gothic cloister. Weingarten also boasts a restored Kornahus at No. 28 Karlstrasse (in which is the Alemanic museum, open Tue–Sat 15.00–17.00, Sun also 10.00–17.00).

In 1094 Weingarten had been given a supposed drop of Christ's blood, and this relic contributed to its fame and wealth. Each year on the Friday after Ascenscion Day ('Blutfreitag') a procession of over 2000 riders celebrates the 'Blutritt'. The monks left Weingarten in 1806, to return in 1922.

*Ravensburg (inhab. 43,200; alt. 449m), founded by Duke Welf IV in the 11C, is 4km from Weingarten, in the valley of the Schussen and still surrounded by its 14C walls, three gates and four towers (the 14C Grüner Turm, the 50m-high Gemalter Turm, with its escutcheons, the 16C round Wehturm, also 50m high and known as the sack of flour, or Mehlsack, and the trumpeter's tower, see below). Ravensburg came under the rule of the Hohenstaufen in the 12C, and then was dominated by the Habsburgs, having achieved the status of a free Imperial city in 1276. The town was called Ravensburc in 1088. In 1380 the Gross Ravensburger Handelsgesellschaft was set up to exploit the profitable linen trade. The town also profited from its close association with Weingarten. Revensburg was annexed to Württemberg in 1810.

The 524m-high **Veitsburg** dominates the town from the SE, once the site of a Schloss where Henry the Lion was born. The fortress was demolished in 1647, though here remains a building of 1750 by G.G. Bagnato (now a youth hostel and restaurant). From it you can see as far as the Alps and the

Bodensee. Close by is an Alemannic burial ground, founded in the 6C and containing more than 800 graves.

In the Marktplatz are the weigh house, 1498 (once the market hall), the Blaserturm (trumpeter's tower) of 1556, and the 15C gabled town hall (altered 1876 and 1930) with an oriel window of 1571. Inside are two fine rooms and wall paintings of 1581. Nearby the town hall rises the sumptuously decorated, Renaissance tanners' house (Lederhaus) of 1514. Markstrasse leads to the Brotlaube, 1625. At No. 36 Charlottenstrasse the 15C Vogthaus houses the town museum (open Wed–Sat 15.00–17.00; Sun also 10.00–12.00). Churches include the 14C Liebfrauenkirche (in Kirchstrasse beyond the Blaserturm), with 15C glass in the choir, a 15C high altar and tabernacle, as well as 15C choir stalls. On the 1380 tympanum of this three-aisled basilica are sculpted scenes from the life of the Virgin Mary, beginning with the Annunciation and ending with her Assumption. The Gothic church of St Jodok (1385), rising NW of Marienplatz, has a mid-century tabernacle and stalls of the same era, its Baroque presbytery built by J.K. Bagnato in 1783. SW of the town the church of St Christina has Gothic vaulting of 1476 and houses a statue of the Virgin Mary c 1420.

Trains run from here to Friedrichshafen and Ulm. Information office is at No. 15 Marienplatz.

The B30 now runs 20km SW to **Friedrichshafen** (inhab. 53,000; alt. 400m), on the **Bodensee** (Lake Constance), because of its situation a major tourist centre. Information office at No. 18 Friedrichstrasse. It dates from 1811, when the Neustadt, created at the behest of King Friedrich of Württemberg, linked the villages of **Buchhorn** and **Hofen**. It profited from passenger traffic on the lake. Count Ferdinand von Zeppelin (1838–1917), a native of Lindau, built his first airship hangar here, launching the first Zeppelin, 128m long, on 2 July 1900. Amongst much fine art from the Gothic era onwards his creation is celebrated with models and photographs in the Städtisches Bodensee-Museum at No. 1 Adenauerplatz, open daily except Mon 10.00–12.00 and 14.00–17.00. Much was destroyed in World War II. The Ducal Schloss of 1830 (adapting an older monastery building of 1654–1701) and its twin-towered church (by Christoph Thumb, 1700, stuccos by the Schmuzers) remain from the old town. The Rathaus dates from 1956 and houses a Zeppelin museum (open except Mon 10.00–12.00 and 14.00–17.00). The town has superb gardens. Trains connect with Ulm and Lindau, boats with Konstanz and Bregenz, buses with Lindau, Ravensburg, etc.

An EXCURSION from Friedrichshafen NW along the **Bodensee** (lacus Brigantinus to the Romans, Central Europe's third largest lake (76km by 14km) and bordering on Austria, Switzerland and Germany). Follow the B31 for 17km along the lakeside through the holiday resort and wine village of **Hagnau**, where you can take steamers across the lake, and admire half-timbered houses and the Gothic parish church of St John Baptist (with its Romanesque tower and a Baroque interior) as far as **Meersburg** (inhab. 5000; alt. 40m), a medieval town of half-timbered houses first mentioned in 988, with orchards and vineyards climbing the steep nearby hill.

The **Neues Schloss**, begun c 1712 and in part designed by Balthasar Neumann, 1750 onwards, with one of his superb staircases was once the home of the Prince-bishops of Konstanz. Its treasures include a hall of mirrors; the staircase and ballroom ceilings painted by Giuseppe Appiani and the trompe l'oeil genius Carlo Pozzi; and the chapel stuccoed by J.A. Feuchtmayr with the ceiling painted by G.B. Goetz, 1741. From the garden terrace are views over the lake and to Mainau. The Neues Schloss houses the Heimatmuseum and the Dornier Museum of Flight (open Easter–Oct 09.30–12.00 and 13.30–17.30). N of the Neues Schloss is the Rathaus of 1551 (with a council chamber of 1582), and the Fürstenhäusle, former home of the poet Baroness Annette Elisabeth von Droste-Hülshoff (1797–1848) and now the Droste-Hülshoff Museum (open Easter–Oct 09.30–12.00 and 13.30–17.30). She is buried in the local cemetery, as is the inventor of mesmerism, Friedrich Anton Mesmer (1733–1815). The Schlossmühle at Meersburg, 1650, driven by an artificial ravine created 1334, is Germany's oldest overshot water mill. The Altes Schloss incorporates the 12C and 13C Dagobert tower and is also a museum; here from 1841 Annette Elisabeth von Droste-Hülshoff spent the last years of her life, her bedroom preserved as she left it (open summer 09.00–18.00, winter 10.30–12.00 and 13.00–16.30). In the Marktplatz is the medieval Obertor, and in the lower town stand a granary of 1505 and a late-Gothic chapel with an altar of the Annunciation c 1490. See also the Wine Museum at No. 11 Vorburggasse (open Apr–Oct Tue, Fri and Sun 14.00–17.00).

Beyond Meersburg the Bodensee branches into the Überlinger See. The route continues to the holiday resort of **Uhldingen-Mühlhofen**, where has been excavated a Stone- and Bronze Age village, 2200–1100 BC (reconstruction on piles in the lake, with the Pfahlbaumuseum Deutscher Vorzeit at No. 6 Seepromenade (open Apr–Oct 08.00–18.00)).

A road leads NE from here to **Salem**, where the Cistercians founded an abbey in 1134, rebuilt by F. Beer, F. Schmuzer and J.A. Feuchtmayr after a fire of 1697 and now transformed into a four-storeyed pink and white Schloss with a Dutch-style gable. It has a Baroque Kaisersaal, an oratory with Wessobrun Stucco and a porcelain Kachelofen, 1735, and the Rococo abbot's study with the swan motif of Abbot Anselm II, 1746–78. The Gothic abbey church, 1297–1414, has Baroque and Classical sculptures, including 27 alabaster altars by Johann Georg Dürer, 1774–84 (also a tabernacle, 1494; choir stalls, 1588–95; ceiling paintings by F.J. Spiegler, 1730; 4 confessionals by J.A. Feuchtmayr, 1752; and a organ by K.J. Riepp, 1766); tours of the church and Schloss (which incorporates a Fire Fighting Museum; Apr–Oct weekdays 09.00–12.00 and 13.00–17.00, Sun and holidays 11.00–17.00). Here with the help of Prince Max von Baden, Kurt Hahn (1866–1974) founded and ran a private co-educational school from 1920 until his arrest by the Nazis in 1933. Further N is the health resort of **Heiligenberg** (inhab. 1100; alt. 788m), with a late-16C Renaissance Schloss, stretching above the trees. Its Rittersaal has a coffered ceiling c 1550, and a chapel, begun 13C, rebuilt 1586, restored 1878–82 (tours Apr–Oct 09.00–12.00 and 13.00–17.00, Sun 11.00–17.00). The park offers views of the Bodensee, the Swiss Alps and the Voralberg).

NW of Uhldingen-Mühlhofen stands the superbly sited former Cistercian pilgrimage *church of **Birnau**, commissioned by Abbot Anselm II of Salem (see above) from Peter Thumb, 1749, stuccoed by J.A. Feuchtmayr and painted by Gottfried Bernhard Götz. On its Bernhardsaltar stands a celebrated Rococo statue known as the Honey-sucker (Honigschlecker), a reference to the honeyed rhetoric of the great Cistercian St Bernard of Clairvaux (1090–1153).

The route continues from here to the fortified town of **Überlingen** (inhab. 13,000; alt. 410–80m), another spa and health resort, with a Kneipp institution and views across the lake to the snow-covered Alps. Its medieval quarter forms a semicircle, facing the lake. The 15C Rathaus has a carved council chamber by J. Ruess, 1490 (open weekdays 09.00–12.00 and 14.30–17.00, Sat 09.00–12.00), and beside it rises the Renaissance Stadtarchiv of

1600. In Münsterplatz rises the Gothic church of **St Nikolaus**. Though a
12C foundation, its present form dates from 1512–86. Inside are Gothic fan
vaulting; a statue of the Virgin Mary on a crescent moon, 1510; a late-Gothic
stone pulpit; statues of Jesus and the 12 Apostles, 1552; and a tabernacle
by J. Zürn, 1611, as is the part Gothic, part Renaissance high altar, 1616.
The rosary altar is by Zürn brothers Martin and David, 1631. Its S tower
carried the Osannaglocke, a bell weighing 6650 kilos.

Überlingen's Heimatmuseum is in the Renaissance Stadtkanzlei of 1598.
The **Städtisches Museum** occupies the 15C and 16C home of the Reichlin-
Meldegg family (the Reichlin-Meildegg'sches Patrizerhaus) and has a
Gothic chapel of 1486, stuccoed in the Baroque style of J.A. Feuchtmayr,
as well as a terraced garden (open Apr–Oct except Mon 09.00–12.00 and
14.00–17.30, Sun and holidays 10.00–12.00). See also in Spitalgasse, N of
Münsterplatz, the 15C Franziskanerkirche (with 18C stucco and wall
paintings and J.A. Feuchtmayr's high altar of 1760), and the Suso House at
No. 10 Suso-Gasse, a museum devoted to the mystic Heinrich von Suso (c
1295–1366) who was born at Überlingen (open Apr–Oct Mon, Tue, Wed
and Sun 10.00–12.00 and 15.00–17.00).

The B31 continues along the lakeside through the wine village of
**Sipplingen**, with its half-timbered houses, the 15C church of  SS Martin
and George (with statues of the patrons by J.A. Feuchtmayr) and the former
Franciscan convent of 1607. The road reaches the resort of **Ludwigshafen**,
created by Grand-Duke Ludwig of Baden in 1826. From here take the B34,
which winds around the NE end of the Überlinger See to reach **Bodman**,
which is set amidst forests at the foot of the Bodanrück height and boasts
the Schloss of the Counts of Bodman, Schloss Freunberg rising 590m above
the town, with a pilgrimage chapel, a museum of children's toys, and the
ruins of 1332 Alt-Bodman. The 18C parish church has a Gothic tower.

The route SW from Friedrichshafen to Lindau also passes alongside the
Bodensee. Leaving Friedrichshafen by the B31 the lakeside route runs SE
for 10km to **Langenargen** (inhab. 5800; alt. 400m), a home of the Montforts
from 1290–1780. Here Wilhelm I of Württemberg built a Moorish castle in
1861. The Baroque church of St Martin dates from 1722. This was the
birthplace of the Baroque painters Franz Anton Maulbertsch (1724–96),
who frescoed the vault of the church, and Andrea Brugger (1797–1812),
and the town has a museum of local art housed in the former presbytery
(open May–Sept daily except Mon 10.00–12.00 and 15.00–17.00).

After 15km the road reaches Kressbronn (camping and tourism), 2km W
of **Nonnenhorn**, with its Gothic Jakobskapelle and a wine press of 1591.
After 2km more the road reaches idyllically sited **Wasserburg**, whose
Fuggers' Schloss, which dates back to the late-13C but in its present form
was built in 1592 is now a hotel. The Lieber Augustin Monument is here
because the novelist H.W. Gliessler who wrote *Der liebe Augustin* lived at
Wasserburg. A Fuggers' column was erected here in 1796, and the
Maulhaus houses the local history museum (open mid-May to Oct daily
09.00–12.00). The Baroque church of St George has Empire-style decoration.

From here Lindau (see Rte 8) and the Austrian border are reached after
6km.

# 20

# Konstanz to Heilbronn

Total distance 272km. Konstanz—52km Radolfzell, through Switzerland—B34, 15km Stockach—B313, 21km Messkirch—17km Sigmaringen—B22, 23km Mengen—B311, 10km Riedlingen—B312, 42km Reutlingen—41km Stuttgart—B27, 16km Ludwigsburg—25km Lauffen am Neckar—10km Heilbronn.

**Konstanz** (or Constance) (70,000 inhab.; alt. 404m; information office: Bahnhofplatz 13) on the Bodensee (see Rte 19) is said to have been founded in the 3C by the father of Constantine the Great, Emperor Constantine Chlorus (283–306). In Alemannic times it became a bishopric, c 590, and enriched itself by the linen trade, prospering as a Free Imperial City from 1192 to 1548, when it became subject to Austria. The Catholic Council of Constance was held here between 1414 and 1418 and attempted to heal the Great Schism between the eastern and western churches. The same Council ordered John Wycliffe's body to be removed from consecrated ground and condemned the Bohemian Reformer Jan Huss to death. He was executed here, along with his friend Jerome of Prague (born c 1370) in 1415, and is commemorated by a huge rock on the Alter Graben inscribed 'Husenstein'. See also the display in the Johannes-Hus-Haus at 64 Husenstrasse, open Mon 10.00–12.00, 14.00–16.00, Sun 10.00–12.00.

The French essayist Michel de Montaigne (1533–92) lived in the Haus Marktstätte 8 (now the Gasthof zum Adler) in 1580, and in Villa Sceheim (86 Eichhornstrasse) lived from 1890 Wilhelm von Scholz (1874–1969), the writer who helped (by his 'Bodensee' and his 'Jew of Konstanz') to make the region famous. Konstanz became part of the Grand-Duchy of Baden in 1805. In 1848 the revolutionary Friedrich Karl Franz Hecker (1811–81) proclaimed at Konstanz the German Republic. A university was founded here in 1966.

Two vestiges of the city's former fortifications still guard Konstanz: the Rheintorturm of c 1300 and the Pulverturm of 1321. The major ecclesiastical building is the Romanesque cathedral of Our Lady, begun in the 11C on the site of a Roman fort. The crypt dates from c 1000. A new cathedral was begun on its foundation in the mid 11C, transformed into a Gothic church in the 14C and 15C and given Baroque vaulting around 1680. Building ended only when the Gothic pyramidical tower was finished in 1856. The west door carvings (ten bas-relief scenes from the life of Jesus) are from the workshop of Simon Haider, 1470.

Inside, the crypt shelters four 11–13C copper gilt panels depicting Christ in Majesty, St John (an eagle), St Konrad and St Pelagius. The *Holy Sepulchre in the Mauritiuskapelle, c 1280, has scenes from the infancy of Jesus and of the 12 Apostles. The 15C crucifix is known as the Gross Hergott von Konstanz. A late Gothic staircase of 1438 (known as the 'Schnegg') in the north transept, has Old and New Testament scenes, 1438. The magnificent choir stalls are, like the portal, from the workshop of Simon Haider, c 1467. The altar c 1660 is by Franz Morinck, and the 17C wooden pulpit by Daniel Schenk. Nave vaulting of 1679–83 rises from 11C arcades, while the classical choir dates from the mid 18C. The organ console dates from 1523; the Margarethenkapelle is filled with fine works of art.

The sacristy and the cloister, with a chapel frescoed with scenes of the Passion, 1472, lead to the 13C Mauritius-Rotunde, which has Renaissance frescoes of 1578 and an octagonal, late Gothic *Holy Sepulchre c 1300, some 5m high. The Kaufhaus on the harbour, 1388, restored 1970, is called the Konzilgebäude, in the erroneous belief that it was the seat of the Council of 1414–18. It is curiously built with one huge hall atop another. Opposite is the Zeppelin memorial to Graf Ferdinand von Zeppelin (who was born here in 1838), a quaint statue with massive wings protruding from his shoulder blades. Across the Stadtgarten on the 'Half Island' you reach the former Jesuit church of Christ (17C Baroque and Rococo, now belonging to the Old Catholics) and the Stadttheater of 1610, at 11 Konzilstrasse, the oldest theatre in western Germany. Opposite on the Dominican Island is the former Dominican monastery, now a hotel which incorporates even the church with its Gothic transept, its early Gothic cloisters 1260–70, and its 16C frescoes in the vestibule depicting the Dance of Death and Virtues. The Blessed Henry Suso (c 1295–1366) lived here in the 14C. He was born at the Haus zur Täsch, 39 Hussenstrasse, now a museum in his memory, open Tue–Sun 10.00–12.00, 14.00–16.00, closed Sun afternoons.

The cathedral square houses a museum of the linen and silk industries (No. 5, Haus zur Kunkel, open weekdays 10.00–12.00, 14.00–17.00) and the city archives in the Haus zu Katze, 1424. Wessenbergstrasse leads S from Münsterplatz with (at No. 41) the city art gallery (open Tue–Sat 14.00–17.00; Sun 11.00–13.00). This street leads to the late Gothic church of St Stephan, 1424–86, whose interior is Gothic and Baroque, and houses Hans Morinck's tomb for his wife, as well as choir stalls and a tabernacle c 1600 by Morinck. Obermarkt is bordered by picturesque houses, including the Hotel Barbarossa of 1419, with inscriptions referring to Barbarossa's peace treaty with the Lombards in 1183, the Haus zum hohen Hafen of 1425, frescoed c 1900, the 13C Malhaus, with its Renaissance oriel window, and the Haus zum groen Merzen, dating from the 14C to the 18C. The city's 14C Rathaus was frescoed in 1864, and has a coffered first-storey ceiling. (It hosts concerts in summer in its interior courtyard.) The Rosgartenmuseum at 3–5 Rosgartenstrasse is housed in a Gothic house once the home of the butchers' guild, and displays sculpture from the 14–18C, regional paintings, local history and Jugendstil works (open 09.00–12.00, 14.00–17.00, closing 16.00 mid-Oct to mid-May). In the same street rises the former Augustinian church of the Holy Trinity, begun in the late 13C Gothic style, modified in the Baroque era, with frescoes of 1417 depicting the history of the Augustinians.

Konstanz has an international Casino at 21 Seestrasse; trains connect with Immendingen and Singen, and boats ply the lake, including a car ferry to the island of **Mainau** with its exotic and tropical plants, including banana trees, a formal rose garden with pergolas and 30,000 roses, dawn redwoods and sweet chestnuts, in a 30-hectare Italian-style park laid out in 1860–80 for Grand Duke Friedrich I of Baden and extended by Count Lennart Bernadotte in the 1930s (open daily Apr–Oct 08.00–19.00). The three-winged Schloss is by Johann Caspar Bagnato, 1739–46, with a Baroque Schlosskapelle, 1734–39, decorated with frescoes by Franz Joseph Spiegler and sculpture by J.A. Feuchtmayr. The façade of the Schloss is decorated with the arms of the Teutonic Knights who owned Mainau for 500 years.

Crossing the mouth of the Bodensee, you can make an **excursion** E from Konstanz to reach the spot where **Reichenau** island in the Untersee is connected to the mainland by a causeway, beside which are the ruins of 10C Burg Schopfeln. On this island in 724 Charles Martel founded the first

Benedictine monastery of Germany. The route reaches first **Oberzell**, with the 9C late Carolingian church of St George. Building continued until 1050. Ottonian **wall paintings c 1000 depict the miracles of Jesus; the late Romanesque crucifix dates from c 1170; in the 9C and 10C crypt are the relics of St George and fragmentary frescoes; and the church also houses a 15C Pietà and Man of Sorrows.

At **Mittelzell** stands the Romanesque former abbey church of St Maria and St Markus, its tower decorated with Lombardic pilasters and friezes. Founded by St Pirmin in 724, and dissolved in 1799, the abbey was rebuilt by Abbot Berno, 1030–48, though some 9C work was retained. The vaulting of the apse is of wood, the chancel is 15C Gothic and the church houses a Rococo screen and an altar of 1477 with relics of St Mark (brought to Mittelzell in 830). The treasury displays early medieval works of religious art in the Gothic sacristy and stands above a Romanesque cellar (open

*The Romanesque tower of the monastery church of St Maria and St Markus at Mittelzell on the island of Reichenau*

June–Sept weekdays 11.00–12.00, 15.00–16.00). The monastic buildings date from 1605–10. At 3 Münsterplatz stands the 13C and 14C half-timbered Rathaus, now a local history museum (open May–Oct except Mon 15.00–17.00). Schloss Konigsegg, 16C with towers and battlements, is now a hotel. At **Niederzell** at the NW corner of the island is the collegiate church of SS Peter and Paul, 9C with 11C towers. Enlarged in the 15C and given a Rococo vault in 1756, it preserves fragments of Romanesque frescoes c 1104. Nearby is the monastic hospice c 1500.

To travel around the S side of the Bodensee from Konstanz means crossing into Switzerland. 3km W of Konstanz is **Gottlieben**, with the Druchenberg House of 1617, and a Schloss of 1250, redone in the neo-Gothic style, 1838, where Huss awaited execution, followed by **Manenbach**, with numerous early 19C Schlösser, the most important of which is a Napoleon Museum, and the medieval town of **Steckborn**, with 14C and 17C small castles, and a Rathaus of 1667, and then **Stein am Rhein**, the most beautiful Swiss medieval town.

Cross back into Germany and drive NE to **Radolfzell** (51km from Konstanz) by way of Gaienhofen where Hermann Hesse (1877–1962) lived from 1904 to 1907. (It is possible to drive directly along the B33 from Konstanz to Radolfzell.) On the site of a hermitage built by St Radolf (9C Bishop of Verona) has grown a town which belonged to Austria until 1805, witness the Österreichisches Schlösschen in the Marktplatz, built for an Archduke of Austria in 1606. In the same square St Radolf lies in a 17C sarcophagus inside the 15C three-aisled Gothic basilica of Unser Lieben Frau, noted for its massive pillars and the Drei-Hausherren-Altar of 1750. Three towers of the medieval fortifications remain. Kaufhausstrasse has Renaissance houses, and in Seestrasse rises the 16C Gothic Spitalkirche, the Fortei of 1619 and two 18C buildings, the Stadtapotheke and the Amstgericht. The writer J.V. von Scheffel made his home here, building the Haus Seehalde in 1873, at 14 Scheffelstrasse. The town is now a holiday and sports resort, with a bird sanctuary and a Kurhaus (in Scheffel's former home) on the peninsula of Mettnau. The city museum is in the Stadtpark (open Tue, Thu, Fri, Sat 15.00–17.00; Wed, Sun also 10.00–12.00). On the third Sunday and Monday in June the three patron saints of Radolfzell are honoured by a naval procession. Trains connect the town with Konstanz, Lindau and Munich, boats with Konstanz, Reichenau and Stein am Rhein.

From Radolfzell the B34 runs N for 15km to **Stockach** (12,700 inhab.; alt. 475m) at the foot of the Nellenburg with its ruined Schloss, famed for the wildness of its Shrovetide Carnival celebrations whose liberties are said to date back to a 14C court jester Kuony von Stocken (hence the Kuony fountain in the Marktplatz). Here in 1799 the French were defeated by the Imperial Army commanded by Archduke Karl Ludwig Johann of Austria (1771–1847). From Stockach the B313 leads N through wooded hills for 21km to **Messkirch** (7000 inhab.; alt. 600m). The basilica of St Martin by L. Reder, 1536, is today neo-classical as a result of the work of F.A. Bagnato in the late 18C, retaining from the earlier building an Adoration of the Magi, 1538, a bronze tomb of Count Gottfried von Zimmern by P. Labenwolf, 1558, and a massive tomb made for Wilhelm von Zimmern by W. Neidhardt, 1599, as well as the St Johann Nepomuk chapel decorated by the brothers Asam, 1734. The Baroque frescoes of the vault are by Andreas Meinrad von Au (1712–82). The 14C Liebfrauenkirche was redone in 1576 by Jörg Schwartzenberger, who also designed the ballroom of the Schloss (now the local history museum, open daily 09.00–12.00, 14.00–17.00). The Rathaus, decorated with coats of arms carved in stone, dates from the 17C. The composer Konradin Kreutzer (1780–1849) was born and died at Messkirch, and the philosopher Martin Heidegger (1889–1976) was born here.

Continue along the B313 N for 17km to **Sigmaringen** (15,000 inhab. alt. 570m), whose Schloss was once the home of the Hohenzollern-Sigmaringen family. Rising impressively on a rock above the Danube and entirely rebuilt in 1893 after a fire, it houses the rich collection of the princely family (open Feb–Nov 08.30–12.00, 13.00–17.30). Close by is the church of St John the Evangelist, 15C with a nave rebuilt 1757 by Johann Martin Ilg, and housing altars by J.M. Feuchtmayr along with the cradle of the local martyr St Fidelis, 1577–1622. The 12C Romanesque church of St Gallus has a 15C choir decorated in the Baroque and Rococo styles. The Josephskapelle of 1629, in the Josephsberg park, has an octagonal cupola of 1739. In Antonjosefstrasse the Runder Turm, once part of the fortifications of the town, is now a local history museum (open from Easter to mid-Oct Tue, weekends 10.00–12.00, 14.00–17.00).

At Sigmaringen in 1944–45 after their retreat from France the Nazis established a 'French Government', and here was interned Marshal Henri Philippe Omer Pétain (1856–1952), leader of Vichy France, after his arrest. The road from Sigmaringen winds E, joining the B32 before Mengen, which is reached after 23km. **Mengen** (9400 inhab.; alt. 580m) has fine half-timbered houses of the 16–18C and a Gothic church of Our Lady which suffered from a fire in the 17C and was then rebuilt in the Baroque style. Its vault was frescoed in 1740 by G.W. Wollmer and J. Sautter. In the choir is a late Gothic Virgin, and the church has a 16C Mount of Olives. Mengen's Alter Fuchs tower was built in 1514 and restored in 1975. This is hiking country and a starting off point for exploring the upper Danube valley.

From here the B311 travels 10km N to **Riedlingen** (8700 inhab.; alt. 540m), set on the left bank of the Danube and still for the most part a picturesque old town, amongst whose fine houses are the mid-15C town hall, with its stork's nest, the former granary of 1686 (called the Alte Kaserne), the 16C inn Zum Greifen and the 16C Grasellisches Haus. The 14C church of St Georg boasts Gothic wall paintings and glass of 1898 by the local glassmaker Albert Burkart. Riedlingen was the birthplace of the Baroque sculptor Johann Joseph Christian (1706–77).

The B312 leads N for 14km to **Zwiefalten** in the wooded Ach valley, where the Baroque monastery church of *Our Lady was built to plans of Franz Beer and Johann Michael Fischer, 1740–65, for the Benedictines. Inside are stucco by J.M. Feuchtmayr, paintings by A. Meinrad and F.J. Spiegler and sculpture by J. Christian. The church also shelters a Byzantine reliquary altar of the 12C. Many domestic buildings of the monastery survive, and the large 17C wing is now a psychiatric clinic.

From Zwiefalten take the B312 NW for 42km to Reutlingen. Potholers should look out en route for Sonnenbühl (to the left of the main road) where the **Bärenhöhle** was discovered in 1949 and then for Honau where the remarkable 380m-long **Nebelhöhle**, with two underground lakes, is open daily from Apr–Oct. The old houses and the valley are dominated by **Burg Lichtenstein**, a Gothic confection rebuilt in the early 1840s by the architect Heidelhoff, with a collection of arms and local paintings (open daily Apr–Oct 09.00–12.00, 13.00–17.00; otherwise Tue, holidays and weekends 09.00–12.00, 13.00–17.30). The rebuilding of the fortress was inspired by the novel 'Lichtenstein' (1826) by the locally born Wilhelm Hauff (1802–27).

**Reutlingen** (96,000 inhab.; alt. 869m; tourist information: 1 Listplatz) is an industrial town (engineering, textiles, tanneries) at the foot of 707m-high

Mount Achalm, whose history began in the 6C when it was founded by the Alemanni. Granted the right to hold a market in 1182, Reutlingen received its city charter in 1209 and remained a Free Imperial City until 1802. As part of the Swabian League the town fought against and defeated the forces of Count Ulrich of Württemberg in 1377, a victory commemorated in Johann Ludwig Uhland's 'Die Schlacht bei Reutlingen'. In spite of much damage in World War II, fine buildings remain. Situated on the River Echaz, the town has preserved parts of its medieval fortifications. In front of the railway station stands a monument of 1863 to the economist Friederich List (a native of the town, 1789–1846), who was born at 4 Wilhelmstrasse. Trains connect Reutlingen with Konstanz, Tübingen and Stuttgart, buses with other places.

Wilhelmstrasse leads SE from the station past the Nikolaikirche of 1358, rebuilt 1948–50, in front of which is the Tanners' and Dyers' fountain, 1921. (These craftsmen lived in the 'little Venice' quarter by the River Echaz.) This street leads to the Marktplatz, with a 14C former Spital and a Spitalkirche, 1333, widened 1555, now a school, and a fountain, the Marktbrunnen of 1570, with a statue of Emperor Maximilian II, as well as the Rathaus, 1966. Wilhelmstrasse continues SE to reach the *Marienkirche, 1273–1343, the finest early Gothic building in Württemberg, which boasts a 73m-high tower built by Peter von Breisach and Matthäus Böblinger, finished 1343. Inside are 14C wall paintings, a late 15C octagonal font, and an early 16C Gothic sepulchre in the choir. Near the church gushes a fountain, the Marienkirchbrunnen of 1561, with a statue of Emperor Friedrich II. Close by is the Baroque Landwirtschaftsschule, 1728.

Continue along Wilhelmstrasse, which is also cooled by the Lindenbrunnen of 1544, in order to reach the town walls. Otherwise walk SW from the Marienkirche to the local history museum, in a building of 1538 (open Wed, Sat 10.30–15.00, Sun 10.30–12.00, 14.00–17.00). Spendehausstrasse leads from here to the Spendehaus of 1518 (formerly the town granary), from which Lederstrasse leads NW to the Tübingen Gate, 1220–40, decorated and half-timbered in the 16C. At the opposite side of the town stands the fortified Garden Gate of 1392.

12km NW is Tübingen (see Rte 23). The road from Reutlingen leads almost directly N for 41km to Stuttgart (see Rte 18).

Leave Stuttgart by the Heilbronner Strasse and the B27 to reach after 16km *Ludwigsburg (85,000 inhab.; alt. 292m; tourist office: 24 Wilhelmstrasse), a town founded in 1709 by Duke Eberhard Ludwig of Württemberg (died 1733) as the chief family seat—which it remained until 1775. Marktplatz was designed by the Baroque architect Donato Giuseppe Frisoni, with arcades and a statue of the founder, by Feretti, 1722, as well as a fountain. On the west side rises Frisoni's double-towered Protestant church of 1726. The single-towered Catholic church opposite dates from a year later.

In Wilhelmsplatz stands a statue of Schiller, who lived here 1768–73 and 1793–94; at 8 Marktplatz was born the poet Justinus Kerner (1786–1862); the poet Eduard Mörike (1804–75) was born at 2 Obere Marktstrasse, next door to the Baroque Amsthaus; the aestheticist F.T. Vischer (1807–78) was born at 12 Marktplatz; and the philosopher and theologian David Friedrich Strauss (1808–74) was born at 1 Marstallstrasse.

On the edge of the B27 at Ludwigsburg is an immense **Schloss built for Eberhard Ludwig in part by the French architect Philippe L. de la Guépière (with other parts by Frisoni and J.F. Nette), modelled on Versailles and consisting of 452 rooms in all, decorated in the Baroque, Rococo and Empire styles. Frisoni added the two pavilions (the Jagdpavillon and the Spielpavillon). After the Schloss had been allowed to fall into a dangerous state of ruin (when Duke Karl Alexander returned to Stuttgart in 1734), it was saved by the architect Thouret at the behest of King Friedrich I. Guided tours of 75 of the rooms, including the hall of mirrors, the portrait gallery and Frisoni's pavilions, take place Apr–mid-Oct 19.00–12.00, 13.00–17.00, otherwise at 10.30 and 15.00.

The vast Schlossgarten with its lake and fountains is the site of a horticultural show—'Blühendes Barock'—from April to October. Part of the park is a game reserve, and the gardens to the north of the Schloss also incorporate Frisoni's Baroque **Lustschlösschen Favorite**, 1715, restored by Thouret 1799–1801, as well as the Rococo **Seeschloss Monrepos**, by Philippe de la Guépière, 1760–65. Concerts and other festivals take place here from May to October. The Kuhländer Archive in the Baroque **Stuttgarter Torhaus** of 1760 is devoted to the history of East Sudetenland, open Sun 10.30–12.30.

The environs of Ludwigsburg include **Marbach am Neckar**, 5km NE, the birthplace of Friedrich Schiller (1759–1802) and the astronomer Robias Meyer (1723–1762). Its 18C Schloss guards a Rathaus of 1762 and the Gothic Alexanderkirche designed by Alberlin Jörg, with a late 15C choir and a belfry of 1481. Schiller's birthplace, a half-timbered house at 31 Nickolastorstrasse, is now a museum (open daily 09.00–17.00), and a greater collection devoted to him is in the Schiller-Nationalmuseum und Deutsches Literaturarchiv at 8–10 Schillerhöhe (open daily 09.00–17.00).

From Ludwigsburg the B27 runs NW across the motorway to reach **Bietigheim** (13,000 inhab.; alt. 220m). Its best monuments are the belfried town hall, 1507; the Hornmoldhaus, 1526; its walls, gates and towers; halftimbered houses; the Ulrichbrunnen of 1549 in the Marktplatz; and the cemetery church of 1390. Bietigheim is followed by **Besigheim** (5500 inhab.; alt. 185m), situated on a ridge between the Neckar and the Enz and defended north and south by two huge round Romanesque towers. Wall paintings of c 1380, representing the Passion, are in the nave of the 14–15C Protestant church, which also has a carved high altar of St Cyriacus by Christoph von Urach, c 1520. The half-timbered mid-15C town hall and a late 16C fountain are in the Marktplatz; and the bridge over the Enz is dated 1581.

This wine road continues through the old villages of Walheim and Kirchheim, reaching, 25km after Ludwigsburg, **Lauffen am Neckar** (9000 inhab.; alt. 172m). Here was born Friedrich Hölderlin (1770–1843), and Lauffen has a monument to him. Parts of the 16C town walls remain. The church of St Regiswinde (once dedicated to St Martin) dates from the 13C, with 16C alterations. Close by, the early Gothic St Regiwindis chapel contains the saint's bones. A stone bridge crosses the Neckar to join both parts of the town. The town hall is the former Unteres Schloss.

After 10km more the B27 reaches **Heilbronn** (113,000 inhab.; alt. 157m), an important town on the Neckar and the Rhein–Neckar canal. Heinrich von Kleist's 'Kätchen von Heilbronn' (1810) brought it literary fame, and its wines also bring renown.

**Information office** in the Rathaus. **Trains** connect with Heidelberg, Schwäbisch Hall, Stuttgart, Karlsruhe and Würzburg, **buses** with Ludwigsburg, Karlsruhe, Schwäbisch Hall, etc.

**History**. Heilbronn's name derives from a pre-Christian holy well—'Heiligen Brunnen', and is first documented in 741. Heilbronn was a Free Imperial City until

1802. Here was born Jules Robert von Mayer (1814–79), who discovered the law of the conservation of energy (monument in Moltkestrasse). Large areas of Heilbronn was destroyed in 1944, though much has been restored and rebuilt. One of the 14C towers of the town fortifications is called the Götzenturm, after the tradition that Götz von Berlichingen was held prisoner there in 1519. Goethe's play has him die here. Another remnant of the medieval fortifications is the Bollwerksturm, at the north end of Untere Neckarstrasse.

Heilbronn hosts a horse fair (Pferdemarkt) at the end of February, a river festival (Neckarfest) in mid-June, even-numbered years only. Alternates with Stadtfest. Late July/early Aug, Unterländer Volksfest (beer) and a wine festival from 8–16 Sept.

The Marktplatz, W of the main railway station, contains the restored Gothic town hall begun 1417, enlarged 1579–82, and partly transformed into a Renaissance building at the end of the 16C. It boasts a stunning astronomical clock, 1580, by J. Habrecht, the maker of that in Strasbourg cathedral, an open-air staircase and a gallery supported by five arches on Ionic columns. At the SW of the square is the birthplace of Kätchen von Heilbronn (with an encorbelled window). S is the church of St Kilian, begun 1013. It has a 15C flamboyant Gothic choir and a delightful and curious Renaissance tower, 62m high and carrying a statue of a medieval soldier with Heilbronn's banner, along with monsters and mocked monks, designed by H. Schweiner and finished c 1530. Inside, the nave is 13C Gothic, the 15C choir is by Anton Pilgram (vaulting by A. Jörg) and the high altar was made by Hans Seyffer, 1498.

Sülmerstrasse leads to the Hafenmarkt, with a tower of 1728, now a war memorial, which is all that remains of the Franciscan church. Kirchbrunnenstrasse leads to the church of the Teutonic Knights (SS Peter and Paul), with its 13C tower, the rest reordered 1721, though basically still Gothic. It is now the city art gallery, open Tue 10.00–19.00, Wed–Sun 10.00–12.00, 14.00–17.00. The theatre at 64 Gartenstrasse dates from 1951. Heilbronn's Historical Museum is at 1 Eichgasse, open Tue 10.00–19.00, Wed–Sun 10.00–12.00, 14.00–17.00, as is the Natural History Museum at 1 Kramstrasse.

# 21

# Stuttgart to Schwäbisch Hall and on to Nuremberg

Total distance 146km. Stuttgart—B14, 27km Schwäbisch Hall—32km Crailsheim—20km Feuchtwangen—25km Ansbach—17km Heilsbronn—25km Nuremberg.

Leave Stuttgart (see Rte 18) by way of Bad Cannstatt and follow the B14 NE for 13km to reach **Waiblingen** (45,000 inhab.; alt. 208m), which has preserved remains of fortifications. Here the church of St Michael, 1480–89, has net vaulting and a pulpit of 1484. The 15C Nonnenkirchlein at 19 Alter Postplatz, by Hans Felber of Ulm, is a chapel above a charnel house. The Städtisches Heimatmuseum is at 25 Kurze Strasse, open Sat 15.00–17.00, Sun 11.00–12.00. Waiblingen was the site of a Carolingian palace and here originated the Imperial Salic line and the later house of Hohenstaufen, hence their Italian name Ghibellines. Continue for 9km to the picturesque town of **Winnenden**, whose former Schloss of the Teutonic Knights is now a psychiatric clinic. It was built in the 13C, reordered in the 18C and contains a 16C chapel. The town also boasts a Gothic church.

After 10km the route reaches **Backnang** (30,000 inhab.; alt. 278m) in the Murr valley, with its early 17C timber-framed Rathaus and Romanesque 13C parish church, with Gothic modifications, and the brasses of Margrave Hermann of Baden and his family, 1515. The 17C Schloss rises on the Schlossberg. The Helferhaus Museum at 8 Stiftshof, opens Sat 15.00–18.00, Sun 10.30–12.30, 15.00–18.00 and displays rustic articles of yesteryear. 6km later the route reaches **Oppenweiler**, with an 18C Schloss serving as the town hall and a late Gothic church. From here the road continues to Sulzbach, where a brief **diversion** E reaches **Murrhardt**, with its notable Walterichskapelle of 1230, with early Gothic alterations, set beside the Gothic parish church of 1434. In the cemetery is the 15C Walterichskirche, with a 17C tower, as well as the tomb of the painter Reinhold Nägele (1884–1972). The Romans built a castrum here to defend the Limes, and traces of the defences still remain. Numerous marked hiking routes take you through the surrounding countryside. Some 15km SE is the **Schwaben-park** zoo, with around 200 beasts, including chimpanzees, elephants, bears, lions and tigers.

The B14 continues NE from Sulzbach for 27km to *Schwäbisch Hall (32,000 inhab.; alt. 270m), a spa on the River Kocher, crossed here by old footbridges.

**Tourist information** at 9 Am Markt. **Trains** connect with Strecken, Heilbronn, Nuremberq and Stuttgart, buses with Heilbronn, Ellwangen and Rothenburg ob der Tauber.

**History**. The town, originally a Celtic settlement, prospered from early times on salt works, was given a charter by Barbarossa in 1156, a royal mint was established, and Schwäbisch Hall became a Free Imperial City 110 years after receiving its charter. Schwäbisch Hall opted for Protestantism in 1522 and became a member of the Schmalkaldic League. Several times captured and pillaged during the Thirty Years War, the town finally suffered from a fire in 1728.

The superb Marktplatz is the scene of annual performances (June to August) of the salt-boilers' dance, etc. on the 53 wide steps of the late Gothic church of St Michael with its huge west tower—the octagonal dome dates from 1573—which is Romanesque apart from the top two sections, added in 1527. The nave is by K. Heinzelmann, finished 1456, while the choir was begun in 1495 by Hans and Jakob Scheyb and finished in 1527. Its high altar has some 50 scenes of the Passion, c 1470, and a crucifix by Michael Erhart, 1494, with a mid-15C tabernacle. The stalls date from 1534. Look out for the 16C Holy Sepulchre; the Michaelsaltar by Hans Beyscher, 1510; and the reredos of the Magi in a side chapel, 1520. The figure of St Michael over the doorway is c 1300.

Opposite in the Marktplatz, with its ancient pillory and Hans Beyscher's Fish Fountain of 1509, set against a wall with statues of SS Michael and George and Samson, is the late Baroque Rathaus (1732–35, the double-headed eagle of the Holy Roman Empire on its façade, alongside patrician houses. Close by are the festival hall, the 'Grosse Büchsenhaus' (arsenal) of 1505–27, and at 8 Untere Herrngasse the medieval Keckenburg, once the home of a noble town family (the Kecks) and now a fine art and historical collection, the Hällisch-Fränkishes Museum (open Tue–Sun 09.00–12.00, 14.00–17.00; opens one hour later in winter). The 13C and 14C church of

St Katharina is on the left bank of the Kocher. Its fine interior, whose choir was built in 1343, contains *stained glass c 1360 depicting Virtues, Sins and SS Catherine, Dorothy and Mary Magdalen, a late 15C choir altar with scenes of the Passion, and a nave rebuilt in 1900. Of the medieval fortifications remain the Diebs Tower on Salinenstrasse and the Malefix Tower in Saümarkt. The suburb of Unterlimpurg retains ruins of its Burg (sung by the lyric poet Johann Ludwig Uhland) and the church of St Urban, 13C and 15C. The Regional Freilandmuseum opens Apr–Oct Mon–Sat 13.30–18.00, Sun and holidays 10.00–18.00.

Unterlimpurger Strasse leads 3km SE to **Grosscomburg** and the 340m-high peak which is dominated by the defensive former Benedictine abbey of Comburg, founded in 1079 by Graf Burkhard II of Rotenburg-Comburg. Designed by Joseph Geising, its triple-towered Romanesque church of St Nikolaus, now the Catholic parish church, has a Baroque interior, 1706–15, with a **Romanesque chandelier 1130; the sarcophagus of Burkhard II c 1220; the *antependium of the high altar c 1140, while the altar itself and its baldacchino are Baroque, 1713–17. The rest of the monastery buildings—in good order and now a teachers' training college—date from the 12C and include the hexagonal chapel of St Erhard, 1227, with early Gothic vaulting and wall paintings of 1562, and the chapel of St Michael. The three gates of its rampart date successively from the 18C, 1575 and the 12C.

Hessemtaler Strasse leads from here a short distance to another former monastery at **Kleincomburg**, again on a hill, founded 1108 as the result of a vow by Heinrich II von Comburg and retaining the Romanesque church of St Gilgen, c 1120, restored 1971, its 12C frescoes restored 1887.

A **detour** 12km E brings you to **Vellberg**, its fortress, razed in 1525, rebuilt in the 1540s, dominating the narrow Bühler valley. Here the church of St Martin has a choir of 1435 and a nave of 1560.

The B14 continues NE from Schwäbisch Hall through **Ilshofen**, with remains of fortifications, a gate of 1609 and a 16C church, reaching **Crailsheim** (25,000 inhab.; alt. 100m) after 32km. Much destroyed in April 1945 at the battle of Crailsheim, this industrial town has a history dating back to a 6C Frankish hunting village. Restored are the 15C late Gothic church of St Johannis, begun c 1280, finished 15C (the high altar and tabernacle c 1490, the Baroque organ 1709), the cemetery chapel, 1580 and the Gothic town hall, whose tower was added in 1717. The Fränkisch-Hohenlohesches Heimatmuseum is at 2 Spitalstrasse.

The B14 runs E, into Bavaria, to reach after 20km **Feuchtwangen** which is on the 'Romantische Strasse' (see Rte 5B).

Continue along the B14 NE, under the motorway to reach in 25km *Ansbach** (40,000 inhab.; alt. 409m; information office: 1 Martin-Luther-Platz) in the Rezat valley and an important railway junction (Prague, Paris, Stuttgart) as well as the point where the B13 and the B14 meet. Originating as the Benedictine monastery of Onolzbach founded 748, it was the home of the Hohenzollerns from 1331; it became the chief seat of the Margraves of Brandenburg-Ansbach in 1460. In the 16C Margraf Georg the Pious (1515–43) spread Protestantism here. Today it is the seat of the Mittelfranken administration and the centre of the Lutheran church of this region. Here was born the poet Johann Peter Uz (1720–96). Queen Caroline of Great Britain (1683–1737), wife of George II, was born here, as was the poet August von Platen (1796–1835). Each year in July, Ansbach, 'the town of Franconian Rococo', runs a Rococo festival as well as an international week of Bach music.

Karlstrasse leads from the railway station NW past (left) the neo-classical Ludwigskirche, 1834–40, through Karlsplatz and across the Promenade to Kannenstrasse (reached by turning left at Neustadt and right again), which leads to the principal architectural treasures. At the end of Kannenstrasse is the Landhaus, on the corner of Martin-Luther-Platz, built by Georg the Pious, 1532, now the Stadthaus and restored in 1928. In Martin-Luther-Platz stands the 15C Gothic triple-towered church of St Gumbertus, Romanesque (the crypt built 1039–42), with a Baroque nave, 1736, a pulpit by P.A. Biarelles, 1738–39, a 15C altarpiece of the apotheosis of Our Lady, and an early 16C Gothic choir. Its north tower was finished in 1594, its south tower a century earlier. The choir, rebuilt 1501–21, incorporates the chapel all 11 tombs of the Knights of the Swan, founded by the Elector Friedrich II of Brandenburg in 1440, with eleven tombs of the members, and a painting attributed to Dürer.

Adjoining the church is the former Hof Chancellery, a late Renaissance building by Gideon Bacher, 1591–1600. From here follow Martin-Luther-Platz W to see the 15C late Gothic St Johannis church, begun in 1441, with two asymmetrical towers. The burial vault of the Margraves under the choir, built 1660, contains 25 of their coffins. To see the Italian Baroque Residenzschloss, built between 1704 and 1738, follow instead Johann-Sebastian-Bach-Platz E from St Gumbertus. Now the offices of the Mittelfranken administration, the Schloss was built for Margrave Carl Wilhelm Friedrich and his cultivated wife Christiane Charlotte, who in 1724 planted the double alleyway of lime trees in its garden. The garden also has a monument to the bizarre Kaspar Hauser, the foundling discovered at Munich in 1828 and mysteriously murdered in this garden in 1833. Details of his life are in the Kreis-und Stadtmuseum, as well as porcelain (open Tue–Sun 10.00–12.00, 14.00–17.00).

Based on plans by Gabriel de Gabrieli, the Schloss utilises parts of an earlier Renaissance building. Gabrieli designed the long façade of 21 bays. Between 1726 and 1741 work was continued by J.W. and Karl Friedrich von Zocha and Leopoldo Retti. Von Zocha designed the southeast façade, Retti the others. Retti also decorated the *interior in the French Rococo style, with its hall of mirrors; a great hall, whose ceiling was painted by Carlo Carlone in honour of Margrave Carl Wilhelm Friedrich, and stuccoed by Diego Carlone; and rooms tiled with 18C Ansbach porcelain, then famous, especially the Kachelsaal and the Gotische Halle. The Hof garden E of the Schloss was laid out in the 16C and remodelled in the 18C. To the N is K.F. von Zocha's Orangery, 1726–43.

Ansbach also has a cemetery chapel of Heiliges Kreuz (1461), a Rathaus of 1623 and streets with 18C Baroque houses. The synagogue dates from the 18C, the Markgrafenmuseum is at 14 Schaitbergstrasse, open except Mon 10.00–12.00, 14.00–17.00, and the Residenz and Staatsgalerie is at 27 Promenade, open summer 19.00–12.00, 14.00–17.00 (winter 10.00–12.00, 14.00–16.00).

From Ansbach the B14 reaches Nuremberg (see Rte 6) after 42km, passing through the resort of **Heilsbronn** where in 1132 Bishop Otto the Holy of Bamberg founded a Cistercian monastery in whose cruciform church—begun 1232, considerably altered over the centuries, restored after World War II—are buried over 20 Hohenzollerns. The wall tombs of Margrave Friedrich, died 1536, and his son Georg, died 1543, have been attributed to Loy Hering; the choir dates from 1280, the south aisle from 1412–33; the tabernacle of 1515 is from the workshop of Adam Krafft; a late Gothic pulpit is carved with the 12 Apostles; the crucifix was carved in 1468; the carved high altar of 1522 depicts the Adoration of the Magi, and the church has another early 15C Nothelferaltar. The 13C building north of the church is the former monastery refectory. Heilsbronn also has a Spitalkapelle, basically Gothic but topped with an 18C half-timbered hat.

# 22

# Stuttgart to the Swiss border via Tübingen

Total distance 170km. Stuttgart—B27, 41km Tübingen—21km Hechingen—40km Rottweil—33km Donauschingen—35km Schaffhausen (Switzerland).

Leave Stuttgart (see Rte 18) to travel S to Tübingen by the B27, passing through the Schönbuch forest to reach **Waldenbuch**, with its 16C and 18C Schloss, and **\*Bebenhausen** set in a 156 sq km natural park with marked hiking paths. At Bebenhausen a Cistercian monsastery was founded in 1185, which became the property of the state in 1806. The buildings are protected by a double ring of 16C walls, in the centre of which is the late Gothic cloister, 1471–96, with fan vaulting, a lavabo and a half-timbered upper storey. The 13C Romanesque church north of the cloister was modified in the 15C and 16C, its spire completed by Georg von Salem in 1409. To the east of the cloister is the chapter house, c 1200, above which is a 16C dorter. South of the cloister stands the Gothic refectory of 1335, used only in summer, the monks eating in colder weather in the 15C late Gothic refectory on the west of the cloister (daily guided tours Mar–Oct at 10.00, 11.00, 14.00, 15.00, 16.00). The kings of Württemberg converted some of the buildings into a hunting lodge in the 19C and early 20C and these now constitute a civic museum of medieval art, open Apr–Sept 09.00–12.00, 14.00–17.00, otherwise opening 10.00.

An **excursion** takes you 7km W where, on a 475m-high hill, is the **Wurmlinger Kapelle**, a little Baroque chapel apostrophised by the poet Ludwig Uhland in his 'Droben stehet die Kapelle', its crypt dating from the 12C.

**\*\*Tübingen** (74,000 inhab.; alt. 322m) lies between the Ammer and Neckar valleys.

**Tourist office**: Eberhardsbrücke. **Central post office**: Europoplatz. **Trains** connect with Stuttgart and Sigmaringen, **buses** with Riedlingen, Rottenburg, Stuttgart and Donauschingen.

**History**. Tübingen, an 11C city, though the region was inhabited in the 7C BC, dating from the building of Schloss Hohentübingen in 1078. It became the capital of the Dukes of Württemberg. Eberhard the Bearded founded its university in 1477, and a Protestant seminary was established here in 1536. Amongst its students was the theologian and ally of Luther, Philipp Melanchthon. The city was occupied by the Swedes in 1638. In spite of expansions as well as several disastrous fires, the old town, with its picturesque houses, remains the heart of Tübingen. Here was born and died Johann Ludwig Uhland (1787–1862). The lyric poet Friedrich Hölderlin lived and died (1770–1843) here.

Leave the railway station and by the underpass reach the city park by the Neckar, ornamented by a nymph group by Joseph Heinrich Dannecker, 1758–1841, and an avenue of plane trees, the Platanenallee, on an artificial island. Follow Uhlandstrasse E to reach the Eberhardsbrücke, and cross the river, turning left into Neckargasse and left again along Bursagasse to reach at No. 6 Hölderlinhaus, the towered house where the poet Johann Christian Friedrich Hölderlin lived from 1807 till his death (open Mon–Fri 10.00–12.00, 15.00–17.00, Sat 15.00–17.00, Sun 10.00–12.00). Further along Bursagasse (on the right) is the classical Bursa, of 1479, rebuilt 1805, once the university faculty of philosophy (Melanchthon was among the teachers here, 1514–18). No. 4B is where the humanist Johann Reuchlin lived when he taught at Tübingen, 1481-96 and 1522.

Continue W, taking Neckargasse, to find the former Augustinian monastery, founded 13C, the Evangelisches Stift, which became the Protestant theological faculty of the university after the Reformation and was graced by such scholars as Hegel, Kepler, Schelling and D.F. Strauss. Opposite the church steps lead to Schloss Hohentübingen, built 1507–40 on the site of the Schloss of 1078. Its elaborate *outer gate was designed by H. Schickhardt in 1606 with sentry posts by Chr. Jelin. There are lovely *views from the terraces, and the cellar has a huge barrel capable of holding 850 hectolitres of wine, made for Duke Ulrich of Württemberg by Simon von Bönningheim.

Between the Schloss and the old monastery buildings runs Neckarhalde with at No. 24 the birthplace of Uhland and at No. 31 the Theodor-Haering-Haus, now the city gallery (until the new Kornhaus museum is completed; open except Mon 14.30–17.30). Return E along this street to join Münzgasse. No. 20 is the former students' gaol (Alte Karzer) 1515. Continue along Münzgasse to reach the Alte Aula, formerly the site of the university festivals, 1547, altered 1777, and then at 32 Münzgasse the exquisitely vaulted Gothic Stiftskirche St Georg, 1470–83. Inside are Württemberg family tombs, especially notable Countess Mechthild's tomb by H. Multscher, 1450, that of Eberhard the Bearded (died 1496), the tomb of Duke Ulrich (died 1550) and that of Duke Christoph (died 1568) and his wife Anna Maria. The church has a rich late Gothic choir screen with a 16C forged metal grille, stained glass in the choir from the workshop of P. d'Andlau and 15C reliefs in the north window openings.

E of the church, across Holzmarkt (with its St George fountain), stands the 15C Pflegehof, the former granary and cellar of Bebenhausen monastery (see above), today mostly students' lodgings. Return across the Holzmarkt and turn N along Lange Gasse to reach on the left Konvikt, where once stood a Franciscan monastery. At the Reformation it became a school. The present late 16C buildings are now the Catholic theological faculty of the university. Lange Gasse leads N to reach on the right Nonnengasse leading to Hintere Grabenstrasse, en route to a park with the 15C Nonnenhaus, a former nunnery.

Return to take Froschgasse and find on the left the church of St Johannes, 1876. Kirchgasse continues from here S to reach (on the right) the Marktplatz with a Neptune fountain of 1617, restored 1948, and the three-storeyed Rathaus of 1435, redone in 1698 and 1872, its façade frescoed in 1876 and restored in 1969. The council chamber is on first floor; the astronomical clock was designed by the astronomer Johannes Söffler, 1511, with Eberhard the Bearded below it; the depiction of 'The Just Judge' is by Jakob Züberlin, 1596. From Marktplatz walk N along Marktgasse to Kornhausstrasse, with the former town granary of 1453. E along Kornhausstrasse appears the 16C vaulted Krummebrüche, surrounded by 18C houses, leading to the church of St Jakob, begun 12C, mostly 15C. From here E by way of Madergasse and Schmidtorstrasse the route reaches Bachgasse and Tübingen's finest half-timbered house, the 15C Frucht-schranne, today the Albert-Schweitzer school.

OTHER MUSEUMS: University collections: archaeology, 9 Wilhelmstrasse, open first and third Sunday in month 11.00–12.30; dentistry, 2–8 Osiander-strasse, open during term time Mon–Fri 08.00–12.00, 14.00–17.00; Egyptian collection, 12 Correnstrasse, admission by appointment; geology and palaeontology, 10 Sigwartstrasse, open Mon–Fri 08.00–12.00, 14.00–18.00; history of medicine, 12 Denzenberhalde, open Mon–Fri 08.00–13.00, 14.00–17.00; mineralogy, 56 Wilhelmstrasse, admission by appointment; zoology, 3 Sigwartstrasse, open Wed, Thu 09.00–16.00 and first Sun in month 09.00–12.00. Temporary exhibitions are mounted at the Tübinger Kunst-happe, 76 Philosophenweg (open Tue–Fri 10.00–20.00, closing at weekends 10.00–18.00).

THEATRES: Landestheater, 6 Eberhardstrasse; Zimmertheater, 16 Bursa-gasse; the small Tübinger Zimmertheater, seating only 90. To the NW is laid out the Alter-Botanischer Garten (open 08.00–16.45).

The B27 continues S to **Hechingen** (17,000 inhab.; alt. 490m), once the chief seat of the Hohenzollern–Hechingen family, where rises the Renaissance church of St Luzen (its pulpit and stalls by H. Amman, 1587–89), and the classical parish church of St Jakob, by Michael d'Ixnard, 1779–83, in whose choir are the bronze tombs of Graf Eitelfriedrich II von Zollern and his wife Madeleine von Brandenburg, by P. Vischer, 1512 and 1496. Villa Eugenia, 1789, in Zollstrasse, with its 19C wings, is set in an 'English' park and haunted by the shade of Franz Liszt. The Hohenzollern collection of art and local history, at 5 Schlossplatz, opens Sun 10.00–12.00 and by appointment.

6km SE of Hechingen on a 856m peak is the walled **Burg Hohenzollern**, founded in the 15C and mostly rebuilt 1850–57 (guided tours at variable times). Remaining from the old castle is the Gothic Michaelskapelle, finished 1461, with three Romanesque sandstone reliefs from an earlier building, 12C, stained glass from the 13C to the 16C and a 15C limewood carving of St George. The building was restored in the mid 19C by the Prussian court architect Stüler and his colleague the military architect von Prittwitz. After World War II the coffins and earthly remains of the Prussian kings Friedrich Wilhelm I (1688–1740) and Friedrich II (1712–86), as well as that of crown prince Friedrich Wilhelm, were transferred here from Potsdam to the neo-Gothic chapel of Christ. They were returned to Potsdam in 1991. The Adlertor gives entrance to the fortress, beside which is an equestrian statue of Elector Friedrich I of Brandenburg. The most evocative room is that used by crown prince Wilhelm of Germany until his death in 1951. The Blue Salon has exquisite marquetry. In the Grafensaal are the royal treasures, including the crown of Prussia (1889).

14km W of Hechingen the town of **Haigerloch** tumbles down a hillside, its restored Schloss—with a chapel c 1600, with Rococo decor, a high altar of 1609, and a Mater Dolorosa of 1755—dating from the 16C and the 17C. In the cellar of the Schloss the Atomkeller-Museum recalls the nuclear experiments of Hitler's scientists at the end of World War II. High above the town is the Baroque pilgrimage *chapel of St Anna by J.M. Fischer, 1750–55, its stucco by Johann Michael Feichtmayr, its frescoes by Meinrad von Ow; on the high altar is a 14C Virgin.

**Balingen** (30,000 inhab.; alt. 490m) lies 20km S of Haigerloch in the valley of the Eyach. Occupied in the mid 9C, given its charter in 1255, the town has a late Gothic hall-church of 1443 by Alberlin Jörg with a powerful tower and an early 16C stone pulpit, the mid-15C Zollern Schloss with its 15C water tower (now the local history museum, open Mon, Wed, Fri 14.00–16.00), remains of the town walls and its own 'little Venice'.

From here the route runs SW for another 25km to reach *Rottweil (24,000 inhab.; alt. 600m; information office: in the Rathaus), founded by Konrad von Zähringen in 1140, a Free City from 1268, a member of the Swiss Confederation from 1463, and notorious for its vicious breed of dogs. In 1643 the French occupied the town. Before Zähringen's foundation the site had housed a Roman camp (*Arae Flaviae*, c 74 BC) and numerous Roman remains have been excavated, especially an Orpheus mosaic, c AD 180, and baths. The old part of Rottweil lies to the right of the Neckar and houses one of the oldest churches in Württemberg, the 11C and 12C Pelagiuskirche. Cross the bridge, with its statue of St Johann Nepomuk, from Bahnhofstrasse and follow picturesque Hochbrücktorstrasse to reach on the right the Kapellenhof with the 14C chapel of Our Lady and its sculpted *Kapellenturm; lower storeys 1330–50, upper sculpted by Aberlin Jörg, 1473. The interior of the chapel was redone in the early 18C in the Baroque style and has paintings by Josef Firtmaier (died 1738).

Continue along Hochbrücktorstrasse to Hauptstrasse. At the crossroads is an allegorical fountain, the Marktbrunnen. Hauptstrasse, with its oriel windows, leads W past the Stadtmuseum at No. 20, with a Roman collection, including the Orpheus mosaic (open 09.00–12.00, 14.00–17.00; closes Fri, Sun at noon). At the end of the street is the Schwarzes Gate, from the Hohenstaufen era, once the sole entry by the inner W wall. Further W, along Hochturmgasse, is the Hochturm, a former city watch tower. Rathaustrasse, in which rises the Altes Rathaus c 1500, leads N from the museum to Kirchplatz and the Heilig-Kreuz-Münster. Begun in the 12C but basically 15C and 16C, the münster houses a 15C tabernacle, Gothic altars brought from other churches, an early 16C crucifix, probably by Veit Stoss, a reredos of the apostles by Cord Borgentrik, a font of 1563 and a 17C pulpit. In Münsterplatz is a Gothic fountain with statues of SS George, Catherine and the Virgin Mary. From here Bruderschaftsgasse leads E to the Protestant Prediger church, once the 13C church of a Dominican monastery, reordered as a Baroque building in the 18C, its roof painting is by Josef Wannermacher, 1755. Continue from here E along St Lorenzgasse to reach the mid-16C Lorenzkappelle, a museum since 1851, with a rich collection of 14–16C religious sculpture (open Tue–Sat 10.00–12.00, 14.00–17.00, Sun 14.00–17.00).

As a holiday resort Rottweil offers swimming, tennis and skiing. Annual events include the Shrovetide Fools' Dance, when masked citizens dance through the streets dressed as clowns. Trains connect with Stuttgart and Villingen, as do buses.

**Schwenningen**, just N of the source of the Neckar, with its Schwenninger Moos nature reserve and clockmakers (clock museum at 16 Kronenstrasse, open except Mon, Fri, Sun 14.00–17.00), lies along the B27 18km S of Rottweil. Its Rathaus is an Expressionist building of 1927 by Herkomer.

After 15km more the route reaches Donauschingen (see Rte 17E) before running SE by way of Blumberg on the southernmost tip of the Black Forest, reaching after 35km **Schaffhausen** (33,500 inhab.; alt. 407m), which after Basel is the chief point of entry into Switzerland and is the capital of the Swiss canton of that name. Here, 150m wide, the Rhine tumbles over a 20m-high waterfall, the largest in Europe. As Mary Shelley exclaimed, 'What words can express—for indeed, for many ideas and emotions there are no words—the feeling excited by the tumult, the uproar and matchless beauty of a cataract, with its eternal, ever-changing veil of misty spray'.

# 23

## The Saar Valley from Saarbrücken to Konz and on to Trier

Total distance 88km. Saarbrücken—B51, 10km Völklingen—13km Saarlouis—
17km Merzig—8km Mettlach—18km Saarburg—15km Konz—7km Trier.

**·SAARBRÜCKEN** (195,000 inhab.; alt. 182m) is the capital of the Saarland
and stands amidst industry and mining country (though also amidst vast
forested lands) where the old Roman bridge crossed the River Saar.

**Information office** by the station and at the town hall. **Main post office** by the station
in St Johanner Strasse. **Trains** connect Saarbrücken with Ludwigshafen, Mainz and
Trier.

**History**. The earliest inhabitants of this region known to us were the Celts, followed
by the Gauls and their Roman masters, who have left in Mainzer Strasse a 3C fort. In
999 the Emperor Otto III presented the Bishop of Metz with a fortress dominating a
bridge, the Sarabrucca, across the river here. Over the centuries the fortress and
nascent city changed hands: the bishops of Metz were supplanted by the Counts of
the Lower Saar, who in turn were succeeded by the Counts of Nassau-Saarbrücken
(1381–1793). So savage were the depredations of the Thirty Years War that Saarbrücken's population declined from 4500 in 1628 to 70 in 1637. A fire of 1677 devastated
the city and its Schloss. Prince Wilhelm-Heinrich in the early 18C presided over a new
era of prosperity, and subsequently the French and the Prussians successively ruled
the city until 1919. The Treaty of Versailles ceded Saarbrücken to France; a commission
nominated by the League of Nations administered the Saarland from 1920 until the
plebiscite of 1935 enabled Adolf Hitler to regain the region for Germany. After World
War II, as the result of a referendum of its citizens, Saarbrücken and the Saarland were
formally returned to Germany in 1957.

N of the main railway station is the suburb of Malstatt. On Heinrich-Koehl-
Strasse is a modern church, St Albert, by Gottfried Böhm, 1954, a pioneer
of churches with central altars. Walk S from the main railway station across
the river to Ludwigsplatz. This is Saarbrücken's finest square, surrounded
by Baroque palaces and centring on the superb, golden Baroque ·Ludwig-
skirche, designed as a Greek cross with rounded corners by Friedrich
Joachim Stengel, 1762–75 (restored), with a partly modern interior, bulls'-
eye windows and statues on the balustrade by Francusz Bingh. W of the
platz is the school of arts and crafts in one of several Baroque buildings
designed by Stengel that border this square. No. 15 is the pre- and early
history museum (open Tue–Sun 10.00–16.00, closes Sat at 13.00, Sun at
18.00) and close by is the Friedenskirche (Peach Church) by Stengel, 1764.

From here Vorstadtstrasse runs SE as far as Schlossplatz and Alt-Saarbrücken, half destroyed in World War II and well restored. Here stands the
Baroque Schloss, a reconstruction by Friedrich Johann Stengel, 1739–48,
of a former Renaissance building, where the Nassau-Saarbrücken counts
lived until the Revolution. It was restored again in 1812 by the classical
architect Johann Adam Knipper after the revolutionary savagery of 1793,

and by Gottfried Böhm after the bombs of 1944. Its garden has fine views, and the Schloss is now the regional history museum (open Tue–Sun 10.00–18.00). The Schloss chapel, 15C and 18C, with graves of the Counts, today the Protestant parish church, was restored in 1958 after war damage; its modern glass is by G. Meistermann. Also restored is Stengel's former town hall of 1760, nowadays the Abenteuer Museum containing the collection of the globe-trotter Heinz Rox-Schulz (open Tue, Wed 09.00–13.00, Thu, Fri 15.00–19.00 and first Sat in month 10.00–14.00).

Hindenburgstrasse contains, just SE of the Schloss, the administrative building of the Saar Landtag. Return along the riverside—passing the old bridge, by H. Sparer, 1549, modified in the 18C—to cross Wilhelm-Heinrich bridge into the finest part of the city, the district of St Johann, crossing Banhofstrasse with its elegant shops to the Rathausplatz, with the monumental, indeed monster, town hall, built between 1897 and 1900 by Georg von Hauberisser in the 15C Gothic style. Opposite it rises a neoGothic church of 1898 by Heinrich Guth.

Bahnhofstrasse leads SE from here to Sankt-Johanner-Markt, with a fountain of 1760 (by Stengel, P. Mihm and the ironworker S. Bockelmann) and at No. 24, in an 18C building, the Saarland Museum (open Tue–Sun 11.00–19.00). NW of the square is the Catholic church of St Johann, by J.F. Stengel, 1752; S of the square is the city theatre. From here Bismarckstrasse leads E, with at No. 11 the Saarland gallery of modern art (open Tue–Sun 10.00–18.00).

SE of Alt-Saarbrücken is the suburb of St Arnual, with an early 14C church of the same name, containing more tombs of the counts and their families, especially Elisabeth von Lothringen (died 1456) and Count Johann III (died 1472). W of Alt-Saarbrücken is the Deutschmühlental, with a 33.8 ha German/French garden, an amusement park, 'Gulliver-land' and, close by, one of the first military cemeteries in Europe (containing c 100 German soldiers who fell in 1870).

The State Theatre is at 1 Tbilliser Platz, the Landestheater at 10 Scharnhorststrasse. Saarbrücken houses the Saarland university 5km NE, at the foot of the 377m-high Schwarzenberg. More than 1000 animals, including a celebrated group of apes, live in the zoo in Breslauer Strasse, NE on the B40 in the direction of St Ingbert, as is the Halberg Schloss, now the HQ of the Saarland Radio.

The B51 leaves Saarbrücken and travels 10km W to **Völklingen** (46,000 inhab.; alt. 200m) in the Köllerbach valley, its wealth from iron and steel works, its health from its site, stadium and sports facilities. The former Rathaus is a Jugendstil building, behind which stands the church of St Eligius, 1925.

From here a brief **excursion** NE for 7km reaches **Püttlingen-Köllerbach**, whose church of St Martin has 15C wall paintings.

From Völklingen travel NW along the valley of the Saar to reach after 13km **Saarlouis**, named after Louis XIV of France at its foundation in 1680, fortified by Vauban, 1681, with walls, gates and a moat—mostly razed in 1889–90, as was much of the town, since restored, in World War II. Saarlouis remained French until 1815, and many of the citizens' names remain French. A plaque at 13 Bierstrasse marks the birthplace of Marshal Ney (1769–1815). The modern Rathaus of 1954 contains Gobelin tapestries. An important museum, with Roman finds, is in Alte-Brauerei-Strasse (open Tue, Thu 09.00–12.00, 15.00–18.00, Sun 15.00–18.00).

An **excursion** N for 2km along the B269 reaches **Dillingen**, whose forges were set up in 1685 by the Marquis de Lenoncourt-Blainville, with a patent from Louis XIV. Dillingen has a 17C church.

The B51 continues NW from Saarlouis, passing through Hilbringen. A **detour** from here, on the B406 NW, brings you to **Perl** on the Mosel Wine Road, the B419, where you can see, Tue–Sun, the excavated Roman villa and Schloss Berg, early 14C and 16C, and on to reach Remich and the Luxembourg border after 31km.

The main route, the B51, 15km from Saarlouis reaches **Merzig** (30,600 inhab.; alt. 174m), a town manufacturing pottery and mosaics and enhanced by wooded surroundings and walks. Its late 12C church of St Peter rises in Propsteistrasse and has a crucifix c 1300, 16C ogival vaulting, a Baroque Pietà and high altar and 19C frescoes. The Renaissance Rathaus by Matthias Staudt, 1647–50, formerly a hunting lodge of Fürst Philipp Christoph von Sötern of Trier, was given a Baroque aspect by C. Kretzschmar. Kretzschmar also built the nearby Staudt-Marxsches-Bürgerhaus in 1782. Merzig's Baroque brewery offices are at 12 Poststrasse, and the town is dominated by the Fellenberschlösschen of 1840. Trains connect Merzig with Saarbrücken and Trier.

From Merzig continue along the B51, reaching after 8km **Mettlach** (13,000 inhab.; alt. 166m), the 'pearl of the Saarland', site of a Benedictine monastery since the late 9C. The church was rebuilt in the 14C, and restored in the 19C, retaining the octagonal tower of 907 under which its founder, St Ludwig, lies buried. The 13C •reliquary of St Ludwig is now kept in the modern Catholic Ludwigskirche. Kretzschmar rebuilt the abbey, 1727–86, constructing a façade over 300m long. When the buildings fell into disuse in the early 19C, they were adapted as the famous Villeroy & Boch ceramic factory. 2km S (an hour's walk) is the ruined **Schloss Montclair** on a 303m-high peak, first built in 1180 by Arnolph von Walecourt to control the traffic along the River Saar and finally brought low by a fire of 1778.

3km SW of Mettlach, at **St Gangolf**, is an octagonal pagoda by Kretzschmar, 1745.

Follow the B51 N for 18km from Mettlach through Serrig to **Saarburg** (6500 inhab.; alt. 148m), where in the middle of the town the confluence of the Saar and the Leuk produces a 20m-high waterfall, the Leukbach. Saarburg has timber-framed houses, and the modern church of St Laurence, built in the Gothic style. A tunnel leads through a peak up to the much pillaged, much rebuilt Schloss of the Electors of Trier. In the suburb of Beurig the pilgrimage church of St Marien has a 13C miracle-working image of the Blessed Virgin.

15km N of Saarburg the B51 reaches the wine centre of **Konz** (the Roman *Contionacum*), where the River Saar joins the River Mosel. The Roman remains here are said to derive from a villa built by Constantine, and the name of Konz certainly derives from the Latin *Contionacum*. The Roman remains are obscured by the modern parish church of St Nikolaus. Cross the river by a bridge first built by the Romans to reach after 7km Trier (see Rte 27) in the Rhineland-Palatinate.

# 24

## Saarbrücken to Homburg

Total distance 31km. Saarbrücken—B40, 13km St Ingbert—18km Homburg.

Leave Saarbrücken (see Rte 23) by the Mainzer Strasse and travel E along the B40 for 13km to **St Ingbert** (42,000 inhab.; alt. 229m) on the Rohrbach (a tributary of the Saar) with its noted brewery tower, its steel works and glass making. There are excursions and marked walks to the S, and you can tour the brewery, which dates from 1927. St Ingbert was almost completely destroyed in 1637; its industries began to develop in the next century. It has a modern church, St Hildegard, by Alfred Bosslet, 1929, and in Kaiserstrasse the Baroque St Engelbert, 1755. At 9 Am Markt is a museum devoted to the works of the Expressionist Albert Weissberger (open weekdays except Mon 09.00–12.00, 13.00–17.00, Sat 10.00–15.00, Sun and holidays 14.00–18.00).

18km further E lies **Homburg** (43,000 inhab.; alt. 233m; information office: Am Rondell), where the university of Saarbrücken's faculty of medicine is established: natural, park. The site, which had been inhabited in the 3C, derives its modern existence from the now ruined 12C Hohenburg, set on the Schlossberg. In 1755 the town came under the suzerainty of the Graf von Nassau-Saarbrücken. Herzog Karl II August built a Schloss here in 1776 which the French destroyed 17 years later, though the ruins are picturesque enough. Artificial caverns, the Schlossberghöhlen, created by sand excavation, can be visited Tue, Thu 15.00–16.00, Sun and holidays 14.00–17.00. Trains connect with Ludwigshafen, Saarbrücken and Zweibrücken.

An **excursion** along the B423 SW in the direction of the French border leads after 12km to **Blieskastel**, with part of a Baroque Schloss, 1680, and Schlosskirche by P. Reheis, 1778, as well as an orangery of 1640. Its 1775 town hall was formerly an orphanage; there is a fountain dedicated to Napoleon Bonaparte. N of the town a pilgrims' chapel of the Holy Cross, c 1680, with a 14C Pietà, is reputed to work miracles. W towards Alschbach stands the **Gollenstein**, a 7m-high, 4000-year-old menhir.

# 25

## Saarbrücken to St Wendel

Total distance 39km. Saarbrücken—B41, 20km Neunkirchen—9km Ottweiler—10km St Wendel.

Leave Saarbrücken (see Rte 23) NE by the A623 and join the B41 to drive N along the Sulzbach valley, which has the largest concentration of factories and population in the Saarland. The mining town of **Dudweiler** on the

A623, 8km from Saarbrücken, is built on a prehistoric site. The inn Zum Brennenden Berg close by the exit from the town stands at the beginning of a hike through the woods to the Brennender Berg—the coal-bearing 'burning montain', described by Goethe. 4km after Dudweiler is **Sulzbach**, where coal has been mined since the 15C. It also has glass works and iron and steel foundries, and produces chemical products and mineral water.

20km from Saarbrücken you reach **Neunkirchen** (45,000 inhab.; alt. 257m), the largest town in the Saarland after Saarbrücken. Coal and steel have been the staple products and support of Neunkirchen for 150 years (iron and steel works dating back in fact to the 18C). The Stumm monument commemorates the steel magnate K.F. von Stumm (1836–1901); the fountain at the end of Stummstrasse the steel workers. Neunkirchen has a zoo—and also boasts Europe's steepest street. Its citizens enjoy a covered swimming pool and other sports facilities, as well as walks and hikes to the Steinwald, Spiesser Höhe.

**Ottweiler** (16,000 inhab.; alt. 262m), 9km N in the Blies valley, marks the end of the dense industrial area and its Altstadt offers the aspect of a medieval German town, with gabled, timber-framed houses. The old town is built around the Schlossplatz and its fountain. SW of this square is Rathausplatz, with the town hall of 1714, and 16C and 17C half-timbered Renaissance and Baroque houses. The tower (the Wehrturm) of the Protestant church NW of Rathausplatz was once part of the town's defences. Friedrich Joachim Stengel designed the Baroque hunting lodge on the Blies, 1759 and the Baroque Witwenpalais, 1760, in the suburb of Neumünster. Tourist information is in Bliesstrasse, where you can ask to visit the local history and carnival museum.

The B41 runs N for 10km to reach **St Wendel** (27,000 inhab.; alt. 282m; information office: 7 Schlossstrasse), named after a 7C Irish missionary, patron of shepherds and farmers, who is buried in a stone sarcophagus, c 1360, behind the high altar of the 14C and 15C *pilgrimage church of St Wendelinus in the Fruchtmarkt. Its choir was built in 1360; the west end was finished c 1400; it houses a pulpit of 1462 given by Nicholas of Cusa; the vaults were painted 1650; and the church shelters 18C sculpture. The church of Our Lady has stucco by K. Zimmermann, 1743, as well as a late Gothic Kreuz chapel (altered 1869) housing the 12C 'Salgau' crucifix and an 18C altar. In the Marktplatz is the Rathaus of 1820, and near the church of St Wendelinus is the former Rathaus of 1803, with a local history museum (open Sat, Sun, Mon 10.00–12.00, 15.00–18.00). St Wendel also has a Mission House, at 50 Missionshausstrasse (open Mon–Fri 08.30–12.00, Sun 14.00–18.00). To the N of the town is the Skulpturenfed, with 14 stone sculptures by modern artists. Trains link with Saarbrücken and Strecke, buses link with Saarbrücken and Oberkirchen.

The B41 runs N to cross the border of the Saarland into the Rhineland-Palatinate. Here and around St Wendel the countryside is less wooded than the rest of the Saarland, growing mostly corn.

# 26

# Mettlach to Saarbrücken via the 'Eichenlaubstrasse', Losheim and Tholey

Total distance 84km. Mettlach—16km Losheim—15km Nonnweiler—B269, 17km Tholey—12km Lebach—B268, 24km Saarbrücken.

The Eichenlaubstrasse, or Oak Tree Route, in the northern Saarland and Rhineland-Palatinate, runs for 72km from Mettlach to Friesen-Ober-kirchen, passing through part of the upper Black Forest and incorporating the most beautiful stretch of the Saarland.

Leaving Mettlach (see Rte 23) travel 16km E by way of Britten to **Losheim** (14,000 inhab.; alt. 300m), whose parish church displays in its crypt Celtic and Roman finds from the neighbourhood. 3km N of the town is the Losheim Lake, with sailing, windsurfing, swimming, camping and a youth hostel. NE of Losheim the route takes 15km to reach by way of Weiskirchen (with its clinics and sanatoria) and passing under the A1 motorway, the health resort of **Nonnweiler** (8500 inhab.; alt. 10m). Here are more clinics and the remains of Celtic fortifications—the Hunnenring on the Dollberg—whose walls at times reach a height of 10m.

From Nonnweiler drive 8km SE along the B269 to **Primstal** whose Baroque church contains a model of the grotto of Lourdes. Dominating Primstal is the 584m-high Petersberg.

The B269 continues SE for 9km to reach **Tholey** (12,000 inhab.; alt. 330m), which Louis XIV ceded to the Palatinate in 1778. Once the seat of a rich Benedictine abbey, a mid-8C foundation that fell victim to the French Revolution in 1795, Tholey has preserved the former abbot's lodgings, now the local presbytery, and the late 12C Romanesque and early Gothic monastery church of St Mauritius, now the parish church—though the abbey was refounded in 1949 and the monks have returned. This splendid three-aisled church with its powerful belfry houses Baroque stalls and a Baroque pulpit. In the choir is the 13C 'Angel of Tholey', which comes from an Annunciation group and smiles beatifically. Underneath the church the remains of the Roman baths have been discovered, for Tholey was a Roman settlement, whose name derives from the Latin *tegula*, i.e. tile. On the nearby **Schaumberg** (527m) is a 40m-high observation tower (ascent daily 10.00–18.00), with a picturesque hill top road, the Schaumberghöhen-strasse passing the peak. Horses are annually blessed here at the feast of the Ascension. On the summit of the Blasiusberg in the suburb of Bergweiler, 3km W, is a pilgrimage church, founded in the 12C though now Baroque. Trains connect with St Wendel; buses connect with St Wendel and Saarbrücken.

From Tholey drive a further 12km SE along the B269 to **Lebach** (550 inhab.; alt. 275m) in the valley of the Thel. Its Gothic church has a 12C font and tombs of the van Hagens. Lebach hosts annual races and a fair on the feast of the Nativity of the Virgin Mary (8 Sept). Tourist information at the Bürgermeisteramt. The B268 leads S for 24km to Saarbrücken (see Rte 23).

# IV  THE RHINELAND-PALATINATE

# 27

# Trier

•••**TRIER** (100,000 inhab.; alt. 130m–370m), a superb city situated on the Mosel 10km from the frontier with Luxemburg and 50km from the frontier with France, is Germany's oldest city.

**Main railway station**: Bahnhofstrasse. **Main post office**: Am Kornmarkt. **Tourist information** in the Porta Nigra. **Trains** connect Trier with Cologne, Koblenz, Saarbrücken, Luxembourg and Paris, **buses** with Mainz, Frankfurt, Kaiserslautern and Luxembourg. **Boats** ply the Mosel to Koblenz and Düsseldorf.

  **Campsites** are found S of the city centre in the Schlosspark Monaise. Trier is surrounded by 3.5 sq km of **vineyards**, with ample opportunities for tasting.

**History**. Julius Caesar conquered Trier in 56 BC during his attack on the Belgae, spotting that this was a major riverside site which also commanded the frontier of the Rhine. Augustus Caesar founded here a Roman town, *Augusta Treverorum*, whose citizens could also become citizens of Rome. Under the Romans trade developed. By the 2C AD this was a major river port and a centre of trade routes. Constantine the Great lived at Trier from 306–14—indeed emperors frequently preferred living here to living in Rome, and Trier became capital of the part of their lands that stretched from Britain south to Spain and from the Danube west. The Roman walls, encompassing four massive gateways and 47 towers, enclosed some 70,000 people, as well as a river bridge, an amphitheatre and a circus.

  Christianity came in the 4C and the first Bishop of Trier was elected in 328. Here was born St Ambrose (c 339–97). Charlemagne elevated the see to an archbishopric. The bishops and archbishops were to become prince-electors in the Middle Ages. The cathedral acquired and still possesses a precious relic, the seamless robe of Christ, displayed rarely (1933, 1959, 1973, see under the Dom, below, rivalled by one in Turin cathedral which is now deemed a fake). The Normans destroyed virtually the whole city in 882. Trier flourished again in the 10C, its electoral privileges confirmed in a bull of 1356. In 1473 the university was founded. In 1512 Emperor Maximilian I called a Reichstag here. Then came a century of decline. Several times Trier was captured: by the Spanish in 1545, by the French twice in the 17C, by Marlborough for the English in 1704, by the French again in 1794. For a time Trier was capital of the French *département* of Sarre and began to blossom again. The Treaty of Versailles ceded the city to the Prussians, and Trier has continued since then to develop, even though a third of it was destroyed in World War II. Here was born Karl Marx (1818–83).

Trier still maintains the layout of the old Roman city: Theodor-Heuss-Allee marks the N boundary; the River Mosel the W; Ziegelstrasse the S; and Bergstrasse, beyond the railway the E. By the main railway station is a fountain in memory of Prince-Archbishop Balduin von Luxemburg (1308–34). Follow Bahhofstrasse NW, which runs into **Theodor-Heuss-Allee**, bordered on the left by the public gardens, to reach •••**Porta Nigra**. This gate—the most important ancient monument in Trier and the largest extant Roman city gate—was given the soubriquet 'black' in the Middle Ages, owing to the colour of the stone (which is in fact grey sandstone). 36m wide, 22m broad and 30m high, its defensive nature is emphasised by the enormous stones with which, without cement, it is constructed and the semi-circular towers which flank its double arch. Built in the 4C AD as the

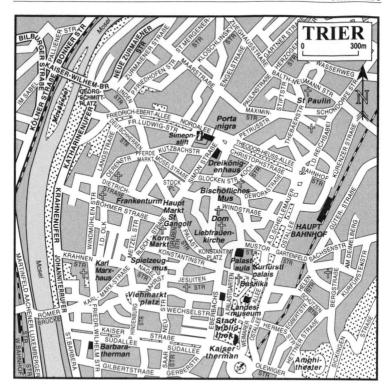

northernmost gate of the city's fortifications, which stretched nearly 7km around the city, over the centuries the Porta Nigra was modified, with the addition even of a double chapel, one part set above the other. The Greek monk Simeon lived and taught in the east tower at the beginning of the 11C. The gate was restored to its original form—apart from retaining a Romanesque apse—by Napoleon Bonaparte, and was further restored 1968–73. The Romanesque wall of the church is adorned with Rococo sculptures.

Adjoining the gate to the right is part of the monastery of St Simeon, the **Simeonstift**, an early Romanesque building begun in 1036. Today it houses a restaurant, the tourist information office and the municipal museum, the **Städtisches Museum**, devoted to local and regional history, textiles and sculpture. Its most celebrated treasure is the Lotharingian Madonna, 1360; here hang paintings by Januarius Zick, 1730–97, and by the abstract artist Julius Bissier, 1893–1965; there is also a sprinking of modern art (open weekdays, except Mon 10.00–17.00, weekends 10.00–13.00). Follow **Simeonstrasse** SW from Porta Nigra to reach the triangular **Hauptmarkt**, passing St Nicolauskapelle, 1761. At No. 7 stands a 16C Renaissance house, and at No. 8 the house owned by the parents of Karl Marx (where he lived 1819–35). At No. 19 stands the 13C house of the Magi, the **Dreikönigenhaus**, with access only by a ladder to the first floor.

To mark the granting of a market to Trier Archbishop Heinrich erected in 958 the stone cross on a granite column in the middle of the Hauptmarkt, whose half-timbered, sometimes gabled houses of different epochs form a delicious *ensemble, its market stalls covered with yellow and green awnings. The Renaissance fountain, with statues of Peter, the city's patron saint and the four virtues (Justice, Prudence, Courage and Temperance) is by Hans Rupprecht Hoffmann, 1595, its Latin inscription declaring that the moral health of the people flows from these virtues as the water flows from the fountain. Medieval Trier grew up around the Hauptmarkt. The four six-storeyed turrets, early 14C, which rise to 62m from the west tower of the church of **St Gangolf** dominate the S side. Built from the 13C to 15C, the church has a Gothic bell tower of 1507, a Baroque doorway of 1732; a stone altar c 1475; an altar of the Virgin of 1603, from the workshop of Hoffmann; and stucco by Michael Eytel, 1746–47.

W of the square is the festival hall of the city aldermen, the crenellated **Steipe** with its pillared arcades. Built in 1430–83, totally destroyed 1944, and restored 1970, the Steipe derives its name from its pillars and is decorated with 15C sculptures of SS Peter, Helena (mother of Constantine the Great and donor to Trier of the seamless robe of Christ and a nail from the cross), James and Paul, with two knights.

From here the Baroque **Rotes Haus** of 1684 (also destroyed 1944 and restored) leads into **Dietrichstrasse** and bears the inscription: Ante Roman Treveris stetit annis mille trecentis/perstet, et aeterna pace fruator. Amen. (Trier existed 1300 years before Rome/May she be granted an equally long life and eternal peace. Amen.) Another inscription adjoins the statue of St Antony of Padua, patron saint of lost property, on the second storey: Auxilium suis confidentibus (Those who trust in him shall find help).

On the left of Dietrichstrasse, at No. 5, is the **Frankenturm**, an 11C house in the form of a tower, its name derived from a former resident, Franc von Senheim. No. 42 is the 17C and 18C **Warsberger Hof**. In the Hauptmarkt to the right of the Steipe are at Nos 15–16 a Baroque house of 1664; at No. 17 a classical house of 1785; and at the entrance 16C half-timbered houses opening onto the **Judengasse** and the medieval Jewish quarter. At 6 Hauptmarkt is Germany's oldest pharmacy, the mid-13C **Löwenapotheke**, mostly rebuilt at the end of the 17C. The arcaded **Palais Walderdorff** to the E side was formed from two canonries, built in 1756 and 1768, and now a gallery of modern art, with emphasis on local artists (open Mon–Sat 10.00–12.00, 15.00–18.00, Sun 10.00–13.00).

Follow **Strenstrasse** alongside this palace to the **Domfreiheit**, surrounded by more canons' houses, and embracing the oldest **Dom** in Germany, built on the site of a Roman palace (revealed 1946). A Christian basilica has existed here since 336, the gift of the Empress Helena, sacked by the Franks in the 5C, rebuilt to be destroyed by the Normans in 882, restored in the 10C, extended in 1030 and in the 12C, the victim of a fire in 1717 and restored by 1729. Parts of the Roman wall still exist on the north side, the 12C building stands over a vast crypt and the nave has 13C ogival vaulting.

**Interior**: 12C Romanesque sculptures of Jesus, John the Baptist, the Virgin Mary and the Twelve Apostles; tomb of Cardinal Ivo, died 1144; Gothic tomb of Archbishop-Elector Baldwin von Luxemburg, died 1354, in west choir; tomb of Archbishop Richard von Greiffenklau, died 1527; tomb of Johann von Metzenhausen, died 1542; monuments to 26 archbishop-electors (especially Johann von Metzenhausen, died 1540); partially reconstructed ceiling paintings from the earlier basilica; Renaissance pulpit, 1570–72, by H.R. Hoffmann, who also created the elaborate tomb beside the third pillar on the right of Lothar von Metternich; Baroque high altar by Johann Wolfgang Fröhlicher, 1699. In the Heiltumskammer, 1702–16, behind the high altar, is kept the Holy Robe (see History). The **cathedral treasury** at 6 Hinter dem Dom displays a 10C \*portable funerary altar of St Andrew, made by Trier goldsmiths and enamellists (open daily 10.00–12.00, 14.00–17.00; closed Sun mornings).

Leave the cathedral by its 13C arcaded cloister, with a statue of the Virgin by Nicolas Gerhaerdt, c 1462, and Roman excavations, especially paintings from Constantine's palace, including St Helena, to find in narrow **Windstrasse**, at Nos 6–8, the **Bischöfliches Museum**, in a classical building of 1830 by Johann Georg Wolff. Here are displayed ecclesiastical treasures from the Carolingian era to the Rococo, including vestments, \*4C frescoes, late 15C and early 16C crucifixes and a monument to Archdeacon Christoph von Rheineck, 1530 (open weekdays 10.00–12.00, 15.00–17.00, Sat 10.00–12.00, Sun and holidays 10.00–13.00).

To the right of the cathedral is the virtually circular (apart from its crossing) **Liebfrauenkirche**, 1235–60, influenced by the contemporary Gothic of northern France and after St Elisabeth, Marburg (see Rte 37) the oldest early Gothic church in Germany. Its shape, a rose of 12 petals, symbolises the Virgin Mary (the mystic rose) to whom the church is dedicated. Its features include richly decorated west and north doorways (the former depicting the Enthroned Madonna, the Annunciation, the adoration of the Magi, the Massacre of the Innocents and the Presentation of Jesus in the temple; the latter the Coronation of the Virgin); an east doorway carved with leaves; an interior (damaged 1944 and well restored) in the form of a Greek cross, with 12 pillars dedicated to the Apostles (their portraits painted very early 16C); and the tomb of Karl von Metternich, died 1636 by M. Rauchmiller c 1675. Next to this church is the episcopal palace of 1786, on the doorway of which are the arms of Georg von Schönbrünn. In front of the church is the **Palais Kesselstatt**, with its pleasing symmetrical façade, built for the Count of Kesselstatt by Johann Valentin Thomann, 1740–45.

From here **Liebfrauenstrasse** runs S to the huge, rectangular brick \*Aula Palatina, the early 4C basilican tribunal of the Roman palace. Built by Constantine around 310 on the site of a ruined 2C palace, it was transformed into an electoral Schloss in the early 17C, when a couple of wings were demolished. The French used the building first as a military hospital and then as a barracks. In 1856 King Friedrich Wilhelm IV had the original tribunal reconstructed. Partly destroyed in 1944, and restored in 1956, the massive and spare 67m by 27m basilica with its coffered ceiling now serves as a Protestant church. The Electoral Palace, the **Rococo-Palais der Kurfürsten**, half Renaissance, half Baroque, with its remarkable inner staircase (a Rococo fantasy by the sculptor Ferdinand Dietz and the architect Johannes Seitz), now stands facing this basilica. The north and east wings of 1623–52 are by Christoph von Sötern; the Rococo south façade was decorated by Balthasar Neumann's pupil Johannes Seitz, 1759–61. The pediment sculpture depicts Ceres, with Pomone and Apollo in a flowery setting. In front of this façade is the 18C palace garden, along one side of which are the remains of the medieval wall, incorporating the Kastil gate, separating the garden from the city library, 1957 (entrance at 25 Weberbachstrasse), which possesses 4000 medieval manuscripts and 2500 incunabula.

**Jesuitenstrasse** leads W from Webernbachstrasse and contains the 15C Gothic **Dreifaltigkeitskirche** (once Franciscan, then Jesuit). It has a 13C choir, while the rest is mostly 18C. It shelters the tombs of Elisabeth von Görlitz, died 1451, and the poet Friedrich Spee, died 1635. Close by is a Renaissance building, once the Jesuit college, built in 1614 with stones from the Imperial Roman thermal baths. Here too is the **Aula** of 1775, now part of the Catholic theological faculty of the university. At No. 44 in nearby Ostalle is the **Rheinishes Landesmuseum**, with archaeological finds including over 150 Roman mosaics, a bronze Mercury, Roman tombs; Celto–Germanic art; Merovingian, Carolingian and medieval art (open Mon–Fri 09.30–16.00; Sat closes 14.00, Sun 13.00).

The huge 4C imperial baths, the **Kaiserthermen**, S of this museum and the palace garden, once measured 260m by 145m and the ruins are still imposing. Begun in the 3C AD and extended by the Emperors Constantine and Gratian, their stones were used as a quarry in the Middle Ages. Visits to the caldarium, the tepidarium and the frigidarium from 20 Mar–Sept daily 09.00–13.00, 14.00–18.00; otherwise closing 17.00.

SE, under the railway passage, in **Olewigerstrasse** is the **Amphitheater**, 1C BC, set today amidst vineyards, its axes measuring 75m and 50m, its seating capacity 25,000, with three entrance towers, one to the arena, two for spectators, as well as 14 arched entrance passages. The upper range of the theatre is a colonnaded walkway (visiting times as for the Kaiserthermen).

Return to the Imperial baths and continue W along **Südallee**, which follows the principal street (*decumanus maximus*) of the old Roman city and now displays a bastion, 1543, of the later fortifications of Trier. At the crossing with Friedrich-Wilhelm-Strasse was the Roman forum. To the left are the remains of the Barbara thermal baths (**Barbarathermen**), dating from the mid 2C AD, and named today after the medieval suburb of St Barbara. Partly destroyed in 1673, their stones used for building (see the Jesuit college, above), these baths cover 4.2 ha of ground. The cold baths alone consisted of eleven pools and were altogether 54m by 10m. The heating system has been reconstructed. (Visiting times as for the Kaiserthermen, though closed on Mon.) In front is a garden, once a Roman exercise park (the Palaestra).

Continue along the Südallee to reach the l90m long, 7.5m wide, eight-arched 11C **Römerbrücke**, based on Roman pillars, much renewed (save for the second, seventh and furthest from the town). Just upstream are the foundations of an even older Roman bridge, dating from the 1C BC. From here you can walk along the quayside towards the Neue Brücke, past old cranes (1474 and 1413) and close by the Baroque church of **St Irmin**, 1771, rebuilt after World War II, when excavations discovered half-timbered 4C AD Roman houses here. The church once belonged to the Benedictines, whose convent is now a hospital. By the Neue Brücke stands the 1626 abbey church of **St Martin**, with (outside) a crucifixion group of 1494. Beyond the Neue Brücke is an 18C fisher- and boatmen's quarter whose origins date from the 7C.

Opposite the Römerbrücke Karl-Marx-Strasse leads into **Brückenstrasse**, where at No. 10 is the house where Marx was born, **Karl-Marx-Haus**, open except Mon 10.00–13,00, 15.00–18.00, with memorabilia and autograph MSS of Marx and his collaborator Friedrich Engels, 1820–95. The 17C **Haus Venedig** is a little further on. Between Brückenstrasse and the Viehmarkt stands the 15C church of **St Antoninus** (pulpit by Ferdinand Dietz, 1762), close by the former Augustinian monastery, 1762 (14C church; bas-relief of Christ, 1142), and in front of the Hercules fountain of 1729. Here too is the municipal **theatre** of 1964.

Brückenstrasse leads into **Fleischstrasse** with on the right the **Kornmarkt**, a fountain of St Georg by Johannes Seitz, 1751 and at No. 21 the former casino, 1825, restored. The city theatre, home of the city orchestra is in Am Augustinerhof. At Nos 4–5 Nagelstrasse is the **Spielzeugmuseum**, with some 5000 puppets and figures.

**Environs**. S of the city, leaving the Hauptmarkt by Brotstrasse, Neustrasse, Saarstrassse and Matthiasstrasse you reach the basilica of **St Matthias**, another Benedictine foundation, 1127–60, transformed variously between the 15C and the 18C; the west tower and its massive clock were rebuilt 1783, after a fire, restored 1967. In the crypt are the tombs of the earliest bishops of Trier; 12C choir; Italianate west doors, late 17C; late Gothic vaulting 1496–1504; 1480 tomb of St Matthias, the Apostle who replaced Judas Iscariot (with his alleged relics, the only ones of an apostle in any German church), as well as those of Trier's first Christian missionaries, SS Eucharius and Valerius. Of the Benedictine abbey for which this church was built, the 13C Gothic cloister has an 18C east wing; it contains many early sarcophagi.

NE of the city, follow Paulinstrasse from Porta Nigra and then turn right along Balthasar-Neumann-Strasse to reach the Baroque church of *St Paulin, by Balthasar Neumann and Johannes Seitz, 1734–54, on the site of a 6C Romanesque church built where the Theban Legion was martyred in 286. (The allegedly exact spot is marked by a cross on the lawn in front of the church.) St Paulinus of Phrygia, to whom the church is dedicated, died in exile in 358 having contested the Arianism of Emperor Constantine II. The first church on this spot was burned down in a fire of 1093; its Romanesque successor was sacked by the French in 1734. Prince-Elector Franz Georg von Schönborn paid for the present building, hence his coat of arms on the choir stalls. Inside also: stucco by J. Arnold and frescos; high altar by Ferdinand Dietz, possibly designed by Neumann; ceiling fresco of 1743 by Chistopf Thomas Scheffler depicting the martyrdom of St Paulinus and his companions as well as that of the Theban Legion; choir screen by J. Eberle, 1767; tomb of Paulinus (Bishop of Trier, 346–58) in the crypt.

From here take Thebäerstrasse back towards the city to find the Carolingian abbey of **St Maximin**, founded in the early 4C by his predecessor Bishop Agritius. The present buildings (now a school) date from 1680–1700, the west façade is Baroque and the Gothic interior has a 10C crypt (whose Carolingian wall paintings are now in the city museum).

9km W of Trier, in front of the village church at **Igel**, rises the 22m-high Igel column, a 3C Gallo-Roman funeral monument of the Secundinus family, with moving inscriptions. Goethe saw it in 1792 and commented, 'One sees here the desire and taste to transmit to posterity the sensible image of a man and his whole entourage, as well as evidence of his work. Here one is in the presence of parents and children at a family banquet.'

At **Trier-Pfalzel**, 5km SE of Trier on the left bank of the river, are the remains of a 4C Roman palace, sheltered in the 17C parish church, which retains remains of its 16C cloisters. The Schloss of the prince-electors of Trier dates from the 12C to the 16C, and the ancient village has medieval walls.

# 28

## Trier to Koblenz
## (via the Mosel valley)

Total distance 143km. Trier—B49, 10km Ruwer—B53, 26km Neumagen—
21km Bernkastel-Kues—23km Traben-Trarbach—25km Alf—B49, 38km
Koblenz.

Leave Trier (see Rte 27) and take the B49 NE travelling along the beguiling
right bank of the River Mosel to reach after 10km **Ruwer**, a town which the
Latin poet Ausonius praised, surrounded by vineyards, lying at the confluence of the River Ruwer and the Mosel. After 5km the route reaches
**Schweich**, the site of a Celtic settlement named *Soiacum*, where the
Romans built a bridge across the Mosel. At Schweich in 1924 was discovered a Roman mosaic of Venus and cherubs. The town preserves a Baroque
Hisgenhaus, 1758, which once belonged to the monastery of St Maximin
in Trier, and a basalt fountain commemorating Stefan Andres, the local poet
and son of a miller.

Cross the modern succcessor of the Roman bridge and take the B53 NE,
reaching after 3km the tiny village of **Longen** with a church c 1400. On the
other side of the Mosel stands next **Longuich-Kirsch**, whose Baroque
church of St Laurentius has a Romanesque tower and, inside, a 15C
Madonna with grapes. NE of Longuich-Kirsch is the town of Riol, birthplace
of Peter Aspelt (died 1300), who lies buried in Mainz cathedral, followed
by **Mehring**, with a church of 1824, based on a Baroque original.

The B53 winds alongside the river, passing through Pölich (the Roman
*pulchra villa*) and **Schleich**, where stands a Schloss of 1700, and through
the ancient wine villages of Ensch, **Detzem**—with its Romanesque church,
and the Baroque Maximinen Hof—and Köverich (where at No. 25
Beethoven's mother was born) to reach Klüsserath, 14km from Schweich.
From here the route continues through **Leiwen**, with its 16C half-timbered
houses and narrow streets, after which another curve in the river leads the
B53 shortly to **Trittenheim**, another noted wine- producing town that stood
here in Roman times, where Roman sarcophagi have been found and where
in 1147 Pope Eugenius II founded the chapel of St Laurence as a gift to the
abbey of St Matthias in Trier. Here was born in 1462 Johannes Trithemius,
successively abbot of Sponheim and of the Scottish monastery of Würzburg.
The plague cross in the town bears the names of those who died of the
plague in 1654; the tower of the parish church dates from 1790.

The B53 continues to follow the bends of the river, crossing again to reach
**Neumagen-Dhron** (3000 inhab.; alt. 120m) after 26km. In Celtic 'magos'
means field, and this was an ancient staging post on the Roman road from
Bingen to Trier. The Emperor Constantine fortified the camp. Ausonius also
sang this spot in his poem about the Mosel (calling it 'Drahomus') and is
rewarded by a memorial in the church of St Peter, 1718, erected on an earlier
building. Here the Romans built a fort against the Germans (a fort destroyed
by the Normans in 822) and Constantine had a villa at Neumagen. Over a
thousand Roman finds from this vicinity are displayed in the Landesmuseum, Trier. Amongst the most remarkable finds is the sculpted
*Neumagen wineboat, a copy of which stands now in front of the church

of St Peter and once marked the grave of a Roman wine-merchant. See also: the Sayn-Wittgensteiner Hof of 1760—the Counts of Sayn-Wittgenstein were the last lords of Neumagen before the French Revolution; the Baroque pilgrimage church of Maria Himmelfahrt, 1793, housing the tombs of Heinrich von Hunolstein, 1485 and Heinrich von Isenburg, 1551; the Martyr chapel, in honour of St Ricius Varus, allegedly slain under Constantine's orders before the emperor became a Christian. Trains connect with Trier and Koblenz, boats with Cologne and Düsseldorf.

3km further along the river the road, which runs by vineyards, reaches the hamlet of Dhron itself and the beginning of the Dhronbach, whose vineyards are noted and the name of whose river (Drahonus) means 'full of fish'. The route now passes either through or opposite famous wineproducing villages and towns: **Piesport**, with its parish church of St Michael, the ceiling painting by J.P. Weber, 1778, celebrated for its Piesporter Goldtröpfchen and Piersporter Treppchen wines; **Wintrich**, with fine timbered houses, a stone cross of 1661 in the Weinberg and a 13C church. On the left bank of the river is **Kesten**, with its Weinhöfe of 1153, and above it Monzel; **Mülheim** (1000 inhab.; alt. 111m), at the entrance of the Veldenz valley, boasts a Protestant parish church of 1668, with a 13C Romanesque west tower, and a Catholic chapel of 1772. The route finally reaches Bernkastel-Kues, 21km from Neumagen-Dhron.

**Bernkastel-Kues** (7500 inhab.; alt. 110m; information office: 5 Gestade), renowned for its dry white and sparkling wines, nestles at the foot of Schloss Landshut. The Schloss was built c 1280 to replace a 7C fortress, and rebuilt in 1693 after a fire. It retains a massive entrance, keep and stairway, and though the rest is partly ruined it houses a restaurant. The town straddles both sides of the Mosel where it is joined by the Tiefenbach. In spite of withstanding numerous sieges and a fire in 1692, Bernkastel, on the right bank, boasts numerous 17C houses and Weinhöfe, particularly in the *Marktplatz, with the late Renaissance town hall, 1698 with a balconied window, its half-timbered houses, its pillory, and the St Michael's fountain of 1606. Two gates survive: the Graacher Tor, rebuilt in the 18C, and 13C St Michael, the French having torn down the town's 13C defences in 1689. The town's late 14C Catholic church of St Michael has works by H.R. Hoffmann of Trier and a 13C Romanesque tower.

A 219m-long bridge of 1905 spans the Mosel to reach Kues, a settlement in Neolithic times. The birthplace of the philosopher and theologian Cardinal Nicolas Cusanus (1401–64) still stands (the Haus zum Krebs, a museum open daily 10.00–12.00). Here in 1447 he founded the hospital of St Nikolaus, or Cusanusstift with a valuable library, a 15C cloister, refectory and Cardinal's room, a late Gothic chapel, with a triptych, c 1450 depicting the Crucifixion, the Crowning of Jesus with thorns and his entombment, and a memorial to the cardinal of 1488, containing his heart, the rest of his body being in St Peter's, Rome. Thirty-three infirm persons are housed here, their number complementing the lifetime of Jesus. The most famous wine of this town, Bernkasteler Doktor, derives its name from reviving a sick Prince-Archbishop of Trier, Boemund II, in the mid 14C. Mosel wine museum. Bus links with Frankfurt, Luxembourg, etc.; boats ply to Düsseldorf, Cologne and Traben-Trarbach.

Here the B53 crosses to the left bank of the Mosel and passes through Graach, with attractive half-timbered houses and a 16C late Gothic church, followed by **Wehlen**, with a famous sundial as well as a heated swimming pool; **Ürzig**, whose Celtic name means House of the Bear, has railway connections with Trier and Koblenz and boats to Bernkastel and Traben-

Trabach. Its Mönchshof of 1574 has a Renaissance façade of 1898. Further on is **Kröv** (2900 inhab.; alt. 105m). The town hall depicts coats of arms relating to Kröv from 755 to 1790, with its own coat of arms, including the double-headed eagle. Kröv produces the noted, delicious, vulgarly named wine, 'Kröver Nacktarsch', a name deriving from the milder word 'Nectar', though its label these days displays a youth being spanked on his bare bottom for having raided the wine cellar, one of his cronies scampering away, the other sitting in a drunken stupor. See the Baroque church of St Remigius, 1725, the three-gabled house of 1658 in Moselstrasse, the Echternacher Hof of 1764 and the mid-17C burial chapel of the Kesselstatts.

The B53 winds alongside the left bank of the river, passing on the right bank the little wine town of **Wolf**, with its church, which has an early 13C tower and choir, and its ruined monastery, to reach 23km after Bernkastel-Kues the town of **Traben-Trarbach** (7000 inhab.; alt. 113m), two united villages spanning the river, with wine merchants, half-timbered houses, the Rococo Haus Kayser, the 1750 Haus Böcking (where Goethe stayed in 1792), now the Mosel museum (open weekdays, except Mon, 09.30–11.30, 13.30–17.00; weekends 09.30–11.30), and two fine churches: the late Gothic Catholic St Peter, whose tower is partly Romanesque, and the Protestant hall-church. Narrow, ancient streets run down to the river. 2km S the ruins of **Burg Grevenburg**, 1350, tower above the river. **Bad Wildstein**, 4km S of Traben-Trarbach, is a thermal spa for sufferers from rheumatism.

The route now winds through Enkirch, Burg, Pünderich, Briedel, Zell and Merl as far as Bullay. Before Enkirch, **Starkenburg** appears 3km to the right, reached by the footpath known as the Moselhöhenweg and on the site of the ruined 11C Schloss of the same name. **Enkirch** boasts numerous half-timbered houses, with balconies, oriel windows and sculptured gables, as well as a cage once used for punishing malefactors, a 13C Gothic Protestant church and a 15C Franciscan pilgrimage church with Roman-esque towers. The town is filled with many Weinstuben, and a local history museum at 20 Weingasse, open Fri 18.00–19.00, Sat, 17.00–19.00, Sun 11.00–12.00. Beyond Burg, on the opposite side of the river—which can be crossed here—a road leads from **Reil** (the birthplace of Gerhart von Ryl, architect of Cologne cathedral) to the Marienburg (see below) and into the Alfbach valley to reach after 6km the Baroque Springiersbach abbey. This was restored after destruction by fire in 1940, and originally built in 1796, with decoration by Franziskus Freund.

The half-timbered houses of **Pünderich** stand by the railway line from Trier to Koblenz. Its finest house is the Fährhaus of 1621. The hamlet is three-quarters of an hour's walk from the *Marienburg which here domi-nates the Mosel, and where the Archbishop of Trier built a castle on a pagan holy site. On the 205m-high peak Abbot Richard of Springiersbach founded a now ruined Augustinian monastery in 1127, part of whose church (the Gothic choir) is incorporated into the present parish church. The restaurant offers superb views.

At Pünderich the River Mosel turns sharply back on itself and runs SE for 3km to **Briedel**, with charming houses and an early 17C Gemeindehaus. At **Zell** (5500 inhab.; alt. 94m) is produced the wine known as 'Schwarze Katz', and a fountain of the Black Cat rises in the Marktplatz. The town has a parish church with an 11C tower and a 13C late Romanesque crucifix. In the classical church of St Peter, 1793, is a 15C Madonna. Some of the former fortifications remain, including a 13C round tower. **Merl** united adminis-tratively with Zell in 1969, has a parish church first built in 1280 as part of a Franciscan monastery, and whose high altar dates from c 1525. In the cemetery is a 12C Romanesque tower (restored 1981), part of the town's former fortifications. Here in 1543 the Bishop of Trier built a town house which is now a hotel with a wine cellar. At **Bullay** (camping, excursions) the B53 crosses a two-tiered bridge to Alf, 25km from Traben-Trarbach. On its hill just outside the town is 12C Burg Arras. **Alf** (1300 inhab.; alt. 95m), at the mouth of the Alfbach, is a health resort with a history dating back to the Celts. Here the route to Koblenz joins the B49.

After 3km the B49 N reaches **St Aldegund**, with lovely *houses, the 12C chapel of St Aldegund and, on the opposite side of the river, gives a view of **Neef**, whose 13C Burghaus, with late Romanesque windows, has a late Gothic oriel and a Renaissance gable. The Romanesque chapel of St Peter rises on the Eulenköpfchen hill, with a Renaissance descent from the cross. **Bremm**, 3km on from St Aldegund, at the foot of sombre cliffs where the river makes an almost right-angled turn, has a 15C Gothic church of St Laurentius, with a Baroque altar, as well as fine houses. Close by are the ruins of the convent of Stuben, built in 1685 for an Augustinian monastery founded in 1137 by monks from Springiersbach.

4km E lies **Ediger-Eller** (1500 inhab.; alt. 92m). Its late Gothic parish church has a Romanesque font and an interment of Christ, 1671. The 16C chapel of the Holy Cross, reached by a 1762 way of the cross up the Ediger Berg, houses the late 17C relief *'Christus in der Kelter'—a crucified Jesus being crushed in a wine press. In Eller, where St Fridolin built a monastery in the 5C, St Hilarius church has a five-storeyed Romanesque tower and a sandstone Lady altar, 1621. See also the late Gothic chapel of St Rochus, the 16C wine cellars and remains of the 14C fortifications. Trains connect Eller with Trier and Koblenz, buses with Cochem and Traben-Trarbach, and boats with Zell and Cochem.

Opposite on the right bank of the river are the ruins of Schloss Beilstein (pulled down in 1668). The fortified town of **Beilstein**, often described as a 'miniature Rothenburg ob der Tauber', has a Baroque hall-church, c 1635, by the wing of a former monastery, housing a late Gothic Madonna, and a Spanish Black Virgin brought here by occupying troops in the 17C. The town hall with a Baroque doorway stands in the Marktplatz, close by the Fachwerk-Zehnthaus of 1577 and other half-timbered buildings.

5km from Eller along the B49 lies the wine village of **Ernst**, after which the road offers views of Kloster Ebernach—the ancient priory is now a psychiatric hospital—and the cliffs above Sehl. Cross the Mosel to see **Bruttig-Fankel**, birthplace of the humanist Peter Schade (1497–1524), otherwise known as Petrus Mosellanus, the house in which he was born still standing beside the river. The Schunksche Haus of 1659 has a Renaissance staircase. The town is followed, as the river turns S again, by **Valwig**, with a chapel of 1643.

5km further is the tourist town of *** Cochem** (7000 inhab; alt. 86m; information office: 1 Moselstrasse), famous for its 11C Schloss, the Reichsburg, set impressively on a vineyard- and tree-clad hill above a bend in the river, which was savagely pillaged in 1689. Well restored, 1869–77, and again after World War II, it preserves of the first fortress the octagonal lower part of the keep (guided tours mid-Mar to Oct 09.00–17.00). In the Marktplatz stands the Baroque Rathaus of 1739, with a fine doorway and oriel. Cochem also has a Capuchin monastery, 1623, to which belonged Father Martin of Cochem, 1634–1710. The parish church of St Martin, with a reliquary bust of its patron c 1500 and mid-15C Gnadenstuhl ('throne of grace'), was restored by Domenikus Böhm in 1851. The town is surrounded by the remains of medieval walls—including four gates, the oldest the

*The medieval Schloss at Cochem, begun in the 11C and restored in the 19C, lours over the River Mosel*

Enderttor, 1332—which encompass gabled half-timbered houses. Trains and buses between Koblenz and Trier; boats trips.

A 45-minute drive NW from the station along the Ender valley reaches the ruined **Schloss Winderburg**, also pillaged by the French in 1689.

After Cochem the river ceases its abrupt windings and flows more directly NE to Koblenz. 4km from Cochem is **Klotten**, at the confluence of the Mosel and the Dortebach. Its late Gothic church of St Maximin, 1525, was restored in 1868. The town's attractions include wine cellars, half-timbered houses, the nature reserve along the Dortebach valley (with Black Sea and Mediterranean flora) and the ruins of 10C Schloss Coraidelstein. The route continues through **Pommern**, a settlement of some 2000 years. Its church has an early Gothic west tower; here is a fortified Renaissance house; and the presbytery was built c 1500. Shortly after Pommern you reach **Karden** just above the Muhlbach confluence, once dedicated to the cult of the Roman god Mars, now blessed by the church of St Kastor, with its three towers, late Romanesque apse and an early Gothic nave. It houses 13C basalt tombs of knights; a terracotta high altar depiction of the Magi, c 1430; 13C wall paintings; the shrine of St Castor, 1490, who brought Christianity here in the mid 4C; a 15C crucifixion; a 17C Entombment; and a Baroque organ chamber. Among Karden's other attractive buildings are the archdeacon's house (Probsteihaus) of 1208, the Zehnthaus (tithe barn) c 1230, the Schultheissen-Burghaus Broy, 1562 and the Stiftschule with 1492 wall paintings.

The road crosses to the right bank of the Mosel after Karden to reach **Treis**, 7km from Klotten, behind which are two ruined Schlösser, the 15C church of St Katharina, with an altar painting of 1552, and the early 17C Zils chapel. The church of St-Johann-Baptist dates from 1831.

From Karden cross the river for an **excursion** of 3km to **Burg Eltz**, the oldest parts of which date from the 12C, the latest from the 16C, all well restored after a fire in 1920. Inside are displayed weapons and furniture (visits Apr–Oct 09.30–17.30, opening 10.00 Sun and holidays).

The route along the left bank of the Mosel to Koblenz includes **Müden**, whose church tower is based on a Roman look-out tower, and **Moselkern**, with half-timbered houses and a Merovingian cross dating from the 7C. The route along the right bank passes through **Burgen**, dominated from the other side of the river by **Burg Bischofstein**, built in 1270, restored after World War II, continuing to reach (14km from Treis) **Brodenbach** (670 inhab.; alt. 75m), where a good two hours' **excursion** can be made E along the Ehrbach valley to see, especially, **Ehrenburg**, once the home of the politician Baron Karl von Stein (1757–1831), the finest ruined Schloss in the region, erected in the mid 12C above the Ehrbach gorge (open Apr–Sept except Mon 10.00–18.00). Further E at **Buchholz** is the 11C Burg Schöneck, now a hotel.

The route along the right bank of the Mosel leads from **Brodenbach** **Alken**, dominated by the 13C Burg Thurand; only two towers and the 16C buildings remain from a French attack in 1689. In **Alken** is the Gothic church of the Trinity, with a Romanesque choir of 1248.

Kattenes, on the opposite bank, derives its name from the chain with which the Romans blocked the river to demand dues of the traffic. The road runs N along the river by way of **Oberfell**. Here you should pause to see the Romanesque tower of the parish church, the 12C pilgrimage chapel on the Bleidenberg, and the medieval house of Countess Jutta von Pyrmont. The route continues through **Niederfell**, where there is a Baroque altar in the parish church.

On the opposite bank at **Gondorf** rise the partly demolished Renaissance Schloss of the Leyen family and Schloss Liebig (1280, restored 1830, now a hotel). Gondorf is now linked with **Kobern**, which boasts the oldest half-timbered house in the Rheinland—the Abteihof St Marien, 1325, alongside other fine houses in the Marktplatz—and the 15C church of the Trinity, in the mountain cemetery. Nearby is the Matthias chapel, a church modelled on that of the Holy Sepulchre, Jerusalem, c 1235, to house the alleged head of St Matthias the Apostle, now in St Matthias, Trier.

To drive directly from here to Koblenz (17km) takes you first through **Winningen**, whose Romanesque church (altered in subsequent years) was founded c 1200, whose witches' fountain is a reminder of the witch hunts of the Thirty Years War and whose vineyards cover 220 hectares. The road then passes through **Koblenz-Güls**, with a 13C basilica and a church, St Servatius, built in the 13C, restored 1833–40. Its three ugly towers have earned it the nickname, the 'Toothpick of Güls'.

On the right bank of the Mosel, 3km N from Niederfell along the B49, lies **Dieblich**, a town built on a Celtic foundation, whose modern church houses a late 14C Gothic painting of the Madonna; see also the Gothic half-timbered Heesenburg. Witches were burnt in the Middle Ages on the nearby Dieblich Berg. From here the road runs for 6km to the wine village of **Lay**, opposite which is a camp site superbly set on the edge of the river. From Lay the route runs for 8km into Koblenz (see Rte 29).

# 29

# Koblenz to Trier via Wittlich

Total distance 123km. Koblenz—A48, 54km Ulmen—A1, 35km Wittlich—B49, 23km Schweich—11km Trier.

**\*\*KOBLENZ** (115,000 inhab.; alt. 65m), sometimes given its French name Coblence, owes its name to its picturesque position at the confluence of the Rhein and the Mosel (Latin *castrum apud confluentes*, the name Drusus gave to the camp he established here in 9 BC on a site already settled by Celts). Close by are the mountainous Taunus, Eifel and Hunsrück.

**Information office** and **main post office**, both opposite the **main railway station**. **Trains** connect with Frankfurt, Trier and the south; **boats** with Düsseldorf and Cologne. **Annual events** include Shrovetide processions and fireworks on the Rhine ('the Rhine in Flames', from Braubach to the S, see Rte 41, as far as Koblenz) on the second Saturday in August.

**History**. The Franks repulsed the Romans but recognised the strategic importance of the spot, and the Merovingians had established a court here by the 5C. An Imperial Diet was held at Koblenz in 843 at which 100 delegates worked out the preliminaries of the Treaty of Verdun which divided the empire of Ludwig the Debonair between his three sons. Heinrich II gave the city to the Archbishop of Trier in 1018, whose successor built a fortress beside the Mosel in 1280. Koblenz became a rich medieval city, developing its trade and its vineyards. Its archbishops became electors, and in 1343 replaced the old Roman bridge across the Mosel with a stone one.

The Reformation brought upheaval, the elector appealing for help in defence of Catholicism to the Jesuits. During the Thirty Years War Koblenz was taken by the French, then the Spanish, then the Swedes and then the Imperial forces. For 20 years after the war Koblenz was ravaged by plague. Two-thirds of the city was destroyed by Louis XIV's artillery in 1689. The city recovered itself during the next century, to be virtually overwhelmed by refugees from the French Revolution who were welcomed by Prince-Elector Clemens-Wenzeslaus. In retaliation the revolutionary troops under General Marceau took the city in 1794. When Marceau was killed in battle two years later he was commemorated in a monument just outside the city, in the suburb of Koblenz-Lützel across the Mosel, inscribed 'Hic cineras, ubique nomen' (Here are his ashes, his name is everywhere).

Koblenz became the chief city of the *département* of Rhine-et-Moselle. The city again began to flourish and in 1815 was assigned to Prussia by the Congress of Vienna. Now Koblenz was walled and moated, these fortifications only to be demolished in 1890. Koblenz remained the administrative centre of the Rhineland until 1945. Over 80 per cent of the city was flattened in World War II, after which the picturesque streets of the former Altstadt were meticulously restored, while in the 1960s an industrial zone was established to the north of the city.

Amongst the natives of Koblenz were the statesman Prince Clemens Lothar Wenzel Metternich (1773–1849), the nationalist, theologian and hater of absolutism Johann Josef von Görres (1776–1848) and the poet and romantic novelist Clemens Maria von Brentano (1778–1842).

Leave the main railway station and follow, directly opposite, Markenbild-chenweg, which leads into Januarius-Zick-Strasse, as far as the quayside. Parkland, first planted here in 1609, runs for 4km alongside the Rhine. Walk left towards the Pfaffendorter Brücke, before which is the **Weindorf** (Wine Village) created in 1925 to represent four typical houses of the region and incorporating restaurants and wine-tasting establishments. Turn left into Julius-Wegeler-Strasse, which passes close by the Congress Hall of 1952 (the Rhein-Mosel-Halle) and right into Neustadt Strasse to find on the right in Schlossplatz the classical **Electoral Palace** (Kurfürstliches Schloss) with a massive portico supported by eight Doric columns and with semi-circular wings. It was built first by Pierre Michel d'Ixnard and then by Antoine François Peyre, 1778–86, though much of the interior was destroyed in 1944. Beyond the Schloss on the right is the city theatre of 1787, in front of which is the Clemensplatz, with its obelisk-fountain, inscribed 'From Clemens-Wenzeslaus, Prince-Elector, to his neighbours, 1791'.

Walk further N along Karmeliterstrasse and Kastorpfaffenstrasse to reach the four-towered Romanesque church of **St Kastor**, founded in 836 by Archbishop Hetti, containing the relics of St Castor (died 450) which the archbishop brought from Kardern where he died. The basilica today for the most part derives from the end of the 11C, its major building finished 1209. The vaulting of the nave dates from 1498. In the choir is a monument to Archbishop Kuno von Falkenstein (died 1388), opposite which is the monument to Archbishop Werner von Königstein (died 1418). In the north aisle is the sarcophagus of St Rizza; pulpit by P. Kern, 1625. The high altar crucifix was created by G. Schweiger, in 1685. Sixteen painted wooden panels, c 1500, remain from the former rood.

The church abuts onto the 'Deutsches Eck', the corner where the Rhine and the Mosel meet, with the remains of the old city wall. Here the Teutonic Knights built a fortress, mostly destroyed in World War II. At the corner stood the monument to Kaiser Wilhelm I, 1897, so badly damaged in World War II as to have been later dismantled; 107 steps rise up the pedestal (inscribed 'The empire shall never be defeated so long as I have your loyalty') on which the monument stood.

Return to the church of St Kastor and follow Kastorpfaffenstrasse, turning right into Rheinstrasse to walk into Firmungstrasse and reach the restaurants and cafés of **Jesuitenplatz**, the site of the former Jesuit college (16C and 17C, now the Rathaus). Its courtyard has a fountain; Renaissance doorway of 1595, with the arms of Prince-Elector Johann von Schönburg; the ceiling of its staircase tower was painted by C.M. Pozzi in 1701. Beside it stands the Jesuit church (rebuilt 1959) with a fine doorway of 1617, and nearby is the Schängel fountain, by Karl Burger, 1940. From here Entenpfühl leads towards the Mosel and reaches Florinsmarkt, where stands the 12C Romanesque church of **St Florin**—a passageway leads to the former monastic cloister and the 13C chapter house. On the N side of Florinsmarkt is the Kaufhaus of 1419 (rebuilt 1963) which along with the adjoining Schöffenhaus of 1530, the Bürresheimer Hof of 1659 and the Galeriebau of 1770 now serves as the **Mittelrhein-Museum** (open Tue 10.00–13.00, 14.30–20.00, Wed–Sat 10.00–13.00, 14.30–17.00, Sun 10.00–13.00). Its displays cover the history of the city; with Baroque works of art, particularly 60 designs by the court painter Januarius Zick (1730–97). Cross the square to see the half-timbered 'Zum Hubertus' and take Burgstrasse to reach the **Alte Burg** or old Schloss, built by Archbishop Heinrich von Vingstingen, 1276–89, to guard the bridge across the Mosel. The burg was enlarged in the 16C and 17C. Here in 1609 the Catholic League was set up in opposition to the Protestant Union. The French destroyed most of the burg in 1688. Reconstructed c 1700, it now houses the city library and archives.

The old bridge of 1343, with 14 arches, was built out of Winningen basalt for Archbishop-Elector Balduin von Luxemburg and bears his name. Three of its ancient arches were replaced with one of concrete in 1973, for the sake of the river traffic. To the right of the Alte Burg the route runs into Münzplatz, in which stands the former electoral mint, by Johannes Seitz, 1763, nearby which, in the Metternicher Hof of 1675, Clemens Wenzeslaus Lothar, Prince Metternich, was born on 15 May 1773. To the E stands the Liebfrauenkirche. Begun c 1200, its choir dates from 1401–31 and the vaulting of the nave was completed in the late 15C. The towers were capped in 1693, and the main doorway was added in 1765. Take the steps S of the square to find the square named Am Plan, on the N side of which is the former town hall; 18C and 19C, with Baroque parts by Sebastiani, 1695–1700, and a stucco ceiling in the staircase hall by Carlo Pozzi. To the W are late 17C houses with oriel windows, including the Feuerwache, once the town hall.

On the opposite side of the Rhine—cross by Pfaffendorfer Brücke and turn left along Pfaffendorfer Tor—you reach the Capuchin church of 1625, its mid-18C Baroque altar by Johannes Seitz, followed by the Kurfürstliche Regierungsgebäude which Balthasar Neumann built, 1739–49, stables by Johannes Seitz, 1762. The Ehrenbreitstein fortifications, which you can reach by chair lift, constitute a fortress built from the 11C over 700 years (the main part today 1816–32), rarely taken by its enemies, and now housing both a youth hostel and the Landesmuseum (much devoted to viticulture) as well as a Rhine Museum (with boats and an exhibition depicting the Rhine in the past), open daily 09.00–17.00 21 Mar–1 Nov. For more history and information see Koblenz-Ehrenbreitstein, Rte 41.

Theatres: theatre of 1787 by Peter Joseph Krah at No. 2 Deinhardplatz; little theatre at 13 Florinsmarkt. Zoos in the Stadtpark and in the suburb of Ehrenbreitstein.

**Stolzenfels**, 5km S on the left bank of the Rhine not far from the village of Kappellen-Stolpenfelz has a Schloss by Karl Friedrich Schinkel, 1836–42, built to replace one destroyed by the French in 1688 (open daily except Mon and Dec 09.00–13.00, 14.00–17.00). 3km further S is Rhens, with medieval fortifications, 16C to 18C half-timbered houses and a halftimbered town hall, c 1560.

NE is **Höhr-Grenzhausen**, with its ruined fortress, and its local history museum (in Kleine Emser Strasse) and its ceramics museum (in Lindenstrasse), open Tue–Sun 10.00–17.00. The town lies at the centre of the 370 sq hectare **Rhein-Westerwald Naturpark**, which has over 70 marked routes. E of Koblenz is the spa of **Bad Ems**, notorious for the Ems telegram which triggered off the Franco Prussian War of 1870–71. The modern Kurpark surrounds the 240m-high Busrkarch heights, with the Bismarck tower. A little further SE at Nassau is the Steinsches Schloss, once the home of the Prussian statesman and reformer Reichsfreiherr Karl vom und zum Stein who was born here in 1757 (died 1831).

W of Koblenz join the A48 to drive 55km SW to **Ulmen** (see Rte 33). The nearby lake (the 'Ulmener Maar') has its origins in a volcanic crater, while to the N is a nature reserve, the **Jungferweiher**, with rare birds. The A1 now leads S for 35km to **Wittlich** (10,000 inhab.; alt. 165m), a town known to the Romans as *Vitelliacum*, on the River Lieser, surrounded by vineyards and tobacco fields, its Marktplatz surrounded by late 17C and Baroque houses. The Baroque Rathaus has a late Renaissance façade. Here is also an 18C town hall and a church of 1709. SW of Wittlich is the last volcano to have been active in the region, the 509m-high Mosenberg. The B49 leads S from Wittlich for 26km to Schweich, to reach **Trier** (see Rte 27) after another 11km.

# 30

# Mainz to Worms

Total distance 45km. Mainz—B9, 18km Nierstein—2km Oppenheim—6km Guntersblum—19km Worms.

**˙˙MAINZ** (188,000 inhab.; alt. 82m), a city of fountains and wine bars, is the capital of the Rhineland-Palatinate. Set on the left bank of the Rhine at the confluence with the Main, the city is the seat of a university and an archbishop.

**Main railway station**: Bahnhofsplatz. **Information office** and **main post office**: Bahnhofsplatz. **Train** links with Basel, Cologne, Dortmund, Frankfurt-am-Main and Saarbrücken, **rail** link with the Rhine-Main airport, **bus** links with Frankfurt-am-Main and Luxembourg, **boats** to Cologne and Düsseldorf.

**Festivals**. Mainz holds a festival at Shrovetide, a wine festival (end of Aug–beginning of Sept), a week-end festival (Johannisnacht) in June, and a children's festival (Nikolausfeier) on the first Sat in Dec.

**History**. Roman legionaries appeared here in 38 BC and set up *castrum Mongontiacum*. For a time in ruins after the withdrawal of the Romans, the city began to blossom in the 8C and the Pope sent first Wynfrith as archbishop and then St Boniface to evangelise the Germans. Mainz became the metropolitan city of Germany. The Archbishop of Mainz became not only patriarch of the German church but from the late 10C chancellor of the Holy Roman Empire. By the mid 13C Mainz was capital of the Rheinish League and known as *Aurea Moguntia*, the golden city. In the mid 15C Gutenberg began printing here. In 1466 the university was founded. After difficulties and decline in the 17C, owing to the Thirty Years War and Louis XIV's depredations, Mainz bloomed again in the 18C. Goethe called it the 'capital of our Fatherland'. In 1792 the city became a republic. For a time French after the Revolution, the city became part of Hesse in 1815, garrisoned both by the Prussians and the Austrians. After World War II, when 80 per cent of the city was destroyed, a new university was established here, and Mainz became the capital of the region. Johannes Gensfleisch zum Gutenberg, inventor of the printing press and printer of the Gutenberg Bible, 1452, was born at Mainz c 1397.

From the main railway station cross Bahnhofplatz and follow Bahnhofstrasse right, crossing Münsterplatz to reach **Schillerstrasse**. On the left is the Baroque **Erthaler Hof**, by Philipp Christoph von Erthal, 1735–43, with its classical pediment and fine staircase tower. Opposite is the 19C ministry of supplies (**Proviantamt**). On the right side of Schillerstrasse at Nos 9–11 is the late Renaissance **Schönborner Hof**, by Philipp Erwin von Schönborn, 1647–73, now housing the Institut Français and the university archaeological museum, close by which is a modern bronze statue of the Mainz wine drinker. Next, at 3 Schillerplatz, is the baroque **Bassenheimer Hof**, by Anselm Franz von Ritter zu Groenesteyn, 1756.

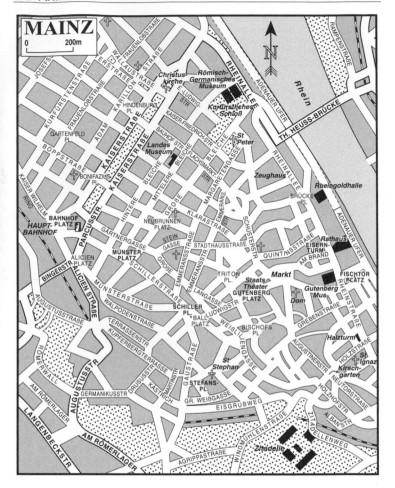

Turn S along Gaustrasse to reach **Stefansplatz**, with its Shrovetide fountain, 1967, and the former Stiftskirche of **St Stephan**, a Romanesque foundation though the present building is 14C Gothic. It comprises a late 15C cloister; a doorway of 1747 and three stained glass windows by Marc Chagall, 1978, representing reconciliation between Christians and Jews. The church also treasures a Byzantine silk cloth c 1100. At the S side of the square stands the late Baroque **Osteiner Hof**, by Valentin Thomann, 1749, rebuilt 1948–62, and boasting a Rococo façade. Close by this building (NW) is the **Dahlberger Hof** of 1710, its doorway surmounted by a 1677 statue of the Virgin Mary. Continue across Eisgrubweg and along Zitadellenweg to the **Zitadelle**, an episcopal palace created 1620–29 by the archbishop out of the former Benedictine monastery of St Jakob.

Return to Schillerplatz. From here Ludwigstrasse, named after Ludwig I of Hesse but once called rue Napoleon, after the emperor who decreed its construction, runs E to **Gutenbergplatz**, in which stands a monument to Gutenberg by Thorwaldsen, 1837. The square also houses the **city theatre**, founded in 1833 and rebuilt in 1950. Behind the theatre, **Höfchen**, the continuation of Ludwigstrasse, contains the former university building, 1615–18 (now housing the European history faculty of the modern university). Höfchen continues to the **Markt**. (Left on the corner of **Schusterstrasse** is an octagonal staircase-tower decorated with a statue of St Barbara, 1717.) Here in 1526 Archbishop Albrecht of Brandenburg erected the Renaissance fountain, commemorating Charles V's victory at Pavia, the first Renaissance fountain in Germany. On the right is the Romanesque church of **St Gothard**, 1137. The Baroque houses with mansard roofs are by Balthasar Neumann's son Ignaz Michael.

Behind them rises the six-towered **˙˙Dom** of St Martin and St Stephan, a Romanesque basilica, successor to the cathedral built by Archbishop Willigis, 975–1009, with a nave and two aisles, to which in the 13C two more Gothic naves were added. The east tower—ruined by Prussian artillery, 1793, rebuilt in a neo-Gothic fashion, 1870—is far plainer than the ornate, later west tower, built at various stages between the 13C and 18C, and as it reaches its 82.5m becoming first Gothic and then Baroque, the upper storey rebuilt by Ignaz Michael Neumann in 1767. The cathedral choir was begun at the beginning of the 12C and consecrated in 1239. Inside are a west choir and an east choir, and here are buried 44 of the 84 archbishops of Mainz, many in superb tombs. In the first chapel left are three early 16C statues—St Willigis, St Boniface and the Madonna known as the 'Schöne Mainzerin'—and a marble tomb of the Christian socialist Bishop Emmanuel von Ketteler (1811–77). In the next chapel is a sandstone entombment c 1495 and the tombs of Archbishop Konrad III (died 1434), Peter Aspelt (died 1320) and Siegfried III von Epstein (died 1249).

The pewter fonts, 1328, are from the former church of Our Lady. The choir boasts two Renaissance altars and a Baroque altar. Rococo stalls are by F.A. Hermann, 1767, above which are monuments to Johann Philip von Schönborn (died 1673) and Lothar Franz von Schönborn (died 1729), both by Balthasar Neumann, 1745. Against the north wall of the crossing is a monument to Bernhard von Breitenbach (died 1497). The late Gothic door to the 'Memorie' (a Romanesque chapel in memory of the dead) was sculpted in 1420. In the nave are three funeral monuments by Hans Backoffen: of Berthold von Henneberg (died 1504), Jakob von Liebenstein (died 1508) and ˙Uriel von Gemmingen (died 1514). The cathedral's neo-Gothic pulpit is by J. Scholl, 1834. The high altar dates from 1960, with a cross by G.G. Zeuner, 1975. The crypt contains the relics of 22 Mainz saints in a modern gold reliquary by R. Wieland, 1960.

The cathedral cloister, 1397–1410, also houses some stone funeral monuments, including one to the Minnesinger Heinrich von Meissen, known as 'Frauenlob' (died 1318). Next to the cloister is the **Diözesan Museum** (open weekdays except Thu 09.00–13.00, 15.00–1800; Sat 09.00–13.00), with a collection of sacred art from the 10C onwards.

Return along Höfchen and turn left at Schöfferstrasse to come to **St Johannis** church, the oldest in Mainz, basically the cathedral baptistery and deriving from an early 10C building, to reach on the right the picturesque **Kirschgarten**, at the beginning of Augustinerstrasse. Here are half-timbered houses, especially the still functioning bakery, and the Mary fountain. Continue along Augustinerstrasse, which virtually escaped damage in World War II, to reach on the left the mid-18C **Augustiner-Kirche**, half-Baroque, half-classical, standing close by the former Augustinian monastery. It has a sandstone façade, and the frescoes inside are by J.B. Enderle, 1772. Do not miss a wooden statue of the Virgin Mary, sculpted in 1420.

At the end of Augustinerstrasse follow Kapuzinerstrasse (E) to reach the Jesuit church of **St Ignaz**, by Johann Peter Jäger, 1763–74, at the entrance to which is a 16C crucifixion by Hans Backoffen. Holzstrasse leads from here towards the Rhine. Where it meets Rheinstrasse stands the 15C **Holzturm**. Turn left along Rheinstrasse to cross Fischertorplatz (near which rises the **Eisenturm**, from the old fortifications) and find the **Rathaus**, by Arne Jacobsen, built posthumously, 1971–74, out of reinforced concrete clad in Norwegian marble. N of the Rathausplatz stands the **Rheingold-halle**, a congress hall holding 3500. Walk from the river back to Markt and turn right along Schusterstrasse to find at Quintinstrasse (on the right) the restored 13C Gothic church of **St Quintin**, inside which is a Rococo pulpit by H. Jung.

Further along Schusterstrasse you reach on the right Karmeliterstrasse which leads to the *Carmelite church, an early 14C Gothic basilica, restored after World War II. Its treasures include frescoes painted c 1400; a Gothic retable of 1517, depicting the Virgin, crowned, between SS Cyril and Jerome; and 15C statues, including Mary with a rosary, c 1420. The courtyard of the former convent has an 18C doorway with a statue of St Joseph and a Baroque cartouche of the coronation of the Virgin.

Turn left at the end of Karmeliterstrasse to reach the former old and new Arsenals (**Zeughaus**, in Zeughausgasse), the first 1604, the second by Maximilan von Welsch, 1740, restored 1958. N of these stands the former headquarters of the Teutonic Knights, the **Deutschhaus**, by Anselm Franz von Ritter zu Groenesteyn, 1730–38, transformed in the 19C into the grand-ducal palace and now the seat of the parliament of the Rhine-Palatinate. Behind it is a replica of the **column of Jupiter** erected in AD 66 in honour of Nero. The Deutschhausplatz is joined by the Grosse Bleiche, a main artery of Mainz, across which is the late 16C Renaissance *Kurfür-stliches Schloss of the prince-electors. Its east wing 1627–78, its north wing 1687–1752, its interior modernised, this is a complex building, now serving as the **Römisch-Germanisches Museum** (open Tue–Sun 10.00–13.00, 15.00–18.00) displaying pre-historic finds and early Roman exhibits.

Follow Grosse Bleiche towards the centre of the city. NW along EmilLudwig-Strasse can be seen the domed **church of Christ**, 1902. Continue along Grosse Bleiche, passing on the left the twin-onion-domed church of **St Peter**, 1752–76, then at Nos 49–51 the former stables (Marstall) of the prince-bishops, now housing the **Mittelrheinishes Landesmuseum** (open 10.00–13.00 and 15.00–18.00; closed Sun afternoons) with pre-Christian remains, and a collection of art and sculpture reaching from then to the 20C. Continue along Grosse Bleiche to find on the right Nebrunnenplatz, with a fountain of 1726.

MUSEUMS: **Gutenberg Museum**, 5 Liebfrauenplatz (open Tue–Sat 10.00–18.00, Sun 10.00–13.00), a museum of world printing, including Gutenberg's 42-line Bible and Gutenberg's Last Judgment of c 1455; plus the history of the book since the 5C AD. **Kupferberg museum of sparkling wine**, 19 Kupferberg Terrasse (open 09.30–11.30, 14.30–15.30); **Natural History Museum** 1 Reichklarastrasse (open except Mon 10.00–18.00).

THEATRES: city theatre, 7 Gutenbergplatz; university theatre; Kammer-spiele, 13 Emerich-Josef-Strasse.

Leave Mainz driving S along the B9 (Liebfrauenstrasse) through the wine villages of **Bodenheim**, with its half-timbered town hall, 1608, and **Nackenheim**, birthplace of the playwright Carl Zuckmayer, 1896–1979, who was the author of 'Des Teufels General', 1946, and whose 'Happy Vineyard' ('Der fröhliche Weinberg') celebrates the spot. Nackenheim has a Baroque church of St Gereon, 1716, and an 18C town hall. 18km from Mainz lies **Nierstein** (6800 inhab.; alt. 89m), whose wine is famous. In its fortified cemetery, with a Romanesque gate, stands the church of St Martin, 1782–87, its bell tower partly 12C, its font 16C, as well as Renaissance monuments. The local Schloss has a 19C chapel. The 18C Baroque church of St Kilian has a Romanesque tower. At the outskirts of the village on the way to Oppenheim were discovered in 1802 Roman thermal baths (the Stronabad).

**Oppenheim** lies 5km S of Nierstein. Known as *Bauconica* in Celtic-Roman times, it was mostly razed by the French in 1688. Oppenheim has retained its Gothic church of *St Katharina, which was begun in 1226; its west towers and choir date from the 13C, the nave from the 14C, the west end from the 15C. Everything was restored 1934–37. Behind the church is the Gothic chapel and charnel house of St Michael, many of its skulls and bones said to be those of Swedes and Spaniards fallen in the Thirty Years War. Oppenheim also has the former Franciscan 14C church of St Bartholomäus, the Gau Gate of 1566 from the medieval walls, the Luther house where the Reformer stayed on his way to Worms in 1521, a Renaissance fountain of 1546, a Gothic town hall of 1689 and a wine museum. A fifteen-minute walk leads up to the restaurant in the Imperial Burg Landskrone (13C, much of it destroyed 1689), with fine views of the local vineyards. Train connections with Mainz and Mannheim, buses with Mainz.

The B9 now continues directly S through vineyards by way of **Guntersblum** (6km), with a Romanesque church and two Schlösser, as well as the Baroque Adelshof, formerly belonging to the Teutonic Knights. To the E is a nature reserve on an island created when the Rhine was straightened in 1829. The route continues S through the wine village of **Alsheim** and, after passing a road to the right which leads for 2km to **Bechtheim** with an 11C and 12C Romanesque church, reaches **Osthofen** (11km). Here the citizens celebrate a wine festival, on the last weekend in September. The town boasts a 13C church on the Goldberg, and 17C and 18C houses. **Worms** (see Rte 31) lies 10km S of Osthofen.

# 31

# Worms to Speyer

Total distance 37km. Worms—B9, 11km Frankenthal—5km Ludwigshafen—21km Speyer.

**WORMS** (80,000 inhab.; alt. 110m), one of Germany's oldest and most impressive cities, is situated amidst fertile vineyards on the left bank of the River Rhine, and profits also from furniture making, sugar refineries, leather goods and light industry.

**Tourist information**: 14 Neumarkt. **Main post office**: Ludwigstrasse. **Train** connections with Bingen, Kaiserslautern, Mainz and Mannheim, **buses** with Ludwigshafen, etc.

**History**. Worms was a Roman garrison and before that the Celtic settlement *Borbetomagus*, a name developing into Vormatia in the Middle Ages and then Worms. The *Nibelungenlied* made Worms the seat of Gunther, king of the Burgundians (and a 19C statue on the Nibelung bridge at Worms depicts Hagen casting the treasure into the river). Emperor Heinrich II gave the city customs rights in 1074. In 1122 the Concordat of Worms brought to an end the investiture controversy between the pope and the emperor. In 1254 Worms allied with Mainz, thus inaugurating the confederation of the Rhine. Over 100 Imperial Diets took place here, in particular the celebrated Diet of 1521 which condemned Martin Luther, declaring that: 'The devil in the habit of a monk has brought together ancient errors in one stinking puddle and invented new ones'. Virtually bankrupted by the Thirty Years War, Worms was almost destroyed during the war of the Palatinate Succession, 1688–97, when its defences were demolished. The city was ceded to the French in 1797 and returned to Hesse-Darmstadt in 1815, when the former great city had been reduced to little more than a small town. Worms began to prosper again, but suffered a further blow when 65 per cent of its buildings were destroyed in World War II. The Biblical and Talmud scholar Salomo ben Isaak (1040–1105) lived and worked here.

Leaving the main railway station, follow Wilhelm-Leuschner- Strasse SE as far as Lutherplatz, with its gigantic monument to the reformer (chiefly the work of Ernst Rietschl, finished by Kietz, Donndorf and Schelling, 1868): the lesser figures are Jan Huss, Wycliffe, Melanchthon, Savonarola, Peter Waldes, Philip of Hesse, Friedrich of Saxony and Johann Reuchlin, as well as statues representing the cities of Magdeburg, Augsburg and Speyer and the coats of arms of the first 24 cities to embrace the Reformation. Take Lutherring right to reach at the crossroads with Andreasring and Andreasstrasse the old Jewish cemetery, the oldest and largest in Europe, part of it 11C, used by the Jewish community that lived here from the 10C. Follow Andreasring to arrive at the city museum, 7 Weckerlingplatz, displaying principally antiquities (open summer 09.00–12.00, 14.00–17.00; winter opens at 10.00 and closes at 16.00). NW past Andreastor is the 12C and 13C church of St Magnus, with a 14C tower, rebuilt 1954. From here en route to the Domplatz you pass some 1.5m of a Roman wall that once was part of the forum.

The massive, towered **\*\*Cathedral of St Peter** was first consecrated in 1018, though the earliest parts of the present Romanesque masterpiece date from the end of the 12C. The east choir was consecrated in 1110, the west end finished 1181. The ogival vaulted nave is entered from the south by an early 14C sculpted Gothic doorway, dominated by a carving of the church triumphant, borne on the heads of the four Evangelists. The interior is 158m long with the dome rising 40m above the crossing. The west end, once reserved for the emperor and leading civil dignitaries, is architecturally more elaborate than the east, with a rose window, an 18C altar and *stalls. The east choir, however, possesses a Baroque high altar by Balthasar Neumann, c 1740, with sculpture by J.W. von der Auwera and two side altars by Johann Peter Jäger, 1750.

The chapel of St Georg is Renaissance; the Gothic baptistery chapel of St Nikolaus was finished in 1325; the chapel of St Anna has two Romanesque carvings (Habakkuk and the angel; Daniel in the lions' den). Other 11C reliefs in the cathedral include Christ among saints; 13C frescoes depict SS Peter, Paul and Christopher; here also are remains of a carved stone cycle of the life of Christ, c 1500. The cathedral also shelters the tombs of Eberhard von Heppenheim (c 1430) and Bishop Theodor von Bettendorf (died 1580).

*Dedicated to St Peter, Worms cathedral boasts four round towers with an octagonal cupola above the crossing*

N of the cathedral is the Kunsthaus Heylshof, housing the rich artistic collection, 15C to 19C, of the von Heyl family (open except Mon and Sun 09.00–12.00, 14.00–17.00; in winter opens 10.00 and closes 16.00), and the garden that formerly belonged to the bishops' palace—bordered to the west by remains of the city walls. Immediately NE of the cathedral is the Lutheran church of the Holy Trinity, 1709–25, rebuilt 1955–59, with modern glass and mosaics representing Luther before the Diet of Worms. Follow Petersstrasse to Torturmplatz, which boasts from the old city walls the Torturm, the Bürgerturm and the Fischerpforte (also called the Lutherpförtchen). Turn N from Petersstrasse along Paulusgasse to reach the Pauluskirche, once belonging to a Dominican monastery. It has 11C towers, though the church is basically 13C with an 18C nave and high altar. Next to it is the 13C and 14C cloister.

From here take Petersstrasse N to reach the Baroque Friedrichskirche, built in 1745, and paid for by King Friedrich II of Prussia, hence its name. Close by is the early Baroque Rote Haus of 1624. Friedrichstrasse leads N to Judengasse (right), where are more remains of the city walls and which leads to the former Jewish ghetto and the oldest synagogue in Europe, deriving from the Romanesque era, almost totally destroyed on the Kristallnacht of 1938, restored 1958–61; open 10.00–12.00 and 14.00–17.00 (closing 16.00 Nov–Apr). It has rich Jewish archives, as well as the Jewish Mikwe of 1186 behind the synagogue, for women's ritual bathing.

Return along Judengasse and continue along Martinsgasse to reach the church of St Martin, 13C, partly rebuilt 18C. Note its finely decorated portals, especially the early Gothic west door, its 13C north tower and the south tower of 1961. St Martin's church borders on Ludwigsplatz, where rises a 24m-high obelisk, erected in 1895 in honour of Grand Duke Ludwig IV of Hesse. Friedrichstrasse leads N to join (on the right) Berlinerring, from which Remeyerhofstrasse followed by Liebfrauenstift wind N to the three-aisled Liebfrauenkirche, 1310–1465, well worth visiting for its sculptures and a 14C painting of the Madonna. The church is surrounded by vines that produce the wine known as Liebfraumilch. The theatre at Worms was built in 1966. See also the Dreifaltigkeitskirche 1725 with a modern interior.

**Environs** include the Bergkirche at **Horchheim**, 2km W, with an 11C crypt and a 12C Romanesque tower; and at **Herrnsheim**, c 4km NW of Worms, the 15C Gothic parish church, whose choir stalls date from 1486, whose late Gothic stone pulpit was created in 1489 and whose tombs include those of the von Dalberg family, as well as a Schloss in a fine park. At **Pfiffligheim**, 3km W of Worms, is the tree under which Luther and his friends are said to have sat while deciding the reject the findings of the Diet of Worms.

From Worms the B9 runs S passing under the Mannheim–Saarbrücken motorway to reach after 11km the industrial town of **Frankenthal** (47,000 inhab.; alt. 96m), whose porcelain factory was famous between 1755 and 1800 and whose history dates back to the 9C. Of the 18C fortifications remain the Worms Gate (1770–72) and the Speyer Gate (1772–73). The classical church of the Twelve Apostles (1820–23) is based on 13C foundations, and the ruined late Romanesque monastery church dates from the 13C and 14C. Frankenthal is 3km N of Ludwigshafen, reached by way of the suburb of **Oggersheim**, where in 1729 the crown-prince of Palatinat-Sulzbach built a Loretto chapel, with sculpted angels by Paul Egell, 1730, dedicated to the Assumption of the B.V.M. The church was rebuilt by Peter Anton Vershaffelt, 1775–77. Behind its high altar is a marble reproduction of the Holy House of Loreto at Ancona, Italy. At Oggersheim in 1782, at 6 Schillerstrasse, Schiller wrote his 'Kabale und Liebe' and worked on his 'Fiesko'. The house is now a Schiller museum (open weekdays except Wed 14.00–17.00; weekends 10.00–12.00).

**Ludwigshafen** (166,000 inhab.; alt. 92m; tourist information: Ludwigsplatz), an important port on the Rhine and the centre of the German chemical industry, developed as a suburb of Mannheim (see Rte 32) in the 17C and is a totally modern city with a fine park and an enormous sports stadium, holding 85,000 spectators. Named in 1843 after King Ludwig I of Bavaria, it boasts a Friedenskirche of 1932 (in Leuschnerstrasse) and the BASF high rise building of 1937, as well as the most modern main railway station in Europe. The Wilhelm-Hack-Museum, 23 Berlinerstrasse, built by Walter and Susane Hagstotz and Peter Kraft, 1975–79, houses medieval to *modern paintings, especially 20C Expressionists (open except Mon 09.30–17.00; Wed till 21.00). Ludwigshafen's main theatre is at 30 Berlinerplatz. The philosopher Ernst Bloch was born here in 1885. Train connections with Kaiserslautern, Mainz, Mannheim, Speyer and Worms; buses with Speyer, etc.

*SPEYER (44,000 inhab.; alt. 104m), its majestic cathedral with six towers and built of sandstone, lies 21km S of Ludwigshafen along the B9, on the left bank of the Rhine. The city dates back to the Celtic-Roman era. In Speyer in September 1861 a bizarre tryst took place, when the future King

Edward VII of England and his bride-to-be Alexandra von SchleswigHolstein-Sonderburg-Glucksburg met and inspected each other prior to their marriage (see below).

**Tourist information** at the town hall, 12 Maximilianstrasse. **Train** links with Saarbrücken and Frankfurt-am-Main, **buses** with Landau and Ludwigshafen.

**History**. Around 10 BC Speyer was the site of a Roman camp, and in the 2nd century AD was known as *Noviomagus Nemetum*. The name Spira first occurs in the 5C AD. Speyer became a bishopric in the 7C, and was made prosperous by the energies of its bishops, so much so that in the early 11C Konrad the Salien made it capital of the empire. A Free Imperial City from 1294, it was the seat of some 50 Imperial Diets between 838 and 1570. At Speyer in 1529 the followers of Martin Luther were first called Protestants. Although the Imperial high court sat here in the 16C and 17C, from the Thirty Years War to the early 19C the city declined rapidly, mostly as the result of wars—the French set fire to the city in 1689, sparing only the cathedral, which accidentally caught alight. The French took the city in 1797 and this time deliberately demolished the cathedral. In 1815 Speyer was ceded to Bavaria.

From the main railway station take Bahnhofstrasse and Glegenstrasse, to pass through the Altpörtel of 1246, whose uppermost storey dates from 1512, rising from four lower storeys built between 1230 and 1250. This 55m-high gateway replaced an earlier wooden one, and its lantern dates from 1708. S of the gateway, by way of Gilgenstrasse, you reach the neo-Gothic, Protestant Gedächtniskirche (the Retscherkirche), 1893–1904, built by Julius Flügge and Carl Nordmann as a memorial to the 'Protest' Diet of 1529. A 1904 statue of Martin Luther, by Hermann Hahn, stands at the entrance.

Walk from the Altpörtal along Maximilianstrasse to the cathedral, passing on the left the old Kaufhaus. The Dom, the largest in Germany—133m by 34m; height 33m—was begun in 1030 and rebuilt by Heinrich IV between 1082 and 1125. The· 11C *crypt—again the largest in Germany—alone remains from this era and is known as the Kaisersgruft, since it contains the tombs of eight rulers, beginning with that of the founder, Konrad II, and his wife Gisela. After the vandalism of the French, Speyer cathedral was rebuilt in the 19C through the generosity of Kings Maximilian and Ludwig of Bavaria. The bronze doorway is by Toni Schneider-Manzell, 1970. The *chapel of St Afra, c 1110, rebuilt in 1850, boasts carvings brought from elsewhere in the cathedral as well as those originally here (Annunciation, c 1470, originally on the outer wall). In front of the cathedral is the so-called Domnapf, a sandstone basin of 1490 which new bishops were expected to fill with wine after their consecration. Opposite the cathedral rises the neo-Baroque Stadthaus, built by Franz Schöbert in 1904.

In the cathedral garden the 13C Heidentürmchen remains from the old fortifications. N of the cathedral, across Edith-Stein-Platz follow Nikolausgasse to cross Sonnenbrücke, dating from the 13C and the sole remaining medieval bridge of the city. Sonnengasse leads from here to Kloster St Magdalenen, in whose church of 1708 are Baroque altars. In this Kloster lived the philosopher Edith Stein, who was killed by the Nazis. Walk left from the cathedral to the church of the Holy Trinity, designed by J.P. Graberand, finished in 1717. It has a Baroque high altar and organ, and the vault was decorated by Johann Christoph Guthbier in 1713 with frescoes depicting scenes from the Old and New Testaments. In this exquisitely austere building on the morning of 24 September 1861 the future British King Edward VII first met his bride, the Danish Princess Alexandra of Schleswig-Holstein-Sonderburg-Glucksburg. Close by is the Läutturm, the remains of the 13C church of St Georg.

The Baroque town hall of Speyer dates from 1712–26. Its architects were J.A. Breunig and J.J. Böhret. Its interior decoration are by Christian Dathan and his son Johann Georg Dathan. On the west side of the town hall square is Speyer's former mint, the Alte Münze, built in 1748 and enhanced with a gable by Heinrich Jester in 1874. Further N, the modern Bernhardus-kirche dates from 1954, was designed by Ludwig Ihm and was built as a symbol of peace with money partly donated by the French. From the town hall square, Salgasse leads NW. Turn left from the street into Grosse Himmelsgasse to find on the left the Baroque Heiliggeistkirche of 1702. Further on Johannerstrasse leads to the church of St Ludwig, built 1266 to 1308, rebuilt 1698 and restored in 1834. Inside is a 15C retable, named after Bossweiler (the village from which it came), which depicts the Annuncia-tion, the birth of Jesus and the visit of the Magi. In a building by Gabriel von Seidl, 1910, at 7 Grosse Pfaffengasse, is the Historisches Museum der Pfalz, its chief treasure a *Bronze Age golden hat, 12C BC, its chief attraction a wine museum (open daily 09.00–12.00, 14.00–17.00). In front of the museum stand two Roman equestrian statues.

# 32

# Mannheim to Zweibrücken via Landau

Total distance 111km. Mannheim—1km Ludwigshafen—B9, 21km Speyer—B9 and B272, 20km Landau—B10, 14km Annweiler—31km Pirmasems—24km Zweibrücken.

**MANNHEIM** (307,000 inhab.; alt. 95m) is situated in Baden-Württemberg on the opposite bank of the Rhine to Ludwigshafen, at its confluence with the River Neckar. Though an industrial town, Mannheim is decidedly attractive.

**Tourist information**: 1 Bahnhofplatz. Mannheim-Neuostheim **airport**. **Trains** link **boats** and **buses** take passengers to Ludwigshafen. Mannheim celebrates the Shrovetide Carnival, hosts a fair in May, the upper Rhine regatta in June and a Christmas market.

**History**: A fishing village existed here in the mid 8C, where in 1606 the Elector Friedrich IV decided to lay out a new town as a bulwark of this strategic position. Although the century saw much destruction of Friedrich's foundations, Mannheim was rebuilt—with the help of Huguenot and Walloon immigrants—in a totally regular fashion whose pattern remains to this day. Although Vauban personally led a French siege on Mannheim in 1689, the town was not ruined by the French wars. In 1720 the Elector Carl Philipp transferred his seat from Heidelberg to here. Early forms of the symphony were developed by the 18C Mannheim School of Composers, the best known of whom was Johann Stamitz, 1717-57. The first German national theatre was established at Mannheim in 1779 and three years later produced Schiller's 'Die Räuber' (Schiller lived in Mannheim 1783–85). Industrialisation began in the late 19C. The 'dandy-horse' bicycle was invented at Mannheim in 1817, and in 1886 Carl Benz demonstrated his first motor vehicle here. Mannheim boasts a massive inland harbour. In the bombardments of World War II the town was seriously damaged.

Leave the main railway station and walk left along **Bismarckstrasse** to reach the Baroque grand ducal Schloss, the **Kurfürstliches Residenzschloss**, 1720–60, one of the largest Baroque palaces in Germany. Its finest features are the great staircase, the knights hall, the Schloss library of 1755–57 and the church. Now used by the university, it fronts the Schloss garden, which stretches to the Rhine and was laid out in the English fashion in the early 19C by F.L. von Sckell. The Schloss can be visited except Mon 10.00–11.30, 15.00–16.30 from Apr–Oct, and from Nov–Dec at the same times on Sat and Sun.

Opposite the Kurfürstliches Residenzschloss stands the **Palais Bretzentheim**, 1782–88, built by P.A. von Verschaffelt and only partly restored after World War II and, further along Bismarckstrasse, the Baroque **Jesuitenkirche** of 1738–60 by Alessandro Galli-Bibiena of Bologna. Finished by F. Rabaliatti and P.A. von Vershaffelt, its dome fresco is by P.H. Brinckmann; a silver Madonna is by J.I. Saler, 1747; and the lovely organ case is by P. Egell. Next to the church is the **observatory** which F. Rabaliatti built between 1772 and 1774 on behalf of the court architect Christian Mayer.

Turn right here to reach the former arsenal of Mannheim, 1777–79, now the **Reiss Museum** documenting the history of the city and its art. As an annex to this museum Mannheim opened a new archaeological and ethnological museum in 1988, in residential block D5, both opening except Mon 10.00–13.00, 14.00–17.00. Turn right again and walk as far as the **Paradeplatz**, laid out in the 18C, with its pyramidical fountain by Gabriel Grupello, 1709–16. Turn left and walk as far as the **Marktplatz**, with its monument to the four elements, 1719, passing the former **Altes Rathaus**, joined by a communal tower with the **Untere Pfarrkirche**, 1701–23.

From here walk SE to **Friedrichsplatz**, with its illuminated fountains, Art Nouveau lamps and the Art Nouveau ('Jugendstil') square constructed in 1907, with a 50m-high cylindrical **Wasserturm** (1886–89), set by the Friedrichsplatz on a grassy terrace which covers the city reservoir. N of this square is the **Rosengarten** with Mannheim's **Kongresszentrum**. The **Städtische Kunsthalle**, or fine arts museum, at 9 Moltkestrasse, displays *19C and *20C painting and sculpture with works by Manet, Cézanne and Beckmann. Open Tue–Thu, Sat, Sun 10.00–13.00, 14.00–17.00 (Fri only 14.00–20.00) it stands to the S of Friedrichsplatz in a Jugendstil building by H. Billing, 1907, fronted by modern works of sculpture.

Follow Friedrichsring N to reach on the right **Goetheplatz**, with the **Nationaltheater** by Gerhard Weber, 1957, opposite the **Luisenpark**, where you are delighted by flamingos, a waterlily pond and a lake with boats topped with yellow canopies. The park covers 41 hectares and contains a 205m-high observation tower and restaurant. The shopping area of Planken, Breite Strasse, Kunstrasse and Fressgasse is pedestrianised and shaded with lime trees. A **Rhine–Neckar Navigation Museum** has been established in a former passenger steam boat, the 'Mainz', from the Rhine's White Fleet. It is moored near the Kurpfälzbrücke, and displays model ships and documents on the Rhine shipping trade (open daily except Mon 10.00–18.00). Mannheim's Planetarium at No. 1 Wilhelm-Varnholt-Allee has displays Tue 10.00 and 15.00, Wed–Fri 15.00 and 20.00, weekends 15.00, 17.00 and 19.00.

Cross the Rhine either by the Konrad-Adenauer Brücke or the KurtSchumacher Brücke to reach **Ludwigshafen** (see Rte 31) 1km W. From here take the B9 S to **Speyer** (see Rte 31). After 9km S the B9 meets the B272. Drive SW for 17km to join the B38 1km from Landau.

**Landau** (40,000 inhab.; alt. 146m), the main wine and tobacco centre of the lower Palatinate, grew from a village into a Free Imperial City in the 13C. Landau hosts a flower festival on the second Sun in Sept.

Much pillaged during the Thirty Years War, Landau passed into French hands in 1648. Vauban fortified the city in 1684. The Imperial forces vehemently attempted to regain Landau which nonetheless remained French throughout the 18C. Given in the 19C first to Austria and then to Bavaria, Landau grew beyond her fortifications, which were demolished in 1876. Of these remain the German Gate, with Louis XIV's motto 'Nec pluribus impar', and the French Gate (both Baroque, c 1690). In Stiftsplatz is a 13C church, close by the monument to Montclar, governor of Alsace (who died in 1690). In Königstrasse is the Gothic Augustinian church, 1407 (now the church of the Holy Cross), with late Gothic font, 1506; late 17C Madonna; 15C cloister; and 18C monastic buildings. In Max-Josef-Platz is the Luitpold fountain of 1892, close by the 14C chapel of St Katharina. The museum of local history, at 8 Marienring, opens weekdays except Mon 09.00–12.00, 14.00–16.00; Sun 10.00–12.30. Information office in the town hall; train links with Karlsruhe, Pirmasens, Saarbrücken and Zweibrücken; buses with Heidelberg, Pirmasens and Karlsruhe.

The B10 continues W through Godramstein and Siebeldingen, passing through the country of the Palatinate forest to reach after 14km **Annweiler** (7500 inhab.; alt. 183m), a health resort founded in the 12C by the Hohenstaufen, with a town hall of 1844; a Protestant church preserving its older bell tower; a Catholic church of 1869; and three medieval Schlösser on the **Trifels** mountain—three peaks c 500m, accessible by foot in an hour. The Hohenstaufen Schloss Trifels, sometime residence of the emperors, dates from the 12C, though it was destroyed in 1602 and rebuilt only in the 20C. Here in 1193 Heinrich VI imprisoned Richard Coeur de Lion, whom he had brought from Leopold of Austria and whom he later released for a ransom.

After 31km the B10 reaches **Pirmasens** (59,000 inhab.; alt. 183m), a town on three hills, once the home of the Landgrave of Hesse and today the centre of Germany's footwear industry, with a biennial footwear fair. The town bears the name of St Pirmin, who founded a monastery at Hornbach near here in the 8C (see below). Its Lutheran parish church was built in 1949. Its former town hall of 1717–74 now houses a shoe museum; open Thur 15.00–18.00 and Sun 10.00–13.00. The B10 runs 24km W through Höheischweiler to reach **Zweibrücken** (39,000 inhab.; alt. 266m; information office: 5 Herzogplatz) at the confluence of the Hornbach and the Schwarzbach. The centre of the town, reconstructed after World War II, comprises the late Gothic church of St Alexander, c 1500, with modern stained glass by Erhardt Klonk; the Herzogs' Schloss, built by the Swedish architect Jonas Erikson Sundahl, 1720–25; and the Karlskirche, which King Karl II of Sweden commissioned from Haquinus Schlang, 1708–11. To the E of the city is the Luitpold park and the famous Zweibrücken rose garden (open Apr–Oct 08.00–20.00). The 18C town exhibition centre in a late 18C building opens Sat 10.00–12.00. Also in Zweibrücken is a famous stud farm and the pheasantry, built by J.E. Sundahl, where the deposed King Stanislas Leczinki of Poland met King Charles XII of Sweden. Trains connect with Homburg, Karlsruhe and Saarbrücken, buses with Homburg and Pirmasens.

The environs of Zweibrücken include the village of **Hornbach**, 9km S, with the ruins of a Benedicine monastery and the grave of its founder, Pirmin. There is also a Pirmin memorial chapel of 1957.

# 33

# The Eifel Massif

## A.  Trier to Cologne

Total distance 176km. Trier—B51, 23km Bitburg—B257, 12km Kyllburg—30km
Schönecken—B51, 8km Prüm—36km Blankenheim—18km Bad Münstereifel—
13km Euskirchen—23km Brühl—13km Cologne.

The Eifel, a plateau dotted by volcanic remains, craters and lakes, has an
occasionally harsh climate, but is rendered charming by its gentle pastures
and thick forests. As part of the Ardennes, it stretches beyond Germany
into Belgium and France.

Leave **Trier** (see Rte 27) by the Kaiser-Wilhelm bridge over the Mosel and
travel through wooded country 23km NW to **Bitburg** (12,000 inhab.; alt.
338m), once a Roman military station (*Beda Vicus*; the B51 follows the old
Roman road from Trier to Cologne) and before that a Celtic settlement.
Almost completely destroyed in World War II, Bitburg retains the Coben
tower from its Roman wall, some 40m of which also remains, the 15C late
Gothic church of Our Lady—its south aisle built in the 16C, the north aisle
in the 19C—and the 16C Kobenhof. The beer fountain honours the town's
celebrated Pils. Information office at 6 Hubert-Prim-Strasse.

From Bitburg take the B257 NE for an **excursion** of 10km, to turn left at
the crossroads for **Kyllburg** (1400 inhab.; alt. 271m), a health resort in the
Kyll valley, though beguilingly situated on the wooded promontory. Its
attractions include the keep of the old Schloss, built for Archbishop Theodor
of Trier on the Malberg; the late 13C Franciscan monastery church of Our
Lady, with Renaissance *stained glass of 1534 in the choir, a Gothic cloister
and a 14C chapter house; and a 20m-high column of Our Lady. On the main
route, drive W and then N from Bitburg for 30km, crossing the Kyll at Erdorf
and passing through Nattenheim, nearby which is the Roman *villa rustica*
at **Otrang**, with a mosaic pavement, baths and a small museum, to
Schönecken on the B51. Here rise the ruins of 13C **Burg Schönecken**. The
B51 continues N to reach after 8km the health and winter sports resort of
*Prüm** (5700 inhab.; alt. 425m). Prüm has a Benedictine abbey, founded
721, today a school, whose present buildings are by Balthasar Neumann
and J.G. Seitz, 1748–65, and an abbey church, the Salvatorbasilika, by
Johann Georg Judas, which has a Baroque façade and a Gothic interior,
housing a Renaissance pulpit, a Baroque high altar and choir stalls, and the
tomb of the Emperor Lothar I, who died in 855. From Prüm the B265 leads
to the Belgian border.

21km further N along the B51 stands the medieval village and resort of
**Stadtkyll**, with the remains of its fortifications. After another 15km the route
reaches charming **Blankenheim** (7500 inhab.; alt. 497m), lying at the foot
of its rebuilt 13C Schloss (now a youth hostel) and near the source of the
River Ahr. Its Gothic parish church dates from 1495–1501, and the town has
pretty 17C half-timbered houses. Follow the B51 18km NE to the walled
spa (mud baths) of *Bad Münstereifel** (16,000 inhab; alt. 280m) on the River

Erft. Attracting many visitors in the tourist season, the town has an 11C Romanesque parish church (SS Chrysanthus and Darius), with a 9C crypt, a 13C dome, medieval tombs, a font of 1619, a 14C Madonna and a tabernacle by F. Roir, 1480. The Windeckhaus of 1644 stands on Klosterplatz. The spa has a 14C and 16C Gothic town hall. Its former Jesuit school is the oldest school in the Rhineland, with a collection of 18,000 schoolbooks. Bad Münstereifel is also defended by four medieval gates and 17 towers along the 13C walls. The local history museum is in a 12C Romanesque house (open May–Oct Tue–Sat 14.00–17.00; in winter Sat 14.00–16.00), said to have been built in 1167. The town hall is a Gothic building dating from the 14C to the 16C.

*At Brühl near Cologne, Schloss Augustusburg is graced by this monumental staircase, designed by Balthasar Neumann in the 1740s, with 1780 frescoes by Carlo Carlone and magical mid 18C stuccos*

At Iversheim, 4km N along the B51, is a Roman lime-kiln with six ovens (visits Sun in summer, 10.00–17.00). The next village, **Kreuzweingarten**, is the site of a Roman villa with excavated mosaic pavements and baths. An **excursion** E to **Billig** reveals the 80km-long Roman canal which brought water to the city of Cologne. 9km N of Iversheim the route reaches the woollen manufacturing town of **Euskirchen** (44,000 inhab.; alt. 165m), a 14C town hall; the church of St Martin, part-12C Romanesque and part-14C Gothic; and remains of the 13C walls. Continue N through Weilerswist to reach after 23km Brühl, by way of '**Phantasialand**', just S of Brühl, 30,000 sq m of fantasy, including a model of Berlin at the time of the Belle Époque, a circus, a 'western express', a pirate ship, a marionette theatre, restaurants and bars, and by way of the **Naturpark Kottenforst-Ville**. At **Brühl** (44,000 inhab.; alt. 65m) stands the Rococo \*Schloss Augustusburg, by Konrad Schlaun, 1725, its interiors by the French architect François Cuvilliés, 1728–40, its staircase by Balthasar Neumann, 1740–48. In the park, designed by Le Nôtre's pupil Dominique Girard, stands the hunting lodge Falkenlust, by Cuvilliés, 1729–40. The Gothic Schloss church of 1493 has a Baroque interior, of 1740–57, with a high altar by Neumann, 1745, as well as bronze doors by Elmar Hillebrand. Open daily (except Dec, Jan) 09.00–12.00, 14.00–16.00.

Brühl lies 13km S of **Cologne** (Köln) (see Rte 43).

# B.   Aachen to Koblenz

Total distance 167km. Aachen—B258, 9km Kornelimünster—25km Monschau—26km Schleiden—20km Blankenheim—32km Nürburgring—26km Mayen—29km Koblenz.

Superb \*\***AACHEN** (243,000 inhab.; alt. 125m), in French Aix-la-Chapelle, stands on the borders of Holland, France and Germany and was known to the Romans as *Aquis Granum*. The city is renowned for its chocolates as well as its textiles, for its jams as well as its pâtés, for its horse races and above all for its cathedral.

**Main railway station, post office**: Bahnhofplatz; **tourist offices**: 4 Bahnhofplatz, Atrium Elisenbrunnen, Friedrich-Wilhelm-Platz. **Trains** and **buses** link Aachen with Cologne and thus with the rest of Germany.

**History**. The 'Granum' of the Roman name derives from a Celtic god. The Romans relished the town as a spa. Here Pepin the Short (714–68) established his court, and his son Charlemagne made the city capital of his empire, and after his death his collection of saintly relics attracted countless pilgrims At Aachen 30 Holy Roman Emperors were crowned. After the Reformation the city was frequently at odds with the emperor. A fire destroyed most of the old city in 1656, hence the Baroque nature of much of its present-day architecture. The War of the Spanish Succession was ended by treaty here in 1748. Aachen ceased to be a Free Imperial City in 1794. The city became part of Prussia in 1815. In 1818 the Tsar, the Austrian emperor and the King of Prussia met at Aachen to set up the Holy Alliance. A bishopric was established here, 1802–21, and again in 1930. Eighty per cent of the city was seriously damaged in World War II.

From the main railway station walk NW along Mirtelstrasse to the **Marienplatz** and the neo-Gothic church of Our Lady, the **Marienkirche**. Take Ullstrasse left of the church to reach the **Marschiertor**, from the 13C walls. Turn right to walk along Franzstrasse and Kleinmarschierstrasse to reach

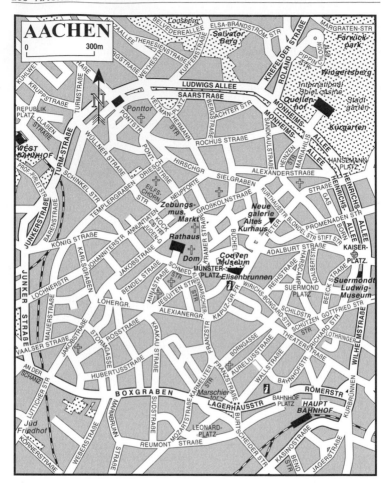

**Münsterplatz** and the cathedral. Aachen *Dom is built in two distinctly different styles: the octagonal rotunda surrounded by a double-storeyed ambulatory of 16 sides, which Odo of Metz constructed in the Byzantine style between 796 and 805 (which was the chapel of Charlemagne's palace), and the Gothic choir, 1355–1414. Around these are chapels dating from the 14C and 15C, the finest being the *Anna chapel of 1449 and the *Hungarian chapel of 1767 on the south side, a gift of the King of Hungary in 1367, redone in the classical style. The rotunda was given its gables in the 13C and the dome was built after the fire of 1656. The base of the bell tower is Carolingian, the upper part 19C. To the cathedral is attached the cloister of 1500 which replaced the previous Romanesque building. The main dorway, the bronze Wolfstür, dates from 800, and is set in a Baroque porch.

   **Interior**. In the entrance hall the she-wolf, a Celtic goddess, dates from c 160 and the bronze pineapple from c 400. The eight pillars came originally from Ravenna, though they were partly renewed in 1854 and all the capitals are reconstructed. Salviati's mosaic on the vault, depicting Christ surrounded by the 24 elders of the Apocalypse, was completed by Schaper in 1902. The great *candelabrum was made in 1165 for the Emperor Friedrich Barbarossa as an idealised model of the heavenly Jerusalem. Charlemagne's bones were exhumed after his beatification in 1165 and in 1215 placed in the superb *reliquary on the high altar. The retable, the ***Pala d'Oro, modelled on that in St Mark's, Venice, was given by Otto III c 1020. The copper-gilt *pulpit was given by Heinrich II c 1101. Charlemagne's former 2C sarcophagus, decorated with the figure of Proserpine, is also here (in the chapel of St Michael), as is his white marble throne, restored 1889. The altar in the 14C chapel of St Nikolaus dates from 1962, the font from the 12C. The **Schatzkammer** (open daily, 09.00–13.00, 14.00–17.00) contains numerous *reliquaries, including the Lothar cross of c 1000, the Marienschrein of 1238 and Charlemagne's reliquary bust of 1349, along with a remarkable number of dubiously authentic relics.

In Krämerstrasse, opposite the cathedral apse, is the church of **St Foillan**, 1657–67. NE of the church is the triangular square known as Hof, where Roman baths were discovered in the 1960s. The Mais Hof (No. 1), with its pointed gable, dates from 1658. At the corner of the Hof and Rommelsgasse the Haus Zum Lindenbaum has a lower storey built in the 17C and an upper built in the 19C. At the corner of the Hof and Krämerstrasse gushes the puppet fountain (Puppenbrunnen), created by Bonifatius Stirnberg in 1975. S of the cathedral across Urselinerstrasse is **Friedrich-Wilhelm-Platz**, in which stands the classical **Elisenbrunnen**, a fountain designed by Karl Friedrich Schinkel, 1825. N of the cathedral is the **Marktplatz**, where Aachen **Rathaus**—almost totally destroyed in 1944 and since reconstructed—was built in 1349 on the base of Charlemagne's palace, of which the Granus tower and the Mark tower remain. On the façade are depicted Pope Leo III and Charlemagne kneeling before Christ. Inside, in the Reichsaal, are five important historical frescoes (out of eight before World War II) by Alfred Rethel, 1816–59. The five have been restored, the rest lost irretrievably. The bronze doors are by the Aachen-born Ewald Mataré, 1965.

NW of Marktplatz at 13 Pontstrasse is the **Internationales Zeitungs-museum** (open weekdays 08.00–13.00 and 14.00–17.00), with a collection of some 120,000 newspapers, not far from the house (No. 177) where Paul Julius von Reuter established his news agency. Grosskölnstrasse leads NE from Marktplatz to pass the restored Gothic church of **St Nikolaus** and turn right into Komphausbadstrasse in which stands the **Altes Kurhaus** of 1782, restored with the addition of an art gallery, 1969. From here walk N along Komphausbadstrasse and Sandkaulstrasse to reach Quellenhof. Turning right here leads into Monheimsallee, on which is the **Neue Kurhaus** in a park stretching to the foot of the Wingertsberg and housing also the congress hall with its casino. The route right continues through **Hanse-mannplatz**, with its monument to David Hansemann, 1888, and S along **Heinrichsallee**, with an equestrian statue of Friedrich III by Lederer, 1911, to reach the church of **St Adalbert**, built by Otto III c 1000 and entirely restored 1873–76.

Turning left instead of right at the Quellenhof takes you into Ludwigs-allee. N on the Salvatorberg is the restored church of **St Salvator**, founded by Louis the Pious and built 814–40. Ludwigsallee leads W to the **Marientor** and a gate, both part of the 14C city walls.

MUSEUMS: **Couven Museum** (architecture, pottery, furniture, from the Baroque to the Biedermeier periods, and a pharmacy dating from 1788, at 17 Hühnermarkt); **Neue Galerie** (modern art, at 19 Komphausbadstrasse); **Suermondt-Ludwig Museum** (art and sculpture since the 14C, including Dutch and Flemish works, in a Renaissance building at 18 Wilhelmstrasse); **local history museum** (at 68 Rehmannstrasse), all open weekdays, except Mon, 10.00–17.00; weekends 10.00–13.00.

THEATRES: City theatre by J.P. Cremer, and K.F. Schinkel, 1825, rebuilt 1900, at 3 Friedrich-Wilhelm-Platz, close by the Grenzlandtheater, at Nos 5–6.

The B258 runs S from Aachen through Brand to entrancing **Kornelimünster** (2700 inhab.; alt. 225m), where you can visit the monastery and church of St Salvator, founded in 814, destroyed by the Normans and by a fire of 1310 and replaced by the present Baroque buildings in 1728. In the Corneliuskapelle is the reliquary of Pope Cornelius (Pope 251–53) from whom the village takes its name.

The route continues through Belgium for 6km, passing the 650m-high Hohes Venn and reaching picturesque **Monschau** (French Montjoie; 11,800 inhab.; alt. 350, rising to 650m) after 25km. Tourist information is at 1 Stadtstrasse; trains connect with Aachen. The ruined medieval Burg, partly rebuilt 1899—with its keep, knights' hall, 16C asses' tower, or Eselsturm, and the Batterie tower—dominates the town, which also has half-timbered houses, and the former town hall of 1654. Monschau's Baroque Rotes Haus, 1765, belonged to Johann Heinrich Scheibler, founder of the Monschau silk industry, and is now a museum, with a Rococo interior (open except Mon 10.00–12.00 and 14.00–17.00). Other delights are the Haus Troistorff, 1783; the parish church of Mariä Geburt, 1649; and the church of St Maria, which belonged to a former monastery, 1726–50.

At Monschau the B258 turns E and runs for 26km to the health resort of **Schleiden** (12,500 inhab.; alt. 350) in the Ettelscheid valley. Its Schloss was frequently rebuilt on a Romanesque original, and the town preserves a fine late Gothic Schloss church, with the Renaissance tomb of Sybille von Hohenzollern and early Renaissance *stained glass of 1525. Its organ case of 1770 was designed by Ludwig König. Close by, the River Ruhr has been damned for hydro-electricity, creating a large artificial lake.

The route now passes through the Schleidener forest, reaching **Blankenheim** (see Rte 33A) after 20km. 32km further SE the B258 reaches the 29km long **Nürburgring** motor racing circuit, set around the health and ski resort of **Nürburg** with its ruined Schloss. The route passes close beside the actual circuit, continuing through the village of **Virneburg** (406 inhab.; alt. 420m), with its 11C Schloss ruined by the French in 1689, its chapel of 1697 and its thatched tithe barn, to reach after 26km **Mayen** (22,000 inhab.; alt. 230m), which the Romans called *Megina* and the Celts *magos* (which means 'plain'). Situated in the valley of the Nette at the foot of the 528m Hochsimmer, Mayen is dominated by Schloss Genoveveburg, 1280, partly ruined by fire in 1891 and rebuilt in 1893, with a Golo tower 32m high. It now houses the Eifeler Landschaftsmuseum (open except Mon 09.00–12.00, 14.00–17.00; Sun 10.00–13.00). At either end of the town stand the Brücken gate and the Ober gate, all that remain of the 14C walls. Marktstrasse leads from the Brückentor to the 14C Gothic church of St Clemens, with a Romanesque south tower and a curiously twisted north spire. Continue along Marktstrasse to the former town hall, 1717, in the Marktplatz (Information Office). Trains connect Mayen with Andernach,

Daun and Koblenz. 4.5km NW, at the meeting point of the Nette, Nitz, Welchenbach and Fraubach valleys, stands **Schloss Bürresheim**, 15C to 17C.

The B258 now passes through **Bassenheim**, with a Schloss of 1614, and the sandstone relief of the 'Bassenheim rider', c 1240, in the parish church, to reach **Koblenz** (see Rte 29) by the suburb of Lützel.

# C. Bonn to Bad Tönisstein via Kelberg and Maria Laach

Total distance 224km. Bonn—B9, 21km Remagen—B266, 9km Bad Neuenahr-Ahrweiler—18km Altenahr—B257, 21km Adenau—8km Nürburgring—17km Kelberg—18km Ulmen—B259, 13km Kaiseresch—10km Monreal—30km Burg Eltz—6km Münstermaifeld—B258 and B256, 44km Maria Laach—9km Bad Tönisstein.

Leave **Bonn** (see Rte 41) and travel on the B9 for 21km S to **Remagen**: for this stretch of the route see Rte 42. 3km S of Remagen the B266 leads right (W) into the Ahr valley. 2km W along the B266 lies the spa of Bodendorf, and after another 7km, by way of the ruined Schloss Landskron and the mineral springs of Apollinaris, the thermal resort of **Bad Neuenahr-Ahrweiler** (28,000 inhab.; alt. 84m), which boasts Germany's biggest Casino and straddles the River Ahr. Information offices: 24 Wilhelmstrasse, 60 Hauptstrasse. Train connections with Bonn, buses with Bonn and Remagen.

In the district of Bad Neuenahr is the church of St Willibrord, founded in 990, with today a Romanesque west tower c 1200, and the Baroque Beethovenhaus, where Ludwig van Beethoven spent his holidays between 1786 and 1792. The l600m-long, 7m-high walls of Ahrweiler were built from the mid 13C to the 15C, and incorporate the Ahrtor, with a 16C relief of the crucifixion, and the Niedertor, with a relief c 1500 of the scourging of Christ. Two medieval cannons guard the Kanonen tower. The Weiss Turm houses the Ahrgau Museum (open in summer Tue, Fri 10.00–12.00, 14.00–18.00, Sun 10.00–12.00). The 13C church of St Laurentius has 14C wall paintings. S of the walls, along Kalvarienbergstrasse, is the 15C Ursuline monastery. The region is noted for its red wines and Bad Neuenahr-Ahrweiler has a wine museum at 86 Himmelsburgerstrasse (open Sun 10.00–12.00, Wed 14.00–19.30).

After 8km the route reaches **Walporzheim**, long noted for its wines and its Kelterhaus (winepress house) of 1717, and then winds through vineyards and the wine villages of Dernau and Mayschoss (with a ruined Schloss) to reach after 10km **Altenahr** (2350 inhab.; alt. 170m), a centre of walking and hiking, especially to Burg Kreuzberg. Built in 1340, destroyed by the French in 1686, and rebuilt in 1760 with a chapel of 1738, this is reached also by the B257 from Altenahr. There are half-timbered houses in Kreuzberg itself. Burg Are above Altenahr, was built around 1100 and destroyed by French soldiers in 1690. Altenahr retains three gates of its old walls, and a Romanesque church, c 1170, with an early 14C Gothic choir.

Continue S along the B257 to **Adenau** (3300 inhab.; alt. 297m), the main town for visitors to the Nürburgring (see Rte 33B) and lying 21km from Altenahr. Adenau has 15C and 16C half-timbered houses in the Marktplatz, and its parish church is an early 13C basilica. From here the route continues for 9km S to the health and sports resort of **Kelberg** (1500 inhab.; alt. 488m), where four small rivers rise (the Elz, the Lieser, the Trierbach and the Üb). Kelberg's finest monument is its Romanesque-Gothic church, with a 15C crucifix and a 16C resurrection.

18km S lies **Ulmen** (inhab. 10,000; alt. 436m) with the ruins of a 12C Schloss. Its new church, on a peak near the crater of an extinct volcano, incorporates an older tower, the tomb of Philipp Haust (d. 1556), a Gothic tabernacle and a Baroque Lady altar. From Ulmen follow the B259 SE and then turn NE for 13km to Kaisersesch, 10km due N of which lies **Monreal**, whose ruined, walled burg was despoiled both by the Swedes in 1622 and by the French in 1689. Nearby are the remains of a Gothic chapel on the Burgberg. A Gothic cross stands in the village, along with a Baroque monument to St Johann Nepomuk and half-timbered houses.

30km SE of Monreal, by a picturesquely twisting route through Düngenheim, Kaifenheim and Pyrmont, you reach **Burg Eltz**, 12C to 16C, restored after a fire of 1920. From here the route leads 6km NE to **Münstermaifeld** (2700 inhab.; alt. 271m), with the former monastery church of St Martin and Severus, finished 1332, with a later Gothic tower. Inside are 12C to 14C wall paintings and the 14C sculpted south doorway is notable. Return to Monreal and drive 29km N and left along the B258, to turn right along the B256 in order to reach (15km) the Benedictine abbey of *Maria Laach*.

Founded in 1093 by the Count Palatine Heinrich II and secularised in 1802, home of the Jesuits from 1863–73, Maria Laach has been restored by the Benedictines and remains a reputed spiritual and liturgical centre. Its Carolingian church was begun in the early 11C, intended with its two central and four side towers to symbolise architecturally the heavenly Jerusalem. The abbey was consecrated in 1156 but not finished until c 1220, and the portico was added in 1225; yet the whole building is harmoniously Romanesque, with friezes and pilasters as well as paint enhancing its decoration. The west choir houses the 13C tomb of the founder. The church's 'paradise' doorway symbolises the Garden of Eden. A late Romanesque canopy shelters the high altar. Maria Laach lies close by the Peeil Edge, a geological fault running along the Maas valley. Here, however, the overnight earthquake of 13/14 April 1992 merely set the monastery's bells ringing.

The nearby lake, Laacher See, was formed by prehistoric volcanic activity, when a mountain exploded: pumice and rock from the site was blown 640km to be discovered as far away as the region of Berlin. The resultant crater has a circumference of 8km and is in parts 53m deep. 9km NE of Maria Laach is the spa of **Bad Tönisstein**, with a ruined Carmelite monastery. The spa lies just E of Burgbrohl, whose name derives from the 11C Schloss, rebuilt in the 18C, and 1.5km from Schweppenburg, guarded by the 17C Schloss Schweppenburg.

# V  HESSE

# 34

# The Rhön in Hesse: Fulda to Bad Kissingen

Total distance 138km. Fulda (and environs)—2km Petersberg—6km Adolph-seck—B27, 13km Hünfeld—B278, 28km Tann—B278 and B284, 23km Wasserkuppe—15km Gersfeld—7km Bischofsheim—28km Bad Neustadt—12km Münnerstadt—22km Bad Kissingen.

**Environs of Fulda**. Petersbergerstrasse passes through the Peters gate and leads 2km NE to the 508m-high **Petersberg**, on which is built the former Benedictine monastery of SS Peter and Lioba, founded by Abbot Raban Maur in the late 8C. Its Carolingian crypt derives from the original church, with wall paintings, 836–47, and the sarcophagus of Boniface's companion St Lioba. The main building dates from 1479, though its portal was added in 1685, and houses 12C tombstones, including one sculpted with representations of Boniface with Charlemagne and Pepin the Short.

6km S of Fulda is **Schloss Fasanerie**, built by A. Gallasini, 1730–50, as the summer residence of the prince-bishops and now a museum (see Rte 12). S and E of Fulda stretches the **Rhön**, the vast remains of an extinct volcano, offering superb opportunities for hang-gliding. Forty thousand hectares of the region—around the health resort of Bad Brückenau, 33km S of Fulda along the B27, also easily reached by the Fulda–Würzburg motorway—has been designated the Hesse natural park, with prehistoric Bronze Age graves, marked access for cars and marked hiking and walking routes.

From **Fulda** (see Rte 12) the B27 runs N for 13km to **Hünfeld** (7500 inhab.; alt. 279m), the 'gateway to the Rhön', much of whose previous architectural history disappeared in a fire of 1888, but whose fine surrounding country-side still attracts many visitors. Hünfeld has the late Gothic hall-church of St Jakobus, with a three-storey Romanesque tower and a late Gothic font of 1496. 3km SE of Hünfeld is **Mackenzell**, with a round-towered Schloss, the Wasserburg, begun in 1253 by Abbot Philipp IV von Erthal.

The B278 continues SE, before turning NE to reach after 25km **Tann** (5300 inhab.; alt. 381m). Here a Baroque fountain of 1686 fronts the red, blue and yellow Schlösser (respectively 1558, 1574 and 1714); the picturesque town gate of 1557 is built of stone and brick and flanked by two round towers with cupolas topped by slender spires; the town is enhanced by half-tim-bered houses, especially in the Marktplatz, with its fountain of 1710. Tann also has the Baroque cemetery church of St Nikolaus, and the Museumsdorf Tann, with its typical regional houses. From Tann drive due S for 18km to Wüstensachsen, passing on the way the powerful ruined Auersburg, 1354, 3km N of Hilders. At Wüstensachsen turn right along the high Rhön ring, the B284, to reach after 5km the health resort of **Wasserkuppe**, with marked hiking routes, and at 950m (*panorama) the highest peak of the Rhön and a major hang-gliding centre. Its aviation memorial and gliding museum are open from May–Oct daily 09.00–18.00.

The route continues W for 15km to Poppenhausen, and the ruins of Schloss Ebersburg, and then E along the B279 to **Gersfeld** (5400 inhab.; alt. 500m), the most popular tourist centre of this region, its charms including thermal springs and mud baths; a Baroque parish church, with a pulpit and organ of 1787 by Johann Michael Wagner; and an 18C Baroque Schloss, with a stucco Festsaal, 1765—now the local history museum (open Wed, Sat 15.00–16.00); marked walks; and a reserve of water birds.

**Bischofsheim** lies 7km SE of Gersfeld, its Renaissance church with a 13C tower. 3km W is the ruined **Osterburg**, while 8km SW rises the 925m-high **Kreuzberg**, a place of pilgrimage whose Franciscan monastery of 1644 has a Baroque church. 28km SE of Bischofsheim you reach the spa of **Bad Neustadt**, situated on the River Saale, surrounded by 13C fortifications, including the 16C *Hohn gate. Inside its Gothic Carmelite convent church is Rococo decoration and an organ of 1732 by Johann Ignaz Samuel Will. The Salzburg fortress retains its curtain wall, a well in its courtyard and the façade of its Gothic palace.

**Münnerstadt** is 12km S, three tower-gates remaining from the walls thrown around it in 1250. Here the Rathaus of 1460 is set on a market hall, while the 13C parish church has a superb *altar of Mary Magdalen by Tilman Riemenschneider, with wings by Veit Stoss, 1490–92. The 18C tithe barn once collected dues for the prince-bishops. The town is overshadowed by the four-winged Schloss of the Teutonic Knights, 13C, 16C and 17C, which now serves as the local history museum, with works by *Veit Stoss (closed Mon). Look out for the Gothic, half-timbered Frühmessmerhaus, with representations of Adam and Eve, 1627.

22km SW the route ends at the spa of **Bad Kissingen**, frequented in the 19C by such European aristocracy as Tsar Alexander II, Ludwig II of Bavaria, Tolstoy and the Empress Elisabeth of Austria. The former Rathaus dates from 1577; the present Rathaus in the Heussleinschen Schloss of 1709; the Jakobikirche was built in 1775.

# 35

# Frankfurt am Main to Heidelberg

## A.  Frankfurt am Main

**FRANKFURT** (634.000 inhab.; alt. 88–212m), on the right bank of the River Main in a large plain bounded by the Taunus Mountains (though its 32 suburbs stretch for 222 sq km on either side of the river), is the commercial centre of western Germany and—because of its trade and banking activities—one of the richest cities in the land, dubbed by some little Chicago, Manhattan and Bankfurt. Since much of the city centre, including some 2000 medieval houses, was razed during World War II, Frankfurt has been rebuilt in a determinedly modern fashion. Apart from housing enormous trade fairs (some 30 a year, with 2.6 million visitors), the city specialises in chemical products, skilled engineering and the electrical industry. It boasts 12 museums, 16 theatres and more than 40 art galleries. There is a race course at Niederad and a swimming stadium seating 90,000 spectators. An underground railway system was set up in 1968.

**Main railway station** (Europe's largest, with 260,000 daily passengers): Am Haupt-bahnhof (with a **post office** and an **information office** facing platform 23). The **main tourist office** is at 52 Kaiserstrasse, with another at 27 Römerberg and a third opposite track 23 at the main railway station. **Main post office**: Grosse Eschenheimer Strasse.

**Bus and rail services** connect with all parts of western Germany; in summer **boats** ply between St Goarshausen, Mainz and Cologne. With 312,000 flights a year and a through-put of over 29 million passengers, the **Rhein-Main Airport** is amongst the busiest in Europe, and is situated ten minutes SW, by the S exit to the motorway. The opening of Terminal Two in October 1994 was designed to raise the airport's annual capacity to around 44 million passengers. An S-Bahn and buses commute from the airport to central Frankfurt, a journey of some 11 minutes. **Motorways** connect with Hamburg, Würzburg, Cologne and Basel. For its own passengers Lufthansa operates an 'Airport Express' to Düsseldorf airport, calling in between at the main railway stations of Bonn, Cologne and Düsseldorf. The same Express also serves Stuttgart to the S. Other air travellers can buy tickets from Deutsche Bundesbahn bureaus to utilise the 'Rail and Fly' service. Transport in the city itself is by U-Bahn, S-Bahn, streetcars and buses.

**History.** Frankfurt is first recorded in the late 8C as Franconofurd (i.e. Ford of the Franks), on the site of a Bronze Age settlement where the Romans had established the castrum Heddernheim. In 1794 a conference of Imperial leaders was called here by Charlemagne, who also established a fair. Louis the Pious built a new palace here in 822 and the city prospered throughout the 9C. Most German sovereigns, from Frederick Barbarossa in 1152, were chosen here. The citizens bridged the Main in 1222. In 1356 the 'Golden Bull' of Charles IV confirmed the city as the permanent seat of such elections. From 1562 the sovereigns were crowned here. Frederick II granted an Autumn Fair in 1240; its Easter Fair was granted in 1330. By the 14C the citizens were emancipating themselves from royal sovereignty, and by the 16C Frankfurt was recognised as a Free Imperial City. Here in the mid 15C worked the printer Johannes Geinsfliesch, better known as Gutenberg.

Frankfurt opted for Lutheranism in 1535. Trading, at home and abroad, increased its wealth. From 1752–63 the French occupied the city. Until the end of the 18C the city was the centre of the German book trade—hence in part its famous 'Buchmesse' today (see below). When the empire was dissolved in 1806 Napoleon gave Frankfurt to the primate of the Confederation of the Rhine, Karl Theodor von Dahlberg. Its 12C fortifications were razed and replaced with pleasant plantations (the 'Anlagen'), so that the city centre is now encircled in a 5km green ring of public parks.

In 1810 the city became capital of the Grand Duchy of Frankfurt and in 1815 one of the four free cities of the German Confederation, as well as the seat of the Diet. The first German parliament met in the Paulskirche in 1848–49. In 1866 the city was incorporated into Prussia, in spite of a vigorous attempt to stave off the annexation. Here the peace treaty between France and Prussia was signed in 1871. The Johann-Wolfgang-Goethe University was founded in 1914, and Rebstock Airport built four years later. During the Hitler Reich most of Frankfurt's Jewish community, which had included the Rothschilds and Anne Frank (born here 12 June 1929, died Belsen 1945), was exterminated. After World War II the German publishing industry made the city its main centre, hence the celebrated annual Book Fair held in the 36-hectare exhibition site near the main railway station, and the fact that the Deutsche Bibliothek, at 4–8 Zeppelinallee, is Germany's main library.

When the large German banks, which had been divided into regional entities at the end of World War II, were allowed to regroup after 1957, the Bundesbank was sited in Frankfurt am Main. In consequence Frankfurt has developed into the most powerful banking centre in Germany. More than any other building, the twin glass and steel towers of the Deutsche Bank, the country's largest, dominate the city—both

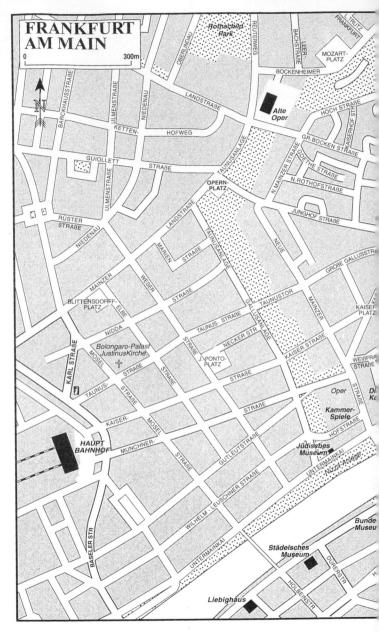

## FRANKFURT AM MAIN

0        300m

Rothschild Park

Alte Oper

OPERN-PLATZ

OBERLINDAU

REUTERSWEG

TRUTZ FRANKFURT

LEER

BACHSTRAßE

MOZART-PLATZ

BOCKENHEIMER

HOCH STRAßE

KAISERHOF

LANDSTRAßE

BARCKHAUSSTRAßE

ULMENSTRAßE

NIEDENAU

KETTEN-

HOFWEG

GR BOCKEN STRAßE

N. MAINZER STRAßE

GOETHE STRAßE

N. ROTHOFSTRAßE

GUIOLLETT STRAßE

ULMENSTRAßE

JUNGHOF STRAßE

RÜSTER STRAßE

NIEDENAU

LANDSTRAßE

MARIEN STRAßE

TAUNUSANLAGE

NEUE

GROßE GALLUSSTR

MAINZER

WESER STRAßE

BLITTERSDORFF-PLATZ

ELBE

NIDDA

STRAßE

TAUNUS- STRAßE

GR TAUNUSTOR

GALLUSANLAGE

MAINZER

KAISER-PLATZ

Bolongaro-Palast
JustinusKirche

KARL STRAßE

MOSEL

STRAßE

NECKER STR.

J. PONTO-PLATZ

KAISER STRAßE

WEIßFRA STRAßE

TAUNUS- STRAßE

STRAßE

STRAßE

Oper

Di Ko

STRAßE

Kammer-Spiele

HOFالسTR

KAISER-

MOSEL

MÜNCHNER-

HAUPT BAHNHOF

Jüdisches Museum

UNTERMAINKAI

Nizza-Anlage

STRAßE

GUTLEUTSTRAßE

Bunde Museu

BASELER STR

WILHELM- LEUSCHNER STRAßE

UNTERMAINKAI

Städelsches Museum

DÜRERSTR

HOLBEINSTR

Liebighaus

---

symbolically and architecturally. Scarcely less visible are the profiles of the two other large German banks, the Commerzbank and the Dresdner Bank, whose tower rises from Jürgen-Ponto-Platz, renamed after terrorists assassinated Jürgen Ponto, chairman of the bank, in 1977. The glass cupola of the Frankfurt stock exchange oversaw a rise in daily dealings in bonds and stocks from 0.2 billion DM in 1980 to nearly 10 billion a decade later. Although there are regional stock exchanges in Munich, Hamburg,

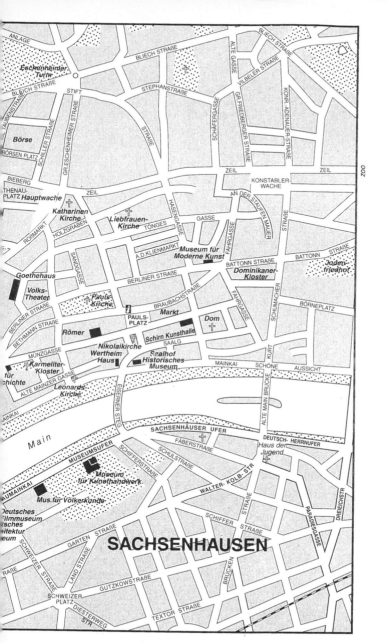

Hanover, Stuttgart, Bremen and Düsseldorf, only the last in any way compares in importance with that of Frankfurt, dealing with around a quarter of the total stock exchange trade, while Frankfurt accounts for nearly three-quarters.

Goethe was born at Frankfurt on 18 August 1749 and recorded in his literary autobiography, 'Dichtung und Wahrheit', how as a young man he loved to walk along the great bridge over the Main, 'watching the arrival of the market boats, from which you could see disembark such varied cargoes and sometimes such extraordinary people'. The philosopher Artur Schopenhauer (1788–1860) moved here from Danzig in 1831. On 26 October 1861 Philipp Reis demonstrated a battery-operated telephone before the Frankfurt physics association. Heinrich Hoffmann (1809–94, creator of Struwwelpeter) and the composer Engelbert Humperdinck (1854–1921) were neighbours in apartments at 95 Grünebergweg in the late 19C. The composer Paul Hindemith, born at Hanau in 1895, died here on 28 December 1968.

Walk SE from the main railway station (built 1883–88) along Wiesenhüttenstrasse to the river and turn left along Untermainkai, passing the Untermainbrücke to reach the initially three-aisled **Leonhardskirche**, which was founded in 1219, from which era date its two Romanesque towers and a Romanesque doorway (now inside, in the north wall). Most of the present church was built between the 13C and the 15C, and two more aisles were added between 1507 and 1536. The choir was completed in 1430, its tracery by Madern Gerthener, the nave in 1500–20. The baptismal chapel (left of the choir) has a window of 1435 and·*hanging vaulting, while Hans Holbein's Last Supper hangs in the north aisle. On the north side is an open-air pulpit. This church was initially dedicated to the Virigin Mary and St George, until it was given a relic of St Leonard in 1323. On the west portal is a stone Madonna of·1395, the original now displayed in the city's Historisches Museum.

W of the church, in Münzgasse, is the **Karmeliterkloster**, founded in 1246, built from the 13C to the 15C, ruined in World War II, restored in 1955–57 and in the 1980s. Its frescoes in the cloister and refectory by Jörg Ratgeb, 1514–23, depict in the refectory the lives of the prophets Elijah and Elias and the history of the Carmelite order (including their persecution by the Saracens) and in the cloister the life of Jesus, beginning with the Annunciation and ending with the Last Judgment. The refectory now contains part of Frankfurt's **Museum für Vor- und Frühgeschichte**, the rest at 1 Karmelitergasse, with finds from the Stone Age, Bronze Age amd Iron Age, especially the accoutrements of an Iron Age warrior. Roman age finds are displayed in the nave of the church, and exhibits from the early Middle Ages in the chapel of St Anne (open Tue–Sun 10.00–17.00, open Wed to 20.00).

E of the church is the 13th and 14C Gothic Cathedral (so-called, though never the seat of a bishop) of **St Bartholomäus**, where from 1356 the German Emperors were elected and where between 1562 and 1792 they were crowned. Rising from Carolingian foundations, begun 852 and restored 1882 and 1950, its principal architect was Madern Gerthener. The transepts, which make the shape of this cathedral a symmetrical cross, were beguin in 1348. The 94.75m-high Gothic *tower was begun in 1415 and finished in 1510, apart from its lantern, which was added in 1877 in accordance with the original plan. (The tower has 383 steps, is open daily 09.00–17.00, and has a fine panorama from the top.) The *carvings of the south doorway date from the mid 14C.

**Interior**. In the choir, 1315–49, are stalls of 1352, with a carving of Emperor Ludwig holding a model of the church and a *frieze of 1407 devoted to St Bartholomew; on the south wall is the tomb of Günther von Schwarzenburg, King of the Romans, who died in 1352; there are 15C representations of Charlemagne and of St Bartholomew on the same wall, 1427; and the high altar dates from c 1470. In the north transept rises the Maria-Schlaf altar (the falling asleep of the Blessed Virgin) with sculptures of the 12 Apostles and a baldacchino, 1434. Above the altar is a rosary window of 1880. Other major altars are the 16C altar of St Anna with the Last Supper, and the altar

of the Sacred Heart, 1505 (both in the north transept), while the sole
Baroque part of Frankfurt's Dom is the altar of Mariä Himmelfahrt, 1728.
In the chapel of the Holy Sepulchre is a 15C altar with an Entombment of
Jesus of 1442. The cathedral houses a 15C triptych of the Passion; a
Lamentation by Van Dyck, 1627; memorials of the Thurn und Taxis family;
and the tombs of Rudolf von Sachsenhausen (died 1393), Gudula Goldstein
(died 1371) and her husband Bürgermeister Johann von Holzhausen (died
1393). In the entrance hall is a *crucifixion group by Hans Backoffen,
carved in 1509. At the crossing is an external relief of St Bartholomew by
Hans Mettel, 1957.

In 1953, when the cathedral was in process of restoration after World War
II damage, a Roman settlement and the foundations of the former palace
of the Carolingians (852–73) were excavated in the **Historische Garten**, in
front of its principle entrance west of the building. In the cloister to the north
is housed the **Dommuseum** (open weekdays, except Mon, 10.00–17.00;
weekends and holidays 11.00–17.00). S of the cathedral in Weckmarkt is
the **Leinwandhaus**, a textile hall built by M. Gerthener in 1396; restored,
and now an art and photographers' gallery.

NE in Kurt-Schumacher-Strasse rises the **Dominikanerkloster**, consecrated in 1269 and built for the Dominicans who had reached Frankfurt in
1233. The church was given its vaulting and its choir by Jörg Ostreicher in
1472, restored 1959–61; high altar reredos by Hans Holbein the Elder.
Opposite the church, behind the flower market, is the former Jewish
cemetery, the **Jüdischer Friedhof**, with funeral monuments from the 13C
to 19C, the oldest 1272, the latest 1828.

Continue a little further E past the cathedral to the **Saalhof**, comprising
three buildings: the Rententurm of 1445, the Bernus House of 1717, with a
Baroque façade, and the Burnitz House of 1840 which incorporates the
Palatine chapel of 1125 (the sole vestige of the Hohenstaufen palace that
stood here). These three buildings, restored 1952–56, now house the
**Historisches Museum** (open Mon–Fri 10.00–13.00). Opposite is the **Haus
Wertheim**, c 1600, late Renaissance and half-timbered, the sole survivor of
nearly 2000 such fine houses, though the Ostzeile in the Römerberg (see
below) and a row of houses in the nearby Rapunzelgasse were meticulously
reconstructed in the 1980s from the style of 15C and 16C bourgeois
dwellings.

The church of **St Nikolai**, begun in the 9C, rebuilt early 13C and 1290;
nave by Eberhard Friedberger, 1458–67; restored 1989, stands to the N at
the corner of the Saalgasse and the square known as the **Römerberg**,
Frankfurt's historic centre. Goethe's 'Dichtung und Wahrheit' vividly de-
scribes how on 3 April 1764, he watched the procession of the newly elected
King of the Romans (and hence the next Holy Roman Emperor) pass
through this square on the way to his coronation in the Dom, and then return
to feast in the Kaisersaal (see below).

On the outside wall of the apse of the church of St Nikolai is a relief of its
patron saint, comforting lepers. Inside is the tomb of Siegfried zum Paradies
(died 1386) and his wife. The Glockenspiel in the tower weighs 40 tonnes
and plays at 09.05, 12.05 and 17.05. The **Altes Rathaus** (the **Römer**), with
five gables and a façade of 1610, stands at the north side of the church in
the Römerberg square and incorporates three houses: the restored Löwenstein (its façade bearing the arms of Frankfurt nobility), the Römer of 1405
(its balcony, tower and carvings dating from 1897) and the Alt-Limpurg
(1495). Two neighbouring houses, the Frauenstein and the Salzhaus,
complete the five gables. Inside are the imperial room (Kaisersaal) where

*Frankfurt's Römerberg, where justice was once dispensed, is fittingly graced by a fountain of justice created in the early 1540s by Benedikt Loscher*

the feasting took place after coronations, with 19C portraits of kings and emperors from Charlemagne onwards, by P. Veit, A. Rethel and E. von Steinle; the Gothic *Römerhalle; a courtyard with a *Renaissance staircase tower, 1627; and the Hercules fountain of 1904 (open weekdays 09.00–17.00, Sun and holidays 10.00–16.00).

The rest of the square, which is Frankfurt's prettiest, incorporates on the N side the **Haus Goldener Schwan** of 1731, with a Gothic hall, and the **Steinerses Haus**, built in 1464 for the silk merchant Joachim von Melen and now an art gallery, and on the S side the **Haus Silberberg**, 1595, as well as other half-timbered houses reconstructed after 1945 (the Grosse Engel, the Goldener Greif and the Schwarzer Stern). The **Schirn Kunsthalle** at 6A Am Römerberg is devoted to 20C art, open Tue–Sun 10.00–17.00, to 20.00 Wed. The square centres on the fountain of Justice, by Benedikt Loscher (1541–43, the statue of Justice added 1610 and today replaced by a copy of 1880). This is the annual venue of Frankfurt's Christmas-tide market, with a 30m spruce tree from Norway, and stalls selling figures made from prunes (Quetschemännchen) and marzipan Bethmännchen.

S of the Römer are modern municipal administration buildings of 1956. W stands the **Neues Rathaus** of 1900–08, built in the Renaissance style with a neo-Baroque wing and a tower 70m high. The Baroque wing overlooks the Paulsplatz, with **Paulskirche**, built 1783–1833, never consecrated and the seat of the parliament of 1848–49. Bombed in World War II, restored 1948 and 1987–88, it now serves as a festival hall. A fresco of 1990 by Johannes Grützke depicts the parliamentarians of 1848 in procession; the north portal has a monument to the victims of fascism by H. Wimmer, 1964. W of the church, in Grossen Hirschgraben stands the birthplace of Goethe, the **Goethehaus**. Though entirely destroyed on 22 March 1944, the furniture was saved and the house reconstructed as it was in 1756. Goethe's house is joined by an arcade to the **Goethe Museum**, with many of his letters, engravings, manuscripts and family furniture (open Apr–Sept weekdays 09.00–18.00, Sun 10.00–13.00; Oct–Mar weekdays 09.00–16.00, Sun 10.00–13.00). This Rococo house was his parents' home, and here he wrote his 'Götz von Berlichingen' and 'The Sorrows of Young Werther'. Leave the Goethehaus and follow Grosser Hirschgraben, which leads by way of Kleiner Hirschgraben and Liebfrauenberg to the Gothic **Liebfrauenkirche**, founded 1308, reordered in the 15C, restored in 1954, with a south doorway by Madern Gerthener, c 1420, and a modern main door by Welker from the 1954 restoration. Inside is a memorial to the writer Wigel von Wanebech, died 1322. In the Liebfrauenberg, the square opposite the church, are a Rococo fountain of 1771 and the neo-Baroque patrician houses Zum Grimmvogel and Zum Paradies.

Liebfrauenstrasse leads shortly NW into the triangular **Hauptwache**, the centre of Frankfurt (in part because the U-Bahn and the S-Bahn meet underground here), once the site of the old municipal guard house—hence its name). The Baroque, arcaded former guardhouse in the centre, founded here in 1671, rebuilt by the city architect J.J. Samheimer 1729 (restored) is now a restaurant, with open-air tables. Behind the building is a neo-classical fountain of 1900, depicting characters created by the Frankfurt doctor Heinrich Hoffmann, in particular his Struwwelpeter. In 1844, unable to find a book suitable as a Christmas present for his son, Hoffmann created Struwwelpeter, with his long fingernails and mad mop of hair, illustrating his tales of young mischief with his own drawings.

On the S side of the Hauptwache is the **Katharinenkirche**, built for Frankfurt Protestants by Melchior Hessler, 1678–81 (restored), where Goethe was baptised and confirmed. From an earlier church on this spot, the 14C chapel of SS Catherine and Barbara, derives the tomb of Wicker Frosch (died 1363), founder of the hospice which it once served. The modern organ has 4400 voices, and Carl Crodel created 15 windows for the church in 1954. The **Zeil**, the pedestrianised central shoppping and commercial street of Frankfurt, leads E from Hauptwache. Entirely rebuilt after World War II (shaded at No. 110 by the post and telecommunications centre of 1951–55, with its 70m-high tower), the Zeil incorporates a massive marble fountain by Lutz Brockhaus, and on the side facing Grosse Eschenheimer Strasse a doorway and pavilions that constitute the sole remnants of the palace built on this spot (to designs of Robert de Cotte) by Wilhelm von Hauberat, 1732, for Anselm Franz von Thurn und Taxis, the imperial postal minister. Note on the doorway Minerva carrying the arms of the Thurn und Taxis (a tower for Thurn, a badger for Taxis). Continue E for some distance to Alfred-Brehm-Platz, where the **Frankfurt Zoo**, founded 1858, occupies 11 hectares (open daily 10.00–20.00, with a 'Nocturnal Animal Exhibition' 09.30–19.00, closing 17.00 in winter). In 1965 here saw the birth of the first baby gorilla in any German zoo.

Schillerstrasse leads N from Hauptwache to the megalomaniac Frankfurt stock exchange, the **Frankfurter Wertpaperbörse**, first established in 1585. The present 109m-long Italianate building is of 1879 by Burnitz and Sommer; restored. Its façade is sculpted with allegories of peace, war, sorrow and prosperity, along with the escutcheons of Berlin and Vienna. A portico of double Doric columns, 32m high, opens into a domed hall, itself 42m high (guided tours during business hours, Mon–Fri 11.30–13.30).

Kaiserstrasse leads S from Hauptwache to the **Rossmarkt**, formerly both a cattle market and a place for executions (including that of Margaret Brand, the Margaret of Faust). The Gutenberg monument in Rossmarkt is by Launitz, 1858. From here continue S along Friedenstrasse for a tour of Frankfurt's 'Anlagen' or boulevards, beginning at the Oper Frankfurt in Untermainanlage (1962, with Marc Chagall's 'Commedia dell'arte' and Zoltan Kemeny's 'Goldwolken' decorating the foyer). This c 5km green ring, laid out in the 19C when the city demolished its fortifications, is best covered by car: Gallusanlage, leading into Taunusanlage, passes right successively the Goethe monument (by Schwanthaler, 1844), the World War I memorial (by Benno Elkan, 1920), the Schiller memorial (by Johann Dielmann, 1864), the Heine memorial (by Georg Kolbe, 1913) and Kolbe's masterpiece the Beethoven memorial (1951).

The Taunusanlage turns right and leads to the Opernplatz, where you find the **Alte Oper**, seating 2500, rebuilt and its classical façade of 1873 restored in 1981 after war damage. N is the **Rothschildpark**, with a notable series of statues by Kolbe, 1954. From here Bockenheimer Anlage leads to the **Nebbiensche Gartenhaus**, c 1810, and to the Gothic *Eschenheimer Turm**, built by Madern Gerthener, 1400–28, strengthened by Wilhelm Dillich during the Thirty Years War and the sole survivor of the former city gates.

On the left bank of the River Main is another survival of medieval Frankfurt, **Sachsenhausen**, which became officially part of the city in 1318. Cross to it by the **Alte Brücke**—the present bridge dates to 1926. On the left of Brücken Strasse is the **Deutschordenshaus**, a three-winged Baroque building once belonging to the Teutonic Knights by Daniel Kayser, incorporating a Gothic church and built 1709–15, its ornamental doorway by Maximilian von Welsch. The whole was restored in 1963, and is now the town art gallery, with Roman remains from nearby Nida. Behind it is the celebrated 'Apfelweinlokale' with pretty fountains. Cider (or 'Ebbelwei' in the local dialect) is Frankfurt's favourite beverage, said to have been first served in Sachsenhausen in 1750. Enthusiastically dispensed here from blue-grey jugs, Ebbelwei accompanies the local dishes: Sauerkraut with a pork chop (Rippchen mit Kraut) or cheese dressed with chopped onions, vinegar and salad oil (Handkäs mit Musik). Sachsenhausen also boasts the 19C Gothic **Dreikönigskirche** with an 80m-high tower, beside which gushes the 18C **Dreikönigsbrunnen**. The sole remains of the town's medieval fortifications, built from 1390 to protect the southern flank of Frankfurt, is the **Kuhhirtenturm** (cowherds' tower) of 1490.

Return to the Alte Brücke and take the Sachsenhäuser Ufer to explore the imaginative **Museumsufer**, created to the W on the river's left bank. Buildings were commissioned from the German avant-garde, such as Oswald Mathias Ungers, to rebuild the Deutsches Architekturmuseum, and the American architect Richard Meier, who designed the Museum für Kunsthandwerk, 1979–85, as well as organising a competition to rehouse the museum of pre- and early history in the Carmelite church (see above), which was won in 1980 by the Berlin architect Josef Paul Kleihaus. In the 1980s not only was the city's oldest museum, the Städelsches Institute of Art and Städtische Gallery, extended, eleven other buildings were also commissioned and a Kunsthalle built for smaller exhibitions, all the buildings set within walking distance of each other along the bank of the river or close to it.

Along the Schaumainkai, you will find the **Städtische Galerie Liebighaus** of antique sculpture (No. 71) opened in 1909 in Baron von Liebig's villa, dedicated as he wished to 'the development of sculpture from many civilisations', the **\*\*Städelsches Kunstinstitut** and **Städtische Galerie** (No. 63), of the world's leading collections, displays 14C to 20C paintings and 19C and 20C sculptures and graphics, including works by Tintoretto, Tiepolo, Stephan Lochner. Hans Holbein the Elder, Jan van Eyck, Roger van der Weyden, Hieronymus Bosch, Hans Memling, Nicolas Poussin, Velásquez, Vermeer, Courbet, Monet, Renoir and Matisse, as well as German masters and 20C art. Both open Tue–Sun 10.00–17.00, closing Wed 20.00. A flea-market is set up on the Schaumankei each Saturday. The **Bundespost Museum** at No. 53 opens Tue–Sun 10.00–16.00, with exhibitions relating both to the development of the German postal service and to international telecommunications; the **Deutsches Architekturmuseum** (No. 43, with a lovely Doric façade of 1912–13 by Fritz Geldmacher, brutally transformed inside by Oswald Mathias Ungers, 1979–84); the **Deutsches Filmmuseum** (No. 41), the **Museum für Völkerkunde** (No. 29), and the **Museum für Kunsthandwerk** (No. 17), displaying Asian and European arts and crafts, all open Tue–Sun 10.00–17.00, closing Wed 20.00.

OTHER MUSEUMS: the Albert Schweitzer archive, 15 Saalgasse (open Mon–Fri 10.00–16.00); the Chaplin archive, 5 Klarastrasse; the Heinrich Hoffmann Museum, 20 Schubertstrasse (open Tue–Sun 10.00–17.00); the Industrial Hoechst Museum, Schlossplatz; the Schopenhauer archive (in the university library); the Struwwelpeter Museum, 47 Hochstrasse (open Tue–Sun 11.00–17.00, Wed to 20.00); Flight Museum, at the Airport (open Mar–Dec 09.00–19.00); the Brewery Museum in the Henninger Turm (beer brewing from the Middle Ages to the 20C, open Oct–Mar daily 10.00–21.00); the Museum of the History of Frankfurt at 19 Saalgasse (open Tue–Sun 10.00–17.00, closing Wed 20.00); the Archaeological Museum, including pre- and early history, at 5 Justinianstrasse, open Tue–Sun 10.00—17.00, closing Wed 20.00.

Frankfurt's THEATRES include the **Oper** in Theaterplatz; the **Kammerspiele** in Hofstrasse; the **Schauspiel** in Bockenheimer Landstrasse; the **Theater am Rurm** in Escherheimer Landstrasse; the **Fritz-Rédmond-Theater im Zoo** in Alfred-Brehmen-Platz; the **Volkstheater Frankfurt** in Grosser Hirschgraben; and **Die Komödie** in Neue Mainzer Strasse. An **English Theatre** (at 52 Kaiserstrasse), presenting plays in the English language, was founded in 1979, and has mounted 235 performances of

Agatha Christie's 'The Mousetrap'. Cabaret is promoted at the **Neues Theater Höchst** at 46a Emmerich-Josef-Strasse, and at 16–20 Heiligk-reuzgasse is the **Tiger Palast**.

A **Palmengarten** was laid out between 1869 and 1874 to the W of the city, acquiring the plant collection of the dethroned Duke Adolph von Nassau. Given to the city in 1922, it now covers 22 hectares, displaying sub-tropical plants, as well as incorporating children's playgrounds, a tropicarium built in the 1980s, a rose garden and the largest and oldest palm house in Germany. The Palmengarten is also the venue of summer concerts (entrances Palmengartenstrasse, Zeppelinallee and Siesmayerstrasse; open daily summer 09.00–20.00, winter 09.00–16.00).

The suburbs of Frankfurt include Bergen-Enkheim to the NE (U-bahn U4 from the Hauptbahnhof and then bus 43), with a medieval square. Its attractions include the local history museum in the medieval Rathaus (open Sun 15.00–18.00, Thur 20.00–21.30); more cider taverns; an annual cattle market—the Berger Markt—beginning four days before the first Tuesday in Sept); and a fine view of Frankfurt.

Incorporated into Frankfurt only in 1928, **Höchst** (10 minutes W by S-bahn S1, 2 and 3 from the Hauptbahnhof) was given its own city charter in 1355 and boasts the remains of fortifications begun in the 14C. The market which sets itself up in the Marktplatz every Tuesday, Friday and Saturday, has been doing so for 600 years. Höchst has finely restored half-timbered houses, a former town hall, rebuilt after a fire of 1586 by Oswald Stupanus and, high above the walls, the Carolingian church of St Justinus, 834, with columned arcades. Also the Höchst porcelain factory, (open weekdays 09.00–16.00; Sun 10.00–12.00) and the Baroque, horseshoe-shaped Balon-garopalast of 1772–75, built for the Italian snuff manufacturers Josef Maria Marcus and Jakob Philipp Balongaro. It incorporates a chapel and a decorated ballroom and has a double-terraced garden stretching down to the river. Overlooking the river rises the Schloss which was begun in 1360 for Bishop Gerlach I. Rebuilt in the Renaissance style for Wolfgang von Dalberg, Archbishop of Mainz, it now houses the Museum of Hochst history and of the 250-year-old Höchst porcelain firm (open daily 10.00–16.00). Höchst celebrates its annual festival on the first weekend in July, beginning Friday. Hoechst AG, set up as a dye factory in 1863 and becoming famous for its medicines, presented its employees with the Jahrhunderthalle in 1963, whose concrete, domed roof has a diameter of 86m and can accommodate 3500 spectators of theatre, opera and concerts.

# B.   Frankfurt am Main to Heidelberg

Total distance 81km. Frankfurt—35km Darmstadt—29km Weinheim—17km Heidelberg.

Leave Frankfurt and drive S by way of the B3 through Neu-Isenburg and Sprendlingen to reach after 35km Darmstadt. Overlooked by a tower raised in 1905 to celebrate the marriage of Grand Duke Ernst Ludwig of Hesse-Darmstadt, **Darmstadt** (134,000 inhab.; alt. 142m), situated amidst extensive forests and at the start of the Bergstrasse-Odenwald Naturpark, is the former capital of the Grand-Duchy of Hesse-Darmstadt and prospers on the electronics, pharmaceutical and chemical industries as well as fine printing.

**Tourist information**: 17 Wilhelminenstrasse and at 5 Luisenplatz; **main post office**: Luisenplatz. **Trains** connect with Basel, Dortmund, Mainz and Munich; **buses** with local destinations; **boats** ply the river to Cologne, Frankfurt and Mainz.

**History**. Settled by an Alemannic colony where Roman roads crossed, Darmstadt first appears in written history in the 11C. Under the Counts of Katzenelnbogen the township continued to prosper. Already a city by 1330, Darmstadt blossomed from the 15C. The Landgraves of Hesse controlled the city from 1479. In the 18C the Landgravine Karoline (Goethe's 'great Landgravine') patronised writers, and it is fitting that today the city is the HQ of the German PEN club and the German academy of literature. Napoleon made Darmstadt a Grand-Duchy in 1806. The dramatist Georg Büchner lived here, 1816–31 and again 1834–35; the city annually presents the Georg Büchner prize for literature. During Büchner's time the architect Georg Möller was giving a classical aspect to many of its buildings. In 1898 the last Grand-Duke, Ernst Ludwig, founded here a suburb of Jugendstil (Art Nouveau) artists. Nearly 80 per cent of Darmstadt was destroyed in World War II.

From the main railway station Rheinstrasse leads to Luisenplatz, in the centre of which is a 33m-high bronze monument to Grand-Duke Ludwig I, by Ludwig Schwanthaler 1844, inside which is a circular staircase. N of the square is the former college of 1780. NE is a monument to the chemist Julius von Liebig (1803–73) a native of the city; to the N is the Regierungspräsidium of 1791. Opposite stands the huge Luisencenter, incorporating both shopping halls and also the new town hall.

Continue across Luisenplatz to reach the huge Schloss, finished by Louis Rémy de la Fosse, whose south façade dates from 1720. This Schloss comprises the 16C Altes Schloss which is connected to the Baroque Neues Schloss by the Glockenbau of 1663–71 (in part rebuilt 1844), containing a carillon of S. Verbeel, 1670, which plays folksongs on the quarter. It now houses a museum, containing the 'Darmstadt Madonna' of 1526 by Hans Holbein the Younger (open except Thu 10.00–13.00 and 14.00–17.00). The east side of the Schloss, beside which stands the Renaissance church, dates from the 1590s. Behind is the Schloss garden (the Herrngarten), containing the burial mound of Landgravine Karoline (1721–74) and a statue of Goethe by L. Habich, 1903, and the technical high school of 1836. Beyond the Herrngarten, the Prinz-Georg-Garten was first laid out in 1625 as a pleasure garden and transformed into a Rococo one in 1720 by Rémy de la Fosse. Its north side surrounds the Porzellan-Schloss of 1720, by de la Fosse, with a rich porcelain collection (open, except Fri, 10.00–13.00, 14.00–17.00; closed weekend afternoons). SE of the Schloss stands the 14C Weisse Turm, from the medieval ramparts.

In front of the Schloss is Friedensplatz and the neo-Gothic Hessisches Landesmuseum, built by Alfred Messsel, 1897–1902. Its contents include prehistory; Roman and medieval art; works by Stephan Lochner and Lucas Cranach the Elder; Flemish and Dutch painters, including Breugel and Rubens; stained glass from the 11C to the 16C; a retable by Riemenschneider; arms and armour; a *Jugendstil collection; and important 20C masters, especially works by *Joseph Beuys and also including Otto Dix, Max Beckmann, Lyonel Feininger and Lovis Corinth. Open except Mon 10.00–17.00; closed Sun 13.00–14.00; opens also Wed 19.00–21.00.

The old town, S of the Schloss, severely damaged in World War II, comprehends the Marktplatz with a fountain of 1780; the town hall of 1599 (restored) with its *Renaissance façade and Ratskeller, and the Protestant parish church. The bottom half of its five-storey west tower dates from 1631, the top half from 1953. The interior consists of a vaulted choir of 1431 and a nave of 1687, redone in 1845. It houses the Renaissance tomb of crown prince Philipp Wilhelm, who died in his first year, in 1579; and an alabaster Renaissance monument to Grand-Duke Georg I and his wife Magdalena, by Peter Osten, 1599. The Catholic parish church of St Ludwig, modelled on the Pantheon, Rome, by G. Moller, 1820, is in Wilhelminenplatz, its 28 15m-high Corinthian columns supporting a dome 33m in diameter.

At Mathildenhöhe, a park E of the city, rises the architectural memorial of the artists' colony set up in 1898 at the invitation of Grand-Duke Ernst Ludwig, the Jugendstil wedding tower (Hochzeitsturm), set up in 1905 to celebrate the Grand-Duke's wedding, by the Viennese Jugendstil master Josef Maria Olbrich, who also designed the Ernst-Ludwig-Haus in Mathildenhöhe and three Jugendstil houses, 1904, on Prinz-Christian-Weg. Here too is the Russian chapel of 1889, decorated in 1914 by Berhard Hoetger, another member of the Mathildenhöhe colony. In 1908 Olbrich also designed the Austellungsgebäude (exhibition building), for the colony, along with its terraces and pergolas. To the E the Platanenheim (a wood of plane trees) shelters sculptures by Hoetger, while further E along Olbrich-weg the Lion Gate (Löwentor, by Hoetger and A. Müller), which gives access to the Rosenhöhe (hill of roses), a park laid out in 1810 and sheltering the Mausoleum of the Grand-ducal family. The City Museum and Art Collection, with more Jugendstil work, is at 1 Europaplatz (open except Mon 10.00–17.00, Wed also 19.00–21.00). At 7 Steinstrasse is the railway museum (open Sun 10.00–16.00). An unusual musem of hairstyling, the Wella Museum, is at 65 Berliner Allee (open weekdays 09.00–12.00, 14.00–17.00).

An **excursion** 8km NE reaches the Renaissance **Jagdschloss Kranichstein**, built for Landgrave Georg I by Jakob Kesselhut in 1578 (guided tours and museum of hunting, open except Mon 10.00–12.00, 14.00–17.00). In the Darmstadt-Kranichstein railway station is a railway museum, with 16 locomotives and 15 carriages (open Sun 10.00–16.00).

The B3 S of Darmstadt is known as the Bergstrasse (and sometimes the 'springtime road'), passing through **Seeheim**, a town of attractive halftim-bered houses and a town hall of 1599; **Jugenheim**, above which towers Schloss Heiligenberg; **Bensheim**, with its 16C wedding house, its classical parish church and to the N the ruined 13C Auerbacher Schloss; and **Heppenheim an der Bergstrasse**. Here the mid-16C Renaissance town hall and the Liebig pharmacy, both with oriel windows, in the delightful half-timbered Marktplatz, as well as a huge neo-Gothic church known as the cathedral of the Bergstrasse, are dominated by the ruined Schloss Starken-burg. The regional museum, S of the Marktplatz, is housed in the Kurmain-zer Amsthof, which has 14C and 16C frescoes (open Tue, Thu, Sat 14.00–17.00, Sun and holidays 10.00–12.00, 14.00–16.30).

From Heppenheim a **detour** W leads to **Lorsch**, with its monastery gate dating from 774–84, belonging to what was once the richest medieval Benedictine abbey in Germany. Founded in 764 it has a Carolingian sculpted *Torhalle, and the church has a 12C nave. The frescoes are Carolingian on the walls and Gothic on the ceiling. The former monastery is now a museum, open except Mon Mar–Oct 10.00–17.00, closing other-wise 16.00. The town's local collection is in the Altes Rathaus, open weekdays 09.00–12.00, 14.00–16.00.

Continue S along the B3 from Heppenheim to reach, 29km after Darmstadt, **Weinheim** (30,000 inhab.; alt. 108m). Its attractions are Schloss

Berckheim (in three parts: 16C, 1725 and mid 19C), whose park includes the oldest cedar tree in Germany; the former Rathaus of 1554; the neoRomanesque church of St Laurentius, 1913, preserving a tower by H. Hubsch, 1850, altars and a pulpit of 1750 and 15C wall paintings. Wieinheim is made yet more picturesque by the remains of 12C Burg Windeck; the Büdinger Hof of 1582; a witches' tower from the old walls; and the Wachenburg, a Schloss of 1913. Its finest ensemble is the 13C tanners' quarter, the Gerberviertel. The local history museum is at 2 Amtsgasse (open Sun 10.00–12.00, 14.00–16.00, Wed, Sat 14.00–16.00). The present Rathaus is in a 16C Schloss, rebuilt 1893.

The Bergstrasse continues through Schriesheim, with its half-timbered Rathaus of 1684, at the foot of ruined Strahlenburg. 4km W is **Ladenburg**, with half-timbered houses, 14C–17C, the 12C Romanesque church of St Sebastian, the Gothic parish church of St Gallus—inside which are the 15C statues of Franz von Sickingen and his wife Margaretha von Dalberg—and the local history museum, in the 16C and 17C Bishofshof (open Sat 14.30–17.30, Sun also 11.00–12.30). 17km after Schriesheim the route reaches **Heidelberg** (see Rte 10).

# 36

# Frankfurt am Main to Fulda

## A. The 'fairy-tale route': Deutsche Märchenstrasse

Total distance 94km. Frankfurt—19km Hanau—B40, 10km Langenselbold—12km Gelnhausen—11km Wächtersbach—15km Steinau an der Strasse—21km Löschenrod—B27, 6km Fulda.

Leave **Frankfurt** (see Rte 35A) E by way of the Hanauer Landstrasse which travels close to the right bank of the Main. After 10km Schloss Rumpensheim, 1680, appears on the other bank. 1km S, shortly before Hanau, appears the French Baroque **Schloss Philippsruhe**, 1712, enlarged 1875–80, now containing the Hanau historical museum (open Sun, Tue 10.00–12.00, 14.00–17.00) and **Wilhelmsbad**, with its spa and health resport. The Kurhaus, built in 1772–82 over a thermal spring, is set in an 'English' park containing a folly, a Hermitage, a ravine with a suspension bridge and a dolls' museum.

After 19km the route reaches the confluence of the Kinzig with the Main and the town of **Hanau** (89,000 inhab.; alt. 108m), whose industries include diamond-cutting, jewellery making and rubber manufacture. In the Marktplatz of the Neustadt is a bronze, unexpectedly stern monument, 1889–96, to the brothers Jakob and Wilhelm Grimm (1786–1863 and 1786–1859), who were born here, hence the name of this route. The Grimm's younger brother, the painter and engraver Ludwig (1790–1863) was also born here. Hanau developed out of the Altstadt, whose former town hall in the Markt (the Deutsches Goldschmiedehaus) was built in 1537. It has a

Rococo sandstone porch, gables, half-timbered upper storeys, steep dormer-bedecked roof, and a museum of gold and filigree work (open except Mon 10.00–12.00, 14.00–17.00). The 14C church of Our Lady opposite has contemporary stained glass in the 15C choir. The Neustadt was chiefly a creation of 17C Dutch and Walloon immigrants. who built its 17C parish church. The town hall of the Neustadt, 1723–33, has a Glockenspiel.

The composer Paul Hindemith (1895–1963) was born at Hanau, though he ran away from home aged 11. Tourist information at No. 41 Nürnbergerstrasse. Trains connect with Frankfurt and buses with local towns and villages. 4km S of Hanau along the B45, on a basalt peak on the S bank of the Main, is **Steinheim** (10,000 inhab.; alt. 115m), its delights the Gothic Schloss on the Bergfried, and the Gothic church of St Johann Baptist.

From Hanau follow the B40 10km NE to reach **Langenselbold** (10,000 inhab.; alt. 122m), set among wooded hills on the River Kinzig and protected by the 18C Schloss of the Fürsten von Isenberg-Birstein. The B40 continues NE for 12km to reach **Gelnhausen** (19,000 inhab.; alt. 141m), which Friedrich Barbarossa made into a Free Imperial City in 1170. On an island in the Kinzig he founded the walled Kaiserpfalz, which was completed by his son Heinrich VI and ruined by the Swedes in the Thirty Years War, as the first seat of the Reichstag. The Kaiserpfalz has been well restored (visits 10.00–13.00, 14.00–17.00, closing 16.00 Nov–Feb). The many-towered *Marienkirche, the model for the Gedächtniskirche in Berlin, was begun c 1170 and finished 1467, with the completion of the chapel south of the chancel. Its *high altar of c 1500 carries a Madonna and SS, and the church houses four other late 15C altars as well as 15C tapestries, an early 13C sandstone rood screen, 14C stalls and and a 14C pulpit.

'Zum Weissen Ochsen' at 12 Schmidtgasse was the birthplace of the poet Jakob Christoph von Grimmelshausen (1622–76), most famous for his 'Simplicissimus' (1689), with its horrific depiction of the Thirty Years War. He is remembered in a museum at 2 Kirchgasse, as is another native, Philipp Reis (1834–74), inventor of the telephone according to the citizens of Gelnhausen (open except Sun 10.00–12.00; Tue, Thu, Fri also 16.00–18.00). A statue to Reis is in the Untermarkt, which has a Romanesque hall of c 1170. In nearby Kuhgasse the Romanisches Haus is the oldest halftimbered house in Hesse, dated 1356. The 13C church of St Peter is in the Obermarkt, reordered as the Catholic parish church between 1932 and 1938. In Holzgasse is a 14C house belonging to the Order of the Knights of St John. The half-timbered former town hall of 1726, at 17 Miroldstrasse, is also a museum (open first Sun in month, 15.00–17.00). Amongst the remaining fortifications are the 15C witches' tower, the brick tower, the Haizer gate and the Holz gate. Tourist information at 8 Untermarkt. Trains connect with Frankfurt.

11km NE along the B40 from Gelnhausen the route meets the B276, which leads 1km N to **Wächtersbach** (10,000 inhab.; alt. 148m), a town of winding streets situated on the Kinzig, surrounded by forests, lying between the nature parks of the Spessart mountains and the Vogelsberg, with a 15C to 18C Schloss, a brewery, a local history museum in a 1495 half-timbered house (open weekdays 10.00–12.00, 14.00–16.00; Sat 10.00–12.00) and a 14C parish church. Follow the B40 a further 7km NE to reach **Salmünster**, whose Franciscan monastery was founded in 1319, and whose 18C Baroque church is by Andreas Gallasini, and then 2km further for **Bad Soden**, a spa overlooked by the ruined 13C Schloss Stolzenberg, where Luther stayed. The spa also has the Renaissance Hutten-Schlosschen of 1536, belonging to the family of the explorer Philip von Hutten (c 1511–46) and his cousin

Ulrich (see below). 8km NE from here on the B40 lies **Steinau an der Strasse** (10,500 inhab.; alt. 173m), where in the Amtshaus, 1562, the brothers Grimm spent their childhood. Documents and manuscripts of their lives are to be found in the Renaissance moated Schloss, built by Asmus of Steinau, 1528–56 (open Mar–Oct 10.00–17.00; otherwise closes 16.00). The Rathaus of 1561 stands in the Marktplatz. Steinau's ecclesiastical buildings include a late 13C Gothic church dedicated to St Catherine of Alexandria; the Reinhardskirche of 1665–76; and a Baroque cemetery chapel of 1616. The town also has a marionette theatre. Tourist information at the Amtshaus.

The health resort of **Schlüchtern** (14,000 inhab.; alt. 206m) lies on the B40 7km from Steinau and boasts a former Benedictine abbey, which retains its Gothic church and cloisters. Most notable inside the church are the St Katharina chapel, c 1100; the Andreas chapel c 1200; the Hutten chapel, 1345; the tomb of Petrus Lotichius (1501–67); and an 8C crypt. The Bergwinkel Museum in the 1440 Lauter Schlösschen has much about Lotichius, as well as more mementoes of the brothers Grimm, and an exhibition devoted to the poet, humanist and headstrong Reformer Ulrich von Hutten (1488–1523), who was born in the now ruined Burg Steckelburg in the suburb of Elm. Other sights are the mid-19C church of St Michael with its 14C tower, and the town hall of 1573. Schloss Ramholz in the suburb of Vollmerz was built by the von Hutten family in the 16C. Tourist information at 10 Grabenstrasse.

The route passes through **Neuhof**, with a Schloss of 1519, to reach after 21km Löschenrod, from where the B27 runs for 6km into **Fulda** (see Rte 12).

# B.  Frankfurt am Main to Fulda via the Vogelsberg

Total distance 197km. Frankfurt—19km Hanau—B40, 23km Gelnhausen—B457, 14km Büdingen—B457, 9km Selters—B275, 18km Gedern—B276, 16km Schotten—B276, 12km Laubach—B49, 34km Alsfeld—B254, 16km Lauterbach—B275, 14km Schlitz—22km Fulda.

Cross to the left bank of the Main at **Frankfurt** (see Rte 35A) to the suburb of Sachsenhausen and follow Darmstadter Strasse, the B3, 3.5km to the Sachsenhaüser Berg. From here take the Landstrasse left through the Frankfurt woods, crossing the B46 after 3.5km and taking the B45 to Hanau and Gelnhausen (see above). From here take the B457 N through the Büdingen woods for 14km to the health resort of **Büdingen** (17,000 inhab.; alt. 133m), which has medieval town walls and three gates protected by water and a town hall of 1458 (with a local history museum, open weekdays, except Mon, 10.00–12.00, Sat 15.00–17.00, Sun 10.00–12.00, 15.00–17.00). Another museum is in the Renaissance and Baroque Schloss, with its late Gothic chapel whose choir stalls are by Peter Schanntz and Michael Silge, 1499, and whose sandstone pulpit is by Conrad Büttner, 1610.

Continue along the B457 for 9km to Selters, to join the B275 NE, reaching **Gedern**, which has a 16C Schloss, after another 18km. From here the B276 leads along the SW border of the Hoher Vogelsberg nature park, named after a once volcanic massif. Decked with oaks and beeches and covering some 38,000 ha, the park includes the winter and summer holiday town of Hartmannshain and the Taufstein (at 774m the highest peak of the Vogelsberg, beating its neighbour the Hoherhodskopf by 9m). After 16km the

B276 reaches the winter sports centre of **Schotten** (10,000 inhab.; alt. 282m) on the River Nidda. Schotten today is a centre for lake sports on the Nidda-Stausee. Here Irish monks in 778 founded a long-disappeared monastery, hence the name Schotten. Its Gothic Liebfrauenkirche, begun c 1300, was enlarged as more and more pilgrims visited the spot. The west doorway is decorated with Adoration of the Magi, Mary and the founders of the church and has late Gothic carvings inside. This church shelters a winged *high altar, c 1375, painted with scenes from the life of the Virgin Mary, a 14C font and an organ of 1782. Schotten also has a half-timbered Rathaus, 1530, and a local history museum at 95 Vogelsbergstrasse (open Tue, Thu, Sun 14.30–16.30, Wed 10.00–12.00; closed winter). This is the site of the motor racing course known as the Schottenring.

Follow the B276 for 23km to **Laubach** on the River Wette, to find a 14C Schloss of the Grafen zu Solms, with an earlier keep. Its Baroque great hall was built in 1739 and has splendid stucco, mirrors and woodwork, while its former mid-16C stables now house a library. Laubach's 13C parish church has late Gothic wall paintings, a nave redesigned in 1702, an organ built by J.C. Beck and J.M. Wagner in 1751 and a tower of 1869. Near the church gushes a fountain of 1589 and in the Markt another of 1780. Laubach also has numerous half-timbered houses and a 15C watchtower, along with an 'English' park with a 16C mill.

From Laubach drive 11km N to the B49 and then drive NE for 23km to *Alsfeld (18,000 inhab.; alt. 264m). The most attractive part of the town is its *Marktplatz with the Wine House of 1538, and the Gothic half-timbered Rathaus rising above a stone market hall, 1512–16. The town hall has oriels and spires and a a decorated council chamber, created in the late 16C and mid 17C. Here too rises the Renaissance Hochzeitshaus, 1564–71, and on the corner with Rittergasse the beautifully half-timbered Stumpfhaus of 1609 (named after the former Bürgermeister Josef Stumpf). Look for the Walpurgis church in the Kirchplatz, 13C and late 14C Gothic, though its nave dates from 1732. Inside are a Romanesque font, late Gothic wall paintings and a 16C altar. The 15C church of the Holy Trinity (Dreifaltigkeitskirche) stands in Mainzer Strasse, with a 14C choir. In Rittergasse are the Neurath-Haus of 1564–71, and the Minnigerode-Haus of 1687 (now the regional museum; open weekdays 09.00–12.30, 14.00–16.30; Sat closes 16.00; Sun opens 10.00). The half-timbered house at Nos 10–12 Hersfelder Strasse, built in 1375, claims to be the oldest in Germany. The Beinhaus, a late Gothic chapel of 1368–1500, was restored in 1982.

Take the B254 SE from Alsfeld for 16km to the health resort of **Lauterbach** (15,000 inhab.; alt, 285m), proud of its massive production of garden gnomes, and equally proud of the late Baroque parish church, 1791–96, with an impressive partly neo-classical tower, 1820. The town's three-winged Rococo Schloss Hohhaus, 1769–73, designed by Friedrich Georg Riedesel, was stuccoed by A. Weidemann, and is now a museum (its greatest treasure the *winged 'Lauterbach altar' of 1480; open except Mon 10.00–12.00, 14.00–16.00; Sat closed afternoons, Sun closed mornings). Lauterbach's former fortress of 1265 was rebuilt in the 18C, retaining a 16C well in the courtyard. Lauterbach hosts a music festival at Whitsun, and an annual pottery market on the first weekend of September, combining the latter biennially with a traditional guild festival. 5km S stands the 14C Schloss Eisenbach, with Renaissance additions and a chapel of 1675 (and today also a restaurant).

From Lauterbach take the sign for Schlitz, which you reach after a 14km drive NE. **Schlitz** (9500 inhab.; alt. 240m) is surrounded by a ring of castles:

the 13C Hinterburg, with its mid-16C Burghaus, formerly part of the town's fortifications; the Vorderburg, 1565–1600, with two wings joined by a tower, and a Glockenspiel which plays at 15.00 and 17.00 (now the local history museum open Apr–Oct 14.00–16.00, except Mon; otherwise only at weekends and holidays); the half-timbered 16C and 17C Schachtenburg; the 1563–1681 Ottoburg; and a youth hostel in the Baroque Hallenburg, which was built c 1760. The parish church of St Margaret dates from the 15C, though its predecessor was founded by the abbey of Fulda in 812, and has a font of 1467 and an organ case of 1718. Schachterburg is also enlivened by numerous half-timbered houses. 4km E is the church of **Fraurombach**, with 14C Gothic frescoes. **Fulda** (see Rte 12) lies 22km directly SE of Schlitz.

# 37

# Frankfurt am Main to Kassel

Total distance 186km (also by motorway). Frankfurt—B3, 32km Niederwöllstadt—B45, 4km Ilbenstadt—B45 and B3, 11km Friedberg—5km Bad Nauheim—10km Butzbach—19km Giessen—18km Marburg—51km Zwesten—2km Fritzlar—34km Kassel.

Leave **Frankfurt** (see Rte 35A) N by way of the Friedberger Landstrasse, the B3, reaching after 10km **Bad Vilbel** (25,000 inhab.; alt. 109m), a Roman town set amongst woods and on the River Nidda, today a spa with 22 therapeutic springs. Bad Vilbel is made more picturesque by the remains of its Wasserburg, 1414; a half-timbered house of 1747; and the parish church of 1697 with a 15C west tower. Following the wide river the route runs 15km to **Kloppenheim**, with its Schloss of the Teutonic Knights, 1714, and for a further 9km to Niederwöllstadt. Here take the B45 right for 4km to **Ilbenstadt**, where Premonstratensian monks built a Romanesque *basilica in the first half of the 12C. Its stone carvings are the work of Italian masons; the dome was added c 1500. Here are late Gothic wall paintings; statues of the Apostles and the Madonna by C.L. Werr, 1700; the organ and gallery were added c 1735; Baroque statues were created for the church by Burkhard Zamel in 1744. Other surviving monastery buildings date from 1707–15, along with the Upper Gate of 1721. Ilbenstadt's Ritterhof was built in 1742.

Return to the B3 and drive N for 7km more to **Friedberg** (25,000 inhab.; alt. 159m), the furthest point N of the Roman empire during the time of Diocletian. Its 54m-high Adolfs tower with four watchtowers dates from 1347 (paid for with ransom money for Adolf of Nassau who was imprisoned here). It probably rises on the site of a 'castellum in the Taunus mountain' described by Tacitus in the mid 3C. Today it contains a local history museum (open Mar–Oct 10.00–12.00, 13.00–17.00; closes winter an hour earlier). Other sights include the Gothic hall-church of *Our Lady, 1260–1410. Its Ziborien altar dates from c 1250, and a late Gothic screen with the sandstone 'Friedberg Madonna', c 1280. In the choir are three panels of the *14C and the three central windows have 15C (or perhaps 14C) stained glass. The sacristy doors are magnificently sculpted with foliage c 1300. A tabernacle of 1482–84 is the work of Hans von Düren. At 20 Judengasse is a Jewish women's ritual *bathhouse, 1260, 26m deep.

Friedberg's burg follows in part the pattern of the Roman fort, and also embraces 16C to 18C houses and the Kavaliershaus, c 1605. The Burg-kirche, classical in style, is by F.L. von Cancrin and Johann Philipp von Wörrishöfer (1738–1808), and to Wörrishöfer is due the fountain of 1738. Behind the church rises the Adolfs tower (see above). The gabled Renais-sance Burgrafenhaus, with its armorial decorations, dates from 1604–10, and the house of the Teutonic Knights beyond it from 1717. Trains connect with Frankfurt, Giessen and Kassel; buses wih Bad Homburg, Laubach, Giessen and Schotten.

Running N, after 5km the B3 reaches **Bad Nauheim** (27,000 inhab.; alt. 144m) in the fertile Wetterau region and surrounded by woodlands. The town developed as a spa when the Sprudel spring erupted in 1846 after a violent storm. The Jugendstil Sprudelhof of 1905–09, now a youth hostel, is by Wilhelm Jost, who also desiged the theatre and concert hall in the 200-hectare Kurpark, which you reach by a bridge across the Usa. Look out for the nearby Raben tower of 1745. Bad Nauheim has a salt museum at 20–22 Ludwigstrasse (open Thu–Sat 15.30–17.30). On the 268m-high Johannisberg rise a Roman tower and the ruins of an 8C church. Bad Nauheim has a national rose museum in the Altes Rathaus (built 1740–42, open Wed 14.00–17.00), and hosts a biennial rose festival in July. The present Rathaus dates from 1740, and the Baroque Wilhelmskirche from 1740–42. Train connections as for Friedberg; buses also connect with Berlin.

The B3 leaves the valley of the Usa, crosses the Frankfurt–Kassel motor-way and passes through rose gardens by way of Steinfurth and Opper-shofen to **Nieder-Weisel**, with its early 13C church, reaching after 10km **Butzbach** (22,000 inhab.; alt. 199m) on the NE slopes of the Taunus. Once a Roman garrison, Butzbach is now a beguiling town making shoes and light machinery. The *Marktplatz contains the encorbelled town hall of 1560 (with a 1630 clock, restored in 1927), a fountain of 1575, the half-timbered house known as the Goldener Ritter and the Alte Post, 1636, and the Goldener Löwe of 1709, which inspired Goethe's 'Hermann und Dorothea'. The town boasts the 14C and 15C church of St Markus, incor-porating 13C pillars and the Markus chapel of 1433. Its organ was built in 1614, and the memorial tomb of Philipp of Hesse-Butzbach in 1622. The church's 15C Michaelskapelle has been fitted out as a museum. A curious survivor in the town is the 15C and 16C chapel of St Wendelin, housing his 16C shrine and with an altar c 1500, the oldest wooden church in Hesse. Butzbach's Solms Schloss dates from 1481, and the Hesse Schloss from 1610.

19km N by way of Pohl-Göns and Klein-Linden is the industrial and university town of **Giessen** (76,000 inhab.; alt. 150m; tourist information: 4 Berliner Platz), situated on the Lahn. Between 1834 and 1852, the chemist Justus von Liebig (1803–73) lived here, and his laboratory is preserved in a house of 1812 at 12 Liebigstrasse (open except Thu 10.00–12.00, 14.00–16.00; Sun 11.00–13.00). The university, founded in 1607, is named after him. Giessen was also the home of the scientist Wilhelm Konrad von Röntgen (1845–1923), who was professor at the university. There is a Röntgen memorial, by E.F. Reuter, 1962, in Berliner Platz, near the city theatre of 1907. In earlier times it was the site of a mid-12C Schloss, and passed in the 13C into the hands of Landgrave Heinrich I, thenceforth to be disputed over by the landgraves and the archbishops of Mainz. The rebuilt 14C Altes Schloss at the heart of the city in Brandplatz was once the home of Landgrave Heinrich II. During the time of Luther's patron, Philipp of Hesse (known as 'the Generous') who also lived here, Giessen embraced the Reformation. Today it serves as the Oberhessisches Museum, with paintings, porcelain and local artefacts (open except Mon 10.00–16.00). The Neues Schloss, with a massive arsenal of 1589 built for Ludwig IV, stands on the NE flank of its courtyard and was built for Philipp the Generous, 1533–39. Nearby is the botanical garden of 1609, laid out for use of the university which Ludwig V had founded two years previously. Covering four hectares, it was joined in 1817 to a forestry garden created in that same year. (Entrance in Sonnenstrasse; open weekdays 08.00–12.00, 14.00–sunset, weekends and holidays 08.00–18.00 in summer, 08.00–12.00 in winter; conservatories open mid-May to mid-August daily 10.00–12.00, 13.30–15.45.)

See also the 14C half-timbered Leibsche Haus restored after war damage in 1977; the 1126 former church of the Augustinians; Schiffenberg, with monastery buildings that include a deanery of 1463 and a Kommanderie of 1493; and the 17C chapel of the old cemetery (in Licher Strasse). The museum of local history at 2 Georg-Schlosser-Srasse is housed in the restored, 14C half-timbered Burgmannenhaus (open 10.00–16.00, Sun 10.00–13.00, closed Mon). Trains connect Giessen with Frankfurt, Marburg and Kassel.

Continue N along the B3, past ruined Schlösser on hilly peaks and through **Staufenberg**, with its Gothic Unterburg and its ruined Oberburg, and **Giesselberg**, with a neo-Gothic Schlosss of 1851, to reach after 28km **MARBURG** (75,000 inhab.; alt. 176m), a delightful old university town with many half-timbered houses in its Altstadt, whose Schloss, standing 400m high in the centre of Marburg, is now part of its university.

**Tourist information**: 1 Neue Kassler Strasse. **Trains** connect Marburg with Giessen, Frankfurt and Kassel.

**History**. Marburg gained renown in the 11C from St Elisabeth of Hungary (see below), and is celebrated for a conference between differing Protestants, called by Philipp the Generous on Michaelmas Day 1529, at which Luther was particuarly charming to the Zwinglians, addressing his opponents as 'my dearest sirs' but refusing to give an inch theologically. Here Emil von Behring (1854–1917), professor at the university from 1895 until his death, discovered a vaccine for diphtheria and for this achievement won the Nobel Prize in 1901.

Leaving the main railway station you cross the two branches of the River Lahn to reach Germany's earliest purely Gothic building, the church of **··St Elisabeth**, built in honour of St Elisabeth of Marburg (1207–31), daughter of King Andreas II and also known as St Elisabeth of Hungary. Married at 14 to Landgrave Ludwig of Thuringia, widowed when he died in a crusade in 1227, she devoted herself to the poor, building for them a hospice here and a chapel dedicated to St Francis of Assisi. Four years after her death Pope Gregory IX canonised Elisabeth and the Teutonic Knights (an order founded only in 1224) came to Marburg to oversee the building of the basilica, which stands over her tomb. The church was finished in 1285, its towers by 1340. The main entrance is decorated with a statue of the Madonna and Child, along with rose leaves (here her symbol) and vines (here the symbol of Jesus).

The interior has restored 15C wall paintings depicting the lives of SS Elisabeth and Catherine of Alexandria. In the north transept is the Gothic chapel of St Elisabeth, with her former tomb, canopied in 1280, while in the sacristy is the 13C ·reliquary containing the saint's bones. The south transept houses tombs of the Landgraves of Hesse, till the 16C. In the chapel under the north tower is the tomb of Field-Marshal Paul von Hindenburg (1847–1934). The choir has a stone high altar of 1290, with Gothic paintings on the reverse side, ** 13C and 14C stained glass, a late 15C *statue of St Elisabeth and a bronze crucifix by Ernst Barlach, 1931.

W of the church is the chapel of St Michael, 1270, restored in 1984. This former funerary chapel of the Teutonic Knights has exquisite early Gothic *vaulting. The knights' Herrenhaus, begun in 1253, is now used by the university, their granary of 1515 is now the Mineralogisches Museum (open Mon–Wed 13.00–16.00, Fri 10.00–13.00). To the S of the chapel is the peaceful former botanical garden of the university.

From the church follow Steinweg, Neustadt, Wettergasse and Reitgasse to reach the university, founded in 1527 by Luther's patron Landgrave Philipp of Hesse (1509–67) as the first German Protestant university. Its present buildings date from 1874–91, save for the 14C church. It houses the largest library in Western Germany (including 1.5m volumes from the Prussian state library, Berlin). Biegenstrasse leads NE to the university art gallery, at No. 11, in the Ernst-von-Hülsen-Haus, with 19C and 20C paintings (open except Tue 10.00–13.00, 15.00–17.00). Continue to climb to the Schloss, at the foot of which is the 13C and 14C Lutheran church, inside which is the 18C tomb of Landgrave Ludwig and his wife. The 13C Schloss boasts a Rittersaal, c 1300, and a Gothic chapel consecrated in 1288, and from it is a lovely *view across the town, the Taunus and Sauerland. It houses a religious history museum (open Mon, Wed, Fri 10.00–13.00). In the park behind the Schloss is an open-air theatre.

As well as the Herrenhaus of 1253 and the headquarters of the Teutonic Knights, c 1483 (see above), Marburg's fine houses include the Brüderhaus of 1254, the 13C Steineres Haus, as well as an early 16C bakery, in Firmaneiplatz. In the Markt is the Rathaus of 1512–27, with the arms of the Landgraves of Hesse, a relief of St Elisabeth by L. Juppe, 1524, a clock with mechanical figures (the Guckelhahn) and a Renaissance gable by Eberhardt Böckwein, 1581. The old university building (Am Rudolphsplatz) dates from 1874 and inside are monumental frescoes depicting the history of the city. The theatre at 15 Biegenstrasse was built in 1969. Marburg's synagogue was destroyed in the Kristallnacht of 1938 and its site has been dedicated as a memorial garden.

OTHER MUSEUMS: ethnological museum (at 10 Kugelgasse, open mornings); cultural history museum (Schloss, open except Mon 10.00–13.00, 15.00–17.00); museum of antiquity (at 11 Biegenstrasse, open Sun 11.00–13.00); Emil von Behring exhibition (at the corner of Kirchplatz in Nikolaistrasse, open weekdays 08.00–16.30).

After Marburg the B3 crosses the Lahn and travels NE through woods by way of Cölbe and through **Schönstadt**, with is half-timbered houses and a Schloss—4km E of which is **Rauschenberg**, again decked out with halftimbered houses, including the Rathaus, 1558, as well as a ruined 13C burg and a Romanesque-Gothic church.

A **diversion** 32km N reaches **Haina** (1600 inhab.; alt. 330m), with an early Gothic Cistercian monastery built between 1216 and 1328, which in 1533 became a hospital for the mentally ill. It is still a hospital, and allows access only to the church and cloister.

Return to the B3 and continue NE. The road skirts the Keller forest and reaches **Zwesten** (3000 inhab.; alt. 240m), 51km from Marburg: a village of old houses, surrounding a church with a tower dated 1506. 12km NE of

Zwesten lies **Fritzlar** (15,000 inhab.; alt. 230m; tourist information at the town hall). Here in 919 Heinrich I was crowned emperor. In the Marktplatz are multi-coloured half-timbered houses dating from the 14C to the 19C, including the late Gothic Rathaus and the Renaissance Hochzeitshaus—the latter a museum of local history opening 10.00–12.00, 15.00–17.00, closed Sat afternoons and Mon—and the Roland fountain of 1564, symbol of the city's freedom. Fritzlar retains 12 watchtowers and most of its 14C fortifications, some late Gothic stone houses and the Romanesque–Gothic *Dom of St Peter, 11–14C, situated where in 724 St Boniface felled an oak sacred to the pagans. The cathedral boasts three crypts. Its oldest monument is a 12C statue of St Peter, the next a reliquary of St Wigbert, 1340. Its also shelters a Gothic Pietà, has Baroque decoration and a Baroque altar, and a 19C spire. Fritzlar cathedral also has a rich museum, its chief treasure the 12C cross of Kaiser Heinrich IV (open 10.00–12.00, 14.00–17.00; closed Sun morning and in winter at 16.00). See also the church of Our Lady and the 13C and 14C former Minorite monastery church (now used by Protestants), both with medieval wall paintings.

11km W of Fritzlar along the B253 is the noted spa **Bad Wildungen**, a town founded in 1242 and frequented for its thermal waters since the 14C. The parish church dates back to the 13C and houses an altar painting of 1403 by Konrad von Soest depicting the Annunciation, Crucifixion and Resurrection, as well as two notable tombs: that of Prince Karl by Markus Krau, 1765, and that of Count Josias II von Waldeck, who died as a Venetian general fighting the Turks in 1669—hence the Turks sculpted on his tomb. The 18C Baroque Schloss Friedrichtein in the suburb of Altwildungen houses a museum of hunting and armour (closed Monday).

16km NW of the spa, along the B485, lies the 29km-long **Ederstausee**, usually dotted with yachts, dominated from a 175-m tree-covered hill by **Schloss Waldeck**, a fortress much restored over the centuries and now a hotel-restaurant. It has retained its St Elisabeth chapel of 1279, a 13C keep, the Grüner Saal of 1577, and a 120m-deep well.

From Fritzlar the route joins the A49 to reach after 34km **Kassel** (195,700 inhab.; alt. 163m). Situated on both banks of the River Fulda, Kassel was until 1866 the capital city of Hesse and until 1945 of Hesse-Nassau.

**Information office**: Wilhelmshöhe Bahnhof; **main post office**: N end of Königstrasse. **Trains** connect Kassel with Dortmund, Frankfurt, Göttingen, Giessen, Marburg, Munich and Mönchengladbach. The city arranges summer **concerts** in Wilhelmshöhe park; and offers **trips** in historic railway carriages pulled by historic railway trains, and boat trips along the river. **Markets**. Its flea-market takes place in Friedrichplatz on the first Saturday of the month from March until November. Here and in Königsplatz is set up the Christmas market. Apart from the Opera and Theatre, the theatre in the Fredericianum has 99 seats.

**History**. In the 10C the town was known as 'Chassala', owing its origin to an Imperial Schloss built here the previous century. The town was granted its city charter c 1180 and became the seat of the Landgraves of Hesse. The Reformation reached here in 1523. After Louis XIV revoked the Edict of Nantes in 1685 French Huguenot refugees fled here and built Upper-Kassel, which became known as the French new town. During the Seven Years War the French occupied the city from 1759–62, and in 1807 Napoleon's youngest brother Jerome ruled the kingdom of Westphalia from here. The Russians occupied the city in 1813, ceding it back to Hesse in 1814. The city became Prussian in 1866. Philipp Scheidemann (1865–1939), first president of the Weimar Republic, was mayor here, 1920–25. After 1945 Kassel became the chief city of the province of Hesse-Nassau.

Kurfürstenstrasse leads from the main railway station SE to Scheidemann-platz where the skyscraper was built by K. Fleischmann and W. Seidel. Ständeplatz, SW of Scheidemannplatz, houses the **Ständehaus** of 1835. A stairway (Treppenstrasse) leads to Friedrichsplatz, with its monument to Landgrave Friedrich II by Nahl, erected in 1783 two years before Friedrich's death. SE of the square is the modern theatre as well as at 2 Steinweg the gabled Ottoneum theatre which Wilhelm Vernukke built in 1606 and Paul de Ry transformed in 1696. This building is now the **Naturkundemuseum**, and displays the Ratzenberger Herbarium of 1556–92, the Goethe elephant on which the sage carried out his jawbone research and the remains of dinosaurs (open weekdays, except Mon 10.00–16.30, weekends 10.00–13.00). It also carries an inscription recording that Denis Papin used a steam engine at Kassel in 1706. On the NW side are what remains of an electoral palace, now part of a modern shop, and the long classical Museum Frederi-cianum with its Doric portico, 1769–76, restored after destruction in World War II, and today hosting temporary exhibitions, including a quinquennial exhibition of contemporary art (open except Mon 11.00–18.00).

The **Karlsaue**, a 150-hectare park with an island, the Siebenbergen, stretches S of Friedrichsplatz as far as the River Fulda. Begun 1568, its present layout derives from a Baroque landscaping, commissioned in 1710 by Landgrave Karl (from which time date the canals, statuary and marble pavilion), and altered in a more naturalistic style in the late 18C. The huge, long Orangery of 1710 once served as the Landgraves' summer residence and is now an exhibition hall.

Due N of Friedrichsplatz is Königsplatz, built in the Parisian circular style in 1766 and approached by six streets, a little way NE of which stands the mid-14C church of **St Martin**. Badly damaged in 1943, in part restored, though not as an accurate reconstruction, it houses the alabaster tomb of Landgrave Philipp and his wife Christine, by E. Godefroy and A. Liquier Beamont, 1572, while in the vault is the tomb of Landgrave Karl, who died in 1730.

Schöne Aussicht leads E from Friedrichsplatz, overlooking the River Fulda and passing SW by the Baroque **Schloss Bellevue**, built by the Huguenot exile Paul de Ry, 1714, and altered by his nephew Simon Louis de Ry, 1790. The Schloss is now a museum of the brothers Grimm (open weekdays except Mon 10.00–17.00, weekends 10.00–13.00), as well as a museum of stringed instruments (open Fri 10.00–17.00). At 1 Schöne Aussicht is the Neue Galerie, a classical building of 1871–74, displaying part of the city art collection, including works by the Kassel artist J.H. Tischbein the Elder (1722–89); landscapes by Caspar David Friedrich and the Nazarenes; paintings by Lovis Corinth; works by J. Beuys, and also a museum on the history of violin music (open except Mon 10.00–17.00).

From here walk beside the park down to the promenade known as An der Karlsaue, W of which is the **Marmorbad**, a swimming pool which the French sculptor Monnot decorated in the early 18C. NE of An der Karlsaue is the **Brüderkirche**, 1292–1396, with a *Lamentation c 1500 over the north door. Close by Schloss Bellevue is the Brüder-Grimm-Platz—the brothers Grimm spent much time in Kassel—with, at No. 5, the Hessisches Landes-museum, including prehistory, an astronomical collection and *Dutch paintings, as well as the German Tapetenmuseum, with wallpapers and hangings (open weekdays except Mon 10.00–17.00; weekends 10.00–13.00). Close by, the Landesbibliothek shelters Grimm archives and also the **Hildebrandlied, a manuscript written by a monk of Fulda c 800.

*One of the grottos of the Baroque park of Wilhelmshöhe at Kassel*

From Brüder-Grimm-Platz take Wilhelmshöher Allee, designed in 1781 by Simon Louis du Ry, which runs for 5km to the new part of Kassel and reaches the classical **Schloss Wilhelmshöhe**, by S.L. du Ry and H.C. Jussow, 1786–1803, housing a gallery of old masters (Gemäldegalerie) including seven paintings by Frans Hals, eight by Rubens and 17 by Rembrandt, as well as Albrecht Dürer's 1499 *portrait of Elsbeth Tucher (open, except Mon, 10.00–18.00, in winter closing at 17.00). The Schloss was the palace of King Jerome Napoleon from 1807–13. Ironically, Napoleon III was imprisoned here in 1870/71. Jerome commissioned the white Ballhaus which rises next to it.

This part of Kassel boasts a superb Baroque park in a stunning site, designed by Giovanni Guerniero for Landgrave Karl after he had visited Villa Aldobrandini at Frascati near Rome in 1699. Amongst its waterfall, cascades and a rose garden planted in 1765, its monuments include a bronze copy of the Farnese statue of Hercules, a temple of Mercury, the Octagon (63m high, supported on 192 Tuscan columns), a glasshouse of 1822, as well as health institutes (Kneipp mud baths). From here visit the Löwenburg, a 'medieval' Schloss built by H.C. Jussow, 1793–1801, for Prince-Elector Wilhelm I, who lies buried in its chapel. The Löwenburg museum opens Mar–Oct 10.00–17.00, closing 16.00 in winter. From here cross the Teufelsbrücke and reach the aqueduct, with its 250m-long water cascade, with 885 steps, ending in the Neptune basin, and enlivened with

52m-high jets of water. See also the Karlskirche by Paul du Ry, 1698–1710, in Karlsplatz. The Elisabeth Spital in Oberste Gasse, c 1300, was rebuilt after war damage, and now shelters cafés and a 15C sandstone statue of St Elisabeth.

9km N of Kassel is the Rococo **Schlösschen Wilhelmsthal**, built by F. Cuvilliés for Landgrave Wilhelm VIII, set in an 'English' park and open for guided tours 10.00–17.00 (closing 16.00 in winter).

# 38

# Giessen to Koblenz

Total distance 97km. Giessen—B49, 15km Wetzlar—22km Weilburg—16km Limburg an der Lahn—20km Montabaur—24km Koblenz.

Leave **Giessen** (see Rte 37) W by way of the B49, passing through Klein-Linden and reaching after 15km **Wetzlar** (52,500 inhab.; alt. 145m; tourist office: 8 Domplatz). 'Pleasantly situated but small and poorly built', as Goethe described the city, Wetzlar has improved since his time. Straddling the River Lahn at its confluence with the Dill, the old town stretches upwards on the right bank. A Free City from 1180 until 1803, from 1693 to 1806 the former Rathaus, 1606–90, was the seat of the highest court of the Holy Roman Empire. Today the town specialises in ironworks and optical goods, cameras, magnifying glasses, telescopes and microscopes. On its peak, the Altstadt is dominated by the interdenominational cathedral of St Maria, begun in the Gothic style in 1225 on an earlier Romanesque church of 897. The Nikolai chapel was finished in 1278 and a new west façade was added in the 14C, from which period also date the naves and the upper part of the north transept. Its massive three-storeyed tower was not completed until the 16C. Of its richly sculpted portals the finest is the Heidenportal (the door of the pagans). Inside are a Pietà of 1380; Christ carrying the cross with the aid of Simon of Cyrene; and a Virgin Mary, c 1500. In the square stands the former Rathaus (see above).

The Spitalkirche in Lahnstrasse is by J.L. Splittdorf, 1755–64. Burg Hermannstein is a 13C ruin. In Schillerplatz is the Jerusalemhaus of c 1700. The Palais Papius, at 1 Kornblumengasse, built 1717–93, was the home of Franz von Pape, known as Papius, assessor at the Imperial court (open 10.00–12.00, 15.00–17.00, except Mon and Sun afternoons). Now a museum of furniture, it is at 8–10 Lottestrasse the former house of the Teutonic Knights—now a Goethe and city museum and known as the Lotteshaus, open except Mon 09.00–12.00, 14.00–17.00; Sun closed afternoon—was the home of Charlotte Buff in 1772, when Goethe came to Wetzlar. When a young philosopher committed suicide out of unrequited love for the already engaged Charlotte, Goethe was inspired by her to write his 'Die Leiden des jungen Werthers', 1774, whereas Goethe's own more successful relationship with Charlotte in turn inspired Thomas Mann's 'Lotte in Weimar', 1939. In the Avemannscherhaus is a museum of the Imperial court (open except Mon 10.00–13.00, 1400–17.00) whose deliberations the young Goethe deemed 'monstrously unhealthy,... the formalities of trial for trial's sake'.

The B49 continues for 10km SW to **Braunfels**, with a thermal spring, the Karlssprudel, half-timbered houses—the Rentkammer, c 1700; some medieval ones in the Marktplatz—and above the town a picturesque Schloss founded in the 13C but now, apart from the 15C tower, the late Gothic hall and the early 18C kitchens, mainly built between 1846 and 1891. (Its museum opens daily 08.00–17.00.) 12km further W lies **Weilburg** (13,500 inhab.; alt. 128m), a town laid out with military precision, once the home of the dukes of Nassau. Weilburg has a Renaissance Hochschloss of 1535–75, enlarged by Graf Johann Ernst, 1703–17, with Baroque stables. Its orangery was stuccoed by C.M. Pozzi. The stucco of the Schloss *church is by A. Gallasini, 1712. At Weilburg J.L. Rothweil designed the Baroque Marktplatz—whose fountain was created by Wilckens in 1709—as well as a hunting lodge in 1713–26. At 1 Schlossplatz is a museum of mining (open in summer daily except Mon 10.00–12.00, 14.00–17.00; closed winter weekends). A 300m-long underground canal was built here, 1841–47.

16km SW of Weilburg the B49 reaches **Limburg an der Lahn** (30,000 inhab.; alt. 122m; tourist information: 2 Hospitalstrasse), set between the Taunus range and the mountains of the Westerwald and retaining a few fragments of its medieval fortifications, the towers of its imposing cathedral overlooking the river. From the railway station follow Bahnhofstrasse to the heart of the city, the Kornmarkt. From here the picturesque Barfüsserstrasse leads left to the 14C former Franciscan monastery church and to the bishops' palace. Inside the former you will find the tombstone of Johannes von Limburg, died 1312, two late Gothic altars, a 15C Pietà, an organ by A. Oehninger, 1685, a Rococo pulpit and a mid-18C ceiling. High on its peak stands the *cathedral, dedicated to St George, founded in 909, influenced by the architecture of Laon cathedral in France and of St Gereon in Cologne. Begun in 1210 and consecrated in 1235, the present Dom bridges the transition between late Romanesque and early Gothic, enhanced by the polychrome restoration of 1971. The towers flanking the façade of the south transept were added in 1863 and 1865. Inside, look especially for the stone rood screen c 1235; 13C to 16C frescoes in the nave (with scenes from the Old and New Testaments, ancient sages, Sibyls and virtues); the 13C tomb of Konrad Kurzbold, who died in 948 and was a founder of this church; a Romanesque font, c 1235; the tomb of Daniel von Mudersbach and his wife Jutta (died 1477 and 1461); a tabernacle of 1496 (renovated 1628); and the modern high altar, 1977. The frescoed dome above the crossing depicts not only St George, patron of the cathedral, but also St Nicholas, patron of the city.

S of the cathedral apse stands the 13C and 14C Schloss of the counts of Lahngau, rebuilt in 1934 after a fire, now the diocesan museum and incorporating a Schloss chapel of 1298. The museum's treasures include a 10C *reliquary of the true Cross—the 'Staurothek', brought by crusaders from Hagia Sophia, Constantinople—and another golden reliquary containing St Peter's staff, c 980 (open in summer 10.00–18.00). Towards the River Lahn, at 5 Fahrgasse, stands the Renaissance Walderdorffer Hof of 1665 with its gate tower and storeyed courtyard, rising above the old 1315 stone bridge across the Lahn. See also the Franciscan church of St Sebastian, with Gothic side altars, a 15C Pietà and a Rococo pulpit, and the remains of Limburg's medieval fortifications.

From Limburg follow the B49 NW through Staffel and Görgeshausen to reach afer 20km **Montabaur** (in the Rhineland-Palatinate), with its 14C and 15C Gothic church of St Peter in Chains, whose wall paintings include a Last Judgment over the chancel arch, a fine Marktplatz and, on a 279m-

*Limburg cathedral, founded in 909 and consecrated in 1235, towers above the River Lahn*

high peak, a yellow-ochre Schloss variously built between the 13C and the 18C, with four domed towers and a 33m-high keep. Montabaur dates back to the 10C and was known as Humbach until in 1221 Archbishop Thierry II of Trier returned from the Holy Land and renamed it 'Mons Tabor'.

From Montabaur the B49 runs SW for 24km to **Koblenz** (see Rte 29).

# 39

# Giessen to Siegen

Total distance 78km (64km by motorway). Giessen—A429, 19km Wetzlar—
B272, 24km Herborn—7km Dillenburg—28km Siegen.

Drive W from **Giessen** (see Rte 37) along the A429 to reach the B277 at
Wetzlar (see Rte 38) after 19km.

The route now leaves the Lahn valley and enters the valley of the Dill,
following the B272 NW by way of Hermannstein, dominated by a ruined
Schloss, and Greifenstein, with the ruins of Burg Greifenstein, 418m high,
for 24km to **Herborn** (108,000 inhab.; alt. 205m), a town of picturesque
alleyways and half-timbered, slate-roofed houses, especially the 16C local
history museum (open Tue, Thu, Sat 15.00–18.00). Built in 1591, two storeys
high with a courtyard and fine staircase tower, this was formerly the town
hall. The present half-timbered Rathaus of 1589–91 is sculpted with coats
of arms. The late Gothic church of St Peter was built in the 16C on the basis
of a Romanesque basilica. At Herborn Protestant theologians set up a
university (1584–1817). The theologians now work in the 14C Schloss (with
its three towers), once the home of the Dukes of Nassau. 2km later, at Burg,
the route meets the B255 from Marburg (see Rte 37).

Continue NW along the B255 and B272 for 5km to **Dillenburg** (25,000
inhab.; alt. 220m), at the foot of a Schloss whose 40m-high Wilhelmsturm
was added 1872–75, and is so named because here in 1533 was born
William the Silent (1533–84), who later was to drive the Spaniards out of
the Netherlands. The mid-13C fortress built by Count Heinrich II von
Nassau (1197–1247), with its 16C and 17C bastions, was partly destroyed
by the French in 1760. A museum in the Wilhelmsturm commemorates
William the Silent (open except Mon 09.00–12.00, 14.00–18.00; closed
Nov–Easter). Part of the town suffered in a fire of 1723, but the parish church
of 1489–1524 survived, and still shelters fifteen tombs of members of the
Nassau-Oranien dynasty, as did numerous half-timbered houses. The town
hall was rebuilt after the fire.

The route now passes into North Rhineland-Westphalia, before reaching
after 28km **Siegen** (120,000 inhab.; alt. 236m), which before the reunification of Germany was the geographical mid-point of the former German
Federal Republic. Situated on the River Sieg, Siegen, surrounded by forests
and good hiking country, was the principle seat of the Nassau family from
the 12C. Here was born (to refugee parents) the painter Peter Paul Rubens
(1577–1640). In 1623 the Nassau-Siegen family divided into a Catholic and
a Protestant wing. The Catholics lived in the 13C to 16C Oberes Schloss,
the Protestants occupying the Unteres Schloss (rebuilt between 1698 and
1714 after a fire) in which is the family mausoleum, 1669–70. The **Oberes
Schloss, modified in the 17C and 18C, houses the Siegerland regional
museum with eight paintings by Rubens and an Orange room with family
portraits (open except Mon 10.00–12.30, 14.00–17.00).

In spite of much damage in World War II Siegen boasts a late Romanesque
(13C) rotunda church of St Nikolaus, with a mid-15C four-storey tower, on
top of which is a wrought-iron, gilded crown (the Krönchen) placed here
in 1658 when Johann Moritz of Nassau was elevated to the status of prince.

The modern bronze doors are by G. Marcks. The Gothic church of St Martin, 1511–17, incorporates from an earlier church on this site a mosaic pavement c 1100 and a Romanesque west door. The Marienkirche is Siegen's sole Baroque church, built in the early 18C for the Jesuits. The Rathaus of Siegen, though founded in 1224, is late 18C and early 20C. Here are two theatres: the Siegenes Theater, 1957, and the Kleine Theater Lohkasten, 1974. Information offices at the main railway station and at the Rathaus at 2 Markt.

# 40

# The Rheingau

Total distance 30km. Wiesbaden—B263 and B42, 9km Eltville—4km, Kloster Eberbach—7km Winkel—B42, 6km Geisenheim—4km Rüdesheim.

The Rheingau is located in the administrative district of Darmstadt in south central Germany, a district created after World War II. Situated W of Wiesbaden on the S face of the Taunus uplands are the chief vineyards of this region, which also spread on the western slopes of the Odenwald along the Bergstrasse.

**Wiesbaden** (270,000 inhab.; alt. 117m), former capital of the duchy of Nassau, chief city of the Prussian province of Hesse-Nassau from 1866 and since 1946 capital of Hesse, is sheltered by the wooded slopes of the Taunus to the N and borders on the River Rhine to the S. A city of parks and gardens, it welcomes to its Kurhaus visitors each May for an international festival, for the Rheingau wine festival in September, and all the year round for its 26 thermal springs.

**Main railway station**: Bahnhofsplatz. **Main post office**: Rheinstrasse. **Tourist office**: Hauptbahnhof, 15 Rheinstrasse.

The **Rhein-Main airport** is half an hour away. **Trains** connect with Basel, Darmstadt, Dortmund, Limburg and Munich; **boats** ply the river to Mainz, Cologne and Frankfurt. **Concerts** by the Hesse State Orchestra take place in the Kurhaus concert hall.

**History**. The site was occupied at the time of Drusus, in the 2C BC, and the Romans, who knew its spa as *Fontes Mattiaci*, built a town here with a temple to Jupiter. In 330 the name Wisibada appears. The town was the site of a Frankish court. The dukes of Nassau ruled Wiesbaden from the 13C (from 1744 it was the Residenz of the Nassau-Usingen line), and Prince Friedrich August (1803–16) and Duke Wilhelm von Nassau (1816–39) in particular commissioned architects who gave the city its classical aspect. The dukes unwisely allied with Austria in her conflicts with Prussia, with the result that in 1866 they were obliged to cede Wiesbaden into Prussian hands, along with the duchy. Between 1919 and 1939 when French and Belgian troops occupied the Rhineland, Wiesbaden was chosen as their administrative seat. The city was much bombed in February 1945. In 1970 an important research hospital was established here. Its Kurhaus reopened in 1987.

Goethe frequently visited the city (an obelisk at Frauenstein commemorates this). Dostoevsky and Turgenev gambled at Wiesbaden. Here Richard Wagner composed his 'Mastersingers of Nuremberg' and Johannes Brahms his symphony no. 3 in F-major. Richard and Clara Schuman lived here. Adolf Hitler's opponent Pastor Martin Niemöller (1892–1984) died here.

The main railway station, built by Klingholtz in 1906, is situated S of the city on its inner ring road, the Ring, which runs in a semicircle SE–NW. W of the station is the **Martin Luther church**. E in Mainzerstrasse are the Hesse state archives, including Nassau documents from the 10C onwards, in a building of 1878, E of which in Wittelsbacher Strasse is the 13-storey **Bundesamt** building of 1955. Cross the gardens in front of Bahnhofsplatz and follow Friedrich-Ebert-Allee to the **Rhein-Main-Halle**, built in 1956, and holding 4000 people. Opposite is the city museum, with natural history, antiquities and paintings, including Cranach and Max Beckmann and the Wiesbaden's adopted member of the 'Blaue Reiter' school, Alexej von Jawlensky, 1861–1941, who settled in the city in 1921; open except Mon 10.00–16.00, Tue also 17.00–21.00.

Rheinstrasse runs W from the museum to reach on the right, Luisenplatz, half-way to Ringkirche. Here rise the Catholic, neo-Gothic parish church of **St Bonifatius**, 1845–49, and a monument to those who fell at Waterloo (an obelisk, set up in 1865). On Rheinstrasse is the state library, with early 16C engravings and 300 ancient manuscripts. At the far end of Rheinstrasse is the Protestant **Ringkirche**, by Otzen, 1892. From the city museum, **Wilhelmstrasse**, filled with shops, hotels and banks, and named after the duke of Nassau who laid it out in 1812, runs N, past the **Warm-DammAnlage gardens** on the right—with monuments to Schiller by Uphues, 1905, and to Kaiser Wilhelm I by Schilling, 1894—reaching on the right the **Staatstheater** and on the left Kaiser-Friedrich-Platz, with its fountain. The theatre has a riotously Baroque interior, created by the Viennese architects Fellner and Hellmer between 1892 and 1894, seats 1041 spectators and stages opera, operetta and ballet. On the right of Kaiser-Friedrich-Platz is the **Kurhaus**, built by Friedrich von Thiersch, 1905–07, and embracing a concert hall, a casino of 1949, which inspired Dostoevsky's (the original of 'The Gambler') and indoor and outdoor restaurants. Tennis courts are found in the **Kurpark**, which in summer is the venue of concerts. N of the Kurhaus is the **Brunnenkolonnade**, 1825, and the **Theaterkolonnade**, 1839.

**Taunusstrasse**, its classical apartment buildings from the Wilhelmine period housing antique shops on their ground floors, leads NW from Wilhelmstrasse. Immediately left is the **Kochbrunnen** hall, which embraces 15 thermal springs capable of delivering 23,000 litres of mineral water every hour. Along Taunusstrasse is an 1870/71 war memorial and the Nerotal thermal clinic, at the foot of the **Neroberg**, whose funicular railway to the park was constructed in 1888. Here are gardens, restaurant and the swimming pool given to the city by the motor car manufacturer W. von Opel, in 1933. On the Neroberg, glimpsed from afar, is the Greek chapel with its five golden domes (open 08.00–20.00; closed Sun mornings). It was built by Philipp Hoffmann in the Russian style, 1848-55, as a mausoleum for the Russian-born Herzogin Elizabeth, who died in 1845 one year after her marriage. Her tomb is by E. Hopfgarten. The Russian Orthodox liturgy is celebrated here.

Immediately left after the Kochbrunnen, Langgasse leads to the Kaiser-Friedrich-Bad of 1913, and then to the Marktstrasse. Follow Marktstrasse left to reach Rathausplatz. The **Rathaus**, built in the German Renaissance style by Hauberrisser, 1884–87, was severely damaged in 1944 and has been perfectly restored, including a Ratskeller. The square also houses the former **schloss** of the dukes of Nassau, built in the classical style by Georg Moller, 1837–71, used by both Kaisers Wilhelm I and Wilhelm II as a royal residence, and now the parliament building, and the Protestant, neo-Gothic **Hauptkirche** by Carl Boos, 1853–62. Boos built in red brick, recalling the medieval Gothic building of northern Germany, and produced a church whose nave measure 60m by 20m, adding five towers of which the highest reaches 90m. In front of the building is a bronze statue of William of Orange.

The Schloss borders onto **Schlossplatz**, with its Lion fountain of 1525 and the oldest building in Wiesbaden, the **Altes Rathaus**, 1609, its formerly half-timbered upper storey rebuilt in stone in 1828. NW of Schlossplatz is the Heidenmauer, the remains of the late 4C Roman defences. The so-called Roman gate was built in 1902.

Wiesbaden's Little Theatre is Am Kochbrunnen. Cabaret and satire are performed in the Parisier Hoftheater in Spielgasse.

**Environs**. NE of Wiesbaden (30 minutes' walk, or drive by the Sonnenberger Strasse) are the valley of the Rambach and **Sonnenberg**, with a Schloss of 1200 ruined in 1689. 4km NE of the town is the hunting lodge **Kranichstein**, built in the Renaissance style, 1571–79, with a hunting museum. 10km S of the city is the ruined 13C **Schloss Frankenstein**, on a 397m peak.

An avenue of chestnut trees leads SW along Rheingaustrasse to reach after 3km **Wiesbaden-Biebrich**, where beside the Rhine stands the Baroque *Schloss Biebrich, built 1699–1706 and embellished and enlarged 1711–45. It now houses the German film institute. Ludwig von Sckell laid out the 'English' garden in 1811. On the park is the Wiesbaden racecourse. At 142 Biebricher Allee the firm of Henkell makes and sells sparkling wines.

The B42 continues W through **Wiesbaden-Schierstein**, with vineyards whose grapes are used to produce sparkling wines. 2km NW is the ruined **Schloss Frauenstein**. The route continues from Wiesbaden-Schierstein reaching (7km from Wiesbaden) **Niederwalluf**, where the River Walluff flows into the Rhine. Here are nurseries, fruit growing and sailing. Pass through Walluf to reach 2km later the oldest town in the Rheingau, **Eltville** (8500 inhab.; alt. 89m). Founded in 1332, the keep of its 1345 Schloss, built for the Archbishops of Mainz, survives, along with an east wing dated 1681. Here too is a 14C late Gothic church of SS Peter and Paul, with Renaissance tombs. Eltville's old houses include the Gothic and Renaissance Hof Langwerth and the Baroque Eltzsche Hof, while the Martinstor is all that remains from the medieval fortifications. The town hosts an annual festival over the first weekend of July.

The wine village of **Kiedrich**, 3km N, was once protected by the ruined 12C Burg Scharfenstein. Underneath the early 16C rood screen of the 15C Gothic church of St Valentin is the Madonna of Kiedrich, c 1350. The church organ, built by Wendelinus Kirchner in 1312 (restored 1653), is the oldest in Germany still playable, and the church choir sings Gregorian chant from a codex of 1260. Near the cemetery chapel of St Michael, 1440, restored in the 19C, is a crucifixion group of 1520.

1km further E from Eltville is **Erbach**, whose monuments are Schloss Reinhardshausen, 1745, and the 15C church of St Markus, and whose glory is the 'Markobrunnen' wine. 4km N is *Kloster Eberbach, a former Cistercian abbey, founded in 1116, whose monks are wrongly said to have brought the vines to the Rheingau. The Romans grew grapes here; the monks greatly developed the skill, and their monastery became the greatest wine-producing centre of Germany. Secularised in 1803 and becoming the property of the state, it remains celebrated for its wines, and the wine producers of the Rheingau use and maintain the building. The restored monastery church, still guarded by its 12C and 13C walls, was begun in 1145 and consecrated in 1186. It houses the tomb of Eberhard von Oberstein, who died in 1331, and the *tombs of Wigand von Hynsperg, died 1511, and Adam von Allendorf, died 1518, and his wife, by Hans Backoffen. The chapter house was built in 1345. The Kloster has wine cellars with old presses, a cloister, and a refectory with a Baroque stuccoed ceiling of 1738. Its 'new' gateway was built in 1774. (Open Mar–Oct weekdays 10.00–16.00, weekends 11.00–16.00; otherwise daily 10.00–18.00.)

Drive S to the wine village of **Hattenheim** (1500 inhab.; alt. 81m), which has a partly ruined Schloss of 1411, and a church of 1740 with a mid-13C bell tower and a Baroque interior. In front of the church is a crucifixion group of 1510. Upstream the 18C Schloss Reichardtshausen is built on the spot from which in the 12C and succeeding centuries boats sailed laden with wine from Kloster Eberbach. 3km W lies **Oestrich**, with the half-timbered Gasthaus Schwan of 1628, the 12C church of St Martin (restored 1508) and a wooden crane of 1652. 3km N of here is **Hallgarten**, its greatest claim to fame a terracotta 'Hallgarten Madonna', c 1420, the Virgin with a pitcher, in the parish church.

The road from Oestrich along the right bank of the Rhine runs through **Mittelheim**, with its Romanesque church of St Ägidius, 1140, reaching after 2km **Winkel**, which has Germany's oldest dwelling, the Graues Haus, c 800, and the 1751 Brentanohaus, so named because the author Clemens von Brentano and his sister Bettina lived here in the 18C. Drive N from here to reach after 3km **Schloss Johannisberg**, built on the site of an abandoned Benedictine abbey by Johannes Dientzenhofer, 1718–25, partly rebuilt in the classical style, 1826–33, restored after war damage, 1946. Reputed wines are sold from the cellars. The former monastery church was also restored after war damage.

Return to the river bank and **Geisenheim** (12,200 inhab.; alt. 96m), seat of the Hesse institute for wine culture. Its Gothic church of 1510 was enlarged by Philipp Hoffmann, 1838–41, who added the towers. Preserving a Baroque high altar, 1700, and 16C to 18C tombs and memorials, this church is known as the cathedral of the Rheingau. Geisenheim also treasures a 600-year-old lime tree, old houses and Schloss Schönborn, 1550, where an end to the Thirty Years War was negotiated in 1547 (a year before the peace of Westphalia). 3km N in the middle of the forest is **Marienthal**, with its medieval monastery church of 1330, restored 1897, outside which is a crucifixion group sculpted c 1520. 4km NW at **Eibingen** is a Benedictine monastery founded in 1148.

Geisenheim is 4km E of **\*Rüdesheim am Rhein** (10,000 inhab.; alt. 90m; tourist information: 16 Rheinstrasse) known to the Romans and famous for its wine. Its most picturesque streets is Drosselgasse (Thrush Street), with 17C and 18C houses. The early 15C church of St Jakob rises in the Marktplatz, with a Romanesque chapel. Rüdesheim has 15C town walls, and the Boosenburg retains its 10C keep despite the transformations of 1828. Other historic buildings are the 16C Adelshöfe, and the Mäuser tower on an island in the River Rhine, built in 1208 by Philipp von Boden on the site of a wooden one set up by the Romans in the 8C BC. Of the town fortifications the Romanesque Oberburg tower dates from 1609. The Adler tower at the E end of the town is 15C. The Rheingau wine museum, at 2 Rheinstrasse, in the early 13C Brömserburg (restored in the 19C), displays 2000 years of viticulture and opens except Mon and Dec–Jan 09.00–12.00, 14.00–17.00. At 29 Oberstrasse in the 16C and 17C Brömser Hof is a mechanical musical instrument museum (open Apr–Oct daily 10.00–22.00), with instruments ranging from the 18C to the 20C. A cable car runs to the Niederwald national monument, with a 10.5m-high figure of Germania, weighing 32 tonnes and created by J. Schilling in 1883 to commemorate the establishment of the Prussian empire in 1871, N of which is the Niederwald hunting lodge of 1764 (now a hotel).

# 41

## The Right Bank: Bonn to Rüdesheim

Total distance 130km. Bonn—B42, 10km Königswinter—17km Linz—22km Neuwied—17km Koblenz—6km Lahnstein—28km St Goarshausen—10km Kaub—20km Rüdesheim.

Along with the journey along the left bank (see Rte 42), this is one of the best known and most romantic routes in Germany. As Byron wrote of the Rhine in *Childe Harold's Pilgrimage*:

A blending of all beauties:
     streams and dells,
Fruit, foliage, crag, wood,
     cornfield, mountain, vine,
And chiefless castles,
     breathing stern farewells
From gray but leafy walls,
     where Ruin greenly dwells.

It begins at the small university city of **BONN** (289,000 inhab.; alt. 56m), which was chosen in 1949 to be the capital of the Federal Republic of Germany and after reunification kept eight of the 16 ministries. Since 1969 the city has embraced the neighbouring communities of Bad Godesberg and Beuel (on the left bank of the Rhine), more than doubling its original population of c 130,000. In 1991, by the narrow margin of 337 to 320 votes, and in spite of the fact that Bonn had commissioned a new parliament building at a cost of 256 millon DM, the Bundestag voted to return to Berlin. Bonn has hotel capacity for 10,600 visitors and its parliamentary hall seems destined to make the city a major international conference centre.

**Information office** at 20 Münsterstrasse. **Trains** connect with Cologne and Frankfurt; **flights** to the sister-capital, Berlin. Bonn hosts a biennial **Beethoven festival**.

**History**. The city stands on a Celtic site, invested by the Romans as *Castra Bonnensia*, to which the Roman Emperor Claudius sent a legion in c AD 44. For the Romans this spot was of great strategic importance, and by AD 69 their legionaries had fortified here Castra Bonnensia. Present-day Adenauerallee follows the route of the Roman road which led to Koblenz from the Roman camp N of the present Rosenthalstrasse. This camp was bisected by the Via Principalis, whose exact route is followed by Römer-Strasse. Bonn was settled by the Franks in the 5C. In 881 the Normans destroyed their fortifications, and the settlement was again decimated by the Hohenstaufens in 1198 and by the Duke of Brabant in 1239. A year earlier the Archbishops of Cologne had made their home here, and they lived at Bonn until 1794. Meanwhile the city had come into the possession of the Kurfürsten of Cologne and joined the Rheinish League in 1677. After becoming part of Prussia with the rest of the Rhineland in 1815, a university was founded here. The historic centre of the city was virtually destroyed in World War II.

    Here were born Ludwig van Beethoven (1770–1827) and the poet Ernst Moritz Arndt (1769–1860). The grave of Robert Schumann (1810–56) and his wife Clara Wieck (1819–96) can be found alongside the central alley of the old cemetery (near the main railway station). Here too are buried Schiller's wife Charlotte and their son Ernst, Beethoven's mother, Ernst Moritz Arndt, A.W. von Schlegel and Otto Wesendonck. The cemetery also houses a chapel of the Teutonic Knights, built c 1250 and brought here in 1846.

W of the main railway station at 16 Colmantstrasse stands the **Rheinisches Landesmuseum**, the museum of the Rhineland, founded in 1820 and rebuilt in 1969. It displays prehistory, *Roman remains, history, art, sculpture and furniture (open weekdays except Mon 09.00–17.00, closing Wed 20.00, weekends 09.00–17.00). From the main railway station follow Poststrasse to Münsterplatz, where rise the 1845 Beethoven monument by Ernst Hähnel, and the former Schloss Fürstenberg. Here stands the Romanesque **Münster**, dedicated to SS Martin, Cassius and Florentinus, and one of the finest late Romanesque churches of the Rhineland. Part of its crypt dates

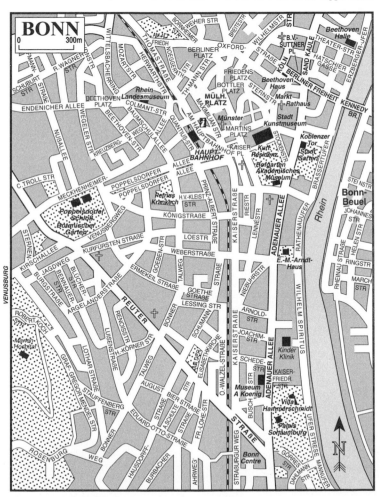

from 1060–70. The west choir was built in the 11C, its exterior finished in the 12C. The Münster has a mid-12C apse with a late 12C vault, early 13C aisles and transepts (the latter restored in the 1880s and in 1934). Works of religious art sheltered here include 13C and 14C wall paintings, a seated Virgin sculpted in the 12C, the tombs of Archbishop Engelbert II of Cologne (died 1275) and Archbishop Ruprecht of Cologne (died 1480), a Renaissance tabernacle in the choir, a bronze statue of St Helen in the nave (created in 1620), a 16C Virgin and Child and 17C marble retables. To the south are the two-storeyed cloisters, 1126–69, open weekdays 10.00–12.00, 13.00–17.00.

From Münsterplatz follow Am Hof NE alongside the university, housed since 1818 in the Baroque **Kurfürstliche Residenz**, which was built for Kurfürst Joseph Clemens by the Italian architect Enrico Zuccalli between 1697 and 1702, and altered by Robert de Cotte in 1715 to make it resemble in certain respects Versailles. Its chapel dates from 1777. The statue of the Virgin Mary, Regina Pacis, at the SE end of the Schloss, was created by Willem and Hendrik Rottermondt in 1750. Behind the Schloss is a **botanical garden**, with numerous rare plants (open May–Sept weekdays 09.00–18.00, weekends and holidays 09.00–13.00; otherwise only weekdays 10.30–12.00, 14.00–16.00). Continue to reach the triangular Marktplatz, whose Rococo **Rathaus** by M. Leveilly, 1737–38, is ornamented with the coat of arms of the Prince-Electors. The Rathaus has an annex of 1954 housing the city art collection, (entrance at 7 Rathausgasse), with important works by the 'Blaue Reiter' and 'Brücke' artists, especially August Macke, and post-1945 works, including pop art (open except Mon 10.00–17.00, Tue, Thu closing 21.00).

There is an extension to the gallery in Friedrich-Ebert-Allee, with emphasis on the poet and German patriot Ernst Moritz Arndt, 1769–1860, who lived and died here. N of the town hall is the 13C church of **St Remigius**, which was built for the minor friars. The Marktplatz centres on a fountain with an obelisk, set up in 1777.

Leave the Marktplatz by Bonngasse to see on the right the Jesuit **Namen-Jesu-Kirche** (Church of the Holy Name), which was built between 1688 and 1717 to the designs of Jakob von Candrea. It has Baroque decoration, two five-storey towers with onion domes, and a *Corinthian façade of 1692. Inside are altars dating from the mid 18C. The high altar is by Bartholomäus Dierix, the side altars by Melchior Jouanny. Beethoven was born at 20 Bonngasse, the **Beethovenhaus**, and this 18C house is now a museum (open weekdays 09.00–13.00, 15.00–17.00, weekends 09.00–13.00, closing earlier Oct–Mar). Its exhibits include various instruments with which the composer tried to combat his increasing deafness, the organ of the Remigiuskirche on which the young composer played, and a large Beethoven manuscript collection. Follow Bonngasse to Bertha-von-Suttner-Platz, across which you take Berliner Freiheit which leads to the 432m-long Kennedy bridge that crosses the Rhine to Bonn-Beuel.

When you reach the bridge, turn left along Erzberger Ufer to the huge congress and concert hall, the **Beethovenhalle**, by Siegfried Wolske, 1959. Brassert Ufer leads right past the city theatre, by Beck-Erlang and Gessler, 1965, to reach the **Alter Zoll**, once the bastion that controlled river traffic and took tolls. Here are statues of Ernst Moritz Arndt and Heinrich Heine. Close by are set out the city gardens. Walk E from Alter Zoll along Konvikt Strasse as far as the **Koblenzer Tor**, a former fortified gateway which was rebuilt in the Baroque stye by Michael Leveilly. From here you follow Adenauerallee S.

On the right is the **Hofgarten**, which Rivert de Cotte laid out in 1720. Here rise the university library, in front of which is a statue by Hans Arp, and at 21 Am Hofgarten the **Akademisches Museum**, founded by August Wilhelm von Schlegel and F.G. Welcker and built by Karl Friedrich Schinkel in 1824 (open except Sat 10.00–13.00; Thu also 16.00–18.00). It houses ancient sculpture and artefacts. At No. 79 was born Ernst Moritz Arndt. His birthplace is now his museum, **E.M.-Arndt-Haus** (open, except Mon 10.00–17.00).

Continue S and SE along Adenauerallee. **Villa Hammerschmidt**, built 1863–65 by August Dieckhoff, the former official residence of the president of the Federal Republic, stands opposite the museum, close by the federal administrative office in **Palais Schaumburg**, 1858–60. Nos 150–164 Adenauerallee house the Institute of Zoological Research and the **Museum Koenig** (open weekdays except Mon 09.00–17.00, weekends 09.00–12.30) with mummified animals, birds and reptiles, northern and local birds and living as well as dead insects. Just beyond the Palais Schaumburg is Bundeskanzler-Platz, with the **Bonn-Center**, and to the left the **Bundeshaus**, the modern parliament buildings. From here Reuter Strasse leads some distance NW to the **botanical gardens** in which stands the former **Schloss Clemensruhe** (also known as the **Poppelsdorfer Schloss**). This imposing building was designed for the prince-electors of Cologne by Robert de Cotte and Enrico Zuccalli between 1697 and 1725. It was completed by Balthasar Neumann, 1744–56, and rebuilt in 1926–30 and 1956. The Schloss now serves as the University Mineralogical and Petrological Museum (open Wed 15.00–17.00, Sat 10.00–12.00). To the W, at 182 Sebastianstrasse, the Schumannhaus was once a hospital, and is so-named because the composer was admitted here in 1854 because of his terrible depressions and died here two year later. Open weekdays 10.00–12.00, 16.00–19.00, Sun 10.00–13.00, the house displays Schumann memorabilia.

Zeppelin Strasse runs S from Poppelsdorfer Schloss to the forest-clad **Venusberg**, with the university medical school, an elegant modern residential quarter and game reserve. The route (20 minutes by foot) to the 125m-high **Kreuzberg**, with its Franciscan monastery and the Kreuzberg pilgrimage church of 1628—whose Baroque chapel of the Scala Sancta is by Balthasar Neumann, 1746–57, and a high altar with statues of electors may perhaps also be by Neumann—runs from Poppelsdorfer Schloss by way of Meckenheimer Allee, Klemens-August-Strasse and Trierer Strasse.

For **Bad Godesberg** see Rte 42.

Cross the Kennedy bridge to **Bonn-Beuel**, to see upstream (N) the double-storeyed Romanesque *church of **Schwarz-Rheindorf**, built between 1151 and 1173, with an upper nave and a lower nave. It has frescoes of 1151 depicting Ezekiel's vision, a 17C Madonna and a Gothic spire. The Theater der Jugend is at 50 Hermannstrasse. The route along the bank of the river (Rheinuferstrasse) leads SE to the B42, passing through **Oberkassel**, where there is an 11C Romanesque church tower. Here was found prehistoric 'Oberkassel man'. After 8km the route reaches Niederdollendorf, from where a road runs 3km left to the ruins of the 13C Cistercian abbey of **Heisterbach**, whose basilica, built between 1202 and 1237, was, apart from the choir, demolished in 1808. Close by is an 18C convent.

2km SE lies leisurely **Königswinter** (37,000 inhab.; alt. 50m), at the foot of the Drachenfels. Along Rheinallee, fronting the river, are open-air cafés and wine-bars. Its parish church of St Remigius, which was built in 1799, has a 14C reliquary of St Margaret. Visitors use the town as a starting point for visiting the Siebengebirge (including Schloss Drachenfels), which can be reached from here by a rack-railway (see Rte 49). The Siebengebirge local history museum is at 11 Klotzstrasse in a Baroque, two-storey building of 1732, and is devoted to geology, wine and paintings by the Nazarene Franz Ittenbach (1913–79).

After 5km the route reaches **Bad-Honnef-Rhöndorf** (45,000 inhab.; alt. 78m), two united towns. In the cemetery of Rhöndorf is buried the former federal Chancellor Konrad Adenaur (1876–1967). The house in which he lived, at 8c Konrad-Adenauer-Strasse, is now a museum (open Tue–Sun 10.00–16.30). Bad-Honnef, situated between the Drachenfels and the Rolandsbogen, dubs itself 'the Nice of the Rhine', and has a late Gothic hall-church dedicated to St John the Baptist, with a 12C west tower and much 16C and 17C reordering. Look out for the chapel of St Servatius, 17C and 18C, with a late Romanesque choir. The Kurhaus, with the Drachen spring providing the waters, stands in a fine park. A bridge leads to the island of Grafenwerth in the middle of the river, where you will find an open-air swimming pool and can take the mineral waters.

Drive a further 6km to Unkel by way of **Rheinbreitbach**, the gateway to the Rhein-Westerwald Naturpark. Its ruined medieval Schloss was the home of the writer Rudolf Herzog (1869–1943), and a plaque on the wall of the Rheinbreitbacher Hof declares that the brothers Jakob and Wilhelm Grimm stayed there in the early 19C while compiling their Kinder-und Hausmärchen. This is a centre for fruit, vegetables and vineyards. **Unkel** (4000 inhab.; alt. 52m) is an important wine centre with half-timbered houses and a parish church dating in parts as far back as the 13C—with an early 13C Romanesque font, a 15C crucifix and tabernacle and Baroque furnishings. The Freiligrath-Haus is named after the poet and democrat Ferdinand Freiligrath (1810–76), who lived there for two years (1839–40). Unkel lies at the foot of the 101m-high basalt peak known as the Erpeler Ley, and 2km NW of the wine village of **Erpel** with its Romanesque church of St Severinus, built in the 13C, enlarged in the mid 18C, half-timbered houses and a Rathaus of 1780.

After another 4km the route reaches the stll partly fortified town of **Linz am Rhein** (6500 inhab.; alt. 60m; tourist information: 13 Burgplatz), which was celebrated by Turgenev in his novel 'Asja'. The fortifications date back to the 14C, with two surviving 15C fortified gates. The town offers a superb view of the river and surrounding countryside. Its delights include painted half-timbered houses and a late Gothic Rathaus of 1392, with a Glockenspiel, as well as a modern statue of a lady selling bread in the Marktplatz. The 13C late Romanesque church of St Martin has contemporary frescoes, and on the 178m-high Kaiserberg is a Gothic pilgrimage church and a Schloss of 1365.

**Bad Hönningen** (6000 inhab.; alt. 65m) lies 6km SE of Linz, and is another point of access to the Rhein-Westerwald Naturpark. This is a modern town with thermal establishments, swimming pools and campsites, as well as several fine inns. 18C Schloss Arenfels rises in its park on the site of a 13C fortress to the N of the town. The view across the river to Schloss Rheineck is stunning. Bad Hönningen runs a wine festival at the begining of June and a summer festival at the end of July. The town offers its guests river trips. 3km SE lies **Rheinbrohl**, a town of Roman remains, since here the Limes reached the Rhine, as well as half-timbered houses. Its mineral springs are dedicated to the Magi.

The B42 now runs through **Oberhammerstein**, at the foot of a 198m-high peak on which is a ruined 10C Schloss where in 1105 Kaiser Heinrich IV took refuge from his son. Oberhammerstein has the 12C Romanesque church of St Georg, and the 16C Burgmannshof. After 6km the wine town of **Leutesdorf** (3000 inhab.; alt. 65m) stretches alongside the river, filled with engaging 16C and 17C half-timbered houses, and half-protected by remnants of the town fortifications. Its 14C parish church has a 12C Romanesque tower and 13C frescoes, while the 17C pilgrimage Heiligkreuz-Kirche has a Baroque altar.

7km further SE by a new Rhine bridge is **Neuwied** (64,000 inhab.; alt. 62m), which was founded in 1653 by Count Friedrich von Wied-Neuwied. Today its industries include chemical and iron works and paper-making.

**Information office**: 50 Kirchstrasse. **Theatre**: 1 Schlossstrasse. **Train** connections with Frankfurt and Cologne, **buses** with Mainz and Koblenz; **boat trips**. At Neuwied lived and worked the cabinet-maker David Roentgen (1743–1807).

Neuwied preserves an 18C Schloss and park with a pheasantry. The municipal museum, which is devoted chiefly to prehistory, is at Raffeisenplatz (open weekdays 10.00–13.00, 14.00–17.00; Sat 10.30–13.00). The Schloss of 1706–56 was stuccoed by A. Gallasini and stands in its Schlosspark. The regular plan of the town derives from its refoundation in 1662, after the destruction of the Thirty Years War, by Count Friedrich von Wied-Neuwied, who brought here Protestant refugees. In consequence you unexpectedly find here a Moravian church of 1783–85 and a Mennonite church of 1768.

Further SE is **Neuwied-Engers**, partly walled, with half-timbered houses, a plague chapel of 1662 and a Schloss of 1759, with a hall of mirrors. Here the Romans first bridged the Rhine. Continue along the B42 to reach (9km from Neuwied) **Bendorf** (17,000 inhab.; alt. 67m). Its chief delight is a butterfly garden (open in summer 09.00–18.00, in winter 19.00–17.00). 2km left is **Sayn**, with an early 13C former Premonstratensian monastery, a ruined Schloss (founded in 1152) on the Burgberg, as well as the ruined 14C Schloss of the Sayn-Wittgenstein-Sayn family which commands the town from a height. Bendorf has a Catholic parish church dedicated to St Medardus, begun in 1204, with a modern Glockenspiel. Trains connect Bendorf with Cologne, Frankfurt and Limburg, buses with Koblenz and Neuwied.

The B42 continues through **Vallendar** (10,700 inhab.; alt. 68m). Here the Catholic church of St Petrus and Marcellinus, built in 1839 by Lassaulx, has a 15C tower. The town has several 17C and 18C half-timbered gabled houses, as well as Kloster Marienburg of 1240 and the Wittberger Hof, c 1700. It also offers visitors Kneipp therapeutic baths. On an island in the Rhine (the Niederwerth) is a 15C former monastery with a frescoed 15C church, and from Vallendar you can see across the river to Koblenz (see Rte 29).

The route along the right bank continues S through Urbar to reach (8km from Bendorf) **Koblenz-Ehrenbreitstein**. Its impressive fortress stands high above the river on the site of a Roman camp and derives its name from a lord named Erembert, who owned it in the 11C. The Archbishop of Trier was in possession of Schloss Ehrenbreitstein in 1153 when he strengthened its fortifications. Successive archbishops enlarged the castle, which was surrendered to the French by Archbishop-Elector Philipp Christophe von Sötern in 1631. Six years later the Germans took back the Schloss and gave it to the Archbishop of Cologne. Schloss Ehrenbreitstein was subsequently powerfully fortified, and in 1688 a French bombardment failed to take it. Only in 1752 did the Schloss once more become French. The Germans took it back ten years later. Starving the garrison into surrender in 1799, the French blew up Schloss Ehrenbreitstein in 1801 before ceding it according to the terms of the Peace of Lunéville. The second Peace of Paris forced them to pay the Prussians 15 million francs for its restoration, which was carried out between 1816 and 1832 by General Ernst-Ludwig von Aster (1788–1855). Today the Schloss serves as a youth hostel and regional museum (open Mar–Oct 09.00–17.00). The fortress has a massive church, and offers a panorama overlooking Koblenz and the schlösser of Lahneck (see below) and Stolzenfels (see Rte 28). The former town hall of Koblenz-Ehrenbreitstein is by Balthasar Neumann, 1749. Beethoven's mother was born here, as was the poet Clemens von Brentano (1778–1842). Hermann Melville declared that 'the finest wine of all the Rhine is grown right under the guns of Ehrenbreitstein'.

**Lahnstein** (20,000 inhab.; alt. 7m), an excellent starting point for river trips, lies 6km S along the B42, at the mouth of the River Lahn. The town is divided into Nieder-Lahnstein at the foot of the 157m-high Allerheiligen-berg, on the peak of which is a 19C neo-Gothic chapel, and Ober-Lahnstein on the left bank of the Lahn. Amongst a profusion of ancient buildings the town's finest include 13C Schloss Lahneck, which was pillaged in 1689 and restored in 1852 in the English neo-Gothic style; the late 13C Schloss Martinsburg, which was altered in the 15C and the 18C; and the 15C Gothic Altes Rathaus, with a rough stone lower storey, timbered gables and a bell tower. A fountain cools the Marktplatz of Ober-Lahnstein. The town boasts two Romanesque churches: St Johannes der Taufer, built in the 10C and 11C, and restored in the mid 19C; and St Martin, which has two Romanesque towers, and a Baroque interior of 1775 which has preserved the 14C choir. Another Romanesque building is the 12C Heimbach house, while the the Salhof dates from c 1150. By the riverside is the Wenzel chapel of 1400. In 1774 Goethe stayed at the half-timbered Wirtshaus an der Lahn, built in 1697, at 8 Lahnstrasse. Tourist information in Ober-Lahnstein, in the Marktplatz. The town museum is in the Hexenturm, Salhofplatz.

The B42 now runs for 4km to **Braubach** (3800 inhab.; alt. 71m). Braubach's 13C church of St Barbara has a tower which once served as part of the town's fortifications. From here a road runs for 2km up to the powerfully defended *Schloss Marksburg*, passing en route the 13C chapel of St Martin, with its rich collection of 16C statues and memorials. Schloss Marksburg's square 13C keep rises in a triangular courtyard created by three 12C to 14C wings. The fortress has also preserved Gothic living quarters and 13C and 14C battlements (open daily 09.00–19.00). Braubach's wine festival centres on the first Sun in October.

Braubach is 6km from **Osterspai**, which is dominated by Schloss Liebeneck, after which the route reaches **Filsen** on a picturesque bend in the river, with a 17C former town hall and half-timbered houses. Kamp-Bornhofen, which lies next on the route (12km away) is dominated by two ruined schlösser known as the enemy brothers—**Burg Liebenstein** and **Burg Sterrenberg**—since they are said to have been built by two brothers at odds with each other. In Kamp are a Gothic church and half-timbered houses, while in Bornhofen are a pilgrimage church of 1435 and a Franciscan abbey of 1680. A museum of rafts, ships and river navigation is housed in the Leyscher Hof of 1594 (open May–Oct Wed 14.30–17.30).

From here the road and river run SE for 12km through the wine village of **Wellmich**, with its little 14C Gothic church of St Martin (which houses a Renaissance tomb of 1545) and the dominating Deurenburg, known as **Burg Maus**, built c 1355, restored 1900–06, to **St Goarshausen** (2500 inhab.;

alt. 74m). Over this picturesque town towers the ruined Schloss known as **Burg Katz**, which was built in 1371 by Graf Johann III von Katzenellenbogen and restored in 1896–98. St Goarshausen has two 14C watchtowers, a neo-Gothic Protestant church, by Eduard Zais, 1860–63, and a neo-Baroque Catholic church by Hans and Christoph Rummell, 1923. Its altarpiece is from the workshop of Lucas Cranach the Elder. The town's Loreley statue was created by Natascha Alexandrovna Princess Jusopov, 1983. Tourist information at 126 Bahnhofstrasse. Trains connect with Cologne and Frankfurt, buses with Koblenz. This is a staging post for Rhine river trips.

2km from St Goarshausen, along the B274, is the 14C **Burg Reichenberg**. 4km SE of St Goarshausen is the **Loreley** rock—sung of by Heinrich Heine in 1824 in a poem set to music by Friedrich Silchers, 1838, which recounts the legend that here mermaids are said to lure sailors to their deaths—followed after 6km by the wine village of **Kaub** (1600 inhab.; alt. 79m). On a height N of the village rises Burg Gutenfels, a 13C Schloss rebuilt in the 19C and now a hotel. Tolls were levied from this Schloss on river traffic from the 12C to the 19C. Here Gustavus Adolphus had his HQ during the Thirty Years War, and here on 1 January 1814 the Prussian Field Marshal Gebbard Leberecht von Blücher (1742–1819) crossed the Rhine in the course of his campaign against Napoleon. At 6 Metzgergasse is a Blücher museum (open Apr–Nov except Tue 10.00–12.00, 14.00–16.00; in winter only mornings). The town has preserved medieval walls, which you can walk around; fine patrician houses, especially in the Marktplatz and Metzgergasse; and a 12C church. In the middle of the river is the exuberant pentagonal island fortress of **Pfalzgrafenstein**, known as the Steinernes Schiff or stone ship and as the 'Pfalz bei Kaub', a toll station built in 1327 by Ludwig the Bavarian with late Gothic defensive walls and a bastion added in 1607. Kaub hosts a wine festival in September. Tourist information at the town hall; train connections with Frankfurt and Koblenz; boat trips.

The B42 continues SE along the river banks to **Lorch am Rhein** (5000 inhab.; alt. 85m), an ancient wine village dominated by the 11C, 252m-high Burg Nollig. Still standing from the Middle Ages is a late Gothic tithe barn, and Lorch am Rhein is further enhanced by half-timbered houses, the Renaissance Hilchenhaus of 1573 (now an inn) and the Gothic *church of St Martin. Basically 13C, the church has a 13C Romanesque crucifix; late 13C choir stalls; a superb painted and carved high altar of 1483; and the tomb of Johann Hilchen von Lorch who died in 1550. The bridge with two round towers over the River Wisper was built in 1556. The vineyards around Lorch produce fine wines, and boat trips sail from its harbour.

9km SE of Lorch is **Assmanshausen**, with remains of the town walls, half-timbered houses and prized red wines. Its Kurhaus has 32.5°C thermal springs, reputed in Roman times. And here stands the 14C church of the Kreuzerhöhung. After another 5km the B42 reaches ***Rüdesheim** (see Rte 40).

# 42

# The Left Bank: Bingen to Bonn

Total distance 123km. Bingen—B9, 17km Bacharach—12km St Goar—15km
Boppard—20km Koblenz—18km Andernach—16km Sinzig—4km Remagen—
14km Bonn-Bad Godesberg—7km Bonn.

Equally entrancing as the journey along the right bank of the Rhine is that
along the left bank, which begins at a superbly sited city. **Bingen am Rhein**
(22,500 inhab.; alt. 77m) rises directly opposite Rüdesheim.

**Tourist information**: 21 Rheinkai; **train** and **bus** connections with Cologne, Luxemburg, Koblenz, Mainz and Kaiserslautern; **boat trips**, including visits to Rüdesheim
across the river (see Rte 39).

A long-established wine-trading town, a Celtic settlement fortified by the
Romans (renamed by them *Bingium*) and lying on the Roman Rhine road,
it bespeaks its antiquity by, for example, the Romanesque Drusus bridge
over the Nahe, which boasts one of the oldest bridge chapels in Germany
and was built on Roman foundations. When the Archbishop of Mainz took
possession of Bingen in 983, he and his successors set about fortifying the
city and building a fortress. Today the city prospers on wine-making, with
a subsidiary investment in Sekt and Weinbrand. On the Rochusberg above
Bingen is the 189m-high Rochuskapelle, built during the plague of 1666,
rebuilt in the late 1880s, and housing a picture of Goethe as St Roch,
presented by Goethe himself.

Burg Klopp is a Schloss of 1875–79, set in a rock garden and built on the
site of the 13C Schloss destroyed in 1711 by the French. Its tower now
contains the local history and astronomical museum (open May–Oct except
Mon 09.00–12.00, 14.00–17.00), and the fortress offers a superb panorama.
The town has preserved 17C and 18C houses, some of its medieval
fortifications, and the parish church of St Martin in Zehnthofstrasse, built
in 1410 over an 11C Romanesque crypt. Its treasures include 13C statues
of SS Katharina and Barbara. Near the festival hall is a monument to
Grand-Duke Ludwig IV, 1913. St Hildegard von Bingen (1098–1179), mystic
and musician and known as the 'Sybil of the Rhine', was abbess of the
nearby Benedictine monastery which she founded at Rupertsberg in 1147.
(It was demolished in the 17C.) Hildegard also founded a daughter house
at Eibingen near Rüdesheim. The poet Stefan George (1868–1933) was born
near Bingen at Rüdesheim, and the Stefan-George-Gedenstättein the
Schulzentrum houses his archive and the library of his great uncle.

Cross the River Nahe, which flows into the Rhine here, by the bridge to
take the B9 NW, noting on cliffs in the middle of the Rhine the 11C–14C
watchtower known as the **Mäuseturm** (mouse tower), where the rapacious
Bishop Hatto of Mainz is said to have been eaten by mice. ('They have
wetted their teeth against the stones, And now they pick the Bishop's
bones', as Robert Southey's poem has it.) In fact the name almost certainly
derives from Mautturm or 'toll tower'. The route runs by **Schloss Rheinstein**,
13C, rebuilt by Prince Friedrich of Prussia, 1825–29, and restored in 1976,
which rises on a 173m-high peak. Inside is a museum of arms and early
Gothic art (open 09.00–18.00, closing at 17.00 in winter). 1km towards the
river stands the 12C Romanesque chapel of St Klemens. From here the route

reaches the wine village of **Trechtingshausen** (1300 inhab.; alt. 74m). Just outside the village is **Schloss Reichenstein**, with its armour and hunting museum (open mid-Mar to mid-Nov 09.00–12.00, 13.00–18.00). The Schloss was founded in the 11C and rebuilt in 1899. Next you arrive at the tiny wine village of **Niederheimbach** which has an 11C church, housing a 17C Madonna and a plague altar, and medieval walls. On the Trechtingshausen side of the village stands 11C **Burg Sooneck**, which was several times restored, particularly in the 15C and in 1840 (visits 09.00–12.00, 14.00–17.00, closing at 16.00 in winter). Niederheimbach is also guarded by Schloss Heimburg, which was rebuilt in 1865.

The B9 continues NW to **Bacharach** (3000 inhab.; alt. 80m), 17km from Bingen, which the Romans knew for its wines. The name Bacharach derives from the Roman *Bacchi ara* (altar of Bacchus). Here in 1356 leading nobles elected Ludwig as the Bavarian emperor. Over Bacharach tower the impressive remains of Burg Stahleck, 12C, though partly razed by the French in 1689. Excellently preserved 14C–16C *walls and towers circle the town, incorporating three fortified gates, the Münztor, the Markttor and the Krahntor. At the foot of the Schloss are the remains of the Gothic church of St Werner, dedicated to a Christian boy allegedly murdered by Jews and canonised in 1428. Begun in the 13C and finished in 1426, parts of the building were destroyed in the Thirty Years War and other parts were demolished in 1689. The town boasts numerous old half-timbered houses (including the Alter Posthof of 1594), especially in the Marktplatz. Its 13C Romanesque-Gothic church of St Peter has a huge castellated tower and a four-storey interior, the whole restored in 1872 and in 1970. The parish church of St Nikolaus, built in 1688, has Baroque altars. Bacharach holds wine festivals on the last weekend in June and the first weekend in October.

Afer 6km the B9 reaches **Oberwesel** (5000 inhab.; alt. 71m). Known to the Celts as *Vosolvia*, it lies at the foot of the hill on which stands the 13C Schloss Schönburg, which was once three fortresses and was mostly razed in 1689, save for the curtain wall and the gatehouse tower. The Swedes and the French pillaged the town in 1639 and 1689. The German national anthem was first sung here in 1843 by its author August Heinrich Hoffmann (1798–1874). Surrounded by 13C and 14C fortifications which include 16 crenellated towers and the late Gothic chapel of St Werner, Oberwesel rejoices in the 'white church', i.e. the church of St Martin of 1303, with 14C sculptures, 15C wall paintings and 16C altars; and the 'red church', i.e. the 14C sandstone church of Liebfrauenkirche on the bank of the river, with a gabled west tower, 72m-high, a stone and iron *rood screen of 1350, the Martha altar of 1503, the *Nikolaus altar, 1506, with scenes from the life of St Nicholas, the tomb of Peter Lutern, who died in 1515, by Hans Backoffen, the tomb of the knights, 1520, a Baroque organ case and a late Gothic cloister. NE from Oberwesel can be seen St Goarshausen on the opposite bank of the river, as well as the Loreley rock (see Rte 41).

The B9 continues NW for 6km to reach **St Goar** (3800 inhab.; alt. 71m). St Goar is dominated by **Burg Rheinfels**, which was built 115m above the river by Graf Dieter III von Katzenellenbogen in 1254, and extended in the 1560s. The French mostly demolished the fortress in 1797 and its former chapel now houses a local museum (open daily 09.30–12.30, 13.00–17.30). From here there are views across the River to the twin town of St Goarshausen, dominated by Burg Katz and Burg Maus (see Rte 41). The 13C to 15C Protestant Romanesque-Gothic parish church of St Goar has a double row of columns supporting the vaulting, a stone *pulpit of 1470, late 15C wall paintings and the 16C and 17C tombs of Landgrave Philipp II of

Hesse-Rheinfels and his wife. This church was built on an 11C Romanesque crypt which is matched in size and splendour only by those of Speyer cathedral and St Maria im Kapitol, Cologne.

The neo-Gothic Catholic parish church, 1889–91, made use of a Baroque tower from the town walls and boasts an altarpiece c 1510. 15km NW of St Goar the road reaches Boppard, by way of **Hirzenach**, whose Romanesque church has a mid-13C Gothic choir, and the spa of **Bad Salzig**, which has mud baths and mineral waters and lies at the foot of the 530m-high Fleckertshöhe.

Still partly protected by Roman and medieval walls with medieval towers and gates, **Boppard** (17,000 inhab.; alt. 70m), whose name is derived from the Roman *Bodobriga*, became renowned in the 10C when it obtained the relics of St Severus, which are still preserved in the twin-towered 12C Romanesque church of St Severus, which has a polygonal choir and a spire dating from 1605. It was colourfully restored in 1967. Inside look for the Madonna of 1300 and the early-Gothic crucifix over the high altar. A Carmelite monastery was founded here in 1265, with a Gothic church begun in 1319 whose nave and north aisle were finished 1444. Look inside for the wall painting of 1407; mid-15C choir stalls; and the Baroque high altar, 1699.

Boppard's 14C burg is now a local history museum (open weekdays except Mon 10.00–12.00, 14.00–16.00, Sat 10.00–12.00, Sun 14.00–16.00). The Thonetmuseum (open daily except Mon 10.00–12.00, 14.00–16.00, Sat 10.00–12.00, Sun 14.00–16.00) in Burgstrasse, is devoted to forestry and woodwork, including furniture by Michael Thonet who was born here in 1796. The Marienburg Benedictine convent, 1738, above Boppard is now a school. A chair-lift rises to the 305m-high Gedeonseck. Information office: 2 Karmeliterstrasse; train connections with Cologne and Mainz, buses to Mainz and Koblenz; boat trips.

The route now passes through partly walled **Rhens**, protected by 14C gates and towers. Its half-timbered houses, dating from the 16C and 17C, include the Rathaus. Above the town is the 14C **Königstuhl** (Seat of Kings) where the electors of Germany would chose their emperor. This curiously modern-looking structure first occurs in recorded history in 1308, was destroyed by the French in 1803 and reconstructed in 1842. On this spot in 1338 the electors decreed that the Pope should no longer have a say in the elections. 3km NW of Rhens (and 15km NW of Boppard) is **Kapellen-Stolzenfels**, with its 14C church of St Menas, rebuilt in the 19C and housing a statue of St Sebastian from Riemenschneider's workshop. On the 95m-high Bergnase was a mid-13C Schloss which the French destroyed in 1689. In 1842 Karl Friedrich Schinkel built the present 'English Gothic' Schloss on the same site for King Friedrich Wilhelm IV of Prussia. Ernst Deger designed the chapel in 1853. A romantic footpath, with a waterfall and aqueduct, leads up to the Schloss (now a museum, open except Mon and throughout Dec 09.00–13.00, 14.00–18.00, closing 17.00 Oct–Mar) and gives views of Schloss Lahneck on the other bank of the Rhine.

In 5km the B9 reaches **Koblenz** (see Rte 29). From here cross the River Mosel and pass through the suburb of Lützel to reach after 13km **Weissenthurm**, with a castle keep dating from 1370. Its white tower, after which the town is named, served from the late 13C as a boundary mark, setting the limits of the territory of Trier. After leading French troops across the Rhine in 1797, General Lazare Hoche (1768–97) died here. His corpse, taken for burial to St Petersburg, was brought back by Marshal Foch in 1919, hence the Hoche memorial (its obelisk by Peter Josef Krahé, its bronzes by Louis Simon Boizot).

After another 5km the route arrives at spacious **Andernach** (29,000 inhab.; alt. 64m), known in Celtic-Roman times as *Antunnacum*. Its former name derives from the Roman *Castellum ante Nacum*, which Drusus (stepson of the Roman Emperor Augustus) founded. Andernach received its civic rights in 1109 and 58 years later became a fief of the Electors of Cologne. In 1253 the city joined the Confederation of Rhine Cities and became the southernmost partner in the Hanseatic League. Andernach was taken over by France in 1794, to be ceded to Prussia in 1815, along with the left bank of the Rhine.

**Tourist information** at 46 Bahnhofstrasse; **train** connections with Cologne, Mainz and Wiesbaden; **buses** with local towns (including Maria Laach, see Rte 33C); **boat trips**.

Of its medieval fortifications survive the 14C and 15C walls, incorporating the 56m-high Runder Turm (Round Tower), built from 1448 to 1532 (once a watchtower, now a youth hostel) as well as the 14C debtors' tower (Schuldturm) and the Rheintor, whose inner door dates from the 12C. The town has a late Gothic town hall of 1572, with an older Jewish ritual bath, vaulted and 13m deep, in its courtyard, and the Catholic church of *Maria Himmelfahrt, which was begun in 1198 and restored 1877–99. This imposing building has four towers, a Gothic tabernacle in the sacristy, a 14C 'plague' crucifix, a tomb of 1524 and an 18C pulpit (from Maria Laach). The ruined Schloss dates from the 15C. The tiny Romanesque cemetery chapel of St Michael was attached to a monastery where St Thomas Becket served.

See also in Andernach the 14C church of the Minorites, now the Protestant parish church, and the church of St Albert by Rudolf Schwarz, 1952. The restored 14C to 17C burg was once a seat of the Archbishops of Cologne. The town museum, decorated with Renaissance caryatids and atlantes, is at 14 Schaitbergerstrasse in the 1620 Haus von der Leyen (open Apr–Oct weekdays 10.00–12.30, 14.00–17.00; closed Fri afternoons).

The route continues alongside the Rhine past the old crane of 1554 (in use until 1911), with a view of the island of **Namedywerth**, with its mineral water spring; the 14C church of St Bartholomäus; and 13C Burg Namedy, restored in the 19C and 20C. Across the river you can see the ruined Burg Hammerstein, before the route reaches, after 7km, **Burgbrohl**. From Burgbrohl the B412 leads SW for 13.5km by way of Bad Tönisstein to **Maria Laach** (see Rte 33C).

The B9 continues to follow the Rhine, passing after 4km through the health resort and spa of **Bad Breisig** (6600 inhab.; alt. 61m), with its three warm springs, its thermal swimming pools, and a park where concerts are held. Bad Breisig hosts an October onion fair. Its 13C church of St Viktor has 13C and 14C frescoes. In **Oberbreisig** are the 18C Baroque church of Maria Himmelfahrt, restored Burg Rheineck, begun in the 12C, and along the riverside half-timbered customs houses. 5km NW lies **Sinzig-Bad Bodendorf** (14,000 inhab.; alt. 71m), still partly walled, with numerous thermal baths and springs, close by the confluence of the Rhine with the Ahr. The Romans knew Sinzig as *Sentiacum*. Secular buildings of interest include the medieval Königshof, remains of the medieval walls, the Zehnthof, 1697–1740, and the 19C neo-Gothic Schloss, which serves as the local history and sculpture museum (open Sun 10.00–12.00). Sinzig also boasts the late Romanesque *church of St Peter, built c 1230, and well restored in 1964, in which are late 13C frescoes, Gothic vaulting and a polygonal apse with a 15C altar.

After 4km the route reaches **Remagen** (15,000 inhab.; alt. 64m), the Celtic-Roman *Rigomagus*. The parish church of SS Peter and Paul, which was enlarged in 1902 by Caspar Clemens Pickel, has a Romanesque nave, a Gothic choir, a 16C Pietà, a 17C west tower and 19C additions. It occupies the site of the Roman fort, some of it still visible below the church. The presbytery has a 12C Romanesque doorway. In the former monastery chapel of the 15C is now a local history museum exhibiting Roman remains (opening times vary). Opposite was erected the Roman Pfarrhof gate in 1902. A Gothic chapel rises in the Am Hof square. Worth visiting on its hill is the pilgrimage church of St Apollinaris, based on a 6C chapel and restored between 1839 and 1857 by Ernst Friedrich Zwirner. At Remagen in 1916–18 on the orders of General Erich von Ludendorff (1865–1937) was built the superb bridge which the 9th American armoured division took on 7 March 1945. It collapsed ten days later, killing 28 American soldiers. In 1980 a museum of peace was established in the tower on the left bank of this bridge (open weekdays 15.00–17.00, Sat 10.00–12.00, 14.00–17.00, Sun 10.00–17.00). Burg Schloss is a classical building by Ernst Friedrich Zwirner, 1839–43.

At **Remagen-Oberwinter**, 4km further, are half-timbered houses, the neo-Gothic Schloss Marienfels and the Haus Ernich, by Ernst von Ihne, 1906–08. The church of St Laurentius, Oberwinter, is neo-Gothic, built by Vincenz Statz in 1866 and incorporating a late Gothic choir. **Rolandseck**, 1km further, offers superb views of the Siebengebirge (see Rte 49) across the river and of the river island of **Nonnenwerth** with its nunnery founded in 1122 (now a girls' school) and thermal baths. A good road leads for 3.5km up to the 105m-high peak on which stands the **Rolandsbogen** (*splendid views), a Schloss supposedly built by Charlemagne's paladin Roland, partly destroyed in 1475, renewed by Ernst Friedrich Zirner in 1839.

Rolandseck lies 6km SE of **Bonn-Bad Godesberg** (75,000 inhab.; alt. 65m), whose spa was known to the Romans, though the present town was founded in the late 18C by the Elector of Cologne. From the central railway station Rheinallee leads to a riverside park, with boats moored for trips on the Rhine, and a car ferry to Königswinter (see Rte 41). Poststrasse leads E from the railway station to the Stadtpark and the Redoutenpark, divided by the Kurfürstenstrasse. In the Stadtpark stand the modern Trinkhalle, the congress hall and the city theatre. Redoutenpark takes its name from the Rococo Redoute, the former Kurhaus, built for Archbishop Max Franz in 1792 by Martin Leydel, finished c 1820 by his son Adam Franz Friedrich Leydel, and now used for concerts and receptions. Here is the new Kurfürstenbad, the thermal establishment called the Draitschbrunnen, and the Hof theatre of 1792, which in the 19C became the town hall. In 1863 Vincenz Statz built for Bad-Godesberg a neo-Gothic Catholic church of St Marien, enlarged 1894. The neo-Romanesque Protestant Rigalsche chapel dates from 1858.

From here Kurfürstenstrasse and the Deutschherrenstrasse lead S to Muffendorf, with its 10C church of St Martin and a house of the Teutonic Knights built in 1254. To reach **Schloss Godesburg**—built for Archbishop Dietrich of Cologne in 1219, ruined on 17 December 1583 by besieging Bavarians, save for a few walls and the 48m-high round keep, restored as a hotel in 1961—from the Stadtpark follow Kirchstrasse and Winterstrasse to climb the hill above the town, passing the partly Romanesque/partly Baroque chapel of St Michael, also damaged in the siege, restored by Archbishop Josef Clemens, 1697–99, and given its Baroque nave. At the foot of the Godesberg is 'Zum Lindenwirtin', an inn rebuilt in 1976. Along with paintings by August Macke (1887–1914, the leader of the 'Blaue Reiter' group), works of post-1945 German painters are displayed in the Haus an der Redoute (open Tue–Sat 10.00–17.00).

Since 1969 Bad Godesburg has been an integral part of **Bonn** 7km away (see Rte 40), which is reached by way of Bonnerstrasse and Kölnerstrasse. En route you find the Gothic **Hochkreuz**, an 11m-high cross set up by the Archbishop of Cologne in 1350. Restored by E.F. Zirner in 1859, it carries a sculpted Christ among angels and the four Evangelists. The city theatre is at 9 Am Michaelshof.

Trains connect with Cologne and Koblenz, buses with Bonn, boats with Königswinter and Niederdollendorf.

# 43

## Cologne

**COLOGNE** (987,000 inhab.; alt. 50m), in German **Köln**, was capital of the Rhine in Roman times. Dominated by the silhouette of its celebrated cathedral, it also possesses a series of remarkable Romanesque churches unsurpassed anywhere else in Germany. Almost totally destroyed in World War II (losing 90 per cent of its inner city—save for its cathedral, in spite of 14 direct hits by bombs—and 70 per cent of the outer suburbs) the city has remarkably rebuilt itself, as well as re-developing its trade. In consequence, what Hermann Melville wrote in 1849 remains substantially true: 'In this antiquated gable-ended town—full of Middle Age, Charlemagne associations—where Rubens was born and Mary de'Medici died, there is much to interest a pondering man like me'. Nine million tonnes of goods are annually loaded and unloaded in the port; Ford-Cologne employs 28,000 workers, Klöckner-Humbolt-Deutz another 17,000 (making diesel engines). The Cologne trade fair (see below) has an annual turnover of 700 million Deutschmarks. Weekly the city creates up to 10,000 million litres of its celebrated perfume *eau de Cologne* ('4711'). Cologne houses the HQ of western Germany's radio and television.

**Tourist information**: 19 Unter Fettenhennen (by the cathedral). **Main railway station**: Bahnhofstrasse. **Boat** connections with Düsseldorf, Basel and Rotterdam. Köln-Bonn **airport** (buses from city centre every 15 mins 06.35–23.35). Underground railway system. Rhine **cable railway** (the only European cable car over a river) with fine views of the cathedral and Old City, daily 10.00–18.00, Good Friday until end October.

Cologne's **festivals** include the Rhine regatta in early June and the Corpus Christi procession along the Rhine. **Carnival** is centred around the seventh Sunday before Easter, Rose Monday and the following Tuesday—most of Cologne is then closed to motor traffic. Cologne's trade fairs occupy the extensive exhibition halls at Messeplatz, NW of Mülheim which were inaugurated in 1922.

**History**. The city in Roman times was called first *Ara Ubiorum* and then *Colonia Agrippinensis* (in 38 BC, when Agrippa was commanding the legions in Gaul). The colony prospered, making pottery and tiles for the empire. Here Trajan was proclaimed emperor in AD 98. The Romans walled the city, which was the centre of a network of fine roads. In the 2C some nameless virgin martyrs at Cologne were commemorated in a 4C or 5C inscription (see below) declaring that a certain Clematius had restored a basilica where they had been put to death, and this fact developed into the legend of St Ursula and her 11,000 fellow virgin-martyrs. (As Byron put it, here are 'Eleven thousand maidenheads of bone: The greatest number flesh has even known'.) The Romans made Christianity their official religion, and here Constantine built a bridge across the Rhine. Cologne became the seat of archbishops, some of whom frequently preferred to live in Bonn. In 795 Charlemagne made his court chaplain Hildebold Archbishop of Cologne. Cologne's twelve superb Romanesque churches, built on tombs and in former cemeteries, indicate the remarkable power of relics over the medieval Christian mind. By the 11C the archbishop had become Chancellor of Italy and by the 14C an elector.

In 1180 a ring of walls far wider than the Roman fortifications was built to defend the population. In the Middle Ages Cologne was an Imperial City and became yet richer as a member of the Hanseatic League—the mercantile alliance of seafaring citizens, set up by Cologne and Lübeck c 1250. In 1288 the citizens won a military victory over the archbishop and assumed political and economic power. In 1360 Emperor Karl IV granted Cologne the right to hold two fairs a year, the start of its present highly successful trade fairs. At Cologne in 1367 the Hanseatic League declared war on Denmark. Twenty-one years later the city's first university was founded.

Cologne's status as a Free Imperial City was confirmed in 1475. From time to time trouble flared between the patricians and the guilds of artisans. The Reformation brought further strife. Luther's works were publicly burnt in front of the cathedral in 1520 by the University faculty of theology. In 1794 the city was taken by French Revolutionary troops. Protestants and Jews were at last allowed to settle here. After the fall of Napoleon the Treaty of Versailles ceded Cologne to Prussia.

In 1881 the medieval walls were demolished to construct wide boulevards around the city. Between then and 1930 the Rhine was twice bridged, and great industrial companies set up here. Nine railway lines today meet at Cologne. After the destruction of World War II an international competition to replan the city was won by Fritz Schaller. By 1985 all twelve of Cologne's Romanesque churches had been restored.

The musician J. Cochläus (1479–1552) taught at the university. The composer Carl Rosier (1640–75) was a native of Cologne, as were Friedrich Schlegel (1772–1929; he taught philosophy here from 1804 to 1809), the socialist politician August Bebel (1840–1913) and the socialist journalist Emil Rosenow (1871–1904). Jacques Offenbach (1819–80) ran the city opera. At Cologne a sudio for electronic music was founded in 1953 under the leadership of Karl-Heinz Stockhausen. The novelist Heinrich Böll was born here in 1917. Konrad Adenauer, Federal Germany's first post-war chancellor, was Oberbürgermeister from 1917–33.

The main railway station is close by the cathedral square and looks out on it through the glass façade of the great shed, which was rebuilt in 1957. In front of the station stands Deichmannhaus of 1911. W of the station Marzellenstrasse leads to the church of **St Maria Himmelfahrt**, designed for the Jesuits by Christoph Wamser of Alsace in 1618. Finished in 1678 and restored in 1964, it has five altars and a pulpit, all early 16C, by Valentin Boltz, a lay-brother who carved himself smoking a pipe on the pulpit. Next door is the former Jesuit college, also by Wamser, and built between 1618 and 1689.

Walk N to Ursulaplatz and the church of **\*\*St Ursula**, built in a Roman cemetery at the beginning of the 12C on the site of a 4C building. On the interior of the south wall an inscription preserved from the earlier church records that a Roman named Clematius built it over the saint's tomb. Legends soon developed about Ursula, an allegedly English queen, and her 11,000 martyred companions (see above), and inside the church are a sarcophagus of the saint, by Johann Lenz, 1659, \*13C and 14C reliquary busts and the 17C Baroque \*Goldene Kammer decorated with innumerable bones. Its chief treasure is a reliquary of St Etherius, c 1170, and there are another 120 bust reliquaries. The church's west tower was extended in the early 13C, and there are late 13C choir extensions. On the Romanesque tower is a Baroque crest, with a crown, supposedly representing that of England.

Still further N the Eigelsteintor, once part of the Roman defences of Cologne, rises in Ebertplatz. A niche in this gateway carries a statue of the 'Kölsche Boor', one of the principal characters of Cologne's Carnival. This gateway is matched at the southern extremity of the old city by the fortified Ulrepforte on Sachsenring, which was transformed into a windmill in the 15C.

Follow the passage underneath the railway line right of the church of St Ursula to reach the church of **\*\*St Kunibert**, the last of the city's

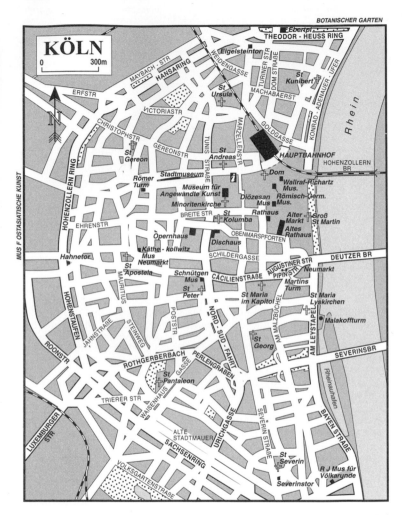

**KÖLN**

0    300m

Romanesque churches, with later ogive vaulting. Consecrated in 1247, it rises on the site of a 9C church built over Bishop Kunibert's 7C grave. Its windows contain late Romanesque stained glass of 1230, depicting a tree of Jesse and legends of SS Kunibert and Clemens. Notable is a stone *Annunciation group by Konrad Kuyn, 1439.

From here follow Konrad-Adenauer-Ufer NE alongside the river to reach, at No. 80, the restaurant Bastei. On one of the bastions built by the Prussians when they razed the city's medieval walls Wilhelm Riphahn built this Expressionist steel, concrete and glass restaurant in 1924. Destroyed in 1943, it was restored by Riphahn himself. Konrad-Adenauer-Ufer leads further NE to the Cologne **Zoo** and **Aquarium**, at 173 Riehlerstrasse, with over 6000 animals of c 600 species (open daily in summer 19.00–18.00, closing in winter 17.00) and the **Botanical Gardens**, which include a swimming pool and miniature railway (open 08.00–21.00 in summer, winter 10.00–dusk).

Across the Hohenzollernbrücke, on the left bank of the river, is laid out the Rheinpark, with its waterfalls and a fountain (the Tanzbrunnen) of 1950. From here a cable car rises 930m to the Zoo, byond which is the Botanical Garden, laid out in 1846 and again after World War II.

Return to the right bank of the river across the Hohenzollernbrücke, to find the cathedral, Germany's most visited building, set on a spacious terrace approached by flights of steps. NW of this terrace has been re-erected a Roman gate discovered here in 1826. Fritz Schaller built the Bank directly W of the cathedral, 1953, in front of which is the pigeon fountain of the same year.

Cologne • • •**Dom**, 'the most beautiful of all the churches I have ever seen or can imagine', in the judgment of Lewis Carroll, is a five-aisled basilica with a triple-aisled transept, its vault carried on 56 pillars. Standing on the site of a Romanesque church, the building was begun under the direction of Master Gerard in 1248, when Archbishop Konrad von Hochstaden laid the first stone, and completed only in 1880, when the two west towers stood, at over 153m, taller than any other buiding in western Europe. In the square is a reproduction of a tower finial 9.25m high, 4.58m wide. Stone was quarried for the building from the Drachenfels (see Rte 48).

The choir was finished in 1322; work started on the transepts in the 14C. Work stopped in 1559. A campaign to finish the cathedral was begun in 1824 and the work was completed at a further cost of 21 million Marks. Bomb damage was repaired by 1956. Northern Europe's largest earthquake, on the night of 13/14 April 1992, amounting to 5.5 to 5.8 on the Richter scale, merely flung some stone decoration from the vaults. The south doorway has decorations designed by Schwanthaler; the north door has four bronze doors by Ewald Mataré, 1948–53. 509 steps lead 95m up the south tower (•view), which houses the heaviest free-swinging bell in the world (ascent daily 09.00–17.00).

**Interior** (144m long, 44.8m wide, 43.5m high). The glass in the north aisle windows dates from the early 16C; that in the south aisle from 1848, and was made in Munich. Of the nave sculptures all are 19C save an Entombment of the 15C and the 1914–18 war memorial, by Grasegger. In the south transept are a stone Madonna, 1420; a statue of St Christopher by Tilman van der Burch, c 1470; and the retable of St Agilolph, 1520. In the north transept are St Ursula protecting her maidens, early 16C; St Peter and the Virgin Mary, both 18C; an altar and octagonal marble tabernacle by Elmar Hillebrand, the first created in 1960, the second in 1964; an organ case by Peter Hacker, 1948; and a statue of the master builder Konrad Kuyn, who died in 1469.

The •choir has the series of •stained glass windows depicting the adoration of the Magi, 1315–29; the three kings (amid 45 others); canons' stalls of 1311; and frescoes c 1322. The •high altar c 1320 was the gift of Archbishop Wilhelm von Gennep (1349–62). Behind it is displayed the • •shrine containing the relics of the Magi (stolen from Milan in 1164), created by Nicholas of Verdun in the late 12C. The shrine is sculpted with prophets and apostles, Jesus's baptism and second coming, and the adoration of the three kings. The surrounding chapels include (beginning from left to right) that of the Holy Cross, housing a Romanesque crucifix from the earlier church (the figure c 970, the cross mid 17C). This chapel also houses the tombs of Archbishops St Engelbert (1216–25), Wilhelm von

*Supported by 56 pillars, Cologne cathedral soars to over 43m*

Gennep (1349–62) and Engelbert von der Marck (1364–68). The chapel gives entry to the chapel of the holy sacrament in which are the Madonna of Milan, 14C, a tabernacle c 1460 and 16C glass. The chapel of St Engelbert to the right houses the early 16C retable of St Georg, the Renaissance tomb of Archbishop Anton von Schauenberg (died 1558), by Cornelis Floris, and modern glass by W. Rupprecht, 1956. The next chapel, of St Maternus, houses the tomb, 1336, of Archbishop Philipp von Heinsberg (died 1191) who, as the design indicates, gave Cologne its medieval walls. Next, in the chapel of St Johannes, is the bronze tomb of the cathedral's founder, who died in 1261, though his tomb dates from c 1320, and the sarcophagus of Queen Richeza of Poland, who died in 1059. The chapel has 13C glass, particularly notable being the *All Saints' window, and 14C wall paintings.

Next is the chapel of the Magi where formerly their relics lay. Its stained glass was fired c 1320, and includes an Adoration of the Magi and the *Bible window. A marble plaque at the entrance covers the heart of Maria de' Medici, who died at Cologne in 1642. Nearby is the tomb, 1460, of

Archbishop Dietrich von Moers (1414–63). The chapel of St Agnes has 1340 frescoes and the Gothic tomb of St Irmgard, as well as glass of 1320 and the 19C. In the chapel of St Michael are an altar triptych of the crucifixion by Barthel Bruyn, 1548, the tomb of Archbishop Walram von Jülich (died 1349), 16C glass and the tomb of General Philipp Bertram von Hochkirchen (killed at Landau in 1703), by Fortini. The chapel of St Stephan houses the 10C tomb of Archbishop Gereon (969–76), preserved from the former church; the tomb of Archbishop Adolf von Schauenberg, by Cornelis Floris, c 1560; and another *Bible window, c 1290. Next is the chapel of the Virgin. Its modern altar is by Willy Weyres, 1956, and its modern tabernacle by Carl von Ackeren, 1956. Its finest work of art is Stephan Lochner's **triptych depicting the Magi, SS Gereon and Ursula, c 1440. When closed, the wings depict the Annunciation. Here too is the tomb of Archbishop Friedrich von Saarwerden, c 1415, as well as modern glass by W. Gayer, 1956. At the entrance are the tombs of Archbishop Rainald von Dassel and Count Gottfried von Arnsberg.

The cathedral **Schatzkammer** displays amongst its many treasures a 12C Byzantine reliquary of the Holy Cross; the Hillinus codex, c 1000; St Peter's staff, variously dated; and a 16C chasuble of St Charles Borromeo (open 09.00–18.00, Sun 13.00–17.30). The **Diözesanmuseum** at 2 Roncalliplatz exhibits religious art from the Romanesque era to the 20C (open Mon–Sat, except Tue, 10.00–17.00, Sun 10.00–13.00).

S of the cathedral at 4 Roncalliplatz stands the *Römisch-Germanisches Museum**, built on the site of a 72 sq m Roman mosaic (open except Mon 10.00–17.00, Wed, Thu to 20.00). Behind the Domhotel is the fountain of the dwarfs, 1900, commemorating the story of little men who used to entertain the citizens of Cologne. Unter Fettenheim reaches Wallrafplatz, with the Cologne broadcasting house, by P.F. Schneider (1948–52), from which An der Rechtschule leads to the *Wallraf-Richartz/Ludwig Museum** at 1 Bishofsgartenstrasse. Built by Rudolf Schwarz and Josef Bernard, 1957, it displays 14C to 16C Cologne artists, especially *Stephan Lochner, and *contemporary works given by Dr Peter Ludwig (open except Mon 10.00–17.00, Tue, Thu to 20.00).

Continue left to reach Kolpingplatz, where you discover part of the Roman aqueduct, and a statue of Adolf Kolping (1813–65). Here rises the **Minoritenkirche**, built between 1250 and 1410, with the modern tomb of Duns Scotus (1266–1308), by Josef Höntgesberg, 1957. Alongside is the **Museum für angewandte Kunst** (open Wed–Sun 10.00–17.00, first Thu in month till 20.00), with applied art from the Middle Ages to the present day. Other works on display are medieval scenes of the life of Jesus, works by Albrecht Dürer (including a self-portrait), the 17C mystical religious paintings of Murillo, as well as Flemish and Dutch paintings, including a Rubens self-portrait and another one by Rembrandt. French sculptors (Maillol, Rodin) are also well represented, as are 19C French painters, with a remarkable collection of Symbolists. Equally fine is the collection of modern American paintings, with a yet more impressive display of 20C German art.

S of the Minoritenkirche stands the chapel of **St Kolumba**, by Gottfried Böhm, 1950, incorporating the remains of a Romanesque church bombed in 1945. Inside are a statue of Our Lady of the Ruins, 1460; Pietà, c 1440; a group consisting of St Anne and the Virgin and Child, c 1500; a statue of St Antony of Padua by Ewald Mataré, 1937; and glass by Georg Meistermann, 1950 and Ludwig Gies, 1954.

From here Herzogstrasse leads to Offenbachplatz, which contains the 1957 Expressionist **Opernhaus** and the 1953 **Schauspielhaus**, both by W.

Riphahn. Between these two buildings runs Glockengasse, so named because of the Glockenspiel on the façade of the house where *eau de Cologne* was first created. Continue along Herzogstrasse turning right at Schildergasse to reach the **Antoniterkirche**, built between 1350 and 1384, and transferred to the Protestants in 1802, thus becoming the first Protestant church in Cologne. Its stained glass includes a choir window of 1520 and aisle windows of 1966 by Alois Plum. The 12C font has a 1934 cover by Wyland. The bronze statue of the commissioning of the Apostles is by Ulrich Henn, 1964, while the organ dates from 1968. The church also houses a cast of the *Angel of death, by Ernst Barlach, 1927—the original having been destroyed as 'degenerate art' by the Nazis in 1937. Its face is that of Käthe Kollwitz.

Return W long Schildergasse to cross Hohe Strasse and walk into Gürzenichstrasse, to reach the **Gürzenich**, built as a concert and exhibition hall by R. Schwarz and K. Band, 1955, where the 15C Gürzenich stood until its destruction in 1943. The exterior has been partly restored. The building abuts onto the ruined church **Alt-St Alban** which, as a war memorial, has a reproduction of 'suffering parents', a statue by Käthe Kollwitz. Gülichplatz, whose Carnival fountain is by G. Grasegger, 1913, lies between the Gürzenich and the old and new town halls. The **Altes Rathaus** boasts a restored early 15C belfry, with a Glockenspiel; the Gothic, richly decorated Hansa-Saal, c 1360; and a Mannerist Vorhalle by Wilhelm Vernukken, 1569. The new building, by Theodor Teichen and Franz Löwenstein, 1955, has a stained glass window by Georg Meistermann depicting the city's history, and the Europe mosaic of Hans-Jürgen Grummer.

Close by are the remains of the Roman **Praetorium** and imperial palace (open 10.00–17.00; entrance in Kleine Budengasse; the visit also includes a rare section of a Roman town sewage system). Under the car park near the old town hall is a ritual Jewish bath, or **Mikwe**, 1150—visits by way of the town hall Mon–Thu 18.00–17.00, Fri 08.00–12.00.

Follow from here Grosse Sandkaul S to reach the Romanesque church of **··St Maria im Kapitol** (consecrated 1065), so named from its site on the old Roman Capitol where in the 8C the stepmother of Charles Martel founded a nunnery. Severely damaged in World War II (the clover-leaf apse partly collapsed in 1948), the church has been entirely restored. *Carved wooden doors of the mid-12C illustrate the life of Jesus. Inside are 12C and 13C tombs, including that of the foundress, Plectrudis, 1180; a 12C enthroned Madonna and Child; a fork-shaped plague crucifix of 1304; and a Renaissance rood screen of 1523. Outside is a weeping angel, by Gerhard Marcks, 1949. N of the church is the late 15C tower of **Klein St Martin**, whose church was demolished 1803.

Walk towards the river, taking first An der Malzmühle and then Rheinstrasse, noting at No. 8 the 13C **Overstolzenhaus**, a Romanesque patrician's house c 1220, restored in 1956. Now the Kunstgewerbemuseum it houses 13 secular frescoes (open Tue–Sun 10.00–17.00). The quayside reaches the Romanesque church of **··St Maria in Lyskirchen**, built in 1220 on the site of a 10C church. It shelters a 12C font and 13C *frescoes with typological scenes from the Old and New Testament (remarkably unscathed in spite of war damage), as well as a 15C 'Sailors' Madonna' and 16C stained glass. The Gothic windows are 17C.

Continue N along the quay to the Deutzer Brücke (1948, where the Romans bridged the Rhine), to find on the left the **Heumarkt** (Cornmarket), with picturesque 16C to 18C houses, dated on the ouside walls, several restored after World War II) and the **Eisenmarkt** (iron market) with

Cologne's marionette theatre. The **Alter Markt** is situated N of Heumarkt, with a fountain whose statue depicts Jan van Werth (died 1651), a general in the Thirty Years War. Towards the river stands Romanesque **••Gross St Martin**, built 1150–1230 on the site of a Carolingian monastery which had been ravaged by fire in 1150. The great tower, totally destroyed in World War II, was restored by 1963. Gross St Martin copies and modifies the clover-leaf apse/choir of St Maria im Kapitol.

The old patterns of the streets have been retained here. To the E of Gross St Martin are the Renaissance houses **Zum Dorn** and **Zum Bretzel** (1580, restored) and the house **Am Hanen**, decorated by Edward Mataré, 1962–65. Unter Seidmacher contains the Renaissance **Gasthaus zum St Peter** (built by Terlaen van Lennep 1563, destroyed in 1945, rebuilt in 1946). Follow Am Leystapel S along the river bank past St Maria in Lyskirchen, turning right at Gross-Witschgasse and continuing by way of Georgstrasse to the Waidmarkt, where stands the Romanesque church of **••St Georg**. Founded in 1059 and consecrated in 1067, it replaced a Frankish chapel which stood on the ruins of a Roman temple. Its vaulting is mid-12C, and the west end was rebuilt c 1190 (the sole part that needed no restoration after World War II). Its Romanesque crucifix is a replica of the original, now in the Schnütgen Museum (see below). The church also houses a 14C forked crucifix, a 16C altarpiece by Barthel Bruyn and stained glass by Jan Thorn-Prikker, 1930.

From here Severinstrasse leads S, along the route of the Roman road, for a 650m walk to the Romanesque church of St Severin, passing on the right first the church of **St Johann Baptist**, a 12C basilica, enlarged in the 14C and the 16C, and restored and modified by Karl Band in 1962, and then (a little distance from Severinstrasse) the **Elendskirche** of 1765–71. **••St Severin**'s church, 13C and 14C, rises on the site of a 4C chapel which stood in the old Roman cemetery, and owes its present form initially to the crypt built for the bones of St Severin in the 10C (and extended in the next). The Romanesque choir was rebuilt in the 13C and shelters a mosaic floor, 13C canons' stalls and 14C wall paintings. Two towers rise at the east end and were finished in the Gothic style in the 14C, while the huge west tower and spire were completed in 1411. The vaulting of the interior and the high windows date from the 15C, when the cloister was also rebuilt. Inside the church look for a Madonna, c 1290; St Severin's present reliquary (behind the high altar), which dates from 1819; and in the sacristy a crucified Christ, surrounded by angels and saints, c 1420. Difficult of access (permission needed from the parish priest) is the **••Romano-Christian cemetery** excavated under the nave of the church.

Severinstrasse continues S to the 13C **Severinstor**, to the E of which is the Bayen tower, again from the medieval walls.

Around St Severin's church are a number of 16C houses. NW from the church follow Kartäusergasse to the Carthusian church, **Kartäuserkirche**, of 1393. Its modern glass is by Carl Cordel, and the modern fittings are by Gerhard Marcks, save for a 15C retable on the north wall and a 15C triptych. Kartäuserstrasse leads into Vor der Siebenburgen, with on the right the Baroque church of **St Maria im Frieden** (built between 1643 and 1716, and restored in 1965), which leads to the Romanesque church of **••St Pantaleon**. Formerly part of a 7C Benedictine monastery which was rebuilt c 950 and consecrated in 980, it has an Ottonian Westwerk. The west façade is 10C, the aisles were added in the 12C, the choir and Gothic windows in the nave redone in the early 17C by Christoph Wamser, with stained glass in the choir of 1622. The 12.80m-high nave houses a •late Gothic rood screen, 1502–14; a 14C branch crucifix; a Romanesque head of Christ; and a

Baroque organ. The ceiling was not restored in its original form after World War II. A sarcophagus of the Empress Theophanu, who died in 991, is by Sepp Hürten, 1965.

From here follow Waisenhausgasse NE, turning left at Köllner-Nord-Süd-Fahrt to reach in Cäcilienstrasse the Romanesque church of *St Cäcilien, which adjoins and houses part of the **Schnütgen Museum** of religious art from the early Middle Ages to the Baroque (and alas was not restored inside with complete faithfulness after World War II, open 10.00–17.00, also the first Wednesday in month 19.00–20.00). Here in 881 was founded a ladies' collegiate church, rebuilt in the 10C, with a further reconstruction in the 12C. St Cecilia with her companions were sculpted over the north door, c 1160; the skeleton sprayed on the west end of the former convent is by the Zurich 'spray-artist' Harald Nägeli. Adjoining this church is St Peter, begun in the 12C, rebuilt in the first half of the 16C. It shelters a painting by Rubens of the crucifixion of St Peter (1642), two wings of a retable of 1525 and a bronze font of the 16C. The church has expressionist frescoes by Hans Zepter and Hans Verbreck, painted 1925–28.

W from the St Cäcilien cross the Neumarkt—Germany's largest medieval square, invaded by handloom weavers in December and always hosting a fine market—to reach the Romanesque church of **St Aposteln, restored and serving as a concert hall. Built in 1020 on a 9C chapel, it was partly rebuilt 1192 after a fire and vaulted in 1219, the date also of the present choir. Its square tower is 12C, and the steeple to the west, with its diamond-shaped spire, is mid 12C. Inside are a painting of the archangel Michael by Friedrich Overbeck, 1850; 13C statues of Christ and the twelve intercessors; a 15C statue of St Michael; woodcarvings of the Twelve Apostles, c 1330; and a *suffering Christ by Tilman von der Burch, c 1450. A modern chapel to the right of the nave has glass by Ludwig Gies, 1955, and other modern glass in the church is by Willy Weyres. To the S along Mauritius-Steinweg is the neo-Gothic church of **St Mauritius**, 1864, restored in 1957.

Walk due N from St Aposteln along Gertrudenstrasse and then follow Sankt-Apern-Strasse to the **Römerturm** (50 BC). To the right along Zeughausstrasse is the brick-built former arsenal, the **Zeughaus**, of 1594–1606, with a Baroque doorway, 1594, by Peter Cronenborch. Now the **Kölnisches Stadtmuseum** (open except Mon 10.00–17.00, Thu to 20.00), its south façade is built on the former Roman wall. The building abutting on the Zeughaus is the former city guard house, the **Alte Wache**, of 1840, restored in 1958. To the S by way of Landgasse is the church of **St Maria in der Kupfergasse**, 1705–15, restored in 1955.

Zeughausstrasse leads further E to the church of **St Andreas, in the centre of Cologne's banking area. Its choir, once 10C, was rebuilt in the late Gothic style of the 15C. It houses the late Gothic *shrine of Albertus Magnus; an early 16C altar by Barthel Bruyn; and 19C glass. The nave and crossing tower were begun in 1200; the side aisles are basically 13C with 14C extensions. The north transept and south transept (with a shrine of the Maccabees c 1527) were rebuilt in the 15C. Modern additions include bronze doors by Karl Winter, 1962, and the present Dominican convent, by Karl Band, 1955.

Return along Zeughausstrasse to Sankt-Apern-Strasse and turn N along Steinfeldergasse to reach the oval-shaped Romanesque church of **St Gereon, built in a Roman cemetery. The well-restored 4C decagon is wrongly alleged to have been built by Constantine's mother, St Helena. This church was altered under Archbishop Anno (1056–75), with the addition of the mosaic floor, a long east choir, which was lengthened in the next century and embellished with two flanking towers. During this era early Gothic windows were added to the decagon, which is closed with ten ribs and a hanging keystone 34m high (completed in 1227). The baptistry was added shortly afterwards, and has medieval wall paintings. The vault of the choir and its Gothic windows date from the 15C, as does the sacristy, while the modern glass is by Georg Meistermann.

OTHER MUSEUMS: **Museum für Ostasiatische Kunst**, 100 Universitäts- strasse (open except Mon 10.00–17.00, first Fri in month to 20.00); the **Police Museum**, 16 Verloerstrasse (open on request); the Beatles Museum, 13 Heinsbergstrasse (open Mon, Wed, Fri and first Sat in month 10.00–19.00); **Rautenstrauch-Joest Museum**, 45 Ubierring (open except Mon 10.00– 17.00, Wed till 20.00); **Theatre Museum** in the Rococo Schloss Wahn (open weekdays 09.00–17.00); a **Brewery Museum** in Küppers-Kölsch Brauerei, 155 Alteburgstrasse (open Sat 10.00–16.00); **Contemporary Ceramics Museum**, 12 Bonnstrasse (open Wed, Thu 10.00–12.00, 14.00–17.00, Sat 14.00–17.00, Sun 10.00–16.00); **Käthe-Kollwitz-Museum**, 18–24 Neumarkt (open except Sat 10.00–17.00, Thu closing at 20.00); and the **Museum für Angewandte Kunst** (Museum for Applied Art) at An der Rechtschule (open except Mon 10.00–17.00, Tue closing 20.00).

OTHER THEATRES: **Theatre am Dom**, 2 Glockengasse; **Theater in Bauturn**, 24 Aachener Strasse; **Volkstheater Millowitsch**, 5 Aachener Strasse; **Kammerspiele am Ubierring**, 45 Ubierring.

OTHER SIGHTS: parts of the 95km long Roman aqueduct bringing the waters of the Eifel to the city; the NW corner tower of the Roman city walls on the corner of Zeughausstrasse and St Apernstrasse; the Rodenkirchen Forestry Reserve (with guided tours daily summer 09.00–20.00, winter closing 16.00); the 266m-high telecommunications tower, the **Fernsehturm**, 1978–80, with a viewing platform and a revolving restaurant; the church of **St Engelbert** on Riehler Gürtel, by Dominikus Böhn, 1930–32; and the church of **Neu St Alban**, 25 Gilbachstrasse, designed by Hans Schilling in 1958 and built of bricks from the former Opera House that was destroyed in World War II.

ENVIRONS: Leave Cologne by driving NE along Konrad-Adenauer-Ufer and then Niederlander-Ufer and left along An der Schanze to turn right and cross the Rhine by the Mülheimer cable-bridge (designed by F. Leonhardt and K. Schüssler, 1949–51) to reach the suburb of **Mülheim**. Once a Frankish settlement, it is an important harbour. Its narrow, tall modernistic church of Our Lady was built by Rudolf Schwarz in 1955. The stained glass was added by Anton Wendling in 1958. Mülheim also has a Baroque church of St Klemens, built in 1692 and restored by Joachim Schürmann after World War II. Its bronze doors depict the saint's life, and were designed by Werner Schürmann in 1960. Another modern church, dedicated to St Theresia, was built by Gottfried Böhm in 1955. To the S is the industrial suburb of **Köln-Deutz**, on the site of a Roman fort, *Castel Divitia*. This suburb today is the HQ of the Klöckner-Humboldt-Deutz factories. Here in 1864 E. Langen and Nikolaus August Otto founded the Deutz motor car factory. The Klöckner-Humboldt-Deutz Motor Museum is at 111 Deutz-Mülheimerstrasse (open weekdays 10.00–16.00). See also the 100m by 14m and 60m-high administrative offices, the Klöckner-Hochhaus by Hentrich and Petschnigg, 1964, and the restored church of St Heribert, 1886, which houses St Heribert's shrine, c 1170. NW of Mülheim stand

Cologne's trade fair halls, with the 85m-high Messeturm, cafés and restaurants and the Rhine park.

### Excursion from Mülheim

Alternatively, leave **Cologne** by driving to the right bank of the river across the Deutzer Brücke and along the B55 to reach after 15km **Bensberg** (44,000 inhab.; alt. 162m), which is dominated by the towers of its ruined 12C Schloss (a building adapted as the town hall by Gottfried Böhm in 1967), and by the Baroque Neues Schloss, built by Matteo d'Alberti between 1705 and 1710, under the inspiration of Versailles.

# 44

# Cologne to the Dutch border: The Left Bank of the Rhine

Total distance 149km. Cologne—B9, 23km Dormagen—13km Neuss—23km Krefeld—B57, 19km Moers—29km Xanten—14km Kalkar—13km Kleve—B9, 11km Kranenburg—4km the Dutch border.

An **excursion** from Krefeld to Kleve by way of Geldern and Kevelaer, 65km. Taking the B57 between Krefeld and Mönchengladbach 20km.

Leave **Cologne** (see Rte 43) N, which offers a view of the highest apartment block in Europe, the 137.3m-high Colonia-Hochhaus, by way of Neusserstrasse, and take the B9 for 16km to **Worringen**. Known to the Romans as *Buruncum*, here in 1288 the citizens of Cologne fought and won against their archbishop and his allies of Brabant. Continue for another 7km to **Dormagen**. Called by the Romans *Durnomagus*, this was the station of their 22nd legion.

2km NE of the B9 lies the entrancing village of *Zons (10,000 inhab.; alt. 36m), on the river's bank. Its 14C walls are the best-preserved medieval fortifications in the Rhineland. Virtually rectangular, they were built by Archbishop Friedrich von Saarwerden c 1373 who used Zons (Roman *Sontium*) as a river toll station. The town has preserved its windmill tower, the Krötschenturm (once a gaol), the Halb tower and the Customs tower. The town is cooled by a fountain of 1577. The museum at 1 Schlossstrasse has a Jugendstil collection (open May–Sept weekdays except Mon 14.00–19.00; weekends 10.00–12.30, 14.00–17.00; other months weekdays except Mon 14.00–18.00). Buses to Cologne, Dormagen and Düsseldorf; boat trips. 14C Schloss Friedenstrom rises beside the Rhine, as does the contemporary Rheinturm, while close by stands the Juddenturm.

Return to the B9 and continue N for 13km to the industrial town and harbour of **Neuss** (150,000 inhab.; alt. 42m), whose town charter was granted in 1190. The finest monument in Neuss is the late-Romanesque *basilica of St Quirinus, with an 11C crypt and a Baroque dome of 1741. It houses a crucifix, c 1350, and a Madonna of 1420. The Obertor dates from c 1300, and houses the Clemens-Sels-Museum (open Tue–Sun 10.00–17.00). The town's former Observaten church, 1640, is now a concert hall.

Also in Neuss are the church of Christ the King, 1955, preserving pre-World War I windows by J. Thorn-Prikker; a botanical garden; and a theatre at 2 Büttget-Strasse.

Tourist information is at 40 Friedrichstrasse; train links with Holland, buses with Aachen, Cologne, Düsseldorf, Zons, boats with Düsseldorf. Neuss hosts an annual festival in late August. From Neuss the B326 crosses the Rhine to Düsseldorf-Süd (6km; see Rte 45).

The B9 continues N, passing en route the B222 which leads W to the new town of **Meerbusch**, where you discover a ruined 17C Schloss, the Haus Meer, and the Haus Dyckhof, 1666. After 22km it reaches the silk and textile manufacturing city of **Krefeld** (235,000 inhab.; alt. 38m).

**Tourist information** is at the main railway station. **Train** links with Cologne, Düsseldorf, Holland; **buses** to Duisburg, Düsseldorf and Venlo (on the border with Holland); **airport** for light aircraft; **river trips**. The town has an ice rink and a racecourse.

Krefeld has a classical town hall of 1893; windmills; patrician houses; and the church of St Klemens, a complex building with a 12C tower, a 14C nave, a 17C south aisle and a 19C east end. Its neo-Gothic church of St Matthias has a 12C Romanesque tower. Restored Burg Linn is now the Niederrheinisches Museum (open Apr–Oct Tue–Sun 10.00–13.00, 15.00–18.00; otherwise closes 17.00) and dates from the 12C to the 17C. Haus Lange, built by Mies van der Rohe in 1929, stands at 91 Wilhelmshofallee and is now an exhibition hall for contemporary art (open Tue–Sun 10.00–17.00). Krefeld's textile museum is housed in a building of 1880 at 8 Andreasmarkt (opening times as the Niederrheinisches Museum). The Kaiser-Wilhelm-Museum at 35 Karlsplatz displays modern art (open Tue–Sun 10.00–17.00).

The B9 leavs the river bank here and travels NW, reaching after 27km **Geldern** (19.000 inhab.; alt. 25m), once the capital of the duchy of Geldre. The remains of its fortifications include the Mühlenturm. Geldern's 15C parish church formerly belonged to an Augustinian monastery whose refectory still stands. 11km NE is the rose-pink brick town of **Kevelaer**, whose mid-17C Madonna and mid-17C shrine developed into a Baroque pilgrimage church, 1654, as the statue's miraculous powers (mocked in Heinrich Heine's 'Die Wahlfahrt nach Kevelaer') became famous. Its present neo-Gothic basilica of St Maria, 1858–64, seats 5000 and annually attracts 500,000 pilgrims. The history of the pilgrimage is set out in the museum at 18 Hauptstrasse (open daily 10.00–17.00, closed Mon Nov–Apr).

Kevelaer is 12km SE of **Goch** (30,000 inhab.; alt. 16m), which has a 14C stone gate whose twin towers are now the town museum, housing 14C and 15C art and a gramophone collection (open Tue–Sun 10.00–12.00, 15.00–17.00). Other sights are the 16C Haus zu den fünf Ringen at 1 Steinstrasse, and the lavish 14C to 16C brick-built *church of St Maria Magdalena with its 15C sandstone tabernacle. From Goch the B9 leads N for 13km to Kleve (see below).

From Krefeld the B57 runs for 19km to **Moers** (103,000 inhab.; alt. 29m; tourist information: 49 Oberwallstrasse). As well as remains of the old fortifications, Moers has a 15C to 17C Grafenschloss at 9 Kastell, now the local history museum (open except Mon 09.00–18.00; weekends opens 10.00). Its mid-15C parish church has a Baroque organ. No. 1 Altmarkt was the birthplace of the hymnologist Gerhard Tersteegen (1697–1769). The town theatre stands at 6 Kastell, while the town museum is in the 17C building at 1 Meerstrasse (open weekdays 13.00–19.00; Sun 11.00–17.00).

The B57 continues for a further 12km due N to **Rheinberg** (27,500 inhab.; alt. 25m). Here the parish church of 1107 has a reredos c 1500; the town hall was built in 1449; and the Zollturm and Pulverturm remain from the medieval walls.

17km NW along the B57 lies *Xanten (16,000 inhab.), once an important Roman garrison town and still preserving its Roman amphitheatre and other Roman remains. This city was beautifully restored after World War II and attracts many tourists. You can visit excavations and an archaeological park at 3 Trajanstrasse (open 09.00–18.00, or dusk if earlier), as well as parts of the medieval walls, their chief feature the double Klever Tor, 1393. The Altstadt retains numerous medieval houses, as well as the town hall of 1786, a Protestant church of 1649 and the Charterhouse of 1646.

The Dom, the collegiate church of *St Viktor, rises on the site of a 4C grave of two martyrs—hence Xanten, i.e. 'Ad Sanctos'. A Gothic five-aisled basilica, with a Romanesque-Gothic west façade, the south tower dates from 1378–79, the north tower (though Romanesque) from 1500. Inside are the oldest choir-stalls in the Rhineland, created in 1250; 14C stained glass fills some windows. The high altar encompasses the golden shrine of St Viktor, 1150, and an altarpiece created by Barthel Bruyn the elder in 1530. The Lady altar of 1535 is by Heinrich Douvermann. The crypt has tombs of martyrs of the Third Reich. Xanten's Dom has retained its Gothic cloister and chapter house, 1543–46. Visit the treasury (open Tue–Sat 10.00–12.00, 14.00–18.00; winter only afternoons). The town has an important regional museum at 7–9 Kurfürstenstrasse, displaying Roman remains (open weekdays except Mon 10.00–17.00, weekends 11.00–18.00).

Tourist information at the town hall. Train links with Duisburg and Kleve, buses with local towns. The *Nibelungenlied* places Siegfried's home here.

The harmonious medieval town of **Kalkar** (11,000 inhab.; alt. 20m), a member of the Hanseatic League and the centre of north Rhenish wood-carving, 1490–1540, lies 14km NW of Xanten along the B57, on the left bank of the Rhine. Its turreted town hall dates from 1444–46 and other 15C brick houses grace the Marktplatz. A 12C Romanesque church of St Clemens serves as the parish church, while the 15C church of St Nikolai has a crucifixion group c 1500 over the north door and magical *furnishings, including a high altar, with wings by Jan Joest, 1505–08; an altar of the Seven Sorrows of Mary by Heinrich Douvermann, 1519; and six other carved altars by the Kalkar school. The church museum opens daily 10.00–12.00, 14.00–17.00. Tourist information at the town hall. Train links with Duisberg and Kleve, buses with other local towns.

At **Kleve** (46,000 inhab.; alt. 46m), 13km NW along the B57, the route rejoins the B9. From here came Anne of Cleves, the fourth wife of Henry VIII of England. The town centres on the former collegiate church of St Maria Himmelfahrt, by Master Konrad of Kleve, 1356. Its nave and west towers were finished in 1426, though the interior was much altered after damage in World War II. Its Lady altar is by Heinrich Douvermann and Jakob Dericke, 1510, and the church shelters 14C to 16C tombs, including that of Graf Arnold II and his wife Ida, 1350. Kleve also has a Minorite church of 1440, with stalls of 1474.

From the 15C Gothic ruins of the Schwanenburg is a splendid *view; and the *garden-park, created by Johann Moritz Fürst von Nassau in 1656, was much frequented by Voltaire. Much damaged during World War II, part of the Schwanenburg has been restored in the 18C style and is now an art gallery (open 11.00–17.00, though only at weekends Nov–Mar). The town also has a zoo; and at 13 Katharinerstrasse stands the Haus Koekkoek, the home between 1861 and 1862 of the painter Barend Cornelis Koekkoek (1813–62). It displays medieval art and works by Heinrich Dovermann (open except Mon 10.00–13.00, 14.00–17.00).

Tourist information at the town hall. Train connections with Amsterdam, Cologne, Düsseldorf, Kranenburg (on the Dutch border) and Klagenfurt; bus connections with Emmerich Geldern, Goch, Kalkar, Kevelaer and Xanten.

11km W of Kleve along the B9 lies **Kranenburg**, 4km from the Dutch border. Kranenburg has a Gothic pilgrimage church; a museum on the Katherinenhof (housed in a former Augustinian monastery) and the nearby Pulvertum, a gallery of 15C to 20C art, specialising in drawings and etchings by Daniel Chodowiecki, 1726–1801 (open except Mon 1400–1700; Sun also 11.00–12.00). The distance from Kranenburg to Amsterdam by way of Nijmegen is 120km.

## Krefeld to Mönchengladbach and Rheydt

From **Krefeld** (see above) the B57 runs SW through Neersen and Neersbroich to reach after 20km the industrial town of **Mönchengladbach** (262,000 inhab.; alt. 50m), an important railway junction whose name derives from a former Benedictine abbey. Though an industrial town, its ancient centre is beguiling. The former abbey church of St Vitus (Münsterkirche), restored in the 19C, has a 13C Gothic choir, finished in 1275 and built on a Romanesque crypt. Inside are a 12C Romanesque font and a late 13C *Bible window in the choir. Its Romanesque altar, c 1160, is now in the treasury, whose other masterpiece is a missal c 1140 (open Sun 10.15–12.15). Nearby in the Alter Markt is the late Gothic church of Maria Himmelfahrt. Other churches include that of Neuwerk, originally 12C, rebuilt in the early 16C, and in the suburb of Wickrath the 12C Protestant church, much rebuilt in the 17C and 18C. Also in Wickrath is an 18C and 19C Schloss.

Mönchengladbach's curvilinear Museum Abteiberg at 27 Abteistrasse was designed by the Viennese architect Hans Hollein, 1972–82. It displays an impressive collection of Expressionism, Dada and Constructivism, Pop and Op art, including works by Rauschenberg and Warhol, and masterpieces by **Josef Beuys, who worked here from 1951 to 1981 (open except Mon 10.00–18.00). The monastery buildings became the Rathaus in the early 19C. SW of the town is **Rheindahlen**, the HQ of the British Army of the Rhine after World War II and also of NATO (Central and N Europe). The theatre is at 73 Hindenburgstrasse. Tourist information at the main railway station.

4km SE of Mönchengladbach the B59 reaches **Rheydt** (110,000 inhab.; alt. 67m), another industrial town, with a Renaissance Schloss built between 1565 and 1585 on medieval foundations and today housing a cultural and weaving museum, whose exhibits also document the history of the town and include Renaissance and Baroque art (open Tue–Sun 10.00–18.00; Nov–Feb only Wed and weekends, 11.00–17.00). Tourist information at 60 Stresemannstrasse.

# 45

# Cologne to Emmerich and the Dutch border: The Right Bank of the Rhine

Total distance 153km. Cologne—B8, 12km Leverkusen—31km Düsseldorf—
10km Kaiserswerth—17km Duisburg—18km Dinslaken—15km Wesel—41km
Emmerich—9km Emmerich-Elten for the Dutch border (en route to Arnhem).

Visit the former Cistercian monastery at **Altenberg. The monastic buildings date from the 13C, though the church was founded in the 12C. It was
rebuilt between 1259 and 1379, after an earthquake, and was restored in
1895. Its interior, 77.7m by 19.5m and 28m high, has 14C stained glass; a
14C Annunciation; a late Gothic tabernacle of 1480; a Madonna created c
1530, and houses the tombs of many of the Berg family. The W window,
18m x 18m is the largest in Germany.

**Leverkusen** (170,000 inhab.; alt. 45m), the home of Bayer AG's dye
factories, welcomed also in 1925 the HQ of its chemical industries, hence
the 122m-high Bayer-Bürohaus of 1921. The Schloss is now a modern art
museum (open Tue–Sun 10.00–17.00). In Kaiser-Wilhelm-Allee is the Agfa-
Gevaert photography museum (open weekdays 09.00–17.00). Trains
connect with Cologne and Düsseldorf, buses with Cologne and Slingen;
boat trips.

The B8 continues to **Düsseldorf-Benrath**. In its 'English' park stands the
richly stuccoed and painted late Baroque/Rococo Schloss Benrath,
designed by the French architect Nicolas de Pigage, 1755–73, who also
designed the waterfalls of the English garden. Its Gartensäle, garden
rooms, were frescoed in the mid 18C with mythological scenes by Lambert
Wilhelm Krahe. Of an earlier Schloss of 1660 remains only the Orangery
designed by Johannes Lolio. The town has a natural history collection and
an aviary at 102 Benrather Schlossallee (open except Mon 10.00–17.00; Sat
opens 13.00; Nov–Mar restricted opening times).

After 31km from Cologne the route reaches **Düsseldorf** (590,000 inhab.;
alt. 38m), situated at the confluence of the 800m-wide Rhine and the Düssel.

Tourist information: 12 Konrad-Adenauer-Platz. Train connections with major
German cities and with Holland; buses with Aachen, Belgium and Holland; boat trips;
Lohausen international airport (6km from city centre) has an aeroplane and flight
museum (open Mar–Dec 09.00–19.00).

The Altstadt is packed for festivals on the Monday before Lent, though Carnival
festivities and balls take place from November to Ash Wednesday, and on 10 November.
The latter date is the eve of the feast of St Martin, when processions of more than
50,000 children carry paper lanterns throughout the city, and in front of the Rathaus
is re-enacted the story of the saint slicing his cloak in two on behalf of a naked beggar.
The Christmas market begins in the Marktplatz at the end of November. Each July
the marksmen's guild of St Sebastian celebrates a festival in the Rhine meadows at
Oberkassel, with a parade and a funfair (attended annually by four million visitors),
which ends with a display of fireworks.

History. As the bones of Neanderthal man reveal, this site was occupied between
150,000 and 50,000 BC. The Romans also invested the spot, but its true founder was
Bishop Swidbert, who established a convent at Kaiserswerth c 700. The name
'Dusseldorp', however, appears first only in 1135. The town rapidly developed in the

early 12C, by the end of which it belonged to the Graf von Berg, becoming the principal family residence in 1288, when Graf Adolf granted it a city charter. In 1348 the city was inherited by the dukes of nearby Jülich. Judicious dynastic marriages eventually expanded the duchy and with it the prestige of its rulers. The greatest of these was the Elector-Palatine Johann Wilhelm II, known affectionately as Jan Wellem, who lived here throughout his long reign (1679–1716) and devoted much of his wealth to expanding its fortifications, adding to the renown of its opera and founding an art gallery. Another princely benefactor was the Elector Karl-Theodor, who at the end of the 18C commissioned Schloss Benrath and also instructed its architect, Nicolas de Pigage, to lay out the Hofgarten.

Napoleon made Düsseldorf capital of the grand-duchy of Berg in 1806. The city became Prussian in 1815. In 1838 the first railway of the Federal Republic ran from Düsseldorf, which led to the expansion of the city's trade and industries. After World War I it was for a time under French occupation. Although 50 per cent of the city was destroyed in World War II, the old city escaped destruction.

The artist Peter von Cornelius (1783–1867) was born in Düsseldorf, as was Heinrich Heine (1797–1856) who observed, 'The city of Düsseldorf is extremely beautiful, and if you think of it when you are in foreign lands and happen to have been born there, strange feelings overcome you'. At various times Mendelssohn, Schumann and Brahms stayed here.

Turn left from Konrad-Adenauer-Platz, in front of the main railway station, and continue W along Karlstrasse across Stresemannsplatz and then along Graf-Adolf-Strasse to Graf-Adolf-Platz, which lies at the S end of Düsseldorf's N–S axis, the ***Königsallee**, so called after a visit by King Friedrich Wilhelm of Prussia in 1851, with its shops, offices and restaurants. Nearly 1km long and known as the **Kö**, the Königsallee was created by C.A. Huschberger in 1804 on the site of the old ramparts and straddling the moat. This part of the Kö is enhanced by a little park, with a 'column of light', the Lichtsäule, created by Günther Uecker in 1981, the statue of the Ballthrower by W. Schott, 1931, and the Knaben fountain of 1909 by Gregor von Bachmann. The interior of the Dresdner Bank was restored in 1982 to its Jugendstil original and its courtyard has a statue of Max Ernst. Another Jugendstil building rises opposite on the corner with Trinkstrasse.

Between here and Blumenstrasse to the right is the massive department store known as the **Kö-Centre**. N rises the Triton fountain created by Fritz Coubillier in 1902, while on the corner with Theodor-Körner Strasse stands the Kaufhof, a very late Jugendstil building of 1909, designed by the Austrian J.M. Olbrich. In the garden here are the statues of a girl playing with a ball (W. Schott, 1932) and the Bergisch Lion (Philipp Harth, 1963). Near the rear of the Kaufhaus is Wilhelm-Marx-Haus, S of Heinrich-Heine-Allee, Germany's first skyscraper, built by Wilhelm Kreis between 1922 and 1924.

Haroldstrasse runs W from the S end of Königsalle, passing the **Schwanenmarkt** with a 1981 statue of Heinrich Heine by Bert Gerresheim and, on the other side of the street, the neo-Gothic **Haus des Landtags** of 1876–80, to reach the bank of the Rhine. Here turn right along Mannesmannufer to find the tall **Mannesmann-Haus** by P. Behrens, 1912. A right turn here, and then left along Berger-Allee discovers on the right the **Stadtmuseum** in the 18C and 19C Palais Graf Spee, which was begun in 1755 (entrance at 7–9 Bäckerstrasse), to find an exhibition devoted to the history of Düsseldorf (open Wed 12.00–20.00, Tue, Thu, Fri 10.00–17.00, Sat 13.00–17.00). The museum has expanded into a new building of 1991 in Berger-Allee.

From the Stadtmuseum, Orangeriestrasse runs NE to reach the former Franciscan church of St Maximilian, known as the **Maxkirche**. This three-aisled brick building of 1734–37 was built for the Franciscans. It has a stuccoed Baroque interior; its lectern dates from 1450 and there are 18C vestment cabinets and vestments in the sacristy. The church also has a stuccoed refectory, with frescoes of the life of St Antony.

Opposite, the 18C Palais Nesselrode is now the **Hetjens Museum** of ceramics, whose exhibits begin with works of the 4C BC and encompass pottery from every part of Europe as well as works from Japan and China (open Tue–Sun 11.00–17.00). Its name derives from its founder, Laurenz Heinrich Hetjens, who not only endowed the museum but in 1908 also left it his own porcelain collection.

From the Maxkirche, Benratherstrasse runs E, passing on the right the late 18C **Palais Wittgenstein**, now a cultural centre with a marionette theatre. Bilkerstrasse runs S from the Palais, with at No. 14 the **Heinrich Heine Institute** (open except Mon 11.00–17.00). The plaque on its façade depicts the Romantic poet Luise Hensel (1798–1876). Follow Benratherstrasse further E, crossing Königsallee, to reach Berliner-Allee. Turn N here and walk to **Martin-Luther-Platz**, which houses the ministry of justice, the Protestant church of **St Johann** (1881, restored) and a monument to Bismarck (1889). Blumenstrasse leads NW from here to **Schadowplatz**, where stands a bust of the artist Wilhelm von Schadow, director of the art academy at Düsseldorf from 1827 to 1846, and the Salinen fountain, by M. Kratz, 1964. N stands Jan-Wellem-Platz, its name derived from the nickname of Kurfürst Johann Wilhelm II, who reigned from 1659 to 1716, with the Thyssenhochhaus of 1959.

W is Corneliusplatz at the N end of Königsallee. It is graced by a basin fountain by Leo Müsch, 1882, a Triton fountain by F. Coubellier, 1902, and a monument to Peter Cornelius by Donndorf, 1879. A subway leads to the **Hofgarten**, a park of c 26 hectares dating back to Nicolas Pigage, 1767, enlarged by Maximilian Weyhe, 1813, and close by a lake known as the Landskronen. This garden is at the centre of several of Düsseldorf's most important cultural institutions. N of the Hofgarten in Jacobistrasse stands the **Jägerhof** by Pigage and J.J. Couven, 1758–63, once the ducal hunting lodge, now the **Goethe Museum** (open weekdays except Mon 11.00–17.00, Sat 13.00–17.00, Sun 11.00–17.00). From here Jägerhofstrasse leads W to the Hofgärtnerhaus of 1790.

On the NW side of the Hofgarten rises the **Tonhalle**, a planetarium, built by Wilhelm Kreis in the mid-1920s. Further N is the **Landesmuseum**, devoted to the local economy, which embraces agriculture, commerce and mines (open weekdays except Mon 09.00–17.00, Wed until 20.00, Sun and holidays 10.00–18.00). The bronze of Heine in front of the museum was created by Georg Kolbe in 1933. Cross Inselstrasse N to reach the museum of fine arts, the **\*Kunstmuseum**, based on the collection of Jan Wellem, including two works by Rubens, as well as 19C and 20C art and Renaissance to 20C sculpture (open Tue–Fri 11.00–17.00).

S of the Hofgarten is the **Deutsche Oper am Rhein**, built in the mid-1870s by E.F. Giese, and reopened after restoration in 1956. Busts of R. Schumann and a monument to Christian Dietrich Grabbe are set at either side of the opera house. The marble **Märchenbrunnen** (fairy-tale fountain) here is by the French sculptor Max Blondat, 1905. W in Grabbeplatz rises the **Städtische Kunsthalle**, devoted to changing exhibitions of modern art (open except Mon 11.00–17.00), fronted by a bronze statue of Habakkuk, based on one created by Max Ernst in 1934.

On the other side of Grabbeplatz the **\*\*\*Kunstsammlung Nordrhein-Westfalen** houses a remarkable collection of modern art, begun in 1960

*Max Beckmann's Expressionist 'Night' (1918-19), in the Kunstsammlung Nordrhein-Westphalen, Düsseldorf © DACS 1995*

with the acquisition of 88 works by Paul Klee (now expanded to 94). Today the collection includes *fauves*, works by Matisse, Derain and Braque, a section devoted to Cubism, paintings by Juan Gris and Picasso and works by Modigliani. Also displayed are German Expressionists, Constructivists and Surrealists, as well as art after 1945, including works by Lichtenstein and Warhol (open except Mon 10.00–18.00).

Heine-Allee runs N from the Kunstsammlung Nordrhein-Westfalen and meets at its N end Ratingerstrasse, leading left by way of the classical Ratinger gate (by A. von Vagedes, 1814) to the old city, with its winding narrow, pedestrianised streets. On the right of Ratingerstrasse is the 15C Gothic **Kreuzherrenkirche**, now part of the nearby art academy museum. Built for the Knights of the Cross, it has a double nave, and was restored in the 1960s. Its address is 5 Ehrenhof, part of a complex running N along the river bank that includes the domed Tonhalle (see above).

On the opposite side of Ratingerstrasse, just before the river bank, stands the basilica of *St Lambert, deriving from the 13C and 14C. Its Italian Baroque interior, 1650–1712, shelters a late Gothic, slender, exquisite tabernacle of the 1470s; the Renaissance tomb of Duke Wilhelm V the Rich by Gerhard Scheben, 1599; the Romanesque reliquary of St Vitalis in the sacristy; and delicate stucco work. Its high altar, created by the workshop of Gabriel de Grupello c 1720, has gilded barley-sugar pillars. To the right is the modern organ (though its carvings match the rest of the church) by Johannes Klais of Bonn, 1950. Another treasure is a Madonna of c 1100, and her infant son holding a cross. The Pfarraltar, created by Karl Matthäus Winter in 1978, houses the shrine (1655) which shelters the remains of St Apollinaris of Ravenna (martyred in the 1C AD), patron of Düsseldorf, the saint depicted rising from death, dressed as a 17C bishop. K.M. Winter also designed the church's stations of the cross, as well as a bronze cover for the 15C font. The side altars include that of the tailors (Schneideraltar), with late 15C statues of SS Lambert and Andrew, and that of the Goldsmiths (Altar de Goldschmeide), with a superb Madonna and Child of 1334. The crypt houses the remains of local lords and ladies from 1592–1819. The belfry was rebuilt in 1817; the main doors were created by Eduard Mataré in 1960. S of this church, in Burgplatz, is the 12C **Schlossturm**, the rest of the Schloss was burned down in 1872, S of which in Marktplatz is the **Rathaus** of 1961. It preserves a façade of 1573 by Heinrich Tussmann, which was in part rebuilt by Johann Joseph Couven in 1749 (visits Wed at 15.00, to see the ceiling of the Baroque gallery, with a painting of the apotheosis of Anna Maria of Tuscany, Jan Wellem's second wife, by Domenico Zanetti, 1694). In front of the town hall prances the Baroque equestrian statue of Kurfürst Johann Wilhelm II by the Dutch sculptor Gabriel de Grupello, 1711. No. 12 Marktplatz carries a Glockenspiel. On the corner with Zollstrasse, with its gabled houses, is a fountain by W. Hoselmann, 1932. (Grupello lived in the 18C house opposite.)

From Marktplatz take Flingergasse and Schneider-Wibbel-Gasse back into the Altstadt to reach Bolkerstrasse where at No. 53 Henrich Heine was born in 1797. The Neander church nearby, 1683–87, is named after the Protestant hymnologist Joachin Neander (1650–80). Take on the left Hunrückerstrasse to reach the Italian Baroque church of **St Andreas**, 1620–29, which contains the mausoleum of seven members of the Neuburg family, 1667 (see in particular Johann Wilhelm II's tomb with a portrait medallion by Grupello) and an altar by Eduard Mataré, 1959. That the church once belonged to the Jesuits is revealed by their typical inscriptions—IHS, signifying Iesus Hominum Salvator; MRA, signifying Maria Regina Angelorum. Opposite the main door is a column with a statue of St Martin by R. Graner, 1965. The former art gallery, destroyed in World War II, has supplied the caryatids by Leo Müsch, 1880, between the church and Grabbeplatz.

Other Düsseldorf churches include the Romanesque **Alt-St Martin**, c 1160, to the S of the city in the suburb of Düsseldorf-Bilk, with its 13C frescoes, and its side-aisles rebuilt in 1881; and the church of **St Margareta** in the suburb of Gerresheim, to the SE, which was finished in 1236 and still conserves its former nunnery cloisters and a crucifix of c 980.

Other features of Düsseldorf are the Nordpark, with a Japanese garden, and the Löbbecke Museum and Aquazoo, both in Kaiserswerthstrasse; the **botanical garden** in Universitätsstrasse (open 08.00, closing at various times of the year 17.00, 18.00 or 19.00); the TV tower, the **Rheinturm**, of 1982, its 174m-high restaurant slowly turning (open daily 10.00–24.00) and the 150-hectare Südpark.

In the suburb of **Kaiserswerth**, 10km NW along the B8, is the 11C and 12C Barbarossapfalz, ruined in the War of the Spanish Succession, 1702, and the collegiate church, founded c 700, rebuilt as a 12C Romanesque basilica and housing the golden shrine of St Suitbertus.

17km further along the B8 is **DUISBURG** (570,000 inhab.; alt. 31m), birthplace of the geographer Gerhard Mercator (1512–94) and the sculptor Wilhelm Lehmbruck (1881–1919), chief port for the Ruhr and the world's largest river port. From the main railway station follow Friedrich-Wilhelm-Strasse E, passing on the left the Niederrheinisches Museum at No. 64, celebrated for its terracottas and excavated Roman remains, with rooms displaying the work of Gerhard Mercator (open except Mon 10.00–17.00, Wed closes 16.00, Sun opens 11.00); and the Wilhelm-Lehmbruck Museum, entrance at 51 Düsseldorferstrasse, whose treasures are works by Wilhelm Lehmbruck (1881–1919) and other 20C sculptors, including Rodin, Moore, Giacometti, Lipchitz, Arp, Brancusi and Barlach (open Tue, Fri 14.00–22.00; otherwise, except Mon 10.00–17.00). At the end of Friedrich-Wilhelm-Strasse turn N to reach Salvatorkirchplatz and the 13C to early 15C Salvator church, which was restored 1903–04 and after World War II. The church houses Mercator's tomb, as well as a 15C hexagonal font and a Renaissance pulpit of 1644. Return E along Gutenberg-Strasse and Kohnenstrasse to the Burgplatz, where you find the eclectically Jugendstil Rathaus by Franz Rätzel, 1897–1902 (restored after World War II), the theatre, the Mercatorhalle concert and congress hall, 1962, and a Mercator monument. The Rathaus has sculptures comparing Charlemagne with Kaiser Wilhelm I. Duisburg also has a museum of German river navigation (Museum der Deutschen Binnenschiffahrt), founded in 1977 and based at 11 Dammstrasse, open daily except Mon 10.00–17.00.

Duisburg's zoo, including dolphins and whales, is on the Kaiserberg. The town is well served with sports stadia. Tourist information at 96 Friedrich-Wilhelm-Strasse. Trains connect with Dinslaken, Wesel and Walsum; buses with Krefeld and Kevelaer; boat trips.

The B8 continues N through the suburb of **Duisburg-Hamborn**, where you can visit an 1170 Romanesque church of a Premonstratensian abbey, reaching after 18km **Dinslaken** (62,000 inhab.; alt. 30m). Here are the remains of medieval walls; the 15C church of St Vincentius; a Protestant parish church built in 1722; a 15C Crucifixion group, the Kalvarienberg; the Burg theatre of 1722; and a local history museum at 31 Brückstrasse (open Tue–Sat 09.00–12.00, 14.00–17.00).

After another 15km the B8 reaches **Wesel** (61,000 inhab.; alt. 27m) at the confluence of the Lippe and the Rhine. Despite enormous destruction in World War II, Wesel preserves its old defences the Zitadelle gate of 1718 and the Berlin gate of 1722, as well as the cathedral church of St Willibrord, a 15C and 16C Gothic church on the base of a Romanesque basilica. The cathedal was restored in 1896, when statues of the Great Elector and Kaiser Wilhelm I were set over the main entrance. The late 19C organ has 67 stops. Wesel has a monument to Peter Minuit, who left for America in 1586, founding New York and Wilmington, Delaware. Its theatre, the Stadtisches Bühnenhaus, stands in Martinistrasse, and its Museum at 14 Ritterstrasse displays gold and silver ware (open weekdays 10.00–20.15, Sat 10.00–13.00).

Finally the B8 reaches Rees and Emmerich. **Rees**, 24km NW of Wesel, preserves from its 13C walls the Mühlenturm and the Toelder gate and a bastion on the riverside. The Protestant parish church of 1624 was restored after World War II. 17km NE of Rees is **Emmerich** (30,000 inhab.; alt. 19m), close by the Dutch border, and a crossing point. This is the chief customs point for German shipping, dealing annually with 200,000 vessels. Almost totally destroyed in World War II, Emmerich now boasts the longest suspension bridge in Germany, stretching for 1228m, the restored church of St Aldigond, 1483 (with a 91m-high tower, well worth ascending for its *view) and the restored church of St Martin, with an 11C crypt; a crucifix, c 1200; 12C wall paintings; and stalls of 1486. In the treasury is the chest-reliquary of St Willibrord, 11C and 15C. The Rathaus of 1939 stands in the main square, the Geistmarkt, as does the Christuskirche of 1715. Emmerich's shipping museum is at 2 Martinikirchgang (open Tue, Wed 10.00–12.00, 14.00–16.00, Thu till 18.00; Fri, Sat 10.00–12.00). Tourist information at the town hall. Train connections with Cologne and Amsterdam; bus connections with Holland; boats cross the Rhine.

For the road to Arnhem, **Emmerich-Elten**, 9km NE along the B8, is the border crossing. Sights are the 93m-high Hohenberg; a 57m-deep Roman well ('the Drususbrunnen'); and the Romanesque St Vitus church, once belonging to a late 10C abbey. Bus connections with Emmerich and Holland.

# 46

# The Ruhr

Total distance 90km. Duisburg—B60, 9km Mülheim an der Ruhr—B224, 6km Oberhausen—A430, 18km Essen—B224, 20km Gelsenkirchen—B226, 19km Bochum—B1, 18km Dortmund.

To visit the populous industrial Ruhr (German Ruhrgebiet), leave its Rhine port, **Duisburg** (see Rte 45), E by the B60, travelling through the Sobald parkland to reach after 9km **Mülheim an der Ruhr** (178,000 inhab.; alt. 37m), where seven bridges cross the River Ruhr with its wide promenades. A warren of twisting streets, Mülheim is dominated by Schloss Broich—on the left of the road from Duisburg as it approaches the Schlossbrücke to cross to the centre of the town—built as a bulwark against Norman invaders in the 11C. Today it reveals 18C alterations, while preserving an 11C tower, 12C walls and the Gothic Rittersaal in the main Schloss. Across the river to the right of Schlossstrasse is the old quarter of the town, with its narrow streets and charming *ensembles of half-timbered houses. Close by each other are the Catholic Marienkirche of 1929, and in Bachstrasse the Protestant church of St Petri, which was begun in the 11C. Today's building has a mid-13C Romanesque west tower and a tower with a gilded cockerel, 1581, most of the Gothic remainder transformed 1870–72. The finest 18C house is at 1 Tersteegen, where the religious poet Gerhard Tersteegen (1698–1769) died. The town boasts a number of 13C towers, the gate of a 13C Schloss, and a former Cistercian convent, Kloster Saarn, founded in the 13C with a Baroque church, 1729–83. The Rathaus of 1911–15 has a 59.7m-high tower. At 1 Leineweberstrasse is the town's art museum; the local history museum is at 1 Tienerstrasse (both open except Mon 10.00–12.30, 15.00–18.00, closing Thu at 21.00). Ships of the 'White Fleet' ply the River Ruhr as far as Kettwig. The race-track is W of the town, in Akazianallee. The 1926 Stadthalle, restored in 1957, is Mülheim's congress centre.

From Mülheim the B224 leads N for 6km to **Oberhausen** (234,000 inhab.; alt. 37m), a town founded around the 1847 railway station in a region of 18C mines, deriving its name from 19C Schloss Overhus, now known as Schloss Oberhauses, which houses the town's collection of contemporary art (open weekdays except Mon 10.00–13.00, 14.00–17.00, weekends

10.00–17.00). In the suburb of **Osterfeld**, N of the town centre, is the moated Schloss Vondern, part 16C, part 17C. Information office in Berlinerplatz.

The A430 leads 18km E to **ESSEN** (660,000 inhab.; alt. 108m; tourist information: in the station), the fifth largest city in Germany and an important industrial centre. Its glory is its cathedral. A small village at the beginning of the 19C, Essen's population has reached over 600,000, largely because of the firm of Krupp. Only the S part of the city avoided industrial expansion. Because of its commercial importance, almost all of Essen was destroyed in 1945.

**Am Hauptbahnhof**, in front of the 1964 main railway station, houses the main post office (1935) and the Haus der Technik (1926). From here the 450m-long pedestrianised Kettwiger Strasse, with its boutiques and shops, bisects the city. At No. 22 is a Glockenspiel with moving figures and 25 bronze bells, which plays at 12.00, 16.00, 17.00 and 18.00. Just beyond the Glockenspiel, on the left of Kettwiger Strasse, is Theaterplatz, with Essen's Schauspielhaus, a theatre built in 1892.

Further along Kettwiger Strasse Burgplatz appears on the right, with the episcopal palace, whose bronze doors are by Ewart Mataré; the Gothic church of St Johann Baptist, founded in 946, reaching its present form in 1471, with a 17C Baroque interior, a font c 1600, an altar by Barthel Bruyn 1525, and the 1770 altar of St Georg; and the *münster. A cathedral only since 1958 when Pope Pius XII set up the diocese, the münster, dedicated to SS Maria, Cosmas and Damien, stands at the heart of the city. Founded c 850 and rebuilt in the 11C to 13C, the main work is late Gothic, 1276–1327, built after a fire of 1275. Between 971 and 1058 its convent waxed great under three powerful abbesses, all members of the Imperial house of Saxony, namely Mathilde, then Sophia, sister of Emperor Otto III, and finally Theophanu, granddaughter of Emperor Otto II.

The Romanesque *west end, with two staircase towers, and the crypt, which shelters the 14C tomb of Bishop Altfrid of Hildesheim, who died in 874, remain from the older building, though the rest was ravaged by a fire in the 13C and rebuilt in the Gothic style. The treasury has 10C and 11C gold treasures, including an 8C reliquary; the 11C *Theophanu cross; the 850 crown of Otto III; and medieval Bibles (open Tue–Sun 10.00–15.30). In the atrium which connects the cathedral with the church of St Johann Baptist is a wooden crucifix, c 1400. The münster houses a **golden Madonna, made in Cologne in 990 for Abbess Mathilde, the oldest Madonna of western Christendom; a *seven-branched candelabrum, c 1100; an early 15C Entombment; a crucifix by Lioba Munz, 1968; and stained glass by H. Campendonck, 1953.

In front of the church of St Johann Baptist is Kurienplatz, with its fountain and garden, leading into Kennedyplatz, where stands a statue by G. Kolbe, 1914. From the church Kettwiger Strasse leads to the Markt, with a church of 1058, badly damaged in World War II. Only the eastern part has been restored, with bronze doors by H. Schardt, 1963. Here too is a statue of Alfred Krupp, set up in 1898.

E of the Markt is Porscheplatz, laid out in 1954 and containing the town hall (by Theodor Seifert, 1972). The domed former **synagogue** of 1911–13 lies on the S side of Porscheplatz, on the corner of Alfredistrasse and Steelerstrasse. It was built by Edmund Körner from 1911 to 1913 and is the largest in Germany (70m long, 30m wide with a cupola reaching 34m). This synagogue contains an exhibition with documents of Jewish history and of the resistance and Nazi persecution in Essen, 1933–45 (open 10.00–17.00, Sun closes 18.00).

S of the main railway station lies the **city garden**, with a lake, the city Opera House—by the Finnish architect Alvar Aalto, completed in 1988, 12 years after his death, and hosting opera, operetta, ballet and drama—and the Städtischer Saalbau, a congress centre and concert hall. This is the home of the Essen Philharmonic Orchestra, which was founded in 1899 and first performed here under the baton of Richard Strauss in 1904. SW at 64–66 Bismarckstrasse is the **Museum Folkwang** which was built in 1960 and displays 19C and 20C French and German art and posters from 1875, as well as the regional **Ruhrland Museum** (both open Tue–Sun 10.00–18.00). Bismarckstrasse leads (by car) to the 70-hectare **Grugapark**, built for the garden exhibition of 1929, enlarged in 1965. The Grugapark houses the Grugahalle, an exhibition hall of 1958, and a botanical garden. S lies the Stadtwald, an ornithological park, with to the E the Schellenberger Wald where you find the 16C and 17C Schloss Schellenberg and restaurants.

Further S by way of Alfredstrasse, the continuation of Bismarckstrasse, stands·**Villa Hügel**, above the 8km-long artificial Baldeneysee—which is devoted to water sports as well as producing hydro electricity. Villa Hügel was built by Alfred Krupp to his own plans, 1869–73, and is the home of the Krupp art gallery (open except Mon 10.00–18.00). Its 75-hectare park is open daily 07.00–20.00 Apr–Sept, otherwise 09.00–19.00. A museum of German industry and trade is housed in the Kleines Haus der Villa Krupp. On the N side of the lake rises Schloss Baldeney, with a late 13C keep, the rest of the building dating from the 18C and 19C. The Deutsches Plakat-Museum in Rathenaustrasse (open daily except Mon 10.00–18.00) houses the most important collection of German posters from the past to the present day.

SW of Villa Hügel is the suburb of **Essen-Werden**, with the Catholic priory of St Ludger, the first Bishop of Münster, who founded a Benedictine monastery here in 794. Its church as it stands today is a late Romanesque bulding of 1156–75 with Baroque furnishings and decor of 1706–18—apart from the Westwerk, which has Romanesque frescoes, some dating from the 10C. The high altar bears the escutcheon of Prince-Elector Johann Wilhelm. St Ludger's relics lie in the circular crypt, along with the tombs of abbots of Werden. The treasury houses a 5C pyx, Ludger's bronze chalice and the bronze Helmsted crucifix of 1060. A wooden reliquary of 1175 was made to resemble the abbey church. Beside the river in Heckstrasse is the church of St Lucius, 995–1003, with 15C alterations. Restored in 1965, it preserves remains of early 12C frescoes and is the oldest parish church in Germany.

The B224 leads for 20km NE to Gelsenkirchen by way of **Bottrop**, whose parish church of the Holy Cross dates from 1957, and whose chief attraction is the 'Dreamland' fun park, and **Gladbeck**, where you find the 13C moated Schloss Wittringen. **Gelsenkirchen** (310,000 inhab.; alt. 54m) on the Rhine-Herne canal is an important inland harbour and mining town, with fine parks, a concert hall and a theatre of 1960, in Kennedyplatz, as well as the 16C and 18C Schloss Berge, in its park with the Berger lake, and the Renaissance Schloss Horst of 1570. At Gelsenkirchen is the Ruhr zoo (open daily in summer 09.00–19.00, in winter closing 17.00), a Safari Park with over 200 animals. The park is situated in Westerholter Wald, E of the town. In Schmalhorststrasse stands the ruined, moated Schloss Horst of 1570, and in the suburb of Buer is an art collection, at 5–7 Horster Strasse (open Tue–Sun 10.00–13.00, 15.00–18.00). Information office in Rathausplatz.

From Gelsenkirchen take the B226 for 19km S to the university city of **Bochum** (430,000 inhab.; alt. 104m). Seat of the Ruhr-Bochum university,

*This bronze head of Jesus, dating from c 1260, is part of the Helmstedt crucifix, now displayed in the priory church of St Ludger, Essen-Werden*

Bochum, though formerly important as a mining town, was from the 14C to the 16C a member of the Hanseatic League. Mining began in the late 17C and rapidly developed, the town prospering until the economic crises of the 1960s threw many of its miners out of work. A good number of them found new work in the Opel factory. The Schauspielhaus, built 1950–53, is the home of the city symphony orchestra, founded 1919. The priory church of SS Peter and Paulus in Brückstrasse has a 14C tower and 16C nave with a 12C Romanesque font carved with five scenes from the life of Jesus, a Gothic crucifix of 1352, a reliquary c 1200 containing the remains of SS Felicitas and Perpetua and a Lamentation c 1530. At 191 Dr.-C.-Otto-Strasse is a railway museum (open Mar–Nov Wed, Fri 10.00–17.00), and at Am Bergbaumuseum a *mining museum (open weekdays except Mon 08.30–17.30, weekends 10.00–12.00). The university art gallery, at 150 Universitätsstrasse, opens Tue–Fri 12.00–15.00, weekends 10.00–18.00. Haus Kemnade is a moated Schloss, begun in the 11C, mostly destroyed by fire in 1589 and exquisitely rebuilt from 1602 to 1708. Inside are Renaissance fireplaces, and the local history museum (open Wed–Fri 13.00–19.00, weekends 11.00–18.00). The 125-hectare Kemnade lake is the venue of regattas.

The city has a festival on 30 April. Bochum Museum is at 149 Kortumstrasse, built by Jorgen Bo and Vilhelm Wohlert, 1979–84 (open Tue–Sun 10.00–20.00, closing 18.00 on Sun); Bochum Theatre at 15 Königsallee; Bochum Zoo in Klinikstrasse. Tourist information is in the railway station.

The suburb of **Stiepel**, S of the town, has a Romanesque-Gothic church, founded in 1008, with 12C to 16C frescoes.

From Bochum the B51 leads N for 7km to **Herne** (188,000 inhab.; alt. 59m) situated on the Dortmund-Ems canal and the Rhein-Herne canal. The town is guarded by the moated, 17C Renaissance Schloss Strünkede, rising to the N of the town in Schloss Strasse. It houses a museum (open Tue–Sun 10.00–13.00, 14.00–17.00). Herne also has thermal baths and a complex leisure park, the Revierpark Gysenberg. The town's annual festival starts at the beginning of August. Information at the town hall.

The B51 continues NW for another 9km to reach **Recklinghausen** (120,00 inhab.; alt. 76m), once a member of the Hanseatic League and before that, in the late 8C, an imperial court of Charlemagne, the plans of whose city can still be seen in the central pattern of the streets. Its 13C and 16C church of St Petrus was founded in the early 13C by the Archbishop of Cologne, Konrad von Hochstaden. Its treats include a Romanesque porch; three Gothic aisles, added in 1522; and a 72m-high tower of 1652–70. Inside is a late-Gothic tabernacle c 1520. Nearby at 2a Kirchplatz, is an *icon museum housing over 600 icons and miniatures from the Eastern Orthodox Church, plus another 100 Coptic works of art (open except Mon 10.00–18.00, weekends 11.00–17.00). Other sights are the 1701 Engelsburg; the Städtische Kunsthalle, which displays German Expressionism (open weekdays except Mon 10.00–18.00; weekends and holidays 11.00–17.00); a former World War II bunker; and the city garden with a Henry Moore statue in front of the 1965 Festspielhaus at 25–27 Grosse Perdekampstrasse (opening times as the icon museum). From the end of May to the beginning of July the Festspielhaus is the venue of the annual Festival of the Ruhr. Tourist information office at 23 Kuniberstrasse.

Not far from Recklinghausen is the Hohe Mark nature reserve. From Bochum the B1 leads for 18km E to Dortmund (see Rte 56).

# 47

# Münster and Environs

## A. Münster

**MÜNSTER** (270,000 inhab.; alt. 62m) lies on the River Aa and the Münster canal and is the chief city of Westphalia. Its Rathaus, with an entrancing filigree façade, rises in Principalmarkt, as does the Lambertikirche and its magnificent Gothic spire, while the stern Romanesque towers of the cathedral are humanised each noon (12.30 on Sun) by the Glockenspiel and performing figures of its astronomical clock.

Münster is the historic capital of Münsterland. Embraced to the N by the Teutoburger forest, by the Lippe River to the S and by the Dutch border to the W, it was ruled by the Bishops of Münster till 1803. Like Holland, it is almost entirely flat, and in consequence Münsterland boasts more cycle tracks than any other part of Germany (with over 14,000 signposts), and its citizens own more bicycles than those living anywhere else in the republic. Münster itself has houses gabled in the Dutch fashion, especially those flanking the cobbled street which curves towards the church of St Lambert. Boats ply its artificial lake (the Aasee). A market is set up beside the cathedral on Wed and Sat.

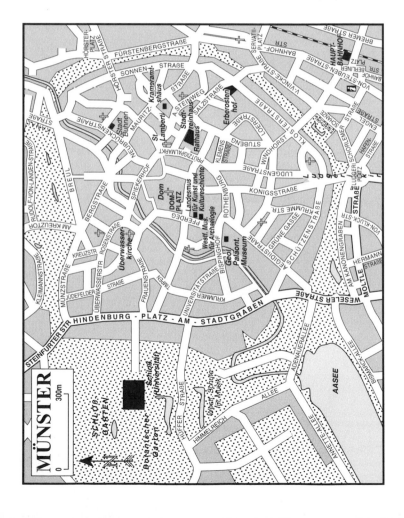

Since in this flat land the nobility was unable to build defensive castles on hill, they defended their fortresses with moats.

**Main railway station**: Bahnhofstrasse (also a post office here). Main **post office**: Domplatz. **Information office**: 22 Berliner Platz. **Trains** to all major cities, and **bus** connections with the Münsterland.

**History**. Charlemagne set up a bishopric here c 800, after the Friesian missionary St Ludger had founded a monastery—hence the name Münster. Around it developed a settlement that was granted its civic charter in the 12C and built its fortifications, of which all that remains is the Buddenturm, c 1200. In the 13C Münster became a member of the Hanseatic League. At the time of the Reformation it was a noted centre of Anabaptists (led by Jan van Leyden, by his step-father Bernd Knipperdolling and by Nernhard Krechting), who espoused polygamy. Imperial troops, urged on by Archbishop Franz von Waldeck, conquered the city and the Anabaptist leaders were tortured and put to death in 1535. Here, and in Osnabrück, was signed the Peace of Westphalia which brought an end to the Thirty Years War.

The city university was founded in 1780, its best-known teacher the philosopher Johann Georg Hamann (1730–88), theologian and a father of the German *Sturm und Drang* ('Storm and Stress') movement. Münster became French and then Prussian in the early 19C. Ninety per cent of its Altstadt was destroyed in World War II; 67 per cent of the rest of the city. Clemens August von Galen, Bishop of Münster from 1933 to 1946, was a noted opponent of the Nazis. Today Münster is once more a major university town, its university, with some 45,000 students, the third largest in western Germany.

To see Münster's oldest church take Bahnhofstrasse N from the main railway station as far as Mauritz Tor, E of which, on St Mauritz-Freiheit, is the collegiate church of **St Mauritz**. Its chapel and three towers were built c 1070. The west tower was capped by a Baroque dome in 1709. The nave was rebuilt by E. von Manger in 1859–61. Return to the station, from which Windthorststrasse leads NE and crosses Klosterstrasse, along which on the right is the **Servatorkirche**. Part of the church dates from the mid 13C, part from c 1500, and the whole was restored and altered in the 18C. It houses a late 15C Lady altar. Continue along Klosterstrasse, passing on the left the Rococo church of **St Klemens**, by Johann Conrad Schlaun, 1754 (its ground plan is the star of David) and turn left into Salzstrasse to find the Baroque **Erbdrostenhof**, also by J.C. Schlaun, 1753–57, followed by the former Dominican church, now the university Catholic chapel. This Baroque church, by L.F. von Corfey, 1725, has a Baroque altar by H. Gröne, 1699, and was restored after World War II. Continue along Salzstrasse to find on the right on the corner of the Prinzipalmarkt the late Gothic *•**Lamberti-kirche**, which was built between 1375 and 1450, and restored 1976–77. Its main door dates from the 15C. It boasts a Jesse tree on the south door. The 99m-high west tower was reconstructed in 1898, with three cages in which were displayed the corpses of the three leading Anabaptists (see above). Behind the church, in Alter Steinweg, is the former grocers' guild house, the brick-built **Krameramtshaus**, 1588. This was restored in 1951 and now serves as the city library.

Turn right from Salzstrasse and walk along Neubrückenstrasse to find on the left the 13C to 17C church of SS **Aposteln**, with its Gothic and early Renaissance decoration, and three bells cast in 1675, and on the right the **theatre**, designed by H. Deilmann, P.O. Rave and M. von Hausen in 1956. Close by rises the Gothic hall-church of **St Martin**, which was begun in the 13C and finished in the next. This church has a Romanesque tower, with a fourth storey added in the 15C and a Baroque top of 1760. Further on along Neubrückenstrasse is the **Zwinger**, a keep set here in 1536 and transformed into a prison in 1730.

Near the church of SS Aposteln, in Hörsterstrasse, is J.C. Schlaun's convent chapel of 1772. Return to Salzstrasse and find, left of the church of St Lambert, the **Prinzipalmarkt**, with its arcades and gabled houses, the **Stadtweinhaus**, a Renaissance 'wine house', by Johann von Bocholt 1615, and the superb gabled façade of the 14C Gothic former ••**Rathaus** (open 09.00–17.00 weekdays, Sat to 16.00, Sun 10.00–13.00). The Rathaus has a Friedensaal (Peace Hall), furnished as in 1577; portraits by J.B. Floris of Angers of those present here for the signing of the Peace of Westphalia in 1648, including Philip IV of Spain, Henri d'Orléans and the Emperor Ferdinand III; late Gothic panelling and a chandelier of 1577, decked with a Madonna of 1520; and lovely fireplaces. Both the wine house and the town hall were restored after World War II.

Leave the town hall and take Michaelisplatz opposite to the twin-towered ••**Dom of St Paul**, a Romanesque and Gothic basilica, built between 1172 and 1265. Its south entrance, known as the 'gate of Paradise', was sculpted in the 13C with a Christ in majesty amongst his apostles. In the narthex are 13C •statues of the Apostles, with a frieze showing secular events. Other features are the Marienkapelle of 1390; a statue of a gigantic St Christopher, 1627; a 1622 reliquary by G. Gröninger; an altar c 1520 and a wall painting by Hermann tom Ring, 1590, in the east transept. In the west transept are a 14C font and a crucifix of 1542; an •astronomical clock, 1420, rebuilt in 1543, with at 12.00 (Sun at 12.30) performing figures (including the Madonna and Child, plus the Magi, and also death), while a Glockenspiel plays 'In dulci Jubilo'. The cathedral has a 1622 high altar in the west choir, with scenes from the life of St Paul sculpted by G. Gröninger; the marble tomb of Bishop C. von Galen, who died in 1678; and modern glass by Max Ingrand. Hitler's enemy, Clemens August von Galen (see above) lies in a magnificent tomb behind the high altar.

Chapels with tombs line the ambulatory, close by which is the Stephanuschor, with a painted wooden cross of 1450, formerly carried in procession in times of plague. The 14C cloister has a Lady chapel of 1390, with an 11C crucifix. In the chapel of the Holy Sacrament, 1667, is a tabernacle designed by M. Gröninger in 1540. The chapter house panelling is by Ludger tom Ring the Elder, 1590. The cathedral treasury (open weekdays except Mon 10.00–12.00, 14.00–18.00, Sun 14.00–18.00) houses •liturgical vestments and statues, including an Entry into Jerusalem by H. Brabender, 1545.

On the W side of Domplatz the early 18C Landsbergsche Kurie houses the university geological and palaeontological museum (open weekdays 09.00–12.30, 13.00–17.00). S of Domplatz at No. 10 is the provincial museum, **Westfälisches Landesmuseum für Kunst und Kulturgeschichte**, built by the Hanover architect Hermann Schaedtler in 1908 and enlarged in 1972. It is devoted to medieval art; Gothic sculpture and religious painting, including works by Konrad von Soest; works by Lucas Cranach the Elder and his contemporaries; and a •collection of 20C paintings (open Tue–Sun 10.00–18.00). Close by rises the **Westfälisches Museum für Archäologie** (open only on Wednesday afternoon and Sunday morning).

Here too is situated the episcopal palace of 1732, opposite which is a monument of 1978 to Bishop Clemens August von Galen (1878–1946, see above). Left of the episcopal palace Spiegel-Turm leads to the Gothic hall-church of Our Lady, known as the **Überwasserkirche**. Founded in 1040, it was rebuilt 1340–60 and has an early 15C tower. The votive tablet at the entrance is by Ludger tom Ring the Elder, 1548. The Baroque altar painting is by Gerhard Koppers, 1763. The font is by W. Gröninger, c 1720. From here walk along Frauenstrasse to the huge **Hindenburgplatz**, on which centre Münster's festivals and its flea markets (the last weekend of each month from April to September). Here also rises the Baroque **Schloss**, built for the prince-bishops by J.C. Schlaun between 1767 and 1773. Built of red brick, with stone facings and an imposing entrance hall, this is now the main university building. Behind the Schloss the city's **botanical garden** takes up part of the **Schlossgarten** (laid out in the 'English' style), and close by is the mineralogical museum (open Wed 15.00–18.00, Sun 10.30–12.30).

Take from here the Promenade S to the water sports centre on the 40-hectare **Aasee**, SW of which is the zoo, set up in 1974, and including a dolphinarium. Continue along Promenade, turning left along Ludgerstrasse as far as the church of **St Ludger**. Built in the 12C and 13C, it houses a high altar of 1961 and stained glass of 1968. By way of Königstrasse, where you find at No. 5 the late 18C **Druffelscher Hof** and at No. 47 the **Heermannscher Hof** of 1564, and Krummestrasse, you reach the church of **St Ägidien**, by J.C. Schlaun, 1724–29. Its font is by A. Reining, 1557; its *Baroque pulpit by J.W. Gröninger, c 1720; its mid-19C wall paintings by E. Steinle.

OTHER MUSEUMS: **Museum Hans Rüschhaus**, with memorabilia of the Droste-Hülshoff family, at 81 Am Rüschhaus, in a building by J.C. Schlaun, 1745–48 (open daily 09.30–12.00, 14.30–17.00); a **Bible Museum** at 7 Georgskommende (open Wed 11.00–13.00, Thu 17.00–19.00, and first Sat in month 10.00–13.00). An open-air museum of the local countryside, the **Mühlenhof-Freilicht-Museum**, has been created SW of the city, past the artificial Aasee and across Sentruper Höhe. The museum displays windmills and the like (open mid-Mar to end Nov 09.00–17.00; otherwise 13.30–16.30, Sun and holidays 11.00–16.30).

10km W is the moated **Haus Hülshoff**, built 1540–45 for Heinrich I von Droste-Hülshoff on a 12C building, but famed as the birthplace and home of the poet Annette von Droste-Hülshoff (1797–1848). It is now the Droste-Museum (open Tue–Sun 09.00–12.00, 14.30–17.00). Between 1826 and 1841 she lived at the Baroque Schloss Rüschhaus, 2km NW in the suburb of Münster-Nienberge, which was built by Schlaun in 1749.

# B.   West of Münster: to Emmerich and to Gronau

## Münster to Emmerich

Total distance 145km. Münster—B51 and B67, 37km Coesfeld—50km Borken—18km Bocholt—13km Isselburg—10km Rees—17km Emmerich.

Leave **Münster** (see Rte 47A) in the direction of Cologne by the B51 to reach the B67 at Appelhülsen after 17km. From here the B67 runs NW for 6km to **Nottuln**, with its 15C monastery church and monastic buildings. Dedicated to St Martin, the church has exquisite tracery rising from round pillars, the ceiling delicately painted. Its organ dates from 1719–21, and it shelters 43 tombs of local nobles. A copy of a painting of 1536 (the original now in the Schatzkammer of Essen-Werden) depicts St Ludger's death. Continue for 14km W to Coesfeld, passing on the left the highest peak of the Baumberge, the Westerburg, on which is a tower 189m above sea level.

Ancient **Coesfeld** (32,000 inhab.; alt. 81m) gained its city rights in 1197, was a Hanseatic town and retains vestiges of its medieval fortifications (the Walkenbrücher gate and the Pulver tower, both 14C). In the church of St Lambert, which is partly Romanesque, though mostly a Gothic building of 1473–1524, is the Gothic Coesfeld cross, which was created in the early 15C and is shaped like a fork. It incorporates a fragment of the true cross, and is carried in procession through the town on Whit Monday. Here too are statues of the Apostles by J. Düsseldorp, 1506–20, and a font of 1504. The west end and Baroque tower of the church were built in 1703 by Gottfried Laurenz Pictorius. Other churches at Coesfeld include the Baroque Jesuit church and St Jakob, which was destroyed in World War II, rebuilt in 1949, and retains a 13C *doorway and remnants of the previous furnishings, including a mid-13C font and an altar c 1520. Old houses survived the war, chiefly in Mühlenstrasse and Welkenbrückerstrasse. The town's open-air stations of the cross, with two chapels, are by Peter Pictorius the Elder. Its local history museums are at 10 Bahnhofsallee (visits only by previous arrangement) and in Letterstrasse (open Sun 11.00–12.30). 5km N is the 18C Schloss Varlar.

Drive 20km NW along the B474 to Ahaus, with its moated Schloss, rebuilt by J.C. Schlaun after an earlier building was destroyed in 1767 during the Seven Years War. Then take the B70 SW for 12km to Stadtlohn. At the centre of the town stands the church of St Otger, dedicated to the 8C Anglo-Saxon missionary sent here by Pope Sergius I, destroyed in World War II and rebuilt. It houses a 17C statue of its patron, and a 15C woodcarving of St Anna. 1km E is the former pilgrimage church of Our Lady on the Hilgen-berg, now largely neglected since its miracle-working image of the Virgin Mary was stolen in the late-19C. 18km further SW along the B70 is Borken, 2km E of which is **Gemen**, with a 15C and 17C Schloss on four islands. **Borken** has three surviving towers from its medieval walls (the Holkken-sturm, the Diebsturm and the Wedemhoventurm, now a youth hostel). The church of St Remigius retains the mid-12C lower part of its west tower, while the rest is mid 15C. Inside are a late 12C Romanesque sculpted font, as well as a 14C forked crucifix and a 15C Entombment. Gemen's local history museum is in the church of the Holy Spirit of 1404 on Heilig-Geist-Strasse, which was badly damaged in World War II (open Sun 10.30–12.00). 6km due S of Borken is **Raesfeld**, with a moated, mid-17C Renaissance Schloss.

The route continues W from Borken along the B67 to reach after 18km **Bocholt** (70,000 inhab.; alt. 26m), an industrial town on the River Aa. Its Gothic church of St Georg, 1415–86, was given its Baroque aspect in the 18C. Its treasures include a wooden 14C Gothic crucifix, a Gothic ciborium of 1470, a 14C diptych representing the crucifixion and the coronation of the Blessed Virgin Mary, and a silver 15C thurifer. The Dutch Renaissance former Rathaus has a stunning gabled façade of 1618–21, restored between 1928 and 1934. Both church and Rathaus were restored after bombing on 22 March 1945 had destroyed virtually the whole town. The Rathaus now houses the municipal archives and etchings by Israhel Van Meckenem (1445–1503). The art gallery is in the new town hall, by Gottfried Böhm, at 1 Berlinerplatz (open daily 10.00–13.00, 15.00–18.00). Bocholt's Textile Museum is at 50 Uhlandstrasse (open Tue–Sun 10.00–18.00). Tourist information at 22 Europaplatz.

After 13km the route reaches **Isselburg**, situated on the River Issel, with vestiges of its 15C fortifications. 3km NW is **Anholt**, administratively linked to Isselburg, a town given its charter in 1349 whose gorgeous moated

Schloss has a 12C keep, with other buildings added in the 14C and 15C, including the staircase tower. The rest was rebuilt in the Dutch Renaissance style in the 17C, and set in a deliberately 'wild' 18C park. Inside are displayed tapestries by L. van Schoor, Chinese porcelain, Renaissance and Baroque furniture, and paintings, including works by Breugel and Rembrandt (open Apr–Sept 10.00–18.00). The Baroque Vorburg is now a hotel and restaurant.

The road now leads by way of **Rees** for 17km to **Emmerich** (see Rte 45) and the Dutch border.

## Münster to Gronau

Total distance 62km. Münster—B57, 38km Burgsteinfurt—24km Gronau.

The B54 leaves **Münster** (see Rte 47A) and runs NW for 7km to Nienberge, 1.5km SW of which is **Schloss Rüschhaus** (see Rte 47A). After another 23km NW along the B54 the route reaches *Burgsteinfurt (32,000 inhab.; alt. 50m), with the moated Schloss of the Fürsten zu Bentheim-Steinfurt, the largest moated Schloss in the region. Begun in the 12C, this Schloss was destroyed and reconstructed in the 13C, added to in the 14C, and rebuilt after the depredations of the Thirty Years War from the 16C to the 18C. Set on two islands of the River Aa, the Schloss still incorporates earlier remains, especially the 12C Romanesque chapel and the 13C knights' hall, restored 1877–79, and the tower-gate. Its most picturesque feature is a Renaissance oriel by Johann Brabender (known as Beldensnyder). Its English-style park was laid out in the 18C, enlivened with mills, grottoes, temples and fountains (in part transformed today into a golf course). The town hall of Burgsteinfurt dates from 1561. Churches include the 15C Grosse Kirche and the neo-Gothic church of St Nikomedes, built in 1885 to replace one founded in 968. Inside are Romanesque altar candlesticks, and the 11C *Heinrich Cross, whose ornaments include the bust of Emperor Heinrich II.

After 12km the B54 runs through **Ochtrup**, which has monastic buildings and a 13C monastery church. Ochtrup lies 12km from **Gronau** (26,000 inhab.; alt. 42m), a town devoted to textiles and nature reserves and close by the Dutch border.

From Ochtrup the B403 runs N for 28km by way of **Bad Bentheim**, whose thermal baths have been in operation since 1711. The town is enhanced by the 15C Schloss Bentheim, with a 12C sandstone crucifixion—the Herrgott von Bentheim—on its south terrace. The route continues to Nordhorn (at the confluence of the Ems-Vechte and Süd-Nord canals). From here the B213 runs for 4km to the Dutch border, 179km from Amsterdam.

From Bad Bentheim the B65 runs NE for 23km to **Rheine** (72,000 inhab.; alt. 40m), which was founded in 838 by Emperor Ludwig. Rheine has gabled houses in the Marktplatz. Its ecclesiastical buildings include the 15C Gothic parish church of St Dionysius, inside which are 12 contemporary stone figures of the Apostles, and the neo-Romanesque basilica of St Antonius, 1899–1905, with a 116m-high tower, the highest in the Münster region. Housed in a mansion probably founded in 838, rebuilt in the 15C, enlarged in 1612 and restored in 1767, is the Falkenhof Museum, which displays arms, paintings and textile history (open weekdays except Mon 09.00–12.00, 16.00–18.00, Sun 10.30–12.30). The zoo is in Salinenstrasse; the town park in Kopernikusstrasse.

4km N is **Kloster-Schloss Bentlage**, a castle which was formerly a 15C monastery, with wings completed in 1653.

# C.  East of Münster: to Paderborn and from Herford to Dortmund

## Münster to Paderborn

Total distance 90km. Münster—B51, 12km Telgte—B64, 15km Warendorf—24km Rheda—3km Weidenbrück—9km Rietberg—12km Delbrück—11km Neuhaus—4km Paderborn.

Leave **Münster** (see Rte 47A) by the B51 and drive E for 12km to **Telgte** (16,500 inhab.; alt. 56m) on the River Ems, a village founded c 800. It has preserved an octagonal pilgrimage chapel of 1647, with a 14C limewood Pietà venerated by medieval pilgrims; and the priory church of 1522. The latter has a 19C tower and inside is a 15C Madonna and a carving of Jesus, c 1200. Telgte's local history museum is in the 1600 parsonage, which was extended in subsequent centuries, at 2 Herrenstrasse (open except Mon 09.30–12.30, 13.30–17.30). Seek here a Lenten veil of 1623 with 33 panels, including scenes of Christ's passion, and numerous Christmas cribs.

The B64 leads SE from Telgte to reach **Warendorf** (34,000 inhab.; alt. 56m), a former Hanseatic town noted for its horses; there is a stud farm here. This is the seat of the German Olympic riding committee, as well as an army sports school. Warendorf's Gothic church of St Laurentius, which was begun in 1404, has a *high altar painted in the early 15C. In the town hall of 1404, one of several 15C and 16C houses, is the local history museum (open weekdays except Mon 15.00–17.00; weekends 10.30–12.30). 4km S is **Freckenhorst**, with a Romanesque *basilica of St Boniface from a former nunnery, which has preserved parts of its cloister. It has a superbly carved 12C Romanesque font; a stone Pietà, c 1520; an early 16C tabernacle; and modern decor by Heinz Gerhard Bücker, 1922.

The B64 continues SE by way of **Herzebrock**, whose abbey was founded in 860, reaching after 24km **Rheda**, with half-timbered houses, a late Gothic 15C and 16C church and the moated Schloss of the Fürsten von Bentheim-Tecklenburg-Rheda. The last dates from the 17C and 18C, though its Kapellen tower is early 13C and the Torhalle was built in 1719. A 15C tower, the Lange Turm, also survives from the past and the Schloss has a Renaissance wing.

3km SW is **Wiedenbrück**, administratively combined with Rheda, which has numerous Renaissance half-timbered houses, especially in Mönchstrasse and Langenstrasse. The oddly built Marienkirche in Mönchstrasse, 19m wide, only 13m long, began life as a pilgrimage church in 1470. The Markt is shaded by the collegiate church of St Ägidien, c 1500. St Ägidien has a 19C choir and tower, and houses a late Gothic font, a tabernacle of 1504 and an early 17C sandstone pulpit.

The road runs NE and then E from Wiedenbrück for 9km to **Rietberg**, whose half-timbered houses include the town hall. The Baroque church of St Johann Nepomuk was built by Johann Conrad Schlaun, 1747–48. From here the route turns SE again reaching **Delbrück** after another 12km. This is a town of half-timbered houses, with a 14C pilgrimage church. After another 11km the B64 reaches **Neuhaus**, at the confluence of the Rivers

Pader, Alme and Lippe. Here is Renaissance Schloss Neuhaus, c 1600, with a monument to the discoverer of morphia, Friedrich Sertürner, who was born at Neuhaus in 1783 and died in 1841. The Schloss now houses part of Paderborn city art gallery (open except Mon 15.00–18.00, Sun also 10.00–13.00). Today the Schloss is also the venue of concerts and an annual Renaissance festival at the beginning of July.

4km SW lies the delightful city of **Paderborn** (115,000 inhab.; alt. 119m), situated on the River Pader between the Eggegebirge and the Teutoburg woods. Two hundred springs created the river, flowing as five streams through the city and meeting outside of the town.

**Tourist information**: 2 Marienplatz. **Train** connections with all major towns.

**History**. Here in 799 Charlemagne received Pope Leo III, who had been accused of adultery, attacked by the Roman mob, formally deposed and escaped from imprisonment. Charlemagne also arranged then his own coronation as Holy Roman Emperor in Rome the following year. Six years later he founded the bishopric of Paderborn (which was raised to an archbishopric in 1930). Charlemagne's first Saxon diet was held here. The city was walled in 1180, and was a member of the Hanseatic League in the 13C and 14C. Though Paderborn for a time became Protestant, at the beginning of the 17C Prince-Bishop Dietrich von Fürstenberg obliged the citizens to embrace the principles of the Counter-Reformation, and he founded its university in 1614. Suffering greatly during the Thirty Years War and the Seven Years War, the city became Prussian in 1802. Paderborn annually hosts an eight-day fair beginning on the Saturday after 23 July.

From the main railway station, Bahnhofstrasse leads by way of Westernstrasse to Marienplatz, where at No. 2 is the early 17C Heisingsches Haus, gabled, with carved figures, its façade restored in 1976, the column of the Virgin Mary dating from 1802. From here Jüdengasse leads to Jesuitenmauer and the Baroque Jesuit church of 1682–84, which was restored after World War II. The route continues from Marienplatz to Rathausplatz, housing the theatre and the *Rathaus of 1613–20. The latter's central gable is flanked by twin gabled oriels rising over Doric arcades. Inside is a natural history museum (open except Mon 10.00–18.00, closes Sun 13.00). The pedestrianised Schildern leads NE by way of shops to the Domplatz. (Alternatively reach Domplatz by the Markt, with the 12C Romanesque church of St Ulrich, known as the Gaukirche, whose delights include a 14C crucifix, a Madonna of 1420 and a Calvary relief, c 1450.)

In Domplatz stands the 13C Gothic Dom, rebuilt after numerous fires (the first in 1058), with a 12C Romanesque west tower. The belfry and corner towers date from the 19C. The cathedral has a late Romanesque north door, and a *paradise doorway on the south side, sculpted c 1250 and depicting a crowned Madonna and child, flanked by SS Peter and Paul, as well as St James the Great (identified by his cockleshell) and St Catherine. Nearby are the remains of the sculpted Brautportal. Paderborn's cathedral has Gothic cloisters, with 16C stained glass depicting three hares, and the Westphalian chapel, with the *tomb of Wilhelm von Westfalen, who died in 1517.

Inside the cathedral are capitals developing from late Romanesque to Gothic; the *tomb of Prince-Bishop Dietrich von Fürstenberg, created in 1618 by Heinrich Gröninger; a late Gothic reliquary altar in the choir, c 1440; the tomb of Bishop Dietrich Adolf con der Recke, 1661; the late Gothic high altar; the pulpit of 1736; and the 12C crypt, with relics, particularly the reliquary of St Liborius, a Romanesque cross and stone tombs of the bishops. The Diözesanmuseum at 17 Markt (open Tue–Sun 10.00–17.00) has a superb collection of religious sculptures, the most celebrated a Madonna of 1058.

Close by the N side of the cathedral is the oldest hall-church in Germany, the chapel of St Bartholomäus, built by Bishop Meinwerk c 1070 and recalling in its architecture Byzantium. The Carolingian imperial palace which stood N of the cathedral has been excavated by Professor W. Winkelmann, 1964–70 (its oldest parts dating from the 8C, its restored parts from the 11C). The Museum in der Kaiserpfalz displays archaeological findings (open except Mon 10.00–17.00). NE of the cathedral in Michaelstrasse stands the Baroque Michaelkloster.

Other important churches in the city are the Franciscan St Josef in Westernstrasse, 1668–71, its Baroque façade by A. Petrini, and in Abdinghof, the Alexius chapel, a rotunda of 1673, and the 11C church of SS Petrus and Paulus, with a magical crypt, alongside half-timbered houses and the city art gallery at No. 11 (open except Mon 10.00–18.00, closes Sun 13.00). In Am Busdorf are the collegiate church and cloister founded by Bishop Meinwerk in 1036. The City History Museum at 7–9 Hathumarstrasse, opens Tue–Sun 10.00–18.00, closes Sun 13.00. Frescoes, archaeological finds, paintings, drawings and coins dating from the 13C to the 18C, are displayed in the oldest house in Paderborn, at 7 Hathumarstrasse, in a 16C building (Adam-und-Eva-Haus) whose façade carries sculptures depicting the expulsion of Adam and Eve from the garden of Eden (open weekdays except Mon 10.00–18.00, Sun 10.00–13.00).

## Herford to Dortmund

Total distance 113km. Herford—B61, 15km Bielefeld—17km Gütersloh—9km Wiedenbrück—14km Beckum—19km Hamm—14km Kamen—11km Lünen (for Cappenberg-Selm)—B54, 14km Dortmund.

**Herford** (68,000 inhab.; alt. 71m), situated at the confluence of the Aa and the Werre, is a former Hanseatic city whose present prosperity derives chiefly from furniture and textiles. The city boasts an Altstadt that grew up around a convent founded in the 8C and a Neustadt founded c 1220. The 13C münster of the former convent has a 16C late Gothic font, Romanesque capitals and Gothic tracery in its windows. Close by the münster are the 14C Jakobikirche, with Renaissance woodcarvings, and the 13C and 14C Johanniskirche, whose stained glass dates from c 1300, and sits alongside a crucifixion window of 1520, as well as fine furnishings. Noble Herford houses include at 4 Höckerstrasse the Bürgermeisterhaus, built in 1583 and the birthplace in 1662 of the Baroque architect Matthäus Daniel Pöppelmann; and at 6 Brüderstrasse the half-timbered Riemenschneider Haus, 1521.

W of the Altstadt in the former village of **Berg** is the 14C collegiate church of Our Lady, Marienkirche, which houses a Madonna c 1340 and a Gothic reliquary altar. The City Museum is at 2 Deichtorwall and displays Romanesque to Baroque sculpture (open Tue, Thu, Fri 10.00–13.00, 15.00–17.00, Wed 15.00–18.00, weekends 10.00–13.00). Tourist information at 16 Fürstenstrasse; good train services; bus links with Bielefeld, Bünde and Detmold.

**Excursion.** 9km W of Herford lies **Enge** (18,000 inhab.; alt. 94m) whose 12C and 14C collegiate church houses a sculpted wooden reredos c 1525 by H. Stavoer, and the 14C sarcophagus of Wittekind (with an 11C graveslab). Wittekind, or Widukind, hero of Germanic legends, was the Saxon adversary of Charlemagne to whom he submitted in 785. The Saxon was baptised at Attigny-sur-Aisne, with Charlemagne as his godfather. Beside the church is the Widukind Haus, a museum of the hero and region.

The B61 leads SW for 15km through hilly country with wild boar hunting, approaching the peaks of the Teutoberg forest, on the N side of which is the industrial and university town of **Bielefeld** (315,000 inhab.; alt. 118m). The twin-towered Neustädter Marienkirche stands in Kreuzstrasse on the S side of the Altstadt. Founded in 1293, completed in 1330 and restored after World War II, it shelters the remains of an early 14C choir screen; a Gothic altar of c 1400 by the same artist who painted the crucifixion altar in the church of Our Lady, Dortmund, see Rte 56; and 14C and 15C tombs, especially the 14C tomb of Count Otto III. The Renaissance Spiegelshofof 1540 is also in Kreuzstrasse. In the Altstadt, at Altstädter Kirchplatz, rises the Altstädter Nikolaikirche, built 1330–40, with a Gothic *altar, probably from Antwerp and carved with over 250 figures. Close by this church is the Renaissance town hall and the fountain of the linen weavers, 1909. At 1 Obernstrasse is the Gothic Cruwellhaus of 1530. In Obernstrasse stands also the church of St Jokodus. Built in 1511, this was formerly the church of a Franciscan convent, with a Black Madonna of c 1220. On the Sparrenburg is a restored 13C Schloss, with a 37m-high watchtower, built by Count Ludwig of Ravensberg 1240–50. In the Markt are the Renaissance Batig Haus of 1680 and the theatre.

Bielefeld has a botanical garden and animal reserve, W of the town. Museums include one at 9 Kantensieck (visits by prior arrangement) dedicated to the celebrated Protestant Pastors von Bodelschwingh—Friedrich, 1831–1910, Fritz, 1877–1946 and Friedrich the younger, 1902–77—founders and fosterers of the German inner mission Bethel homes, begun by Friedrich the Elder, 1887 and today housing 8000 incurables. The Bauernhaus Museum stands at 82 Dornberger Strasse and is devoted to farming from the 16C to the 19C (open Tue–Sun 10.00–13.00, 15.00–18.00; Nov–Mar 10.00–13.00, 14.00–17.00). The Kulturhistorisches Museum at 61 Welle is housed in a 16C building and displays porcelain and silver (open except Mon 09.00–12.00, 15.00–18.00; Sun 10.00–13.00). The City Art Gallery (the Kunsthalle, otherwise known as the Richard-Kaselowsky-Haus) is at 5 Artur-Ladebeck-Strassse. Built in 1966–68, it has a library of 30,000 volumes and Expressionist and Cubist works of art (open weekdays except Mon 11.00–18.00, Thu 11.00–21.00, Sat 10.00–18.00). The Ravensberg spinning mill, 1855–57, stands by the Rochdale park, named after another great European spinning town, which is twinned with Bielefeld.

The Stadttheater, venue of opera and operetta, is at 27 Niederwall; the Theater am Alten Markt is for plays; the Rudolf-Oetker-Konzerthalle is in Stapenhorsstrasse. Tourist informationat 6 Am Bahnhof and at 47 Bahnhofstrasse.

The B61 continues SW, crossing the B68 (Osnabrück–Paderborn) after 3km and reaching Gütersloh 9km later. **Gütersloh** (50,000 inhab.; alt. 94m) is a centre of the German publishing and silk industry, and is enhanced by half-timbered houses. 9km SE the route reaches **Wiedenbrück** (see Rte 47C). En route to Beckum, which lies on the B61 24km SW of Wiedenbrück, is **Oelde-Stromberg**, at 156m the highest place in Münsterland, with a ruined medieval Schloss and the church of the Holy Cross, which was built in 1344. **Beckum** (40,000 inhab.; alt. 110m) has inside its parish church of St Stephanus, built from the 14C to the 16C, the *shrine of St Prudentia, 1240, and a 13C octagonal Romanesque font.

**Hamm** (179,000 inhab.; alt. 63m), 19km SW of Beckum, is the westernmost part of the Ruhr, an important iron manufacturing community and, in its suburb Bad Hamm, a health resort with thermal baths, a congress hall and a Kurpark. The 13C and 14C three-aisled Pauluskirche rises in the Marktplatz. The Gustav-Lübcke museum at 2 Museumstrasse (open except Mon 10.00–16.00, closing Sun 13.00) houses works of art from Greek to modern times, including Egyptian remains and coins. In the suburb of Heessen is an open-air theatre (with performances from May to September) and two moated schlösser: 16C Heessen and 17C Oberwerries. Tourist information in Bahnhofsplatz. Train connections with Dortmund and Soest; bus connections with local towns.

At **Kamen** (45,000 inhab.; alt. 62), 15km SW along the B61, is the classical Pauluskirche, 1844–49, built on Romanesque foundations and incorporating a 12C tower capped in the 14C. The B61 continues to **Lünen**, 12km N of which at **Cappenberg-Selm** is a 13C Romanesque church begun in 1127 and still preserving its late 14C Gothic vault. It once belonged to a former Premonstratensian monastery. Inside is the 12C Cappenberg crucifix, as well as the Gothic double-tomb of the founders, Gottfried and Otto von Cappenberg, created c 1330, and choir stalls of 1509–20. In the treasury is a gold-plated **••reliquary bust of Friedrich Barbarossa**, made in Aachen 1155–71. The monastery buildings date from 1708, though this was originally a Carolingian fortress taken over by the monks. Now known as Schloss Capppenberg, with mid-19C gatehouses and set in a park laid out by the Prussian statesman Karl Freiherr von und zu Stein, who died here in 1831, it houses a museum of art and culture with furniture from Gothic to Jugendstil, Kachelöfen and porcelain (open Apr–Nov except Fri 10.00–18.00).

Two superb moated castles are nearby. At **Nordkirchen**, 6km NE of Selm, is 'the Versailles of Westphalia', Baroque Schloss Nordkirchen, its pink and grey walls and wings built in the early 18C on the site of a medieval fortress by Pictorius, its gardens laid out by Schlaun. **Burg Vischering** is at Lüdinghausen, 10km N of Selm, surrounded by water, begun in the 13C and rebuilt after a fire of 1521. It houses the Münsterland museum (open except Mon Mar–end Oct 09.30–12.30, 14.00–17.30; otherwise 10.00–12.30, 14.00–15.30).

From Lünen the B54 runs for 14km S to **Dortmund** (see Rte 56).

# 48

# The Hill Country of the Weser

Total distance 160km. Minden—B65, 10km Bückeburg—B83, 31km Hameln—55km Höxter—5km Godelheim—9km Beverungen—B80, 50km Hannoversch-Münden.

**Minden** (84,000 inhab.; alt. 46m) lies 7km N of the Minden Gap, known as the Porta Westfalica (with a monument of 1896, by B. Schmidt, to Kaiser Wilhelm I, who is blessing the country), and at the northernmost edge of the hill-country of the Weser ('Weserbergland')—mountainous country on either side of the River Weser, seldom reaching 500m but marked by deep ravines. At Minden Charlemagne established a bishopric at the turn of the

9C. The city received its charter in 1220 and became a member of the Hanseatic League.

Its Romanesque **Dom** of SS Peter and Gorgonius, founded in the mid 10C and restored after destruction in World War II, has a lofty belfry with two staircase towers. The present building has a Romanesque chancel, 1210, and a nave of 1290 which includes a superb Westwerk. Inside are an 11C bronze crucifix; 13C reliquaries; part of the late 13C choir screen, now set against the south wall of the transept; and a high altar in part painted by G. von Loen at the end of the 15C. The north transept has a rose window c 1300, the 1622 altar of the Holy Spirit, and modern stained glass of 1957. The cathedral treasury houses the bronze *Minden cross, c 1070, and a late 11C shrine of St Peter (open Mon, Wed, Fri 15.00–17.00, Sun 10.00–12.00).

Minden has houses dating from the 13C to the Renaissance, the finest in Backenstrasse and Papenmarkt. At the highest point of the upper city stands the Marienkirche of the 12C and 14C, with a massive 57m-high tower and a late 16C font. Minden's Rathaus, arcaded with Gothic arches, is basically 13C, though much restored, with an upper storey added in the 17C. Also to see are the 14C church of St Martin, with its late 15C choir stalls, its bronze font of 1583 and a tomb by A. Stenelt, 1615, and the Minden museum of local history at 23–31 Ritterstrasse (open Tue–Fri, Sun 10.00–17.00). In Martinikirchhof rises the Alte Münze (former mint), begun in the 12C with 13C windows. Opposite the mint is a group of corbelled houses built in the 16C. Other buildings surrounding the church of St Martin are the Corn Market, a classical building of the mid-1830s, and the neo-Gothic Heeresbäckerei of 1832–34.

N of the city is the Mittelland Canal, served by a brilliant system of locks, the largest (the Schachtsleuses) 85m long and 10m wide. A canal bridge above the Weser (this 375m long and 24m wide) enables 211km of canal to join Münster and Hanover without a change of level. Boat trips ply the water. Minden has a Museum of Rivercraft and Shipping at 1 Am Hohen Ufer (open Apr–Oct 09.00–17.00). Information office at Grosser Domhof.

10km from Minden along the B65 is **Bückeburg**, with a *Schloss built c 1300 and rebuilt in the mid 16C in the Renaissance style, only to be rendered Baroque in the next century, though preserving its former keep. It has a superb coffered ceiling in the Goldener Saal. Its chapel of 1396 was restyled in the 17C, with a princes' stall and Renaissance woodwork (open daily for guided tours 09.00–12.00, 13.00–18.00). In the Schloss park is the mausoleum of Fürst Adolph zu Schaumburg-Lippe, by Paul Baumgarten, 1911–14, the biggest of its kind in Europe and built at a cost of 1m Goldmarks (open Apr–Oct daily 09.00–12.00, 13.00–18.00). Johann Gottfried Herder (1744–1803) was court chaplain and preached from 1771–76 at the parish church, built 1611–15, its bronze font by A. de Vries, 1615; its Baroque organ restored in 1962. The local history museum is at 22 Lange Strasse (open daily 10.00–17.00) and Bückeburg also has a helicopter museum at 6 Sabléplatz (open daily 09.00–17.00).

The B83 leads for 31km SE to **Hameln** (51,000 inhab.; alt. 68m), known in English as Hamelin because of Robert Browning's poem about the Pied Piper, whose legend, dating from 1284, is daily performed here from May to September. In spite of Browning's assertions, Hameln is not near Hanover and is in Lower Saxony, not Brunswick. It does stand on the right bank of the Weser, on the site of an early 9C monastery, founded by the Abbot of Fulda. In 1259 the Bishop of Minden secured sovereignty over the town. Between 1426 and 1572 Hameln was a member of the Hanseatic League, embracing Protestantism in 1540. The town's two remaining medieval defences are the Pulverturm and Haspemanthturm.

In Münsterkirchhof stands the 13C münster church of St Bonifatius, a Gothic hall-church with an 11C crypt and a Romanesque late 12C octagonal tower. Inside are a relief of the coronation of Our Lady, 1415, and a Gothic tabernacle. From here the old town with its charming narrow streets is reached by way of picturesque Kupfermiedstrasse, where at No. 9 stands the Steinhaus, at No. 10 the Renaissancehaus and at No. 11 the Eckhaus, the last two both built in 1591. The church of St Nicolas in the Markt is basically Romanesque, 1220–30. Enlarged c 1300, it was later given a Baroque aspect, and was rebuilt after World War II. The Demptersches Haus at No. 7 was built for Tobias Dempter in 1607.

In *Osterstrasse are the so-called Rattenfängerhaus (Ratcatcher's House), 1602 (now a café and wine bar), the early 17C Hochzeitshaus, the beautifully half-timbered Stiftsherrenhaus, 1558, and the Renaissance Leistsche Haus, 1589. The last is now the local history museum (open except Mon 10.00–17.00, weekends 10.00–13.00) and houses some 11,000 tin soldiers enacting the battle of Langensalza between the Hanoverian army and the Prussians in 1866. At the end of Osterstrasse rises the Garrison Church of 1712. Other half-timbered houses flank *Bäckerstrasse and Bungelosenstrasse particularly the Rurie Jerusalem and the magnificent Rattenberg built by Cardinal Tönniesic, 1568. Hameln's Gemäldegalerie Hohensee, in a Jugenstil house of 1898 at 37 Lohstrasse (open Wed and Sat afternoon), displays 19C local art and caricatures.

Due S of Hameln is the health resort of **Bad Pyrmont**, known for its healing springs in the 1C AD, with a Kurhaus, a Kurtheatre, and the 360m-high Pyrmonter Berg.

The route continues S along the B83 for 55km to reach the walled town of **Höxter** with its painted, half-timbered 16C and 17C houses, on the left bank of the Weser. Its *deanery in the Markt dates from 1561, while its half-timbered Renaissance Rathaus dates from 1613. In its oriel is a Romanesque relief. The Altstadt of Höxter has numerous Renaissance houses. The 11C church of St Kilian, in An der Kiliankirche, has a 15C south aisle, an early 16C crucifixion group, a pulpit of 1597 and an 18C font. To the E of the town beside the Weser is the former monastery of *Corvey, founded in 822, where Widukind wrote the history of the Saxons. This was the home of the poet Hoffmann von Fallersleben (1798–1874) from 1860 to 1874, who was court librarian here, wrote the German national anthem and is buried in the graveyard. Although the abbey was rebuilt in the Baroque style after the Thirty Years War, the Westwerk of 873–85, with a contemporary fresco, remains the oldest building in Westphalia. The abbey's Gothic church of 1671 contains the Benedictus chapel of 1772 and the Lady chapel of c 1790. Its Baroque interior was almost all restored after World War II.

The Schloss at Corvey was built out of part of the monastery buildings between 1699 and 1721, and is now the Museum Höxter-Corvey (open daily, Apr–Oct, 09.00–18.00). Its medieval library disappeared during the Thirty Years War, after which the Landgraves of Hesse-Rotenburg began to build up a new one. The bibliomaniac Viktor Amadeus (1799–1834) transformed it into a remarkable collection of belles-lettres, including a collection of virtually every novel published in English between the 1790s and the 1820s, along with German and French Romantic novels, all rebound and shelved in 107 glass-fronted bookcases. By the time Hoffmann von Fallersleben died (see above) the library comprised almost 67,000 volumes.

On the other side of the river is the region of Solling, famous for its game, especially wild boar. 10km NW of Höxter stands the Benedictine abbey of **Marienmünster**, with an organ of 1738. The B83 continues for 14km through Godelheim to reach **Beverungen** (6000 inhab.; alt. 100m), with an early 14C moated burg, the late 17C church of St John the Baptist and several half-timbered houses.

9km further on from here take the B80 for 50km to Hannoversch Münden, now known simply as **Münden** (20,300 inhab.; alt. 141m), at the confluence of the Weser with the Werra and Fulda, a place still boasting that Alexander von Humboldt regarded it as one of the finest in the world. The Weser is here spanned by a stone bridge first built in 1329. The splendidly restored Altstadt is crammed with half-timbered houses. The Welfenschloss of 1560–80 is decorated with *Renaissance frescoes and is also a local history museum (open Tue–Fri 10.00–12.00, 16.00–18.00; weekends 10.00–12.00). In Kirchplatz is the church of St Blasius, with a 13C east end. Work continued west until the completion of the building in 1519. The tower was added later, finished in 1584. Inside is a 13C chandelier, as well as a bronze font by N. von Stettin, 1392; a pulpit of 1493; an organ case of 1645; and a Baroque altar of 1700–10. G. Crossman incorporated into his gabled, Renaissance new town hall (1603–09) parts of an earlier Gothic building.

# 49

# The Siebengebirge

**Königswinter** (see Rte 41) is the best point of entry to the seven extinct volcanic peaks that make the picturesque Siebengebirge, and whose stones built Cologne cathedral and its Romanesque churches. There are in fact about 30 peaks in the c 50 sq km range, but the name arose because only seven can be seen from Bonn, namely the *Grosser Ölberg, the Löwenburg (455m), the Lohrberg (435m), the *Petersberg, the Nonnenstromburg (336m), the Wolkenburg (325m) and the *Drachenfels (whose crag, as Byron put it, 'Frowns o'er the wide and winding Rhine'). This is Germany's oldest natural park with over 200 marked hiking routes furnished with resting places.

The top of the 321m-high **Drachenfels** can be reached by foot, motor car or Germany's oldest rack railway, 1883. On it perch the modern Schloss Drachenburg and the early 13C Schloss Drachenfels, built by the Archbishops of Cologne in the 12C and 15C, invested and ruined by the Swedes in 1632. Its chapel was rebuilt from 1700 onwards. Half-way up is the cave of the dragon, celebrated in the legend of the Nibelungen where Siegfried slays the beast and washes himself in its blood to become invincible.

Buses run to the 331m-high **Petersberg**, where there is a modern hotel. The highest of the seven peaks is the 461m **Grosser Ölberg**, reached by cable-car and then on foot (20 minutes) through woods and graced by the ruined Schloss Löwenburg.

The Siebengebirge Museum is at 11 Klotzstrasse, Königswinter.

# 50

# The Bergisches Land: Wuppertal to Düsseldorf

Total distance 55km. Wuppertal—B51 and B229, llkm Remscheid-Lennep—
B229, 10km Solingen—B229, 14km Langenfeld—B8, 9km
Düsseldorf-Benrath—B8, 11km Düsseldorf.

**Wuppertal** (418,000 inhab.; alt 157m), straddling the River Wupper and
sheltered by a range of low hills, was formed in 1929 from the union of
Barmen, Elberfeld, Beyenberg, Vohwinkel, Cronenberg and Ronsdorf. The
textile industry was well established here by the 16C. Between 1898 and
1901 an overhead railway 13.3km long was built to join Elberfeldt, Barmen
and Vohwinkel. Here was born Friedrich Engels (1820–95), Marx's collaborator and patron. The Engels Museum is at 10 Engelsstrasse (open Tue–Sun
10.00–13.00, 15.00–17.00). Wuppertal was also the birthplace of Johann
Carl Fuhlrott (1803–77), the discoverer of Neandertal man. The Fuhlrott
natural history museum is at 20 Auer Schulstrasse (open at the same times
as the Engels house, with some extensions). A university was founded here
in 1927, reached S of the city by the Kiesbergtunnel, Europe's sole two-storey motor car tunnel. At Barmen in 1934 Protestant opponents of Hitler
made a celebrated declaration of the spiritual independence of the church
from the state.

The church of St Lawrence in Friedrich-Ebert-Strasse is a classical church
built by Adolf von Vagedes, 1828–32. 20C buildings include the swimming
complex, the Schwimmmoper, 1956, the Schauspielhaus in Bundesallee,
built by G. Graubner in 1966, in front of which is a statue by Henry Moore,
and the opera house of 1956 in Friedrich-Engels-Allee. Older buildings
include Barmen town hall, 1912–22. Elberfeld also has a zoo, founded in
1881 and now sheltering 3500 animals, and the **∗∗Von-der-Heydt Museum**
at 8 Turmhof. It displays 16C and 17C Dutch artists; 19C paintings, including works by the Norwegian Edvard Munch and the Impressionists; ∗20C
German and French paintings, including the Blaue Reiter school, especially
works by ∗Ernst Ludwig Kirchner; and German Realism or *Neue
Sachlichkeit*, especially Otto Dix's ∗∗'To Beauty', 1922, and his 'Portrait of
Karl Krall', 1923; works by the Wuppertal-Elberfeldt born Carl Grossberg
(1894–1940), including his 'Machine Room', 1925 and his 'Bridge over the
Schwarzbachstrasse', 1927; a riveting ∗∗'Half Nude', 1929, by Christian
Schad (b. 1894); sculptures by Rodin, mobiles by Alexander Calder; and
1920s French art, especially works by Picasso, Léger and Juan Gris (open
Tue–Sun 10.00–17.00). In Barmen are the botanical gardens.

OTHER MUSEUMS: are the Clock Museum at 11 Poststrasse (open weekdays 10.00–12.00, 16.00–18.00; Sat 10.00–12.00), the Cinema Museum is in
Friedrich-Engels-Allee, displaying old movie cameras and rarities of film
history; same opening times as Clock Museum, and the Missions Museum
at 9 Missionsstrasse (open weekdays 08.00–16.00). The Toelle tower in
Barmen offers panoramas. Tourist information at pavillon Döppersberg in
Elberfeld.

9km E of Wuppertal is the 5.2km-long Klütert cave, reputed to heal asthma.

Take the B51 S from Wuppertal to reach **Remscheid-Lennep** (135,000 inhab.; alt. 370m) on the B229, its prosperity deriving from the manufacture of precision tools. Wilhelm Conrad Röntgen (1845–1923), the discoverer of X-rays, was born at Lennep, and the Röntgen Museum is at 41 Schwelmer Strasse (open Sun–Thu 14.00–17.00, Fri 10.00–14.00). The regional museum is in a Baroque house of 1778 at 2–6 Cleffstrasse (open Wed–Sat 09.00–13.00, 14.00–17.00; Sun 10.00–13.00).

The Bergisches Land is named after the former Dukes of Berg, whose artistic and cultural collection is partly preserved at **Schloss Burg an der Wupper**, 7.5km SE, which was founded in the 12C and rebuilt in 1887. Its museum is devoted to regional history (open Mar–Oct 09.00–18.00, Mon 13.00–18.00; winter closed Mon and at 17.00 other days). The Schloss chapel has wall paintings, and you should not miss the *Festsäle. Tourist information at Remscheid town hall.

The B229 leads 10k W of Remscheid-Lennep to reach the industrial town of **Solingen** (177,000 inhab.; alt. 224m). En route the River Wupper is crossed by Europe's highest railway bridge (107m high, 550m long). Solingen makes cutlery and swords and has a museum, the Deutsches Klingenmuseum, with swords and weapons from the Bronze Age onwards, at 160 Wuppertaler Strasse (open except Mon and Thu 10.00–13.00, 15.00–17.00). In the 18C market square is a Protestant church of 1718. The Catholic parish church of Solingen-Gräfrath dates from 1690, the theatre (at 71 Konrad-Adenauer-Strasse) from 1963. Tourist information at Cronenbergerstrasse.

14km from Solingen along the B229 is Langenfeld (29,000 inhab.; alt. 44m), where you join the B8 to reach after 9km **Düsseldorf-Benrath** (see Rte 45) and after another 11km **Düsseldorf** (see also Rte 45).

# 51

## Hamburg

**HAMBURG** (1,600,000 inhab. alt. 17m), Germany's second largest city after Berlin and one of the premier European ports (serving 200 shipping lines, with 15,000 ocean-going vessels docking annually to transport over 50m tonnes of cargo), is situated on the right bank of the River Elbe and around the basin of the Alster, 104km from the North Sea. Hamburg is proud to be a city of 2400 bridges (compared with Amsterdam's 600 and Venice's 450). Its daily fish market (in the St Pauli quarter from 06.00 to 10.00), its extensive parks, its scandalous Reeperbahn, its Beatles memorabilia (though their Star Club at 39 Grosse Freiheit is no more) and its lakes, make up for the slightly brutal nature of the rebuilding after some 80 per cent of the city was destroyed in World War II.

**Main railway station**: Steintorplatz. **Main post office**: Stephansplatz. Every post office facility is also found in Münzstrasse, close by the main railway station. **Information office**: in the Bieberhaus am Hachmannplatz (named after Bürgermeister Gerhard Hachmann, 1838–1904) and at the Kirchenallee entrance to the Hauptbahnhof. Hanse-Viertel **Information office**: Shopping arcade, Poststrasse. Fuhlsbüttel **airport**, 11km from the city centre, with an **information office**, is served by buses running every 20 minutes and reaching after 25 minutes the city's main railway station. In the city itself **transport** is provided by a single company which runs the U-Bahn, S-Bahn and river boats. Hamburg hosts sailing **regattas** and an annual folk **festival** in November and December.

**History**. Late Saxon remains of the 7C and 8C have been discovered in the vicinity of Hamburg and in the Altstadt. Here Charlemagne founded first a church and then a fortress to keep back the heathen, thus creating its name 'Burg am Hemmis'. In 831 Emperor Ludwig the Pious founded the bishopric; 14 years later the Vikings plundered and burned the city. Hamburg was again razed in 983, to be rebuilt under the inspiration of Archbishop Unwan, 1013–29. The city now began to prosper again and by the 12C was a rich trading centre, in the next century helping to set up the Hanseatic League and damming the Alster river to create its celebrated lake. In the mid 14C Archbishop Bezelin ordered the construction of the city walls. In the next century the city came under the control of the Danes.

In 1529 the city turned Protestant, under the influence of Luther's ally, the scholarly Johannes Bugenhagen. The Hamburg stock exchange was instituted in 1558 and the Hamburg bank founded in 1619. As Bulstrode Whitelock wrote in the mid 17C, 'It may be said of this towne, that God hath withheld nothing from them for their good'. Recognised as a Free City by the emperor in 1618, Hamburg gained a seat on the Imperial Diet in 1770. After the dissolution of the Hanseatic League in the 18C Hamburg kept a special relationship with two other Hanseatic cities, Lübeck and Bremen. Savants of the calibre of Friedrich Gottlieb Klopstock (1724–1803) and Gotthold Ephraim Lessing (1729–81) brought the city fame at this time.

By the beginning of the 19C Hamburg was amongst the richest cities in Europe. Between 1816 and 1818 Heinrich Heine worked here in his father's bank. French occupation in 1803 (which blocked trade with England and caused swift British reprisals), hampered her trade and in 1810, after three brief years of freedom, Hamburg was incorporated into the French empire. The city regained its free status five years later. Devastated by a fire in 1842, Hamburg was rebuilt. (The British architect Gilbert

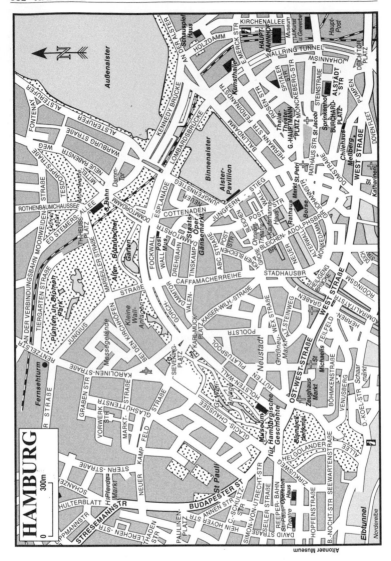

Scott won the competition to design the Nicolaikirche.) In 1860 Hamburg guaranteed to its citizens freedom of the press, of religion and of assembly.

By the beginning of World War I Hamburg was the world's third most important port—after London and New York. The university was founded in 1919. In 1921 the city set up a new constitution and a democratic assembly. Once more devastated in World War II—in 1943 British bombers demolished all but the tower of Gilbert Scott's Nicolaikirche—Hamburg has since that time both restored some of its old quarters and also built a modern city. Hamburg became a separate Land of West Germany in 1949.

A severe flood ravaged the city in February 1962. In January 1975 the 500m-long Elbtunnel, for pedestrians and vehicles, was officially opened.

Hamburg prospers on engineering, ship building, car manufacture, beer and chemicals. Today it is the HQ of the North German radio and TV company, the Norddeutscher Rundfunk, and the publishing house of Axel Springer.

Hamburg was the birthplace of the composers Felix Mendelssohn-Bartholdy (1809–47) and Johannes Brahms (1833–97). C.P.E. Bach died here in 1778. The city boasts an internationally renowned symphony orchestra. The opera company, founded in 1678, is the finest in Germany.

Glockengiesserwall leads NW from the main railway station (built by Moeller, Reinhart and Süssenguth in 1906) by way of the **Kunsthalle**, the city art gallery (built in the Italian Renaissance style, 1868, 1886 and 1907; see **Museums** below) to the Binnenalster lake which is separated from the Aussenalster by the Kennedybrücke and the Lombardsbrücke, built along the line of the former ramparts. Cross the Lombardsbrücke, decked out with wrought-iron candelabra of 1865, to reach Stephansplatz, with the main post office (and a post office museum, open Tue–Fri 10.00–14.00). To the N is the **Botanischer Garten** and then the park known as **Planten un Blomen** (dialect for plants and flowers), which covers 38,000 sq m and incorporates a miniature railway, a tropical house, a congress centre, the trade fair, the Ernst-Marck hall and the 272m-high TV tower, the **Fernsehturm**, of 1968, with a revolving restaurant. To the NE of the park in Edmund-Siemers-Allee is the university.

From Stephansplatz Dammtorstrasse leads S, with on the left the opera house, the Hamburger **Staatsoper** of 1817, which was rebuilt in 1955, to the Gänsemarkt, the centre of Hamburg's antiquarian quarter. On the SE corner of the Gänsemarkt is a statue of Lessing, created by Fritz Schaper in 1881, and Hamburg's first opera house, which was founded in 1678. The present building is by Gerhard Weber, 1955. Left of the Dammtorstrasse the fashionable shopping street of Jungfernstieg leads to the embarcation point for sailing on the Binnenalster and the Aussenalster. Beside the lake is the **Alsterpavillon**. Continue to the end of Jungfernsteig and turn right into the **Alsterarkarden** along the Kleine Alster, taking the road on the right to cross the Michaelbrücke and reach in Michaelistrasse the late Gothic church of **St Katharina**, 1380–1425, which has north and south Renaissance doorways. Its bulbous Baroque tower, 115m high, added by Peter Marquardt in 1659 (and restored in 1957), is topped with a statue of St Catherine and her wheel. The Baroque façade of the church is by Johann Nikolaus Kuhn, 1732–37. Inside are a statue of St Catherine of c 1400; a 13C crucifix; and the monument by Gerhard Marcks for the victims of the 'Pamir', which sank in 1957. The writer Johann Melchior Goeze (1717–86) was once pastor of this church; and in 1720 Johann Sebastian Bach performed for two hours here to an audience including the 90-year-old organist J.A. Reinicken, who exclaimed after the master had extemporised for half an hour on *An Wasserflüssen Babylon*, 'I believed that such artistry was dead; I perceive it lives on in you'.

Close by is Hamburg's '**Speicherstadt**' (warehouse city). This is a port within a port, with a curious history. From 1189 until the second half of the 19C, when Otto von Bismarck decided to change the political face of Germany, Hamburg had been a duty-free port. Bismarck enticed the city into the Prussian Customs' Union by offering it a special, duty-free trading quarter, the warehouse city, which survives to this day. A remarkable example of industrial architecture, the Speicherstadt was built between 1885 and 1910. Threaded by canals, this is the largest warehouse complex in the world, with its blocks of exotic red-brick warehouses sheltering coffee, tea, oriental carpets, silk, cotton and rum. Six, seven and eight storeys high, with little towers and balconies, the buldings seem more like medieval palaces than warehouses. Thus, evading the custom's duties of its rivals, this city prospered (one consequence being that its university was founded only in 1919, since Hamburg merchants didn't want their sons to espouse unprofitable book-learning).

From St Katharina take Ost-West-Strasse to reach on the left the Baroque, oval-shaped church of *St Michael, which was built by Ernst Georg Sonnin and Leonhard Prey, 1751–77, was restored in 1907–12 by J. Faulwasser, H. Geissler and E. Meerwein, and restored again after World War II by Gerhard Langemaack. This is undoubtedly Hamburg's finest building, indeed one of the supreme Baroque churches in northern Germany. Its tower, Hamburg's symbol, rises to 132m, from which there is a splendid *view of the city. Musically, this is hallowed ground. Brahms was baptised here in 1833; Georg Philipp Telemann was musical director of St Michael (1721–67); Carl Philipp Emanuel Bach is buried in its crypt. The statue of Michael killing the dragon on the doorway under the tower dates from 1912; that of Luther (in bronze north of the tower) is by Otto Lessing, also created in 1912. In the entrance is the Sonnin memorial by Oscar Ulmer, 1906. The Steinmeyer organ dates from 1962. St Michael has two other organs. Every mid-day the church bountifully provides for Hamburg's spiritual and aesthetic needs with a free organ concert, but the doors are locked spot on twelve o'clock. The church has a marble font of 1763 and an Italian pulpit and high altar of 1912. In the crypt an exhibition documents the tribulations of the Michaeliskirche, and here too is the tomb of the composer Carl Philipp Emanuel Bach. From the pulpit of St Michael after World War II until his death in 1986 the anti-Nazi resistance leader Helmut Thielicke brought new renown to this church by his preaching.

S of this church, in 1671, Hamburg merchants built an exquisite group of almshouses (the **Krameramtswohnungen**) for 22 of their widows. Two- or three-storeyed, half-timbered and overhanging a narrow passage, they continued to fulfil their original purpose until 1960. Today shops, restaurants and bars have taken over, though the windows are still filled with stained glass and the decor in which visitors drink punch remains authentic and charming. One of the buildings now houses a museum dedicated to the redoubtable old ladies who once spent their aged days here.

Behind the church at 10 Krayenkamp the Mercers' Guild in 1670 set up widows' charitable homes. Continue along Ost-West-Strasse to reach the **Zeughausmarkt**, whose 34m-high Bismarck monument was created by Lederer and Schaudt in 1906. The Elbe park lies on the W side of the Zeughausmarkt and houses NW of Zeughausmarkt, at 24 Holstenwall, the **Museum für Hamburgische Geschichte**, the city history museum, built by Schumacher, 1913–21 (open Tue–Sun 10.00–17.00, closing Sat 13.00).

Walk S through the park to reach the river bank and the St Pauli Hafenstrasse. From here the Elbtunnel leads to the pleasure quarters of **St Pauli** and the **Reeperbahn** (bars, cabaret, night clubs, the Panoptikon waxworks, etc.). Beside the St Pauli-Landungsbrücken, close by Hamburg's fish market, stands a melancholy monument, set up in 1985. A sculpted mother crouches on top of it, mournfully gazing out to sea. The inscription is by Joseph Conrad, and reads, 'To the immortal sea, the ships which are no more and the simple men whose days will never return'. Next door is the 19C **Fischmarkt**, on the spot where not only fish fresh from the trawlers but also live poultry, rabbits, fruit, vegetables and clothing have been sold since 1703. Follow Königstrasse W from the Reeperbahn to reach the former Prussian village of **Altona** (an independent town until 1937), whose church of the **Holy Trinity** was restored after World War II. Also worth visiting are the 18C **Christianskirche** in Klopstockstrasse and the neo-classical palaces in **Palmallee**. The Altona **Fischmarkt** opens each Sunday morning, selling also live birds, flowers, antiques and second-hand goods. Altona's Jewish cemetery dates from 1611. Its imposing Rathaus was begun in 1844 and finished in 1898. Continue along Königstrasse and then take Museumstrasse to find at Nos 21–23 the **Altonaer Museum**, which is devoted to the history of Schleswig Holstein and the lower Elbe (open Tue–Sun 10.00–17.00; closing Sat at 13.00).

Return to St Pauli Hafenstrasse and continue E as far as the **Schaar** gate and then the **Deichstrasse** with, at No. 35, Hamburg's oldest surviving house, 1641, and from here to No. 49 a row of fine 17C and 18C gabled houses, the **Nikolaifleet**, half-timbered where they face the water. A plaque on Baroque No. 42, built in 1760, recalls the fire which raged overnight on 4 and 5 May 1842, and destroyed most of the inner city.

Just beyond, in Hopfenmarkt, the 147m-high neo-Gothic tower from Gilbert Scott's **Nicolaikirche**, built between 1864 and 1874, is all that remains of the church after World War II (see above). It now serves as a memorial of victims of the Nazis. Where once rose its crossing is a wine museum, the **Weinkeller unter St Nikolai**, open for sampling, weekdays 13.00–18.00, Sat 09.00–13.00.

The Schaar gate adjoins the Rödingsmarkt, which leads to the **Börse**, stock exchange, whose present neo-classical building is by F.G. Forsmann, 1841. Close by, in massive Rathausmarkt, rises the Renaissance **Rathaus** of 1886–97, with a 112m-high tower, the sixth in the city's history, the whole built by numerous architects under the supervision of Martin Haller. Its façade includes statues of 18 emperors and the saints commemorated in Hamburg church dedications. The **Ratsweinkeller** was decorated with a statue of Bacchus by the Swiss sculptor Mannstadt in 1770. Inside, amongst no fewer than 647 rooms, is a great Festival Hall, 46m by 18m and 15m high, enlivened with paintings by Hugo Vogel, 1909. In the courtyard is a bronze fountain set up in 1892 to commemorate 8605 persons who perished in a plague of 1892 (guided tours hourly Mon–Fri 10.15–15.15, weekends 10.15–13.15). S of the town hall stood a monastery which furnished Hamburg with its first school.

From here take Mönckebergstrasse—named after Bürgermeister Johann Georg Mönckeberg, 1839–1908, with the Mönckeberg fountain, by Georg Wrba, 1926—to see the 12C **Petrikirche**, in origin Hamburg's oldest church. It was rebuilt by Alexis de Châteauneuf and H.P. Fersenfeldt between 1844 and 1849, and the architects preserved the lion's head of 1342 on its doorway and a 133m-high tower of 1342. The octagonal crown was added to the tower in 1877. You climb to the top by 550 steps. Inside this three-aisled, brick Gothic church is a stone Madonna of c 1470.

In Jacobihof stands the Gothic **Jakobikirche** with its 124m-high tower. The church was begun in the 14C and faithfully rebuilt in 1959 after destruction in World War II. This is architecturally a curious mix, its west façade built in 1742, its south entrance neo-Gothic and dating from 1869, its spire a post-war creation. The church's treasures include a St Luke altar in the aisle, built by Hinrich Bornemann in 1499; an altar in the baptistry chapel, c 1500; the 16C Trinity altar; a Baroque pulpit by Georg Baumann, 1610; and a completely restored Baroque *organ by Arp Schnitger, 1689–93, with four manuals, 60 speaking stops and some 4000 pipes—which prompted J.S. Bach to apply for the post of organist in 1720, though when it was offered him, he turned it down.

S of the church in Burchardplatz are found two noted 20C buildings: the **Chilehaus**, by Fritz Höger, 1922–24, and the **Sprinkenhof**, by Höger and his collaborators, the Gerson brothers, 1930. The Gersons were also responsible for the **Messberghof**, 1924, in nearby Pumpenstrasse. (The Expressionist statues in the entrances are by Ludwig Kunstmann.)

Hamburg's Ohlsdorfer cemetery contains a Memorial to the World War II Air Raid Victims of Hamburg, created by G. Marcks in 1951. 24km SE of Hamburg Neuengamme has a richly decorated hall church, begun in the 13C, finished in the 19C, with an independent belfry in wood. Here too is a former concentration camp (the KZ-Gedenkstätte Neuengamme) in Jean-Dolidier-Weg, open daily except Mon 10.00–17.00, in which were imprisoned 106,000 persons, only half of whom survived.

MUSEUMS: * * *Kunsthalle, the museum of fine arts, in Glockengiesserwal, displays medieval retables; Dutch and Flemish art, including Ruisdael and Rubens; 17C French art; 18C Italian works, including Canaletto and Bernini; 19C German and French works, including Caspar David Friedrich; 20C German works, including Max Liebermann, Lovis Corinth and Max Slevogt; Matisse and Picasso; Munich Jugendstil, including Kandinsky and Jawlensky; Max Beckmann, Oskar Kokoschka, Georg Grosz, Christian Schad, Otto Dix; and Pop Art (open Tue–Sun 10.00–18.00); the **Museum of Folk Art** is at 14 Binderstrasse (open Tue–Sun 10.00–17.00); a **Brahms Museum** is found at 39 Peterstrasse (open Tue, Fri 12.00–13.00, Thu 16.00–18.00); the **Planetarium**, Wasserturm is in the Stadtpark (open Sun–Fri 10.00–15.30); a **Museum of Tobacco** and its history is at 51 Parkstrasse (open by appointment); the **University Theatre Collection** is housed at 45 Rothenbaumchaussee (open weekdays 09.30–16.00, Tue until 18.00). SW of the city, at 284 Curslacker Deich, is an **Open-air Museum** with windmills and a farmhouse of 1663. The * *Museum für Kunst und Gewerbe (Steintorplatz) displays sculpture and paintings from the Middle Ages to the present day, as well as antique art, art from the near and far east, and a collection of etchings; open except Mon 10.00–17.00.

THEATRES: As well as the Staatsoper, the **Operettenhaus** in Spielbudenplatz, Hamburg's theatres include the **Theater im Zimmer** at 30 Alsterchaussee, the **Schauspielhaus** at 39 Kirchenallee, the **Thalia-Theater** in Gerhardt-Hauptmann-Platz, the **Ernst-Deutsch-Theater** at 60 Mundsburger Damm, the **Neue Flora** in Stresemannstrasse and the **Hamburger Kammerspiele** at 11 Hartungstrasse.

ENVIRONS: N of Hamburg, at 4 Tierparkallee in the suburb of Stellingen, is *Hagenbeck Zoo, established 1848 and reconstituted 1945–52 (open 08.00–19.00, closing 16.30 Nov–Mar), with most of the 2500 animals, comprising more than 300 species, roaming in open settings. Here too are a Troparium and Dolphinarium.

The B431 leads W from Hamburg for 14km to the fishing village and modern, fashionable suburb of Blankenese, by way of **Klein-Flottbek**, with a museum of the works of Ernst Barlach. **Blankenese**, which belonged to Denmark until 1864, boasts the 80m-high Süllberg (with a magnificent *view) and the 87m-high Bismarckstein. The heart of Blankenese offers narrow streets and climbing terraces, as well as a beach lined with restaurants and cafés.

# 52

# Hamburg to Hanover

Total distance 127km. Hamburg—B4, 15km Harburg—B75, 11km Nenndorf—9km to the junction with the B3—B3, 17km Wintermoor—23km Soltau—22km Bergen—23km Celle—7km Hanover.

An alternative route via the A7 motorway (148km) offers stupendous views of Lüneburg Heath (see Rte 53).

Leave **Hamburg** (see Rte 51) S by the Bilorner Brückenstrasse, crossing the river by the New Elbe Bridge, built between 1883 and 1887, to reach Veddel, where the motorway to Hanover begins. Continue over the canal into the industrial suburb of Wilhelmsburg, to cross the river again by a 470m-long bridge. Drive along Hanoversche Strasse, Moorstrasse and Wilhelstorfer Strasse to reach after 15km Harburg. **Harburg** was already settled in the 12C and became a chartered city in 1297. It was the seat of a branch of the Lüneberg-Celle family in the 16C and 17C, and was taken over by Hanover in 1705 and by Prussia in 1866, before becoming a suburb of Hamburg in 1937. Although most of the old city was destroyed in World War II, Harburg retains a fine park, an open-air theatre, and borders onto Lüneburg Heath (see Rte 53). An archaeological and local history museum at 2 Museumsplatz opens Tue–Sun 10.00–17.00.

The B75 continues 20km SW through Nenndorfto join the B3, which then runs 17km S across the Heath, much of which is here a nature reserve, with no motor traffic, up to Wintermoor. The route now descends to the Böhme valley and, after 23km, **Soltau** (18,000 inhab.; alt. 68m). Known as *Curtis salta* in the early 10C, Soltau's Johanniskirche has wall paintings by Rudolf Schärer commemorating the victims of World War II. The town has managed to preserve some half-timbered houses. 22km further S lies **Bergen** (18,000 inhab.; alt. 70m), just outside which is a memorial to the victims of the concentration camp of Bergen-Belsen (signposted 'Gedenkstätte'). Bergen's local history museum is in a 300-year-old farmhouse at 7 Am Friedensplatz (open weekdays 09.30–12.00, 15.00–17.00; closed Fri afternoons and weekends). The African Museum at 9 Buhrstrasse is open by arrangement. NE of Bergen is **Hermannsburg** with a church dated 972.

The B3 continues for 23km, passing 3km W seven megalithic tombs from the New Stone Age, the 'Sieben Steinhäuser', before reaching \***CELLE**, the former residence of the Dukes of Lüneburg and situated where the River Aller is navigable.

**Tourist information** at 6a Schlossplatz. **Train** and **bus** links with Brunswick, Hamburg and Hanover.

**History**. *Kellu* or 'riverside settlement' appears first in written history in a charter of 990. It flourished because of the river trade, and in 1292 Otto the Severe refounded the town, with a new Schloss 3km downstream. Celle became the capital of the Lüneberg Duchy in 1378. In 1526 under Herzog Ernst the Confessor the town embraced Protestantism. Celle continued to prosper, as is indicated by its many fine buildings—which escaped destruction in World War II. Becoming part of the Electorate of Hanover in 1705, Celle was chosen as the seat of a court of appeal in 1711 which later became the supreme court of this province. The royal stud farm founded in 1735 by George II of Great Britain and Ireland, who was also Elector of Hanover, is still flourishing, with some 300 horses.

At Celle in 1666 was born Sophie Dorothea, who married the future King George I of Great Britain and Ireland and was grandmother of Frederick the Great.

From the main railway station Bahnhofstrasse leads by way of Westcellerstrasse to the moated ducal **Schloss**, which faces onto Schlosssplatz. Traces remain of the 13C foundation, though the present gleaming white late-17C building is substantially due to Herzog Georg Wilhelm. The Gothic *Schloss chapel, built in 1485, was rebuilt in the next century in the Renaissance style and boasts paintings by the Dutchman Martin de Voss—see especially the crucifixion on the altar. The 1685 Italian-style theatre in the Schloss is the oldest surviving in Germany, has its own company and is lavishly stuccoed and decorated (visits daily 09.00–12.00, 14.00–16.00; Sat closes 12.00).

E of the Schloss across Schlossplatz are the main post office and the **Bomann Museum**, which is devoted to the history of Celle and Lüneburg Heath, with a model of a Lower Saxon farmhouse of 1571; portraits of the ducal family; and 19C Hanoverian army uniforms (open daily 10.00–17.00; closes Sun 13.00). The old town stretches further E, with numerous half-timbered houses. Vast Stechbahn was formerly the spot for jousts and has a Renaissance pharmacy, Zum Löwen, of 1537. It leads to the market place with the Protestant parish church. Built in the 14C, the church has a tower 74.5m high. Its extensive Baroque alterations date from 1675 to 1698, though it still shelters an altar of 1613. Amongst its Renaissance and Baroque tombs of the ducal family, those in the crypt are especially fine, particularly the 17C one of Duke Wilhelm the Younger and his wife Dorothea of Denmark. You can climb the 234 steps of its tower for a satisfying view.

Kalandgasse leads N from the Stechbahn to the old Latin School of 1602. Zöllnerstrasse leads E from Stechbahn to the former **Rathaus**, rebuilt by Jakob Riess in the early Renaissance style, 1561–79, its classical façade added in the 18C. Richly gabled, the Rathaus overlooks the Markt, and on this façade is inscribed the Biblical text, 'Unless the Lord protect the city, their labour is but lost that guard it'. The east front has an ogival doorway, over which is the coat of arms of Duke Wilhelm the Younger and Dorothea.

Other historic buildings in Celle include the former stables, the Altes Reithaus, of 1664, its gable decorated with the escutcheon of Duke Georg Wilhelm (who died in 1705). At 14 Grosser Plan rises the Baroque Stechinelli Haus of 1675, with a classical façade of 1795. Zöllnerstasse is also crammed with splendid houses, and at 8 Poststrasse, a continuation of Zöllnerstrasse, stands the *Hoppener Haus of 1532, which was built for Simon Hoppener, the chamberlain of Ernst the Confessor. The finest half-timbered house in Celle, the Hoppener Haus is decorated with sculpted figures, including angels, gods and an Amazon. To the S of Celle are a French Garden, the Französischer Garten, with a monument to Queen Caroline Mathilde of Denmark, who died in 1775 and whose lover Struensee was beheaded in 1772, the Lower Saxon institute of bee research, the Bienenistilvt, and the stud farm (the Niedersächsische Landgestüt).

11km SE of Celle along the B214 is the 13C and 14C former Cistercian convent **Kloster Wienhausen**, founded by Agnes, the daughter-in-law of Henry the Lion, in 1231 and after the Reformation a convent of Protestant women. Inside are wall paintings, stained glass, a tabernacle of 1445 and a nuns' choir. The church was frescoed in 1335 and has statues of the foundress Agnes, 1280, of the Virgin of Wienhausen and of the Risen Jesus, both 13C. Its gilded and sculpted reredos of 1519 is magnificent, dedicated to the Blessed Virgin Mary, its panels around the Madonna portraying scenes from her life. The Gothic cloister has some masterly sculptures.

The B3 continues S for 7km to **HANOVER** (German **Hannover**; 557,000 inhab.; alt. 56m), the capital of Lower Saxony. Despite several exceptionally fine buildings in the city centre, Hanover's chief delight must undoubtedly be the Herrenhäuser Gärten.

Main **railway station** and main **post office**: Ernst August-Platz. **Tourist information**: 8 Ernst-August-Platz. **Airport** at Langenhagen, N of the city. Hanover is served by an **underground railway**; **trains** connect with every important German city. The Saturday **flea market** sets up on either side of the River Leine, principally along Am Hohen Ufer.

History. An industrial city situated on the Mittelland canal and in the valley of the River Leine, Hanover appears first in recorded history in 1100. Henry the Lion established his residence here in 1163, and in 1241 Duke Otto confirmed Hanover's civic rights. The son of Frederick Barbarossa destroyed the city in 1189 and then rebuilt and fortified it. In 1386 Hanover became a member of the Hanseatic League. Its future prosperity was enhanced in 1526 when Cord Broyhan created the light ale which became renowned throughout the region. The city opted for Protestantism in 1533, and the Catholic church council moved to Hildesheim. During the Thiry Years War the city was occupied by the Danes and a third of the citizens died of the plague.

In 1658 Princess Sophie of England, grandchild of James I, married Duke Ernst August. Under the Elector Ernst August (1679–98) the city continued to prosper and underwent a cultural renaissance. Gottfried Wilhelm Leibniz (born Leipzig 1646, died Hanover 1717) became court librarian in 1676. The elector Georg Ludwig united Hanover to Great Britain and Ireland when he became George I in 1714, a union which ended only in 1837 when Ernst August became king of Hanover and over the next 14 years gave the city a classical face through the work of his architect Georg Ludwig Friedrich Laves. Before then French troops had occupied Hanover for a decade after 1803, though Hanoverian soldiers escaped to Britain and contributed to Napoleon's defeat at the battle of Waterloo. The city expanded industrially in the 19C, its street gas lighting in 1826 the first on the European mainland, its first railway train running to Lehte in 1843, its railway station the first transit station in Germany. The city was taken over by the Prussians in 1866.

By 1873 over 100,000 people lived here. Five years later Hanover founded the first German football club, and in 1887 the Hanoverian Emil Berliner invented the gramophone. Kaiser Wilhelm II opened the new Rathaus in 1913, and three years later the Mittelland canal between the city and the Rhine was inaugurated. In 1934 the Machsee leisure lake and park were planned (see below), completed two years later.

Over half the city and 80 per cent of its centre were destroyed in World War II. In 1946 Hanover became the capital of Lower Saxony, and its first export trade fair took place a year later. In 1952 the Hanover Langenhagen airport opened to civilian traffic. The underground was inaugurated in 1975.

The astronomer and musician Friedrich Wilhelm Herschel, who discovered Uranus in 1781 and the following year became private astronomer to George III, was born here in 1738 (dying in Slough, England, in 1822). Other natives of Hanover were the writers August Wilhelm Iffland (1759–1814), who was born in the Leibnizhaus, August Wilhelm von Schlegel (1767–1845) and Karl Wilhelm Friedrich von Schlegel (1772–1829), as well as the artist Kurt Schwitters (1887–1914).

Opposite the main railway station is the huge Ernst-August-Platz, with a monument to Queen Victoria's uncle, King Ernst August (1837–52). Follow Bahnhofstrasse SW, noting the **Passerelle**, a sunken shopping street 750m long, to another huge square, **Kröpcke Platz**, with the skyscraper-store known as the Hanover Kröpcke Centre. Bahnhofstrasse runs into Karmarschstrasse, which boasts the *Altes Rathaus, 1410–55, restored in 1875 and rebuilt 1953–64. Nearby is the **Leibniz Haus** of 1652, with a Renaissance façade. On the right in Am Markt rises the brick Gothic **Marktkirche**, which is dedicated to SS Georg and Jakob. Built between 1340 and 1360, this hall-church was restored after World War II. The tower, four-gabled and

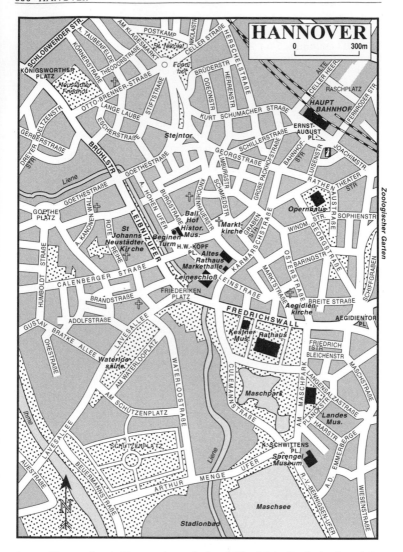

topped by a spire, is Hanover's symbol and 98m high. Its choir glass dates from c 1400, the sculpted altar from c 1490 and the bronze font from c 1500. The bronze doors are by Gerhard Marcks, 1958.

Continue to the bank of the Leine and take Leinestrasse NW to reach Heinrich-Wilhelm-Kopf-Platz and the **Leineschloss** which overlooks the river. The Schloss was begun in 1637 for Duke Georg von Calenberg, restored between 1816 and 1826 by Georg Ludwig Laves, who gave it the classical portico, and restored again after World War II. In its chapel is the tomb of George I of Great Britain, who died in 1727. The Schloss is now the seat of the Lower Saxon parliament. Opposite the Schloss in Dammstrasse is the 1850 extension of the old town hall, popularly known as the Doges' Palace.

Continue NW along Leinstrasse to reach Ballhofplatz, with the *halftim-bered ***Ballhof**, 1649–64. One of Hanover's most attractive buildings, the Ballhof was once an indoor tennis court and theatre, and now serves as the civic theatre. Kreuzstrasse leads N from the Ballhof to the **Kreuzkirche**, which dates from 1433, has a mid-17C tower and was completely rebuilt after World War II. Inside there is a font of 1450, an altar painting by Lucas Cranach the Elder, icons in the chapel of St Anne (which is used by the Serbian Orthodox congregation) and the 17C Duve chapel, built by the entrepreneur Johann Duve, who also paid for the tower—hence the dove it carries. Today the church is at the centre of an entirely modern quarter of Hanover, which the citizens have proudly dubbed their Goldener Winkel (the golden corner).

Return to Ballhofplatz by way of **Burgstrasse**, amongst whose halftim-bered houses the 1566 Traufenhaus at No. 12 is the oldest in the city. Then turn right into Rossmühle to reach the river by way of the old stables' gate, incorporated into the Remy de la Fosse's **Rathaus** of 1714, the city's second. Turn left at the river bank to find the former arsenal, the **Zeughaus**, built 1643–49 and partly demolished in 1886. The **Beginenturm**, close by in Pferdstrasse, dates from the 14C and was the most powerful of the city's former defences. The **Historisches Museum** of the Hohes Upfer, in a building by Dieter Oesterlen, 1960–66, incorporating the Beginen tower and the former arsenal is devoted to city history, history of Lower Saxony and ethnology (open Tue–Sun 10.00–17.00). The ***Niedersächsisches Landesmuseum** at 5 Am Maschpark, built by Hubert Stier 1897–1902, contains prehistory, geology, ethnology, medieval art, and a rich collection of paintings from Cranach the Elder to the 20C, including works by Caspar David Friedrich, the Impressionists, Max Beckmann and Paula Modersohn-Becker (open Tue–Sun 10.00–17.00).

Cross the river by way of Schloss Strasse and the Schloss bridge, continuing W along Calenberger Strasse, with various ministries, to reach the Neustädter Markt, whose church, dedicated to **St Joannis**, is by the Venetian H. Sartorio, 1660–70. Its tower of 1700 was rebuilt in 1872, and again after World War II. Inside the church is Leibniz's tomb. The Baroque church to the N is the 1711–18 **Clemenskirche**, by another Venetian, Tommaso Giusti, with a dome added after World War II. Archivstrasse leads SE from here, passing on the left the state archives and the National library, by Remy de la Fosse, 1712–25, opposite which is a monument to General Carl Graf von Alten, who died in 1764.

Continue along Archivstrasse to **Waterlooplatz**, with the 47m-high **Waterloosäule**, a column of 1826, on which a goddess of Victory commemorates 800 Hanoverians who fell at the battle of Waterloo.

Return NE along Lavesallee and then SE along Friedrichswall to reach on the right the **Neues Rathaus** of 1900–13, with a domed tower 100m high, incorporating a curving lift to the top. Inside are three models of the city, as it was in 1689, 1939 and 1945. There are frescoes by Hodler in the Hodlersaal. Built by Hermann Eggert and Gustav Halmhuber, the Rathaus stands in marshy ground and is supported by 6026 beech piles. Civic fathers, ministers, churchmen, saints and monsters are carved on its façade, as well as a frieze of nine scenes depicting the city's history.

Behind the town hall is the **Maschpark** and a 74-hectares artificial lake, the **Maschsee**, created in the 1930s for water sports and sunbathing. The

Hanover broadcasting house stands to the W of the lake. NW of the lake is the Lower Saxon stadium, seating 6000 spectators (built by Richard Konwiarz and Heinz Goesmann in 1952 and modernised in 1974). Friedrichswall contains Laves's 1832 **Wangenheim Palais**, and the house he built for himself, the **Laveshaus**, 1822–24, now the tourism and congress office. Friedrichswall continues E as far as Aegidientorplatz, where you find the 14C **Aegidienkirche**, ruined but retained as a memorial to war dead. It has a kneeling woman by Professor Lehmann, and a peace bell, a gift of Hanover's twin city Hiroshima in 1985. The **Kestner Museum**, founded 1889, rebuilt 1958–61, housing the collection of August Kestner (a son of Goethe's friend Charlotte, née Buff), who was the city's representative at the Vatican from 1817–53 is at 3 Trammplatz (open Tue–Sun 10.00–16.00, times occasionally extended). The collection includes a bust of Akhenaten, c 1359 BC, the husband of Nefertiti.

From here take Georgstrasse NW to reach the **Opernhaus**, by Laves, 1845–52. Georgstrasse continues through the Kröpcke—turning to the left you find fashionable shopping, banks and street theatre—reaching the square **Am Steintor**, with another skyscraper to the N, the **Anzeiger-hochhaus** by Fritz Höger, 1928).

*A detail of the fifty hectare Baroque Herrenhausen garden, laid out northwest of Hanover between 1680 and 1714*

Follow the continuation of Georgstrasse, Lange Laube, on the other side of the square to reach Königswortherplatz. From here the pedestrianised Herrenhäuser Allee, laid out with 1400 lime trees in 1734, leads 2km NW to the Baroque **•Herrenhauser Gärten**, passing en route the university—in the former royal Schloss of 1857–66, the **Welfenpalais**, begun by Heinrich Tramm. The **Herrenhausen Museum** in the Schloss at 14 Herrenhäuser Strasse, built in 1721 for the illegitimate daughter of Georg I, houses 17C to 20C paintings from the royal household (open Apr–Sept 10.00–18.00; otherwise 10.00–16.00). Most of the garden Schloss was destroyed in World War II, though the Galeriegebäude of 1698, with its Baroque frescoes escaped. The Baroque geometrical **Grosser Garten**, restored in 1945, a rectangle 800m long, with its fountains, garden theatre, formal French garden maze and orangery, was laid out between 1666 and 1714. Surrounded on three sides by a canal, its conception was that of Sophie, wife of Ernst August, who had spent much of her youth in the Netherlands and sent her gardener Matin Charbonnier to study there. The main hedged parterre is bisected by a central axis, the whole divided into smaller gardens each with a different pattern. A star-shaped bosquet with an 80m water jet is surrounded by ornate lateral bosquets. A cascade created in 1676 has a *buffet d'eau* whose waters tumble over open shell work.

The botanical **Berggarten** to the N began as the kitchen garden, gained an orangery in 1686 and became the recipient of rare plants collected by Sophie, developing as a botanical garden only after 1750. Its greenhouses saw the first flowering of *Victoria amazonica* (Queen Victoria's water lily) and in 1893 the African violet. This garden surrounds the royal mausoleum, built by Laves in 1842. Grosser Garten opens daily 08.00–sunset; Berggarten daily 07.00–sunset; the greenhouses 08.00–sunset.

In the 18C Georgengarten to the left is the Palais Wallmolden, now the **Wilhelm Busch Museum**, which is devoted to the humorous works of Wilhelm Busch (1832–1908, creator of 'Max and Moritz') and the satirical sketches of Heinrich Zille (1858–1929).

The 112-hectare Deer Park (**Tierpark**) laid out in 1678 as hunting grounds for Duke Johann Friedrich, has some 200 fallow deer, as well as boars, wild horses and ancient trees. Hanover's swimming pool, the **Stadionbad**, was built between 1964 and 1972 by F.F. Grünberger, and the **Bundesleistung-szentrum Nord** by W. Ziegemeier and H. Pfitzner between 1974 and 1977. This is a training centre for top athletes, with public tennis courts.

OTHER MUSEUMS: The **Kunstmuseum**, in Kurt-Schwitters-Platz (open Tue–Sun 10.00–18.00); connected with the **Sprengel-Museum**, also in Kurt-Schwitters-Platz, built by Peter and Ursel Trint and Dieter Quast and opened in 1979, displaying 20C art (open Tue 10.00–22.00, Wed–Sun 10.00–18.00); the Veterinary Museum at 15 Bischofsholer Damm (open Mon, Tue, Fri 14.00–16.30 and by arrangement).

ENVIRONS: E of Hanover is the 650-hectare forest of **Eilenreide**, with the Annateichsee on the E side, and containing 300-year-old oaks, the **Hanover Zoo** and numerous restaurants. The zoo was founded in 1865, and has more than 1400 animals, with Indian elephants and the largest variety of antelopes in Europe, plus a seal house and a jungle house for the apes. SE are the **Stadthalle**, by P. Bonatz, 1913, with seats for 3700, and the impressive and huge industrial exhibition complex, the 970,000 sq m **Messegelände**, with the 83m-high Hermes tower and restaurant (found by taking Messeschnellweg E).

Further afield are the neo-Gothic **Schloss Marienburg**, 1860–68, 20km S via the B3 just before Nordsemmen; and 30km NW the **Steinhuder Meer**, off the B441, an extensive 32 sq km lake with sailing, swimming and surfing, and an island fortress built 1761–65 for Herzog Wilhelm von Schaumburg-Lippe. The village of **Steinhude** has a museum of toys and the world of children (open 08.00–19.00, closing 16.30 in winter). NE of Hanover, via the B188, the **Burgdorf** district offers extensive moors, fens, heathland, lakes, ancient half-timbered farmhouses, watermills and marked routes for hikers, cyclists and horseback riders. Burgdorf itself was rendered virtually to ashes by a fire of 1809, but it still has some halftimbered buildings, the finest being the Schloss and the Rathaus, and a 16C Baroque organ built by Hans Scherer in the church of St Pankratius.

# 53

# Lüneburg Heath

Total distance 151km. Hamburg—B5, 17km Bergedorf—10km Geesthacht—11km Schnakenbeck—B209, 22km Lüneburg—B4, 15km Bienenbüttel—20km Uelzen—56km Gifhorn.

Lüneburg Heath (Lüneburger Heide), once covered with forests, is today attractive heathland enhanced by scattered junipers and rosy heather. Long neglected as scrubland, it was discovered and celebrated by 19C writers and painters and today is a wildlife park, a favourite holiday and recreations region of Germany and prohibits motor cars and buses. It comprises the Naturschutzpark Lüneburger Heide, which covers some 200 sq km, the Naturpark Südheide covering some 460 sq km and the Naturpark Elbufer covering some 600 sq km.

Adenauerallee and Borgfelderstrasse lead SE out of **Hamburg** (see Rte 51) from the main railway station to **Hamm** whose Holy Trinity church was built by Reinhard Riemerschmid in 1957, and on to **Bergedorf** (on the B5), a town founded in the 9C whose moated and gabled Schloss, in Bergedorfer Schlossstrasse, dates from the 13C. The present buildings, mostly 16C, 17C and 19C, now house the museum of the region, with costumes, toys, furniture and household utensils (open Sun, Tue, Thu 10.00–17.00). Bergedorf's half-timbered guesthouse, the *Gasthof Stadt Hamburg, at 2 Sachsentor, dates from the 17C. See also the church of SS Peter and Paul, which was rebuilt on a mid-12C foundation in the 16C and has a tower of 1759. The town also has an observatory, of 1915.

  The environs of Bergedorf are known as the Vierlände, since they comprise four separate parishes, and are given over to market gardening. One of the parishes, **Curslack**, has an interesting open-air museum of the countryside, the Vierländer Freilichtmusueum Rieckhaus, at 284 Curslacker Deich (open Apr–Sept weekdays 08.00–17.00, weekends 10.00–18.00; winter Tue–Sun 10.00–16.00). Among several fine buildings stands the superb Rieckhaus itself, built in 1533 and renovated in 1663. The 14C St Johanniskirche of Curslack was rebuilt in part in 1600 and in 1801. Standing apart from the church is its lovely Baroque wooden belfry 1761.

The B5 continues 10km SE to reach **Geesthacht**, with its 18C church and fine views from the high bank of the Elbe. 11km further is Schnakenbek, from where an **excursion** further along the B5 takes you 4km E to **Lauenburg** (13,000 inhab.; alt. 45m) marking the SE point of Schleswig-Holstein, a town founded between 1230 and 1260 by Duke Albrecht I of Saxony. Lauenburg, sited at the confluence of the River Elbe and the Elbe–Lübeck canal, grew rich off the salt-trade. Here is a bridge for the railway and road traffic across the Elbe. There are 16C and 17C half-timbered houses in the lower town, while in the upper town are the remains of the Schloss of the Dukes of Sachsen-Lauenburg, which was partly burnt down in 1618. The oldest half-timbered house, built in 1573, stands in the Markplatz, close by the chuch of Maria-Magdalena, which was founded in the 13C and rebuilt in part in 1598, to be restored again in 1827. Inside are ducal tombs, with 18 sarcophagi in the crypt. A museum devoted to the navigation of the Elbe is housed at 59 Elbstrasse (open Mar–Oct weekdays 10.00–13.00, 14.00–17.00, weekends 10.00–17.00; in other months closing at 16.30 and lunchtime at weekends). From Lauenburg the Elbe–Lübeck canal, dug 1896–1900 along the lines of a late 14C canal, runs to Lübeck.

At Lauenburg the main route crosses the River Elbe and takes the B209 to reach after 22km the red-brick town of **LÜNEBURG** (65,000 inhab.; alt. 17m), lying in Lower Saxony on the E side of Lüneburg Heath—where the German High Command surrendered on 4 May 1945. This part of Germany is a land of strong traditions, especially in the countryside, though with the coming of modern methods of farming some of these have disappeared. 'About Lüneburg,' according to Sir James Frazer's *Golden Bough*, 'the woman who binds the last corn is called the Corn-goat'. Alas, women no longer bind the last corn at Lüneburg.

Lüneburg's thermal institutions treat sufferers from rheumatism and related diseases in a Kurzentrum set in a 32-hectare Kurpark. In the centre of the square called 'Am Sande' is the 14C brick Johanniskirche, with a massive 106m-high leaning spire; 16C stalls; an organ case of 1715; the organ of 51 registers and 4500 pipes by Georg Böhm; splendid chandeliers; and a *high altar dated 1430–85. Its reredos by Heinrich Furnhoff depicts SS John Baptist, Cecilia, Ursula and George. Am Sande houses numerous gabled buildings, with beautifully patterned brick, including at No. 1 the Schwarzes Haus of 1548, and a 17C gabled Baroque house at No. 16.

The Rathaus, the largest surviving medieval town hall in Germany, stands in Marktplatz and dates from the 12C, though most of it was rebuilt in the 14C and 15C, while the Baroque façade was added in 1720. Its loggia dates from c 1330, and was painted by M. Jaster in 1530. Lüneburg's Rathaus is flanked by 15C and 16C rooms still preserving their original decor, including the 15C Fürstensaal. The **main council chamber was built in the Renaissance style, 1566–84, panelled, with sculpture by Albert von Soest. The town hall also incorporates a tribunal, with paintings of the school of Memling and early 14C frescoes and stained glass, as well as a Baroque state room built in 1706 (guided tours Tue–Sun 10.00–15.00). Marktplatz is cooled by a 15C and 16C bronze fountain topped with a statue of Diana. East of the Marktplatz, at 14 Rotehahnstrasses, rises the three-gabled, half-timbered Stift Rotehan.

Other sights at Lüneburg include, to the N of Markplatz in Lüner Strasse, the 15C Gothic Nicolaikirche with its late 19C tower. Inside are a bronze font c 1300, the St Lambert altar by Hans Snitker the Elder, c 1450, and a high altar of 1448 by Hans Bornemann; a medieval crane of 1420; and Kloster Lüne, formerly a Benedictine house, standing on the outskirts of the

*Gabled houses, built of brick, enhance the main square (Am Sande) of Lüneburg. Note the medallions decorating a magnificent 16C building, and a crane poking out from one of its upper storeys*

city at 4 Bundesstrasse, which was built between 1379 and 1412 and possesses fine late 15C tapestries, a Renaissance pulpit of 1608 and a baldacchino of 1524. Its cloister is 16C. Today it is a Lutheran ladies' institution (guided tours Apr–Oct weekdays 09.00–12.00, 15.00–18.00, Sun 11.30–13.00, 14.00–18.00). In the street known as Am Berge rises the Glockenhaus, a former factory built in 1482, while in nearby Bäckerstrasse stands the lovely Renaissance Rathapotheke of 1598, its brick façade enhanced by a sandstone portal. In Johann-Sebastian-Bach-Platz stands the three-aisled hall-church of St Michael, 1376–1418, in whose crypt are the tombs of dukes of Brunswick-Lüneburg.

Cross the Ilmenau by the Lünebrücke to reach the district of the former port, the Wasserviertel. Here stand the Alter Krane of 1797 and the Altes Kaufhaus, the former merchant house, only its façade of 1745 original, after a fire in 1959.

The Ostpreussisches Landesmuseum at 10 Ritterstrasse is devoted to regional culture (including silverware and pottery), to regional natural history and to east Prussian art (opens weekdays 10.00–12.00, 15.00–17.00, weekends 10.00–12.30). The Deutsches Salzmuseum in Sülfmeisterstrasse is dedicated to all aspects of salt (including its commercialising), the trade which made Lüneburg rich (open weekdays, except Mon, 10.00–18.00, weekends 10.00–17.00). The Museum für das Fürstentum Lüneburg at 10 Wandrahmstrasse opens weekdays, except Mon, 10.00–16.00, weekends 11.00–17.00, displaying religious art, chiefly of the 15C, local history and customs as well as prehistory and local ethonography. There are also two reconstructions of ancient peasant living rooms. The Kronen-Brauerei-Museum is at 39 Heiligengeiststrasse. This fine patrician house was transformed into a brewery in 1845. The Stadttheater at 3 An den Reeperbahnen hosts plays, opera, ballet and operetta. Information office at the town hall.

From Lüneburg take the B4 SE for 15km to the summer resort of **Bienenbüttel** in the Ilmenau valley. You here find a Gothic reredos c. 1520 in the parish church. 11km SE is the small spa of **Bad Bevensen**, with modern facilities as well as Kneipp cures, with Kloster Medingen, a Cistercian monastery founded in 1336 and rebuilt in the Baroque style after a fire of 1781, as well as a natural history museum (the Museum Schliekau in Kurze Strasse, open May–Sept Mon and Thu 16.00–18.00). Drive 14km SW to **Ebstorf**, to find a Benedictine abbey of 1160, with a Gothic cloister, a 14C church and the reproduction of a 13C map of the world whose original has unfortunately perished.

**Uelzen** (25,000 inhab.; alt. 35m) is 12km SE. 'Near Uelzen, in Hanover, the harvest festival begins with "the bringing of the harvest goat"', Sir James Frazer noted in 1922, explaining that the woman who bound the last sheaf was wrapped in straw, crowned with a harvest-wreath, and brought in a wheel barrow to the village, where a round dance took place. Today Uelzen is noted for its two markets—the Griepemarkt and the Kiekemarkt—and its half-timbered houses as well as its Gothic Marienkirche, which was built in the 13C and rebuilt after World War II. Inside is the 13C nave, known as the 'Goldener Schiff', as well as a 15C chandelier, the memorial tomb of Prior Stillen, who died in 1702, and a mid-18C Rococo organ. Heiliggeistkapelle, 1321, in Lüneburger Strasse, has a 15C stained glass window and a 16C altar of the Virgin. The local history museum is at 36 Lüneburger Strasse (open in summer Tue–Fri 15.00–17.00, Sat 10.30–12.30). Information office at 43 Veersserstrasse.

An **excursion** 16km E, is to **Suhlendorf**, where there are numerous windmills, visitable save Monday.

The B4 now runs for 56km to Gifhorn, passing half-way there—(B244) on the left towards **Wittingen**, with its half-timbered houses and 16C church **Hankensbüttel**, where you find the church of St Pankratius and a brewery museum (open Wed and Sat 14.00–18.00, Sun 10.30–12.30). 1km S stands **Kloster Isenhagen**, a monastery of 1243, with a winged altar of the Virgin, 1520, and a Baroque font and pulpit, both dating from 1621. **Gifhorn** (30,000 inhab.; alt. 65m), situated at the confluence of the Ise and the Aller and boasting half-timbered houses and in the Hauptstrasse the Kavalierhaus of 1540, was rebuilt after a fire of 1519. The Guelph fortress had been transformed into a Renaissance Schloss by 1581, with a chapel of 1547, restored in the 17C and 19C and now a museum (local history, opening times vary at present). The Baroque parish church of St Nikolaus was built between 1733 and 1744. Here is an international windmill museum (open 10.00–18.00, closing earlier in winter).

# 54

# The Harz

## A.  Seesen to Brunnbachsmühle

Total distance 47km. Seesen—B243, 7km Münchehof—B242, 8km Clausthal-Zellerfeld—26km Braunlage—6km Brunnbachsmühle.

**Seesen** (23,000 inhab.; alt 250m) lies at the beginning of the so-called Harz high road (Harzhochstrasse), in the W parts of the wooded Harz mountains. Founded as Sehusa in the 10C, the town retains the 16C Renaissance part of a moated Schloss founded in the 13C, as well as a Kurpark with lakes. Here was born the piano maker William Steinway, who in 1835 gave this park to the town. The Baroque church of St Andreas was built between 1673 and 1702, though its tower was added only in 1956. Inside is an 18C altar with a baldacchino. The local history museum in Wilhelmsplatz (opening times vary) is housed in a half-timbered 18C hunting lodge, and other half-timbered houses line Lange Strasse and Am Markt. Burg Sehusa in Wilhelmsplatz was first built in 974, rebuilt in the Renaissance style in 1592 and modified in 1699. Finally, a couple of new wings were added in 1870 and 1885. Trains connect Seesen with Brunswick and Hildesheim.

From Seesen the B243 runs for 7km S to Münchehof, a summer resort, alt. 210m, meeting here the B242, which leads SE for 7km to where a diversion 2km SW leads to Bad Grund. **Bad Grund** (3300 inhab.; alt. 350m), the oldest of the hill towns of the Harz, stands at the foot of the 563m-high Iberg, and is noted for its winter sports, its thermal and mud baths, and the stalactites and stalagmites of the 150m-long Iberg cavern, which was discovered in 1874 (visits May–end Oct 09.00–17.00, otherwise 10.00–16.00). Here too children can be diverted in the so-called 'Indian village' and the 'fairy-tale valley'. In the Marktplatz rises the church of St Antonius, 1640, its tower square, its dome octagonal, surrounded by half-timbered houses.

8km from Münchehof the B242 reaches **Clausthal-Zellerfeld** (16,000 inhab.; alt. 560m) situated amidst woods and 66 mountain lakes. Its *parish church is an unusual treat. Dedicated to the Holy Spirit, it was built of spruce wood between 1639 and 1642, and has an oak tower and dormer windows. This is Germany's largest wooden church, and boasts a clock tower, a Baroque pulpit sculpted by Duder in 1642 and a Baroque organ and altar. Nearby rise the Bergamt of 1727–31, with a Rococo salon, and the Berg-apotheke of 1674. The town has swimming pools; an open-air theatre; is given to summer and winter sports; and has a Technische Universität with a *mineral collection (Mineraliensammlung) at 2 Adolf-Römer-Strasse (open Mon 14.00–17.00, Tue–Fri 09.00–12.00). A celebrated mining school and a museum of mining, the Oberharzer Bergwerksmuseum, can be found at 16 Bornhardtstrasse in the suburb of Zellerfeld (open Tue–Sun 09.00–13.00, 14.00–17.00). See also in Zellerfeld the 17C church of St Salvator, which was rebuilt in the Gothic style in 1863. Numerous buses service the town. Information office at the Kurverwaltung at 5a Bahnhofstrasse.

The Harz high road continues 26km SE towards Braunlage, passing the Sperberhaier Damm Haus from which the B498 leads for 5km to **Altenau**.

This is a summer and winter sports centre, with an 18C wooden church, close by the **Brocken**, with its 114m-high peak, the highest in the Harz. The health resort of **Braunlage** (7000 inhab.; alt. 560m), with its ice stadium and monster ski-jump lies close by the 972m-high **Wurmberg**, the highest peak in western Germany, and the 926m-high **Achtermann**. Peaks are reached by a cableway. Buses connect with neigbouring towns. Information office at 17 Elbingeröderstrasse. 6km further the Harz high road reaches **Brunnbachsmühle**.

# B.   Hildesheim to Hohegeiss

Total distance 156km. Hildesheim—B243, 11km Gross-Düngen—14km Bockenem—16km Seesen(—24km Bad Gandersheim)—12km Gittelde—10km Osterode am Harz—B241, 13km Katlenburg—B247, 25km Duderstadt—20km Herzberg—20km Bad Sachsa—5km Walkenried—6km Zorge—4km Hohegeiss.

**HILDESHEIM** (103,000 inhab.; alt. 89m) stands on the NW side of the Harz mountains on the Mittelland canal and has been an episcopal see since 815, founded under Emperor Ludwig the Pious.

**Information Office**: 5 Markt. The nearest **airport** is at Hanover (50km). **Trains** connect Hildesheim with Brunswick, Hameln, Hanover, Goslar, etc.

**History**. Legend has it that out hunting, Ludwig left a reliquary concealed in a rose bush, which—as a result of divine pique—froze, even though the season was high summer, hence Ludwig's foundation, as an act of penitence. A market town since the 11C, Hildesheim prospered so that a new town was founded c 1220—and not finally united with the old town until 1803. After the deliberate destruction of the medieval inner city in an air raid of 22 March 1945, the cathedral, and the churches of St Michael and St Andreas in particular, have been splendidly restored.

The huge market square, SE of the main railway station and post office, houses the rebuilt Gothic Rathaus, which was founded in the 13C, and the Tempelhaus, a building of 1457 which escaped destruction in World War II. It is decorated with a Renaissance oriel of 1591. Beside it stand the Wedekindhaus of 1598, with a decorated oak façade, the üntzelhaus of 1755 and the Baroque Rolandstift whose magical entrance was spared destruction in 1945. Other fine buildings in the Marktplatz include the Backeramtshaus of 1800, the Knochenhaueramtshaus (built in 1529 and now part of the Roemer Museum), the Rokokohaus of 1757, the Stadtschenke of 1666 and the Wollenbergildehaus of 1600. The Marktplatz centres on a fountain set up in 1402 and embellished in 1540.

From here Hoher Weg leads S to the nearby Gothic church of St Andreas, whose dimensions are 78m by 35m, with a middle nave 28m high. Built in the 14C and 15C, the church was rebuilt after World War II. The choir, originally 14C, has an ambulatory. The church's Romanesque lower tower was raised to its present height of 114m in the 19C. Inside is the second largest church organ in Germany (cf. the Stephansdom in Passau), on which Georg Philipp Telemann studied.

Continue S by way of St Bernward's hospital and Hinterer Brühl, with the half-timbered Wernesches-Haus of 1606, to reach in Brühl Godehardplatz on the S side of the moated old city the Romanesque basilica of ˚St Godehard. The only church to escape the bombardment of March 1945, St Godehard was built between 1133 and 1172. It boasts an octagonal, pointed tower. On the north door is a tympanum of Christ and two saints, c 1205. The interior has Romanesque *capitals and mid-15C Gothic choir stalls, as well as an ambulatory and a Benediction altar of 1518. In the treasury is the 12C Albani Psalter and a 13C chalice. The surrounding streets contain most of what remains from the half-timbered houses of the old city and include the sole remaining tower of the old fortifications, the Kehrwieder-turm of 1465.

From the Kehrwiederturm walk E along Kesslerstrasse and then N to pass the 15C Lambertikirche and reach the Neustädter Markt. NW of the Neustädter Markt the route leads to the Heiligkreuzkirche, once a city gate and transformed into a church by Bishop Hezilo in 1079. As it stands today the church is complex, with a Baroque façade of 1712, a Romanesque nave, a Gothic south aisle, a Baroque north aisle, while the galleries, transept and choir remain Romanesque. Its rarities include a 13C stone Madonna, a font of 1529, an 18C organ, a Baroque pulpit and the altar of the Virgin Mary which was created in 1700.

Walk W along Kreuzstrasse to the Domhof and the Romanesque *Dom of St Maria. Destroyed in 1945, Hildesheim's Dom was well rebuilt in its original style. Its artistic treasures are rich. The Ottonian bronze doors of 1015 display 16 reliefs from the Old and New Testaments. Bishop St Bernward (who died in 1022) gave the 3.80m-high Christ column, which weighs seven tonnes and carries scenes from the life of Jesus and John the Baptist. The Hezilo chandelier was made in 1061 and was given by Bishop Hezilo (1054–79). The bronze *font, supported by four kneeling figures representing the rivers of paradise, dates from c 1230. In the Romanesque cloister is a rose tree that has blossomed here since the 13C. The cathedral treasury (open Sun 12.00–17.00, Wed 10.00–19.00, Sat 10.00–16.00) houses the silver cross of St Bernward, 1007, and the mid-12C Oswald reliquary. Hildesheim cathedral was given its Baroque decorations under Prince-Bishop Joseph Clemens, 1724–30.

Continue W to reach the *Roemer-Pelizaeus Museum at 1–2 Am Steine, one of the best endowed in Germany. Its ancient Egyptian collection, is fabulous, perhaps its finest piece a statue of Prince Hem On, c 2600 BC. The museum has an equally fascinating prehistoric collection, as well as works from ancient Rome and the Graeco-Roman era (open Tue–Sun 10.00–16.30). Take Dammstrasse by way of the Damm gate further W to reach the Romanesque Mauritiuskirche in Moritzberg, built between 1058 and 1068 by Bishop Hezilo. This church has a Romanesque crypt and 12C cloisters. The upper part of the tower was completed in 1765. Its Baroque decorations date from 1744. It also shelters Hezilo's tomb, which was carved in the late 17C.

Return along Dammstrasse and turn N along Burgstrasse, which leads to the extremely fine church of **St Michael (in Michaeliplatz), with its six towers and double apse. Bishop Bernward (died 1022), who is buried in the crypt, founded the church in 996. The main church was finished in 1033, the choir added in the late 12C. Its architecture is mathematically complex, the square of the crossing repeating itself 16 times in the rest of the church. 15C late Gothic windows adorn its south aisle. The church has a 13C late Romanesque painted wooden ceiling, including a Jesse tree and possibly the earliest depiction of Adam and Eve, and a sculpted font of 1618.

Leave Hildesheim by the Alfelder Strasse and drive SE on the B243 for 11km to Gross-Düngen. Here, an **excursion** 2.5km S leads to the forest health resort of **Bad Salzdetfurth**, with its mud and salt baths and campsites.

The B243 continues through the Hildesheim forest for 16km before reaching **Bockenem** (12,000 inhab.; alt. 102m), with its Gothic church of St Pankratius, its motor museum (open Apr–Oct weekends and holidays 10.00–12.00, 13.00–18.00) and its steeple clock and local history museum (open Fri 16.30–18.00, Sun 10.00–12.00). Follow the B243 another 16km S to **Seesen** (see Rte 54A).

**Excursion** The B64 leads 24km W from Seesen to the thermal resort of *****Bad Gandersheim** (12,500 inhab.; alt. 125m), the home of Germany's first woman poet, the nun Roswitha von Gandersheim (935–1001). Its former collegiate church of SS Anastasius and Innocentius was founded in 852, though the present building is 11C Romanesque with two 15C towers, five 15C chapels and an exceedingly impressive Westwerk. Inside you find five armed bronze candelabra, c 1425; a Bartholomäus altar, c 1490; the Lady altar of 1521; the 15C altar of the Magi; and a mid-18C tomb in the Andreas chapel. E of the church is the mid-11C chapel of St Michael. The Renaissance abbey buildings are the work of Heinrich Overkate, 1599–1600, with a Kaisersaal built in 1730. The 15C church of St Georg is built on a Romanesque foundation, with a high altar of 1711.

Bad Gandersheim also possesses numerous half-timbered houses, especially surrounding its Marktplatz, a 16C Schloss, a *****Renaissance town hall of c 1580, and the former Benedictine monastery church of SS Maria and George, with a Lübeck altar of 1487. The local history museum is housed in the town hall (open Apr–Oct Mon, Wed 10.00–12.00, Fri 16.00–18.00). Train connections with Brunswick.

26km due N of Bad Gandersheim is **Lamspringe**, where a Benedictine monastery was founded in 847. Its church, 1670–91, is now the Catholic parish church, has a *****high altar by Johann Mauritz Gröninger, 1695, altar paintings by Hieronymus Ses of Antwerp and choir stalls by Heinrich Lessen the Elder.

From Seesen the B243 continues SE through **Gittelde**, which is reached after 12km. 10km further on from this town of 18C half-timbered houses, lies another health resort, **Osterode am Harz** (32,00 inhab.; alt. 230m), its name perhaps deriving from Ostara, the goddess of spring. Two towers, the Pulvertum and the Sonnenturm, remain from its fortifications of 1233. Osterode's 1552 Rathaus, with a polygonal oriel and a Baroque cupola, is close by the traffic-free Kornmarkt, with its 16C half-timbered houses.

The town's church of St Aegidien, with a powerful bronze belfry, was built in the 13C, burned down in 1545, and rebuilt from the mid 16C to the mid 20C. Its font was created in 1589; it shelters tombs of the Herozöge von Grubenhagen; it boasts a Baroque altar 1660; and it rises in the Marktplatz. The former Schloss church of St Jakobi, in Jakobitorstrasse was built in 1218 and next belonged to the Cistercians. St Jakobi was restored in the 18C and in 1976. Osterode has a Kornhaus in Eisensteinstrasse, dating from 1719–22. N of the Kurpark stands the church of Our Lady, which was begun in 1258, rebuilt after a fire of 1430 and restored in 1658. Inside is a late Gothic Lady altar of 1517. Tilman Riemenschneider lived here as a young man. The local history museum is at 32 Rollberg (open except Mon, weekdays 10.30–16.00, weekends 10.00–12.00). Train and bus connections with Hildesheim. Information at the Kurverwaltung. The nearby Söse reservoir is Germany's largest (for drinking water).

Take now the B241 for 13km SW to **Katlenburg**, at the confluence of the Rhume and the Oder, where you find a 16C ruined Schloss, and then the B247 SE along the Rhume valley, reaching after 25km *****Duderstadt**. Still

walled with the Westertorturm (towered gate), Duderstadt offers a remarkable ensemble of some 400 half-timbered houses. Amongst the finest is the
13C Rathaus, which was repeatedly enhanced until 1533 and boasts
arcades, asymmetrical spires, a half-timbered upper storey and a Glockenspiel in the west spire (playing at 09.00, 11.00, 13.00, 15.00, 17.00 and
19.00). Close by the Rathaus in Marktstrasse rises a Mariensäule (or column
with the Virgin Mary) near to which is a Renaissance house of 1620 (No.
84).

Many more half-timbered houses grace Apothekenstrasse. An especially
beguiling one stands at 6 Marktstrasse, while the Steinernes Haus of 1752
rises at 91. Another half-timbered house serves as the local history museum,
built in 1767 at 3 Oberkirche (open except Mon 10.00–12.00, 15.00–18.00;
closed Sun afternoons).

The town's priory church of St Cyriakus was begun in 1394 and finished
in the 16C. It has a mid-19C high altar, 15 Baroque figures on the pillars
and a Baroque organ by Johann Kreutzberg, 1733–37. Duderstadt also has
the Gothic church of St Servatius, which was burned down in 1915 and
rebuit 1917–18. Nearby (10km NW) stretches the Seeburger See, with
swimming and water sports facilities.

From Duderstadt drive N by way of **Rhumspringe**, with Germany's most
prolific sping, to reach after 20km **Herzberg** (18,000 inhab.; alt. 245m), with
its 12C Schloss and its pedestrianised quarter lined with half-timbered
houses. The town is dominated by a 16–17C Schloss, begun in 1286, which
now houses a forestry museum and a museum of lead figures. Do not miss
nearby the 400m-long Einhorn cavern, where Goethe claimed that the
ancient bones discovered in the cave were those of unicorns.

From here the B243 runs 20km SE to Bad Sachsa. The route passes S of
Germany's oldest Kneipp health resort, the holiday centre of **Bad Lauter-
berg im Harz**. The heart of the spa is the church of St Andreas, built in 1536
and rebuilt in 1736. St Andreas is surrounded by half-timbered houses.
Outside the town rises ruined Schloss Scharzfels, built in 952, and there is
a chairlift to the Hausberg.

The health resort of **Bad Sachsa** (9500 inhab.; alt. 325m), close by the
650m-high Ravensberg, is a noted winter sports centre and boasts the
Baroque church of St Nikolaus and a Jugendstil Rathaus. It lies 5km NW
of **Walkenried** (2950 inhab.; alt. 275m), which retains the ruins, including
the cloisters, 1294, of a Cistercian monastery destroyed by Thomas
Münzer's followers during the Peasants' War. From Walkenried the route
runs N by way of the wooded health resort of **Zorge** (1700 inhab.; alt. 340m),
which is famous for its charcoal, reaching after 10km **Hohegeiss** (1600
inhab.; alt. 642m), one of the highest spots in the Harz and noted for its fir
trees.

# C. Hameln to Bad Harzburg

Total distance 102km. Hameln—B1, 23km Elze—8km Heyersum—10km
Hildesheim—B6, 33km Salzgitter Bad—15km Goslar—5km Oker—8km Bad
Harzburg.

Leave **Hameln** (see Rte 48) and drive 23km E along the B1 by way of
**Coppenbrügge**, with its ruined Schloss and mid-16C late Gothic church,
with a Baroque reredos of 1685, to the industrial town of Elze, and another

18km through Heyersum, N of which is **Schloss Marienburg**, a neo-Gothic building of 1860–68, to **Hildesheim** (see Rte 54B).

33km E of Hildesheim along the B6 is the health resort of **Salzgitter Bad** (116,000 inhab.; alt. 138m), with a former Benedictine monastery church, built from 1504 to 1694, the tower added a year later. This church was extended c 1790, and its Rococo interior shelters a wooden crucifix of c 1000. The Protestant parish church of St Jakobi dates from the mid 18C. The city museum is in the 17C Schloss, which stands in Hinte dem Knick and was built mostly by Paul Francke in the early part of the century (open Tue–Sun 10.00–17.00). Train connections with Bad Harzburg, Brunswick and Hanover. Tourist information at the railway station. In the region are mined Germany's richest veins of iron ore.

15km further SE is **GOSLAR** (53,000 inhab.; alt. 320m), lying on the northern rim of the Harz, a winter sports resort exploiting the 726m-high **Bocksberg**.

**Information Office**: 7 Marktplatz. **Trains** connect Goslar with Bad Harzburg, Brunswick and Hanover; **buses** to other localities.

**History**. Goslar was already prosperous in the 10C, since the nearby Rammelsberg was rich in silver, copper, lead and zinc. Emperor Heinrich II made it his capital in the early 11C, and here in 1056 Pope Victor II and Henrich III staged an historic meeting, and when Heinrich died on 5 October of the same year, the pope was entrusted with the care both of the empire and Heinrich's five-year-old son. Goslar joined the Hanseatic League in the 13C, when it also became a Free Imperial City. Although the city fathers quarreled over religion with the powerful Dukes of Brunswick in the mid 16C, only in the 17C and 18C did the city fall into relative decline. Savagely attacked during the Thirty Years War, Goslar next suffered two devastating fires, in 1728 and 1780. Annexed to Hanover between 1815 and 1866, the city then became part of Prussia. As a hospital-city during World War II, happily Goslar completely escaped destruction.

Leave the main railway station, crossing the square and reaching Rosentorstrasse. To the left is the powerful Achermann tower (1501), behind which is the richly decorated *Neuwerkirche, a Romanesque former Benedictine abbey church completed in 1186. The church boasts 13C west towers; Byzantine-style wall paintings, 1230, including a Madonna enthroned; and a stone rood screen of 1230, with statues. Close by is the hospice of 1719.

Follow Rosentorstrasse, looking left down Mauerstrasse for the remains of the medieval fortifications—the **Weberturm** and the **Teufelsturm** (Devil's Tower)— to Jakobikirchhof and the **Jakobikirche**. Founded by Bishop Hezilo of Hildesheim, this 12C Romanesque church was Gothicised in the 15C. Inside are 13C and 16C frescoes, as well as a Pietàin painted limewood by Hans Witten of Brunswick, c 1520, and 17C Baroque altars carved by Heinrich Lessen. The font dates from 1592, the pulpit from 1620 and the organ from 1640. To the S side of the church is Jakobistrasse leading to the 1528 **Mönchehaus** at 1 Mönchestrasse, which is now a museum of modern art (open, except Mon, 10.00–13.00, 15.00–17.00; closes Sun afternoon), with works by Max Ernst, Alexander Calder and Joseph Beuys. At No. 15 a house of 1612.

Rosentorstrasse leads by way of Fischemäkerstrasse to the **Marktplatz**, with its bronze fountain of 1230 surmounted by the imperial eagle. Here the former drapers' guild house, the **Kaiserworth** of 1494, is decorated with Baroque statues of eight German emperors and mythical subjects—notably Hercules and a Renaissance naked man called the 'Dukatenmännchen', symbolising in his crude fashion the city's right to mint its own money. A

**Glockenspiel** was set up on the façade of No. 6 in 1968 to commemorate a thousand years of silver mining (chiming at 09.00, 12.00, 15.00 and 18.00). Close by rises the twin towered Romanesque-Gothic **Marktkirche** of SS Cosmas and Damien. Its 13C stained glass depicted the martyrdom of the patrons; its bronze font by Magnus Karsten, 1573; the pulpit was created by Hans Seck in 1581, with biblical scenes from Adam and Eve to the Ascension of Jesus; and altar painting of 1659 by Andreas Duder. This church's asymmetrical towers were rebuilt in the mid 19C. Goslar's **Rathaus** stands E of the church. Built from the 11C to the 17C, this is mostly late Gothic, with arcades, gables and an open-air staircase of 1537. Its late Gothic *council chamber has wall paintings c 1500 and the Rathaus incorporates a tiny frescoed chapel of 1506 (visits in summer 09.00–18.00; winter 10.00–16.30). In front of this town hall gushes a Romanesque fountain, its two bronze basins set up in the 13C, on top of which is the imperial eagle—the emblem of Goslar.

Opposite the twin towers of the church, at the corner of Hoher Weg and Bergstrasse, is the bizarre house known as the **Brusttuch**, with satirical and biblical carvings by Simon Stappen. It was built in 1526. In a house built 1510 at 5 Hoher Weg, is the **Museum für Musikinstrumente mit Puppenmuseum** (open Apr–Oct 10.00–18.00, otherwise closing at 14.00) with over 500 musical instruments of diverse kinds, as well as toys, puppets and figurines. To the N of the church of SS Cosmas and Damien, **Schuhhof** contains fine old houses, as does nearby **Münzstrasse**—at No. 10 for example the former 15C and 16C mint, and at No. 11 the 17C 'Zum Weissen Schwan'. Hoher Weg leads to all that remains of the Dom, which was pulled down in 1820, namely the mid-12C narthex, with the 11C imperial throne on which Kaiser Wilhelm I sat to announce the Reichstag of 1871. The **Domvorhalle**, the best preserved remnant of the cathedral, in Kaiserbleek (open Jun–Sept weekends 10.00–13.00, 14.30–17.00; winter weekends 10.00–12.00).

To the W of the cathedral remains, in the vast square known as Kaiserbleek, is the imperial palace—the *Kaiserpfalz*—built under Heinrich II (1039–56), with the great hall, decorated with late 19C frescoes and the early 12C chapel of **St Ulrich**. The lower part of this chapel is a Greek cross, the upper part an octagon. The whole was restored in the 19C (open May–Sept 09.00–18.00; otherwise 10.00–16.30). The Kaiserpfalz was the home of eleven German emperors from 1050 to 1253. Heinrich III's heart is buried in the chapel.

Other delights are the **Siemenshaus**, the family house built by an ancestor of the inventor Werner von Siemens in 1693 (museum open weekdays 09.00–12.00); the **Kleines Heiliges Kreuz**, a hospice founded in 1254 and rebuilt in 1686, which has a doorway of 1510 and a chapel sheltering a Gothic tomb and a Baroque crucifix; and the Romanesque **Frankenberger Kirche** of SS Peter and Paul. This was begun in 1108 and has 13C ogive vaulting. Its Baroque west tower dates from 1786. Inside are 13C frescoes, depicting Abraham meeting Melchizedek, Jesus judging the world, David and Solomon, the Archangel Gabriel and the Madonna and Child. Inside too are Baroque carvings, including an altar by H. Lessing the Elder.

The ramparts, with remarkable views and including the 16C wide gate on **Breites Tor**, and the powerful tower known as **Zwinger**, which dates from 1517; the birthplace of Marshal Hermann Maurice of Saxony (1696–1750) at 95 Breite Strasse; the ruined 11C hospice of St Peter; the 15C hospice of St Ann add to Goslar's charm. **Stephanikirche**, which was rebuilt in 1730, after a fire and has an 18C altar. The **Goslarer Museum** at 1

Königstrasse (open weekdays 09.00–13.00, 14.30–17.00; Sun 10.00–13.00) has exhibits relating to 100 years of local history.

Continue SW along the B6 to reach **Oker**, 5km from Goslar, with its ironworks and chemical factories, as well as the Romkerhalle waterfall, which tumbles 6km S. After another 8km the route ends at the health resort of **Bad Harzburg** (27,000 inhab.; alt. 300m) at the beginning of the Radau valley, surrounded by the peaks of the Rabenklippe(555m), Kästeklippe (602m) and Burgberg(483m). The ruined Schloss from which the town derives its name was built by Heinrich IV in 1065. Bad Harzburg is a spa enhanced by the 11C and 12C Martin Luther Kirche, and by the 14C St Andreaskirche, which has early 17C modifications. Train and bus connections with Hanover, Goslar and Brunswick. Information at the Kurverwaltung.

# 55

# Hanover to Helmstedt

Total distance 101km (via the motorway 82km). Hanover—B5, 42km Peine—11km Vechelde—B1, 12km Brunswick—21km Königslutter am Elm—8km Süpplingen—7km Helmstedt.

Alternative route from Brunswick to Helmstedt. B4, 10km Wolfenbüttel—13km Schöppenstedt—B82, 15km Schöningen—B244 11km Helmstedt.

By the Hans-Böckler-Allee leave **Hanover** (see Rte 52) E to join the B65, which runs for 42km to the industrial town of **Peine** (28,000 inhab.; alt. 80m), with its many oil rigs. 11km E of Peine is Vechelde, where the B1 leads right for 12km to **BRUNSWICK** (German **Braunschweig**). Brunswick (262,000 inhab.; alt. 72m), the second largest city in Lower Saxony, lies between two streams of the River Oker, close by the Mittelland Canal and in the midst of the fertile Lower Saxony plain.

The main **post office** and **information office** are in the main railway station. **Trains** connect Brunswick with Hanover, Helmstedt and Hildesheim.

**History**.Brunswick was founded in 860 by Bruno and Dankward, the two sons of Ludolf of Saxony. Henry the Lion (Heinrich der Löwe, 1129–95), who made the city his permanent home in 1166 (and died here), gave Brunswick its city charter, and in 1247 the city joined the Hanseatic League. Around 1300 the citizens managed to free themselves from ducal control. At the time of the Reformation Brunswick supported the Protestants. In 1671 Duke Rudolf August von Braunschweig-Wolfenbüttel became ruler of the city. His successors resided here from 1753 to 1918, though the city was part of the Napoleonic Kingdom of Westphalia from 1803–13, and in 1834 the citizens again gained the right to run their own affairs. In World War II destruction was colossal. A new main railway station was built in 1960, and in 1974 the city took in 22 surrounding suburbs.

The jester Till Eulenspiegel, was born c 1300 SE of Brunswick at Schöppenstedt (see below). The first performance of Goethe's 'Faust' was given here in 1828. Gottfried Ephraim Lessing (1729–81) is buried in the graveyard of the Magnifriedhof. The novelist Wilhelm Raabe (1831–1910), whose pseudonym was Jakob Corvinus, was born at Eschershausen and settled in Brunswick in 1870, remaining in the city until his death.

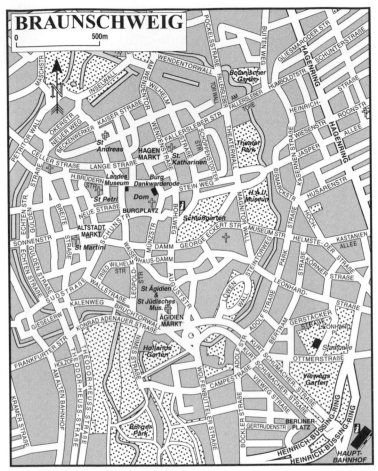

Walk NNE from the main railway station along Altewiekring to find on the left the Stadthalle, to the W of which is the main cemetery, where are buried Gottfried Ephraim Lessing (born 1729, died in Brunswick 1781) and the novelist Friedrich Gerstäcker (who died in Brunswick 1872). Continue along Altewiekring and turn left into Leonhardstrasse, where stands the **Wilhelm Raabe Museum** (open Wed, Fri, Sun 11.00–13.00).

From here Steinweg runs W to the Ruhfäuchtenplatz, which houses **'Burg Dankwarderode**, at the centre of the old city. The Schloss, said to have been built by Dankward in the 9C, was rebuilt by Henry the Lion in 1170. It was restored in the Romanesque style in 1873 after a fire, and again after World War II. Its Knappersaal houses medieval art and sculpture from the Herzog-Anton-Ulrich-Museum (see below; visits Tue–Sun 10.00–16.00). To the W of the Schloss the bronze lion set up in 1160 by Henry the Lion stands on its pillar. (This is Germany's first free-standing sculpture.)

S is the Romanesque *Dom of St Blasius (1173–1250) which Henry the Lion founded on his return from the Holy Land. The cathedral is remarkable above all for its mid-15C twisted pillars and nave vaulting. Its Westwerk has two octagonal towers. The side aisles of 1340 were extended by more aisles in 1469. The south transept dates from 1894. Inside is Henry the Lion's tomb and that of his wife Mathilde. The daughter of Eléanor of Aquitaine, she died in 1189, and her tomb was sculpted c 1250. Other tombs include that of Duke Otto, died 1344 and his wife Agnes of Brandenburg. The cathedral also houses a seven-branched candelabrum made for Henry the Lion; the wooden *Imerward crucifix, c 1160, inscribed 'Imevard me fecit'; Romanesque wall paintings; and tombs of the Dukes of Brunswick from 1687 in the crypt, which has *wall paintings, 1220–40.

To the E stands the neo-Gothic **Rathaus**, built by Winter in 1899 with a 61m-high tower, as well as the magnificently sculpted Guildehaus of 1536, the **Veltheimhaus** of 1573 and an 1804 building housing the Brunswick **Landesmuseum** (open daily 10.00–17.00), with extensive displays relating to regional culture and history, as well as collections devoted to music, churches and theatre. From here continue E into the huge Schlossplatz with the 13C and 14C **Magnikirche**, which was modernised after World War II, by which is a fountain (1931) in memory of Wilhelm Raabe. Behind the church are half-timbered houses. From Schlossplatz walk along Am Magnitor and into Steintorwall to reach at No. 14 the Stadtmuseum (open Tue–Sun 10.00–17.00), whose collection relates to the city's long culture, particularly the work of its goldsmiths. Continue N by way of the Steintorwall into Museumstrasse. No 1 is the **Herzog-Anton-Ulrich-Museum**, named after Duke Anton Ulrich (1633–1714) who gathered together its collection of works by Rubens, Rembrandt and Vermeer van Delft. In addition the museum houses Italian Renaissance and Mannerist sculpture, paintings by Giorgione and Veronese; an arm reliquary of St Blasius; and Italian majolica (open, except Mon and religious holidays, 10.00–17.00, Wed closing 20.00). To the N is laid out the **Museumpark** and the **Theaterpark**, between which stands the **Staatstheater**, built in the Florentine Renaissance style in 1861, restored in 1948.

Take Steinweg W from the theatre and then turn right along Bohlweg to reach the huge **Hagenmarkt**, where you find the 13C and 14C **Katharinenkirche**. Begun by Henry the Lion c 1200, it was restored after World War II, and boasts a Gothic tower and a Baroque organ of 1620. The square centres on a fountain and statue of Henry the Lion, 1874. E of the square is the Romanesque *church of **St Andreas**. Built in the 12C, it was gothicised in the 13C and 14C, and has a 92m-high tower added between 1518 and 1532. From this church Alte Waage leads S to the 13–15C church of the Brothers (Brüderskirche). Its 15C Gothic stalls were painted by Reinhold Roggen, 1597, and include portraits of fathers of the Reformation as well as of 4C fathers of the church. The high altar was sculpted in 1420.

From this church the street called Hintern Brüdern reaches Bäckerklimt the **Eulenspiegelbrunnen**, with a statue of Till Eulenspiegel, 1906, whose drolleries tormented a baker in Bäckerklimt. Close by is the **Petrikirche**, founded in the 12C and extended in the next two centuries, with a tower of 1260–70 and 1960s stained glass.

Follow Breite Strasse S to reach the **Altstadtmarkt**, with the 15C Gothic fountain of Our Lady and the superb *Altstadt Rathaus. It dates back to the 13C and 14C; its statues are c 1460 (they depict Saxon and Guelph princes as well as dukes of Brunswick); and it was restored after World War II. S of the square are the **Gewandhaus** (Cloth House) of 1250, with a **Renaissance gable of 1590–91 by Hans Lampe, and the former customs house (**Zollhaus**) of 1643. W of the square stands the late 12C church of **St Martin**. This was modelled on the cathedral, though altered during the 13C and 14C. Its font, held up by four figures symbolising the rivers of paradise, was designed by Bartold Sprangken in 1441, as was the late Gothic chapel of St Anna.

Walk SE from the square to find the former Benedictine church of **St Aegidien**. Begun in the 12C, rebuilt in the 13C, its west end was finished in the early 14C. Inside is a late Gothic pulpit with reliefs by Hans Witten. Some 12C buildings remain from the former convent, including the chapter house. See also the city's natural history museum, the Staatliches Naturhistorisches Museum, at 10a Pockelsstrasse (open Tue–Sun 09.00–17.00, closing 19.00 on Wed. The oldest such museum in the world, founded 1754, it has a remarkable collection of tropical and other fish, as well as birds, reptiles and insects.

The late Baroque **Schloss Richmond** in Wolfenbüttelerstrasse, built by K.C.W. Fliescher, was commissioned by Duke Karl Wilhelm Ferdinand for his English wife Augusta in 1768. (Visits can be arranged through the tourist office.) The house of Wilhelm Raabe is at 29 Leonhardstrasse (open Wed, Fri, Sun 11.00–13.00).

Brunswick also has a **Botanischer Garten** (in Bültenweg), an ice stadium and a football stadium seating 32,000 spectators (both in Hamburger Strasse).

Continue E from Brunswick along the B1 for 21km to Königslutter am Elm by way of **Hornburg**, which has over 200 half-timbered houses, a former Rathaus of 1744 and the parish church of Beatae Virginis, 1616. The last houses a font of 1581, a reredos of 1660 and an organ console of 1715.

**Königslutter am Elm** (17,000 inhab.; alt. 123m), with its Marktplatz surrounded by half-timbered houses has an entrancing view of the Elm hills and forest. Its former cathedral was founded by Emperor Lothar in 1135 as the church of a Benedictine monastery. Look inside for its 12C Lombardic frieze in the apse; 14C vaulting; the 15C Gothic west end and Gothic spires; a 17C font; 17C vaulting in the nave; the tomb of Lothaire III von Süpplingenburg (d. 1137), by Michael Helwig, 1798; wall paintings of 1894, based on earlier work; and the *north cloister. The mineral and fossil collection of the textile magnate Otto Klages is housed at 1 Sack (open weekday mornings). The route continues 8km E through Süpplingen, 2.5km N of which is Süppplingenburg, the birthplace of Emperor Lothar.

Follow the B1 7km E to reach **Helmstedt** (28,000 inhab.; alt. 140m). As neolithic tombs, the Lübbensteine, on the St Annenberg to the W of the town indicate, Helmstedt has been inhabited for millennia. An important Christian settlement in the 9C and 10C, Helmstedt flourished between the 16C and the early 19C, when it was the seat of a Protestant university (the 'Juleum') whose late 16C Renaissance buildings still grace Juliusplatz. From the medieval defences survives the Hausmann tower, c 1500, in Neumärker Strasse.

The so-called double-chapel of SS Peter and John the Baptist in the Passhof began as a Carolingian chapel topped by an 11C Romanesque one, but today dates essentially from the 12C and 13C. It has medieval wall paintings and a dome of 1666. Initially this church belonged to a Benedictine monastery founded in the 9C. The monastery church of St Ludger was restored after World War II, with a Felicitas crypt. In Klosterstrasse is the former nunnery church of St Marienberg, blessed with a Romanesque nave and a Gothic choir of 1488, Romanesque stained glass in the north transept, wall paintings of 1250, and an *antependium c 1250 (which is displayed in the convent buildings).

The Brunnen theatre, founded in 1815, the present building dating from 1924–27, is at 7 Brunnenweg. The Kreisheimatmuseum (local history museum) is at 2 Bötticherstrasse (open weekdays 09.00–11.00, and on Mon, Sat 15.00–17.00, Sun 11.00–12.30).

Train links with Hanover and Berlin. Information office at 2 Lindenplatz.

## Alternative route from Brunswick to Helmstedt

10km S of Brunswick by the B4 lies **Wolfenbüttel**, where the dukes of Brunswick lived from 1432–1753 and Lessing was ducal librarian. Here was born Anna Amalia (1739–1807), Goethe's Weimar patron. Henry the Lion built its Schloss, though its present aspect dates from the 18C. It retains a Renaissance tower of 1614; the Renaissance hall of 1570; ducal apartments decorated by Hermann Korb, 1695; and 18C tapestries and furniture (open Tue–Sun 09.30–12.30, Wed, Sat also 15.00–17.00). The Herzog-AugustBibliothek, in a building of 1883–87 at 1 Lessingsplatz can also be visited (open Tue–Sat 10.00–13.00, 14.00–17.00; closed Sat afternoon), displaying the Gospels of Henry the Lion, incunabula; medieval manuscripts and maps; and 16C volumes, many in uniform pigskin bindings. In Schlossplatz the late Baroque house of 1781 where Lessing finished his 'Nathan der Weise' is now a Lessing museum (open Tue–Sat 10.00–13.00, 14.00–12.00).

These in no way exhaust the delights of Wolfenbüttel. Its Stadtmarkt is flanked by lovely half-timbered houses. E of the Stadtmarkt at 3 Kanzleistrasse rises the Alte Kanzlei of 1588, today the home of the Lower Saxon regional archives. In Klosterstrasse is the superb Renaissance *Hauptkirche Beatae Maria Virginis, work of the architect Paul Francke between 1607 and 1623. Finally, do no miss, on the E side of the town the Ludgerikloster, a monastery, the crypt of whose Romanesque chapel of St Peter and St Johannes is mid-8C Carolingian, while the monastery boasts another Romanesque church founded in the 11C.

**Schöppenstedt** lies 13km E, the birthplace of Till Eulenspiegel. Its museum is in Nordstrasse, with over 400 exhibits and a library of 1800 volumes (open weekdays 10.00–17.00, weekends 10.00–12.00). Schöppenstedt also has half-timbered houses of the 18C and 19C, and the 12C tower of the Stephanskirche. 15km further the B82 reaches the oldest town in the Land of Brunswick, **Schöningen**, which was founded in 748. Its 11C church of St Lorenz has nave vaulting added in the late 15C. In the Marktplatz rises the Gothic church of St Vincenz, 1429–60, renovated in 1644 after a fire. Its Baroque interior shelters an altar of 1647 and a pulpit of 1652. The Marktplatz is also enhanced by the Anna Sophianeum of 1593—the seat of a Latin school founded by Duchess Anna Sophia in 1623—and a Baroque tribunal of 1767.

Schöningen's Renaissance Schloss of 1569 has four irregular wings and two square, late medieval towers. In addition the town has 16C and 17C half-timbered houses.

**Helmstedt** (see above) lies 11km NE, on the B244.

# 56

# Hanover to Dortmund

Total distance 207km. Hanover—B217, 10km Weetzen—15km Springe—20km Hameln—B1, 15km Griessen—15km Blomberg—10km Horn-Bad Meinberg (—B239, 13km Detmold and the Hermann monument)—5km the 'Externsteine'—13km Bad Lippspringe—8km Paderborn—12km Salzkotten—7km Geseke (—13km Büren-Wewelsburg)—13km Erwitte—17km Soest—8km Ostönnen—6km Werl—16km Unna—17km Dortmund.

Leave **Hanover** (see Rte 52) by Deisterstrasse, taking the B217 SW for 10km to **Weetzen**, a point of entry into the hill country of the Weser (see Rte 48), W of which is the hilly range of the Deister. Drive for 15km more to reach **Springe** (15,000 inhab.; alt. 113m), a summer resort, with half-timbered houses and views of the 345m-high **Saupark** and the 419m-high **Osterwald**. On the corner of the Markt and Burgstrasse the Eckhaus of 1619 is entertainingly decorated with sculptures, while the Marienbrunnen in the Markt is an unusual blend of a Baroque fountain with a Judenstil top of 1903. At the W end of the Markt stands the former Rathaus of 1685 and the tribunal, a beguiling half-timbered late Baroque building of 1775.

**Bad Münder**, 5km W, has superb half-timbered houses, most of them Renaissance, including at 3 Kellerstrasse the Wettbergenschen Hof, a Renaissance building with an oriel window, its upper storey half-timbered. The Wettbergenschen Hof houses the local history museum (open Sat and first Sun in month). The classical Rathaus dates from 1815. 20km SW from Springe the B217 reaches **Hameln**(see Rte 48), having passed the 437m-high **Süntel** peak.

The B1 leaves Hameln SW, crossing the Weser and reaches after 15km **Griessem**, close by the 258m-high **Klüt** peak, with a view tower and restaurant. Griessem is a health resort boasting a superb Kurpark. After 15km the route reaches **Blomberg** (15,000 inhab.; alt. 235m), a gentle spot noted for its medieval half-timbered houses. On the S side of the old part of the town, the Niederntor remains from its former fortifications. Blomberg also has a Schloss begun in the 12C, set in a park with a 1000-year-old lime tree, and a Rathaus of 1587.

Beyond Blomberg, 18km from Hameln, lies another health resort, **Horn-Bad Meinberg** (18,000 inhab.; alt. 210m). S of the suburb of Horn is the •'Externsteine', a striking group of five sandstone rocks (one 3.75m high), carved with pagan motifs which were later transformed c 1120 into a carving of Jesus being lifted down from the cross. There is a chapel in the rock. We are now in the region of the Teutoburg woods, which mostly comprise oaks and conifers.

**Excursion**. 13km NW of Horn-Bad Meinberg lies **Detmold** (315,000 inhab.; alt. 134m), a furniture manufacturing city in the Werre valley and on the N slopes of the woods. Written history records Detmold as *Theotmalli* in 783. Here Charlemagne defeated the Saxons. Receiving its municipal charter in the 13C, Detmold was from 1613 to 1918 the principal seat of the Grafen (later Fürsten) zur Lippe. Today it is the home of the North German Music Academy. Here were born the poet Ferdinand Freiligrath (1810–76) and the dramatist Christian Dietrich Grabbe (1810–36).

Detmold's Marktplatz houses the 15C Erlöserkirche, with its 16C tower, topped with a Baroque bulb and sheltering a Baroque organ of 1795, a fountain of 1901 and the classical Rathaus of 1830. Freiligrath was born at No. 5 in the half-timbered Unter der Wehme; Grabbe died at No. 7. The princely Schloss was rebuilt by J. Unkair and C. Tönnis between 1551 and 1557, though they retained its medieval keep. Inside the Schloss are eight tapestries woven to designs by Jan Frans van den Hecke of Brussels in 1670 (visits Apr–Oct daily 09.00–12.00, 14.00–17.00; otherwise daily at 10.00, 11.00, 15.00 and 16.00).

Other museums are also fine buildings. Detmold's Baroque Neue Palais, which dates from 1706–18, now houses the North German Music Academy. Its garden, initially laid out in the French style, was transformed into an 'English' garden in 1865. The Lippisches Landesmuseum is at 4 Ameide, housed in a 19C classical building, which is linked to 16C half-timbered buildings (open Tue–Sun 09.00–12.00, 14.00–17.00), its collection expounding the region's past bourgeois and religious life, as well as its crafts and costumes.

Trains and bus connections with Herford and Osnabrück. Tourist information at the town hall.

S of Detmold a group of peasant and farm houses have been reconstructed, in 80 hectares, at the **Krummes Haus** (open Apr–Oct 09.00–18.00).

6km SW of the city is the 386m-high Grotenburg, where Ernst von Bandel erected the **Hermannsdenkmal** in 1838–75. It commemorates the legendary defeat of the Romans by the chieftain Arminius in 9 AD. Almost 20m high, Arminius brandishes a 7m-long sword. You can visit the monument in summer 08.30–18.30, in winter 09.30–17.30, and from it is a fine panorama of the Weser mountains and Detmold. At the foot of the hill is the **Vogelpark** (open daily spring–autumn 09.00–18.00), with some 2000 indigenous and exotic birds.

The B1 continues SW from Horn-Bad Meinberg, reaching after 13km the thermal resort of **Bad Lippspringe** (10,000 inhab.; alt. 150m), situated at the Senne, heath land on the S side of the Teutoburg woods. Bad Lippspringe has an open-air swimming pool and a ruined Schloss, as well as two sources of the River Lippe—hence the name of the spa. Tourist information at the Kurverwaltung. 8km SW is **Paderborn** (see Rte 47B).

Leave Paderborn SW by the B1, reaching after 12km **Salzkotten**, with its 13C ruined Schloss and half-timbered houses. After 7km in the same direction the B1 reaches **Geseke**, with its 12C and 13C nunnery church.

A **diversion** 13km S leads to **Büren-Wewelsburg**, where stands a Schloss, built in the Weser Renaissance style between 1604 and 1607 and now serving as a local history museum, with grim memorials of the Niederhagen concentration camp, run by the SS from 1933 to 1945 (open Tue–Sun 10.00–12.00, 13.00–18.00). Less forbidding monuments here are the 12C church and the 18C church.

The B1 continues from Geseke SW, arriving after 13km at **Erwitte**, with its 12C church of St Laurentius and a moated Schloss. **Lippstadt** lies 7km N on the B55. A former Hanseatic town founded on the River Lippe by Bernhard von Lippe in the 12C, its architectural treasures include the 13C and 15C Marienkirche, with a Gothic reredos on a Baroque altar as well as a painted ceiling. Lippstadt also has a ruined 14C Augustinian monastery. The Haus Goldener Hahn of 1566, at 12 Lange Strasse, is the oldest in Lippstadt. A half-timbered former brewery stands at 12 Rathausstrasse. The town's museum is in the partly Rococo Haus Köppelmmann, at 13 Rathausstrasse (open Tue–Sat 10.00–12.00, 15.00–18.00, Sun 10.00–13.00).

17km SW of Erwitte is **Soest**, a town of narrow winding streets and seductive ancient houses. Once a leading member of the Hanseatic League, the site was inhabited long before then in the 7C BC, but the foundation of the present city dates back to the 7C AD. Converted to Christianity under Charlemagne, Soest was placed under the rule of the Archbishops of Cologne, to whom its leading citizens were continually insubordinate, finally emancipating themselves in 1449. In 1531 Soest became Protestant, a Lutheran oasis in a Catholic land. The Dukes of Cleves, Princes of Brandenburg, determinedly attempted to suppress the city's independence, and this task was completed by Frederick the Great in 1751.

Encircled with walls in the 16C, Soest now utilises the *Osthofentor as a museum of arms and local history (open Apr–Sept weekdays except Mon 14.00–16.00, Wed also 14.00–16.00, Sat, Sun 11.00–13.00, Sun also 15.00–17.00). Its other bastion is the 16C *Katterturm. Soest retains its (restored) cathedral-collegiate church of St Patroklus. Begun in 954, its present aspect dates from c 1100 to the late 12C. Its glory is its Romanesque tower. Inside are the 11C Westwerk, 13C Romanesque stained glass and in the choir some traces of Romanesque frescoes dating from 1165. Ovr the high altar is a 15C crucifix. The Dom Museum is at 2 Propst-Nübel-Strasse (open Sat 10.30–12.30, 14.00–16.00, Sun 11.30–12.30, 14.00–16.00, when you can also visit the cloister).

In the same square rises the five-aisled 12C and 13C Petrikirche, with its 13C–15C *frescoes (restored in 1950), a Westwerk, a 15C crucifix and Gothic vaulting. A third church retaining Romanesque wall paintings is Maria zur Höhe. Built in 1225 it shelters a *high altar enriched with paintings of the Passion, c 1480.

In Thomässstrasse stands the 12C Nikolaikapelle, with an altar painted by Konrad of Soest as well as more Romanesque frescoes. The church of Maria zur Wiese, built in the 14C with 15C towers, and finished in the 19C, rises in Wiesenstrasse and has late 14C *stained glass—whose Last Supper is renowned for its setting in a typical Soest tavern, offering beer, ham and local Pumpernickel—and an altar by H. Aldegrever c 1520. Aldegrever's engravings are displayed in the Galerie Wilhelm Morgner Haus, at 3 Thomästrasse (open Mon–Sat 10.00–12.00, 13.00–17.00, Sun 10.00–12.30).

The local history museum is in the Burghof at 22 Burghofstrasse, which is partly 1559, partly early 13C Romanesque (open except Mon 10.00–12.00, 15.00–17.00, Sun 11.00–17.00). See also the 16C Haus zur Rose in Marktstrasse.

**Werl** (30,000 inhab.; alt. 90m), which lies 14km SW by way of Ostönnen, is notable for its 12C Romanesque church. Werl also has a Gothic priory church of St Walburga with a Romanesque tower. It boasts a calvary group of c 1520; 15C and 16C altars; and a 17C Pietà. Seek out also the 18C pilgrimage church of the Capuchins; a 13C Madonna and Child in the Franciscan church of 1903–05; and a local history museum at 1 Am Rykenberg (open Tue, Wed, Fri 14.00–16.30, Thu 16.00–18.30, weekends 10.30–12.30). The Franciscans run a missionary museum at 15 Meisterstrasse (open weekdays 09.00–12.00, 13.00–17.00, Sun 11.00–12.00, 15.00–17.00).

After 16km the B1 reaches **Unna** (55,000 inhab.; alt. 103m), an important coal and industrial centre of the Ruhr, with salt and thermal baths in the suburb of Unna-Königsborn. Its Protestant parish church, built between 1322 and 1467, has an ambulatory, a tabernacle of 1451 and a Baroque pulpit of 1667. Unna's late 17C Schloss was renovated in the 19C and 20C;

the local history museum, known as the Hellweg-Museum, is in an 18C Schloss at 8 Burgstrasse (open weekdays except Mon 10.00–12.30, 15.00–17.00, Sat 11.00–13.00, Sun 11.00–13.00, 15.00–17.00).

Unna is 17km from the former Hanseatic city of **DORTMUND** (618,000 inhab.; alt. 87m), the largest and one of the oldest cities in Westphalia, with a harbour on the Dortmund-Ems canal covering 192-hectares, and including nine docks, whose role as a centre of sporting events has been increasingly developed, whose beers are renowned.

**Tourist information**: 6 Südwall and 8 Königswall.

**History**. First known in the 9C as *Throtmanni*, when the Carolingian kings established here a settlement to guard the rich Hellweg, Dortmund developed into a Free Imperial City in 1220 and a member of the Hanseatic League, defended by mid-13C fortifications—marked today by the circle of streets named Königswall, Burgwall, Ostwall, Südwall and Hoher Wall. The Thirty Years War ruined its trade and Dortmund began to prosper again only in the mid 19C, when its iron and steel works were massively developed, as well as its breweries—the most productive in Germany. After World War II 90 per cent of the city had to be rebuilt. Dortmund university, 3km SW, was founded in 1968.

In front of the main railway station climb the steps to Westenhellweg (with fine shops, such as are also in Ostenhellweg) to find the three-aisled Petrikirche. Built in the 14C and restored in 1963, it has a 115m-high tower, and a huge **high altar—the largest in Westphalia—created in 1521 by Master Gilles of Antwerp, with 633 gilded statues, carved out of oak depicting 48 scenes. The rear of the altar has paintings of the legend of St Emerentia, held to be the great-grandmother of Jesus. Continue S to the Propsteikirche on Schwarze-Bruder-Strasse. It was built in the 14C, and the church and cloister were restored in 1965. It shelters a winged altar by Derick Baegert, 1480, with a view of Dortmund in one panel; a 15C tabernacle; a sandstone Madonna, 1420; and the Rosenkranz altar created by Master Hildegardus of Cologne, 1519. Next comes the Marienkirche on Ostentorwall. Built from the 12C to the 14C and restored in 1957, inside are a 12C painted oak Madonna and Child; an altar c 1390 and another by Konrad von Soest c 1420; late Gothic choir stalls of 1523; and 1970s stained glass by Johannes Schreiter.

Adjoining the Marienkirche is the *Reinoldikirche, dedicated to the patron saint of Dortmund. Founded in the 11C and rebuilt in the 13C, the Reinoldikirche was restored in 1956. Its 105m-high Baroque tower was finished 1701, having tumbled down in 1611, and carries the heaviest set of bells in the Land. Other delights in this church are the 15C statues of Charlemagne and St Reinold; the font of 1469 by J. Winnenbrock; its late Gothic high altar; and the modern stained glass windows in the choir by Gottfried von Stockhausen.

Walk along the W side of Marienkirche to reach the Markt, with the Westphalian Civic Library (Haus der Bibliothek, 1957). The civic theatre, 1958–66, is on Hansastrasse.

**Museums**. The Museum am Ostwall displays works by 20C artists (Erich Heckel, Max Beckmann, Ernst Ludwig Kirchner), particularly those reviled by the Nazis (open except Mon 09.30–18.00, Sun 10.00–14.00); the Natural History Museum at 271 Münsterstrasse (open except Mon 10.00–18.00, Thu to 20.30); a Brewery Museum at Märkische Strasse 95 (open except Mon 10.00–18.00); and the City Art and History Museum at 34 Ritterhausstrasse (open except Mon and Sat 10.00–17.00).

Other sights are the **Volkspark**, SW of the city at 25 Am Kaiserhain, whose Westphalian Halls of 1925 (rebuilt in steel and glass by Walter Hötje in 1952) seat 24,000 and whose stadium seats 54,000. Annual events include show jumping in March and races in October. The complex comprises an ice rink, a rose garden (with 3200 varieties) and a running track. S is the 70-hectare Westfalenpark, whose TV tower, the 'Florianturm', (220m-high) has a revolving restaurant (137m-high). The park leads SW to the botanical gardens and the zoo, in Rombergpark, whose Schloss Romberg dates from 1682. Further S is the Bittermark forest.

Dortmund's southernmost suburb is **Syburg**, whose Hengstey lake has been devoted to water sports. Nearby are two panoramas, from the Kaiser Wilhelm memorial and the Saxon *Schloss Hoheynsburg, which Wittukind ceded to Charlemagne in the 8C, and whose church dates from the 12C. Syburg is also blessed by the 13C church of St Peter.

# 57

# Hanover to the Dutch border via Osnabrück

Total distance 186km. Hanover—B65, 28km Bad Nenndorf—13km Stadthagen—14km Bückeburg—10km Minden—23km Lübbecke—21km Harpenfeld—B51, 24km Osnabrück (—B51, 15km Bad Iburg)—B65, 40km Rheine—16km Schüttorf—5km Bentheim—8km Dutch border—175km Amsterdam.

The B65 leads W from **Hanover** (see Rte 52) reaching **Bad Nenndorf** after 25km. This spa (4200 inhab.; alt. 71m) lies on the slopes of the Süntel (part of the hill country of the Weser, see Rte 48) and has sulphurous springs and mud baths. The panorama from the 146m-high **Rodenberg** is impressive.

Continue W along the B65 for 13km to reach the old town of **Stadthagen** (17,000 inhab.; alt. 68m), whose 16C gabled town hall in the Marktplatz is set amid other 16C houses. Other delightful survivals from past times are the 16C half-timbered Amtspforte, and the 16C Schloss in Obernstrasse, which is built in the style of the Italian Renaissance. In the Schloss garden stands a late 16C summerhouse, while in front of the Schloss is the 16C Kavaliershaus.

Stadthagen has also preserved some early 15C fortifications, and the church of St Martin, at 3 Am Kirchhof. Begun in 1318, with 15C and 16C extensions, the church has an altar of 1585; a 16C pulpit; and late 16C panelling and tombs. The Baroque *mausoleum adjoining the church was built for Fürst Ernst von Schaumburg and his family by J.M. Nosseni, 1609–25, with sculptures by A. de Vries, including a marble **Resurrection. The local history museum in Obernstrasse opens Wed, Sat 15.00–17.00, Sun 11.00–12.30.

The B65 now runs SW through (14km) **Bückeburg** (see Rte 48) and (10km) **Minden** (see Rte 48). 23km W of Minden is **Lübbecke** (11,000 inhab.; alt. 100m) at the foot of the 319m-high **Wurzelbrink** (which is topped by a tower). Lübbecke has a Renaissance town hall; a ruined 13C Schloss; and a local history museum in the 16C Burgmannshof, in the market square (open Tue–Fri 10.30–12.00, 15.00–16.30, Sat 10.00–12.00).

21km W of Lübbecke along the B65 is Harpenfeld. 1km S on the wooded Wiehengebirge, the western extension of the hill country of the Weser, lies the spa of **Bad Essen** (3000 inhab.; alt. 190m) with its salt springs and its 13C church. The B65 now runs 24km SW into **Osnabrück** (160,000 inhab.; alt. 64m), situated on the River Hase and the third richest economic centre of lower Saxony.

**Tourist information**: 22 Markt. Osnabrück hosts a summer music festival and a picturesque children's peace parade on 25 October.

**History**: After Charlemagne had overcome the Saxons in this vicinity in the year 783, he built a church on the site of the present cathedral of Osnabrück, around which the city developed and prospered. By the end of the next century Osnabrück was minting its own money and an important trade centre. Its fortifications were built under Frederick Barbarossa in the mid 12C. A new town had developed, centred on the church of St Johann, and this was merged with old Osnabrück in 1306. Osnabrück became an important member of the Hanseatic League. Here, and in Münster, the preliminary negotiations took place which in 1648 led to the end of the Thirty Years War.

After the peace the Bishops of Osnabrück were alternately Protestant and Catholic. The prince-bishops who ran the city developed strong diplomatic and dynastic relationships with France in the 18C, relationships that have left artistic traces on Osnabrück. Numerous émigrés escaped here from the French Revolution. In the last quarter of the 19C Osnabrück again began to expand, and most of its fortifications were demolished. Much was destroyed in World War II, to be carefully restored or rebuilt. The university was founded in 1970.

Here was born the novelist Erich Maria Remarque (1898–1970), author of 'All Quiet on the Western Front'.

From the main railway station Möser Strasse (named after the historian and statesman Justus Möser, 1720–94, who was born and died at Osnabrück) leads NW past the main post office, and reaches Schillerstrasse. The **Herrenteichswall**, which abuts onto Schillerstrasse, contains the remains of the old fortifications—the Helling Wall, the Pernickel tower, now in a garden, and the two Helling towers.

Left of the Herrenteichswall can be seen across the Hase the three towers of the **Dom**, badly damaged in 1944, but restored by 1952. Dedicated to St Peter, this cathedral, founded by Charlemagne in the late 8C and destroyed by the Saxons, was begun again in the 11C, with an octagonal tower added in the early 12C. The nave and choir were rebuilt between 1218 and 1277, after a fire. Twenty-eight altars were built in the 14C. The northwest tower was added in the 13C, the ambulatory in the 15C and the southwest tower in the 16C. In the nave are eight splendid sandstone statues of the Apostles, 1525. Other treasures include a cross c 1250; a bronze *font of 1225, depicting the baptism of Jesus and the apostles Peter and Paul; 16C statues of the apostles; a tomb statue of Bishop Konrad von Diepholtz, who died in 1482; a 15C Pietà; the Baroque pulpit which J.A. Vogel designed in 1751; and in the south transept the tomb of Ferdinand von Kerssenbrock, which was designed by J.C. Schlaun in 1754. The choir stalls date from 1900.

The **Diözesanmuseum** houses a cross of c 1050 and the largest collection of chalices in Germany (open weekdays except Mon 10.00–13.00, 15.00–17.00; weekends 10.00–13.00). In front of the cathedral is the episcopal chancellery, the Bischöfliche Kanzlei, by F. Schädler, 1783, and a bronze statue of Justus Möser, created by Drake in 1836.

Across the Domhof is the three-sided **Markt**, with the late Gothic
*Rathaus, 1487–1512, from whose open-air staircase the Peace of West-
phalia was proclaimed. The town hall is enriched with sculptures of
German emperors and kings, including Charlemagne. Inside is the Peace
Hall, where the treaty was drawn up. The council chamber furnishings date
from 1554 and the Rathaus has a 16C wrought-iron candelabrum. The
**Schatzkammer** (open Tue–Fri 10.00–13.00, 15.00–17.00, Sat, Sun 10.00–
13.00) includes a 14C 'Imperial goblet' (the 'Kaiserpokal'), with Renaissance ornamentation.

Opposite the town hall is the 14C Gothic **Marienkirche**, bombed in 1944
and well restored. It has a gabled west end, with sandstone statues, and a
Bride's doorway. Inside you find the tomb of Justus Möser; an Antwerp
retable of the Passion, 1530, above which hangs a cross c 1320; and a font
by Johann Beldensnyder, 1560.

Return to the cathedral and walk N along Hasestrasse to the **Vitischanze**
of 1636 (now a restaurant) and the **Barenturm** of 1471, a tower from the
former fortifications. From here follow the site of the fortifications SW by
way of Hasemauer to reach the 1519 Bürgerhorsam tower, which once
served as a gaol, opposite which is the former **Dominikanerkirche** dating
from the 14C. From the Dominican church cross Rissmüllerplatz.
Bierstrasse, which leads from here back to the Markt, boasts old houses,
especially at No. 24 the **Walhalla** of 1690. Continue S to find the **Bucksturm**,
a tower now housing a museum of torture, with instruments that have
tortured among others Anabaptists and witches. Outside is a World War I
memorial by Hosaeus, 1922. Further S is the **Hegertor**, a monument to the
dead of Waterloo set up in 1817. At 27 Heger-Tor-Wall are Osnabrück's
**Museum für Kulturgeschichte**, its paintings including works by Jan
Brueghel the Elder and Jan Vermeer, and the Natural History Museum
(both open weekdays except Mon 09.00–17.00, Sat 10.00–13.00, Sun 10.00–
17.00).

Continue S along Heger-Tor-Wall and turn left along Katharinenstrasse
to find the 14C church of **St Katharine**, with its 103m-high tower. S of this
church in Neuer Graben rises the 18C **Schloss** of the prince-bishops, built
by P. Carato, rebuilt after a fire in 1945, and now a school. Follow Neuer
Graben E to reach the Neumarkt, from which **Grosse Strasse**, with its
Baroque houses, leads N, and Johannissstrasse leads S to the Gothic
**Johanniskirche**. Built between 1256 and 1291, it has mid-15C sandstone
sculptures of Christ, his mother and the apostles; a tabernacle, c 1440; and
a carved altar of 1511.

See also the Romanesque church of **St Gertrud**, in Gertrudenberg, N of
the city, which was begun in the 13C as the church of a Benedictine
nunnery; the abbess's house, 1757–65, also survives.

Osnabrück's civic theatre, in the Domhot, is a Jugendstil building of 1909.
The football stadium is at 10 Schlosswall, the central sports complex in
Ernst-Sievers-Strasse.

**Environs.** 4.5km N are to be found two **prehistoric tombs**, the great and
the small Karlsteine; 4km E are two more; the Teufelsteine and the
Hermannsteine. 14km E is the moated **Schloss Schelenburg**, built by J.
Unkair, 1528–32, who preserved a Romanesque keep.

15km S of Osnabrück the B51 reaches the spa of **Bad Iburg**, devoted to
Kneipp cures, with a hill-top Benedictine abbey, founded in 1070, though
the church was rebuilt in the 13C and 15C. It has a stucco ceiling by J.
Geitner, the 11C tomb of Bishop Benno and a chapel of 1665. The present

abbey was designed by J.C. Schlaun, 1751–53). Bad Iburg's further architectural pleasures include the Protestant church of 1607, and the 17C
prince-bishops' Schloss, which was decorated by the Italian A. Aloisi, and
has a knights' hall of 1656, designed by J. Crafft, as well as the 331m-high
Dörenberg.

From Osnabrück to the Dutch border the B65 runs for 40km to **Rheine** (see
Rte 47B). After 17km you pass through the industrial town of Schüttorf,
reaching after another 5km **Bentheim** (14,500 inhab.; alt. 50m). Here has
stood a Schloss since the 10C, rebuilt for the Princes of Bentheim in the 15C
and 17C, but retaining its 13C chapel and towers. On the terrace stands a
sandstone *crucifix dating certainly from the 12C and perhaps from the
11C. (Bentheim quarries were for centuries an important source of sandstone and supplied the builders of Bremen town hall.) The town museum
is at 28 Schlossstrasse (open daily 09.00–17.00). To the N of the town is a
popular spa and casino. Tourist information at 2 Schlossstrasse. Trains
connect Bentheim with Hamburg and the Hook of Holland.

Bentheim is 8km from the Dutch border.

# 58

# Hamburg to Emden via Bremen, Oldenburg and Wilhelmshaven

Total distance 319km. Hamburg—B4, 15km Harburg—B73, 9km Neugraben-
Fischbek—12km Buxtehude—10km Horneburg—13km Stade—B74, 28km
Bremervörde—29km Osterholz-Scharmbeck—9km Burgdamm—B6, 13km Bre-
men—B75, 13km Delmenhorst—25km Oldenburg—B69, 13km Rastede—19km
Varel—37km Wilhelmshaven—B210, 12km Jever—8km Wittmund—25km
Aurich—B72, 11km Georgesheil (—B90, 16km Norden)—16km Emdem.

Jever—11km Schloss Gödens. Jever—Carolinensiel-Harle, the islands of
Wangerooge and Spiekeroog, and the other East Frisian islands—total distance 20km, excluding the trips to the islands.

Leave **Hamburg** (see Rte 51) S by the B4, reaching after 15km **Harburg**
(see Rte 51). From Harburg drive W along the B73 through hilly woods. At
Neugraben-Fischbek, the route borders to the N on the Altes Land, a
vegetable, cherry and apple region whose fertility and old farmhouses were
created by Dutch settlers in the 12C and 13C and whose main towns include
the pretty little village of **Jork**, c 11km N, with its 17C church and a 17C
Rathaus.

12km W of Neugraben-Fischbek is the former Hanseatic town of **Buxtehude** (32,000 inhab.; alt. 5m), the chief town of the Altes Land which is set
beside the Este, a tributary of the Elbe. Buxtehude appears in a document
of 959 as Bouchstaden and became a member of the Hanseatic League in
1363. Amidst its picturesque streets stands the 12C church of St Peter, which
was reordered as a brick North German Gothic church in the 14C Its pulpit
dates from 1674, its high altar from 1710. You can explore here the
excavated foundations of a former Benedictine cloister; restored medieval
houses; the 'Marschtorzwinger' from the old fortifications; and the local

history museum in a mid-17C building at 9 St Petriplatz (open, except Jan, Tue, Wed, Fri 11.00–16.00, Sun 11.00–15.00).

The route now enters the strawberry, plum and cherry country known as the **Lühe**, reaching after 10km Horneburg and then running NW for 13km to reach **Stade** (45,000 inhab.; alt. 7m), another former Hanseatic town. Stade once lay on the Elbe, since when the river changed course, so that the present harbour is on a tributary 5km from the main waters. Destroyed by the Vikings in 994, Stade was rebuilt by the local counts. From 1648–1712 Stade belonged to Sweden; from 1712–1715 to Denmark. Its chief glories are the 13C church of SS Cosmas and Damian, noted for its Baroque spire of 1682 on the crossing. Its barrel-vaulted nave was built in the 13C. Its furnishings are late 17C, save for one 15C altar, with a pulpit of 1663 and a carved marble font of 1665. The high altar of 1674 is by C. Precht. the *organ, the first work of Arp Schnitger, was completed in 1688.

SS Cosman and Damian stands next to the late Gothic hall-type Wilhadikirche, dating back in parts to the 12C, with groin vaulting; a Baroque organ by E. Bielfeldt, 1735; and the tomb of Johannes Pahlen, who died in 1686. Half-timbered houses shade the Altstadt. The finest secular buildings of Stade are the medieval *Burgermeister-Hintze-Haus, with a *Baroque façade added by Mayor Heino Hintze in 1621; the house of the Brauerknechte, built in 1604; the Rathaus of 1668, with its 15C Gothic cellars and on its façade the sculpted coat of arms of the Swedes; and the Arsenal of 1698.

Museums include at the picturesque, restored harbour the Schwedenspeicher Museum, built in 1705 situated on Am Wasser West, and devoted to prehistory and medieval history (open Tue–Sun 10.00–17.00) and the Alte-Stade in Baumhaus, in a farmhouse of 1773 on the site of an earlier one of 994, situated on Am Wasser Ost (open Mar–Oct Sat 15.00–18.00, Sun 10.00–12.00, 15.00–18.00; otherwise Sun 15.00–18.00). The local history and open-air museum is at 12 Inselstrasse (open May–Sept Tue–Sun 10.00–12.00, 14.00–17.00). Trains connect with Bremen and Hamburg. Tourist information at the town hall.

From Stade the B74 leads SW through peat and cattle country for 18km to reach **Bremervörde** (18,600 inhab.; alt. 4m) on the River Oste. Its museum at 8 Amstallee is devoted to the pre- and early history of the district (open weekdays 08.00–12.30; Sun 14.00–16.30). At Bremervörde are the remains (stables) of former Burg Vörde. The tourist authorities have laid out 78 marked walks and hikes through the moors and woods, and the town has modern swimming pools. The route continues on the B74 to the end of the Teufelmoor to **Osterholz-Scharmbeck** (29km, see Rte 60) and then for 9km to Burgdamm, joining here the B6 which runs 13km S to **Bremen** (see Rte 60).

From Bremen the B75 leads 13km W to the industrial town of **Delmenhorst** (78,000 inhab.; alt. 18m), which has modern swimming pools and a modern sports complex. You can ascend the tower of the Jugendstil town hall, which was designed in 1910–13 by Heinz Stoffregen. Delmenhorst has a 17C and 18C parish church. Tourist information at the railway station. 25km W of Delmenhorst lies **Oldenburg** (137,000 inhab.; alt. 7m), the administrative seat of Weser-Ems, set on the River Hunte. A university town, as well as an industrial centre, its old city has been preserved, at least in so far as it remained intact after a fire in 1676 (see below).

**Tourist information**: at 3 Lange Strasse. **Trains** connect with Bremen, Emden, Hamburg and Wilhelmshaven; **buses** with Bremen, Aurich and Wilhelmshaven.

**History**. Oldenburg first appears in written history in 1108 as *Aldenburg*. The Counts of Ammerland chose it as their family seat in 1150, and Oldenburg received its municipal charter in 1345. After the death of Count Anton Günther (1603–67) Oldenburg passed into the hands of the Danes. The plague devastated the city in the following year, and in 1676 almost every old building was burned down in a disastrous fire. The Grand-Dukes of Holstein-Gottorf lived here from 1773–1918. Oldenburg was a free state from 1918 to 1945. Its university was founded in 1970.

From the railway station follow Bahnhofstrasse SW and then Gottorpstrasse S to reach the Grand-Ducal Schloss. Medieval in origin, rebuilt in the late 16C, partly rebuilt in the 18C and 19C, it remains an impressive late Renaissance palace. The Holmerscher wing was added in 1778, the theatre in 1899. The Schloss now serves as the Landesmuseum für Kunst und Kulturgeschichte (open except Mon 10.00–13.00, 15.00–17.00; closes Sun 13.00), with a large collection of works from the Middle Ages to the 20C. Johann Heinrich Wilhelm Tischbein (1751–1829) the first Galerie-Inspektor of the Dukes, visited Rome with Goethe and their *Idylls* are commemorated in a cycle of paintings in the Tischbein Room. In the 18-hectare Schlossgarten, laid out in 1806, is the 19C neo-Renaissance Elisabeth-Anna-Palais. Follow Dammstrasse SE to reach the Museum für Naturkunde und Vorgeschichte (open weekdays except Mon 09.00–13.00, 14.00–18.00; weekends 09.00–13.00). Return to Schlossplatz and find NW the Gothic church of St Lambert, restored in the 18C and 19C, 12 pillars supporting its cupola. W of the church, Theaterwall leads to the Staatstheater 1893.

Other sights include, in the Markt, the Haus Degode (built in 1618, restored in the 19C), opposite which is the Rathaus of 1887. In Lange Strasse at No. 76 is the 17C frescoed house of Count Anton Günther and at No. 3 Oldenburg's oldest building, the Lappan, built in 1468 as part of the former Heiligen-Geist-Spital, with its tower and a golden clock. The exhibition hall, Weser-Ems-Halle, was built in 1954. The botanic garden is laid out NW of Oldenburg. In the Gertruden cemetery is a chapel, the Grand-Dukes' mausoleum, with 15C wall paintings.

12km NW of Oldenburg is the 3km by 2.5km **Zwischenahner Meer**. The local spa of Bad Zwischenahn has thermal establishments and mud baths.

From Oldenburg the B60 leads N, reaching after 13km **Rastede**, a health resort with an 11C church of St Ulrich, which boasts a 15C belfry; a mid-13C stone font; a pulpit of 1612; and in the crypt a very early 12C sarcophagus of a princess of the Schleswig-Holstein-Beck family. Rastede's *schloss park was laid out in the English style in the 19C, when the Schloss was given its classical aspect. After 16km the route reaches a road that leads right for 3km to **Varel** (25,000 inhab.; alt. 13m) on the Jadebursen. Varel has a 13C Schloss church, in which you can enjoy 15C frescoes, an early 17C *altar and a font and pulpit by Ludwig Münstermann. The local history museum is at 3 Neumarkt (open Tue–Sun 15.00–18.00). 6km to the N, **Dangast** is a bathing resort that was founded in 1797.

Return to the B60 and drive 24km N to **Wilhelmshaven** (105,000 inhab.; alt. 12m), lying at the western end of the Jadebusen.

**Tourist information**: 29 Virchowstrasse. **Train** connections with Bremen, Hamburg, Hanover, Oldenburg and Osnabrück; **buses** with Aurich, Emden and Oldenburg; **boats** with Heligoland (see Rte 60).

**History**. Wilhelmshaven was founded in 1853 by Wilhelm I of Prussia as the chief base for the Prussian navy, and in 1869 it took his name. In 1937 Wilhelmshaven merged with Rüstringen. In spite of much damage in World War II and industrial reconstruction, this remains a popular seaside resort. The construction of the 1958 pipeline with Köln-Wesseling has made Wilhelmshaven Germany's largest oil port.

The Rathaus, orginally that of Rüstringen, 1927–29, was built by Fritz Höger and has a 50m-high belfry. In Heppenser Strasse stands the 16C Heppenser Wurt church, with a pulpit of 1633 by L. Münstermann. See also the garrison church of 1872; the Nordsee-Aquarium (open 10.00–18.00); two museum ships moored at Kaiser-Wilhelm bridge; and the ornithological museum in the Heinrich-Gätke-Halle at 21 An der Vogelwarte (open Tue 09.00–13.00, Thu 13.00–17.00). The Küsten-und-Schiffartsmuseum (open, except Mon, 10.00–13.00, 15.00–18.00, Sat closed in the afternoon) is at 10 Rathausplatz. N of the town is **Schloss Knyphausen**.

Follow the B210 W across E Friesland to **Jever** (12,400 inhab.; alt. 5m). Here is a 14C to 18C hunting Schloss, with an *audience chamber of 1560 (now the local history museum, open Tue–Sun 10.00–13.00, 15.00–17.00). The town hall is by A. von Bentheim, 1616. Jever's 18C church, with a Frisian *funeral chapel of 1511, has a marble Renaissance monument to Edo Wiemken (died 1511) designed by Cornelis Floris in 1560. Tourist information at the town hall.

**Excursions.** 11km S of Jever is the moated **Schloss Gödens**, 1669, though begun in the 14C. It has an Audienzsaal by the Antwerp-born Cornelis Floris (guided tours Tue–Sun, Mar–Dec). Jever's gabled Rathaus was built 1606–16. Just W of Jever a road leads 20km N and then W to **Carolinen-seil-Harle**, from where boats serve the **East Frisian islands** of **Wangerooge** (9km by 1.5km) and **Spiekeroog** (8km by 2km), whose church contains fragments of a wrecked galleon of the Spanish Armada.

The other six East Frisian islands are, from W to E: **Borkum**, the largest at 36 sq km, with 7800 inhabitants, with a 6km promenade and a sandy beach, a Kurhaus and a 63m-high 16C lighthouse. Boats reach Borkum in two hours from Emden, by air takes 20 minutes; **Memmert**, 11.5 sq km, and Germany's largest bird sanctuary, is attainable by foot from the island of Juist at low tide.

**Juist**, 17km by 1.5km, with a population of 1500, possesses a nature reserve, a sandy beach and an island lake. Juist has its own airfield and is also reached by boat from Norddeich. **Nordeney**, 15km by 2km, with a seaside resort—Germany's oldest—founded in 1797, has a population of 7800, a 5km-long promenade, forests and sand flats. Connections with Norddeich.

**Baltrum**, the smallest island (6.5 sq km) with a population of only 850, has 8km of sandy beach. **Langeoog**, at 19 sq km the island with the highest dunes, is a North Sea health resort, with a gull colony, 14km of sandy beach, a population of 300, beds for nearly 7500 visitors and boat connections with Bensersiel.

The B210 leads 8km W to **Wittmund**, whose Schloss was ruined in 1674. This is a starting point for woodland excursions. Another 25km brings you to **Aurich** (34,000 inhab.; alt. 8km), administrative centre of East Friesland. Here in the 13C the Counts of Oldenburg built a church. The Schloss was founded in the following century. The present Schloss, housing the administrative offices, dates from 1852, with 18C stables. The East Frisian Landschaft is housed in a neo-Renaissance building of 1897–1900. The church of St Lambert, 1832, boasts an early 16C carved altar from Antwerp. In a five-storey windmill is a museum devoted to the history of mills (open

Apr–Sept Tue–Sun 10.00–12.00, 15.00–17.00; Sun closed afternoons). Aurich hosts a major cattle and horse market. Tourist information at the Pferdemarkt.

The B72 runs 11km W from here to Georgsheil, from where the B70 runs for 16km NW to **Norden** (25,000 inhab.; alt. 8m). Norden has a church of St Ludger, 1445, with a free-standing bell tower, set in the exquisite tree-lined Marktplatz. Inside are eight mid-13C sandstone statues, the 16C tomb of Unico Manninga, and * *Arp Schnitger's finest organ, built 1685–88. The 1000-year-old Theelacht (peasant landowners' association) still meets in the Rathaus of 1542, which also houses the local history museum (open Wed, Fri, Sat 15.00–17.00). In the Markt is also a house of 1662 now used as a Mennonite church. The gabled Schöningh Haus in Oberstrasse dates from 1576.

From Norden the B70 continues to the North Sea health resort of **Norddeich**, with boat excursions to the islands of Nordeney, Juist and Baltrum (see also above).

Close by Norden is **Schloss Lütetsberg**, rebuilt in the 16C Renaissance style after a fire of 1959.

From Georgsheil the B72 runs SW for 16km to **Emden** (52,600 inhab.; alt. 4m), at the mouth of the Ems and possessing on the Dortmund-Ems canal Lower Saxony's largest harbour.

**Tourist information**: 2 Gräfin-Anna-Strasse. **Train** connections with Bremen, Hamburg, Münster and Norddeich.

**History**. The town was trading as early as the 9C and by the 16C was one of Germany's major ports. When the Ems changed course the prosperity of Emden disastrously declined, to revive again in the 20C with the digging of the canal and the building of a new harbour. Today it constitutes the third biggest port on the North Sea.

Worth seeing are the medieval church of SS Cosmas and Damian, ruined as a result of World War II and the Calvinist New Church in Brückstrasse, dating from 1643–48. Emden's Rathaus (1576) was built by the Dutch architect Laurenz van Steenwinkel. 13–16C sculptures and 16–19C paintings, as well as the work of East Frisian gold and silversmiths, are to be found in the Ostfriesisches Landesmuseum at the Rathaus am Delft (open 10.00–13.00, 15.00–17.00, weekends 11.00–13.00; closed Mon Oct–Apr).

# 59

## Hanover to Göttingen

Total distance 102km. Hanover—B3, 14km Pattensen—16km Elze—7km Banteln—12km Alfeld an der Leine—15km Einbeck—18km Northeim—9km Nörten- Hardenberg—11km Göttingen (—6km Nikolausberg).

Drive S from **Hanover** (see Rte 52) along the B3, reaching after 14km Pattensen, with fine views of the Diester and Osterwald hills and the Weserbergland; see Rte 48. After 16km the route reaches Elze.

Continue through **Banteln**, with a Schloss in a park, reaching 19km from Elze **Alfeld an der Leine** (15,500 inhab.; alt. 93m). Its town hall dates from

1584–86; the old grammar school, half-timbered and brick, was built in the 16C and has coloured carvings of classical as well as Old and New Testament characters. Banteln also boasts a steel-framed shoe factory by Walter Gropius and A. Meyer, 1911–14, as well as the Romanesque and Gothic church of St Nikolaus. The local history museum and exotic zoo are at 5 Am Kirchplatz (open weekdays 10.00–12.00, 15.00–17.00; weekends 10.00–12.00). A private zoo supplies imported animals world-wide.

15km SE of Alfeld an der Leine lies the partly fortified town of **Einbeck** (23,000 inhab.; alt. 114m), an unusually ravishing town in the valley of the Ilse. Founded by Count Dietrich II von Katlenburg around 1080 and a former member of the Hanseatic League, Einbeck possesses over one hundred sculpted Renaissance houses, including the public weighhouse, the Ratswaage, of 1565, the Bakers' House (Brodhaus) of 1552, the Ratsapotheke of 1562 and the Rathaus with its three tiled spires of 1593. This town also boasts the oldest brewery in Germany, dating back to 1378—from 'Einbeck' possibly derives the term 'Bockbier' (the beer now dubbed 'Ainbocksch Bier'). The ancient breweries can be spotted by the openings in the roofs designed to dry hops. The town's church of St Jakob, though founded in the 13C, is today chiefly 17C Baroque. Its finest features are the west façade, the pulpit and furnishings, and the 65m-high west tower which was completed c 1500.

The Münsterkirche, dedicated to St Alexandri, derives from the 13C and 14C, with remains of the 12C church (and its choir stalls of 1288). The font was carved in 1427; the reredos of SS Erasmus and Guy, c 1500. In its crypt a reliquary enshrines a drop of Jesus's blood given by Richenza von Katlenburg, the wife of Emperor Lothair III.

Einbeck has a bicycle museum at 1 Papenstrasse, and a town museum at 11 Steinweg (open weekdays 10.00–12.00, 14.00–16.00, Sat 10.00–12.00). In the 16C chapel of St Bartholomäus is buried Friedrich Setürner (1783–1841), who discovered morphia and worked here as a pharmacist, 1806–20.

The B3 travels 18km SE along the Leine valley to reach **Northeim** (25,000 inhab.; alt. 121m), another former Hanseatic town and like Einbeck still partly fortified and possessing many half-timbered Renaissance buildings. Other important architectural remains include Benedictine monastery buildings (1474 and late 16C), incorporating the Münsterkirche; the 1500 hospice of the Holy Ghost at 32 Münsterplatz; the late Gothic *hall-church of St Sixtus, its choir built 1464–78, its nave finished 1496. This last has late 15C stained glass; a high altar of 1430, with a Gothic tabernacle and statues of the Virgin Mary, the Apostles and four other saints; two early 16C altars; a font of 1509 by Heinrich Mente of Brunswick; and a organ case c 1740. The local history museum is on Am Münster (open Tue–Sun 10.00–12.00, 15.00–18.00). Tourist information at 12 Markt. Train connections with Basel and Hamburg.

From here the B3 runs due S through **Nörten-Hardenberg**—which has half-timbered houses; an 18C and a modern church; and nearby a ruined 11C Schloss—to reach after 20km **GÖTTINGEN** (130,000 inhab.; alt. 150m).

**Tourist information** at the railway station and the Altes Rathaus. Göttingen hosts an annual Handel **festival**, an international organ festival and a Christmas market.

**History**. 'Famed for its sausages and university', as Heinrich Heine declared in 1824, Göttingen first appears in written history as *Gutingi* in 953, when Emperor Otto I granted the hamlet to a monastery in Magdeburg. Flourishing as a market because of its position where the River Leine could be forded and where two trade routes crossed, the town was granted its municipal charter. In 1351 the city became a member of the Hanseatic League, remaining such until 1572. In 1387 the burghers emancipated themselves from the control of the duke by destroying his Schloss. Prosperity declined with the fall in 1547 of the Lutheran Schmalkaldic League, which Göttingen had joined, to the forces of the Holy Roman Emperor Charles V. Göttingen suffered severely during the Thirty Years War.

A new period of importance was inaugurated when Elector Georg Augustus of Hanover founded the university in 1734, dedicated to theology, philosophy, law and medicine. Amongst its teachers have been Freidrich Wöhler, who discovered aluminium in 1827, and Karl Friedrich Gauss (1777–1855), who discovered the magnetic field in 1833. Otto von Bismarck was a student here from 1832–33, living in a tower on the city wall which is now known as Bismarck Cottage. In 1772 in a grove ('Hain') at Göttingen a league of Romantic poets, the 'Hainbund', came together to reform German poetry. In Göttingen is buried Max Planck (1858–1947), who conceived quantum theory, and Göttingen became the headquarters of the Max Planck Society after World War II.

Cross into Berliner Strasse from the main railway station and walk S, following Goethe Strasse, to turn left into Groner Strasse, reaching on the left the 14C church of Our Lady. Its bell tower dates from 15C, and it houses painted 16C altar panels, sculpted by Bertold Castorp. Next to the church is a gatehouse adjoining the 14C house of the Teutonic Knights, who endowed the church. Papendiek leads NE from Groner Strasse, from a corner of which Johannisstrasse runs E to the oldest church in Göttingen, St Johann. Begun in the 13C, its important features include a Romanesque north doorway and two asymmetrical 15C towers. (You can ascend the north tower to view the city.)

This church lies on the S side of the Markt, whose 1396–1443 Altes Rathaus, first built as a trading centre c 1270, is itself in two unequal parts. It includes a Ratskeller; a guard house; Gothic heating system; and a Great Hall, decorated by Hermann Schaper 1883–86 with the coats of arms of 56 members of the Hanseatic League and murals depicting local life. The brewery was installed in the Rathaus in 1345. In front of the town hall is Göttingen's goose girl fountain, 1901, by tradition kissed by each university postgraduate who obtains a doctorate. A half-timbered house of 1553, NE of the Markt, contains the old pharmacy, which was founded in 1332.

From the pharmacy follow Barfürstrasse to reach at No. 5 the decorated Junkenschänkeof 1549, decorated with Renaissance medallions, and at No. 12 the Bornemann Haus of 1536. Barfürstrasse continues as far as the 'Aula', the former great hall of the university, built 1835–37, with a pediment sculpture by Ernst von Bendel. Continue E to reach the 15C church of St Albanus in Geismarstrasse, in which is an altar depicting the beheading of the saint and scenes from the life of the Virgin Mary, by H. von Geisman, 1499. From this church proceed N to Theaterplatz, noting at No. 11 the Deutsches Theater, by Schnittger, 1890. From here follow Wall, the site of the former fortifications, to the botanical gardens, laid out in the 18C.

The chief shopping street of Göttingen, Weender Strasse, leads S from Wall back to the Markt, passing on the way the delicious Gothic church of St Jakobi, begun 1350, completed 1433, and rebuilt after a fire of 1555. Inside is an *altarpiece of 1402, depicting the coronation of the Virgin, who is surrounded by apostles and saints. This church's 72m-high tower was built by Hans Rutenstein of Hildesheim, 1427–33. The picturesque St Johannes quarter of the city (restored in the 1970s) shelters the Paulinerkirche, built in 1331 for the Dominicans and now housing part of the university library.

Museums in the city include the University Art Gallery at 10 Hospitalstrasse, with its Renaissance and Baroque art (visits by arrangement); the Städtisches Museum at 7–8 Ritterplan, which displays medieval to Baroque religious art (open Tue–Sun 10.00–13.00, 15.00–17.00; closes Sun afternoons); and the University Zoological Collection at 28 Berlinerstrasse (open Sun 10.00–13.00).

The Junges Theater is housed in the mid-19C Otfried Müller House at 1 Hospitalstrasse.

6km NE of Göttingen on the **Nikolausberg** stands the 12C former abbey church of Augustinian nuns, with a high altar c 1490 and a north altar c 1400. From here is an impressive *view of Göttingen.

# 60

# Hanover to Heligoland via Bremen

Total distance (excluding ferry to Heligoland) 245km. Hanover—B6, 24km Neustadt am Rübenberge—24km Nienburg(—5km Hoya—3km Bücken)— 14km Verden—A27, 20km Bremen—B6, 13km Burgdamm(—B74, 9km Osterholz-Scharmbeck—18km Worpswede)—45km Bremerhaven—44km Cuxhaven(—ferry to Heligoland—45km). Cuxhaven—B73, 8km Altenbruch—9km Otterndorf—9km Neuhaus).

Leave **Hanover** (see Rte 52) by way of the Herrenhäuser Gärten taking the B6 for 24km NW to **Neustadt am Rübenberge** (13,000 inhab.; alt. 37m), once the seat of the Dukes of Calenberg, whose chief architectural monuments are Schloss Landestrost of 1570 and the 13C collegiate church of St Peter.

The route continues through woodland a further 24km NW to reach **Nienburg** (30,000 inhab.; alt. 25m) on the River Weser. Amongst several half-timbered houses is the arcaded Renaissance *rathaus in Lange Strasse, c 1590. Nienburg has a late Gothic church of St Martin, 15C (with a modern belfry); the Stocktower, from a former 15C Schloss; and a local history museum at Nos 4 & 7 Leinstrasse, a classical building of 1821 (open Tue–Sat 10.00–12.00; also Wed, Thu 14.00–17.00). Tourist information at 39 Lange Strasse. Train connections with Bremen and Hanover.

At **Marklohe**, 5km NW, is a 13C Romanesque church with an altar of 1420, late 15C wall paintings and an early 16C tabernacle.

From Nienburg take the B215 N for 19km to Hassel.

An **excursion** 5km W of Hassel, across the River Weser, brings you to the town of **Hoya**, with a 14C Schloss, seat of the Counts of Hoya from 810 to 1582. The Schloss chapel is now the local parish church of St Martin, and you can still see the coats of arms of the counts on its stalls. 3km S of Hoya lies **Bücken**, with a 12C and 13C Romanesque *church, housing a triumphal cross of 1270 and 13C stained glass in the choir.

The B215 continues N from Hassel to reach after 14km.**Verden** (24,000 inhab.; alt. 23m) on the River Aller (where you can take boat trips and hire canoes), close to its confluence with the Weser. Once an Imperial and Hanseatic city, Verden was the see of a bishop from 786 and today hosts an important horse fair in April, July and October each year. The Deutsches Pferdemuseum at 7 Andreasstrasse has a fascinating collection, including a section devoted to the horse as soldier (open Tue–Sun 09.00–16.00). The 11C *Dom, extended and reordered in the Gothic style 15C, has three naves and a copper roof, a Romanesque font, an early 14C Gothic sedilia, and numerous tombs including that of Bishop Philipp Sigismund (died 1623).

In the neighbouring church of St Andreas, in Grüne Strasse, is the oldest surviving monumental brass in the world, to Bishop Yso of Verden, who died in 1231, as well as early 18C pews and a curious Baroque altar. The Johanniskirchein Ritterstrasse is North Germany's oldest brick church. Begun in the 2C, it was enlarged and Gothicised in the 15C. Inside are a 15C triumphal cross and tabernacle; medieval wall paintings; and a stuccoed Last Judgment.

Vestiges of the old fortifications, particularly the Johanniswall and the Nikolaiwall, survive on the circular boulevards of the town. Verden also boasts a 'Märchenland' (fairy-tale land) with electrically operated models (open Apr–Oct 09.00–18.00). The local history museum is in a house dated 1708, at 10 Grosse Fischerstrasse (open except Mon and Thu 10.00–13.00, 15.00–17.00; Sun only 14.00–17.00). Tourist information at 7 Ostertorstrasse. Train connections with Bremen, Hanover and Rotenburg.

On the Halse 2km N of Verden are 4500 stones, the Sachsenhain, commemorating 4500 Saxons massacred by Charlemagne's troops in 782.

From Verden take the A27 for 20km NW to **BREMEN** (558,000 inhab.; alt. 5m). Germany's oldest seaport and lying on either side of the Weser, so that one's first impression is that of a seafaring town.

Main **railway station**: Bahnhofstrasse. Main **post office** Domsheide. **Information office**: 29 Bahnhofsplatz. Bremen has an international **airport** and is served by inter-city **trains**. **Annual events** include ice-sports on 6 January; a traditional banquet in the town hall in February; and a market held since 1035 in the weeks of October.

**History** Charlemagne established a bishopric here in 787 and the episcopal cathedral was built two years later, its importance being enhanced as an archbishopric in the next century. Bremen gained market rights in 888, and under Otto the Great in 965 the right to mint its own coins and dispense justice. Archbishop Adalbert (1043–72) enlarged its influence and prestige. The city joined the Hanseatic League in 1358. In 1525 the citizens opted for the Reformation. Bremen became a Free imperial city in 1646. After suffering greatly during the Thirty Years War, at the Peace of Westphalia the archbishopric was united with that of Hamburg and the see transferred there. Peace did not ensue: the Swedes attacked Bremen in both 1654 and 1666. Napoleon took the city in 1810, but Bremen regained its independent republican status by the Treaty of Vienna and joined the German League.

When silting of the Weser jeopardised its trade in the 19C, the merchants of Bremen first founded Bremerhaven and then, between 1886 and 1895, vigorously deepened and regulated the river so as to open up the port once more. Much of the harbour was destroyed in World War II, its importance paradoxically recognised by 175 air attacks. Reconstructed, the port now serves 140 shipping lines—with a large container harbour, constructed 1973.

Today Bremen is the capital city of the Land of Bremen. Its university was founded in 1970.

The main railway station is flanked by the city library and the **Museum Übersee**. Founded in 1896, the museum is devoted to ethnology and palaeontology (open Tue–Sun 10.00–18.00). From the main railway station Bahnhofstrasse leads by way of Herdentor across the gardens with which Altmann replaced the moat in 1805, along the site of the old fortifications, as far as Sögestrasse. To the left of Herdentor can be seen Bremen's sole surviving windmill. To the left of Sögestrasse stands the **Liebfrauenkirche**.

Its first stones were laid in the 12C. The church has a Romanesque south tower, a west tower of 1229 and three aisles. Inside is a Baroque tomb of 1686 and a pulpit of 1709 sculpted by Gerd Rode. the stained glass of 1960–73 is by Alfred Manessier. Left of the church is the **Marktplatz**, in which is the 10m-high **Roland statue** and pillar, now the city's emblem. Set up in 1404, on the shield is inscribed 'Vryheit do ik ju openbar'—'Freedom do I give you liberally'. The statue, symbol of civic freedom, faces the cathedral, whose archbishops had threatened the citizens' privileges.

The **St Petri-Dom** stands on the spot where Bishop Willehad built a church in 787. The present building was begun in 1043. It boasts a remarkable Romanesque double crypt, with a Romanesque bronze font, c 1220, an enthroned Christ, c 1050, and the 'Bleikeller', or Lead Cellar, with mummified bodies (visits May–Oct weekdays 09.00–12.00, 14.00–17.00; Sun 09.00–12.00). The west façade and towers were completed in the 13C, followed by the south aisle chapels (14C and 15C) and the late Gothic north aisle. The *organ gallery is by H. Brabender, 1518. The twin towers, c 100m high, were restored in the Romanesque and early Gothic styles in the late 19C.

Next to the cathedral stands the Gothic *Rathaus of 1405–09; its Renaissance façade of 1609–12 is by Lüder von Bentheim. It is adorned with statues of Charlemagne and seven electors, carved 1409–10. It has a superb Gothic chamber. The upper chamber is partly Renaissance. The splendid *Güldenkammer is decked with early 16C Renaissance frescoes and Renaissance carvings (hourly guided tours Mon–Fri at 10.00, 11.00 and 12.00; Mar–Oct also Sun 11.00 and 12.00). The modern part of the town hall dates from 1909–12. The Ratskeller of 1408, with 18C barrels, has reputedly 400 local wines on sale.

The bronze statue by the town hall represents the Bremen 'musicians' (a donkey, dog, cat and cock, by Gerhard Marcks, 1961) from a story by the Brothers Grimm.

Opposite the town hall is the **Schütting** (dialect for 'money making'), i.e. the guild house of the Bremen merchants, with a façade by Johann den Buscheneer of Antwerp, 1538, a late Gothic west gable and a Renaissance east gable. The doorway and balustrade are 19C. Today it houses the chamber of commerce. The Marktplatz also contains several patrician houses and the modern parliament building, the **Haus der Bürgerschaft** of 1966 (visits Mon–Fri 10.00, 14.15). In Langenstrasse, which runs between an 18C house and the Schütting is the office of weights and measures, the **Stadtwage** of 1587–88, which was destroyed in World War II and rebuilt in 1961.

To the S of the Markt is the narrow *Böttcherstrasse, an old street of craftsmen's shops, which Ludwig Roselius, the founder of Kaffee Hag (producers of the first caffeine-free coffee in 1907), had redesigned 1926–31, using especially the sculptor Bernhard Hoetger (1874–1949). The **Roselius-Haus** of 1588 houses Ludwig Roselius's own collection of art from the Gothic to the Romantic eras, with weapons (open Mon–Thu 10.00–16.00; weekends 11.00–16.00); the **Paula-Becker-Modersohn-Haus** has paintings by Paula Becker-Modersohn and modern art exhibitions (open weekdays 10.30–12.30, 15.00–19.00; weekends 10.00–14.00). The house is by Hoetger 1927, with his sculptures on this and other façades.

Also in Böttercherstrasse are the Robinson-Crusoe-Haus; a porcelain carillon on the Haus des Glockenspiel which plays at noon, 15.00 and 18.00; the Kammerspiel theatre; and a Casino.

Böttcherstrasse leads to Martinistrasse and the 13C **Martinikirche** on the bank of the Weser, rebuilt after World War II. Its windows are filled with modern stained glass. Inside is a Bockelmann organ of 1619 with a 1604 case by Hermen Wulff. The carillon in the tower plays at 09.15, 12.15, 15.15 and 18.15. Close by here is the **Martini-Anleger**, the landing stage for boat trips along the Weser, around the harbour, to Worpswede and to Heligoland.

Martinistrasse leads E to the 14C Gothic hall-church of **St Johann**, at the centre of the district known as *Schnoor. Here rise 15C, 16C and 18C houses, as well as art galleries and restaurants. N of the church the street called Am Landherrenamt leads past Domsheide to Ostertorstrasse, to find at 207 Am Wall the **Kunsthalle**. Its rich collection is particularly strong in 15C to 20C paintings and drawings (open except Mon 10.00–16.00; Tue, Fri also 19.00–21.00). Next door, at No. 208, is the **Gerhard-Marcks-Haus**, a museum devoted to Expressionism (open Tue–Sun 10.00–18.00).

Continue E to find in Goetheplatz the city theatre and at No. 24 **Villa Ichon**, a cultural centre built 1852 and 1871, restored 1982.

In the suburb of Schwachhaus, at 240 Schwachhauser Heerstrasse, is the **Focke-Museum**, partly housed in a building of 1768. This museum records daily life in Bremen and North German history (open Tue–Sun 10.00–18.00). The local history museum is in the moated Schloss Schönebeck of 1660, situated at 3–5 Im Dorfe (open except Mon and Fri 15.00–17.00; Sun also 10.00–12.30). The Bremen Broadcasting Museum is at 85 Findorffstrasse (open weekends 10.00–12.30). The Windmill in Oberneuland is worth visiting (open Tue–Fri 09.00–12.00, Sun 10.00–13.00).

See also the Renaissance House of the Guild of Artisans, the **Gewerbehaus** of 1619–21, in Ansgaritor Strasse.

**Excursion**. The B6 leaves Bremen NW, crossing the Weser and after 13km passing through Burgdamm, from where the B74 leads NE to reach after 13km **Osterholz-Scharmbeck** (24,000 inhab.; alt. 8m). Here explore the 12C Romanesque monastery church; a traditional farmstead; stone graves; windmills and watermills; and the local history museum at 32 Rollberg (open except Mon, weekdays 10.30–16.00, weekends 10.00–12.00).

From here drive 18km E across the Teufelsmoor to the artists' village of **Worpswede** (800 inhab.; alt. 51m) on the slopes of the 57m-high Weyerberg. Worpswede was made famous in the early years of this century by Rainer Maria Rilke, Paula Becker-Modersohn, Berhard Hoetger and Heinrich Vogeler, all seduced by its charms, and in consequence is filled by art galleries.

45km N of Burgdamm, by way of the Garlstedter Heide, marshland and sandy ridges, the B6 reaches **BREMERHAVEN** (142,000 inhab.; alt. 3m).

**Tourist information**: 58 Friedrich-Ebert-Strasse. **Train** connections with Bremen, Hanover, Cuxhaven, Bremervörde and Stade; **buses** connect with Cuxhaven; **boat trips** to Heligoland and Bremen.

Bremerhaven was bought from Hanover in 1827 as an alternative port by Burgermeister Johann Schmidt of Bremen when the silting of the Weser threatened his city's economy. Its eleven docks and over 12km of quays (including the 1250m-long Columbus Quay) help to make it the busiest passenger and fishing port of Germany. Bremerhaven incorporates the suburbs of Geestemünde, which is reached first from Bremen, Wesermünde and Lehe.

The fishing harbour, with its vast fish markets (auctions begin at 07.00), lies SW of the main railway station. To the right at 6 Kaistrasse is the

Morgenstern Museum, devoted to prehistory, local history and folklore (open weekdays except Mon 10.00–16.00; Sat 10.00–13.00, Sun 10.30–12.30). Close by, at 12 Handelshafen, is the **Nordseemuseum** North Sea and Fishing Museum; (open weekdays 08.00–18.00; weekends 10.00–18.00). Enter Geeste Strasse, passing the radar tower (rising to 116m, with a panoramic view), to reach the National Museum of Navigation, the **Deutsches Schiffahrtsmuseum**. Built by Hans Scharoun in 1970, with an entrance in Von-Ronzelen-Strasse, this is devoted to the whole history of German shipping (open Tue–Sat 10.00–18.00).

Other museums in Bremerhaven include the **Kunsthalle**, museum of 20C art at 4 Karlsburg (open except Mon 15.00–18.00; Sun only 11.00–13.00), and the Verkehrsmuseum (travel museum), housed in a building at 17 Hansastrasse dated 1912 (open weekdays 08.00–12.00). The institute of marine research beside the harbours has a diorama depicting undersea fauna (open weekdays 08.00–16.00). Bremerhaven also has the Zoo Am Mer—Zoological Caves and the North Sea Aquarium (open daily 08.00–16.30). N of the town at **Speckenbüttel** is an open-air museum with reconstructions of Lower Saxon houses of the 16C and afterwards (open daily, except Sun and Thu 09.00–11.00, 15.00–17.00).

43km further N from Bremerhaven along the B6 is Cuxhaven, the road to which runs not far from the coast. Resorts along this coast include **Wremen**—7km W of Cuxhaven, with mini-golf, etc., connected to Bremerhaven and Cuxhaven by train and to Bremerhaven and Dorum by boat—and the health resort of **Sahlenburg**—4km W, with a 3kmlong beach at the foot of the wooded Wolfsberg. 1km N of the road to Sahlenburg the B6 reaches **Cuxhaven** (62,000 inhab.; alt. 3m), on the 15km-wide mouth of the Elbe. Cuxhaven, now part of Lower Saxony, belonged to Hamburg from 1394 to 1937, and with its two fine beaches has been renowned as a thermal sea spa since 1816. In Schloss Ritzebüttel is the town's historical museum. Set in a small park, the brick-built Schloss has a late 13C Gothic keep (open daily 10.30–12.30). After Bremerhaven and Altona this is Germany's largest fishing port (auctions begin at 07.00). Its emblem is the Kugelbake beacon. The suburb of **Döse** has a church dated 1528. Tourist information at the Kurverwaltung. Trains connect Cuxhaven with Hamburg and Bremerhaven; boats with Hamburg and Heligoland.

Boats leave Cuxhaven for the 1700m x 600m red limestone island of **Heligoland** (German **Helgoland**), 45km away, sailing from the pier known as Alte Liebe (derived from the name of a ship, the *Olivia*, which sank here in 1732). Heligoland offers bathing, cliff walks and duty free goods. Other excursions can be made to the islands of **Neuwerk**, with its 600-year-old lighthouse, attainable by horse carriage along the mud flats, and to **Scharnhörn**, with a bird sanctuary. Neuwerk is best reached from the seaside resort of **Duhnen**, situated 5km from Cuxhaven along the B73.

8km E of Cuxhaven on the B73 lies **Altenbruch** (4500 inhab.; alt. 3m), a seaside resort with a twin-towered Romanesque church of St Nikolaus, Gothicised and then rendered partly Baroque. Its high altar dates from 1480, and it has a Baroque organ. Just beyond Altenbruch a road leads 1km right to **Lüdingworth**, where you find a Romanesque stone church.

Continue E along the B73 for 9km more to the walled town of **Otterndorf** (6200 inhab.; alt. 5m). Here is a town hall of 1583; half-timbered and gabled houses, including the Kranichhaus of 1696 which contains the local history museum; the ruined Schloss of the Dukes of Lauenburg; the church of St Severin, built in 1261; and the house of Homer's translator, the poet Johann Heinrich Voss, who taught in the grammar school (1614) from 1778 to 1782. 9km further W is Neuhaus, close where the River Oste flows into the Elbe.

# 61

# Hamburg to Lübeck

## A. Via Ahrensburg and Bad Oldesloe

Total distance 58km. Hamburg—B75, 23km Ahrensburg—6km Bargteheide—
14km Bad Oldesloe—15km Lübeck.

Leave **Hamburg** (see Rte 51) NE on the B75 through the suburb of
**Wandsbek**, where the poet Matthias Claudius (1740–1815) lived, and who
is buried close by the market place in the cemetery of the Christuskirche.
This church houses the classical mausoleum, 1782–91, of Count H.C. von
Schimmelmann. After 16km the route passes the open-air village museum
of **Volksdorf** (open save Tue and Thu 09.00–12.00, 14.00–18.00).

7km further the B75 reaches **Ahrensburg** (25,000 inhab.; alt. 40m). On
the N edge of the city rises the moated Renaissance Schloss Ahrensburg
and its Schloss church, both of which were built by Count Peter Rantzau,
c 1595. Its Baroque alterations date from 1759 to 1782, beginning in the
year that the Schloss came into the possession of a treasurer of the King of
Denmark named Schillelmamm. The building also encompasses a 19C
ballroom, and displays valuable *Saxon porcelain (open Tue–Sat 10.00–
dusk). Tourist information at 39 Rathausplatz.

4km N lies **Bargteheide**, with its Schloss Hotel Tremsbüttel and a 13C
church. The B75 continues for 14km to reach **Bad Oldesloe** (20,000 inhab.;
alt. 17m) at the confluence of the Rivers Trave and Beste. A church has
existed here since the mid 12C. No longer a spa, though the Kurpark
remains, with fine sports facilities, Bad Oldesloe was treasured for its
springs by Henry the Lion. The town was the birthplace of the composer
Dietrich Buxtehude (1637–1707). The present Baroque church building,
which rises on the site of the first, dates from 1757–64, its tower added in
1886. The neo-classical town hall dates from 1806. Close by here (1.5km
N, on the road to Bad Segeberg) is **Menno-Mate**, refuge of Menno Simons
(1496–1561), founder of the Mennonites.

The B75 continues NE for 15km to reach the entrancing city of
***LÜBECK** (220,000 inhab.; alt. 11m), entering by the Moislinger Allee,
which runs as far as the central railway station. Amongst many architectural
gems, Lübeck is a city of brick medieval churches, none of which should
be missed.

Main **railway station**: Am Bahnhof. Main **post office**: Marktplatz. **Information office**:
14 Rathaushof and at main railway station. **Trains** and **buses** connect Lübeck with
major towns and cities, **ships** with Denmark, Finland, Sweden and Trellenborg. Lübeck
has an **airport**.

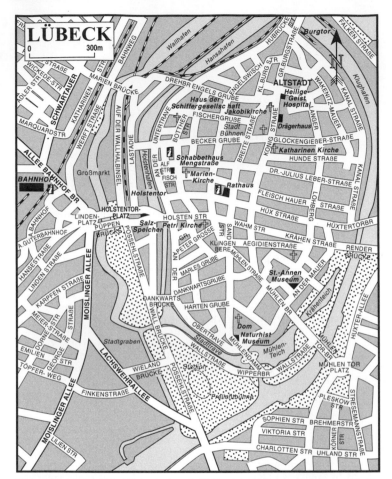

**History**. Count Adolf II of Holstein founded Lübeck in 1143, on a spot once settled by
the Wends where the River Trave meets the Schwartau. Henry the Lion took possession
of the town in 1159, setting up a mint here. In 1160 the bishopric of Oldenburg was
transferred to Lübeck, a sign of the city's growing importance. Frederick Barbarossa
ratified the city's privileges in a charter of 1188, and Friedrich II gave the city more
rights in 1226. Lübeck escaped the domination of Denmark and in the early 13C began
building its city walls and gates as a symbol of that freedom. Declared a Free Imperial
City in 1226 by decree of Emperor Friedrich II, Lübeck's favourable position on the
Trave, only 20km from the Baltic Sea, enabled it to prosper and become one of the
three dominant members of the Hanseatic League—in effect the leader, and for a time
the largest German city after Cologne.

Between 1300 and 1350 Lübeck rebuilt all five of its main churches in the Gothic
style. The last meeting of the League in 1630 consisted only of Lübeck, Bremen and
Hamburg. Lübeck's fortifications spared her some of the atrocities of the Thirty Years
War. After a period of decline, mitigated in part by the wine trade, during which
Lübeck was the theatre of struggles between the two sides of the French Revolution
and became in 1810 capital of the French *département* of Bouches-de-l'Elbe, the city

began in part to prosper again. Lübeck joined the German Confederation in 1815 and the North German Confederation in 1867. After Napoleon's defeat, Lübeck, Bremen and Hamburg had united as three Free Hanseatic towns, a status lost only in 1937 when the city voted to become part of Schleswig-Holstein, whereas Bremen and Hamburg have remained Free Cities within the united Germany.

Further prosperity has come from the establishment of new industries at nearby Schlutup and the construction of the Elbe–Trave canal, opened 1900. The city was severely damaged in World War II in an air raid of 29 March 1942, and has been splendidly restored. Today its port has twelve docks.

Here were born the former West German Chancellor Willy Brandt (1913–1992), and the novelists Heinrich Mann (1871–1950) and Thomas Mann (1875–1955). Thomas's first major work, 'Buddenbrooks' (1901) depicts the the decline of a Lübeck bourgeois family throughout the 19C. Addressing the citizens of Lübeck in 1926, he declared that the city represented a 'spiritual concept of life', which defended the principles of humanity 'against all extremists, both of right and left'.

Lübeck's marzipan is famous. Restaurants serve a red wine (Rotspon), which has been aged for four years in oak barrels.

From the main railway station follow Bahnhofstrasse E across the **Puppen-brücke**—decorated with statues by Dietrich Jürgen Boy, 1778, one of which, Mercury, inspired a noted poem by Emmanuel Giebel, 1815–84—to reach the city's symbol, the **\*\*Holstentor**, a splendid medieval fortified gate, built 1469–78 by Heinrich Helstede, which now houses an historical museum (open Apr–Sept 10.00–17.00; closes winter 16.00). The motto 'CONCORDIA DOMI FORIS PAX' ('Harmony inside, peace outside') was added in the 19C. On the city side the letters SPQL (i.e. 'Senatus Populusque Lubecensis') were engraved on the gate in 1871. To the right of the Holstentor are former salt barns, the **Salzspeicher**, dating from the 16C and the 17C.

Cross the Holstenbrücke (right the Upper Trave, left the Holsten harbour) to reach the Markt, passing en route on the right the 12C and 13C Romanesque **Petrikirche**. Built with a nave and two aisles in the 14C, two more aisles added in the 16C. The church burned down in 1942 and has been beautifully restored. A lift ascends the 50m-high tower which was crowned with its spire c 1430, and also restored after 1942. The tower offers a splendid view of Lübeck. The **Museum für Puppentheater** at 4–5 Kleine Petersgrube (open Tue–Sun 09.30–18.00) documents, with many exhibits, German puppet theatres. The exquisite street known as **Grosse Peters-grube** boasts numerous Gothic, Renaissance, Baroque and classical half-timbered houses.

In the Markt is situated the **\*\*Rathaus**. The oldest part of its brick Gothic façade dates from 1230 and was ornamented further in 1434. The Rathaus has a Renaissance loggia of 1570, with a 13C Ratskeller. A south wing was built from 1298 to 1398, with long Gothic arcades, a wing further embellished in 1442. Inside this wing is the War Hall, whose furnishings were destroyed in the 1942 air raid. This building was yet further enriched by a lavishly decorated Dutch Renaissance open-air staircase and bay window of 1594 (in Breite Strasse).

In Breite Strasse is also the main entrance to the town hall, with two brass side panels, cast in 1452, depicting the enthroned emperor and a wild man whose shield bears the Lübeck eagle. Bronze mountings on the double doors depict the emperor amidst the seven electors. Tours of the interior (on the hour from 10.00 to 16.00 weekdays, 11.00 and 12.00 weekends) reveal the late Baroque Audienzsaal chamber (1754–61), with a Renaissance doorway, by Tönnies Evers the Elder, 1573; paintings by the Italian Stephan Torelli, 1754–60; the cellars, with Romanesque pillar, 1220–26; various halls—including the Bridal Chamber, whose fireplace of 1575 is

*Lübeck's fortified Holstentor, built in the second half of the 15C, with, on the left, the spires of one of the city's five medieval churches the Marien-kirche*

inscribed in low German, 'Many a man sings loudly when he brings home his bride; if he saw into the future, he would weep'); and the Bürgerschaft-shalle with 17C and 18C portraits of the city fathers.

A passage leads from the corner tower of the town hall (1425) to the part Gothic, part Renaissance Kanzleigebäude (Chancellery). Initially dating from 1480–85, it was extended in 1588 and 1614, and has wall panelling by Tönnies Evers the Younger. The modern wing of the town hall, by way of the *north façade, 1887, is flanked by a garden and leads to the Gothic, three-aisled, brick-built *Marienkirche. Destroyed in World War II, this magnificent church has since been meticulously restored, under the direction of the architect B. Fendrich. The choir was finished in 1291, the west end in 1337. The two towers, each 125m high, were built from 1304 to 1310. The nave measures 70m by 40m.

Inside are 13C roof paintings, discovered after the conflagration of 1942. The font of 1337 is by Hans Apengeter. The church's bronze gilt **aumbry was created by Nikolais Grude (the brazier) and Nikolaus Rughese (the goldsmith), 1476–79; its Madonna was added by C.J. Milde in 1855. Behind the high altar is a late 15C altar of the Annunciation. Another masterly work of ecclesiastical art is the bronze tomb of Godhard Wigerich (d. 1518), and his four wives, by Peter Vischer of Nuremberg. In a side chapel a Falling Asleep of the Virgin dates from 1518; the high altar bronze crucifix by Gerhard Marcks from 1959. In the south tower is a bell as it lay smashed after the air raid of 1942.

To the W of the Marienkirche, in Mengstrasse, is the **Buddenbrook Haus** at No. 4. Originally built in 1239 and rebuilt in 1758, from which era dates the façade, the house in one form or another has served merchants since 1289. It belonged to Thomas Mann's family, 1841–91, and here the Mann brothers were born. Today it is a Mann museum (open daily except Mon 10.00–17.00). Return along Mengstrasse towards the harbour, passing several old houses and at No. 49 the baker's Schabbelhaus—built in the 13C and 14C, given a Baroque interior, and now a restaurant.

From here walk N and then E along Fischergrube to reach, at 2 Breite Strasse, the gabled **Haus der Schiffergesellschaft**, set up as a house for sailors in 1535. This too is now a restaurant, with inside: intricate models of sailing vessels; a painting of Lübeck's largest flagship, the *Adler*, which was built in 1566; and wall paintings of biblical stories. No. 6 Breite Strasse is the merchants' company house, **Haus der Kaufmannschaft**, a neo-Gothic building of 1819–39 which rises on the site of a building constructed in the 15C. Inside are 16C and 17C furnishings, especially the superb panelling by Hans Dreger, 1572–83, with 1035 mythological and biblical figures. Since the panelling was brought here in the 19C from another Renaissance house (the Fredenhagen Haus), the salon housing it is known as the Fredenhagen room.

Opposite the Schiffergesellschaft is the 13C and 14C *Jakobikirche. Its flèche dates from 1623, while the top storey of the tower was added in 1636, and the city architect Kaspar Walter added the slender Baroque spire in 1658. St Jakobi's treasures include pillar paintings of the mid 12C; a font by Klaus Grude, 1466, supported by three kneeling angels and depicting the twelve apostles; an exquisite small organ, built in 1515 and 1636; a larger organ of 1504; a spiral staircase to the west gallery, built in 1619; a 1698 carved altar by Jakob Budde; Renaissance choir stalls; a Baroque high altar of 1717 by Johann Hieronymus Hassenberg; and the *Brömse altar, 1498–50, whose sculptor also made the four stone reliefs of the Passion on the trellis work of the choir. In the north chapel under the tower is the wrecked vessel the *Pamir*.

Walk E to find across the road the **Heiligen-Geist-Hospital**, an old people's home, founded c 1230, and thus one of the earliest of its kind in the world. The present building dates from 1276–86, its façade enchantingly incorporating three gables and an octagonal tower. Inside the hospice is a chapel with early 14C wall paintings, Gothic altars, star vaulting of 1495, a five-arched screen with an early 15C frieze depicting 23 scenes from the story of St Elizabeth; a 16-branched chandelier, 1673; and the Long House, 88m-long, whose roof trusses date from the 13C with 170 small rooms (or cabins) for the pensioners, built in 1820. The hospital archive has 15C Gothic wall cabinets, and the warden's room has a fireplace of 1672.

From here follow Grosse Burgstrasse N to reach Lübeck's other gate, the five-storeyed **Burgtor**, the lower four storeys from the old fortifications of 1230, the fifth built by Nikolaus Peck in 1444. The cap-like roof replaced a slender spire in 1685. To the right is the former customs house of 1571, with a terracotta frieze by Statius van Düren.

Return past the Heiligen-Geist-Hospital to find on the left the classical **Behnhaus**, built in 1779–83 for the city father Peter Hinrich Testorf. It now is an art gallery with works by such important German masters as Franz Overbeck, Caspar David Friedrich, Emil Nolde and Schmidt-Rottluff (open Apr–Oct except Mon 10.00–17.00; winter closes 16.00). Close by, at 9 Königstrasse, the continuation of Grosse Burgstrasse, is the **Museum Drägerhaus**, in a late 18C building, housing memorials of the Mann brothers (opening times as the Behnhaus gallery). Beyond it on the corner of Glockengiesserstrasse is the 14C former Franciscan **Katharinenkirche**. Its asymmetrical façade was begun in 1335. This church shelters a late 15C triumphal cross; Gothic choir stalls; in the niches of the west façade *three terracotta created figures by Ernst Barlach in 1947 ('Woman in the Wind', 'Beggar' and 'Singer'); and six figures by Gerhard Marcks, 1949. On the inside south wall is a Raising of Lazarus by Tintoretto.

Continue S to find right Aegidienstrasse, leading to Lübeck's brick Gothic church of **St Aegidien**, whose earliest building, 1227, possessed a single nave. St Aegidien was extended in the 14C to become a hall-church with three aisles. Its *organ has an early Baroque case, 1624–26, by Michael Sommer, following the specifications of Hans Scherer of Hamburg, with reliefs and mosaics by Baltzer Winne, 1626, and foliage and trumpeting angels of 1715. The font was cast by Hinrich Gerwiges in 1453, with the font cover and trellis-work added in 1710. The pulpit dates from 1706, with figures by H. Freese. The rood screen was made by Tönnies Evers the Younger, 1586–87. The Gothic wall paintings were discovered in 1907.

St-Annen-Strasse leads SW from here and contains at No. 15 the **St-Annen-Museum**, formerly an Augustinian convent, 1502–15, and now devoted to the history and treasures of Lübeck. Probably its finest work is the *crucifixion altarpiece by Hans Memling, from the cathedral (open Apr–Oct except Mon 10.00–17.00; winter close, 16.00). Built into the museum is a Baroque hall of 1736 from Glockengiesserstrasse.

Take Mühlenstrasse to reach Fegefeuer Strasse—Purgatory Street, leading in theory from the hell of the city to the 'paradise' north entrance of the cathedral, 1250, but at present a one-way street running the other way—along which you reach the *Dom*, begun when Henry the Lion laid the foundation stone in 1173 and finished in 1247, with two 120m-high towers, partly Romanesque, partly Gothic. Buxtehude was organist here, and a modern plaque shows Bach learning from him. From the bombardment of 1942 escaped a 17m-high triumphal cross made by the Lübeck painter and sculptor Bernt Notke in 1477, the bronze font by Lorenz Grove, 1455, a Schöne Madonna of 1509, a mid-15C Virgin Mary crowned with stars and the Renaissance pulpit of 1568, its railings dating from 1572. So did the high altar and the Lady altar (both 15C and made in Antwerp). But Notke's *Totentanz* was lost and is now represented by a modern stained glass window depicting the scenes. The cathedral museum opens at the same times as the St-Annen-Museum. The Naturhistorisches Museum der Hansestadt Lübeck is at 1–3 Mühlendamm (open Mar–Oct 10.00–17.00, except Mon; closing at 16.00 Nov–Feb).

# B.  Via Ratzeburg

Total distance 90km. Hamburg—B5, 18km Bergedorf—B207, 20km Schwarzenbek—21km Mölln—B207 and B208, 8km Ratzeburg—B208 and B207,
11km—Gross-Sarau—4km Gross-Grönau—8km Lübeck.

Leave **Hamburg** (see Rte 51) SE to reach Bergedorf by way of the B5.
Continue E along the B207 to reach after 20km Schwarzenbek.

For an **excursion** take the B404 from Schwarzenbek through the Saxon
woods in the direction of Trittau, reaching after 6km the signposted **Schloss
Friedrichsruhe**, in the heart of the forest. Destroyed in 1946 and subsequently rebuilt, this was the Bismarck family retreat and has the Bismarck
mausoleum, completed in 1889, with the mortal remains of Otto von
Bismarck and his wife (visits save Monday 09.00–17.00). The health resort
of **Trittau** (5500 inhab.; 17m) lies along the B404 16km from Schwarzenbek.

From Schwarzenbeck drive for 21km NE along the B207, the route of the
medieval salt road between Lübeck and Hanover, crossing the
Elbe–Lübeck canal, to reach **Mölln** (15,500 inhab.; alt. 18m), is a town
surrounded by lakes, with picturesque houses, including a Gothic Rathaus
in brick— with a staircase gable of 1373—and, near the Markt, the 13C and
15C church of St Nikolaus. Romanesque, with a Gothic tower, St Nikolaus
has a seven-branched candelabrum of 1436; a font created by P. Wulf in
1509; a triumphal cross of 1504; Gothic frescoes in the choir; a 1658 Baroque
organ by Peter Scherer; and a pulpit of 1743. On the church wall is the 16C
memorial stone of the merry jester Till Eulenspiegel—depicting an owl and
a mirror: 'Eule' and 'Spiegel'—who is said to have died of the plague here
in 1350. He is remembered in the local history museum, at 2 Am Markt
(open Apr–Oct weekdays, except Mon 09.00–12.00, 15.00–17.00, weekends
09.00–12.00). Mud baths and a Kneipp centre have made this a renowned
health resort. Trains and buses connect with Lübeck, Lüneburg and Ratzeburg, buses also with Hamburg. Tourist information at the Kurverwaltung.

Mölln is at the start of the natural park of the Laurenburg lakes, 440 sq
km, with 330km of marked hiking routes.

Continue along the B207 for 6km, turning E along the B208 for 2km to
reach **Ratzeburg** (13,000 inhab; alt. 16m) on a promontory of the Ratzeburger See and picturesquely almost surrounded by water. In 1154 Henry the
Lion founded its bishopric and cathedral, one of the oldest in Germany.
Completed in the 13C, with a powerful west tower, the cathedral was rebuilt
in 1954 and is the chief architectural attraction of Ratzeburg. The exterior
is patterned in yellow and red brick. Inside are the gravestones of 23
bishops, a Romanesque triumphal cross, flanked with statues of Mary and
John, Romanesque choir stalls, a Gothic ducal pew, a sculpted oak pulpit
of 1567, a Baroque altar in the south transept, 1629, the mid-17C tomb of
August and Katharina von Sachsen-Lauenburg by Gerhard Jürgen Titje
and an organ of 1881 restored in 1954. The cathedral cloister has medieval
wall paintings, the treasury religious art from the Middle Ages. Outside is
a copy of the bronze lion set up by Henry the Lion in Brunswick.

In the Domplatz are the Andreas Paul Weber Museum, with a collection
of his satirical lithographs and drawings, and the regional museum, housed
in a Rococo house built 1764–66 for Duke Adolf Friedrich von Mecklen-
burg-Strelitz (both open Tue–Sun 10.00–13.00, 14.00–17.00).

Because the old town was razed by King Christian V of Denmark in 1693, its oldest secular buildings are the Kreis house and the Weigh house in the market square, c 1700. Close by is the classical parish church of 1787–91, whose neighbouring, c 1840, presbytery was the home of the sculptor and poet Ernst Barlach (1870–1938) from 1878–84. It is now a Barlach museum (open Tue–Sun 09.30–12.00, 15.00–18.00). Barlach is buried in the cemetery on the E bank of the Ratzeburger See (over the Königsdamm), his grave marked by a copy of his statue of a singing choirboy.

Trains connect Ratzeburg with Kiel, Lübeck and Lüneburg, buses with local places. Tourist information at 9 Am Markt.

Return to the B207 and travel N along the Ratzeburger See, passing **Einhaus**, with a 2.8m-high stone cross commemorating the martyrdom of Abbot Answerus, who was stoned to death by the Wends in 1066.

Continue through the villages of Gross-Sarau and Gross-Grönau to reach after 23km **Lübeck** (see Rte 61A).

# 62

# Hamburg to Kiel

Total distance 95km (by motorways A7 and A215, 90km). Hamburg—B4, 46km Bad Bramstedt—19km Neumünster—12km Bordelsholm See—18km Kiel.

Leave **Hamburg** (see Rte 51) NW by the Kieler Strasse, passing through the suburbs of **Eimsbüttel**, with its 19C church, and **Stellingen**, 0.5km E of Hagenbeck Zoo, to reach by the B4 after 46km **Bad Bramstedt** (10,000 inhab.; alt. 14m), a spa with peat and saline baths. The modern health centre, reputed for its treatment of rheumatic diseases, lies 2km S of the town. Bad Bramstedt has a Gothic church of St Mary Magdalen, with a 14C altar. A 1693 copy of a late 16C statue of Roland (the protector and symbol of the citizens' rights), dressed as a Roman legionary, stands in front of the Baroque Kavalier house. This was built in 1633 by the Danish King Christian IV (1588–1648) as a gift to his third wife, who was born here.

Tourist information at the town hall. Trains connect the spa with Hamburg and Neumünster.

**Neumünster** (81,000 inhab.; alt. 22m) lies on the B4 19km N of Bad Bramstedt. The name derives from the new monastery which Bishop Vicelin founded here in 1127, in a small settlement called Wippendorf. All of the monastic buildings were destroyed in air raids in World War II, along with most of the old town. Today Neumünster is a modern textile and metal-working town. Sights include the neo-classical church of St Vicelin, with a green domed tower, by F. Hansen, 1829–34; the Baroque Caspar-vonSaldern Haus built by the statesman Caspar von Saldern in 1746; and the zoo, which is set in the city forest, NW of the town, and has over 400 animals and an aquarium (open 09.00–dusk). The textile museum illustrates spinning and weaving from the Iron Age onwards (open weekdays 07.30–16.00, Sun 10.00–13.00).

Tourist information at the Stadthaus. Train connections with Bad Oldesloe, Flensburg, Hamburg and Kiel.

12km N along the B4 is the Bordesholm See, on which lies the village of **Bordesholm**. Its Augustinian monastery, founded in 1332, later became a college which was the basis of Kiel university. The only building remaining from the monastery is the late medieval Gothic church, which has a tomb inscribed by J.H. Voss; choir stalls of 1509; and the bronze tomb of Herzogin Anna von Holstein-Gottorf, who died in 1514. The Bordesholm altar by Hans Brüggemann, 1666, is now in Schleswig cathedral.

Continue N through the Obereider valley to reach in 18km **KIEL** (250,000 inhab.; alt. 5m), on the Kiel fjord which gives shipping access to the Baltic.

**Tourist information**: 18 Augusta-Viktoria-Strasse. **Boats** ply to Bagenkop, Göteborg and Oslo; **trains** connect with Flensburg, Hamburg and Lübeck.

**History**. The name Kiel derives from the city by the spring ('kyle') founded by Count Adolf IV von Schauenburg in 1242. The settlement prospered, became a member of the Hanseatic League in 1283 and established a thriving market and stock exchange. The city voluntarily chose Christian I of Denmark as its ruler in 1460, one of whose descendants, Herzog Christian Albrecht of Gottorf, founded the university in 1665. Kiel was where the provisional government of Schleswig-Holstein sat in 1848 to declare its opposition to Denmark. The city became Prussian and a major naval base, a role continued under the German empire. In 1895 its naval resources were enhanced by the opening of the Nord–Ostsee canal, known then as the Kaiser-Wilhelm-Kanal.

In 1917 the city was made capital of the Prussian province of Schleswig-Holstein. Here in 1918 a naval mutiny began the November revolution. The damage suffered by Kiel in World War I, though severe, was far outweighed by that of World War II, when 80 per cent of the city was destroyed. Kiel has recovered, redeveloped its shipbuilding industry, built a new city and, since 1945 been capital of the federal province of Schleswig-Holstein.

The most celebrated son of Kiel is the physicist Max Planck (1858–1947), who formulated the theory of quantum mechanics in 1900. Here in 1728 was born Karl Peter Ulrich who became Tsar Peter III of Russia and was assassinated in 1762. Kiel has twice hosted the Olympic Games Water Sports, in 1936 and in 1972.

Close by the main railway station is the **Sophienhof**, a cultural centre opened in 1988 and housing a municipal gallery with temporary exhibitions, as well as works by the Kiel Expressionist Heinrich Ehmsen (1886–1964). Follow pedestrianised Holstenstrasse NE to the **Alter Markt**. Here rises the 14C and 15C church of **St Nikolaus**, partly modernised during its restoration after World War II, but still retaining its bronze font cast by Johann Apengeter in 1344, the patriarch's altar of 1460, a triumphal cross of 1490 and a Baroque pulpit of 1705 rising from a statue of Moses. The church's modern stained glass is by Heinz Lilienthal. Outside the church is Ernst Barlach's bronze 'Spiritual Fighter' of 1928. The former Schloss, in Schlossstrasse, much damaged in the war, has been rebuilt in the 16C Renaissance style and is now a cultural centre, with a concert hall, a radio and TV centre, an art gallery, with works by Caspar Dietrich Friedrich and Van Gogh, and the regional library, plus a Heimatmuseum (open weekdays except Mon and Wed afternoons, 10.00–13.00, 15.00–19.00, Sun 11.00–13.00). The Schloss has a splendid garden.

Of the former **Franciscan monastery** in Falckstrasse a little further N have survived the mid-13C refectory, now students' lodgings, and the cloister—with the tombstone of Adolf IV von Schauenburg, who died in 1261). In Kleiner Kiel, W of the Alter Markt, stands the restored red-brick **Opernhaus**, by Christian Heinrich Seeling, 1905–07. Kleiner Kiel also boasts Heinrich Billing's Jugendstil **Rathaus** of 1911, with its 106m-high copper-covered tower, standing on a tributary of the fjord at 9 Fleethörn. Two statues by Ernst Barlach flank its staircase (visits daily 10.30 and 11.30,

May–Sept). Here too, at 1 Düsternbrooker Weg, is the art and archaeological collection (open Tue–Sun 10.00–13.00, 15.00–18.00; closed Sun afternoons).

Other museums include the geological and palaeological collection and the theatre, both at 40–60 Olsenhausenstrasse (open Wed 14.00–18.00). The university zoological museum is at 3 Hegewischstrasse (open Tue–Sun 10.00–17.00, closing Sun at 13.00). The Warleberger Hof at 19 Dänische Strasse houses the **Kieler Stadt-und-Schiffartsmuseum**, with numerous model ships (open mid-Apr to mid-Oct daily 10.00–18.00, otherwise, except Mon 10.00–17.00). Kiel's theatre is in Holtenauer Strasse. The **Kunsthalle**, with works beginning in the 16C and specially fine in 19C artists (Slevogt, Liebermann) is at 1 Dünsterbrooker Weg (open, except Mon, 10.00–13.00, 15.00–18.00; closed Sun afternoon).

The Olympic centre and Olympic harbour, used for the Olympic Games of 1936 and 1972, are on the outer fjord in the suburb of Schilksee. In the suburb of **Rammsee** 6km S of the city is the **Schleswig-Holsteinisches Freilichtmuseum**, with reconstructed farmhouses and workshops (open Tue–Sun Apr–15 Nov 09.00–17.00). The environs of Kiel include 19km N by the Marine-Ehrenmal, the German naval war memorial at Laboe, by G.A. Munzer, 1927–36.

# 63

## Lübeck to Kiel

### A.   Via Bad Segeberg and Neumünster

Total distance 85km. Lübeck—B206, 28km Bad Segeberg—B205, 27km Neumünster—B4, 12km Bordesholm See—18km Kiel.

Leave **Lübeck** (see Rte 61A) by the Fackenburgen Allee, taking the B206 W through attractive woodlands to reach after 28km **Bad Segeberg** (15,000 inhab.; alt. 52m), a town built by Emperor Lothar III in the 12C as a bulwark against the Slavs. The fortress Lothar built here was destroyed during the Thirty Years War. This is the major town of the scenic region known as 'Holstein Switzerland' (see below), and is picturesquely situated between a lake and a mountain. The town's development as a spa dates from 1884. The 91m-high Kalkberg E of the town is today a protected national monument, and includes a limestone cave with nine chambers sheltering uniquely developed species both of animal and plant. Bad Segeberg has an open-air theatre, 1934–37, seating 10,000, and hosts an annual Karl May theatre festival.

At the foot of the mount rises the brick and gypsum Romanesque church of Our Lady, with its splendid tower. Begun in 1160 and restored in the 19C and 20C, it has a bronze font of 1447; a late Gothic altar sculpted in 1515; a triumphal cross of 1515; and a Renaissance pulpit of 1612. And do not miss a plaque of 1596, designed by Heinrich Rantzau in honour of Adolf von Schauenburg, who was killed by Harwig Reventlow in Bad Segeberg in 1315. Heinrich's grandfather, Gert Walstorp, also has a tomb in this church.

Harmonious Lübecker Strasse has numerous 15C and 16C half-timbered houses, including at No. 15 the 16C local history museum (open daily 10.00–12.00, 15.00–18.00).

The B205 continues a further 27km NW to **Neumünster** (see Rte 62) from where the route runs N along the B4 for 30km by way of the Bordesolm See to **Kiel** (see again Rte 62).

# B.   Via Bad Schwartau, Eutin and Plön

Total distance 73km. Lübeck—B206, 7km Bad Schwartau—14km junction with B76—B76, 8km Eutin—15km Plön—13km Preetz—16km Kiel.

Leave **Lübeck** (see Rte 61A) N in the direction of Bad Schwartau (20,000 inhab.; alt. 16m), reaching the spa after 7km. Close by this little town of mud and salt baths, Blücher surrendered to the French in 1806. After a further 14km the route reaches the junction with the B76. This road runs NW through the hilly *'Holstein Switzerland'* for 8km to the lakeside town of **Eutin** (17,000 inhab.; alt. 43m). Founded in 1156 by Gerold, the first Bishop of Lübeck, Eutin was for many years the home of subsequent bishops—one of whom, Prince Bishop Adolf Friedrich, became King of Sweden in 1750). Here was born the composer Carl Maria von Weber (1786–1826), 48 Lübecker Strasse. Herzog Peter Friedrich Ludwig, who ruled from 1785 to 1829, generously patronised artists such as Homer's translator Johann Heinrich Voss, the poet Friedrich Leopold Graf zu Stolberg and the painter J.H. Wilhelm Tischbein. Herder was tutor to his son.

Voss's house with a façade of 1784–1802 is now a hotel. N of Markplatz rises the late Romanesque Michaelskirche. Begun in 1230, it has a Gothic choir of 1317. Inside the church are a triumphal cross dating from 1256; a candelabrum of 1444 by Hinrich Sodebotter; a Madonna in a Lantern, 1322, restored in 1740; a 1511 bronze font; and a pulpit of 1653. The Marktplatz also houses several half-timbered houses, the gloomy Stadtpalais of 1786, built for the widow of Duke Friedrich Augustus, and the classical town hall of 1788–91.

Schlossplatz is dominated by the Schloss, which began life as a 13C fortress and was enlarged, after a fire of 1689, by the bishops in the 17C and 18C. Its trapezoid courtyard is flanked by classical façades, as well as the Gothic towered entrance. Inside are princely portraits, tapestries and work by Tischbein, while the Schlosskapelle of 1615 is Baroque (tours Tue–Sat 11.00, 15.00 and 16.00 May–Sept). The Schloss park, set out in the 'English' style in 1758, with temples and an orangery has hosted an annual Carl Maria von Weber festival since 1951. At 17 Lübeckerstrasse stands the former St George-Hospital of 1770, built by Georg Greggenhofer. You find the local history museum at 17 Lübeckerstrasse (open Jun–Aug, except Mon 10.00–13.00, 15.00–17.00, Sun 10.00–12.00, 15.00–17.00).

Tourist information at 9 Am Markt. Trains connect Eutin with Hamburg, Lübeck and Kiel, as do buses; boats ply the lake.

The **Bungsberg**, 16km N, at 164m is the highest peak of Schleswig-Holstein.

Continue NW on the B76 for 15km through forests and lakeland to **Plön**
(11,500 inhab.; alt. 25m), which lies seductively between the Grosser Plöner
See (31 sq km) and several smaller ones—hence its devotion to water sports.
Long ago Plön was a Slavonic settlement. Seat of the Dukes of Schleswig-
Holstein-Sonderburg-Ploön from 1623, when their line died out in 1761 the
town became a summer residence of the Danish royal family. The three-
winged Schloss, now a boarding school, was built for Duke Joachim Ernst
von Schleswig-Holstein, 1633–36, and retains Italianate stuccoed rooms
and a Rococo panelled library. In the entrancing Schloss park is the Rococo
*pavilion called the Prinzenhaus, 1747–50, with wings dated 1896, while a
little peninsula juts out into the lake.

Plön's regional museum is at 1 Johannisstrasse (open May–Sept 10.00–
12.00, 15.00–18.00; Sun 15.00–18.00; winter Tue–Sat 10.00–12.00). In the
Altstadt the Gothic Nikolaikirche was built in 1868. The Rathaus of 1816 is
by C.F. Hansen. In the Neustadt stands the half-timbered Johanniskirche
of 1685, with (on the outside wall) the tombstone of Christian Gottlieb, a
'Moor' brought from Africa in the late 17C to serve as trumpeter in the ducal
regiment.

To the E of Plön is the Max Planck hydro-biological institute. 1.5km N of
the town rises the 64m-high Parna, with a hotel and view-tower.

Tourist information at 12 Bahnhofstrasse. Trains and buses connect Plön
with Kiel and Lübeck.

The route continues NW between the Small Plön See and the Trammer
See to reach after 13km **Preetz** (16,000 inhab.; alt. 34m). The 13C abbey,
around which the town developed, was founded in 1211, but its present
buildings date partly from the 17C, with a 14C abbey church—whose
Knorpelwerk-Altar was created by Hans Gudewert the Younger in 1656.
At the heart of the town stands the partly Romanesque, partly 17C and 18C
Baroque parish church. The two styles are divided by a wall; the organ was
built by Nicolas Plambeck in 1734; and the walls are decorated by coats of
arms.

From Preetz the B76 runs 16km NW to **Kiel** (see Rte 61), passing through
**Rastorf** (3km NE of Preetz), where in a park stands an entrancing Baroque
Schloss, with stables, all created between 1723 and 1729 by Rudolph
Matthias Dillon.

# 64

# Lübeck to Puttgarden

Total distance 107km. Lübeck—B75, 16km Travemünde—the Bäderstrasse
5km Niendorf—3km Timmendorfer Strand—7km Haffkrug—5km Süsel—
B207, 8km Neustadt in Holstein—2km Merkendorf—13km Lensahn—8km
Oldenburg in Holstein—11km Heiligenhafen—12km Grossenbrode—22km
Puttgarden.

Leave **Lübeck** (see Rte 61A) NE by way of the Burgtorbrücke and then
along Travemünder Allee past a large military cemetery. After 5km the B75
reaches the B104 (which leads E for 4km to reach Schlutup, whose pastor
in Thomas Mann's 'Buddenbrooks' was particularly amorous). 16km from

Lübeck the B75 reaches **Travemünde** (13,000 inhab.; alt. 3m), a port founded in 1178 by Count Adolf von Schauenburg. Travemünde was bought by the citizens of Lübeck in 1329 for 1060 Marks, and Thomas Mann described it as Lübeck's loveliest daughter. Today an elegant bathing and health resort, situated on the Baltic where the River Trave empties itself into Lübecker Bucht, Travemünde has a casino, golfing, camping sites, the four-masted sailing ship *Passat* (visits May–Sept 09.30–12.30, 14.30–17.30) and, in the oldest part of the town, several half-timbered houses and the church of St Lorenz. Built in 1557, with a tower of 1620, St Lorenz has a Baroque altar by Hieronymus Jakob Hassenberg and a pulpit of 1735. The nearby police station is housed in the brick, gabled Vogteigebäude of c 1600. Travemünde's lighthouse, built in 1539, was restored after a fire in 1829. The central Strandbad is an immense bathing establishment, with saunas, massage and Kneipp therapy. Travemünde also has a Kurpark with a Kursaal of 1962.

Tourist information at 1b Strandpromenade. Train connections with Hamburg and Lübeck, buses with Lübeck and the Bäderstrasse (see below). Boat trips in the bay and to Scandinavia (Gedser, Trelleborg, Bornholm, Helsinki), with a car ferry to the promontory of Priwall on the right bank of the Trave. Since 1899 Travemünde has hosted an annual summer regatta with more than 1000 yachts participating.

The Bäderstrasse now follows the coastline W and N from Travemünde, reaching after 5km the small seaside and fishing resort of **Niendorf**, with a 4000m-long sandy beach, after 3km more the larger, elegant **Timmendorfer Strand**, with an even longer beach and pine woods; tourist information at 73a Strandallee, and then—after respectively 4km and 3km more—the family-oriented resorts of **Scharbeutz**, and **Haffkrug** (tourist information at 134 Strandallee), all with good train and bus connections.

After 5km W the Bäderstrasse reaches Süsel. From here take the B207 for 8km NE to **Neustadt in Holstein** (16,000 inhab.; alt. 4m), a port and bathing station on Lübecker Bucht founded c 1200. Its Gothic parish church dates from 1238–44, with a west tower of 1334. Look inside the church for its Gothic wall paintings and an *altar of 1643, which was designed for Schleswig cathedral. The Heliggeistpital dates from 1408, the Kornhaus from 1830. The Kemper Tor of Neustadt in Holstein, sole survivor of the medieval fortifications, now houses the local history museum, including works by the local painter Adam Hölbing, (1855–1929) and a steamship of 1850 (open May–Sept weekends 14.00–17.00, with the same times weekdays July, Aug). 4km N on the road to Schönwalde is the village of **Altenkrempe**, with a 13C Romanesque basilica.

Tourist information at the Kurverwaltung. Train connections with Hamburg, Cologne and Lübeck; local bus services; boats to the other resorts on Lübecker Bucht.

**Excursion**. The B207 continues for another 2km to Merkendorf, from where NE along the coast are more bathing resorts. The first, reached after 9km, is Grömitz. After 6km more comes **Cismar**, with a 13C and 14C former monastery church. 3km further is Kellenburg; and after a further 3km Dahme, with a bathing pool using heated sea-water.

The main route, the B207, continues NW from Merkendorf by way of **Lensahn** (13km). Here is a Gothic parish church, with a 15C carved altar, and nearby rises Schloss Güldenstein. After another 8km you reach **Oldenburg in Holstein** (16,000 inhab.; alt. 4m), which was founded by the Slavs and given a bishopric in 940. The little city is flanked by two lakes and you can explore numerous megalithic tombs in the vicinity. Its cathedral of St John the Baptist dates from 1146. In two 18C barns, reconstructed in a park overlooking three lakes, is the Wallmuseum (open daily 10.00–17.00).

Continue NE for 11km to **Heiligenhafen** (10,000 inhab.; alt. 3m), a bathing resort on the Baltic. The town was founded in the mid 13C as a fishing port. It now protects a nature reserve for seagulls and other coastal birds. 12km NE of Heiligenhafen is **Grossenbrode** (2000 inhab.; alt. 3km), a resort noted for its seagulls' egg dishes. The town has pleasant beaches; boats to Gedser; trains to Lübeck and Puttgarden; local buses.

The B207 now runs NE for 22km to the port of **Puttgarden** on the island of **Fehmarn**, crossing en route the 963m-long bridge across the Fehmarn-sund. The island (185 sq km) is farmed by some of its 14,000 population, has many beaches and three towns. In **Burg** is the frescoed convent of St Jürgen, 1439 and the Peter Wiepert local history museum (open Jun–Sept Mon, Wed, Sat 14.00–18.00) near the 13C and 15C church of St Nikolaus. Inside St Nikolaus is a bronze font of 1391, a reredos of 1443, a Gothic statue of Mary Magdalen and a Renaissance statue of St John. The town of **Landkirchen** has the 15C church of St Peter, which is worth a visit to see a votive ship of 1617 and the octagonal font of 1735. Finally, **Lemkenhafen** has a windmill of 1737. 4km N is the Niobe memorial, in memory of 69 sailors lost with the sailing ship *Niobe* in 1932.

From Puttgarden, trains run to Hamburg and Lübeck, buses to Kiel and Neustadt in Holstein, and ships sail to Denmark.

# 65

## Kiel to Flensburg

Total distance 70km. Kiel—B76, 14km Gettorf—13km Eckernförde—Fleckeby–8km Haddebey—2km Schleswig—25km Oeversee—8km Flensburg.

Leave **Kiel** (see Rte 62) by the Eckernförder Allee, driving NW along the B76 through the Danish woods and crossing the Nord–Ostsee canal by the Levensauer bridge, reaching after 14km **Gettorf**, whose 13C to 15C early Gothic *Church has a bronze font of 1424; a carved altar of c 1510; and a 1598 Renaissance pulpit by H. Gudewerdt the Elder.

The B76 continues in the same direction for 13km, running scenically alongside the Eckernförder Bucht, to reach **Eckernförde** (25,000 inhab.; alt. 5m), a town known in the late 13C and lying at the W end of the bay. Eckernförde was virtually destroyed in a fire of 1416 and began to flourish again only in the 16C. It became noted for its pottery in the 18C and was developed as a seaside health resort in the 19C.

Sights include the 15C brick hall-church of St Nikolaus, with superb interior decor. Its Baroque *altar of 1640 is by Hand Gudewerdt the Younger. The bronze font supported by four lions was created by Michael Dibler in 1588. The pulpit dates from 1605. Eckenförde's 14C town hall in the fine Rathausmarkt has a staircase of 1588. The local history museum is also in Rathausmarkt (open Tue–Fri 15.00–17.00, weekends 10.00–17.00).

The bathing suburb of **Borby** boasts an early 13C Romanesque stone church with a contemporary font. The altar is perhaps by Gudewerdt the Younger, and was made in 1686. Local history museum at 59 Kieler Strasse (open Wed 16.00–18.00, weekends 10.00–12.00). Boats to Denmark; trains to Kiel and Lübeck. Tourist information at the Kurverwaltung.

From here drive W along the B76. The road runs at first along the fishing lake called the Windeber Noor and passes the 97m-high Hüttener Berg. You pass through the villages of **Fleckeby**, notable for Schloss Luisenlund, now an international school, and Haddeby, close by which was the Viking setlement of **Haithabu** (now with a museum devoted to the Vikings; open daily Apr–Oct 09.00–18.00; Nov–Mar weekdays except Mon 09.00–17.00, weekends 10.00–18.00), whose 10C rampart follows the banks of the fishing lake known as the Haddeby Noor. Nearby stands a Romanesque church, c 1200, with a superb Gothic altar and a 13C Romanesque crucifixion scene.

20km from Eckernförde is **SCHLESWIG** (29,500 inhab.; alt. 14m), a city rich in architectural treasures, particularly its cathedral. It lies at the end of a long narrow bay stretching 30km NE into the Baltic and known as the Schlei.

**History**. Schleswig developed out of *Haithabu*, and appears in written history in 808 as Sliesthorp. Its bishopric was established in 947. The bishops of Schleswig and the Dukes of Schleswig-Holstein helped to enrich the city from the Middle Ages until 1720, for many years dependent on the Danish archbishopric of Lund. Its prosperity was sealed when Duke Adolf of Holstein (1533–86) made Schloss Gottorf his principle residence in 1544, and Schleswig attained its cultural peak under Duke Friedrich IV (1659–1702). In 1721 the town again fell under Danish hegemony. In 1866 Schleswig became the chief town of Schleswig-Holstein, retaining that status until 1945. Schlesiwg remains the seat of the supreme court of this region. Its welcome to tourists has included building a holiday centre—'Port Viking'—an apartment block 85m high.

From the main railway station walk N to Friedrichstrasse to find at Nos 7–11 the Von Günderoth'sche Hof, built for Herzog Friedrich III as the ducal guest house, 1633–35, and today serving as the city museum (open, except Tue 09.00–17.00, closing Sun 13.00). N of this guest house stands Schloss Gottorf, the largest ducal Schloss of Schleswig-Holstein and the residence of the Schleswig-Holstein-Gottorf family from 1544 to 1713. Its round tower dates from 1574, the north wing from 1570–90, and the south wing from 1698–1703. Schloss Gottorf underwent a Baroque conversion, c 1700, and was also given an 18C façade and central tower. The Schloss also boasts a 17C dolphin fountain. Its chapel, begun c 1500, was finished in 1590. Chapel furnishings include a Renaissance *prie-dieu* of 1608–14, and biblical scenes painted by Marten Van Achten, 1590–93. Heinrich Kreieber created its pulpit in 1590, and its altar of 1666 is by Hans Lembrecht of Hamburg. The Schloss has a Königsaal of c 1520, with some fine furnishings dating from the first half of the 17C.

Schloss Gottorf now houses the Landesmuseum für Kunst und Kulturgeschichte and the Landesmuseum für Vor-und Frühgeschichte. The first has superb medieval–to 19C works of art, as well as furniture and kitchenware. The second is the home of a celebrated 'bog man' and the **Nydam-Boot, a 4C ship 23m x 3m, excavated in 1863 from the Nydam marshes (both museums open Apr–Oct 09.00–17.00; winter 09.30–16.00).

From here walk NE along Lollfuss to find the Amstgericht, built by C. Friedrich Heespen in 1754. At 53 Lollfuss is the Landestheater of 1892. The continuation of Lollfuss, Stadtweg, leads N to the **Dom of St Peter, in Süderdomstrasse at the centre of the Altstadt. Founded in the 11C, St Peter's cathedral was rebuilt in 1440 as an imposing three-aisled Gothic hall-church. Its tower dates from the 19C. Look first for the Christ in majesty surrounded by the symbols of the Evangelists on the tympanum, carved c 1180. It houses a 12.6m-high *altar by Hans Brüggemann, 1514–21, which in 1666 was transferred to here from Bordesholm on the orders of Duke Christian Albert and has 392 sculpted statues in wood, depicting the life of Jesus. The cathedral wall paintings date from the 14C (and were restored in 1938).

Other treasures are the altar of the Magi, c 1300; the choir stalls of 1512; the 1644 Kielmannseck altar, whose paintings are by J. Ovens; and the funeral monument of Kielmann von Kielmannseck, 1573. Other delights are the restored 15C rood screen and the 16C choir screen, as well as 17C and 18C chapels containing the ducal tombs, with a Baroque entrance to the Schacht vault. In the north choir is the memorial tomb to King Frederick I of Denmark who died in 1533 (he was also Duke of Schleswig-Holstein), created by Cornelis Floris, 1551–55. The 15C cathedral cloister has 13C wall paintings.

N of the cathedral at 15 Norderdomstrasse stands the Königstein'sche Hof, built in the 15C and enlarged in 1702 by Baron von Mönigstein. The Rathaus in the Markt just E of the cathedral is a classical building of 1794, and in the same square is the court pharmacy of 1517. On the Schlei, SE of the town hall, stands the former Benedictine *convent of St Johann, begun in the late 12C. The choir is late 16C; there is a late 15C tabernacle; also a 17C altar of St John the Baptist, with his sculpted image; a pulpit of 1717; an 18C canonesses' choir; and a vaulted cloister and refectory; It is now a Protestant convent and situated in the former fishermen's quarter of Holm; see also the 17C and 18C houses in Lange Strasse.

Tourist information at 7 Flensburgerstrasse. Trains run between Hamburg, Flensburg and Neumünster; sailing trips in summer. Schleswig hosts a July regatta on the Schlei.

25km NW of Schleswig along the B76 lies the village of **Oeversee**, with a 12C Romanesque stone church. Near here the Austrians fought the Danes on 6 February 1864, a battle commemorated by a war memorial. This is a centre for potholing and hiking.

The B76 runs N for 8km to reach **FLENSBURG** (88,000 inhab.; alt. 3m) on the 36m-long Flensburg fjord.

**Tourist information**: 6 Norderstrasse. **Trains** to major cities of Schleswig-Holstein; **boats** to Denmark.

**History**. A busy port that first appears in written history in the 12C, Flensburg obtained a city charter in 1284, became Danish in 1460, suffered severely during the Thirty Years War and began to prosper on the rum and sugar trade in the 18C. The town was Prussian in 1864 and became the home of a naval academy. By a popular vote in 1920 Flensburg opted to remain German, and at the end of World War II served as the seat of Admiral Doenitz's three-week-long government after Adolf Hitler's suicide. Germany capitulated here on 7 May 1945.

From the main railway station take Bahnhofstrasse to the Südermarkt, passing the library and concert hall of the Deutsches Haus of 1929 (see below). Südermarkt contains, as well as half-timbered houses, the Niko-laikirche, a building dating from 1390. Its west tower was begun in 1516 and given a neo-Gothic aspect in 1877. The pulpit dates from 1570; the organ case of 1604 is by H. Ringerrinck; the altar was built in 1749.

Take Angelburger Strasse E of the Südermarkt, and over the railway bridge, to reach the 12C church of St Johann. Flensburg's oldest church, St Johann was begun in the 12C and enlarged in the 14C. The dome was added c 1500, the west tower in 1741. Its interior, restored in the 19C, has late Gothic frescoes on the vault. It shelters a 1500 statue of St John the Baptist and a pulpit of 1587 by Hans von Bremen.

Return to the Südermarkt and walk N along the Holm, with its shops and at No. 13 an 18C pharmacy, to find the town hall. Grosse Strasse continues N to the Heiliggeistkirche of 1385, with its Baroque gable and an octagonal lantern of 1761. The church has 15C frescoes and services here are held in Danish. Continue as far as the Nordermarkt, with its arcaded Schrangen Haus of 1595 and its Neptune fountain of 1785. On the N side of the market square stands the Marienkirche, built in brick in the 13C and given a neo-Gothic tower in 1880. The chief monuments inside are the Renaissance tomb of Anna von Buckwald, who died in 1597; a pulpit of 1579; a 1591 bronze font by Michael Dibler; the Renaissance high altar by H. Ringering, 1598; and a modern stained glass window devoted to the Virgin Mary and designed by Käte Lassen in 1953.

Continue N along Norderstrasse, another shopping street, to find at No. 8 the Alt-Flensburger Haus of 1780. This was the birthplace of Hugo Eckener (1869–1954), who flew the first Zeppelin across the Atlantic. The symbol of Flensburg, the brick Northern Gateway, Nodertor, of 1595, with the city arms and those of Christian IV of Denmark, is at the end of Norderstrasse.

**Museums** Naturwissenschaftliches Heimatmuseum der Stadt Flensburg at 40 Süderhofenden has information on regional plants and animals; the Städtisches Museum at 1 Lutherplatz; and the Schiffahrtsmuseum at 39 Schiffbrücke (all three open, except Mon 10.00–13.00, 15.00–17.00, closing Sun afternoons). The Deutsches Haus, a concert hall of 1929–30 is in Dr Todsen-Strasse.

The B76 reaches the Danish border after 7km.

6km NE of Flensburg by way of Mürwik with its naval officers' academy, lies **Glücksburg**. Splendid, moated Schloss Glücksburg was built for Duke Johann the Younger by Nicolaus Karies of Flensburg between 1582 and 1587. Its interiors are Baroque, apart from the white room which is contemporary with the foundation. The Schloss chapel dates from 1717 (visits Tue–Sun Jun–Aug 10.00–16.30, otherwise 10.00–12.00, 14.00–16.00). To swim or sunbathe, visit the sandy beach at the nearby health resort of **Sandwig**.

# 66

## Flensburg to Itzehoe

Total distance 108km. Flensburg—B76, 8km Oeversee—25km Schleswig—B77, 7km Jagel—21km Rendsburg—8km Jevenstedt—39km Itzehoe.

Follow the B76 for 33km from **Flensburg** to Schleswig (see Rte 65). From Schleswig take the B77 S for 7km to reach **Jagel**, to the E of which have been excavated the foundations of the wall built by the Danes as a defence against Charlemagne in 808.

Continue along the B77 to cross the River Eider and reach after 21km the industrial town of **Rendsburg** (34,000 inhab.; alt. 7m), which has preserved an attractive Altstadt and an unusual Italian Baroque suburb. Rendsburg first appears in written history in 1199 as *Reynoldsburg*. Long disputed between Holstein and Denmark, it was rendered prosperous by a canal dug in 1784. Its iron and steel works are today served by the Kiel canal. A tunnel (1961) carries traffic under the canal to the W. To the SE is the huge high-level Rendsburg bridge (42m high, built 1911–13) carrying rail and other traffic over the canal. Here are based the main theatre companies of Schleswig-Holstein.

The old city, based on an island in the River Eider, houses in the Markt the half-timbered former Rathaus of 1566, with a porch of 1609 carrying the city coat of arms and a Glockenspiel which hourly plays local tunes from 10.00 to 20.00). In the Markt also rises the church of Our Lady, which was founded in 1287. Its belfry was completed in 1454. There are 14C paintings in the vault. The Renaissance pulpit of 1621 is by Hans Peper. In 1649 the Baroque altar was created by Henning Claussen. The church houses 16C and 17C tombs, as well as stained glass by Käte Lassen. Nearby at 3 Schleifmühlen Strasse rises Rendsburg's oldest house, the half-timbered 'Zum Landsknecht' of 1541. The hospice of the Holy Ghost was built in 1758 in Schlossplatz, on the site of the former Schloss.

Find the Italian Baroque suburb of Neuwerk S of the Altstadt by way of the Jungfernsteig, which stretches along the city park. Neuwerk was created between 1690 and 1695 by Domenco Pelli, who was born at Lugano in 1656. Its Paradeplatz boasts Baroque houses by Pelli, as well as the Christuskirche (formerly the garrison church) of 1685–1700. Christuskirche has a Baroque interior and an altar of 1663, as well as an organ of 1716 and the 1720 funeral monument of Andres von Fuchs. Nearby in the Stadtpark is the former Arsenal, its lower part built 1696–97, upper part in 1740.

Rendsburg's regional theatre is at 7 Jungfernsteig. The local history museum is located in the Arsenal (open, except Mon, 10.00–12.00; also Fri–Sun 15.00–17.00). Tourist information at 25 Herrenstrasse. Train and bus connections with Flensburg, Hamburg, Husum and Kiel.

The B77 continues S by way of **Jevenstedt**, 8km away with a fine view of the high level railway bridge, and for another 39km to **Itzehoe** (see Rte 67).

# 67

## Itzehoe to the Island of Sylt

Total distance 133km. Itzehoe—B204, 38km Albersdorf—14km Heide—B5, 17km Lunden—9km Friedrichstadt—15km Husum—5km Hattstedt—12km Bredstedt—23km Niebüll—motorail by way of Klaxbüll for the island of Sylt.

**Itzehoe** (38,000 inhab.; alt 7m) lies on the River Stor where Charlemagne established a bulwark against the Danes c 818. To its chagrin, the town was Wallenstein's HQ during the Thirty Years War suffering greatly during the fighting. Later much was destroyed during a fire of 1657. Itzehoe's chief treasures begin in Am Markt with the Baroque Rathaus of 1685, which was extended in 1893 (note especially deliciously ornamented porch), and the brick, Baroque church of St Lawrence. Begun in the 12C, the church was rebuilt in 1716. It shelters numerous fine tombs, the finest those from the 18C and 19C in the crypt. Its altar and pulpit date from 1661, the organ case from 1718. The small church of St Jürgen, built in 1657, still preserves its paintwork of 1672.

Other notable sights are a Bronze Age grave, at Am Lorsenplatz, of c 1200 BC; the remains of a mid-13C Cistercian monastery; and—5km SE of the town—**Schloss Breitenburg**. Wallenstein demolished its predecessor, a 16C Schloss belonging to the Counts of Rantzau-Breitenburg, and the present building dates from 1750 and was in part rebuilt in 1898. It has a well of 1582 and a chapel of 1634. The local history museum of Itzehoe is in a 17C building (the Prinzesshof) at 20 Viktoria Strasse (open daily, except Mon 10.00–12.00, 15.00–18.00). Tourist information at 8 Bahnhofstrasse. Train connections with Hamburg and Husum.

The B204 runs 27km N from here to Hademarschen, and then W for 11km to **Albersdorf** (7000 inhab.; alt. 6m). Here is a church with a 15C font. To the S is the Brutkamp, a neo-Stone Age megalithic tomb; to the N the Schalen stone, with curious carvings, covering another megalithic tomb.

**Heide** (22,000 inhab.; alt. 14m; tourist information: 1 Postelweg), 14km NW, has the largest market place in the former Federal Republic. Its Gothic church of St Jürgen has an altar of 1515, a pulpit of 1570 and a font of 1640. Heide's Carl-Diem Hall seats 500, and the town is well equipped with sports stadia. The Klaus Groth Museum at 48 Lüttenheid is devoted to the poet Klaus Groth (1819–99), who was born here and became a Professor of German Language and Literature at Kiel (open Mon–Sat 09.30–12.00; afternoons except Wed, Sat 14.00–16.30). The local history museum is at 8 Brahmstrasse (open Apr–Sept, except Mon and Sat, 09.00–12.00, 14.00–17.00; winter closed mornings).

**Excursion**. From Heide the B203 leads SW for 20km to the North Sea health resort of **Büsum**, whose citizens enjoy crab fishing, long walks along the tidal flats and boats to Heligoland. Büsum has an institute of maritime research. 10km N of the town is **Wesselburen**, the birthplace of the dramatist Friedrich Hebbel (1813–63), The Hebbel Museum is at 6 Osterstrasse (open daily, May–Oct 10.00–12.00, 14.00–18.00, Sun closes 17.00), and there is a monument outside his home at 49 Süderstrasse. See also the Baroque church of St Bartholomäus, built by J.G. Schott in 1738.

From Heide the B5 continues 17km N to **Lunden**, whose church dates from the 12C to the 16C. The holiday resort of **Garding**, W of Lunden on the Eiderstadt peninsula, is reached by the B202 through Tönning. From Tönning follow the B5 for another 9km to reach **Friedrichstadt** (2700 inhab.; alt. 4m), where the River Treene meets the Eider, a town built by Dutch Protestant refugees welcomed here by Herzog Friedrich III von Gottorf in 1621, and now a health resort with many sporting facilities. The former mint of 1626 has a Dutch Renaissance façade; the town also has a shared Catholic and Protestant church, built between 1643 and 1649. Trains run to Hamburg and Westerland; boats ply to Heligoland and the Halligen.

The **Halligen**—a group of nine islands once attached to the coast (detached by a storm and floods in 1634) and including Hooge, Langeness, Gröde, Süderoog, Nordstrand, Pellworm—whose Romanesque church has 12C wall paintings and an 18C organ by Arp Schnitger—and Südfall, some of them connected again to the mainland by causeways. Their inhabitants breed cattle, welcome tourists, and fish commercially.

The principal point of departure is the animated town of **Husum**. On the N side of its Markt is the Rathaus of 1702, next door to the 15C and Rococo Herrenhaus. No. 9 Am Markt is the birthplace of Theodor Storm (1817–88), with a museum in his memory (open Apr–Oct 14.00–17.00; otherwise Tue, Wed, Sat 15.00–17.00). Husum's Marienkirche dates from 1827–29. Follow Schlossgang, N of the market square, to find the Dutch Renaissance Schloss vor Husum, 1577–82, now the venue of concerts and exhibitions (open Mar–Oct daily, except Mon, 10.00–12.00, 14.00–17.00), with the Renaissance Torhalle of 1612 in the Schlosspark. The Nordfriesisches Museum is at 25 Herzog-Adolf-Strasse (open Apr–Oct 10.00–12.00, 14.00–17.00, otherwise closing 16.00).

After 5km the B5 reaches **Hattstedt**, from which a 2.5km causeway runs to the island of Nordstrand. Continue 12km N along the B5 to **Bredstedt** (5600 inhab.; alt. 5m), which hosts both an agricultural market and the North Friesland nature centre. The route continues across the Bordelum Heath (10km E of which is the Kalkerheide nature reserve), by way of Klaxbüll and the 11km-long Hindenburg Dam, built 1923–27, reaching after 23km **Niebüll** (7000 inhab.; alt. 5m), from which trains serve both Hamburg and (including a motorail) the island of Sylt. Niebüll has a museum dedicated to the painter and sculptor Richard Haizmann (1895–1963), in Rathausplatz (open Apr–Oct, mid-Dec to mid-Jan, Tue–Sun 10.00–12.00, 14.00–16.00,) a local history museum at 76 Osterweg (open Jun–Sept 14.00–16.00) and the museum of natural history at 108 Hauptstrasse (open 21 May–11 Sept daily 14.00–18.00; otherwise 10.00–12.00). A branch line leads to **Dagebüll**, the port for the islands of **Amrum** and **Föhr**, the latter's chief town being Wyk, a seaside resort since 1819. Here is the Carl-Haeberlin Frisian Museum, with its botanical and geological collection (open Mar–May, Sept–Oct, Tue–Sun 10.00–12.00, 14.00–18.00; Nov–Jan Tue–Sun 10.00–17.00).

**Sylt**, at 102 sq km the largest of the North Friesian Islands, has a beach almost 40km long on the W coast. Its villages include **Hörnum**, with dunes and fishing, and boats sailing to Hamburg and Cuxhaven; **Kampen**, with sandflats and the Abessina naturist beach; **List**, at the N tip of Sylt, from which boats sail to Denmark; the health resort of **Wenningstedt**, whence Angles, Saxons and Jutes set sail for England in 449; and the main town, **Westerland**, was founded in the 15C. Today it is a sophisticated holiday resort, with health baths; a sanatorium; a 'graveyard of the homeless', for those drowned at sea and washed up here; and a church dated 1635 (part Romanesque, part Gothic). The resort also boasts a casino, an aquarium and more naturism. Tourist information at the railway station and the Kurverwaltung.

# A NOTE ON BLUE GUIDES

The Blue Guide series began in 1918 when Muirhead Guide-Books Limited published Blue Guide London and its Environs. Findlay and James Muirhead already had extensive experience of guide-book publishing: before the First World War they had been the editors of the English editions of the German Baedekers, and by 1915 they had acquired the copyright of most of the famous 'Red' Handbooks from John Murray.

An agreement made with the French publishing house Hachette et Cie in 1917 led to the translation of Muirhead's London guide, which became the first 'Guide Bleu', Hachette had previously published the blue-covered 'Guides Joanne'. Subsequently, Hachette's Guide Blue 'Paris et ses Environs' was adapted and published in London by Muirhead.

In 1931 Ernest Benn Limited took over the Blue Guides, appointing Russell Muirhead, Findlay Muirhead's son, editor in 1934. The Muirheads' connection with the Blue Guides ended in 1963, when Stuart Rossiter, who had been working on the Guides since 1954, became house editor, revising and compiling several of the books himself.

The Blue Guides are now published by A & C Black, who acquired Ernest Benn in 1984, so continuing the tradition of guide-book publishing which began in 1826 with 'Black's Economical Tourist of Scotland'. The series continues to grow: there are now more than 50 titles in print, with revised editions appearing regularly, and new titles in preparation.

# INDEX